THE WORLD OF EARL HINES

Also by Stanley Dance
THE WORLD OF DUKE ELLINGTON
THE WORLD OF SWING

VOLUME TWO
THE WORLD OF SWING

THE WORLD OF EARL HINES

STANLEY DANCE

CHARLES
SCRIBNER'S
SONS,
NEW
YORK

ILLUSTRATION CREDITS

Copyright © 1977 Stanley Dance

Library of Congress Cataloging in Publication Data

Dance, Stanley.
    The world of Earl Hines.

    Bibliography: p. 312
    Discography: p. 313
    Includes index.
    1. Hines, Earl, 1905–   2. Jazz musicians—
United States—Biography.   I. Title.
ML417.H5D4   786.2′1′0924 [B]   77-2269
ISBN 0-684-14935-4
ISBN 0-684-15030-1 pbk.

Material from *The Night People*, © 1971
by Stanley F. Dance, is reprinted by permission of
Crescendo Publishing Co., Boston.

1 3 5 7 9 11 13 15 17 19 V|C 20 18 16 14 12 10 8 6 4 2
1 3 5 7 9 11 13 15 17 19 V|P 20 18 16 14 12 10 8 6 4 2

Printed in the United States of America

CONTENTS

Introduction   1

Earl Hines   7
Piano, bandleader and singer
    A Bird Out of a Cage   7
    A Tree Full of Owls   33
    See No Evil   57
    A Long Way from the
      Leader House   103

Lois Deppe   131
Singer and bandleader

Charlie Carpenter   142
Lyricist and manager

George Dixon   160
Trumpet and saxophones

Walter Fuller   166
Trumpet

Quinn Wilson   171
Bass and arranger

Wallace Bishop   175
Drums

Irene Kitchings   179
Piano and songwriter

Teddy Wilson   183
Piano, arranger and bandleader

Milt Hinton   187
Bass

Freddy and Irving Goodman   193
    Trumpets

Jimmy Mundy   197
    Arranger and tenor saxophone

Budd Johnson   202
    Saxophones, clarinet and arranger

Trummy Young   220
    Trombone

Willie Randall   228
    Saxophones and arranger

John "Streamline" Ewing   235
    Trombone

Billy Eckstine   238
    Singer and trumpet

Franz Jackson   246
    Tenor saxophone, clarinet and
        arranger

Dizzy Gillespie   254
    Trumpet and bandleader

Cliff Smalls   261
    Piano, trombone and arranger

Dicky Wells   273
    Trombone and arranger

Road Stories   277

The 1946 Band   285
    Capsule Biographies

Appendix   290

Chronology   293

Bibliography   312

A Representative LP
    Discography   313

Index   316

LIST OF ILLUSTRATIONS

Duquesne, Pa., steelworks	6
Earl Hines's mother	8
Earl Hines: school days	11
Earl Hines at the Leader House	17
Lois Deppe's Symphonian Serenaders	20–21
Local No. 471, Pittsburgh, 1922	24
Hines family	27
Eubie Blake and Earl Hines	31
Joseph "Boots" Hines	32
Nancy Hines	32
Earl Hines, a newcomer to Chicago	37
Earl Hines, 1926	38
On the Oakland–San Francisco Ferry, 1926	40
On tour with Carroll Dickerson, 1926	41
Poster of Carroll Dickerson's Syncopators	43
The Carroll Dickerson Orchestra	44
Ad for the Sunset Café	44
Louis Armstrong's Stompers	51
Zutty Singleton	53
Earl Hines, 1928	59
The First Grand Terrace band	60
Valaida Snow	64
Earl Hines and his orchestra, 1932	66–67
Earl Hines and his orchestra, 1935	68
The Earl Hines orchestra at the Apollo Theatre	71
Ann Jones and the Nicholas Brothers	74–75
Darnell Howard	77
Omer Simeon	77
Earl Hines and his orchestra, 1939	78–79
Earl Hines displays his initials in diamonds	87
Earl Hines on piano	87
The Earl Hines and Louis Armstrong bands	90
Earl Hines, 1940	94
Madeline Green	94
Earl Hines and his orchestra, 1943	96–97
The Bluebonnets and Sarah Vaughan	98–99
Earl Hines and his orchestra, 1946	100
Earl Hines and Muhammad Ali, 1975	101
Joe Louis and Earl Hines, 1947	101
Goodbye, Grand Terrace!	102
Louis Armstrong, Jack Teagarden, Earl Hines	105
Louis Armstrong and Sid Catlett	106
Louis Armstrong, Earl Hines, Mantan Moreland	106–7
Arvell Shaw, Earl Hines, Velma Middleton, Sidney Catlett	107
Earl Hines, Kid Ory, Louis Armstrong	108
Tommy Potter, Art Blakey, Jonah Jones, Earl Hines, Benny Green, 1952	109
Earl Hines, Benny Green, Tommy Potter, Jonah Jones, Ocie Johnson, Aaron Sachs, 1953	109
Club Hangover, San Francisco	110
Joe Sullivan, Earl Hines, Muggsy Spanier	111
Earl Hines and band at the Hangover	112–13
Earl Hines with basketball stars, 1954	112–13
Tosca, Earl, Janie and Janear Hines, 1966	114
In Rome, 1966	115
"Fatha" Hines meets Pope Paul	115

Rehearsal for Russia, 1966   117

Earl Hines in bowling league competition   118

Marva Josie   119

Earl Hines, San Francisco   121

Earl Hines plays Scott Newhall's gift   121

Earl Hines and Duke Ellington   123

Earl Hines and Oscar Peterson, Buenos
    Aires, 1969   124

Earl Hines and Dave Brubeck, 1975   125

Earl Hines, Harley White, Rudy
    Rutherford, Eddie Graham, 1975   124–25

At the White House, 1976   127

Earl Hines and his father, 1935   128

South American poster   129

Lois Deppe, concert program   130

The *Great Day* company, 1929   138–39

Earl Hines and Lois Deppe, 1951   141

Lois Deppe   141

Louis Dunlap and Charlie Carpenter   143

Buck and Bubbles   145

Ed Fox   151

Banquet at the Theresa Hotel in Harlem   159

Billy Eckstine, Franz Jackson, Earl Hines,
    George Dixon   163

Roy Eldridge, Alvin Burroughs, Lotus Per-
    kins, Rozelle Claxton, George Dixon   164

Lois Deppe, Earl Hines, George Dixon   165

Walter Fuller   167

Billy Franklin, Omer Simeon, Charlie
    Allen, Lawrence Dixon, Wallace
    Bishop, Earl Hines, Walter Fuller   169

Quinn Wilson   173

Earl Hines and Wallace Bishop, Paris,
    1949   176–77

Earl Hines and Wallace Bishop, Antwerp,
    1965   178

Irene Wilson   180

Kathryn Perry and Irene Wilson, 1936   181

Irene Wilson's orchestra at the Vogue   182

Teddy Wilson and Earl Hines, New York,
    1959   185

Duke Ellington's seventieth birthday party
    in the White House   189

Cassino Simpson's band, 1931–32   192

Irving Goodman   196

Earl Hines and his orchestra, 1935   199

Jimmy Mundy with Jimmy Rushing, Nat
    Pierce, Coleman Hawkins, 1958   201

Budd Johnson   205

Leroy Harris, Willie Randall, Budd John-
    son, Madeline Green   214

Thomas Crump, Budd Johnson, Scoops
    Carry, Buddy Hills, Ernie Wilkins,
    Woogie Harris, Willie Cook   215

Budd Johnson and Earl Hines, South
    America, 1969   215

Sarah Vaughan and Earl Hines, 1943   218

The Little Theatre concert, 1964   219

Earl Hines's musicians, 1937   223

Trummy Young and Kid Ory, Hawaii, 1971   226

Reunion of the Hines alumni, 1971   231

Willie Randall and his orchestra   233

Trummy Young, Earl Hines, Streamline
    Ewing, 1971   236

Billy Eckstine with the Earl Hines
    orchestra, 1940   239

Billy Eckstine with the Earl Hines
    orchestra, 1942   242–43

Earl Hines, Billy Eckstine, Dizzy Gillespie,
    Bobby Tucker, Wolf Trap, 1976   244

Dizzy Gillespie, Earl Hines, Billy
    Eckstine, Wolf Trap   245

François Moseley's Band, 1927   247

Earl Hines and his orchestra, 1941   249

Franz Jackson, 1966   250

Frank Newton's band in Boston   252

Franz Jackson and the Original Jass
    All-Stars   253

Dizzy Gillespie   256

Earl Hines and his orchestra, 1943   258–59

The Carolina Cotton Pickers   263

Earl Hines and Count Basie   265

Cliff Smalls, Cleveland, 1944   267

Earl Hines and his orchestra, 1943   267

Earl Hines's brass, 1945   268

Ira Pettiford   268

Cliff Smalls, Art Tatum, Sonny
    Thompson, Earl Hines   270–71

Earl Hines, Carl Pruitt, Shadow
    Wilson, Leroy Harris, Jerome
    Richardson, Dicky Wells, Gene
    Redd, 1954   274–75

Sarah Vaughan, 1943   283

Sarah Vaughan and Earl Hines, 1973   283

Scoops Carry   286

Arthur Walker   286

Lord Essex   287

Dolores Parker   287

Jazz programs   288–89

Three Maniacs of Rhythm with Earl
    Hines orchestra   289

Alvin Burroughs   291

Jazz collage   292

Kermit Scott   303

Sonny Thompson welcomed to the El
    Grotto, 1945   303

Old friends: Earl Hines and Benny Carter   305

Earl Hines/Benny Carter ad   305

Departure for Europe, *Jazz from a Swing-
    ing Era* tour, March 1967   307

Earl Hines and Truck Parham, 1971   309

Fatha and friends at the Rainbow Grill,
    1975   311

The Grand Terrace and the Sunset Café,
    1976   311

Recording for M-G-M in 1960   312

Recording for Contact in 1964   315

Recording for Flying Dutchman, 1970   315

Recording for Ducretet-Thompson, 1965   315

Recording for Swaggie, 1972   315

INTRODUCTION

Like its two predecessors, *The World of Duke Ellington* and *The World of Swing*, this is a book of oral history, although unlike them it contains an autobiography of its central figure. When I began to collect the material, I thought it would encompass even more of the Chicago scene than it actually does, but Earl Hines and his associates take the reader to many different areas—musical, geographical and temporal. Pittsburgh, from which other great musicians like Roy Eldridge, Mary Lou Williams and Erroll Garner came, has never, for example, received much attention in jazz histories, but Earl Hines and Lois Deppe show it to have been fertile soil for the music at a very early period.

Jazz in Chicago is a much bigger subject than is perhaps generally realized. Often chronicled have been the exploits of the Original Dixieland Jazz Band, King Oliver, Jelly Roll Morton, Louis Armstrong, Freddy Keppard, Jimmie Noone, Tommy Ladnier, Johnny and Baby Dodds, Bix Beiderbecke, Benny Goodman, Mezz Mezzrow, Eddie Condon, Bud Freeman, Dave Tough and Gene Krupa, but the perspective has sometimes been one-sided. "You heard about the Austin High School," Milt Hinton told Whitney Balliett, "but not much about Wendell Phillips High School." This despite the fact that out of the second came musicians like Eddie South, Nat Cole, Ray Nance, Hayes Alvis, Happy Caldwell and Hinton himself. There can be little doubt that Wendell Phillips made as impor-

tant a contribution to jazz as Austin High, but the former was black, the latter white.

There was, of course, an early intermingling of black and white *jazz* musicians in Chicago, although blacks had their own strong, autonomous union local, which had been originally chartered in 1902. It had the same wage scale as the white local and was an active competitor. Alongside the musical world with which this book is primarily concerned, two others existed. One was the world of white dance bands which played at most of the more expensive hotels and ballrooms. The interviews with Freddy and Irving Goodman therefore provide an alternative viewpoint on Chicago jazz, in addition to individual memories of two of the Swing Era's major figures. While Benny Goodman was interviewed in *The World of Swing*, Bunny Berigan received scant attention. He was a sensation when he appeared with Goodman in 1936 at the Congress Hotel in Chicago, and many regard him as the greatest white trumpet player in jazz history. Irving Goodman's warm memories explain why Berigan is still recalled with such affection by those who knew him.

The other world, like a basic stratum, was that of the blues artists and groups who entertained emigrants from the South in the idiom to which they were accustomed. It existed throughout Earl Hines's reign in Chicago, just as it does to this day, and it gave the South Side roots of a character and strength quite different from those of Harlem. In the chapter on Chicago in his autobiographical *Music Is My Mistress*, Duke Ellington wrote of "apparently broken-down neighborhoods where there were more good times than any place in the city." But he was also very much aware of the *togetherness* of the South Side and the achievements of its black community.

It should perhaps be pointed out here that the terms "colored," "Negro" and "black" are used rather inconsistently in this book, sometimes in accordance with the age of the speaker, sometimes with the date of the interview, and at others with the time frame of the reminiscences. But it is interesting to recall that Robert S. Abbott, the indomitable editor of the famous black newspaper *The Chicago Defender,* was resolutely opposed to the use of "Negro" and insisted on "Race" so long as he lived. To him it was not the disparaging adjective latter-day writers unanimously suppose it to be.

Everyone is familiar with the capsule history which has jazz marching through the streets and tinkling in the bordellos of New Orleans. Then, a little later, it gets on the riverboats and stops at Memphis and St. Louis before arriving in Chicago for the great sunburst of talent that makes the city all too briefly the Jazz Capital of the World. After a few years New York becomes the magnetic centre and Chicago pales into insignificance.

But it wasn't like that really. Many musicians much preferred the lifestyle of Chicago to that of New York. Had fine players like Omer Simeon, George Dixon and Walter Fuller succumbed to the lure of New York, they would in all probability have received greater national and international fame. Even the Hines band, with very few equals in the land, was regarded, according to Jonah Jones, as a "western" band by musicians in the East. Certainly, it never received much benefit from New York's propaganda mills.

Chicago, however, was an influential and powerful broadcasting centre, and radio was a far stronger force than records in the '30s, stronger even than television today so far as *music* was concerned. It was Chicago radio

that made a hit of *Christopher Columbus* and brought Fletcher Henderson back into prominence in 1936. Musicians in Kansas City heard the Earl Hines band broadcasting from the Grand Terrace, were impressed and inspired. In due course Kansas City was to throw down its own challenge to New York and further upset the simplicity of historical geography.

To simplify historically is often to falsify. After examining the evidence before him, the historian passes judgment on characters and events. He may not have all the evidence. He may be prejudiced. His moral values and artistic standards may be those of a later generation. As he reduces in order to simplify, falsification, whether intentional or accidental, is all too likely to occur. The method adopted in this book and its predecessors leaves *interpretation* to the reader. Different speakers variously confirm, contradict or clarify. The same incident is seen from different viewpoints, and this sometimes involves repetition, but such emphasis aids in assessing significance. It is valuable, I believe, to see a major artist like Earl Hines both as he sees himself—he is franker than most—and as he is seen by some of his close associates. What is understated or by-passed in one interview will usually appear in sharper relief in another.

The introduction to *The World of Swing* discussed the effect of theatrical values on Duke Ellington and Earl Hines at the Cotton Club and Grand Terrace, where their reputations were respectively built. Ellington gained invaluable experience at the Cotton Club, but it was not an especially happy period in his career. The band was underpaid, and not until 1938 was Ellington permitted the artistic gratification of writing the show's music himself. The jazz purist or near-purist would not, in fact, have been in a seventh heaven at either the Cotton Club or the Grand Terrace, because he would have had to endure considerable show-business ham, theatrical singers and stagey presentations. The most rewarding periods were those when the band played for dancers—acts, chorus line and public—and came alive rhythmically.

In the '30s jazz musicians labored generally under a variety of inferiority complexes, some stemming from the fact that many of them were not by any means good readers, others from the unorthodoxy of self-acquired techniques. If playing the *Poet and Peasant Overture* or *Rhapsody in Blue* gave no real scope to an improvising genius, frequent performance of such works in theatres and the bigger clubs nevertheless led to higher standards of musicianship and the relatively accurate interpretation of arrangements. For the inspired soloist whose reading ability was somewhat doubtful, room was found elsewhere. Duke Ellington liked to quote the reply of one job applicant: "Yeah, I can read, but I don't let it interfere with my blowing!"

I first became aware of Earl Hines in 1928 when his Okeh records with Louis Armstrong were issued in England on the Parlophone label. His piano solos followed and, much impressed, I subsequently obtained every available record on which he played. In 1937 I heard him with his band at the Apollo Theatre in New York and was disappointed. It was unfortunate that I did not hear them playing for dancers at the Savoy Ballroom, because at the Apollo, much to the delight of the audience, the band presented a fast, flashy show. The faster the leader's fingers moved over the keyboard, the more the applause mounted. He played *Canadian Capers* and this was not what I had expected to hear from the intense, dynamic pianist of *West End Blues* and other classics. Having yet to differentiate between what might be called the public Hines and the private Hines of the record studio, I was mystified.

After World War II he came to Europe for the first time with Louis Armstrong, and again a decade later as joint leader with Jack Teagarden of a small group. Although his fortunes had waned in the U.S., he was everywhere acclaimed, for he was obviously playing as well and inventively as ever. In between tours he and I corresponded. His "letters" came on seven-inch tape reels recorded in the San Francisco radio studio where he presented a weekly record program. Always a reluctant writer, he found this a convenient method of replying, and if he ran out of things to say he would fill up the tape with a piano solo. At a time when he was seldom recorded, these solos served a double purpose. They gave great pleasure while demonstrating that he remained the best of all jazz pianists, and I voted for him as such in magazine polls like *Down Beat*'s annual International Critics' Poll. This provoked a certain amount of ridicule from those who had not heard him and were convinced that anyone who made his name in the '20s was inevitably *passé* three decades later. Pianists, of course, knew better. "When you talk about greatness, you talk about Art Tatum and Earl Hines," Erroll Garner declared. "Why, Earl can go on for ninety years and never be out of date," Count Basie told Ralph Gleason. "You get bruised running up against a cat like that." Nat Cole, who as a boy used to stand in the alley by the Grand Terrace and listen, said, "Earl Hines had a tremendous influence upon my own piano stylings." Another bandleader, Stan Kenton, affirmed that Hines's "ability to swing and his fantastic sense of originality are a constant source of wonderment to me." And Lennie Tristano summed up for the profession when he said, "Hines is great, immense, unique."

In 1958 I was in New York recording a series of albums for British Decca's Felsted label (since reissued in the U.S. by Master Jazz). Yannick Bruynoghe, the Belgian critic and a trustworthy friend, was going to San Francisco and I authorized him to record a session by Hines. The album side that resulted alerted the more discerning critics to the pianist's continuing power and creativity.

Six years later critic Dan Morgenstern and his friend Dave Himmelstein had obtained the use of the Little Theatre in New York to present jazz concerts on Friday and Saturday evenings. They began splendidly with Coleman Hawkins and were looking for another strong name to follow.

"How about Earl Hines?" I asked.

"Will he come?" Morgenstern replied.

"I can call him."

Hines was on the point of quitting the music business. His second venture in club ownership, this time with "international" entertainment at Music Crossroads in Oakland's Jack London Square, had not proved financially successful, and he was tired of the Dixieland context he had endured in San Francisco while his two daughters were growing up. He was doubtful now about the advisability of coming to New York. The resources of the two entrepreneurs were limited, and the money they could offer not particularly tempting.

"It could lead to other things," I suggested.

"Well, I don't know . . ."

"I think it's worth trying, and it's only a couple of days."

"I've never played a concert by myself."

"It's a small, intimate theatre. *You* won't need to worry."

The three concerts Hines gave were a remarkable success and could scarcely have been better timed, for New York's jazz critics were unanimous in their praise. A live recording from the first concert on Focus, and subsequent albums on Victor and Columbia, led to renewed interest in him. Even more influential was a lengthy profile in *The New Yorker* by Whitney Balliett. Suddenly Hines found himself in demand again. Since that time he has worked steadily, usually with a quartet, both here and abroad.

When this new phase began, his quartet included Budd Johnson, the great saxophonist and arranger, who had contributed so much to his earlier big bands and who had also played briefly at the Little Theatre concerts. The group's musical policy emphasized jazz, but the number of clubs where an unadulterated jazz program could be played continually diminished, and eventually the addition of a girl singer was unavoidable. After Budd Johnson left in 1969 Hines employed a number of capable musicians (although none of Johnson's stature), and with the acquisition of Marva Josie, an effective and good-looking vocalist, he was able to present a miniature show that echoed his experience at the Grand Terrace and in theatres.

Despite the acclamation received for solo appearances in the U.S., Europe and South America, he continues to insist that he thinks of himself as a band pianist, not a soloist. Nevertheless, he very well knows what he is capable of and always seems to have reserves to draw upon to fit the occasion, as he twice showed in the East Room of the White House, once when he played at Duke Ellington's seventieth birthday party there, and again in his own seventieth year when he performed following a state dinner for President Giscard d'Estaing of France.

During the last twelve years I have been considerably involved in the business side of Hines's career, becoming in effect an amateur equivalent of what is known in the trade as a "manager." After unsatisfactory experiences following exclusive contracts with two different agencies he had regained his independence, but while he was touring abroad, or working on the other side of the continent, future bookings had to be correlated, and ultimately this responsibility became mine. Thus I was introduced to the business conditions prevailing in jazz, conditions which are exacting, often to a point of inadmissibility.

Hines is a realist who recognizes the need for a flexible attitude. He is prepared to bend, but not to crawl. Sometimes, however, as Charlie Carpenter points out, "Earl will tell it like it is when he ought to duck." It is not just a matter of pride or ego when he rebels; after fifty years as a professional he believes that artists are entitled to a just salary and fair working conditions.

He devotes whatever time is necessary to press, radio and television interviews and will go out of his way to appear at schools, particularly in poor neighborhoods; but televised baseball, football and boxing have high priority, too. Sport and physical fitness are, in fact, extremely important to him, and he has a number of very beneficial ways of exercising hands and fingers.

In the last twelve years he has been recorded as extensively—in terms of playing time and titles—as during the whole of the four previous decades. His genius as an improviser is heard at its best in the record studio. When recording alone, the vast majority of his performances are made in one "take." If a second is done, it is usually to try an entirely different approach or tempo, not merely to seek a more precise, polished (and mechanical) interpretation of the original.

He taped most of his autobiography unassisted in his Oakland home. The two decades when he led a big band (1928–48) were unusually rich in incident, and in some cases the sequence of events may be clarified by reference to the chronology at the back.

I wish to express my gratitude to all the musicians interviewed for their generous cooperation, and particularly to Lois Deppe and George Dixon, who submitted so patiently to innumerable questions. I owe special thanks to Louis Vaes, who did not hesitate to drive from Antwerp to Soest in Holland in order to interview Wallace Bishop on my behalf. I was fortunate in being able to confirm the accuracy of many details with my wife, who was in Chicago during the '30s. She is also responsible for the interviews with Irene Kitchings, Streamline Ewing, Freddy and Irving Goodman. And I am again indebted to Mrs. W. J. Boone for her unfailing care in transcribing and typing taped interviews.

STANLEY DANCE

Rowayton, Connecticut, 1976.

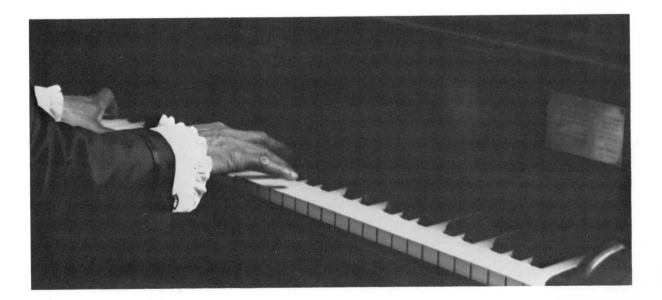

Earl Hines

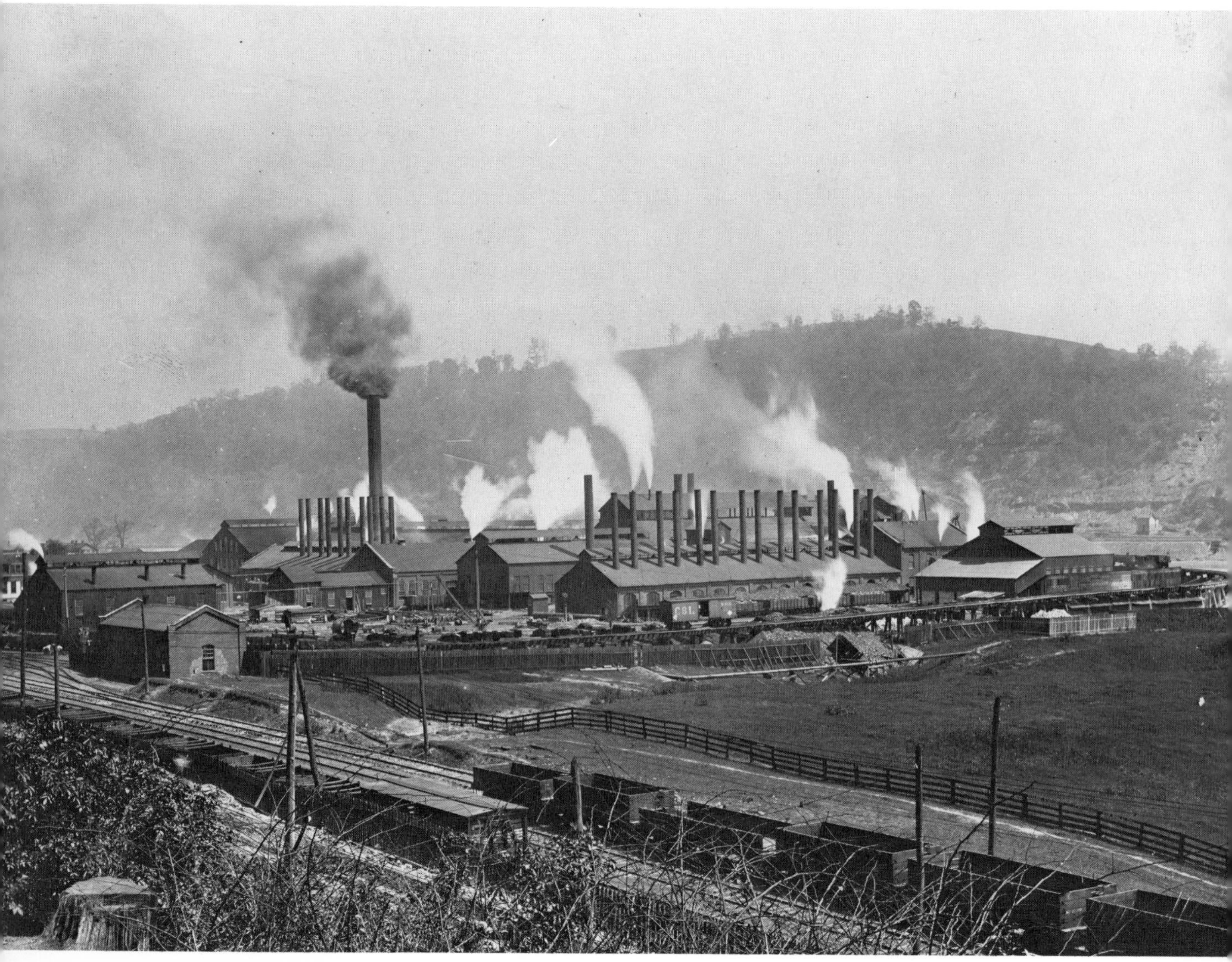

PIANO, BANDLEADER AND SINGER

A BIRD OUT OF A CAGE

I was born on 28 December 1905, in Duquesne, Pennsylvania, a suburb of Pittsburgh. Nowadays, I understand, it's just called a part of Greater Pittsburgh, but when I was a kid it was twelve miles out from the city. McKeesport, where the airport is now, was just a mile away, across the bridge.

We lived at the extreme end of the town on Grant Avenue, about fifty feet from the town line, in a twelve-room house—my dad, my stepmother, my grandfather and grandmother, my two cousins and their parents, and an uncle who wasn't married. My mother died when I was three, and I was really raised by my stepmother, who did a great job. Later on, I had a half sister and a half brother.

We had two large dogs, an English bulldog that used to roam the front yard, and a great big collie that used to roam the back and keep the other animals in their proper places. We had two cows back there, so you can imagine how big this backyard was. It was like a miniature farm because they had chickens and hogs on one side and a garden on the other where they grew all kinds of vegetables. We needed to buy very little so far as food was concerned, because we raised nearly everything we ate. I often saw the meat that was butchered and how they did it. At first, when I was a child, it kind of made me sick, but after seeing it year after year I began to get used to it. Sometimes

the hogs were shot in the middle of the head with a rifle, and sometimes they were hit with the blunt end of an axe. My two girl cousins used to sit out there with me and watch.

Duquesne is a rather hilly place and we lived at the top of a hill. Our school was at the bottom of Grant Avenue, about twenty-five blocks away. It was quite a distance, for they were some large blocks; but rain or snow, it didn't make any difference, and oftentimes I was frozen or soaked on my way down to school. But we didn't mind, because we were healthy and full of vitality and always ready to eat a big dinner in the evening. We carried a little lunch to school, because it was too far for us to walk home and back in the middle of the day.

We used to have to pass a Catholic school about eight blocks from my home, and there wasn't a day passed that we didn't have some sort of an entanglement and fighting. It wasn't racial fighting, just the Protestant children, white or colored, fighting the Catholic children. In the wintertime we had snowball fights, and in the summer we threw sandbags at one another. We also had fist fights. Everybody felt like they were all good friends, and it was a funny thing how after we'd had our fight we would help each other up!

There were only twelve colored families in Duquesne, out of a population of about nineteen thousand. Everyone there seemed to have the same feeling about raising children. They were all trying to see that everyone knew right from wrong, and anyone's child, white or colored, would be chastised by any adult who saw them getting out of line. If you told your parents about it, you got another whipping, because there was this understood agreement among all the families.

I remember once I was filling paper bags with sand when a fellow came riding along on a motorcycle. I threw a sandbag and it hit him in the forehead. Later, I realized what damage it could have caused. He stopped his motor-cycle and gave me a good whipping. I was afraid to tell my dad, but when this gentleman came home from work he told him, and I got another whipping. So we were always on our P's and Q's, even when we were playing. "There's your mother over there," I might say, "so we'd better be careful." Or one of my friends would say, "Look, Earl, that's your fa-ther. We got to watch out for him." We weren't saints, of course, but we mostly stayed on the right path. We did a lot of little things when nobody was around, but we respected the parents and never had any bitterness in our hearts in regard to each other. We didn't know anything about a racial situation, be-cause it was an understanding neighborhood and the kids all lived and played and had a ball together. When I look back now, it makes me feel good to think that I had an opportu-nity to see real people that understood people as people, who helped with your education and bringing you up, who helped you to go out in the world and protect yourself and also to know how to help others.

One time when I was nine, a friend and I went into an undertaker's to watch him doing embalming. He left the room to get some cuff-links to put in the shirt of the corpse he was dressing. An arm the undertaker had left rest-ing on the corpse's stomach suddenly slid off, and a lot of air escaped from the body in a loud "Aaah!" We were so scared, and as we rushed out of the parlor in terror we knocked over some expensive caskets. The undertaker was a friend of my father's, and when he com-

The only existing photograph of Earl Hines's mother.

plained about the damage done I was questioned. When I told my dad what happened, he said, "Well, I guess I would have been out of there even faster than you were!"

The school picnics in the summer were a lot of fun, and they all called on Dad and his band to play. He played the cornet, which is a smaller instrument than the trumpet they have today, but it had a larger tone. My uncle on my mother's side played all the brass instruments, and he was a terrific musician. My auntie, also on my mother's side, was a light opera singer, and my stepmother played the organ, so I heard music night and day.

My father had about fourteen men in his band, the Eureka Brass Band, and we would go out to the picnics in Kennywood Park in four or five streetcars. They'd have them all lined up, and my dad and his band would sit in the first car, with as many children as could possibly get around them, and they would play music all the way out to the park with the other streetcars following. They were summer cars, with the running board along the side, but no windows. All they had in case it rained was something similar to the Venetian blinds we have today. You could still get a bit wet through them if it rained hard.

The second car would usually be full of children, and the parents and their baskets would be in the others. When we got to the park the fathers would help the mothers off and everybody would head for the luncheon area where the tables were all lined up. They'd open up the baskets and spread out all the food, and you were welcome to eat anyone's, anything you saw that you wanted. What a meal that was! Everybody had to lie down for about an hour afterwards, because nobody could move! Then the mothers would start gossiping about what happened in the past, and how times had changed, about how the children were growing up, and what have you. We'd begin running about to find the places where we thought we could have the most fun for the least money. We'd have a few tickets, and there'd be some rides, like a merry-go-round and a roller coaster. Then we'd have to decide whether to play horseshoes or to get ready for

the baseball games. All the people from the different sections, like McKeesport, Braddock, Homestead and Duquesne, joined in this picnic, and each of them had a team, so this was one of the day's highlights. After the game, my dad's band played, and this gave the baseball players a chance to rest.

In the evening, when everybody got through with their supper, which was really a very big dinner, the mothers would put on their dancing clothes and get ready for the dance that usually started at 8 P.M. The children were boxed off on one side of the hall upstairs with matrons to watch us until the dance was over. My interest was watching the band, and I used to sit up there the whole time looking at the different musicians and listening to what they were playing. Sometimes I'd look at the formation on the floor, all going in one direction. It was usually rather warm, and the men showed their respect for the ladies by using handkerchiefs, so that if their hands got sweaty they didn't soil the ladies' dresses. The ladies had respect for themselves, and this naturally made the men toe the mark.

You very seldom saw a fight at the picnic, and if you did it was just a plain fist fight; and after it was over they'd get up, drink beer, and laugh it off. Nearly everybody went away happy and full of beer, although there were some stronger drinks too. You'd see some men being picked up and helped along so that they didn't miss the streetcars when the dance was over. To us youngsters, the beauty part of the whole evening was seeing how the people used to dance. We always wanted to dance, and I wanted to play music.

It seems to me now that people then tried to see how much fun they could have, and they tried to make it a great evening for *everyone*. Today I think there is a more destructive and envious feeling at affairs like baseball games and dances. There's animosity today because people living next to them are in a better position, have a better home or clothes. They're envious if they have a better car, and this forms a bit of malice that is very, very bad! It makes me say, "Well, I'm happy to

have been born in those days when I really
knew what living was."

The big horses they used to have to pull the
beer trucks impressed me very much as a kid.
They were giant animals and I loved to watch
them going up the street. When automobiles
came in, we could just never believe that you
could ride around without a horse attached.
We'd heard about them, of course, but they
hadn't come to a little town like Duquesne.
Then the Rev. Woods, the minister of our
Jerusalem Baptist church, had four or five automobiles brought out to his church one afternoon and said we were going to take a trip
around the world. It was twenty-five cents for
the kids and fifty cents for the grownups. They
took us from one end of the town to the other,
and back to the church. That was the first ride
I had in an automobile. It was very big and I
think it was a Pierce-Arrow. It had right-hand
drive, a sort of convertible top with leather
straps to hold it down, and to us, of course, it
looked as amazing as an airplane does to the
average person today.

At home, I used to watch my stepmother
playing the organ. She'd have her music set
up, and I'd imitate her by putting paper on a
chair and playing from the chair. I still remember my dad saying to her, "Do you think
he might like music?" The next thing I knew,
there was a piano moved into the house. My
first teacher was Emma D. Young, and she
was very learned as an instructor, but liking
music as much as I did I couldn't wait for her
to come. I kept turning the pages and sometimes I'd be two or three lessons in front when
she came. It got to the place where she told
my parents there was nothing more she could
teach me because I'd gone past her grades. So
she recommended a German teacher, a very
strict fellow whose name was Von Holz. He
didn't want me to play baseball. After I was
cracked on the knuckles a couple of times and
hit on the end of the finger, I saw why he
tried to stop me from playing baseball. He got
upset and told my parents, "I don't want your
money; I just want results." That is what he
got, because I loved music and studied hard.

While I was studying, I was taken to see
several of the shows that traveled from coast
to coast, playing theatres in big cities. I had a
good ear and a good memory, and I'd be playing songs from these shows months before
song copies came out. That astonished a lot of
people, and they'd ask where I heard these
numbers, and I'd tell them at the theatre
where my parents had taken me.

My cousin, Pat Patterson, and a friend of
his across the street realized that I could really
play the piano and play by ear. My teacher
had no idea I was playing show tunes. He
thought I was continuously studying out of his
exercise books, but on the side I was playing
the songs of the day. To my cousin and his
friend, this was like having a Victrola, or
what a record player is to the average youngster today. When he was going out and having his fun with the young ladies, he'd carry
me along as a musician. In fact, I was in
charge of the entertaining! Although I didn't
know what was happening, I thought my
cousin liked me well enough to take me along
with him. But everywhere we went, there was
always a piano of some kind. They'd ask me to
play, and they'd bring me a girl, and other
girls would come and stand around me. They
were girl friends of my cousin and his friend,
and much older than I was. My cousin would
say, "In order to keep him playing, just give
him a little kiss and a hug." That is what they
did, and I'd play all night, not knowing what it
was all about until a few years later.

Now I come to the time when World War I
broke out. Pittsburgh, Pennsylvania, was the
steel centre and the mills were very busy.
They were in the section between the
Monongahela and the Allegheny rivers, and so
much steel was needed that there wasn't
enough manpower. My father was a foreman
on the coal docks, and he was in charge of the
large cranes that took the coal from the trucks
and loaded it on the barges to go down the
river, the Allegheny and the Monongahela,
and from there to the Mississippi and different
parts of the country. Because of the need for
more manpower, we began to get any number
of people from the South, Negroes who migrated to all sections of Pittsburgh in order to

go into the mills. A lot of them were probably people who were lying around not doing anything, and naturally they wanted to get out to see the different territories. A lot of them were good people who were looking for a new place to live and wanted money. But along with them were a lot of roustabouts who had no good intentions at all, and when they came north and found a freedom they hadn't had, they began to get excited. Although there were not the same restrictions they knew in the South, there were people in the North ready to take advantage of their illiteracy.

There was a family with a sort of confectionery store where they sold sandwiches and what they called Jamaica Gin. These new Negroes used to come in there, and the owner had his daughter in the store. She would be friendly with these young men who were working in the mills, and not having any experience like it before they just spent their money right and left in that store, thinking they would get somewhere with the girl. The owner was making a whole lot of money off them, and then he went to the people in

charge of the payrolls at the mills and arranged for these fellows to tab whatever they wanted. He'd have them sign the slips and then he'd take them to the pay officer, so he never had to worry about getting the money from the men. And they signed many a slip showing off before this girl, trying to get to first base with her!

These people from the South changed the whole picture of life in Duquesne. We didn't know what it was to lock doors before they came. You could walk around all hours of the night and nobody bothered you. If one of the fathers got intoxicated on payday, the police would come along, pick him up, take him home and say, "Here's your man! Put him in the house and let him get some sleep." Nobody would have bothered him about money.

The people who had been living around Pittsburgh really didn't know how to cope with the situation that the migration brought. Somebody who represented the mills and this big industry ought to have seen that the Negroes from the South were briefed before they left home, so that they knew about the dif-

School days: Earl Hines at extreme left of second row.

ferent conditions in the North. If they'd known about the laws, rules and regulations they had to abide by, I don't think we would have had the trouble this sudden change brought, but no one took any interest in anything like that. Everybody was interested in one thing, and that was the American dollar. I don't mean that nice families didn't come up from the South, but for most of the people it was a complete change, getting out from under the hammer. Why, they were like a bird out of a cage!

There was a Mrs. Jennings who had a boarding house on the opposite side of the street. She had married a second time and her son's name was Phil Windear, and he was the friend of my cousin that I mentioned. My father used to talk to the fellows who lived in this boarding house, and he tried to get them interested in the little athletic club he had started with the idea of keeping youngsters together. He tried to arrange a baseball team out of the group there, but he was careful not to go into Mrs. Jennings's place because then the mill people would have thought he was infringing and trying to take men away from them. The mills had already made contact with boarding houses like this and had made arrangements about expenses and money that was borrowed. They had a record of everything, and it became impossible for my dad to put his progressive ideas into practice. He and some of the elders thought there should have been schools to train some of these new men for important jobs in the mill, and they wanted to get them to go to church and the picnics.

Instead, there were stores like the one I've talked about, and others opened up where things went on after hours that they tried to keep the police from knowing about. Girls had been accustomed to being out at night, walking around and crossing the bridges we had there, and, of course, they were attacked. So the police were busy trying to straighten out things like that.

We moved from Grant Avenue down across the tracks to Fourth Street. The reason for that was that segregation had gotten so strong they were pushing most of the colored families across the tracks. It happened practically all over the country. They called the railroad the stem, and most of the colored people were across the tracks. In Pittsburgh, there were many foreign people living there, too. Some were here without the government knowing, and they were not naturalized citizens. They had to learn to speak English, but they moved in across the tracks where there wouldn't be much searching for them. There were Hungarians and Austrians there, and I used to go to their houses selling newspapers when I was ten or eleven. The odor of the type of food they cooked, and the smell in their houses, was too much for me, and I used to get a long stogie, light it, and have that in front of me when I went in. It helped an awful lot!

At the time, I didn't realize what it was all about, and even now I don't know if I can explain the changing relationship between whites and the blacks properly. My father built this little club house behind our house, and all the kids who used it would gang together, until the older boys said we were going to have two organizations, the Inner Circle and the Outer Circle. The boys in the Inner Circle were supposed to be the executives, and the others were just members. Although the club house was built by my dad and was in our backyard, and although I had been on the ground floor since the thing started, I found I wasn't going to be in the Inner Circle! At first they said I'd have to work up to it, and then they came out with the fact that it was just because I was "a different complexion"! It started there.

Then there was a fellow named Kirk we had any number of fights with going to and from school. One day I asked him, "Why do you constantly pick fights with Isaiah Hughes and myself?" Now Isaiah and I were very good athletes in school, and Kirk and another boy were the only two who could challenge us. I could really run at that time, and he was envious because we had a track in our gymnasium. Well, he told me his parents had only recently realized that he had to quit running around with me because I was not on a par with him or any of the white race! He told me this to my face. "What are you talking about?" I said. "We never had any talk about this white race thing before." Then he told me there had been many discussions about it in his home. Now these people never thought anything about this until the migration planted the poisonous seed. This boy Kirk naturally grew up with all this in his mind, and there was no way I could change it. I'm quite sure my parents didn't know this was brewing and were just as puzzled as I was. Some of the other boys met the same thing, and Isaiah said, "Man, we don't need him. We can outrun anybody." But then when I was on the football team at high school I met it in a different form. We'd be in some other city, and we'd go in a restaurant, and the people would say, "We'll wait on the rest of them, but we can't wait on this boy." Then the whole team would get up and go out.

During this time, I was learning to be a barber. I started with a fellow named Giles as a shoeshine boy. There was no other barber for blocks, so all the foreigners went to him, and he was very good, just as good at cutting white hair as black hair. He had a rough time keeping another barber there, however, especially at weekends, because it was wild territory. The men were making so much money at the mills and there was a lot of heavy drinking, and good barbers didn't want to get mixed up with these characters. So Giles decided to make a barber out of his shoeshine boy.

"Earl, would you like to be a barber?"

"Yes," I said, not knowing what I was getting into. He knew I would be there all the time, since it was my hometown, not like other barbers he had had who came from other cities.

He started me with a razor on the back of my hand, and I finally got to the stage where it was a matter of wrist movements and clippers at the same time. One day a fellow came in who was in an awful hurry and had to have a shave. He took a chance and I shaved him very good. I was the kind of guy who, if I went into something, went in for all it was worth. And I had watched Giles and learned

how to cut white hair as well as Negro hair, and I shaved some of those Hungarians and Austrians. They had very, very tough beards, because, like the Negroes, they worked at the furnaces, which burned their skin. You had to have a terrific razor to give those guys a real clean shave. Anyway, I got to be a very good barber, and I had a chair of my own and was making quite a bit of money.

During this time, Lois Deppe came to see me and wanted to know if I'd do some gigs. There was a fellow named Arthur Rideout up the river in, I think, Monongahela City. He had a barbershop, but he was a pianist and had a little group that used to go around playing dances. Lois used to sing with him. Now at that time I didn't know anything about what they called the "blue vein society." There were a lot of people around there who were very fair—Negroes mixed up with Caucasians—and this fellow used to use all fair-looking people. Lois was all right so far as complexion was concerned, and Rideout asked him about me. Lois told him he didn't think I could play their dance program, but then Rideout said, "I understand he barbers." I went up there with all intentions of playing in the group, but I found I had to stay in Rideout's barbershop while he played the gig! That was a new twist for me, but nevertheless I got nice money and transportation back.

While I was working in that barbershop during the war, there was a terrible influenza epidemic in our section of Pennsylvania, and they made me wear a bag with garlic in it on a string around my neck. It had a terrible smell to it, and it was supposed to keep the 'flu away. Although I was working among all kinds of people doing different things, I never got the 'flu, so it must have had some effect.

During that time, too, I remember going down to the station when trainloads of black soldiers who had been drafted were leaving. The whistles would be blowing from the boats on the river and the steel mills, and the band would be playing and marching. Everybody was crying and kissing their loved ones. The following day the same thing would go on when the white soldiers left. This happened several times until they got their quota from our part of the state. My dad was drafted, but the war was over before they got to him.

When the first soldiers came home on leave, very sharp in their uniforms and with their shoes shining, they were the most popular guys in the town. But segregation still existed, and there were plenty of restaurants where the colored soldiers couldn't go. It was like the Deep South, and there was no argument because there was no effective action taking place. I do know that there were white businessmen who said, even then, that if there was a law to protect them they didn't see anything against a Negro eating or staying in their places. People who were born in Pittsburgh, like my family, had to have the reason for things that were being done then explained to them. As for our family doctor, Dr. Martin, although he never had much to say, there was no such thing as segregation in his heart, and he was white.

After I was doing well as a barber, my dad decided he would open a barbershop of his own, because Giles was having marital troubles, and sometimes he was at his place and sometimes he wasn't. I did all right for a time in my dad's place, but I was still only a kid, and I was only there half the time. He would come by and find me gone and lock the shop up. Finally, he gave up on that and opened a little restaurant. We used to catch a lot of people coming from the mills at all hours of the night, but our biggest trouble was giving credit. And then, of course, I was probably eating all the profits! Everybody would give me a story, and I'd be giving credit, making one fellow a sandwich and another an omelette. "Yeah, let 'em have it," I'd say. So we closed that up, too. I ended up in a tailor shop and learned how to clean and press. They were washing clothes and hanging them up at the back of the shop. The steam press came in later, but then we used a gas iron. The guy that owned this shop was colored, but I noticed that a lot of white people were very friendly and thought the world of him. These were people, too, in better positions, with bigger goals in mind. That was when I first no-

ticed that it was illiterate people with little education that did more discriminating among themselves.

The barbershop and the restaurant were not successful, but my dad's little athletic club was. It's one of the reasons I have the health and strength I have today. Thank goodness for my father's forethought. Dr. Martin, who looked after us, gave us a bit of advice I've been using all my life. He said if you keep your stomach in good condition you'll very seldom get sick, and that most sickness comes from the stomach. I know we've been very fortunate, and that there hasn't been anyone sick in our family in I don't know when. My children had the kind of illnesses all children have, but after that no sickness at all.

Of course, exercise is very important, too, and I started exercising as a child. Any animal when it first gets up will stretch. People should do likewise. Stretch, even if you're not vigorous enough to exercise for a half-hour. Ten minutes can mean a lot in getting your blood circulating.

I was growing up, around ten or eleven, when I began to play the organ in the Baptist church I belonged to. Because of my studies with the German teacher, who had had me go through Czerny and big books of composers like Chopin, I didn't find church music very hard, although I had a problem reaching the pedals at first. But the church people really took advantage of me! I played for Sunday School, for the 11 o'clock service and the night service. Oftentimes we had a 3 o'clock service for visiting ministers; and there was also a young people's program called the D.Y.P.U. I did all these for three dollars a month, and some people thought they were paying me too much, especially if I was away for just one performance. On Sundays, parents used to go to the parks with their kids, and I wanted to go too.

My dad sympathized with me, and I had several arguments with the people in charge at the church. As I grew older, I began to make my own decisions, and I found out about the concert field in other towns in the area. Homestead was, I'd say, about eight miles from Duquesne. Braddock was seven miles across the river, and McKeesport was just a mile away. Von Holz had all this territory, and when he gave concerts I began to travel. All I would get was a pat on the head, a box of handkerchiefs, and maybe "The boy's a genius." One of those things. But I loved the piano, and there was competition. There was a very talented girl from Homestead, and we used to compete every year. I was fortunate to come out on top. I remember one year I was playing at a concert and my music teacher was turning the pages that I was supposed to have memorized. I got down to about the twenty-fifth page and I didn't know where I was, so I put together some of my own ideas until I caught up with the music again. The teacher noticed it and afterwards he said, "You gave a wonderful performance, although all the time I've been playing and teaching that particular piece I've never heard that passage you put in there of fourteen bars." All I could do was laugh, but he was quite impressed because I had been able to think up the passage that I inserted.

When I began to win prizes and get publicity in the paper, other families became envious of my mother and father, and they made their children play piano, which was a very big mistake. I think they should have let them choose what they wanted to do. One particular family I remember, the Jordan family, had two boys and a girl, and the girl had a marvelous voice. She was terrific and could really sing, but the father insisted that she play piano. They had to come home, do the chores, do their homework, and then go to the piano. He was very strict about it and they had no opportunity to go out to play. One of the boys, Emmett Jordan, didn't want to play piano at all, and he insisted on playing violin. They finally gave way and got him a violin, and he turned out to be very good on it. Yet the whole of Duquesne wanted to put their children up there as *pianists*. I think that was quite wrong, that parents should watch to see what they are most interested in, and then help them with what they feel they can do.

My two children, for instance, wanted to play piano. I got a piano and a teacher, and they learned for about a year. When they became teen-agers, they began to use the phone quite a bit, and lie around on the floor talking, and what have you. While the teacher was there, they did their lessons, but they wouldn't use the piano until he came back. I told them I didn't want anybody playing half an instrument. "If you don't want to play piano," I said, "you don't have to." I stopped the teacher coming, and the reason I stopped him was because my dad always told me, "If you're going to be a thief, be a good one. You get as much time for ten dollars as for a thousand." I think they realized what I meant a year or two later, and they did go and pick at the piano now and then, but they both chose other fields. My older daughter is in drama, and the younger is taking ballet.

Of course, as I went around at home I discovered people studying other instruments. A boy in Homestead, Harry Williams, was learning to be a drummer, and a distant cousin had a big, six-string guitar. It was the first time I'd seen this instrument, and I thought it was great. I still didn't know anything about jazz. All I knew was finding these popular songs, and playing them, and getting what I could out of them. I still had what you might call a classical type of feeling, and it wasn't until I started going to theatres with my parents and relatives that I began to realize these numbers had soul in them, and then I tried to get as much feeling out of them as I possibly could.

The first of these numbers I really remember playing was *I'll See You in C-U-B-A*, and it was brought to me by Lois Deppe, the man who started me in show business. He happened to be visiting my relatives in East Liberty. He had this little song under his arm, and he gave it to me. I ran through it so fast it excited him, and he never forgot me. The next numbers I learned were *Squeeze Me* and *Panama*.

I was staying with my auntie, Sadie Phillips, and going to Schenley High School then. As I said before, she was in light opera, and she was acquainted with many of the greats of the day, like Eubie Blake and Noble Sissle.

Luckey Roberts, that great pianist, was another friend of hers, and they'd come out to her house when they were playing in Pittsburgh. She would keep them waiting so that I could hear them play. I was exposed to a whole lot of talent, but I still didn't realize what jazz was.

This Phil Windear who lived across the street from us was a sort of playboy. He and Pat, my oldest cousin, were both working by now, and their biggest thrill was to drive into Pittsburgh to a nightclub. It was a wild town at that time, especially on Wylie Avenue. I was going on fifteen and was tall and lanky, so one night they put some long pants and a big old diamond ring on me and took me into Pittsburgh in a Case automobile they had. They were showing me the big time because of when I used to play for them and their girls all night long. We were sitting in a restaurant, eating big steaks like I'd never had before, and I was reacting to the glamour of the waitresses, when I heard this music upstairs. It had a beat and a rhythm to it that I'd never heard before, and everybody seemed to be enjoying themselves. "Oh," I said, "if only I could just get upstairs and see what they're doing—see what kind of music that is!" A few weeks later, we came back into town and they slipped me upstairs. Of course, the laws weren't too strict. All people in Pittsburgh wanted to know then was who was spending the money! Well, Phil Windear had the money, and he was sort of in charge, so they told him he could take me up since I had long pants on, but to crowd me in so I wouldn't be seen.

A little humpback sort of fellow they called Toadlow * was playing. He had very small hands and what he was playing was *Squeeze Me*. It had another title to it then, which I won't mention here, but this was the first time I heard it. There were girls, too, going from one table to another, singing and picking up money. There were no microphones and they and the men singers all used megaphones. Toadlow would play just whenever *he* wanted to, but I don't think he was too popular, and most of the money was made from tips the girls picked up. After going there a couple of times, I became very interested in that sort of life.

One day my little drummer, Harry Williams, and I were walking down Wylie Avenue. We had just left Homestead, where he lived. Although I was only a youngster, I liked to be around and listen to the guys' conversation and watch the girls on Wylie Street. Show-business girls were like the stage lights in the theatre. They glittered and excited me. So now we ran into Lois Deppe.

"What're you fellows doing?" he asked.

"Just walking around."

"Would you like to have a job?"

I told him we were too young, but we found out he was being accompanied by a pianist who played by ear. He could only play in strange keys like B natural, A natural and E natural, and Lois sang in F and E flat and C. Lois had also picked up a C-melody saxophone, and he thought if he got somebody who could play he would buy all the late compositions and learn them early, rather than having to struggle to teach them to someone when he didn't know them himself. He made me an offer, but we just laughed, and Harry and I went along back to our respective homes in Homestead and Duquesne.

Lois Deppe approached my father about my coming to play with him, and he also spoke to my auntie about it, and between them it was agreed. I went to work with Lois in the Leader House on Wylie Avenue, and that's where I really started to gain experience. I witnessed so many things there that were advantageous to me later. Lois would be playing his C-melody sax—he could play piano parts without transposing on that—and after a time we had Harry Williams playing the drums.

---

* Everyone who remembers this pianist seems to have a different way of spelling his nickname, but there is reason to support Don Redman's reference to him as "Toodle-oo" Johnson. "Toodle-oo" was commonly used after World War I as a substitute for "goodbye," and Duke Ellington supposed it to be derived from *"tout à l'heure."*

Opposite: Earl Hines at the Leader House.

Lois would pick up the megaphone and sing out the window, the way they used to do for publicity on Wylie Avenue. There was another club down the street, Collins Inn, where a high tenor named Bob Cole used to do the same thing. He and Lois tried to outdo one another, and this was the way we drew people in. After the people came, the girls would go around the tables and pick up money.

We lived in this Leader House and had our meals there, two meals a day. I remember that I really went for their apple dumplings. I was getting fifteen dollars a week, and I began to glamorize a bit and smoke cigars, although that had really begun when us kids used to smoke corn silk in Duquesne. We did very good business, because Lois Deppe got all the latest tunes and we played them right away. The other clubs couldn't keep up with us, for they had musicians who only played by ear.

We decided to augment the group with Emmett Jordan, the fellow whose parents had wanted him to play piano. By now he was playing very good violin. Suddenly, Pittsburgh became a place where all the big bands and big shows came, and a fellow named Vance Dixon came through. He was the first I ever saw who could play two clarinets at one time, one at each side of his jaws, his left hand playing one clarinet, his right the other. He was rather exciting and the people thought this was the greatest thing they had ever seen. He wanted to settle in Pittsburgh, so we hired him and added him to the organization.

We stayed at the Leader House about two years, and while we were there I ran into a pianist named Jim Fellman. This was before we augmented. I'd go around with him after we finished at night, and there were a lot of little houses where the piano players used to make nice money. Bob Cole, the singer down the street, would also go out at night to these houses, where the landladies had him sing beautiful tunes that everybody seemed to like then. But it was Jim Fellman who interested me, and he was one of the finest pianists I had heard up to that time. He had a wonderful left hand. He didn't use his fifth finger, but

stretched his fourth finger to make tenths, and this was the first time I had seen or heard of the tenths. I found out that there was a lot of harmony and rhythm being carried as well as the bass. When he showed me this, my hands were too small and I couldn't do it. I had to eliminate or jump these tenths and play smaller chords, but I was learning, and he showed me how to stretch my fingers so that in time I could make tenths. I used to sit and listen to his playing beautiful soft piano, and I wanted to find out how I could do it. Although I was making only fifteen dollars a week, I made him a proposition. Out of what change I had, I would buy him tobacco or beer, whatever he wanted. He knew I was only getting a small salary, and he was very nice about it: "Oh, just give me some Mail Pouch chewing tobacco and a few bottles of beer, and some afternoon we'll go up and sit down and I'll show you a few things." That's what we did, and that was just one side of my piano playing.

Then a fellow came to town from Detroit, named Johnny Watters. Now he kept stretching the tenths with his *right* hand, and it was the first time I saw that. His hand was so large he was playing the melody with his middle fingers and using his thumb and last finger for the tenths. He played some of the prettiest things I ever heard. He was very fast executing with his right hand, and this was fairly simple to me because of my classical training, but I couldn't make the tenths and use the middle fingers the way he did. I had to go on stretching like he and Jim Fellman were telling me. Johnny was a guy who loved Camel cigarettes, and his beverage was gin. Between the two of them at different afternoons, I spent what little money I had; but by putting their two styles together I think I came up with a style of my own. I also used to listen to Elzy M. Young from Detroit, a piano player whose small hands caused him to play a lot of close-chord harmony. He's living in Buffalo now.

Being in Pittsburgh, I did an awful lot of getting around town. I had no real goal in mind. I just wanted to do like all the other youngsters and enjoy myself the best way I could, even if it put me out of touch with the pianists to some extent. I had got myself one room in a boarding house on Wylie Avenue, a block from Townsend, and I'd got a baby grand in it. It was a beautiful instrument and I used to get up in the morning and play it. You can imagine how pretty a grand could sound early in the morning, and I would play no matter what was going on outside. I never noticed that everything seemed to stop while I was playing, until I came down the stairs one day and was met by the landlady.

"Why did you quit?" she asked. "Everybody was listening to you."

"I didn't notice I was causing a commotion," I said.

"That wasn't a commotion," she said. "That was a pleasure!"

That and running around on the streets was the way I relaxed.

We used to meet at the Leader House for breakfast, and by now I had come in contact with people from all walks of life, because gamblers and sporting women were always around when I was playing at that club. One of the things I loved to do was play pool, and when you're laying over a pool table your profession is forgotten—so far as piano playing is concerned. They only allowed boys of my age to use the poolroom in the morning, to perfect our strokes and concentration, but I used to hang out there every day until I began to become something of a pro. The real pros and gamblers taught us how to make an easy living when they found out that we were perfectionists, too. They used to wait for strangers to come to town, or for some of the people who worked in the mills and were around in the morning after their pay night. The gamblers would bring them in, and it was our duty to get them in a game. While we were playing, we'd look around and say, "Would you like to play a game?" Naturally, they thought we're just youngsters who don't know too much about pool, and when we finally played we would almost win, and then just lose. Sometimes we would win by just one point, and this later was known as "lemon" pool. The gamblers would be betting on the side as one

game led to another, but when the stranger figured he had us trapped and that there was good money to be made, the betting began to get rather high. So then we would win all the games, and the gamblers would give us a percentage of the winnings afterwards.

Bojangles Robinson used to come to that poolroom when he was appearing at the theatre. He'd bring his valet, a special stick, a scorekeeper, and I don't know what else. There were any number of pool sharks around that laid and waited for him, because they knew he had money. He'd play for as much as a thousand dollars a game, and everybody had to be quiet then. As well as he knew me, he didn't want to have to say anything to *anybody* when he was shooting pool. There had to be complete silence.

I guess I had a wild streak in me, and meeting people like the poolroom gamblers brought it out. The territory I roamed was all within ten blocks of Wylie Avenue, north, south, east and west. Like the other boys, I indulged in some of the things we constantly heard these characters talking about. Because of the men working in the mills, there were any number of nice-looking, attractive girls about—streetwalkers. I was young, wild and crazy, and I got tied up with one of these little girls who used youngsters like me to keep men away who were demanding money from them. They knew all we wanted was to dress nice, be on the Avenue, and not have to worry about breakfast and dinner! That gave me a little more money to hang out with Jim Fellman and Johnny Watters, too. I almost forgot about classical piano till I went home some mornings, and then I played classics continuously.

All this was happening in the summer, and my auntie didn't know I was doing these things. She didn't know where I was living and she tried to trace me several times, but she couldn't find me. Although I was tall, I was still under age, so if anybody asked for me at my landlady's house they would say they didn't know where I was.

When I went back to Schenley High School in the winter, I concentrated more on the piano, and it seemed I could break off from anything, just as I can now. I would never go down the Avenue in the wintertime. I was really in it for all I could get so far as piano was concerned, and I was so far advanced from watching Fellman and Watters play. They'd never heard of a tenth in the left hand or the right hand at that school. I was doing a lot of things that put me at the head of the class, and they thought I was a kind of genius. Even during school, I would play in some of the clubs at night.

As a kid at home, I used to pick my dad's cornet up. I wanted to play it, but in those days they didn't have the no-pressure system, and I used to put it to my mouth, fill my jaw up with wind, and blow, which some of the guys are still doing. I did that until it hurt me behind the ears, and for that reason I decided I didn't like the cornet. After I learned the piano and got into jazz, the idea came to me to do on the piano what I'd wanted to do on cornet. That went into my style, too, with this guy's left hand and that guy's right hand, until I got to the stage where I began to feel myself. And while we were playing the Leader House, a whole lot of musicians and bands came through Pittsburgh. There was a boy there at one time who played some of the finest trumpet I ever heard in my life. I never before heard a man play an open horn with just a coconut shell and get a velvet tone, almost like a human voice. I just couldn't believe it. It was Joe Smith, and I followed him everywhere in the world he went. He used to go to a lot of these parties with Jim Fellman, and sit in. He was a very handsome boy and the women all went for him, so it was a pleasure for him to go around and play for kicks. If you had money, all right. All you had to do was pay the rent, get the suit pressed, and have enough to eat next day. He didn't have to worry about such things. Those young ladies saw to that! I sat and listened to him whenever I could, and marveled at his style, and wanted to play what he played on trumpet. It gave me a lot of new ideas and it is too bad so few people realize today what a great musician he was. He was in a class by himself,

and nobody else could get his kind of expression out of the horn. We tried to get him to join our little band up at the Leader House, but he was persuaded by other musicians to go out with them and play at these dances, so we lost him. Because we were tied to the club then, we couldn't play the dances, too.

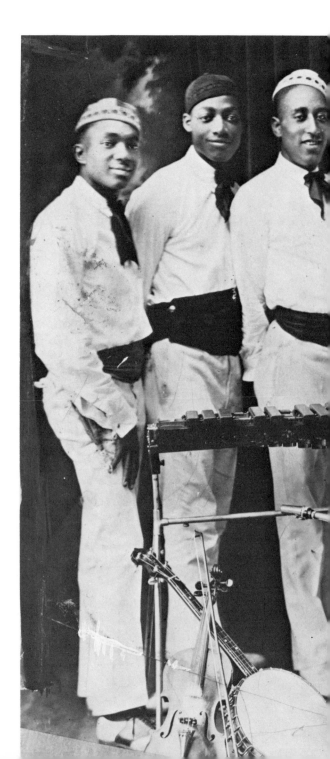

We played a couple of afternoon programs and had such big crowds that Lois Deppe began to think about having a big band, and that was what we all decided to do. We had Emmett Jordan, Vance Dixon, Harry Williams, Lois and myself to start with, and then the Shorter Brothers came through. The younger Shorter played all sorts of instruments, including the violin. The older one played the bass horn and was responsible for putting colored lights in the bell of the instrument as well as in saxophones. We kept adding musicians until we got too big for the Leader House and had to pull out. Lois

Lois Deppe's Symphonian Serenaders. Left to right: Frank Brassfield, trombone; Emmett Jordan, violin; Thornton Brown, trumpet; Harold Birchett, banjo; Earl Hines (the only one to forget his cummerbund); Lois Deppe; Vance Dixon, reeds; Silas Brown, banjo; Harry Williams, drums.

Deppe got around the country himself getting publicity and putting up placards. There was a newspaper for Negroes called the Pittsburgh *Courier* which was powerful even then. Through this paper we got to play any number of engagements, mostly one-nighters. We had competition from another band organized around the same time as ours, the Broadway Syncopators. Don Redman was their leader, and that was the first time I heard of him. Joe Smith joined them and got so good he went to New York and ended up with Noble Sissle and Eubie Blake. Another band I remember coming through there was the Tennessee Ten. Gus Aiken, a very good trumpet player at the time, was with them. He had a little knot at the side of his mouth when he was playing. Darnell Howard, who played with me years later in Chicago, was also in that band.

After we'd played around Pittsburgh, we went into West Virginia and played in Wheeling and a lot of little towns around there. Then we went to Springfield, Ohio, where Lois Deppe's people lived. From there we reached out to Columbus and a lot of Ohio towns. It got so we had three or four months of work, not long engagements, nearly all one-nighters. As long as we had fun and a few dollars for food, we weren't particular how much money we made. We were all young and we drove in automobiles. A fellow called Dan Cane had a big Pierce-Arrow, and we had another car, a great big old Packard. They had running boards then and we had instruments on the side, on the top and everywhere. It was something! Because it was so much easier to carry than a sousaphone, a bass saxophone was used much more in those days.

I remember we slid off the road once in an awful lot of mud. It was raining like mad and everybody was scrambling for their lives. When I got out I found myself next to the cello player.

"My baby is in there," he said, with tears in his eyes.

"What in the world are you talking about?" we asked.

Come to find out he was worrying about the cello. We were lucky we could walk away from there!

After we'd been out for a while, my father thought it was time for me to have an automobile. I badly wanted one, because in those days everybody used to drive up for the evening and park their cars on the main stem, Wylie Avenue. That was before parking meters, but you still might have trouble finding a place. The style then was for silk or *crêpe de chine* shirts, as bright as you could get and with your initials on them. You'd also wear a gold chain with a gold dollar or a watch on the end of it—anything to attract attention. All the glamour boys used to wear Edwin Clapp shoes, and they had a little tag at the back to pull them on like a boot. They'd leave the tag sticking out, and when they crossed their legs everybody could see they were wearing Edwin Clapp shoes. Men used to like gold teeth in those days, and one came around with two diamonds stuck in his front teeth.

Of course, in the morning we'd wear ordinary clothes and do things like the average kid—play pool or baseball. In the late afternoon we would go home, clean up, change our clothes and come on down the Avenue. We'd park our cars, let everybody see them, and stand around. Sometimes the cars would sit there all the evening while we ran up and down the street. This was one of the ways musicians got work, because there was no such thing as a union. Whoever wanted to hire a man would come up the Avenue and say, "Is there a drummer here?" or "Is there a piano player here?" or whatever he wanted. You made your own price and charged whatever you thought you were worth. That's why it paid to be dressed up, because you never knew when somebody was going to call. There were two regular big bands and a couple of others that carried seven or eight pieces. The general public knew that all the other musicians would be hanging around on Wylie Street.

When my dad told me where I was to go to pick up my car, I took Dan Cane with me to drive it, because I didn't know how. You didn't have to have a license to drive then. You merely had to own the car. I took the money out, they gave me the papers, and Dan drove back and parked right in front of the

Leader House. After I finished work there that night, I told everybody, "Come on, take a ride with me!" I had never driven before, but I'd watched Dan shifting gears and I'd asked him a lot of questions. Now I took those people all over Duquesne, up and down those hills. I was lucky and I guess the Man Upstairs was with me. When we got back, they said, "Earl, you did all right. How long have you been driving?" When I told them it was the first time, everybody fell out!

I started to use the car to carry the band. With Lois Deppe, Dan and I driving, we could make it. I remember one time we were coming from Columbus, Ohio, which isn't very far, but it took me two days. I had I don't know how many blowouts, because the tires were worn down till they were like paper. We put rags in what was left of them and coasted along at about ten miles an hour. By the time we got to Pittsburgh, we'd spent all our change on gasoline. People heard about that trip and it was written up in the Pittsburgh press.

There weren't many arrangements made for bands in those days. It was a bit later that stocks became common. Mostly what we played were head arrangements, or something like what would be called Dixieland now. This left a lot of liberty to musicians, and the one who had a fast mind, could think far ahead in regard to the chords coming up, and was good on his instrument—he was used for the "hot" solos. He didn't have to worry about the section. We just had him there to take a solo for two or three choruses. Guys like Joe Smith and Coleman Hawkins were used in that way at first. Then they had first and second men playing in the sections, playing together. When King Oliver had his band, he played the lead trumpet and whoever was playing second trumpet, like Louis Armstrong did, had to sort of harmonize with him, and they would figure out what they call a riff today. They'd go over it again, and the second trumpet would try to put harmony to that, while the trombone worked out a part for himself. This was the beginning of a head arrangement. The reed section would do something similar. If one guy started on C, the second started on A and the third on F. They would begin the passage with one guy a third or fifth lower, and another a third or fifth higher, and that way you'd end up with harmony in it.

Big bands became very popular in those days when *everybody* loved to dance. There were still small groups for the smaller places. I think it was musicians and theatrical people who first began to change the strictly segregated way of life. People in Pittsburgh began to forget about discrimination as we began to play in more places and make friends. At least, it lightened up to a certain extent. People tried to hang out with us, especially those who wanted to find out how and what we were playing. They went to our theatres, too, to get ideas. All this caused more mingling and more understanding in the theatrical and music worlds, so that soon there was less discrimination and envy there than elsewhere. I often think back to how musicians used to stay over at each others' homes if they got caught after dark in the Wylie Avenue clubs. The sporting world didn't catch on so quickly as the theatrical world in cutting out discrimination. Football wasn't so popular then, but people loved baseball. Nobody even dreamed of integrating baseball, because there were such large and wonderful Negro baseball teams with their own regular circuit. They had fine pitchers, wonderful catchers, great batters, and minor leagues, too.

It was different in the theatrical world, where it got so we played in the same houses. People knew Negroes had the feeling and the comedy they wanted, and they loved the blues especially, because they sang them with so much soul. They knew the Negro had a heart, and they knew he was singing about everyday life's toils and turmoils, singing about situations he couldn't help but was just making the best of. Years later, when I was traveling with my big band, we'd go to territories where people were really hungry and barely living, but they were whistling and singing. White people sometimes asked me, "Earl, how can these people sing, dance and tell jokes when they haven't a penny in their pockets? I can't understand how they can be happy." They really couldn't understand what

Membership of Local No. 471
American Federation of Musicians

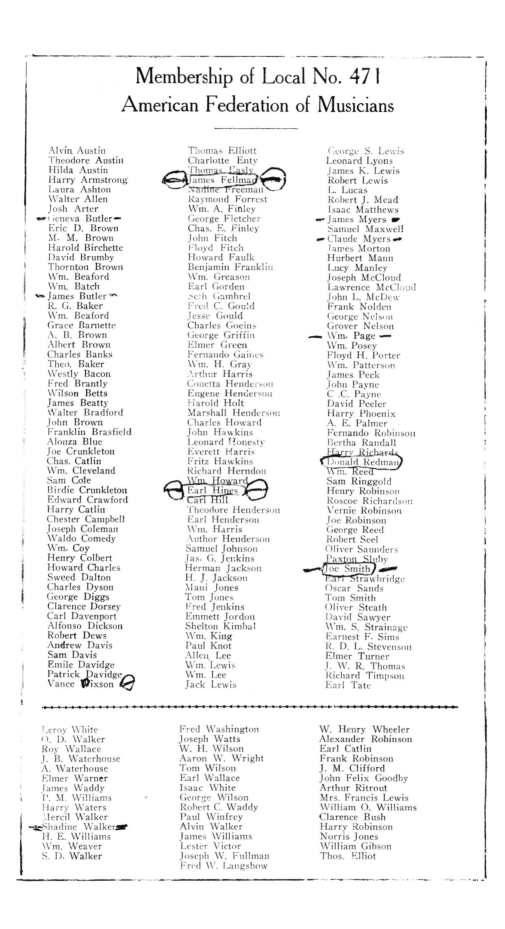

Alvin Austin	Thomas Elliott	George S. Lewis
Theodore Austin	Charlotte Enty	Leonard Lyons
Hilda Austin	Thomas Easly	James K. Lewis
Harry Armstrong	James Fellman	Robert Lewis
Laura Ashton	Nadine Freeman	L. Lucas
Walter Allen	Raymond Forrest	Robert J. Mead
Josh Arter	Wm. A. Finley	Isaac Matthews
Geneva Butler	George Fletcher	James Myers
Eric D. Brown	Chas. E. Finley	Samuel Maxwell
M. M. Brown	John Fitch	Claude Myers
Harold Birchette	Floyd Fitch	James Morton
David Brumby	Howard Faulk	Hurbert Mann
Thornton Brown	Benjamin Franklin	Lucy Manley
Wm. Beaford	Wm. Greason	Joseph McCloud
Wm. Batch	Earl Gorden	Lawrence McCloud
James Butler	Seth Gambrel	John L. McDew
R. G. Baker	Fred C. Gould	Frank Nolden
Wm. Beaford	Jesse Gould	George Nelson
Grace Barnette	Charles Goeins	Grover Nelson
A. B. Brown	George Griffin	Wm. Page
Albert Brown	Elmer Green	Wm. Posey
Charles Banks	Fernando Gaines	Floyd H. Porter
Theo. Baker	Wm. H. Gray	Wm. Patterson
Westly Bacon	Arthur Harris	James Peck
Fred Brantly	Conetta Henderson	John Payne
Wilson Betts	Eugene Henderson	C .C. Payne
James Beatty	Harold Holt	David Peeler
Walter Bradford	Marshall Henderson	Harry Phoenix
John Brown	Charles Howard	A. E. Palmer
Franklin Brasfield	John Hawkins	Fernando Robinson
Alonza Blue	Leonard Honesty	Bertha Randall
Joe Crunkleton	Everett Harris	Harry Richards
Chas. Catlin	Fritz Hawkins	Donald Redman
Wm. Cleveland	Richard Herndon	Wm. Reed
Sam Cole	Wm. Howard	Sam Ringgold
Birdie Crunkleton	Earl Hines	Henry Robinson
Edward Crawford	Carl Hill	Roscoe Richardson
Harry Catlin	Theodore Henderson	Vernie Robinson
Chester Campbell	Earl Henderson	Joe Robinson
Joseph Coleman	Wm. Harris	George Reed
Waldo Comedy	Author Henderson	Robert Seel
Wm. Coy	Samuel Johnson	Oliver Saunders
Henry Colbert	Jas. G. Jenkins	Paxton Sluby
Howard Charles	Herman Jackson	Joe Smith
Sweed Dalton	H. J. Jackson	Earl Strawbridge
Charles Dyson	Mani Jones	Oscar Sands
George Diggs	Tom Jones	Tom Smith
Clarence Dorsey	Fred Jenkins	Oliver Steath
Carl Davenport	Emmett Jordon	David Sawyer
Alfonso Dickson	Shelton Kimbal	Wm. S. Strainage
Robert Dews	Wm. King	Earnest F. Sims
Andrew Davis	Paul Knot	R. D. L. Stevenson
Sam Davis	Allen Lee	Elmer Turner
Emile Davidge	Wm. Lewis	J. W. R. Thomas
Patrick Davidge	Wm. Lee	Richard Timpson
Vance Wixson	Jack Lewis	Earl Tate

Leroy White	Fred Washington	W. Henry Wheeler
O. D. Walker	Joseph Watts	Alexander Robinson
Roy Wallace	W. H. Wilson	Earl Catlin
J. B. Waterhouse	Aaron W. Wright	Frank Robinson
A. Waterhouse	Tom Wilson	J. M. Clifford
Elmer Warner	Earl Wallace	John Felix Goodby
James Waddy	Isaac White	Arthur Ritrout
P. M. Williams	George Wilson	Mrs. Francis Lewis
Harry Waters	Robert C. Waddy	William O. Williams
Mercil Walker	Paul Winfrey	Clarence Bush
Shadine Walker	Alvin Walker	Harry Robinson
H. E. Williams	James Williams	Norris Jones
Wm. Weaver	Lester Victor	William Gibson
S. D. Walker	Joseph W. Fullman	Thos. Elliot
	Fred W. Langshow	

we had lived through. But now education has changed the situation, and the Negro has found out that he is an American, because he was born here, and that he is entitled to a better life and wonderful things that other people have.

It got so with me that I was making so much money I became careless with it. When we were traveling in our cars we used to play for picnics, and after one of them we got sixty-five dollars apiece. I thought I was at the end of the world! Lois Deppe's was the first Negro band and I was the first Negro pianist to play on KDKA in Pittsburgh.

By this time we were getting to hear a lot of recordings that were made mostly in New York. The first blues records I remember were by Ma Rainey. Then came Lucille Hegamin with Fletcher Henderson. She had a pretty style and a lovely, soft voice. These singers would make tours on the T.O.B.A. circuit of black theatres in towns like Pittsburgh, Detroit, Chicago and Cleveland. The white theatres didn't think too much of the Negro actor or the Negro musician in those days, but a lot of stars of theatrical life began in those black theatres, like Ethel Waters and Bojangles Robinson. When the white race began to realize that there was so much fun and activity in these little theatres, a special midnight show was put on for them, and people would line up for blocks to get in. It got so popular, they had to put on two shows and start at 11 o'clock. The Negro comedians were very successful. Their funny comments on everyday life, and on what happened in the Southland, were all mixed up with references to segregation that were particularly funny to us Negroes who knew what it was all about. It was a relief to the distress and the turmoil and the obligations we always had, and that is where a lot of that great soul feeling came from.

Then theatrical people used to sit out back of the theatre on beer boxes and soda boxes. The sun would bake down the alley, and they'd fan themselves and fan the flies away. The dressing rooms were small and terribly hot, for there was no air conditioning then and few electric fans.

Some of the bigger stars, traveling from town to town, finally got to the place where they were fortunate enough to have a regular sleeping car on the railroad. The car would be unhitched and left to sit on the tracks until they finished their engagement, when they would go down, get into their car, and sleep on their way to the next engagement. If it was for a week, of course, they'd get a room in a hotel.

Not all people in show business had what you'd call good intentions. In one particular instance I know the whole show owed the hotel a lot of money. The people took their clothes over their arms to the theatre as though they were going to change costumes. When they'd been gone a couple of days, the hotel manager went to the theatre to find out where they were and learned the show had finished. "Those people can't have left," he said, "because their trunks are still upstairs." When they went up to move them, he said, "See how heavy they are; they must be full of clothes." But when he got a locksmith he found they were empty and just nailed to the floor!

We heard many performers in those shows, although the bands were small, usually a trumpet, saxophone, piano and drums. Sometimes just piano and drums. That was all that was needed for the tap dancers and blues singers. It was when they got chorus girls as well that whites began to realize what talent Negroes had, and they began scheming how to commercialize it.

As Ethel Waters got to be a big headliner, and we heard more and more records, we realized that you had to go to New York to get the stamp of approval, no matter how good you were. It was the Mecca then, and most of the records came from there. That was how I first heard the name of Fletcher Henderson. He had a group of four or five pieces that backed the singers on records. Because Lois Deppe thought we should try to get on some of these records, he and I went to New York on the train, traveling by coach. I guess I was fifteen or sixteen then.

We had met Luckey Roberts at my auntie's

place, so we went to see him first. He had three rooms in his apartment with nothing but pianos sitting in them. One reason for this was that he had very strong hands and could break anybody's piano down. He had fingers as big as my thumbs, and I remember him playing for us on a torn-out piano, and the keys were flying out as he played! There was one piano there he liked best when he was writing something drastic, something rhythmic. Another one he liked better for its tone when he was writing more melodic tunes. Then he had one he wouldn't let *anyone* play except himself. He wrote so many compositions for different shows. One show I never forgot—oh, years ago—was *Go, Go*, and two numbers in it were *Isabel* and *I Want Some Molasses*. Mostly, he wrote songs with flowers or girls' names in the title. He got so busy he had to have a co-writer to do the lyrics, but he always amazed me the way he could write music and talk to people at the same time. He used to bring a society-type band to Pittsburgh. He was in with millionaires, and later on he'd take bands from New York for dates in Chicago, and get a lot of money and all transportation paid. His wife was an operatic singer, and a great one.

After a while he decided to show us the town, because I'd never been to New York before. We were walking down Broadway and I was looking up. "Don't look up unless you actually see something," he said. "If you look up and don't see anything, and you stop the traffic, there's a twenty-five-dollar fine!" What I was looking at was a zeppelin or a big airship coming over, and I'd never seen anything like it before. "I'm glad you saw something," he said, "because everybody was looking at you." And sure enough, the traffic had really stopped!

He took us to a little club downtown where Duke Ellington and about five pieces were working. I just met them casually and said, "Hi," and listened to the music, but that was the first time I saw Duke and Sonny Greer. I thought their weird, strange sounds were very good, and Bubber Miley was playing an unusual type of trumpet. Then we went uptown to a club that belonged to a fellow called Broadway Jones, a singer. Fletcher Henderson was there, although the band was led by a violinist. That was the first time I met Coleman Hawkins. He had just joined, and he was starring, turning his back to the rest of the reed section. I had never heard so much horn in my life. From there we went to Happy Roane's nightclub, where I was amazed by the colored lights which flickered all night long. Our reason for going there was that Don Redman had left Pittsburgh and had the band there.

Of course, we overdid it in New York and spent so much money that we ended up eating in little hamburger stores. We had to get out or be stranded. We thought we were going to record for a company there, but nothing came of it.

Back in Pittsburgh, Lois Deppe made arrangements for the whole band to record for the Gennett Record Company in Richmond, Indiana. Recording then was so different from what it is today. We went into a sort of steam room, with towels hanging on the walls to deaden resonance, and we took our shirts off. Each instrument played into an individual horn. Although the equipment didn't pick up the bass or drums, they had horns just the same. We played for hours, one tune after another. I had written a number called *Congaine*, and Lois sang Luckey Roberts's *Isabel*. We made four records and when they came out in Pittsburgh they were quite a sensation. People said we had rung the bell! They began to talk about us, and we got around as much as possible, playing big dances and big parks. My style was recognized as unusual, but the band was so large that I had to figure out a way to be heard, because they were constantly drowning me out. So I started to use the octaves, and with octaves I could cut through the sound of the band. We had no amplification then and everybody was singing through megaphones. Later on, people considered what I did a *style*, but it was great for me then, because I could play the technician with my fingers or use the octaves when I wanted to be heard above the others. I began to get a little cocky, I guess, and Lois Deppe, being older, sometimes thought I was getting too big for my britches. Although people liked my piano, Vance Dixon was very good with his clarinet and he acted as musical director. An argument came up when we were in Springfield, Lois's hometown, and I decided I'd had it. So when we got back to Pittsburgh I put my notice in.

I got such a lot of stage experience while I was with Lois Deppe, and I've always been grateful to him for it. He taught me so much about the voice and how to accompany a singer. I had to know his limits from bass to soprano. I used to see how high he could go, and before doing a concert he would exercise his vocal cords. When doing low notes he had to sing from the stomach, and when doing high notes, why, naturally, it came from his head. It all gave me a lot of confidence in coaching my own band vocalists in later years. While I was around Pittsburgh, I even tried

singing myself, but I gave it up later and decided it was best to stick to the piano.

While I was still with Lois Deppe, I got involved with Mary Robinson, a prostitute. "Why work?" she said. "I can give you enough to buy clothes and eat!" But it was no life for me. There's no rest in the pimp's life anyway. At all hours of the day or night they're coming home saying, "Let's have a drink!" So all of a sudden I knew I was making a mistake. I decided to leave her and go back to the piano.

Before I left Lois Deppe's band, I ran across Laura Badge, who came from Alabama. She was a singer in a show at the Star Theatre on Wylie Avenue, and she was neat, brown-skinned and young. We were attracted to one another, and she decided to go around with me because I was popular and it could help her find work in the clubs. I also knew that all the guys up and down the Avenue were shooting at her, as they did at all the new girls who

Hines family picture. Left to right: (top) Laura Badge, Earl Hines's father and stepmother, Grandfather Phillips, Aunt Sadie Phillips; (bottom) Earl Hines, half sister Nancy June, Cousin Hilton.

came to town, and I felt they were just going to destroy her future. At the time, I didn't know she was as smart as she was. Anyway, I used to play for her and go around different places until we became really infatuated with each other. One day Lois decided he wanted to get married, and he asked us if we would stand up for him. So we did, and after having a few drinks we decided we would get married, too! From then on she called herself Baby Hines, and she began to get very popular. She could sing and she was a very pretty girl, but later I learned she was hooked up with the wrong people. She started running around with characters who were using women for a livelihood. These guys always had one girl they wanted to be with, not commercially, but for romance. She was caught in that web by a fellow whose mother was running a house with a whole lot of girls in it. They weren't allowed on the street, and the men who put them in there were only allowed to see them once a week, when they collected the money they were entitled to. I learned about it by accident when I decided to go to the theatre one day. "Let's take in a show this afternoon," I said to a girl who this guy was actually commercializing. She and another girl decided we would, and while we were at the theatre the other girl said, "You got a lot of nerve going out here with another woman's husband." The answer to that was, "Well, she's with *my* man!" I was so upset, because that was the first I heard of it. When I spoke to my wife, she was honest and told me all about it, and that was a turning point in my life so far as marriage was concerned. Later on, I learned she had married me for a purpose, to use me and my little reputation to help her singing. My playing helped her an awful lot, and she stayed advanced in comparison with other singers around. But she had bigger ideas. She thought it was something to be with people like that, who were living an easy life and running around in big cars.

We kept the room where we lived, but she was going her way and I was going mine. I would be there one part of the day and she'd be there at another. I remember we had saved up four hundred dollars to buy her a Hudson seal coat, a terrific fur coat at that time, but I had become so angry with her that I took all the money and went out. When I came back and told her, all she said was, "So what?" She just forgot about it. And then we really separated. She was a fine girl, but just on the wrong track. After I went to Chicago she realized how sincere I had been about her, and that she had been misled by all the notoriety and advantages of being around with those well-known guys on the Avenue. She finally joined a show and left Pittsburgh with it.

For a time I tried to run and book a band myself. That ended when we got stranded in Wheeling, West Virginia. I persuaded the man to let the band play in the park and charge a penny admission. We drew fifty people!

Harry Collins ran a club down the street from the Leader House called Collins Inn, and he was using five or six men with Vernie Robinson, a good violinist, as musical director. Vernie asked me if I would play with them weekends, and he got highly excited about my playing in contrast with the pianists who worked there the rest of the week; so he insisted I work there all the time. He had a man there named Harold Birchett, and he was the one who really taught me how to keep tempo. After playing a lot of classical music, with no set tempo, I found a big difference in nightclubs, where you had to have a rhythm and a tempo back of singers. You couldn't run away with the music. You know, the very first tune I played in a band I read so fast I finished 'way before the rest of 'em. I sat back laughing, waiting for them. "Well, I beat you all that time," I said. They laughed, too, wondering what I was trying to do. They thought I was kidding, I found out later from Birchett, but I was sincere. He was an unusual fellow. He had a banjo, and he was forever taking it apart, no matter how new it was. He tried to make it sound like a harp before they ever thought of guitars in bands. He had a six-string banjo, and it had a lot of strength in it, but the way he strummed it he got a sort of harp effect, which is what he was after. He had all kinds of things like screwdrivers and monkey wrenches stuck in the back of it, to take certain sounds away and to add others. People used to admire what he did very much, and musicians would come up and say, "Good gracious, what makes the banjo sound like that?" The only unfortunate thing was that right in the middle of a solo the doggone thing would sometimes fall apart, and there would be screwdrivers and nuts and bolts all over the place. Of course, I would have to continue playing while he was putting it together. He was getting such a great tone, people just laughed and said, "We'll have to wait till he's fixed it to hear some different things." He did perfect it to a certain extent eventually. The way he helped me was strange, too. He would be rocking his own thing, set up against the tempo we were playing, but if I tried to get fancy he would say, "Hold it, hold it! You're getting out of tempo now. Relax. Take it easy!" He got me to the position where I really knew what tempo meant.

Entertainers from all over used to come to Collins Inn. There was a girl named Corinne, who was married to a great pianist out of Detroit, Bart Howard. He wrote a number for her called *Has Anyone Seen My Corinne?* I had never met anyone quite like her. She was a very pretty girl, around 5'6", and she had a wild way of entertaining. Now the club had two rooms upstairs with a sort of a hallway in between. The bandstand was right in the middle, and she would have to go around the stand to get to the people sitting on the other side. There were very small salaries at this place, so everybody had to depend on the tips. Vernie Robinson had the band and Corinne would sing in front, and she might end up with two hundred dollars in two fist-fuls of bills, which she had to divide up, a hundred for herself and a hundred for us. Vernie finally woke up to the fact that when she went around back of the band to the other side she would stash some of the money away, so he told her she had to pay off first on one side and then on the other. He used to get off the stand to play his violin and he caught her sometimes stuffing bills down between her breasts. So then he told her to keep her hands away from her body altogether while she was entertaining, and that's how we kept up with her. We made so much in tips there that sometimes our salaries amounted to nearly two hundred dollars a week. When the proprietor found out, he said, "I'll tell you what I'm going to do. I'm not going to pay you a salary anymore, but I guarantee you a hundred and fifty dollars a week. If the money doesn't amount to that, we'll make up what the loss is." We were all discouraged about it because it put us on a flat salary. It didn't make any difference how hard we worked, we didn't get any more than our tips had been.

I had a lot of liberty, and I was running around with Corinne Howard. My auntie got to hear about it and she sent word to the place where I was staying that if I didn't get out of there she was going to have it raided. The landlady was uncertain what to do, but she had me move in the end and I went back to East Liberty. Meanwhile, I had decided to leave Collins Inn and go out on my own. After I left a trumpet player from Baltimore, much older than I was, came in there, and Corinne fell for him. I went in there one night and saw her on his lap, and that upset me so much I really turned my corners.

I had made a lot of friends there and I went to different clubs, including an after-hour place in Homestead. Actually, it was a front. The club was upstairs and there was gambling downstairs. We'd sit there and entertain when people came in. It was similar to the way it is in Las Vegas, where they have entertainment just to bring people in to gamble. The law was supposed to know nothing about it, but some of them did and were being paid off. It was another experience that proved advantageous to me, because the entertainers there would all want me to play in their different keys. This helped acquaint me with *all* the keys on the piano, which is something I was very proud of later.

The next thing was that I got a little group of my own together and went into a place called the Grape Arbor. I had Benny Carter on baritone saxophone, Cuban Bennett on trumpet, Emmett Jordan on violin, and Harry Williams, who was Maxine Sullivan's uncle, on drums. I ran across Benny on the street, and I knew he was from New York, but I didn't know how he happened to be there. I found out that he had relatives in the area and that his mother had let him come, although he was only a teen-ager, in Billy Page's band along with his cousin, "Cuban" Theodore Bennett, who was one of the fastest trumpet players I ever heard. We had a lot of fun together at the Grape Arbor, because the owner wasn't familiar with nightclubs and didn't know when or how long or what we were supposed to play! We stayed there until they decided to close the club, and then I was running back to Collins Inn or back to the Leader House.

By this time I'd seen a few prizefighters, among them Jack Johnson, who had been in the club when I was playing. When he came to Pittsburgh, of course, he was the talk of the town, and when he came on the Avenue he was the centre of attraction, just as Bojangles was. They'd have their big cars, their broad-stripe silk shirts, their Edwin Clapp shoes and their big diamonds—anything to show! That was the way of staying on top with the young ladies and keeping ahead of the game. One time he went to a little club on Fifth Street in Pittsburgh, and some of the heads of newspapers were with him. They came and got me, and from there we went to a place in McKeesport, where I got fooling around in a back room and lost all my money! I had to walk the mile home to Duquesne across the bridge at 3 o'clock in the morning. When I got there my people were so surprised to see me knocking on the door and getting into bed!

When I left next morning to go back to Pittsburgh, everybody wanted to know what I was doing. They jumped on my father, telling him his boy was never going to be a success. "You're going to be sorry," they said, "letting him hang around with all those underworld characters!" My father said, "Listen, he's chosen his field and that's what he wants to do. I told him when he left here at the age of twelve that I'm not a millionaire. I don't have a lot of money, but we live nice."

He had told me "the facts of life" when I was twelve, and I always remember him saying, "If you make twenty dollars, save ten." He really told me right from wrong. He told me about the different types of women I would run into, and the different snares I'd meet. He told me he didn't have anyone to get me out of jail, and that if I got in I had to get out the best way I could. I remembered that many times in Pittsburgh. I was at the Calloway Hotel one time. I just happened to walk in, and friends were having a little party in a room upstairs. Sometime later, I heard a lot of knocking downstairs, and then the law came upstairs, knocked, opened the door, said, "You're under arrest," and took all of us off to jail. I had to call Lois Deppe that time, and he came down and got me out.

Anyway, I wanted to get out of Pittsburgh now, but about this time Joe Smith came back. He'd been to New York and he was in a show called *Bamville* with Noble Sissle and Eubie Blake at one of the downtown theatres. Those shows really helped to get me wrapped up in music, and they made me feel there was a big future in it. Liking my auntie so much, Eubie Blake had heard me play at her place several times.

"This boy is a genius," he told her. "He has no business staying here."

"Where am I going to send him?" she said. "None of the people in this operatic work I'm doing know anything about nightclubs."

"I'll see what I can do about it," he said.

He used to wear a raccoon coat and a derby, and he always carried a cane. He was the first one I ever saw playing piano with one hand and conducting with the other. He used to lift his hands high off the keyboard, which was one of my first lessons in the value of showmanship. He and Sissle were all the rage when they came to town, and Joe Smith would be with them. To show you how popular this young man was, how much his horn meant to the musical world, they would put him on stage after the show ended to play what they called "walking-out" music as the people left the theatre. He was up there with his coconut-shell mute, and a big band, strings and all, below in the pit. They had to stop it

Eubie Blake and Earl Hines at the Hines home in Oakland, March 1971.

because people got jammed in the doors listening, and nobody could get out until he finished playing. What a musician! But he was a
wild character, too. He got in an argument
with one of the chorus girls and hung her with
a belt strap. They fired her and kept him, naturally.

Noble Sissle and Eubie Blake used to come
back quite often, and the next time I saw him
Eubie said, "If I catch you here again I'm
going to take this cane and wrap it around

your head. Do you realize you can stay in
Pittsburgh the rest of your life and still be the
same boy you are now? You've got to get away
from here."

The opportunity came when Vernie Robinson was invited to go to Harry Collins's new
club on State Street in Chicago, called Elite
No. 2. Harry Collins said, "Would you like to
come back to the club or would you mind
going to Chicago?"

I didn't know what in the world to say. I'd

never been out of the Pittsburgh area except to places like Wheeling, Columbus and Springfield. But Chicago . . . I'd heard so much about Chicago. I was up a tree. I asked my auntie.

"Yes, you go," she said. "If you run into trouble, you can always wire home, and I'll see you get money to come on back."

There was one other person helped me make up my mind to go, a great tap dancer named Lovey Taylor. He ran around with me in Pittsburgh because he liked the work I was doing, and we all got a kick out of watching him dance. He could do more with his feet than some people could do with their hands. I could play all the licks that he was doing on the floor as a kind of background for him, and he was always after me to travel with him. He was interested in my career apart from that, and he kept pushing me. When he heard about the offer in Chicago, he came to see me.

"Now, Earl, I'm telling you something worthwhile," he said. "My wife's an entertainer, and I've just come from Chicago. I went to look the territory over and see what was happening. If you do have an opportunity to go and don't take it, I think you'll be making a big mistake."

Half brother Joseph "Boots" Hines.

Half sister Nancy Hines.

A TREE FULL OF OWLS

I came into Chicago the back way and didn't like it at all. Railroads always seem to go a long way in cities past the backs of houses where people have their clothes hanging out, and I found this discouraging. I guess I was a little like the kid in the story who was going to London and expecting to see streets of gold. But we were met at the station by Harry Collins, who took us where we were to stay. It was a place on Prairie Avenue, a big, wide street, wider than any I'd seen before. I hadn't paid any attention to apartment buildings in New York, but here they seemed different, more of a condition of living on the South Side of Chicago. It wasn't as congested as New York either, and some of the apartment buildings on Prairie Avenue had little lawns in front. I soon began to feel that this city was built differently from others I'd known, and that the planning of it was very fine.

After we'd unpacked our bags and cleaned up, Harry Collins came back to take us to give the club the once-over. We went through downtown Chicago like lightning, and he didn't give us a chance to stay long because he had other business to attend to and calls to make. He took us back to our place and told us to get a rest and to get acquainted in the neighborhood. He would come back later that night for us. His club didn't open until midnight. Now I'd been accustomed to going to work around 9 or 10 o'clock in Pittsburgh, although nothing much happened until 11 or

12. You were just there in case somebody stopped by. This place opened at 12 and ran to 6 in the morning.

It was what they called an after-hour club, and it was frequented by musicians and entertainers after the other clubs closed. There were a lot of underworld people there, too. When I went in there it seemed everybody was looking at me, a thin, lanky fellow. I didn't have much weight on me then, and here I was being introduced to all these men and pretty girls. I would never think of remembering all the names.

I noticed that a lot of the fellows there had their hair glossed so it looked almost like patent leather. "Goodness gracious," I said to myself, "this is something I've got to do." When I went to the barbershop, the barber said how happy he was when we came in to see we hadn't had our hair changed like all the other boys. He had a fit, said it was a shame when I told him that that was what I'd come in for him to do. "Well, I've got to look like everybody else," I said.

I really was impressed and astonished to see all the fellows so neat and well dressed around Chicago. That was right down my alley, because I always did like to dress anyway. I practically lived in the barbershop, getting manicures and massages, as well as having my hair fixed.

Before we opened at the Elite No. 2, we decided to have a little rehearsal, but Collins said we didn't need it. "Just go up there and play like you played at the club," he told Vernie Robinson, who made up his mind we would get new things as we went along. Well, when we opened I was all eyes, you know, like a tree full of owls. I could always play piano without looking at the keys, so I was looking everywhere to see what was going on. They gave me two or three solos to play, and the people recognized that I was playing a strange style they hadn't heard before.

The most prominent pianists in Chicago at that time were Dave Peyton, who had an orchestra, Teddy Weatherford, who played in Erskine Tate's theatre orchestra, and Jelly Roll Morton, who was the most popular underworld pianist around. Jelly Roll was a fair-complected man and sort of handsome. Nowadays you'd say he was overdressed, but he was the kind of fellow who carried his pearl-handled pistols with him and had plenty of money in his pocket at all times. If anybody tried to put him in a corner or push him aside or outdo him, he'd say things like, "I've got more suits than you've got handkerchiefs!" or, "I've been further around the world than you've been around a teacup!" He had written any number of tunes and everybody thought a lot of him. Whenever he needed money, he'd write a tune and sell it to one of the downtown publishers like Melrose for fifty or seventy-five dollars. Tunes like *Milenberg Joys* were very popular, and when the bands began to play them he made a lot of money. King Oliver had a band at the Plantation, and he was playing Jelly Roll's compositions. I don't know whether Jelly Roll ever had a contract, but he had his name on his records, so he had to have some return from royalties. Music wasn't his only source of income, because he was very well thought of as a gambler. As a pianist, he had good tempo, and he used to write things that went well with a nice, slow, easy tempo. He used to go around all the nightclubs and parties, and he'd get a lot of ideas that way.

After our opening, I began to attract attention among people in the music world who were out after hours. Word of mouth helped. "Did you go down and listen to that lanky boy play piano?" they'd say, and then they'd talk about my unusual style. And Lovey Taylor, the tap dancer, came to town, and he was so pleased to see me he became like my publicity agent. He'd tell everybody I was the world's greatest piano player, and I'd look at him and think he was losing his mind. Bandleaders came to see me, and one in particular, Carroll Dickerson, hung around and just haunted me. He was always telling me to join his band. So many people came in just to hear me play that Vernie Robinson began to get a little jealous of me. After he'd had a few drinks, Vernie would put up all sorts of arguments to Harry Collins, and Harry finally let him go. So then there was just Jimmy Hayes, me, and a guitar player who had an unusual, homemade instrument of the kind they used to have in the Southland. I can't explain it, but it had a guitar tone. We made so much commotion there with this little trio that first Teddy Weatherford came down, and then Jelly Roll Morton. There was another good pianist across the street called Glover Compton, and he used to keep a cigar in his mouth all the time like Willie "The Lion" Smith. Glover was in an after-hour place run by a woman named Mamie Ponce, and they used to call it "a bucket of blood." Glover would play you anything you wanted him to play, always smoking his cigar. Next door to them was Dreamland, which had a band and a show. Carroll Dickerson was working at the Entertainers Club on 35th Street, and Sammy Stewart was at the Sunset Café, also on 35th. King Oliver, at the Plantation, was on the other side of that street. And the Nest was a little place up the street across from the Sunset, an after-hour place where musicians used to hang out. Anybody could go in there and play. There was no regular group then. Guys from the Sunset and the Plantation used to go in sometimes to sort of keep up with the times on their instruments, especially those who played in the sections and didn't get many solos.

Since I didn't have to go to work till 12, it gave me a chance to go to these clubs and see the shows they put on around 9:30 and 10. They were real productions, and I felt so happy to have been born and able to actually see them in person.

The club where I was working brought in, as I said, a lot of underworld people, and among them many pimps. They used to hang out there until their girls finished working at 2 or 3 o'clock. Then they'd bring them there and thrash out whatever went on during the day. The big-time pimps had Packards and Pierce-Arrows, and I often wished I could get a car like they had. They were dressed up at all times, and they were very patient with their girls. They saw to it that they were the best-dressed girls in the city, and they kept them in jewelry and fur coats. They would send the more experienced girls, who had seen all the business, to check on others who were completely green. They would train them as though it was a school for nurses! The pimps might have five or six girls, but they always had one who was more like a girl friend, for relaxation, and to take around, mostly. They picked these girls out of the the-atrical and other professions.

There were several bad men around who didn't have any ambitions at all. They didn't care nothing about nobody, and they would take advantage of every situation. Anybody who wanted to live naturally got along with them! One in particular I remember was "Shug" Burroughs, a very rough fellow. In a club where everybody had to wear a tie and collar, he'd walk in without either one. No-body said anything to him and he did what-ever he wanted to. If he wanted to pay the check, he paid it; if he didn't want to pay it, he didn't have to. But he would work as a bouncer and keep order. I don't know why, but he took a liking to me, and I found out later he wasn't as bad as a lot of people painted him. "I won't take any nonsense from these people," he told me. "There are so many here who have a few dollars because of their complexion or because they're more handsome than I am, and they've tried to ride roughshod over me. I let them know I was a man, a full-grown man, and nobody was going to take advantage of me." He lived that way, and he broke several necks and killed two or three people. The gangsters were afraid of him and the police were afraid of him.

There was also a real rough woman around there called Tack Annie. She was just about the roughest woman I saw in my whole life. It would take several men to hold her. She had a couple of girl friends who looked after her, and, like Shug, she wasn't as bad as they painted her. But she wasn't a nice-looking woman and she was a loud type of person, so she had to back that up some way, and that's what turned her out to be bad, period.

There was an awful lot of racketeering in Chicago, and as they went on the gangsters got into bigger clubs and theatres like the Grand Theatre, if I'm not mistaken. It was similar to the one they had in Pittsburgh, and part of a circuit. Some of the great stars of the day used to appear at the Grand, where Dave Peyton played piano in just a small group at first. Musicians like Freddy Keppard were in Chicago at the time, and they were all gigging around, playing dances and in and out of these theatres. Erskine Tate was across the street at the Vendome Theatre, where they showed movies—no sound—and had live musicians. He used to get script and music sent him with the film. There would be several themes about eight or sixteen bars long, which were used for changes of scene, as when a door closed and the characters went outside. These were known as one-finger theme, two-finger theme, three-finger theme, four-finger theme, and so on. If he held out his fourth finger, it meant they had to go to the fourth theme for, say, cloudiness in the sky and to get ready for a rough section of the music. The third finger would be for birds flying before a love scene. The themes let us know we were going into a different type of music. All this music was sent in, and the reason I'm talking about it is that I eventually ended up playing with Erskine Tate after Teddy Weatherford left. Watching him was how I learned to conduct an orches-tra. He was my coach, and what a way he had of conducting! His arm and finger movements, his concentration—he was terrific and it was beautiful to watch him. I used to sit right under him. Louis Armstrong and I were there

together, and from the Vendome we went to
our regular work. But I must go back to the
Elite No. 2.

Harry Collins had gambling in the back
room, and he had sharks working for him. He
had crap-shooters that were sharks who rolled
the dice evenly, and he had others who knew
every spot on the cards. In fact, he was a sort
of shark himself and after he closed at night
there was almost no need for him to pay the
people who worked there. He used to set up
drinks and sandwiches, and there were always
chorus girls hanging around who would keep
you there. First thing you know, you were
caught in one of those traps where he didn't
have to pay you your salary because you had
blown all your money playing the games back
there. Collins was a little short fellow and a
very rough guy. His English was very bad and
he couldn't carry on a decent conversation.
He liked all kinds of sports and he bet on anything. He liked my piano playing, too, and
he took a liking to me. He thought I should
be top, and he really paid me a wonderful
salary.

The place I was staying at was very home-
like. Mrs. Liggins and her husband were both
in their '50s, and she was accustomed to show
people. She'd cook breakfast for us in the
morning and dinner in the evening. The El
trains ran all the way out there, and it was a
thrill to me to be able to jump on one of them
and be downtown in the Loop in twelve minutes. I enjoyed looking around Chicago. The
buildings weren't as tall as in New York, but
the atmosphere was different altogether.
There seemed to be more night life, maybe
because it was more centralized. In New York
it was spread out quite a bit.

Most of the action on the South Side was
around the junction of two streets, 35th and
State. From the Grand Theatre in the north to
the Savoy Ballroom in the south was not much
more than sixteen blocks. Nearly everything
in that section was run by Negroes, even the
bank on State Street. There were fine restaurants and theatres, and there may have been
hotels, but I was not interested in them then
because I was so comfortable in that home on
Prairie Avenue.

People of that neighborhood were walking
and talking all night long on the corner of 35th
and State. Many times I ran into Jelly Roll
Morton, Glover Compton and Lovey Taylor
there. Like Glover, Lovey was always smoking cigars, a brand that sold three for fifty
cents. He always had a big one stuck up in his
mouth. He was sort of a sharpie around there,
but he was a great dancer. He wouldn't dance
for nothing, though. You had to pay him. And
he didn't care too much for gambling.

The three of them were the loudest fellows
I ever heard. When they were standing on the
corner, you could hear them for blocks. We
used to go to ball games together, and you
didn't have to know where they were sitting
because you could hear them all over the
White Sox park. They'd be betting and arguing:

"Why they got this guy pitching?"

"What in the world they want to put a man
like that at bat?"

"This guy's average is real low!"

If I came to the game late, I just followed
their voices and found them. They were great
company for me, and I learned a lot from
them because they were older and experienced.

My drummer at the Elite No. 2, Jimmy
Hayes, was a dry sort of fellow who didn't go
around much that I knew, but Lovey Taylor's
wife liked him. She was a very pretty woman
who worked tables, singing in nightclubs. She
was very fond of me through Lovey, but she
was having some difficulty with him. One day
she said to me,

"Earl, we're going to have a party at the
house. I want you and the drummer to come
up after you finish."

"Well," I said, "we don't get off until 6
o'clock in the morning."

"That will be time enough. They'll all be
getting there about then."

We went, and she was there with a very
pretty girl from the Sunset Café called Kittens
Ellison, nobody else. "Where's the party?" we
kept asking, but it turned out that Lovey's
wife just wanted to get to the drummer. Next
thing I knew I was hung up with this girl, Kittens, and she became one of my girl friends.

Earl Hines,
a newcomer
to Chicago.

Because of her, I began to find I was running into trouble. She was one of those chorus girls underworld characters used to romance with, and her fellow saw me leaving the Elite Club and said, "This has got to stop." We ran around secretly after that, but I knew I had to take it easy, because I still didn't know much about Chicago night life.

In those days, we all worked seven nights a week. There was so much going on that no-body paid any attention to the time of the day. You'd go to work, get on the stand, play, come off the stand, go outside, get into all sorts of arguments, go back, play again, and so on like that through the night. Then they started going to roadhouses on the outskirts of the city. My sort of sponsor there was this dancer, Lovey Taylor, and there were several other little guys around town who were sort of spon-sors for Teddy Weatherford. They wanted to find out whether or not I played better than Teddy. There was nothing out there. It was just a matter of driving out and having break-fast and maybe sitting around listening to other musicians in a jam session. Then they'd say to me, "Come, play a number for us." So I'd get up and play, and then they'd ask the same thing of Teddy. It got so we were meet-ing there quite often; and finally they gave it to me, said I was in a class by myself.

Now Teddy would come up and say, "Earl, how do you do this? How do you do that?" Anything I had I would show him, and we were closer together than musicians are today. He had bigger hands than me, but he couldn't play tenths. We'd sit down and show one an-other our ideas, and we'd use whatever we liked or found interesting. We became very good friends and we used to run around together, call each other, have parties, lun-cheons and dinners.

The biggest trouble I had in Chicago was when I went to the musicians' union. I knew I had to get my card, but they gave me a hard way to go because they didn't want any strangers or outsiders there. They wanted to preserve all those nightclubs for musicians liv-ing in Chicago, and there was quite a number of them, because they'd come from all directions, including New Orleans. They said I'd have to stay in Chicago six months before I could get a working card, and they actually didn't want to give me that. They had no real basis for treating me and my little drummer like this, and we didn't find out until later that they were trying to get even with Collins the best way they could. They didn't like him because he'd told them, "If you guys don't want to work for me, I'll get my little band out of Pittsburgh." They knew he was a good payer.

In fact, we were getting higher salaries than anybody around there. So long as I was drawing people, he didn't care what he paid me, because the place was a playhouse for him and a front for the other things he wanted to do. I had a great time while I was at the Elite No. 2, and I stayed another six months after I got my card.

Meanwhile, Carroll Dickerson kept asking me to join his big band, and when I eventually agreed he had me go down to a rehearsal.

Earl Hines, 1926.

They were all sitting there, very curious, trying to figure how much I knew and whether I knew what they liked to play. They were putting me on the spot, and they brought out all kinds of music. They knew that many of the musicians around there then, most of them from New Orleans, were very ordinary readers. They didn't have any idea of the training I'd had, but when I quickly ran through everything they had, then they decided to let me alone. Carroll Dickerson was just as happy as he could be when he realized the type of musician I was.

When we went into the Entertainers, the union began to give him trouble for using me, a "traveling" musician. Every time he moved they would fine him fifty or twenty-five dollars, and another twenty-five when he opened his mouth! "I don't care what they do," he said. "They're trying to discourage me, but I'm going to keep you with the organization." So I stayed with him, although other bands wanted to see if I'd join them. It looked like he was trying to front for me at a time when nobody else in the city, with the exception of Lovey Taylor, was in my corner. Since I'd left his place, Harry Collins didn't want to have any more to do with me.

At the Entertainers, I was working with a group of chorus girls for the first time. I was having a picnic watching them dance, and trying to keep from looking like I was imported or had just got off the boat. The girl from the Sunset found out I was down there, and she had to come running to see what I was doing, which made me feel a little important. But the Entertainers didn't have good management behind it. They got behind with payments to the band several times, and I was surprised anything like that could happen in Chicago. One of the managers came up to me and said:

"You're a week behind, and you'll be two weeks behind next week. Do you want a little money now?"

"Oh, no, if you're going to pay . . ."

That's where I made a big mistake. Others had drawn some money, and I wished I had, because the following night when I went to work I found the place was padlocked. I couldn't get my money and I was stuck, but I told Carroll Dickerson about it and he had a little money of his own, so he saw me through.

"We're going to keep the band together," he said, "and we're going to travel."

I didn't pay any attention to what he was saying, because I thought he was just giving me a line of noise. The union said nobody else could open up at the Entertainers, and no other musician could go in there until we were paid our money. Almost the next day I heard that the band and all the help had gone down to the club, broken in, and taken everything out, including the piano. By the time I got there, the only thing I could lay my hands on was a box of napkins!

Carroll was a hustler, however, and somehow or other he made contact with one of the representatives of the Pantages circuit. This circuit had a chain of theatres that ran from Chicago to the Coast and back again. (I understand the Keith circuit was even larger and ran from New York to Chicago to California.) They used to audition acts and rehearse in Chicago, and we did about five auditions in our costumes before we got an engagement for forty-two weeks. There were four other acts besides our band. We traveled in a Pullman car that was fixed up for us, and we'd play in each of the theatres for a week. We had a road manager with us, and we slept in the Pullman car at night as we moved from one city to another. When we reached the next place, we would go right to the theatre. When you walked in the back door the stage manager would point to a blackboard and you'd find out where your dressing room was. Then, in your dressing room, on the mirror, you'd find details of where your hotel was, the room they'd secured for you, the time of the shows and the time of the rehearsal.

At the theatre there would be errand boys to bring whatever you wanted if you didn't want to go outside. They didn't give them a salary, but you tipped them for what they did. There was usually a little anteroom with a great big table on which you could eat, but mostly that was where we sat around and passed the time between acts and shows. The band was the last act on, and what I remember now is the wonderful way everybody helped each other so that we could make the train, because it always seemed to be scheduled immediately after the last performance. Everybody would hang around till we finished, then jump in and help, tear the bandstand down and pack the instruments. Our dressing trunks were kept at the theatres, and they would already have been packed and gone. All we kept was a bag to put our costume in when we changed into a suit afterwards. Most of the time you changed at the theatre anyway, not in the hotel.

Nobody was trying to outdo one another in the show, because the Pantages representatives routined it, made the spot for you, and had it work up to a climax. We had fourteen men in the band, a girl singer, and three boys who did a charleston act. It was the time when the charleston was the big dance, and the show was called *Carroll Dickerson's Charleston Revue*. We wore smocks, ordinary smocks, all in bright yellow, and we had tams on our heads something like the berets the French wear. We had ribbon ties and if it was cold we kept our coats on, but if it was warm we'd leave the coats off and just wear the smocks. We also wore our regular street trousers. What was most important was that our shoes had to be shined!

Carroll Dickerson wore a velvet smock with circular rhinestones on the back, as well as a tam like ours. He would very seldom turn around to the front and he was a very strict guy so far as playing instruments was con-

On the Oakland–San Francisco Ferry, 1926. Left to right: Mancy Cara, a Charleston dancer, Earl Hines, another Charleston dancer, Tubby Hall.

cerned. He wanted everything to be just right.

He used to get on us for being a little frightened sometimes onstage, and he was always telling us how to act, so we began to get on him for not playing anything. "Carroll," the guys said, "you should play something, a popular number, to show why you're the leader of the band. The people out front want to know whether you play the violin or are just standing up there holding it!" So I fixed up *Tea for Two* for him, with the verse, and he was supposed to memorize it and take a solo. The first time we played it, he never did get into the verse and he never did get out of it. He could never get together on it. He had stage fright so bad, we had to take him out of it, and all the guys gave him the devil about that. From then on he gave me more respect, because I

had to play the whole number myself as a solo. We used to tell him, "Straighten up and fly right! You're afraid to turn around and face the audience, and you jump on us for the least little thing we do wrong. If we mix any notes or passages, you give us hell." His answer to that was nearly always the same: "You have a union card. I don't know what you're doing with it if you can't play things as they're supposed to be played." We hadn't heard that before, but we'd feed it back to him whenever he looked hard at us: "You've got a union card, too!"

We all got along together in the show, despite little arguments of that kind, but we always seemed to be broke. Tubby Hall was the drummer in the band, a good rhythm drummer, and he and I ran together. We didn't want to take a back seat to anyone when

On tour with Carroll Dickerson, 1926. Left to right: Carrie Williams, Earl Hines, Willie Hightower, two Charleston dancers, Stanley Brown (solo dance act), Dave Brown (alto sax) and (kneeling in front) another Charleston dancer and Carroll Dickerson.

it came to playing black jack, but there were a couple of slickers in the band who kept us broke all the time. When we got to San Francisco, we had twenty-five cents between us on Christmas night. As we went down the street, we looked through restaurant windows, and we would stand there and watch all these people eating turkeys. It made us so hungry, and we ended up eating salted crackers and drinking water. I'll never forget that as long as I live. After that I told Tubby, "From now on just one of us gambles. If one loses, at least the other will have some money!" He was a happy-go-lucky fellow and I could always count on him. Since I was thin and he was stout, I always had an advantage in good times with our lady friends.

There was a good bit of discrimination in California at that time. There were no laws about where you couldn't go, but the doors were not opened readily to us. We'd go to a hotel and they'd say, "Do you have a reservation? No . . . Well, we're sorry . . ." In San Francisco, we finally wound up at a Japanese hotel.

One section we were to go to in Canada would be very cold, the Pantages people told us, and they advised us to get some heavy underwear. I'd never been accustomed to wearing that. Maybe it was because I had thick blood, but I used to feel warm all the time. Nevertheless, I got this long underwear and wore it. While we were playing onstage, between the heat of the spotlights and the drinking I'd done backstage, I fell out. They had to pull the curtain down and carry me off before they could finish the show. Carroll told me later he made a speech and said I suffered from dizziness. When I spoke to a doctor about it, he said, "Your blood can't take those heavy clothes."

The one who would really drink it up was Carroll himself. Sometimes, when he got to play his violin, he didn't know whether he was using the front or the back of the bow. We'd be wondering why he couldn't get a sound out of his instrument, and then he'd turn the bow over! Other times he would continue directing the band after we finished the music. After

I realized what was happening, I would continue playing the piano. The first time I did that, he came downstairs to me with the manager.

"That was a nice thing you did," Carroll said.

"Yes, it was," the manager remarked. "You saved the act."

"I kind of lost my place in the music," Carroll added.

"No, it wasn't that," I said. "We shortened the arrangement and hadn't told you."

That's how we got out of that.

The tour was a wonderful experience for me, and I really got to know how things were done on the theatre stage. There were some interesting fellows in the band, like Honoré Dutrey, the trombone player, who had sinus trouble. When we were in higher altitudes he had difficulty breathing, and we had to find ways to pep him up. Then there was Dave Brown, who played alto sax, a very attractive boy with great big eyes. Women just fell over him left and right. He stayed out in California somewhere, and later a jealous husband killed him. Willie Hightower, the trumpet player, used to write his wife every day, and she used to write him every day. His wife was secretary of the union in Chicago. On the road, he never asked anybody for anything, because he had everything he wanted. "Never leave home," he told me, "unless you have everything you need, including matches." He smoked cigars and used a cigar holder. He told me how to control a wife if I got married:

"You know what I did my first night of marriage? My wife fixed a dinner and set it all on the table. When I sat down, I pulled the tablecloth, the dishes, the whole thing on the floor."

"What did you do that for?" I asked him.

"I wanted to let her know who was master of the house."

She had to tell him about every penny she spent, and have it all itemized. But writing those letters was all he did between shows, and sometimes, when the mail caught up with him, there'd be two or three from her, and that was his biggest kick. He'd be reading

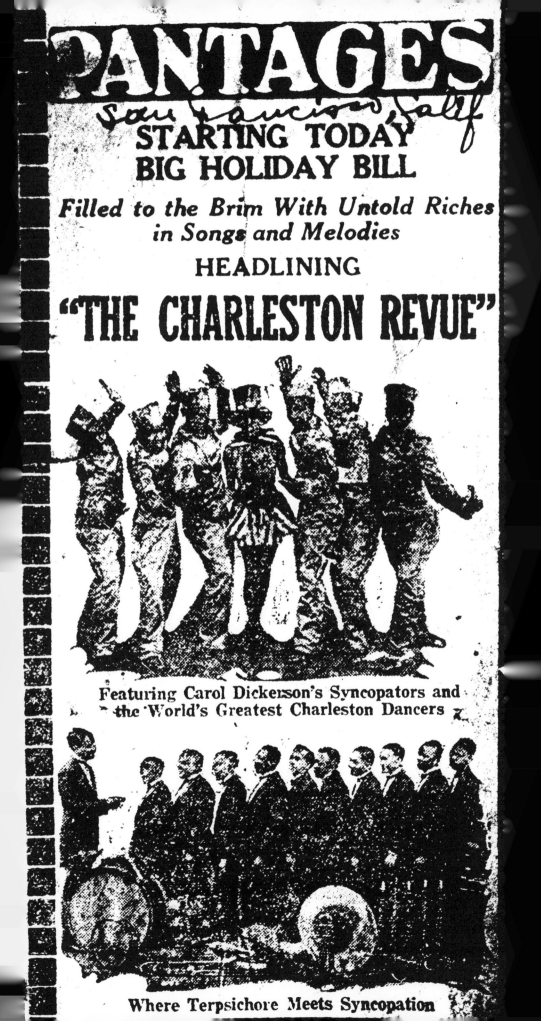

TOURING PANTAGES CIRCUIT

The CARROLL DICKERSON ORCHESTRA.

F. HALL. J. HALL. M. CARR. D. BROWN.
H. DUTREY. W. H. HIGHTOWER. E. HINES. C. IRWIN.
A. DOMINIQUE. CARROLL DICKERSON. E. BROWN.

them backstage, and I might be thinking of smoking a cigar myself, but I'd be afraid to ask *him* for a match because he would say, "Remember what I told you: always be prepared."

In our forty-two weeks on the Pantages circuit, we went all the way to Los Angeles and all the way back to Chicago. The tour, the first of that kind by a big band from Chicago, greatly increased Carroll Dickerson's popularity, and it wasn't hard for us to secure a steady engagement. The people at the Sunset Café were having trouble with Sammy Stewart, who had the band there, so the arrival of our band offered them a way out. Sammy had been there a long time, and they thought he was getting stagnant. The Sunset was owned by Joe Glaser's mother, and Ed Fox and Sam Dreyfus leased it from her. (Joe was just a sort of man-about-town at that time.) When they secured Carroll's services, we naturally wanted to go in there with the best musicians we could pick. Some who had been on the tour we didn't want to keep, and Dave Brown, who played alto, hadn't returned. In the three weeks before we opened, others got sort of scattered out, so Carroll had to reorganize the band. Tubby Hall stayed with us, and Dutrey and Hightower. We had a little, short fellow called Stumpy Evans, who everybody was trying to get, and who could really play that tenor saxophone. Darnell Howard played alto and clarinet. Big Green was on trombone, and he was another good one. On trumpet we had Natty Dominique; and Zutty Singleton came in for Tubby Hall at the tail end of the engagement. I can't remember the others, but, most important, we had Louis Armstrong!

I met him in 1925 at the musicians' union, Local 208, on State and 39th in Chicago. They had a kind of pleasure place up on the second floor where you could hang out, play cards, have a few drinks and tell jokes. The union had become much stronger since the time I was at the Elite No. 2, and I got along with them better now that I was in an established band. Carroll Dickerson did, too, because his reputation had grown and everybody looked up to him. Anyway, it was at the union that Louis and I first got talking to one another, in

the poolroom. I'd heard of him, of course, and he told me he had heard me playing out at the roadhouse with Teddy Weatherford.

A month or so later, they had finally put a piano in at the union, and I was running through some tunes downstairs when he came in. He took his horn out and began to blow. I always remember that first tune we played together. It was *The One I Love Belongs to Somebody Else*. I knew right away that he was a giant. Nobody could play the horn the way he played it. He really knew that trumpet. From that time on, we began to hang out together. The union was one of our main meeting places until I found he lived just around the corner from me at 421 44th Street. I was on Vincennes, and I'd go to his house and pick him up, or he'd come around to mine. Sometimes, we'd call and say, "See you down at the union." He was a very happy-go-lucky guy, and we used to have so much fun, telling jokes and so on. We had a lot in common, but we didn't work together commercially until we started making records, and many of those dates came out of meetings at the union.

One day, when I was going to a rehearsal with Carroll Dickerson's band, I ran into Louis. He was on his way to a rehearsal with King Oliver, and we stopped in the middle of the street.

"Why don't you come on over with us young fellows?" I asked him.

"I already promised Joe Oliver," he said.

"Yeah, but you would do better to come with us."

Because of all the running around we'd done together, Louis could see where it would be a great thing and a lot of fun for us both. So he came with us and the band opened at the Sunset.

The band at the Sunset was very good at reading music, and that was important, because we had to play big shows. They were produced by Percy Venable. He was the guy who created ideas for them, and everybody liked him. Although the club was on the main stem of the Negro neighborhood, it drew white as well as colored. Sometimes the audience was as much as ninety percent white. Even the mixing of white girls and colored pimps seemed to be an attraction. People came in big parties from Chicago's Gold Coast to see these shows. They had never seen tap dancing and comedy like we had there. The comedians were *really* funny, and there were plenty of girls in all sorts of costumes. For beautiful picture numbers, the producer would find very hard music, like *Black Forest Overture, Poet and Peasant Overture* and *Rhapsody in Blue.* You had to know your instrument and you had to know what you were doing, because it was never all written out. We might start on page one, jump over to page seven, play eight bars, come back to page three and play all of it, and then turn back to page two. This could be very confusing.

Percy Venable used to rehearse the girls and then have two band rehearsals, but we never really had a finale rehearsal the whole time we were there. We'd get the finale together backstage just before the show started. He'd come back there with it all written on paper. He knew all the tunes we had in the book, and he'd say, "Give me sixteen bars of this, segue, slow the tempo along, give me eight bars of that, and then sixteen bars of this." So the finale was often produced the evening when a new show opened.

There was more excitement among the girls and boys waiting for their costumes. It often looked as though the costumes would never get there in time for the show, which would always be a half-hour or an hour late going on. Then the costumes would arrive for the first section, and they had three seamstresses back there sewing and patching before getting the costumes ready for the middle number. I remember how excited the girls were when they tried on the big, beautiful blue costumes for that first show. They were walking around, happily showing their dresses to us, until they found some of the shoes mixed up, and then the girls with large feet got mad. Oh, opening night could be a real madhouse, the scariest thing you could want to see!

One night Shug Burroughs came in with a message for Carroll Dickerson, who was in the back after the show. He was in a hurry to catch him before he went out the back door, and on the way he bumped into Joe Eadey. Joe was a thin fellow whose wife Irene was a good pianist, and she later married Teddy Wilson and wrote some fine songs.

"You think you can run over everybody just because you're Shug Burroughs," he said.

"I'm sorry," Shug said, "but I'm going back there to deliver this before Carroll gets out."

"You can run over everybody else, but I ain't going to let you run over me!"

One word led to another until Shug got sick of it, knocked him down under a table, and went on back to catch Carroll and give him the note.

The waiters picked Joe up and took him to their dressing room downstairs. He said he was going to get his pistol, and then come back, which he did. Meantime, Shug had delivered the note, and he came back through the club.

"Shug," I said, "you better get out of here, because that boy's really gone to get his pistol."

"What do you think I've got?" he said. He was in his shirtsleeves as usual, and he opened his shirt and showed me his pistol.

So I went on out the front door. The club was closing and it began to be daylight. I went across the street to the Apex and went upstairs. Percy Venable looked out and saw Shug standing behind a whole lot of cars. Then Joe Eadey came in the Apex, looking for Shug and crying, "I'm gonna kill him!" We tried to catch him and stop him, but he ran back downstairs and out on the street, where Shug walked up to him.

"Gimme that gun," he said, and he'd been in the habit of taking guns from guys. He'd take the gun, slap the guy, and hand it back to him. But Joe backed away, raised the gun and shot Shug one time. Then Shug took good aim and shot him. They took this boy to the hospital and he died at 4 A.M. Shug got in a cab and went to a hospital. The first one he went to wouldn't do anything for him. Joe had had an automatic steel-jacket gun and Shug had a hundred holes in his intestines. He died at 7 A.M.

Shug was a racketeer, a gambler, and he had a girl that was crazy about him. He thrived on gambling and on people who used him for protection. He walked upstairs one night where there were four pimps who were going to beat me up because I was going with a girl of one of the pimps.

"I understand you want to take advantage of a personal friend of mine," he said. "If one hair in his head is hurt, they'll never see any one of you again."

So they never bothered me, and I didn't learn about that happening until two or three weeks afterwards. He was always around, and he was good to have as a friend. I was really sorry he was killed. It was sort of stupid, but during those days everybody tried to be half bad, and everybody had a gun.

Thirty-fifth Street was a bad street, and when I first went to Chicago I thought it was the worst city in the world. Pittsburgh was no heaven either. I knew how to duck and dodge there, and I did the same thing in Chicago, but at first I didn't realize how dangerous 35th Street was. It was lit up at night like Paris, and there were some of the most dangerous people in the world on it. That's why Jelly Roll Morton carried his pistol and was so loud-mouthed. You had to *act* bad, whether you were bad or not. Somebody was always getting hurt, and you had to have a certain amount of courage to work in those clubs. You had to know how to talk to Tack Annie, for instance, because if you didn't she'd have you beat up, or beat you up herself. It took four cops to put her out of the Sunset one night.

There was a dance act over at the Plantation, three boys who all carried knives. They did little contract jobs for the gangsters. All the gangsters had to say was, "We don't like this guy so-and-so," and the guy would be found all cut up. The police paid no attention to those kind of things, and nobody knew who was responsible, but later on they began to find out.

Thirty-fifth and State was like, you might say, 125th and Seventh Avenue, or 125th and Eighth Avenue in Harlem. Calumet was a block down on 35th, just a block over from South Parkway. State Street was five or six blocks over, and when they figured it had gotten too bad down around that section, night life moved up towards South Parkway. The Elite No. 1 was at 31st and State, and when things grew worse there they moved to where I was at the Elite No. 2 between 35th and State Street. For a time, 35th Street was *the* street. They had four big clubs on it with big shows and big bands. They wanted to keep them all open, because the more clubs the more people the street drew. Why, when the Sunset caught fire, all the people from the Plantation ran over there and tried to help put the fire out, because they didn't want the Sunset to go down. At weekends both places would be jammed with people who went from one club to the other.

I got a world of experience in directing a band from watching Erskine Tate and Carroll Dickerson. Carroll was with us five or six months, but unfortunately he did too much drinking and they had to let him go. He would never play his violin, and all he would do was conduct. Sometimes he'd start the band off and leave the stage without telling any one of us to take the band over, and it got so the band seemed to be actually doing better when he was off the stand. That went on till he came in one night so bad off that the proprietor fired him. So they decided to give the band to Louis and have me act as director. That's where it came in handy knowing how to conduct. And I used to go down when Percy Venable rehearsed the girls and listen to the music the rehearsal pianist was playing. By the time the band had to rehearse, I practically knew the whole routine. After a time, we got a second pianist, Willie Hamby, but at first I had to jump around from conducting to playing. That was where the rehearsals helped. I knew where it was possible for me to conduct and where I had to sit down and play piano. We really perfected that show with such good characters as Stumpy Evans playing beautiful tenor sax and the giant of jazz, Louis Armstrong, blowing that trumpet.

When he got through blasting his horn, and all the rest of us came up with him, that band was really swinging! And so was the show!

Of course, we had competition, especially from King Oliver across the street at the Plantation, because he was another guy who could really play that horn. There were only two big clubs on the street now, because while we were out on the Pantages circuit the Entertainers burned down. They claimed it was an accident, but we believed it was done purposely. Those people just outsmarted everybody, and there was nothing we could do about the money they owed us.

They had all sorts of great talent at the Sunset. That was where I first met Buck and Bubbles and Sammy Vanderhurst. Sammy and Bubbles were both terrific dancers, and when they got together in contests you can imagine the kind of tap dancing that was going on. They did things with their feet that looked impossible. Then we had an act called Brown and McGraw. She was very cute and he was a handsome little fellow, and later on they got married. They were both short, but he had sharp uniforms and she was well developed and always wore a pretty dress. They had a riff they used that later became very popular with big bands. It used to go *bomp-bomp-bomp-bu-bomp, bomp-bomp-bomp-bu-bomp*, and Louis used to take his trumpet and do it right with them. So people began to realize what it was all about. Later, all the acts used to have the bands making the licks they were doing on the floor, especially the tap dancers. This was when the public and the clubs began to understand how effective the band could be behind acts like that, as well as singers. Then the acts didn't want to go anywhere but places where the band could feel their act like we did. Arrangers began to come into their own, writing those things for them so that they could get the same effect in any houses they played. I must say Louis gained a lot of popularity from doing that thing with Brown and McGraw. Of course, that was his heart. He just got a kick out of it.

Sometimes the chorus would steal the show at the Sunset, and Louis used to get a great kick out of backing them up, too. We had parade girls there that were just for the picture numbers. The smaller girls—"ponies" we called 'em—were the ones that did the dancing, and they danced with all their heart and soul! They were so popular, we always had a waiting list of girls wanting to work there.

We were still using megaphones. There was no amplification then, but you could usually hear clearly, because they tried to make sure the rooms they used had good acoustics. Sometimes it got rather loud, because there was no way to hold the heavy bands down. The amount of business we were doing there meant that it was jammed every night, and the number of people in the room would absorb a lot of sound. People made reservations and just kept them there month in and month out. The newspapers were playing up the clubs on the South Side till they were the talk of the country, and the Sunset and the Plantation were famous long before the Cotton Club became the big place in New York.

The Sunset also became quite a hangout for musicians. We played seven nights a week till 3:30 or 4 in the morning and we never had a night off. Most of the clubs and hotels where the white musicians played closed between 1 and 2 o'clock, and they'd come down either to King Oliver at the Plantation or where we were. Benny Goodman used to come with his clarinet in a sack. Tommy Dorsey was there with either his trumpet or trombone, because he hadn't decided then which one he wanted to specialize on. His brother, Jimmy, would come with his alto and clarinet. Muggsy Spanier, Joe Sullivan, Whitey Berquist, Jess Stacy, and I don't know how many different musicians came to sit in and jam with us. Whatever section they wanted to sit in, why a musician would step out from his chair. We all got a kick out of listening to each other, and we all tried to learn. We sat around waiting to see if these guys were actually going to come up with something new or different. Bix Beiderbecke was a versatile young man who played trumpet and piano. At that time he was thinking a lot about writing tunes, and one where he used chords that were unusual then later became quite well known. It was called *In a Mist*. He played very good trumpet with Paul Whiteman, and it was like a hobby with him to go some place where he could play piano as well. Working in a big band and in a section, you have only a certain amount to play each night, and when you do that constantly you can get a little rusty on your instrument. So guys look for a place where they can get new ideas, stretch out, and really get over their horn. Another musician with Paul Whiteman who was a sensation during those years was Frankie Trumbauer. He had an unusual tone and people loved to hear him. He made records with a little group of his own like we were doing with Louis Armstrong. Yet another musician that would drop in when he was at the Vendome Theatre was Fats Waller. He used to take over on Hamby's piano and we'd play duets. I also remember a fellow who often came in and wanted to sit down and jam with the guys, but all he wanted to play was a sweet old number he had written. Nobody at that time wanted to hear it. "Look," the guys said, "get this cat off that piano so we can go to town!" But he was constantly playing his new composition and trying to make everybody listen to it. It was *Stardust*, and he was Hoagy Carmichael. We all loved him, and now we all know that he really did something for our music world, but at that time everybody wanted to get at his horn and blow and hear what the other cats had to offer.

Louis Armstrong and I were inseparable at this time. We hung out together and we started what we called a Christmas Fund, putting all the money made on the floor into it. It got so large some of the guys became a little leery of the treasurer we had. They thought the temptation would be too much for him, so they said, "Man, give me my money now!" But Louis and I kept it up and around Christmas we had three or four hundred dollars apiece to spend. We went around buying our girl friends presents. We had a lot of fun going in those department stores, picking out lingerie and things we thought a girl would like, and all the time hoping we'd get a present in return!

Louis used a certain salve on his lips to keep them from becoming dry or cracked after playing a lot. Sometimes, if we were out rather late, he would just fall out and lie down wherever he was. Maybe next day he'd have a little scab on his lip, and if he were picking at it I'd ask him:

"How're your chops?"

"Well, they're *rare!*" he'd say, grinning.

He was always a trouper. He knew how to get by, but many times I knew he must have been playing in pain. He never showed it. He was all smiles.

Louis and I were both at home sitting up there on the bandstand, but we didn't realize what that floor meant. Louis had never had an opportunity to be out on the floor, and when he went out for the first time to sing with Mae Alix he was frightened, and he wasn't sure of his lyrics. Also, although she didn't know it, he really liked Mae, and that probably made him a bit nervous. A number called *Big Butter and Egg Man* had been written for them. She'd sing part of it, he'd sing a part, and then he'd blow his horn. Now Mae was a very good-looking girl, and she really had a lot on the ball. As a singer, she was one of those shouting-type girls. She knew Louis was timid and she just took advantage of him. On opening night, when Louis went out there, he forgot the lyrics and everything else. He was just looking at Mae. Not having any experience on the floor, and being out there with a finished artist, it just took all the run out of him. He didn't know whether to sit down, stand up, or what, but Mae got a kick out of it and had fun with him, and the whole house cracked up. He got accustomed to it finally, but when she used to put her arms around him and look at him and sing "I need a big butter-and-egg man," he would stand there and almost melt, and everybody in the band would get up and shout, "Hold it, Louis! Hold it." Of course, a big butter-and-egg man was a playboy, a guy with a lot of money, and it was a number Brown and McGraw used to do, too.

Blanche Calloway, Cab's sister, had a very good way of entertaining. She was wild and wiry in certain things, and very sensitive when it came to balance. To me, she had a better voice than Cab, and although Cab may not say this himself I think all of his style was hers. She came to Louis and me at the Sunset and said, "If you can do anything for Cab, I'd sure appreciate it, because I can't keep him in school." We asked her what he did and she said he played drums and sang. The show had no room for another drummer, and he didn't really get into show business until after the club closed, but we coached him to a certain extent. Being around there with his sister, and watching shows nightly, he became educated so far as nightclubs and entertaining were concerned. Like any youngster, he was soon imitating a lot of people.

Red Simmons came to the club, too. He used to dance, similar to Fred Astaire—hat, cane and all that business. He was very good with that cane and he did a lot of tricks with it. But he was one of those guys who would talk himself in and talk himself *out*. He talked himself into the Sunset, but soon Ed Fox and his partner were saying, "Look, this guy's all right, but he's going to run our business sooner or later, and we don't want nobody like that around here telling us what to do." So he got angry with them and went across the road to the Plantation. Although Joe Glaser didn't have anything to do with running the club then, the place belonged to his mother and he was always around. He ran about town with show people and had good ideas, and we listened to him. It was when *he* said, "This guy's *too* smart," that they let Red go. Now somehow or other Red and Cab Calloway got into a heated argument, each saying he could outshine the other as an entertainer. When it came to blows eventually, the waiters at the Sunset said, "Well, we'll do better than that. Let's use this hall behind us here, put some boxing gloves on you guys, and we'll find out who *is* the best!" That's what they did, and everybody went over there to see the fight. Simmons knocked Calloway out, and that was the end of it.

Johnny Dunn came to Chicago one time with his horn, a long stretched-out trumpet like a coaching horn. He came through town in a show, and he used to sit in the pit with the bell of this thing resting on the stage. It was a new thing, a gimmick, and of course everybody went for that. He was supposed to be a great blues trumpet player, so one night he came out to the Sunset Café. After those long shows, Louis and all of us used to relax as much as we possibly could. Every chance I could, I'd get off the stage and leave the piano to Hamby. Louis would do the same if some trumpet player came in who wanted to jam. If we had to play a third show, we'd be really tired, and Louis would sit there with his horn on his knee. He was plump then, not fat, and full of personality. He wasn't smoking but half a cigarette at that time, and he did very little drinking. We had only two trumpets and one trombone, so a lot of the weight was on him. The night Johnny Dunn came in he was sitting there, holding his horn, a handkerchief across his lap, and we were bumming around, just playing anything. Everybody knew we had a hot, swinging band, but the guys liked to cool off for a few minutes with some of those standard tunes. We'd give one guy three choruses to play, another guy four choruses, and that way we would get a little rest. Well, Johnny walked up and reached for the horn on Louis's lap, and Louis very obligingly gave it to him, and got up, thinking that this was his chance to rest. Johnny went out on the floor and, boy, he was blowing! He had people with him from the theatre, and he was known about Chicago because he was in a big show, so when he mentioned his name and the show everybody applauded like mad. Oh, he was in a seventh heaven! Now he had heard about Louis, but he didn't know him, and he'd never heard him stretch out. After he got through playing the blues, he handed Louis's horn back to Natty Dominique, the second trumpet player. When the applause died down, Louis came back and sat down in his chair. We had to play a dance set, and we started to play a little tune called *Poor Little Rich Girl*. Nobody said this was a cutting contest, that Louis was going to try to outplay this man. We went into the tune at up tempo, and Darnell Howard played several choruses, Stumpy Evans played several, I played several choruses, and when it came Louis's turn I don't know how many choruses he played, but every time he played a new one he just kept going higher and higher. That was the end of the trumpet for that night! The place broke up. People ran up and grabbed Louis. Johnny came up and said, "Man, I didn't know you played that much horn!"

When Louis went to New York, I think Johnny Dunn was the cause of his getting a lot of publicity, because Johnny was always trying to get him to join him in jam sessions. He'd invite Louis to different places, and Louis outplayed him everywhere until people recognized Louis for the giant he was.

Punch Miller was a friend of Louis's from New Orleans, and he came into the Sunset one night. He walked up to Louis during intermission, when we were changing music and talking to some song-pluggers who wanted us to play their tunes.

"Let me play some of these things," he said

Louis Armstrong's Stompers at the Sunset Café, 1927. Standing at left: Tubby Hall, Honoré Dutrey, Earl Hines. Willy Hamby, second from right. Louis Armstrong, sitting.

to Louis as we passed out the sheets of the arrangements.

"Man, you can't play this music," Louis said. "Everybody is reading in this band."

"I can read now."

"Are you sure?"

"Yes, I can read."

"All right," Louis said, "you go ahead and play if you think so."

I got off the stand, because Fats Waller was up there on the second piano. I wanted to hear Punch Miller, because I'd heard so much about him. Louis came off, too, and we stood at the back of the room.

"All right," said Fats, "let's stomp it off!" And he stomped it off.

Punch evidently couldn't get it together, but there was a little strain he thought he was familiar enough with to take a solo on. Well, he got into the strain, but he couldn't get out of it, and that's when Fats came up with an expression that would make musicians crack up for years afterwards:

"What key are you struggling in?" he hollered. "Turn the page!"

Chicago was a wide-open town at that time. The churches were trying to close it down, and the police department thought they would co-operate. Of course, a lot of money passed under the table, but the police would raid the Sunset and we would all have to get into the patrol wagon and go down to the police station every night. All we did was sign up and go back to finish the rest of the night. I stood up in the wagon so often on those trips, I finally decided to *run* and get a seat when the police came.

The association with Louis all through this period was very inspiring to me. He was called "Satchelmouth" and I was called "Gatemouth." We were very close and when we were playing we would steal ideas from each other. Or, rather, I'd *borrow* an idea from him, and say, "Thank you." Then he'd hear me play something he liked, borrow it, and say, "Thank you." A lot of people have misinterpreted the whole thing and said that I just got my style from Louis, but I was playing it when I met him. Eubie Blake and Tom

Whaley, pianists older than I am by several years, have often told people that. Apart from the pianists in Pittsburgh I mentioned, I was very strongly influenced by Smitty's (Joe Smith's) style. He was playing a type of thing very similar to what Louis was doing at that time, but it was smoother, and it didn't have the punch Louis had. Now, of course, you couldn't be around Louis as much as I was without catching some of his spirit and drive.

Everybody knows how Louis brought high-note playing into prominence. Nobody else played in the upper register then like he did, and it was important to him to hit those high ones with a good tone and a lot of feeling. With all the ideas he had, he *also* had a beautiful tone. That's one of the reasons why ordinary people who were not musicians appreciated him so quickly. When we were playing together, it was like a continuous jam session, like when we made that record of *Weather Bird Rag*. Now when people talk of my "trumpet style," I think they usually mean when I play phrases in octaves like a trumpet player would play, but I used tremolo to give an effect like his vibrato, too. I'd reduce the weight of the note and use the sustaining pedal as the sound of the note thinned out.

Making records was something we loved to do. We hardly thought about the money. Ideas used to come to us in the studio, and we were getting our kicks without thinking about making our reputation by records. But I think the public realized that we were really playing from the heart. When Louis and I listened to what we had done, we'd grin when we heard something we liked, but we were also quick to criticize our own work to each other.

57 Varieties was really an accident. Louis and I were resting, but it was a cold day and I went to the piano just to keep my fingers warm. I was fooling around with *Tiger Rag*, hardly thinking, when a girl came out and whispered to me to finish it. I had no idea they were recording, but when I heard it I asked them what they were going to do with it.

"What shall we call it?" was all they wanted to know, and after a lot of talk they came up

Zutty Singleton.

with that title. The Heinz people in Pittsburgh, who made ketchup and pickles, used it in all their advertising at that time, so we borrowed it from them, but I never played that again!

My Monday Date got its title as a sort of gag. Louis would sometimes forget we were going to meet, or Lil, his wife, would take him off somewhere, and I'd wait and he wouldn't show up. So the next time we would be going to get together, I'd say something like "Don't forget our Monday date that you promised me last Tuesday." Out of that we got a tune and a title for one of our record sessions.

After we left the Sunset, Louis, Zutty Singleton, and I got an automobile that cost eighty or ninety dollars. It was such a terrible looking thing, we called it "The Covered Wagon." It was so bad, nobody wanted it left in front of his house. We'd leave it sitting in the street somewhere, but not near where we lived. We kept it because we wanted to run around to clubs and places after we finished, and this was our means of transportation when we weren't working. We had some gigs then that paid only three or four dollars a night. Louis's wife was booking us at that time, and we played some dances where the average good-thinking person wouldn't even dream of going. But we couldn't be choicy, and we had to play wherever she booked us. Sometimes we got our money and sometimes we didn't. It was one of those darned situations where I might have to ask Lil for two or three dollars. We'd drive into garages in the Thing and say, "Give me one," meaning one gallon. But sometimes Louis was very proud of it. He'd ride to church in it, sitting up there just as big and proud as you like. When Zutty and I wanted to get rid of it, Louis took it, and he and Lil would drive to church in that, all dressed up. He didn't go very often, but he did go. I saw him one Sunday morning, and I remember him telling me:

"Man, I had to go, because she's in some kind of club."

"Well, what did you do?"

"Sat up there and looked like all the rest."

I remember one time when Louis was driving The Covered Wagon we hit a real big bump. I was riding in the front with him, and Honoré Dutrey was in the back. Dutrey was always a very sharp, sort of fastidious dresser, and he was wearing a derby. He flew out of his seat and that derby was jammed down over his eyes and ears so hard that we had to help him out of it.

Zutty was always full of fun and jokes in those days. He'd come up to some girl he knew and say, "Gee, you look beautiful today, but where did you get those pimples?" Or he'd be walking along the sidewalk, his face would light up with a big smile, he'd fling his arms wide like he was going to greet a long-lost relative, and then he'd sweep right past some surprised person who just didn't know what to think. Then sometimes when we were going home to bed in the early morning it would still be gray, cold and dark, and we'd meet men hurrying to work with their heads down into the wind and their lunch boxes under their arms. Zutty would look at them, all smiles, and ask them, "Where's the picnic?"

When the Sunset closed in 1927, Louis, Zutty and I had formed like a little corporation, and we agreed to stick together and not play for anyone unless the three of us were hired. We even tried to run dances ourselves at Warwick Hall, but the Unholy Three were out of luck there. I made a short trip to New York, and while I was away Louis and Zutty joined Carroll Dickerson's band when the Savoy Ballroom opened in Chicago. They had Clarence Black's band on one side and Carroll's on the other. When I got back I was very disappointed that our little pact was broken and they had gone off and left me.

During the time we hadn't been working much, Ethel Waters came to Chicago. She always used to stay with a comedy act called Butterbeans and Susie, and sometimes she would just rest up at their house. If she had an

engagement she would call me, because she liked the way I accompanied her. In fact, I played for her any number of times. When a person's in the spotlight, and you're accompanying, you're always supposed to be *under* what the artist is doing. I'd always listen to what she did, and listen to the changes she made, so that the next time I could really follow the channel she was in. Some nights she'd come in not feeling so good, and she'd say, "Well, Earl, let's put it in a lower key, and take it a little slower. My throat is sort of clogged up." Sometimes she'd start a tune out and automatically slow it down. I'd feel what she was doing and do likewise. "I'm at home when I'm singing with you," she told me. "I don't have to worry about the accompaniment."

When she was at the Regal Theatre one time, Dave Peyton had the band, and he wanted to show it off and he brought up the embellishments loud. When she came off the stage she used a lot of language I won't repeat here, and told him:

"Look, you got all afternoon to show off this band. When I'm out there, I'm supposed to be the one doing the starring. You musicians are always trying to show yourselves off. When we had the rehearsal, I didn't tell you to play all that stuff. Don't ever let me catch you playing louder than me! And you on that piano, you play that backroom piano for other people, not for me. You're the leader, but you're just a piano player to me!"

It was the same with Bojangles Robinson. Some nights he would come out there feeling good and say, "We're going to pep it up tonight!" And I'd say, "All right, you set your own tempo out there, Bo, and I'll catch you." Some nights, the same tune, he would slow it down, and then the next night he'd be going at a heck of a pace.

I never forget when we were playing for him in Pittsburgh, years later, during World War II. I hadn't my regular drummer then, because they kept going to the war. Bojangles was out there dancing, dancing very light, *each* tap to be heard. That's how strict he was, and that was why he liked me. I never interfered with him on the piano. I kept the piano so soft, yet still loud enough for him to hear and feel the tempo. The drummer was playing along very lightly on the cymbals, when all of a sudden he went BOOM with his bass drum. So Bojangles stopped right there in the middle of the whole thing and said, "Look, there'll be no bombs dropping today! From now on, you just lay out. Just let Mr. Hines play for me. I'm not used to a drum anyway."

Now I always knew about the importance of softness from the time when I used to go across the street to the Plantation and listen to King Oliver. "Let me hear those feet," he'd say, when he was playing a tune like *The Pearls* by Jelly Roll Morton. "I want to hear the shuffle of feet!"

While Louis and Zutty were at the Savoy, I used to drop in the Apex Club on 35th Street. It was the same small place that had been called the Nest before. I had a girl friend who sang there, and sometimes I would sit down and accompany her. I happened to be there one night when the boy who usually played piano for Jimmie Noone couldn't make it.

"Earl, will you come in with us for a week?" they asked.

"I don't mind," I said.

At the end of the week, Jimmie asked if I'd stay, and I'd been there three months when Louis and Zutty came after me and said, "Come on, we want you to come up with us." Then I was a little sarcastic.

"No," I said, "you guys left me in the rain and broke the little corporation we had, so I'm going to stay down here with Jimmie Noone."

That's when we separated. I was so warm about being left out of that band, but I did go to see them one time. That was when Zutty had just got a xylophone. He didn't have but one note to play at the end of a number, but everybody was going up there to hear him play this xylophone. He had put a piece of paper on the note he wanted to hit, but during intermission somebody moved it, so when the band finished he hit a note completely out of tune. Everybody fell out on the floor, and he didn't know what to say. Zutty almost quit the band right then.

I guess I was with Jimmie Noone almost a year. We worked from midnight to 6 A.M., and when we got off we'd get in the car and go out to Jackson Park as day was breaking. Jimmie's wife was a golf pro who mostly taught women, but she did a lot for us, too. She showed us how to hold the club properly, how to drive, and everything. She was a very pretty girl, a Creole from New Orleans, I think, and she would play all the champions around. We still had to contend with the racial thing, but the man there would let us play until 9 when the clubhouse opened. Sometimes we'd play eighteen holes, sometimes only nine if we were tired. Then we'd go home, take a shower, and sleep the rest of the day, because we didn't go to work till 12 at night. Jimmie was very good at golf, but we went out more for exercise than scores. After being among smoke and whiskey all night long, it was a good thing to do. The banjo player, Bud Scott, didn't go at all, and Joe Poston only went occasionally; but Jimmie, his wife, the drummer, and I went all the time when the weather was good. The drummer, Johnny Wells, was the most unorthodox golf player I ever saw. He never paid any attention to instructions Jimmie's wife gave us. He had the most unorthodox way of driving, and he could drive farther than any of us. He could really hit the ball, and straight, without slicing like the average golfer often does.

I used to play tennis, too, at Jackson Park. There were a couple of fellows in the same building, and I saw them going out to play in the morning a lot, and I wanted to see if I was still as good as when I was real young. I always liked sports, but the problem when you get in a band is finding someone you want to go out with. Because they fool around all night and sleep all day, most musicians never think of going bowling or playing golf. When I was with Louis at the Sunset, we used to go out and play baseball in the morning. In the afternoons we'd have teams, and play with a hard ball, too! In later years when I was driving my car, I always used to carry my bowling ball in the back, hoping to find people I could go bowling with. The kind of bookings I get now mean I have to use planes instead of a car.

Going back to the Apex, I have to say that Jimmie Noone was a very fine clarinetist, but he was sort of a jealous fellow and he didn't want anyone to get more applause or consideration than he did. I'd made a lot of friends at the Sunset, and they would come in to hear me. They'd stand around behind the piano to listen to me play, and Jimmie didn't like that too well. Then the proprietor wanted to fire Jimmie and hire me, and the musicians' union wanted to fine me, because they said I was taking over Jimmie Noone's band, which I wasn't. I didn't want the band, and I wanted to quit, but the union wouldn't let me quit. Finally my contract ran out, and I just walked off the place, although the people that owned it begged me to stay. "You've got the place as long as you want to stay here," they said.

One incident that I always remember at the Apex had to do with *Rhapsody in Blue.* I had been playing it in the Sunset because they had a show built on it, and because I had played it so long I really knew it backwards. We used to get some very prominent musicians and theatrical people in the Apex, and I used to sit up there on its very small bandstand and play this piece with quite a lot of success. One night, after I finished playing it, I went to the men's room.

"You play *Rhapsody in Blue* very well," a gentleman said.

"Thank you," I said.

When he went out, the attendant asked if I knew who he was.

"No."

"That was George Gershwin."

You known that really upset me. You never know who's listening to you.

While I was walking around not doing anything, I got a call from the Q.R.S. people to go to New York and make eight sides for them. They were an established piano-roll company, but they didn't know much about the record business and put out all eight sides at one time, so the records didn't go over too well. During those days you put out a record and waited three months before you put out another. I think I made a couple of piano rolls for them, too, but nobody has ever been able to trace them, so I guess they didn't issue them. What is strange, though, is that I got a call from the Q.R.S. people when I was playing at the Statler-Hilton in Buffalo in 1975! The company had moved to Buffalo and they had me cut piano rolls of *Blues in Thirds, Rosetta, My Monday Date* and *Boogie Woogie on St. Louis Blues.* I was surprised to know people were still making and selling piano rolls. I'm sure the process has been much improved, but they are not so easy to make as ordinary records.

When I went to New York with Lois Deppe the first time, I met Willie "The Lion" Smith and played something like *Twelfth Street Rag.* I don't think it impressed him much. He just roared, "I'm the Lion!" and then went back to the piano and tore it up. In 1928, after playing *Rhapsody in Blue* and music like that in Chicago, I got a little more recognition from him, but he was twelve years older than I was, so I was really in awe of him. A few years make a big difference when you're young.

SEE NO EVIL

Percy Venable, the producer, had a boy who used to work with him and run errands. His name was Lucius, and sometimes he was known as Lucius Venable, but later on he was better known as Lucky Millinder. He was said to be Percy Venable's nephew, but I don't believe he was a relative at all. I think Venable just allowed him to use his name. Anyway, he was taught to dance, to memorize all the steps and different dances that the chorus line were given by Venable. It was very important to have somebody to remember the routines, because Percy Venable was producing shows at several different clubs, and after a time Lucius became a real pro and could rehearse and take a whole show down for him. He also became well acquainted with the music the guys were playing at that time.

Ed Fox was getting ready to open a new club at Oakwood and South Parkway in 1928. It had been an old movie house and it had a sloping floor, not like the Sunset, which had a regular flat floor. They took the balcony out, built different levels like terraces where the customers sat, and called the place the Grand Terrace. I hadn't heard anything about this, but Fox had hired Percy Venable to produce the show. They were trying to find somebody with some sort of name that could open the Grand Terrace as a bandleader. It was Lucius who said, "The one person I know is Earl Hines." And he called me while I was still in New York for Q.R.S.

I didn't actually have a band at that time

but a group of us had been rehearsing in the hope something would turn up, and now it did. I think we opened with twelve men, and those I remember are Shirley Clay and George Mitchell on trumpet; Billy Franklin on trombone; Lester Boone and Toby Turner doubling on alto clarinet; Cecil Irwin, arranger and tenor sax, doubling clarinet; Claude Roberts, banjo; Hayes Alvis, bass; and Buddy Washington on drums. I think we started with ten chorus girls, whom we called "ponies," and four or five acts. Later we had sixteen chorus girls and eight parade girls in the show. The place wasn't really finished and it wasn't completely carpeted. It had an upright piano. Everybody thought Ed Fox was losing his mind opening a club like this in the heart of the South Side, but he called us all together before it opened, the waiters, the band, the chorus and the acts.

"I have a hundred thousand dollars," he said, "and I'm going to run this place for one year. Whether anybody comes in here or not, you're going to get your money."

He was true to his word, too. He used to sit at a ringside table, sometimes by himself, sometimes with his family. The whole show had to go on, because he was a stickler about time. It went on at 10:30 whether there was anybody there or not, and we had to do the show exactly like we would if the house was full. Whatever else I may say about him, I have to say he was one of the finest nightclub managers I ever ran into. He had a good system and he stuck to it. It was the same with the club's menu. Everything on it was always available, regardless of what business he was doing.

"If you're going to ask these people for money," he said, "you've got to give them a good show."

He went all over the United States to find people of the right calibre for his shows. We had Bojangles Robinson, Buck and Bubbles, Ethel Waters, and the Four Step Brothers. By the time work on the club was finished it was a beautiful place. There were stairs coming down each side of the bandstand, and six parade girls used to pose on those stairs while the chorus line was tearing it up on the raised dance floor in front of the band. There were a whole lot of mirrors with blue lights on them that gave a starlight effect at the bar, which was at the back of the room so that it was never too much of a distraction. The acoustics were very good, but we didn't have any amplification yet. On Saturday nights, especially, you used to get customers far gone with liquor who were rather loud, and the waiters would go around trying to keep them quiet. But that didn't happen too often after a while, because people realized we were putting on really good shows, and they had to be quiet to enjoy them. Percy Venable's name was a guarantee of a good show in Chicago at that time, and when we opened it was at the top of the marquee, the acts were in the middle, and the band was at the bottom. By the time I finished there in 1940, the band had been at the top for a long time.

We opened at the Grand Terrace on my birthday, 28 December 1928, and we began to record for Victor early in 1929. As a matter of fact, I was on the Victor staff as a pianist for three years in Chicago and recorded with all kinds of groups and singers. I never forget a session one snowy morning with a hillbilly group from Louisville led by a violinist named Clifford Hayes. The producer assured me the records wouldn't be issued, but they were. I was sitting in a restaurant with Louis and Zutty about 5 o'clock one morning when one of these records was played on the radio.

"Man, that cat sounds so much like you,"

Louis said, "he could be your twin brother!"

We all stopped to listen, and then he said, "That *is* you!"

"Oh, you're kidding," I said. "You know I wouldn't be playing with a group like that!"

"Well, he sure has got your style. That's the closest I've heard anybody play like you."

During the course of the record I realized it was me, but I never told Louis. If he had seen that band, I would never have heard the end of it. The trombone player's slide was bent up so it looked like he was playing around a corner, and the violinist held his violin down where his chest was. The Victor people used to call me up in the morning, and I'd go down to record with people I'd never seen or heard of in my life. I may very well have recorded that *Blue Yodel No. 9* with Jimmy Rogers, and I can definitely remember recording with a harmonica player around that time.

Louis went to New York soon after we opened at the Grand Terrace, and I never forget the postcard he sent me when he got there. It read like this:

"Man, everybody up here is trying to cut one another. It's got so bad that when we were at a party one night a guy with a bass horn on his shoulder came and knocked on the door. 'Anybody here I can cut?' he asked."

Gangsters came into the Grand Terrace about two years after it opened. They just walked in one day. One man went to the cash register, one stood out front, and one on either side of the building. The lieutenant went to the back.

"We're going to take twenty-five percent," he said.

"You must be losing your mind," Ed Fox said.

"Well, you need protection."

"I've been doing all right for two years and I don't need protection."

"You're going to have protection. You have a nice family and you wouldn't want anything to happen to your boys, would you?"

So they practically ran the place, and while they were there the police never came in, so I guess there was some finagling going on. If

Opposite: Earl Hines, 1928.

The First Grand Terrace band. Left to right: (back) Billy Franklin, Toby Turner, Shirley Clay, Claude Roberts, George Dixon; (front) Cecil Irwin, Hayes Alvis, Buddy Washington, George Mitchell, Earl Hines, Lester Boone.

anybody was unruly, the floorwalkers that belonged to the gangsters threw them out front, and the police picked them up from there. From time to time different gangs would come in and try to outspend one another, and a whole lot of money was made that way. Mae Alix used to run across the floor and do a split, and every time she did it they gave her money, which she used to divide with the band. We had a comedian named Billy Mitchell, and he had a way of turning his foot almost completely around. They liked that so much, they'd keep him out there thirty minutes sometimes, and then they'd give him money which he'd share out with us, too.

They told us no harm would come to us so long as we did what we were supposed to do and let them handle what they were supposed to do. It was a case of the three monkeys: See no evil, hear no evil, speak no evil. I used to hear a lot of the appointments and arrangements they made while sitting in the kitchen. Trucks of beer to be run from this place to that place, and things of that sort. If a detective asked me what they were talking about, I'd say, "I don't know."

"Well, you were sitting right next to them back there."

"I sit next to people on the El and the bus, and it's none of my business what they're talking about."

I knew and everybody else knew that if you had anything to say about the way the club was being run, why the first thing the department would do was stick your picture in the paper, and the next thing you'd be found dead in Jackson Park someplace. I knew the police knew every move they were making, so why should I be the fall guy?

Along with so many of the bad traits people said Al Capone had, he had some good traits, too. He used to run a restaurant twenty-four hours a day where poor people could get free meals, and he took over real estate where these same poor people could move in and live. He used to come by the club at night, and if I met him by the door he might put his hand up to straighten my handkerchief, and there would be a hundred-dollar bill. Or he might give me a handshake and put a twenty-dollar bill in my hand. Some nights the heads of his organization used to come in and tell Ed Fox to close up. "This is our night," they'd say, and give him a thousand dollars. They would always pick a slow night, too, so Fox loved that. We'd play one show, and after that everybody used to come off the stand, and then you didn't know what you were, a musician, a show person or a gangster. Everybody was mixing, having a great time. So there was fun along with the headaches during the reign of the racketeers.

Guns were often drawn at the Grand Terrace—even the waiters had guns—but no shots were fired because of the risk of hitting innocent customers. Rival parties from different parts of Chicago would fight sometimes, and throw ice and bottles at each other. I remember getting under the piano one time, and by then we had a Bechstein grand. I found a lady already there.

"What are you doing here?" I asked.

"I'm a guest. What are you doing here?"

"This is my place. I work here."

Business improved in the club so much that Ed Fox sent me downtown one day to pick out a new piano. When I went in the showroom, I saw this beautiful, white Bechstein standing there. I played it, and it sounded as good as it looked. "This is it," I said. The people called Ed Fox, and he said, "Yes, let him have whatever he wants!" But when he got the bill, he hit the ceiling. "Three thousand dollars!" he said. "Are you crazy?" But I think he was proud of it, and for a time he used to have his son sort of stand guard over it on the floor. It made a big difference to me, because a good piano makes me feel like playing and inspires me.

When I went out on the road with the band the first time, Al Capone appointed two bodyguards to go with me, because he felt rival gangs might try to injure me to injure him. He thought of me as a "property" in which he had a whole lot of money invested because of the Grand Terrace. Those guys followed me everywhere and would even camp outside my hotel-room door. Eventually I protested.

"I don't need them," I said.

"You don't?" Capone answered. "I've got thirty of them."

I was in a music store a block away when the St. Valentine's Day massacre occurred. There were so many cops in the area right afterwards I thought some celebrity was visiting.

The gangsters had a meeting one night when I was in the Grand Terrace kitchen, and one of them came rushing through and tossed a package in my lap.

"The heat's on!" he shouted as he went out the back.

I opened it up later and found there was $12,000 in the package. I counted it and hid it, because I knew I'd have to have it when they asked for it.

"You got that stuff?" they asked a week later, and gave me five hundred for my trouble.

This kind of thing didn't happen only in Chicago. Hayes Alvis, the bass player, went to New York after he left me, and he worked at the Cotton Club with the Blue Rhythm Band and Duke Ellington. He told me Owney Madden kept carrier pigeons on the roof of the club and the boys used to send things by pigeon that would have been illegal by mail. At the time when they were having trouble with Dutch Schwartz, Hayes was told not to go up on the roof, but one nice night he went up anyway and found two guys with machine guns trained on the entrance!

Things like this went on in the background. The public wasn't aware of them, and the shows and music took all their attention. They were exciting times all the same, and I think some of the excitement got into the music, but maybe it just came from the kick we got out of making those "ponies" dance harder and faster. We certainly played more up tempos in those days than bands did later on, and that shows on the records we made in the '30s for different labels.

After we'd been at the Grand Terrace about three years, they kept having trouble with m.c.'s, so Percy Venable said, "I'm going to make an m.c. out of Earl." I thought that was the greatest thing in the world! I knew practically everybody that came in the place just from seeing them there night after night, and I thought I was well prepared to be an m.c. But just like Louis Armstrong at the Sunset, I found it was an awful distance from a foot-high bandstand to the floor. I didn't realize that till opening night.

"He can't talk," Ed Fox said. "Don't let him be an m.c."

"These m.c.'s come in here and work just as long as they want to," Percy said, "but when they don't feel like working the show is stuck and nobody knows what to do. Earl has the band here every night, and he's got to be here, so we wouldn't have to worry about an m.c. Is it okay with you, Earl?"

"Sure," I said, "think nothing of it."

Although Ed Fox told me what to say, he knew show business, too.

I came confidently down the staircase onto the floor, and when I got to the microphone it was just as Fox expected. I couldn't remember what I had to say, I couldn't open my mouth, I couldn't even say, "Good evening." I was tongue-tied. Fox was standing at the side sort of hissing at me.

"Goddammit, say something!" he said. "Say something!"

In the end I learned to be an m.c. Working under several different directors and producers, I got a good conception of show business and could almost produce a show myself. I knew how to set a show up and get contrasts in it. I studied stage deportment, and I paid a lot of attention to vocalizing, to those who were getting the best reception because of the *tone* of their voices.

We started broadcasting out of the Grand Terrace just after the third year. We used to play on a small station that they called the Cadillac station. They'd play records and talk all night long. After we'd made arrangements to put the remote in, the engineer would call from the station and say, "Whenever you're ready." Dave, the captain of the floormen, was a pretty well educated fellow. He knew the show backwards and he knew all the people who came in, so as soon as they turned it on he would start talking about what was going on in the club, and often he'd give a running commentary for as long as three hours. When we were playing a dance number, he'd say who was dancing on the floor. People would come up to the mike and say things like, "Be home very shortly, Mom." Or, "We're having a grand time!" Or, "Hello, honey, how are you?" They'd hear the band playing and he would tell the names of the people in the show and what they were doing. It may have been corny, but people liked it, and it was a good advertisement. Of course, microphones were not very good or strong then, and he'd just be sitting at a table with the one from the radio station.

This went on until larger stations began to get interested. NBC had two stations, WMAQ and WENR, and they had what they called a blue line and a red line. The blue line went to New York and the red line from Chicago to California. So we would sign on in Chicago to New York at 11, play a half hour, sign off, and then sign right back on the red line going to California. This red line took in quite a bit of Canada, so when we toured Canada there was just as much enthusiasm. It got to the stage where we were broadcasting every night and people were waiting up to hear us. We played our jazz numbers, but we also played tunes of the day and even waltzes. We did a little bit of everything and became very popular. I think we had more air time than any other band in the U.S.

Guy Lombardo came into vogue around this time with his "sweetest music this side of heaven," and that kind of music kept his place jammed every night. But he used to come down to hear us, because his band couldn't play jazz like we were playing it. "I come down here to be reborn," he told me once.

I was lucky to have Cecil Irwin playing tenor saxophone in the band. He was a wonderful arranger who had really studied music. He had read any number of books on harmony and arranging, and he was really ahead of his time. Most bands were playing the stock arrangements put out by music houses, so Cecil's gave our band a touch of individuality. He

was a calm, likable fellow who didn't care about gambling or anything like that, and he never got into any trouble. He was a very good friend of mine, and I liked him because he was so serious about his work. He was a stickler for good music and wanted things exactly right.

The first girl singer I had in the band was Geneva Washington from Pittsburgh. I didn't have another till Valaida Snow. She had been to Shanghai, China, with Teddy Weatherford in Jack Carter's band. Teddy stayed, but she came back.

Valaida was very versatile and very musical. She could sing, dance and produce a show. She could play trumpet, violin and piano. Walter Richardson, one of the great baritone singers of that time, introduced me to her. She had come in the Sunset with Kathryn Perry and her husband. Walter liked Valaida and she didn't pay much attention to me. Later, he got attached to Kathryn. I was living at 51st Street then, and I got a strange idea. I had the lady who owned the house cook a dinner and invited them over. I hadn't the slightest idea I was ever going to get mixed up with either one of those girls, but I did, with both of them.

Both of them were very pretty. Kathryn was much smaller, and Valaida is harder to describe. She had all the physical attractions you could want in a girl, and she made a heck of an appearance. All this came out after she had begun working at the Sunset, and I thought she was the greatest girl I had ever seen. In her act she had seven different pairs of shoes set out front, and she'd do a dance in each of them—soft shoes, adagio shoes, tap shoes, Dutch clogs, and I don't know what else, but last of all Russian boots. She'd do a chorus in each, and on the tap number she tapped just like Bojangles. Louis Armstrong had a fit when he saw her. "Boy, I never saw anything that great," he told me. She broke up the house every time.

About the time I was going into the Grand Terrace, she was going with one of the Mills Brothers, who were just getting started then. Later on, she was going with one of the Jones

Boys. She was a girl like that. She just loved a good time, and she had to have the best of everything.

After the Sunset closed, she went on the road and was in several big shows. The last time I saw her before she came back to Chicago again, she was with Noble Sissle and Eubie Blake in a show called *Rhapsody in Black*. They had about thirty musicians and she directed the whole band in the first part of the show. Then she had her own spot, and after that she did a number with the Berry Brothers. When that show finished, Ed Fox got in touch with her and had her come to the Grand Terrace. I can't remember who was headlining, but she came next after a great dance couple from Cuba. She was what we called an *ingenue* then, in front of the chorus. She sang *The Very Thought of You* and that kind of number. I always remember, too, how she used to sing *Brother, Can You Spare a Dime?* She'd come out dressed all raggedy and wearing an old cap on her head. During the Depression she would break the people up with that song.

I was broadcasting a lot by then, and after hearing her sing Fox asked me:

"Why don't you let her sing a number on the radio with you?"

"Fine," I said, and when I asked her about it she immediately said, "Yeah." We had an arrangement all ready and it went over very well.

When the club closed for the summer, Fox thought it best to send her out on the road with us, and that's when she and I became *very* close friends. When we came back, they were having trouble with producers and directors.

"Valaida," Fox said, "do you know anything about producing?"

"Sure," she said. "I can put the show on for you."

After all, she could dance and she could sing and she knew what to do. She put that show together herself. She saved him an awful lot of money, too, because whenever a new

Valaida Snow sings *Brother, Can You Spare a Dime?*

show went on there had to be a lot of new arrangements for it. She was so talented. She
picked out numbers from the band's book that
could be used, memorized them, and
hummed or scatted them to the chorus. Then
when we came in, the rehearsals were very
short, because the girls already knew the
band's routines. *Bubbling Over* was one of the
numbers she produced. Beer and wine had
come back after Prohibition, and that was the
inspiration for the song. She always knew
what she wanted and nobody could fool her.
There was still no legal whiskey, gin or hard
liquor.

She had a Mercedes and a chauffeur, and
she used to send him to pick me up and take
me home. That was one way she had of keeping track of where I was and what I was doing!

"Dammit," I'd say, "I've got my own car
right here!"

"Yes," the chauffeur would say, "but I have
to follow orders."

She used to dress luxuriously and look very,
very glamorous. She was just a beautiful and
exceptionally talented woman. I remember
one time when we were playing together at
the Regal, just the two of us, as we often used
to do at the Grand Terrace. She had been in
an accident and she had about a dozen stitches
in her head. When she blew a high note on
the trumpet, a stitch popped and blood began
to run down the back of her head, and a doctor had to fix her up when we got through.
But all the time she was onstage she continued to smile, and the audience never knew
what trouble she was in. It was the same when
her mother died. The funeral was on Sunday,
but Valaida was back at work Monday, entertaining the people as though nothing had happened.

After she left the Grand Terrace, she went
to Europe for the first time, and she had gone
back there when World War II broke out. The
Nazis put her in a concentration camp and
treated that wonderful woman so badly I don't
think she ever really recovered, physically or
mentally, although she kept working until she
fell sick and died in 1956. I was playing the
Apollo when she came back from Europe, and

Jack Carter brought her by, and I didn't realize who it was.

"Don't you remember Valaida, Earl?" he
said.

She was one of the greatest.

After Valaida left, we had to find another
girl, and we found Kathryn Perry. She'd been
at the Sunset, too, in a dance act. She was a
very charming, pretty girl. She had a good
voice and played violin. She became such an
important part of the show at the Grand Terrace that when Fletcher Henderson came in
she stayed and sang with him. In the meantime, I had been divorced and she had become my common-law wife. We lived in a big
apartment and her parents stayed with us.

Back in the '20s and '30s, waiters took far
more interest in the clubs they worked in than
they do now. There was an awful lot of competition in Chicago—between twenty-five and
thirty nightclubs that had big attractions and
shows—and they wanted their club to stay
open and wanted people in it. They heard a
lot of singers and bands, and saw people dancing, and really got a darn good conception of
what an artist could do on that floor. Proprietors used to listen to what waiters said, especially when new acts opened. Fox knew I had
had a lot of experience at the Sunset, and he
used to consult me. I did so many things that
were successful, but when new singers came
in he got in a habit of huddling up with the
waiters, asking what they thought.

Alberta Hunter had made a bit of a name as
a blues singer and then went to France. When
she came back, she tried to sing all standard,
popular tunes, some of them in French.

"She's singing like she's got marbles in her
mouth," the waiters at the Grand Terrace
said, "and we can't hear the words. Why don't
she sing them blues like she used to years
ago? That's what you hired her for."

Fox went to her and said, "I want to hear
you sing them blues." But one thing led to
another, and finally he cut her salary. She was
getting $750 a week, a whole lot of money for
a single then, but he finally cut it down to
where she was getting only $200. "You quit

whenever you get ready to quit," Fox told her, but she stayed until the show ended.

The waiters criticized me in the same way when I brought Trummy Young in there. He was learning to hit high notes on his trombone then, and they were going around saying, "Why don't you get that musician out of here?" Fox told them I was the bandleader in charge and knew what I wanted. When Trummy turned out to be good, and to have an original style, the waiters all said, "I knew that boy had it in him!"

Sundays, the Grand Terrace was let off to social clubs from 4 to 7 o'clock. The band and show would go on for them in the usual way. Sometimes the crowd would be sitting around a bit drunk when the waiters wanted to set up tables for the 9 o'clock show. If he couldn't get rid of the people, the owner would turn on the air conditioner full and freeze them out!

Ed Fox knew music all right, because he'd been in show business all his life, but he knew very little about *bands*. We used to get very angry because he was listening so much to what the waiters had to say. Not satisfied with that, he was always asking other bandleaders what they thought of the band and making slighting remarks about it. It didn't make any difference to him that we had the best arranger in Chicago at that time. He used to bring in other bands on Sundays, like Erskine Tate's, and have them play a few numbers, and I think Fox thought Erskine had a better band than ours. He asked Guy Lombardo what he thought about Erskine's band, and Guy laughed at him and told him it was ridiculous to make the comparison. Another time Paul Whiteman came in with Mildred Bailey and Roy Bargy.

"Are you out of your goddamned mind?" Whiteman asked him. "You've got the world's greatest piano player."

"You make a change," Bargy said, "and you'll lose all the business you get from other entertainers."

Gradually Fox came to realize that our band was an asset to the place, but he wouldn't give me more than a year's contract. It wasn't till the gangsters moved in that I got a lifetime contract at the club. Meanwhile, the radio was making us known around the country.

"You can make a lot of money with this band in the East," Willie Bryant told Ed Fox. "Everybody's listening to them!"

Earl Hines and his orchestra, 1932. Louis Taylor, Billy Franklin, trombones; Charlie Allen, Walter Fuller, George Dixon, trumpets; Earl Hines, piano; Wallace Bishop, drums; Omer

I wish he had told us, because we didn't know that, and it was the first time Ed Fox knew. He sold us down the river, but when he sent us out we thought it was something new. We'd get a dinner on the train, and that was a big deal, but I was getting $150 a week and the boys were making $75, $80, or $90. Fox was getting $3500 a week for the band when he was paying us that so he really made money. The first theatre we played when we left Chicago was the Pearl in Philly. We had played Balaban and Katz theatres around Chicago by this time, so we were not new to the stage.

The same thing was happening with the song-pluggers. They used to give us a few dollars for playing their songs, and then one time I refused to play a guy's tune because it was a real dog. He wanted to know why.

"Look," he said, "I gave Fox fifty dollars to play our tune. You're playing everybody else's!"

"Well, now," I said, "I didn't know *that*."

So from then on I was on the ground floor, although we had to split it. The arranger got twenty-five and so did I.

The first time we went to Pittsburgh after the band had become a success in Chicago and people had heard our broadcasts, they had a great big parade for us, and they put the whole band in the Elks Lodge. We got a great reception, just like the astronauts when they came back!

Another time, on my way to the Lafayette in New York, I brought the band to play in Olympic Park in McKeesport. (Kennywood Park, that I mentioned earlier, was between Duquesne and Homestead.) Now as a youngster, my feelings had often been hurt in the matter of color. My grandfather, on my stepmother's side, was white. Many of the relatives were light-skinned and belonged to what was called the "blue vein society" up river from McKeesport. I had often been shunned, excluded, and made to feel unwelcome by these relatives, but now that I was famous they were all over me. They all came to Olympic Park, told me they were going to have a party afterwards, and asked me to come. "Sure," I said, but I asked my valet to find me the ugliest black girl he could. After the dance I introduced her to my "blue vein" relatives as my girl friend. They were taken aback by her manner and appearance. They said they would

Simeon, Darnell Howard, Cecil Irwin, saxophones; Lawrence Dixon, banjo; Quinn Wilson, bass.

rent a car to take her and me out to the party. I just laughed and said, "Forget it!"

In Chicago, Louis Armstrong and I had also met up with "blue vein society" when our color prevented us from joining Sammy Stewart's band. It consisted entirely of light-skinned musicians at that time. Stewart's guitar player, Lawrence Dixon, who later worked for me, was white in appearance.

that he knew and we went and played them. After we got to them, he found out what was happening in the neighborhood. We didn't need too much advance publicity, because everybody knew us from the broadcasts, and they wanted to see what we looked like. All they wanted was a week in front of the date. We stayed out there close to six months with Harry Squires and a rented bus. We even

Earl Hines and his orchestra, 1935. Left to right: (back) Walter Fuller, Warren Jefferson, George Dixon, trumpets; Wallace Bishop, drums; Quinn Wilson, bass; (front) Kenny Stewart, Trummy Young, Louis Taylor, trombones; Lawrence Dixon, guitar; Earl Hines, piano; Omer Simeon, Budd Johnson, Darnell Howard, Jimmy Mundy, reeds.

When we first went out on the road in a bus, it was with a guy called Harry Squires. He had heard the band broadcasting while he was in New York. He was working out of the William Morris agency, but they didn't have a section for bands then. So he decided to go out on his own. He came to Chicago and sold Ed Fox a bill of goods. "When you close up in the summer," he said, "let me take the band on tour." We used to say he carried his office in his hat, because he had two or three towns

found out we were popular in Canada, where they had been listening to us on the red network. Harry was the kind of fellow who knew just how to conduct himself with all the guys. He carried papers with phone numbers all written everywhere.

I remember one time we had to cross a bridge, and when we got to the other side they wanted to collect so much for the bus. Harry came in and told us to give him just the pennies we had, nothing but pennies. This made the people at the bridge think the band was hungry and didn't have any money, so they let us through! Harry did a lot of little things like that, and I appreciated the way he worked for us. He finally became a concert booker and opened up a department for bands at William Morris. I never forgot him, because he gave us all the experience we needed in traveling when we first went out with a bus.

Later on, we'd rent our own bus, usually from the Newark Bus Company for about twenty-eight cents a mile. If you had a strange bus, you had to have a license to get into New York, and half the time other bus companies wouldn't have it. Of course, there were different ways of coming into the city where they wouldn't be checked on, and some drivers knew just how to slip into New York.

When we were in Philadelphia one time, we parked the bus at a gas station. When we came back, all of our clothes and some of the instruments had been stolen. Later on, I ran into the local head man—the leader of gangsters, I'll call him. They were real tough boys there, but he and I became friends and he said, "Let me get all your things back together." Do you know, he finally got practically *every*thing that had been stolen given back to us. And after that we stood in good with those guys and never had any more trouble in Philadelphia.

The bus drivers were usually very congenial. Sometimes we'd stop on the highway and play baseball. If we met another band with baseball equipment, we'd all get out and play while the drivers slept. We had one driver, though, who just *wouldn't* sleep. We stopped one day just off the highway, and the boys were going to gamble while he slept. I found out he was right in the middle of the game— no sleep at all! Those drivers were so accustomed to driving that they thought nothing of five hundred and even seven hundred miles.

When we had a terrible accident in 1935, it wasn't our driver's fault. Cecil Irwin, my closest friend, was killed instantly when a loaded grain truck hit the bus. We had finished an engagement in Des Moines and the bus was on the way to Minneapolis. It was a bad night,

raining, turning to hail and snow, and I had tried to tell the road manager, Philip Aiken, not to send the bus through. Our driver was smart and pulled off to one side on a narrow road, but the truck had bulging sides and it just gouged into the side of our bus, threw my little tenor saxophonist to the back and broke his neck. Aiken, Kathryn Perry and I were traveling by train, but somehow George Dixon caught up with us at Iowa Falls.

"We have had an accident," he said.

"What!"

"Cecil . . . I think Cecil is dead."

It upset me so much that I didn't know what to do. The pit orchestra kept playing overtures over and over, waiting for the band to come in. They had had to stop at a hospital and be bandaged up, and I didn't want to go on at all. Besides Cecil, Billy Franklin, Omer Simeon, George Dixon, Walter Fuller, Wallace Bishop, Louis Taylor, Trummy Young, Louis Dunlap the valet, and an entertainer named Bobbie Frazier were all injured. I drank two bottles of the hardest whiskey I could find, and it didn't faze me. I was so angry with that manager.

You can imagine how we looked on that stage. Some of the guys had to be carried on, their faces all greased up so the marks didn't show. We put on a terrific performance, although I felt very bad when we played arrangements Cecil had made especially for our tour. Billy Franklin was so badly injured he could never play slide trombone again, but he had been singing with us and he decided to go to a classical teacher later on and he did very well in the classical field afterwards.

A year or two later, we were in another accident in the Cumberland Mountains when the bus went off the road at a corner. Wallace Bishop broke his ankle there trying to jump out the door before the bus landed. When we got to the hospital we were all whispering and he got very alarmed. "Talk out loud," he said. "Stop whispering back there! What's happening?" He was afraid he was more seriously injured than he was.

Another time when we were traveling, the bus suddenly made a very sharp turn and stopped. The guys were all drinking and one of them was standing in the aisle with a bottle of strawberry pop. For some reason, the lights went out, but when they came on again he looked at his shirt and cried out, "I'm dead! Look at the blood! I'm dead!" Nobody could convince him otherwise until we showed him the bottle.

We used to play in Natchez, Mississippi, quite often, because George Dixon had relatives there, and people were very nice. So we always used to take every chance to rest up in Natchez a day or so. One year, we had played there and were supposed to make a return engagement for some high school kids, but they couldn't come up with the agreed money so we didn't play it. Walter Barnes and His Royal Creolians played instead, and we were working just a few miles away. The whole place burned down and only Walter's vocalist and a couple of the boys were able to get out. Someone must have been watching over us that time.

A third accident happened years later when I was driving myself. I had a new Chrysler Newport, canary colored with red upholstery and red wire wheels—a very attractive car. It was summertime, so naturally I wanted to drive it with the top down. We had played a dance in San Anton', and the guy who gave it wanted us all to go by a club he had there, so it got very late. A doctor I knew had asked if I'd take his daughter with me to Fort Worth, where I was going to stop. When we drove off, I'd had hardly any sleep, and I must have dozed, because the next thing I knew I was in hospital. I think the girl had grabbed the wheel, but they told me I'd hit a truck and been thrown out of the car. My head struck a rock and glass ground in my eye because I was wearing sunglasses. Luckily for me, the surgeon was just leaving the hospital when they took me in, and he decided to stay when he heard who I was. I had fifty-two stitches in my eyelid and three in my eyeball, and it cost me $2000 to save my right eye. I came out of the hospital too soon. I should have stayed longer. The doctor said he was afraid of what might happen if I didn't take treatment. Ever since then I've had trouble with that eye when I'm in a room full of smoke or when strong lights are shone on me. It gets sore and I can't see too well with it. My friend Clark Terry was in the London House once, and he thought I was ignoring him, but I didn't see him to recognize him. It's a shame I didn't stay longer in the hospital, but the bookers were canceling engagements left and right, and I couldn't afford to let them do that, for the band's sake as well as my own.

Several years later, Duke Ellington was in an accident. He was coming down in an elevator when one of the dome lights fell out and cut the back of his hand. I was off at the time and he called me and asked if I would fill in for him at the Adams Theatre in Newark for a week. That was an experience I shall never forget. It was the strangest thing about Duke's band: when you saw them they looked like they could never get it together, but when they *hit*, the whole roof would come down! Each man was an artist, and they did a lot of things like other bands, but when they came together and hit, that was a real machine, a real band. Rex Stewart came late one time and he slid onstage just in time to play the high notes at the end of *C Jam Blues*.

When we were out on the road, I always used to feel fine till we got to New York. Then my feathers fell. It was such a rat race there. Anybody who didn't live there was considered a damn fool. I used to hate it when I first went there, and I still do.

"Well, you're in the Big Apple now!" Ralph Cooper would say, very grand, when he was m.c. at the Harlem Opera House.

"What does that mean?" I'd ask. "Chicago is a hell of a town, too!"

We used to play a four-week tour that was known as "Round the World." We played in Philly (first at the Pearl Theatre, then at the Lincoln and the Grand), in New York (at the Harlem Opera House, the Lafayette, and then the Apollo), in Baltimore at the Royal, and in Washington at the Howard. Ristina was the leader of the No. 1 chorus at the Apollo, and I always asked for her and Dusty Fletcher, the comedian, for the whole trip.

As I said earlier, I made very little money as a leader the first few years when I went out on the road. We were being taken, and I didn't know it. It was because of this that I am the way I am today, a fact that some of the agents may not realize.

Now we soon got in the way of using certain comedians, who worked best with us when we went to cities like New York, and Dusty Fletcher always worked with us there. This particular time, when we went back to the Apollo, Dusty came to me when we were at rehearsal Thursday night and said, "They've canceled me out of the show!" Then the producer came and said, "Now, look, you're going to play in the pit."

We had white suits that were very pretty, and we had some heavy fellows in the band, like Darnell Howard. The pit was so small and so difficult to get in and out of, I was afraid we

The producer called the manager, and he came and said, "You *are* going in the pit!"

I told all the boys to pack up then, and we left the show standing there. Next morning I went to the theatre and said, "Well, what about it?" The stage manager said, "We've got you set up on the stage."

Then the owner of the theatre, Frank Schiffman, came by. He had a fit. "Nobody works with me, the so-and-so's," he said.

"This man held the band up," the stage manager said, "and we had to have a show, didn't we?"

Anyway, we didn't go in the pit, and from then on any number of bands started working on the stage.

While we were there, Dusty Fletcher came to me and said, "Earl, you should be getting more money. They're paying $3500 for the band."

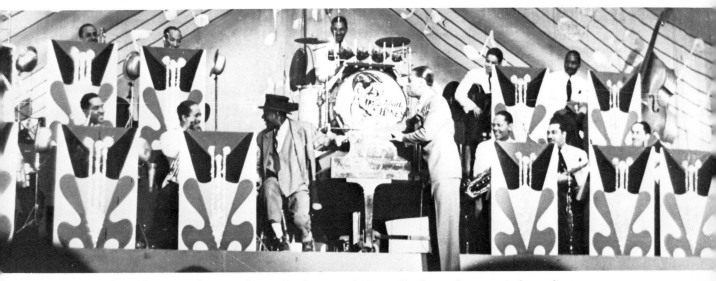

The Earl Hines orchestra at the Apollo Theatre with Dusty Fletcher at the piano. Left to right: (back) Trummy Young, Kenny Stewart, Louis Taylor, trombones; Wallace Bishop, drums; Lawrence Dixon, guitar; Quinn Wilson, bass; (front) Walter Fuller, Milton Fletcher, George Dixon, trumpets; Budd Johnson, Omer Simeon, Willie Randall, Darnell Howard, reeds. Earl Hines, standing.

were going to get our clothes dirty. We had to play the show from the pit and then go up onstage for our specialty. I had written three weeks before we got there that we wanted to wear the white suits and be onstage all the time, and they had agreed.

"I'm not going in the pit," I said, getting salty.

So then I went to Ed Fox. "Look, directing the band, playing in it, being a master of ceremonies and setting up the shows," I said, "I think I'm entitled to more money." He didn't want to do it, but I insisted, and eventually I went to the musicians' union.

"You're supposed to collect your own money, Earl," the union delegate said. "Nobody's supposed to collect it for you." They had made it a union rule that it had to be that way, and I was paid the full amount. I was given five hundred dollars a week, which was very nice, but it left me skeptical from then on.

I knew that bands were growing, that dancehalls were getting larger, and that I had to keep up with the pace set by bands that didn't have a location back of them like I had. So every time I came off the road, I'd come back with another member of the band. I first met Jimmy Mundy in Washington. He had five arrangements he said he would sell me for five dollars apiece. We laughed about it, but I put him in the band as a tenor saxophonist, and he was a very good one. The next time I went back there I got Trummy Young. Everybody was telling me about this boy playing trombone, and although he was criticized at first he eventually proved himself.

It got so the Grand Terrace was no Grand Terrace without us, because we were there so long. When people came to Chicago and the club was mentioned, they naturally thought of us. At first, Fox had closed the place during the bad months, but then he found out that Chicago was a convention city and decided to stay open. So when we were out on the road, he brought in other bands. First, Erskine Tate's, then Fletcher Henderson's, and later Count Basie's for a little while.

When Fletcher came in, he wasn't doing so hot at first, but he had a little sign-off theme that everybody raved about. Mrs. Fox suggested that he use it as his theme song when the band was on the air. It was *Christopher Columbus*, and overnight he jumped from a $400-a-night band to a $1000-a-night. He played the Grand Terrace several years until he decided to go out with an agency.

"Fats" Waller was one of my best friends, and we'd always get together when he came to Chicago. He was one of those people who got a kick out of others having a good time. If you didn't have a good time, he wanted to know why, and he'd create some kind of comedy, pull off a funny gag or something, just to start

you laughing. That's why he used to do those things in his songs, as much as to say, "I'm not a singer, but everybody thinks I am!" He did that until people started saying, "Look, sing seriously. You've got a nice voice." He had, too, and he could sing. He wanted to be out and around people all the time, and, of course, his biggest habit was drinking. We tried to keep him from that when we realized how detrimental to his health it was, but it was as impossible with Fats as with other alcoholics.

He was very serious about music, though, and he always wanted musicians to pay attention to what they were doing and *learn* their instruments. He had the *biggest* hands, and he was a guy who could really read any kind of music. He was also one of the finest organists I've ever known. He was swinging on an organ long before these guys today knew what an organ was, and he taught me a few tricks on the Hammond. People didn't pay too much attention to the instrument then, because of the difficulty of carrying it around. He used to carry it with him, though, and he'd rent two rooms at the hotel, one of them for his Hammond organ and one for himself. One Christmas, we were all there sitting up in his room, and he was playing all the Christmas hymns, like *Holy Night*, and everybody was crying in their beer and I don't know what all! The next morning the people who were in charge of the College Room in the Sherman Hotel, where he was playing, called me.

"Where's Fats?" they wanted to know.

"I don't know. He's not in his room."

The next morning I got a wire which said, "I'm on my way to New York. Call the College Room. Fats."

What had happened was that he'd gotten to drinking and crying so much as he played those Christmas songs that he began to think of his family, especially of his sons, and he just got up and left and went home to New York.

I didn't see him for months after that. He'd run in and run out, always laughing and jovial. Lots of times he said things that were true and people didn't believe him. He could be stubborn, too, and I remember him saying sometimes, "I'm not going, and nobody's going to make me go!" And he wouldn't go, no matter what the affair was. But as an individual, person to person, he was one of the nicest guys you'd want to meet. You'll never find a better.

When he was onstage, he'd have a boy standing offstage with his bottle, ice and chaser on a tray. He'd tell the audience, "I'm going to cool myself off now!" The boy would pour him a drink, and he'd come back making noises in his throat like he'd had a drink, and say, "Oh, boy, that was good! And so *refreshing!*" Sometimes he'd be standing out back of the theatre between shows, and the boy would be there with his tie on, with his tray, ice, liquor and jug of water, just waiting until whenever he got ready to drink again. At some dancehalls he'd have his bottle sitting right up on the piano.

He got me into a situation which made him laugh when I told him about it. He had told Una Mae Carlisle to look me up, with the idea that she could play intermission piano at the Grand Terrace. We both got drunk one night, and I was in bed with her when Cab Calloway's band arrived unexpectedly, including her boy friend, a guitar player. This guy got a chair and was waving his knife through the transom. He couldn't see the bed, but he could see my watch beside it. We were on the third floor, and I got out the window and inched along a narrow ledge until I came to another open window. When I stepped in, an old lady was just hoisting up her pantaloons. As I passed through her room, I think she fainted.

When I first heard Art Tatum in 1931, he was already outplaying everybody, although he was not getting the attention he should have had. At that time he used to do imitations of Fats Waller, James P. Johnson and me. As compared with Fats—the most jovial fellow I ever ran across—Art was a little more serious. He didn't know anything but playing the piano, and that's all he wanted to do. He lived with the piano, day and night. Every time he saw one, he was playing. I don't think he really knew how much he could play. He was certainly one of the greatest and most in-dividual pianists I've ever heard in my life. He could do as much with his left hand as most people could do with their right. He was one of those guys who like company. He didn't like to go to bed, didn't like to close his eyes. When I had the El Grotto in Chicago we had an after-hours club there we called the House of Blue Lights. If he was working downtown, he'd come up there about 4 A.M. and sit there all through the night—at the piano. I'd come down the next morning to check my secretary out, and he'd still be there, with a group of people around him—and he was paying all the bills! I never did try to have a jam session with him, because I knew exactly what this man could do. There are many who are sorry that they did! I shall never forget him as a friend. One reason I loved Fats Waller so much was because of the way we exchanged ideas. Art was another one who thought nothing of taking time out to show you what happened in certain passages and how he played them.

You may have noticed that nearly all pianists have a pet phrase or passage they play first when they sit down at a piano after being asked to play at a party or an informal get-together. It may be four or eight bars. With me, it's four bars of *You're Lucky to Me.* I don't know why my mind always runs to it, but I remember playing it with Ethel Waters. She used to have a way of talking the verse before going into the chorus. I remember one time—and this was 'way back—I didn't realize what was happening until she turned around and said, "You're in the chorus, son!"

So many things happened during the Grand Terrace years that it is difficult to remember them in the right order. As the band got bigger, I was thinking more and more of myself as a band pianist, not as a soloist, although I took solos like everybody else. The trumpet style really cut through the band, and besides the tenths in the left hand I used to carry a pretty steady, heavy rhythm that held my rhythm section together. Teddy Wilson had heard of me while he was in Detroit, and he used to come by all the time. In fact, he lived at my house for a while till he could get him-

At the Grand Terrace. Ann Jones, inspiration of the song *Ann*, at far left. The Nicholas Brothers at far right.

self situated in Chicago. He turned out to be a fine musician and a very wonderful guy. Then he married Irene Eadey, who was also a very good pianist.

Another guy who stayed in my house was Reginald Foresythe. Walter Richardson, the singer, had been to England, where Reggie accompanied him. Walter brought him back to this country.

"Earl, you got a place where you can keep Reginald?" Walter asked me.

"Yes, if he wants to stop over the house with us."

"Just long enough till I can get him placed," Walter said.

He stayed with us several months and he and I wrote what became the band's theme song together—*Deep Forest*. I took him around with me and sort of coached him on some of the things he wanted to learn. This was about the time Paul Whiteman was appearing at one of the big, fine hotels. He often used to come down to the Grand Terrace with Mildred Bailey.

"If you were only white . . ." he said to me one night. I didn't pay much attention to that then, but later on I realized what he was talking about.

Anyway, I introduced Reginald to Paul Whiteman, and Paul took him right away, because he was a very good, well-trained musician. He could play any overture you wanted to hear, and he had memorized works like *Rhapsody in Blue*. He wrote and arranged numbers like *Serenade to a Wealthy Widow* and *Dodging a Divorcée*, and for a time he did very well with Whiteman, who recorded our *Deep Forest*. The titles give you an idea of the kind of sophisticated guy he was. He had been indignant about the poor piano in the club, and so had the radio personnel.

Reginald was colored, but very English in the way he spoke and acted. America was strange to him, and a very big thrill at first, but eventually he went back to England. When I knew him, he had no habits, but over there I understand he became something of an alcoholic. It was too bad, because he was a wonderful boy. I remember a funny story about him.

There was a girl he was crazy about singing in a club, and we were all sitting around there one night. The girl didn't have any eyes for him, but didn't want to insult him. So just to have fun, they asked him to have some chocolates, and he just enjoyed himself eating candy while we were all talking. He must have eaten half a box, and those chocolates were the kind they first made as a laxative, Ex-Lax or some such name.

The next morning, Sunday, he had an appointment to do a radio show with Walter Richardson. He came back that night and told us he had had the most "disturbing" day he

ever had in his life. "I don't know what it was, what I ate," he said, "but I couldn't sit still five minutes without going to the lavatory. They were so discouraged with me. They had to hold up the program, but I really never knew when I'd have to leave!"

It was after we started using *Deep Forest* as a theme that I got my nickname, "Fatha." By this time we had a very music-minded announcer named Ted Pearson. They used to bring this remote control box with dials on it and set it up on a table in the Grand Terrace. He was really an engineer as well as an announcer, because he knew how to adjust those dials while talking into a carbon mike, and do justice to muted trumpet and low-register clarinet solos. Unfortunately, he liked wine, Italian wine, and was what we'd call a wino today. The head of NBC became very dissatisfied with him, and they were threatening to fire him. The whole band was crazy about him, because when we had soft, muted trumpets or clarinet, or something like that, he

knew just what to do. So this particular night they said I ought to go down and talk a little seriously to him, which I did. We played the show and then there was a fifteen-minute intermission before the broadcast. One of the boys came to me and said, "Well, he's out again!" I went down to his table and we had to use ice, wet towels, and I don't know what all to bring him to. Now he *thought* I was reprimanding him, and he figured he would get back at me. So when I went on the stand and was about to go into our theme, his voice came over the air saying, "Here comes Fatha Hines through the Deep Forest with his little children!"

Everybody thought that was nice and catchy, especially NBC. "Leave it in," they all said. It was okay to have a nickname, because there was "Duke" and "Baron Lee" and, in a year or two, "Count," but the problem with mine was that I was so young to be called "Fatha." They didn't know we were spelling it that way, and when it got to be "Father" in the papers I ran into a lot of trouble, especially when we started playing through the South. The bus would pull up and there'd be people lined up for blocks. I'd get out to go past them into the hotel or rooming house where we were staying, not knowing what it was all about.

"When is Father Hines coming out?" they'd ask the bus driver or the valet.

"He's gone."

"Don't tell us that! We've been standing here looking all the time, and we haven't seen him."

I even worked dances where the promoter wouldn't pay me because of that. They'd get hold of the road manager and then say to me, in front of him, "You're not Father Hines. You two are working in cahoots!" Sometimes they didn't say anything until the end of the engagement, and sometimes when they wouldn't pay we had to leave it to the agency to collect.

One night in Chicago, I was late going to work. I couldn't get my car started, and I got in one of those jitney cabs that would take you anywhere on the boulevard for fifteen cents.

"39th and South Parkway," I said.

"Oh, that's where the Grand Terrace is," the cab driver said.

"Yeah."

"You ever seen Fatha Hines?" the fellow sitting next to me asked.

"No," the cab driver said, "You seen him? What's he look like?"

"Yeah," the fellow said. "I've seen him. He's a little, short, fat fellow, and he's got the worst disposition! You don't want to go in there. He won't even speak to you."

So when they put me out at the corner where the club was, one of the waiters was standing there.

"Hi, Fatha," he said, "how you feelin'?"

Both of them like to crack up in the cab, but they followed me all the way to the door, because they wanted to apologize.

Another time when I was in the men's room, a guy was giving me the devil, saying this, that and the other thing about Earl Hines, the Fatha, the so-and-so . . .

"You know this fellow?" the boy in the washroom asked.

"No, I don't know him," he said.

"Well, you just saw Fatha Hines," the boy said as I went out the door, and the two of them got into a terrible thing in there.

Henri Woode was a boy I met in Kansas City. He had good ideas, but nobody wanted to bother with him around his hometown. You know how it is in your hometown. Everybody says, "Ah, he don't know nothin! He hasn't anything to offer." We were the cause of his leaving Kansas City, and he traveled with me a little while. He was crazy about a girl called Rosetta. Whenever I wanted him, or asked the guys where he was, they used to say, "He's with Rosetta." Finally, I got a bit mad, and told him to have Rosetta come where we were playing, and she could eat and drink and I'd pay for it. Then he heard a little phrase I made one night on the piano, and he worked it into a tune we wrote together. We dedicated it to her and called it *Rosetta*, and it became a big hit when we recorded it with Walter Fuller singing. Walter even named his daughter Rosetta. We wrote it as a ballad, but later it was played in all kinds of ways, as a waltz, as a Latin number, as a brass section number, and so on. It's been very good to both of us. Henri went to New York, and I think he's still around, but I've not seen him in a long time.

Before I go any further, I want to say a word about the personnels of my bands in the '30s. A few years ago, Willie Randall got together with Leon Washington, George Dixon and Joe McLewis, and came up with a wonderful chart that showed the various changes. So far as my memory serves, it is accurate, and I think it will be useful to the reader to give the main details here.

The personnel at the time of the first bus accident was: George Dixon, Walter Fuller, Charles Allen, trumpets; Louis Taylor, Billy Franklin, Kenneth Stewart, trombones; Omer Simeon, Darnell Howard, alto saxophones and clarinets; Cecil Irwin, Jimmy Mundy, tenor saxophones; Lawrence Dixon, cello and guitar; Quinn Wilson, bass; Wallace Bishop, drums.

Budd Johnson and Trummy Young took

the places of Cecil Irwin and Billy Franklin in 1935 after the accident in which Irwin was killed and Franklin severely injured.

In 1936, Milton Fletcher replaced Charlie Allen and Willie Randall replaced Jimmy Mundy. Allen left to teach and to promote his mouthpieces, and Mundy joined Benny Goodman.

In February 1937, Ray Nance replaced Milton Fletcher, and Leon Washington replaced Budd Johnson. Johnson joined Gus Arnheim's band as arranger, and Fletcher left because of family problems.

Late in 1937, Trummy Young left to join Jimmie Lunceford and was replaced by Joe McLewis. Walter Fuller, Omer Simeon and Darnell Howard left to join Horace Henderson at the Rhumboogie and were respectively replaced by Leon Scott, Budd Johnson (on alto) and Leroy Harris. Wallace Bishop left to go on location in San Diego and was replaced by Oliver Coleman. Lawrence Dixon wanted to remain in Chicago and was replaced by Claude Roberts. "Pee Wee" Jackson was added to the trumpets in October 1937, making four in all, although George Dixon doubled on alto and baritone saxophones.

For a road tour in January 1938, Milton Fletcher returned to replace Leon Scott, and John "Streamline" Ewing and Ed Burke replaced Louis Taylor and Kenneth Stewart.

After further changes in May 1938, the personnel was: George Dixon, Freddie Webster, Ray Nance, Pee Wee Jackson, trumpets; Streamline Ewing, Joe McLewis, Ed Burke, trombones; Budd Johnson, Leroy Harris, alto saxophones; Julian Draper, Willie Randall, tenor saxophones; Hurley Ramey, guitar; Quinn Wilson, bass; Oliver Coleman, drums.

Much should be written about each of these men, but you will find more about most of them in other sections of this book, so I will limit myself to a few memories and appreciations.

Omer Simeon was a very quiet sort of fellow, and serious about his work. He always stayed by himself and didn't hang out with the wilder guys. But whenever we went to New Orleans, his people used to open the doors, and we'd have a great time at his home.

I naturally knew what Darnell Howard could do when he came with me, because he had been at the Sunset, playing alto sax, violin and clarinet. He didn't care too much about

Darnell Howard, 1957.

Omer Simeon.

saxophone, but he loved the violin and his clarinet. If he made a mistake playing violin or clarinet, he would always cover it up by making a comedy of it. We knew it was a mistake, but the audience thought he was doing something funny. He had great ideas on the violin, and many people—even Eddie South—got ideas from his playing. Eventually, he gave it up and played only clarinet. He never cared much for sports. All he wanted to do was to make radios and fix cameras. He was a camera bug and was always taking pictures of everybody everywhere we went.

George Dixon was a great addition to the band because he doubled on trumpet and baritone sax, and played both of them well. So we didn't have to hire another saxophonist, and baritone is a hard instrument to do well. He also used to do a little singing. He was one of the guys who started the muted trumpet business, and everyone liked to hear him playing it when we were broadcasting. (Incidentally, he's still playing that horn.) He has a lovely personality and is still married to the girl he met in the South. He was always a great support to me, and he's now doing a wonderful job in Chicago, where he has good connections downtown.

Wallace Bishop was a drummer that could do anything you wanted to hear him do, and he was always right behind me. It made no difference what I would start out on, I could always count on the drums being in there very shortly. He knew practically everything I was going to do. We didn't see much of him during the daytime, but he was always around. He got in a little marital mix-up one time, but we kind of got him straightened out on that.

Walter Fuller was a delightful boy with great ambitions. Everybody at that time was working toward one end, and that was to have a good band. Walter used to blow his brains out, and work just as hard when nobody said too much about who was doing what. We were glad to hear guys like him blow, and happy to see them get recognition from the audience.

Louis Taylor was one of the few guys in those days playing what we'd now call the

Tommy Dorsey type of horn—very smooth trombone. We always used him in first position, first chair, and we all listened to him, because although he didn't try to play too much he really knew what he was doing.

Charlie Allen was the man in the band who made mouthpieces, and he was hitting those high notes before most people realized what it was all about. But what he didn't realize was that this could be done by other people. We went to 'Bama State to play a dance, and before we went on the other band—all youngsters—was playing. I never heard so many high notes before in my life. They were hitting them all over the ceiling! This sort of tamed Charlie, and after that we could get along with him until he left a few months later. The guy who was doing most of the blowing that night was, of course, Erskine Hawkins.

Jimmy Mundy was a jovial type of fellow, but very sincere about his arranging, and eventually he made a career out of it. He also had a habit of falling in love overnight, and we

Earl Hines and his orchestra, 1939. Left to right: (standing) Ed Simms, Walter Fuller, Claude Roberts, Quinn Wilson, Alvin Burroughs, Ed Burke, John Ewing, Joe McLewis, Budd Johnson; (sitting) Milton Fletcher, George Dixon, Leroy Harris, Omer Simeon, Bob Crowder.

used to have to straighten that out constantly. Before he went with Benny Goodman, he wrote some wonderful arrangements for us. The background he wrote for three clarinets and tenor on *Everything Depends on You* was so pretty. When he gave up playing for arranging, we lost a very good tenor player!

But we used to have our problems when we broadcasted. People would call up and say I was playing too much piano and there was not enough band. Others would say there was too much band and not enough piano. I had discussions about that time and time again, although I never professed to be a soloist. I would just sit down and play whatever came out of my heart and head. I can thank the world for liking the things I've done, for standing behind me and giving me courage. I'm very appreciative, but I always wanted to be a *bandleader*. That was my first love. So I would play two or three choruses, but I still

wanted to feature other people in the organization.

Budd Johnson was a wonderful youngster. When he first came with me, he said he could arrange, and we decided to let him try. The first tune he brought down to the Grand Terrace was called *Buckets*, but we never did get together on that! He finally picked up the books Cecil Irwin·had had, and he got many good ideas from them. Practice makes perfect, they say, and Budd soon progressed to the point where his arrangements were always up to par. On and off, he has probably been with me longer than anybody. He's a very good saxophonist, and still very much underrated. He always tried to stay up with modern ideas, but without getting too far out.

I should say here that some of our biggest hits were from "head" arrangements—that is, arrangements that were not written down but carried in our heads. We did *Boogie Woogie on St. Louis Blues* for the first time in the Oriental Theatre, and I just sang the brass riffs for the band to play. We cooked up the last chorus of *G. T. Stomp* to walk the dancers off the floor and up the stairs. This was done at a time when the musicians were really enthusiastic and thinking like a team in the World Series. It was a band that would add to any arranger's blueprint, and I always used a lot of different arrangers. I wanted variety and didn't want to be trapped in a style the way some bands were. We had a big book and could play whatever the occasion required.

When Louis Armstrong left Chicago, he said to me, "I've got a boy here who is valeting for me. I want you to take care of him and look out for him." This was Charlie Carpenter, and the first time we went out after that he came with us. I wasn't making but a little bit of change with the group I had then, but after we'd played an engagement in Gary, Indiana, we went to a restaurant for dinner. Everybody in there was getting bacon and eggs, but Charlie had to have a steak. The steak cost me $2.50, which was a whole lot of money in those days. Everybody fell out laughing about the expensive valet I'd got. But Charlie stayed with me and really learned show business, till he became very useful. He was a guy who was always looking forward to bigger things, and could write very good lyrics. He became so active around the band that I moved him up to secretary and made his friend, Louis Dunlap, the band valet. Louis used to like to write songs, and he and Charlie collaborated on several numbers with me, including *You Can Depend on Me*. I never will forget when Herb Jeffries first joined the band. Dunlap took him off to one side and said, "Look, I don't think you're going to make it, singing like a girl. You've got to lower that voice—if you possibly can."

Ed Fox was a man who didn't want to pay out any money, so I couldn't buy stars like other bands coming through Chicago used to have. It was Duke Ellington who said to me, "Why don't you *make* your own stars?" That's

when I started making them right out of my own band. As we traveled back and forth, we were in contact with all sorts of vocalists and all sorts of musicians. One reason, too, why bands had to be continuously enlarged was that we were playing in places like tobacco warehouses in the Southland. They had no air conditioning and the portable amplification wasn't so good. The band could only be heard just so far. So every time a bandleader made a couple more dollars and had the opportunity, he added another instrument. I ended up with eight brass, five reeds and four rhythm. Some bands had nine brass, and it got so some had ten. That was because you had to be heard.

There should be more big bands today. At the time we're talking of, they helped keep down child delinquency. Youngsters had idols in the different bands, and they were always looking for big bands to come through their particular town or city. Some had an idol in the brass section, and some had an idol in the reed or rhythm section. They would sit right under these different musicians, and you would be surprised what big bands did for the youngsters. It kept them off the streets, and a whole lot of rehearsal halls opened up so they could learn to become musicians. It led to their getting little groups together and developing vocalists. In those days, too, when there was so much dancing, they created dance teams and groups, and got on the stage. There were scouts looking for good dancers, ballroom dancers, and many of them came from small cities where youngsters hadn't the slightest idea of ever coming in contact with show business. Musicians also began to try to play more than one instrument, so that they would be more versatile and more in demand. I don't think big bands will be back in the way we knew them then, because we haven't got the facilities in the first place, and because the cost of living is soaring. Hotels are charging more. Restaurants are charging more. And in order for a musician to stay on the road today, he has to have an enormous salary to live decently. Taxes are heavy, and he has to take care of his home as well as his road expenses. Other countries look up to the American musician and I think it is high time America realized it is the home of jazz. With the exception of those in sports, the musician has probably done more than anyone else in the U.S. to help create good relationships with other countries.

I don't want to overlook the fact that my band was among the first Freedom Riders, because we were riding through the South many, many years ago, and creating all kinds of excitement. Most of the members of my organization at that time were northerners, and it was unusual for the white southerner to see Negroes all over a Greyhound bus! They had restrictive signs at railroad stations, bus stations, on streetcars and all kinds of transportation. When they wanted to board *our* bus, the driver would say, "This is a private bus." Of course, he and these people would get into all kinds of arguments.

I always used to tell the guys, and even the girl singers, to make sure they had *everything* they were going to need when we went out on those tours. When we went into those southern towns, we'd pull into what we called the "main stem," and that's where all the black people were—all on one side of town, usually near or across the railroad tracks. If we were going to play a white dance, we'd stay there till time to go and all would board the bus and leave at the same time. Afterwards, we'd all come back to the main stem. In the early days, there were no hotels available to us and we had to stay in private homes. Doctors and lawyers would open up their houses and allow us to stay there.

Eventually, it got to the stage where there were so many bands going south to play dances that people began to get wise—the colored people, that is, who were housing musicians. They'd ask if you were a musician, and if you were with a prominent organization all the prices went up. Sometimes we'd get there in the afternoon after riding all night and half the morning. We'd be tired, so the first thing the guys would do would be to get pajamas

out of their bags, drop in bed, and try to sleep until time to go to dinner. After dinner, we'd go to work, and then come back to bed again. So there were times when the landladies tried to charge them for two nights.

"We just slept one night," the boys would say.

"Well, you had two sleeps!" the landlady would answer.

They used to have different prices in restaurants, too. A fried chicken dinner would normally be a dollar, but when we came to town it was $1.50. I remember once in Texas I was transacting some business and went in behind the boys. They were all sitting at the counter, and I sat at a table because there was no more room there. They were charging them $1.50 and $1.75 for their dinners.

"I won't charge you like I charged them," the girl who waited on me said.

"No," I said, "because I'm the valet."

"Fine," she said, "I'll just charge you seventy-five cents."

"Oh, I sure appreciate that."

"I know how it is," she said, "but we *have* to charge these bandleaders and musicians more, because they're making so much money!"

This young lady came to the dance that night, and when she saw me sitting at the piano—well, I can't use the language she used to me! I ended up giving her three or four dollars to keep her quiet.

When we traveled by train through the South, they would send a porter back to our car to let us know when the dining room was cleared, and then we would all go in together. We couldn't eat when we wanted to. We had to eat when they were ready for us.

If there was a disturbance at any of those dances in the South, two policemen could handle the whole hall in those days. They used to beat up on the women, but so long as they were cutting each other up the police didn't pay much attention. "Oh, there's old Sadie," they'd say; "she's cutting up so-and-so . . ." And they'd pick 'em up and take 'em to the hospital, but they didn't worry about it.

One colored dance we played, they didn't have a piano.

"What in the world do you think I'm playing?" I said.

"Well, we thought you were bringing your piano with you."

"You must be kidding!"

They ran around town and borrowed what was supposed to be a very fine piano from a doctor's house, but it was *all* out of tune. It was terrible.

"This is a brand new piano," they said. "Nobody's touched it!"

I ended up not playing that night. I went away and let the boys run the band. I was supposed to have got such a bad headache that I had to leave.

We played one night in Corpus Christi, a damp hall quite a bit out from town, on a levee like, and there was water all around the place. Billy Eckstine and Madeline Green used to sit in front of me, alongside the band. To start my theme song, I used to run my hand up the piano, and when I did that, dirty water flew out of the piano all over everybody. Billy and all of them had a fit.

The pianos in some places would be so bad that I would be playing in one key and the band would be playing in another! People used to say to me, even when I didn't have a mike in the piano, "You don't sound like the records." Or, "You don't sound like you did when you were broadcasting from Chicago." They didn't realize that in Chicago I was playing on a beautiful $3000 Bechstein piano.

In Fort Lauderdale, a policeman and another fellow had been standing right in front of the piano watching me play.

"Can you boys play *Honeysuckle Rose*?" the policeman asked.

"Yes, we can."

"Will you play it?"

"Yes, we'll play *Honeysuckle Rose*."

We played another number or two and then went into it. Meanwhile this policeman had gone to the men's room.

"When you going to play *Honeysuckle Rose*?" he asked when he came back.

"I played it."

"You're a liar."

"I'm not. We played *Honeysuckle Rose*. Ask this gentleman," I said, pointing to Endicott Johnson's son, who was down there on vacation. (We had played a town in Pennsylvania called Johnson City that his father owned.)

"Yeah, they played *Honeysuckle Rose*," Mr. Johnson said.

"No such thing," the policeman said, and he began to use bad language and get very offensive about race.

So I went to the proprietor, who was a northerner, and he called the captain, who came down and found out his man was drunk. Nevertheless, he said the best thing was for us to pack up and leave after intermission, and that's what we did.

There were a lot of situations like that, and I could just keep on. They couldn't understand our being so well dressed, nor the way we carried ourselves. It was beyond them then. That's why I say we were some of the first Freedom Riders. There were so many illiterate people in the South—on both sides—and they were the people who constantly caused commotion. I think the bands saw the beginning of the change in the South, and then later when sports began to be integrated everyone began to see there was something to think about.

We played a lot of places in the South where they had ropes down the middle of the hall, dividing black from white, but the first place I saw them dancing together was in San Anton'. That was because dark-complexioned Mexican Indians had protested, saying they were not Negroes.

Some of the boys decided they just didn't want to go south any more. It was too much for them to take, the way they were treated. To get sandwiches, they might have to go to a little back entrance of a bus station. At one place, the manager went in with a list of sandwiches that we were going to eat on the road to save time. When the owner of the restaurant saw us in the bus, he threw all the sandwiches in the trash basket.

"I don't serve colored people!" he said.

"We're taking them out anyway," the road manager said.

"I don't care where you're taking them, so long as you get out of here."

That was in Ohio, and I wouldn't want to make it seem that such attitudes were met only in the South.

One time in Kentucky, the weather was very hot and I wanted to buy some thin silk shirts and underwear. The town we were in was very much segregated, and no Negro would normally go into a white store downtown. When I went into this particular place, a fellow stood 'way back in the back, and there was nobody else in the store but me.

"Well, what do you want, boy?" he asked.

"I'd like to see some silk shirts and underwear, if you have any here."

He came and pointed to a few things.

"Oh, I don't want anything like that," I said. "Is this the best you have?"

"Can you afford the best I have?"

"Let me see what you have."

After I looked at the shirts and underwear, I said, "*Now* you're beginning to show me what I want."

"You're not from down here, are you, boy?"

"No, and for another thing I'm *not* accustomed to being called 'boy.' We're here on a tour and my name is Earl Hines."

"Oh, yeah, I read something about that, boy."

After I had bought about $150 worth of clothes, he was so overwhelmed he said he was going to come to see the affair. He gave me a ten percent discount and told me to tell anyone else in the organization to come on down.

While I was buying the clothes, there were colored people who lived in the town all up against the window, looking in. You'd have thought I was some sort of sideshow man.

"You know, ain't no boys 'sposed to go in there," they said when I came out. "No colored people go in there!"

"Well, *I* was in there," I said.

After another engagement down there, I remember the people running the dance told me, "We don't pay no Negroes. Ain't you got a white man traveling with you?"

"Yes, we have," I said, "but he's getting the group together at the present time."

"Well," they said, "send him back here if you want your money."

The fellow I had was from Detroit, and he disliked the South, too. They were against him on account of his being a Jew, but he went back there and told them, "Look, it's this man's band. I'm just the manager, and I want him to collect his money. So I'm going to stay here and see he gets it. Give it to *him*, not to me! I'll be here, but give it to him."

"We'll never use him again," they said, "if we have to pay this darky."

"So far as 'darky' is concerned," the manager said, "when we get the money, that's all we want with you."

They gave it to me.

There were always things happening on the road. I was trying to relax in Omaha, Nebraska, on a Sunday. This was when Ray Nance was in the band, and they were all having a grand time. Early that morning I got a phone call saying to come down to the police station.

"What police station?" I asked.

"Here, in Omaha."

"What's the trouble?"

"We've got half of your band down here. They told me they belong to your band and they gave us your number."

So I went down, and there they were, all back behind the bars with a long tale. After pulling out cards and letters of all descriptions to prove who I was, I persuaded the police to let them all out. They didn't want any drinking on Sunday, and they'd been drinking and raising quite a bit of Cain at the house where they were staying.

After I got them all out, I looked for my valet.

"Where's Red?" I asked.

"He's back at the house," they said. "He's knocked out and they didn't take him in. They left him there."

When we got back, I found he had my white suit on, which I hadn't worn. He just got juiced so that he fell out and laid up in my white suit! So I'm over there trying to get him together and to get my suit off him, when here come the police again! They wanted to take us *all* in.

"I just came here to get this valet," I said. "I told you who I was. He's drunk, and you didn't take him before."

"Yeah," one of the policemen said, "that's the guy we didn't take before."

"I came here to get him and take him home," I said.

"If you let one of 'em go," another policeman said, "you have to let 'em all go."

"Well, just let me get out with this boy, because I don't want to be caught here if anything happens later on."

They let us all go, but I told the guys, "If the police catch you here again, you'll have to stand on your own."

That wasn't so bad as when we were in Denver and two of my trumpet players were chasing after the same girl. Finally, one caught the other having a good time with her, and they were shooting at each other at 3 o'clock in the morning. The hotel people made us all move out at that hour, at that time of the night, and it was *snowing!*

I remember when Jack Hylton came over from England in 1935. He had a famous big band there, but the union here would only let him use his key men—his first trumpet, first trombone, first alto, and so on. The rest had to return to England. He brought Alec Templeton, the blind pianist, with him, too, to play at the Blackstone Hotel in Chicago. It irritated Jack to be treated that way, and when he went back he fixed it so that American bands got the same treatment in England. But there were more than thirty big bands around Chicago at that time, and George Olsen got all the bandleaders together to give a banquet to welcome Jack Hylton to Chicago and the U.S. Then Jack turned around and gave a banquet for us. He and I became good friends, and he asked me to come down to the hotel one day and have a talk. He told me he had heard a lot of my records in England, and had always wanted to meet me.

I went in the front door of the Blackstone and went over to the desk. "My name is Earl Hines," I said, "and Mr. Jack Hylton is expecting me."

"Fine," the clerk said, "you take the elevator over there."

When I got to the elevator, the starter said, "You can't go up on this elevator."

"Why can't I?"

"You use the freight elevator."

"I'm down here to see Jack Hylton. I live in Chicago and I don't take anybody's freight elevator!"

We got into a heated argument, until Jack's secretary and some members of his band came in and saw me standing there.

"Jack's expecting you," they said. "Have you been up?"

"No, because these people want me to ride the freight elevator!"

The secretary called Jack, and he came down and threatened to give up the engagement altogether. But then the manager came and said the fellow had overstepped his bounds, and the whole thing was passed off when Jack began to cool down; but he was very, very angry.

The first time we went to California, an FBI man came to me as soon as we got off the train and said, "You have so-and-so and so-and-so in your band," and he named all those who were smoking pot, and those who weren't. "You tell them to watch their P's and Q's, because we know all about them." So I called a band meeting that night. "Look, fellows," I said, "the man met us at the station and he told me all about you—who's using and who isn't. Now you guys be careful!"

When Don Redman was at the Zanzibar in New York, he and I were standing out on the corner during intermission discussing music and arrangements. A police detective who knew Don joined the conversation and asked Don if he had a cigarette. Don happened to have some stuff already wrapped up, but mixed with other cigarettes, and the detective picked the wrong kind.

"What kind of cigarette is this?" the man asked. "I never tasted one like this."

"Maybe I gave you one of those doggone handmade cigarettes," Don said.

After we talked some more, I found out he was a detective, so I eased away from them! But Don told me later that the guy never found out what it was he smoked.

Years later, I was playing at a little club in Oakland. They had a bar, and behind the bar, near the back, was a dressing room with no windows. I was sitting out at the bar with two policemen, and I kept smelling this marijuana smoke coming out from under the door. "Oh, my goodness," I ran back and told the guys, "you can't smoke that stuff around here, because I'm sitting out there with two policemen!"

"We're not smoking," they said.

"Don't tell me that! It's coming out under the door."

They gave up, but they were afraid to open the door, and I managed to talk the policemen into going out on the street.

One way of keeping the guys in the band on their toes was a system of fines we worked out. I was a stickler for making time, and I let them know that the contract depended on being on time, as well as on behavior onstage when we were in a theatre. It meant almost as much to be on time as to do a performance. So we fined latecomers. It was twenty-five dollars when you missed a curtain in a theatre, and five dollars for every minute afterwards. When we were traveling by bus, there was a five-dollar fine for each person who wasn't ready at the hotel or rooming house when the bus was due to leave. We even fined the bus driver if he came late with the bus—a dollar for every minute he was late. They also had fines in the band among themselves, in the different sections. There was a fine of twenty-five cents for each mistake made, and each section leader had a writing tablet on which he noted mistakes during the performance. They paid close attention, and whatever tune we were playing they would note the title, the number in the book, the time, and the particular spot in the arrangement. Every Saturday night we'd have a meeting of the whole organization at the Grand Terrace, downstairs in the "hole" as we called it. They would bring up all those things, and each member had to be responsible to the others. Sometimes it would happen a guy would say, "Now, look, man, read your part, because I'm tired of paying out all this money!" We got to the stage

where we had an awful lot of discipline, and because of those fines there was great interest in the quality of the band's performance.

In later years, I always had four or five changes of uniforms for the musicians, and we had a band valet who had to take the uniforms out of the trunk and put them back again. They were particular about not being seen after the performance in their uniform. They had to take it off right there on the bandstand, unless we were late, and then they'd have to sit in the bus in them. You'd be surprised how careful the guys were about taking their coats off and hanging them up, and sitting in such a way their pants didn't get wrinkled. All the bands tried to outdress one another, but, with Jimmie Lunceford's and Duke Ellington's, we were considered the best-dressed band on the road. It meant an awful lot, because appearance was almost half the battle.

The stage fines—and there weren't many of those—used to go into my pocket. I used to buy something with them and wear it onstage, and walk by whoever had been late, and say, "Thank you, man!" When some of them found out about that, they decided they didn't want to dress me up. The other fines went into a jackpot, and at Christmas time the boys in the band divided up the money, and sometimes there might be seventy-five to a hundred dollars apiece, or even more. The bandstand fines between the sections got so they didn't amount to much, but the bus fines ran into a lot more money.

Whenever they played particularly well, acted well, and made time, I would show my appreciation by giving a dinner in some hotel when we had a night off. Then they'd have anything and everything to drink they wanted. It meant a lot to the musicians, and they appreciated the fact that the leader thought something of them. I think I was a bit different from the average bandleader anyway. I liked to associate with my men and be on the ground floor with them. I liked to know what they were thinking, and to be in a position where they were not afraid to ask me questions. That way, when you went up on the stand in front of the band, you got a lot of smiles, rather than the kind of look that suggests a musician would like to throw his instrument at you! I'd hang out with them in bars and restaurants near where we were working. I'd stand around in their dressing room, too, and they'd offer me all kinds of liquor, because they drank everything from coal oil up. They didn't call me "boss" very often. Just as they used nicknames among themselves, they called me "Gate," which was short for "Gatemouth," the name I got at the Sunset when Louis was "Satchelmouth." They dropped "mouth" in his case, too, and he became "Satchmo" or "Satch."

Tempo was always a very important thing in the big band days. When it was a vocal number, I told all the guys to watch me directing; but when it came time for dancing I had to have an understanding with the drummer as the main man. "Don't you set the tempo," I used to say. "The people and dance acts set the tempo and you keep it." Some nights they don't feel like dancing too fast, and I always had the music arranged with the people in mind. I used to tell arrangers like Jimmy Mundy to make it flexible, so if we wanted to change the tempo it would still have the same feeling. In directing for my vocalists, I was always out front and watching, almost looking down their throats! I watched the singer's mouth and his expression, and I watched the people's feet. That's why we were considered a good show band at the Grand Terrace by the artists, and a good dance band by the dancers.

When we got a new pop song, I'd sit down at the piano with the singer and we'd go through the song just as it was to see if he got any feeling out of it. I had to be careful here about tempos, too. Billy Eckstine was a balladeer and never good on up-tempo tunes. Sarah Vaughan could do something a little faster than the average tempo. We'd run the number down, decide on the key, and then mumble around with it. That's when the arranger used to help out sometimes. "I think it might be more effective if you'd put just a little bit of tempo in there," he'd say. "I can give you much more of a lift with the brass section." Then, if it wasn't comfortable, he would strike out the brass section altogether and change the arrangement completely around. If you were going to arrange for a tap dancer, it would depend on what he was doing. You take a boy we used to have who danced up and down steps like Bojangles. When he got ready to do that, there would be a slight drop in tempo to make those steps clear. After coming off the steps, he'd pick it back into the tempo he wanted to dance on the floor. We'd have to follow him. Once you got the idea, you'd *feel* along with them, dancers and singers.

I've always told all my singers never to look at an audience, but to look *over* it. They're nearly always nervous when they're starting out. "Just look *over* them," I'd say. "They think you're looking at them anyway, although you're not." A producer told me about that originally. "Look straight at the back of the house," he said, "and just look from one side of the room to the other, but don't see anybody." What so many don't realize is that you're entertaining all sorts of people. Somebody's got a bad tooth, somebody's just left his wife, somebody just lost a lot of money— you're entertaining all these people and they come to the club to forget their troubles. But if you see the looks on their faces, you'll think, "Gee, I must be bad! What am I doing wrong?" It's like when you're playing music and you make a mistake. If you stop and think about it, you'll make three or four more.

There used to be a time when I wanted a whole lot of music behind me before I'd go out and say something. Now it doesn't bother me. I just go out and say, "Good evening, ladies and gentlemen," and say whatever I want to say. I learned the importance of confidence from one of my directors when he was producing a show. "Once you gain that confidence, Earl, you couldn't care less about anybody, and the people relax." That's what he said, and it's true, because when a guy comes out

Opposite: It was sometimes suggested that Earl Hines had had the webs between his fingers cut to improve his dexterity at the keyboard. He offers proof to the contrary here and displays his initials in diamonds on a ring given him by a Chicago jeweler.

sheepishly you feel for him, and you say to yourself, "Oh, God, what is *this!*"

Smiling is something else. I was on a tour once in Europe with another pianist who never smiled. "What's the matter? Are you having your teeth fixed or something?" I asked him. He was playing a helluva lot of piano up there, and he said, "Well, I don't have to smile." "Yes, you do," I told him. "You should let people know you enjoy playing for them."

I had the same trouble when Ida James first came with me. The producer of the show at the Grand Terrace was talking to her one day and he came to me and said, "Man, she's got a pretty set of teeth! Make her smile, Earl." Then when we played the Palace in New York, first thing a reporter came back and said, "Why don't that girl smile?" So I had a talk with her, and next time I saw her, after I let her go to the bandstand—hey, she was grinning all over her face!

It means so much onstage. People often say to me, "Earl, you set up there smiling like you're enjoying yourself." And I tell them, "I really am. I'm having a ball!" But one day, up at the Apollo Theatre, I smiled so much that when I got offstage I couldn't get the smile off my face.

"You're off the stage now, Fatha," a cat said, when I walked off during the drum solo.

"Man, I know that, but I can't get this thing off!"

It was as though the muscles froze, and they kept working on them till the side of my face relaxed. I knew not to do that again. I had gone too far. I was really giving them the ivory!

Sometimes you have the opposite problem. Guys in the band get moody and don't feel like smiling at all. The audience may drag them, or they let the effect of what happened at home come over them. I've seen bandleaders come stomping offstage, saying, "Every time I get out there, something seems to happen." Duke Ellington used to put up with some solemn faces, but you'd never know he even saw them so long as he was onstage. That's how a leader has to be.

Opening night, of course, is never a good night to be ˙critical. It frightens some people.

Ethel Waters used to have a beautiful colored handkerchief—light purple, light green—and she'd tie it around her wrist, and play with it, she was so nervous. Ella Fitzgerald's the same way. You see her backstage at some club where she's been going for years. Opening night, she'll tell you she's a nervous wreck.

One way or another, I led a big band for nearly twenty years, and there were a lot of fine musicians, personalities and singers in and out of it during that time, so now I'm going to try to remember some more of them.

I first heard of Ray Nance when he had a sextet at a little club in Chicago whose owner was trying to take advantage of him. Ray came to me about it, and by this time I was well known in the city because of the Grand Terrace engagement. "I think you have six of the best musicians in Chicago," I told that club-owner, "and I think they're entitled to more consideration than you're giving them." He paid attention to what I said, and he kept Ray working until 1937 when Ray was in the mood to travel. Most of the other members in his group wanted to stay home in Chicago, so they broke up and Ray came with me, playing trumpet and violin. He was with me until 1939. A bit later, Duke Ellington came to Chicago, woke me up about 3 o'clock in the morning, and came up to my hotel room.

"Say, Fatha, you know a guy named Ray Nance?"

"Sure."

"How does he read?"

"He reads fine."

"And he plays violin?"

"Yes."

"I'd like to have him."

"If you're that game," I said, "you can have him!"

So he got Ray Nance* to take the place of Cootie Williams, who was going with Benny Goodman, and Ray proved a great asset to him, the second one I helped Duke with, because I had to talk Ivie Anderson into auditioning for him some years before. She had a

---

* For more details of Nance's career and experiences with Hines, see *The World of Duke Ellington.*

boy friend at the Grand Terrace and really didn't want to leave.

Scoops Carry was a brilliant saxophone player, a great musician, and I was very proud of him when he ended up as one of the finest lawyers in Chicago. He should have been a lawyer from the start, because he was always outsmarting everybody! If he went in a store and thought he could get away without paying, that would make him happy. "Well, I beat them that time," he'd say. He liked sports, liked to play ball, but he was also efficient and reliable as strawboss of the band, and as director when I was off the stand.

Willie Randall, a well-schooled saxophone player and arranger, was another reliable man when it came to business and organization. He married Madeline Green when she was singing with the band, but they're both remarried now. He used to be in the trio we called the Three Varieties, along with Budd Johnson and Leroy Harris. They did vocal backgrounds on numbers like *Everything Depends on You* and *I Got It Bad*. Willie also acted as manager of the band.

Buggs Roberts was another *very* talented arranger. We were playing the Plantation in St. Louis when I ran across him. I was planning on doing some concerts, but when they told me about him I wasn't sure whether he could do what I had in mind. He was a timid guy, and I think this upset his married life and may even have caused his early death. But he had studied and knew what he was doing when it came to arrangements. He knew how to voice all the instruments and make them sound real good. He knew how to write straightforward jazz arrangements, but he also did great concert-type work on medleys from musicals like *Show Boat*. I always remember what he did on *Make Believe*—a beautiful waltz thing which Essex Scott sang.

I didn't have too much dealing with Buster Harding. He was friendly with some of my musicians, and he'd come down to a rehearsal and bring one or two arrangements and we'd play them. He wrote some good ones like *Call Me Happy* and *Windy City Jive*.

Bob Crowder, who we called "Little Sax," played tenor and also wrote some good arrangements while he was in the band. He was always a gutbucket man. His wife used to travel with us on the road and when he got his own group she played piano in it. Another good tenor player in the band who arranged for me was Franz Jackson. He did *Comin' in Home* and *Yellow Fire* among others.

By the time we got into the '40s, and World War II was on, there were a lot of changes, as there were with all the bands. At any time there are guys who want to travel and guys who marry and want to stay home. Now there was the extra complication of guys going into the Army and Navy. It was during this time that I engaged the services of Dizzy Gillespie and Charlie Parker. I'd seen Charlie a couple of years before when we were in Detroit. He had come over to the hotel and we talked. He was dissatisfied with the band he was in.

"If you ever have an opening, let me know," he said.

"I'll be happy to," I replied.

I meant it, too, because I'd never heard a man play an alto sax like he did. During the war, there was a place on 116th Street in New York called Minton's where all the musicians from the different bands used to go—a jam-session place where they would try to cut each other. I went there one night with Count Basie because one of my saxophonists told me to go and listen to this boy who was playing alto. It was Charlie, but what we needed then was a tenor, not an alto player.

"I can play tenor," he said.

And he really could! I went out and bought him a tenor, and he could just about run anybody out of the country with it! Little was heard about that because after he left the band he went back to alto. He was a brilliant musician. We'd rehearse, and everything we rehearsed he would play that night without music. It was too bad he got mixed up with the wrong crowd. He was a fine boy and there was nothing wrong with him at all when it came to his character. All the harm he did, he did to himself.

All Dizzy was thinking of in those days was getting over his horn. He never thought too much of tone. I used him on up-tempo numbers, but for tone I would use somebody else

Birthday party at the Royal Theatre, Baltimore, and a reunion between the Earl Hines and Louis Armstrong bands.

in the trumpet section. Same way with Charlie Parker. He didn't have the tone on alto that you'd like to hear in playing a ballad. He sacrificed that to get over his horn. Nowadays, Dizzy uses a mute and that uptilted horn, and that takes some of the piercing quality away from the audience. He is concentrating more on tone.

Dizzy's humor and high spirits were good for the band, and he used to do quite a bit of writing then. One of his numbers became famous as *Night in Tunisia*, a title I suggested because World War II was raging and there was a lot of action in Tunisia. Dizzy also did a vocal on *Salt Peanuts*, the two words of the title! He was very serious about music and he

and Charlie Parker were always working on the exercise books they had accumulated.*

Years before, most of the trumpet players like Joe Smith and Gus Aiken tried to be as close to the sound of the human voice as they possibly could. I used to love to hear Joe, sitting in a room, because he sounded just like somebody singing. It was *pleasing* to hear him. They forget about "tonation" today. They have a different embouchure and they get a different vibrato. All they want to do now is to be heard, and a lot of them never took time to find out what *tone* actually was.

You take Tommy Dorsey. Miff Mole stopped him from playing hot trombone, and when he wanted to play trumpet, Louis

---

* See Appendix, items 2, 3 and 4, for further references to this period. The Hines band of that time is often referred to as the "incubator of bop." Duke Ellington once told me that the seeds of bop were in Earl Hines's piano

style. Ellington had a way of saying serious things about music casually, but at first I thought he was kidding and then I realized he had in mind the revolution Hines effected in the function of the jazz pianist's left hand. S.D.

Armstrong stopped him from playing that! So he went in the "woodshed" and came out with that "tonation," using his horn as a voice, making a sound people loved right away. Some musicians put their horn up to their mouth and only a certain amount of vibrato comes from their lips. Others, like Louis Armstrong, would use their wrist, wavelike on the valves, for wrist tone. Jack Teagarden used his slide to get the vibrato he wanted. Then the non-pressure system came in, and there was a teacher in Chicago I used to send trumpet players to. He would hang a trumpet up in the air, and he could walk up and play it without holding it. That was a good way of learning how to play the horn. Wild Bill Davison is a guy who can pick up his horn and play without any setting up at all. So can Bobby Hackett. He has a natural tone that he has developed, a beautiful straight tone with very little use of the hand apart from the fingers. Then, recently, I heard a kid who plays just like Dizzy. He's got a piercing tone and he'll be great for the Latin-type thing they're doing now, for running up and down, doubling up on chords, and hitting high notes. But for something pleasing, of course, on a standard tune, like Bobby Hackett does—he can't make it, with that kind of approach.

In a reed section, I saw to it they didn't use the vibrato. They followed the first saxophonist, and everybody used a straight tone. Same way with the trumpets. They wouldn't use the vibrato system when they were playing together. They all sustained the notes the same length of time, and made the passages the same in one breath. You couldn't match four different vibratos! The reason some vocal quartets sound so very good is because they throw out the vibrato and just try to sing in straight tones. Then they all sound even. Otherwise, maybe one has a fast vibrato and one a slow vibrato, and you wonder why they don't sound good. The sax sections got to the stage where they were practically perfect, like Jimmie Lunceford's. The trumpets had to play the same, so did the trombones, and we never did allow a guy to use that vibrato when tuning up.

Joe Smith was a *natural*. He didn't know

anybody to go to, but he was crazy about tonation, and when he picked up that horn I imagine he adjusted his mouth to get the sound he wanted. Johnny Hodges was another one, just a natural—just pick up his horn, and a beautiful sound! I think you do that yourself. Paul Desmond, the saxophonist with Dave Brubeck, had a certain way of getting that weird sound from his horn. I don't think people like that learn it from anybody. It's a natural tone they perfect themselves.

Jonah Jones has to use the vibrato system with his hands. Dicky Wells is a trombone player who was great on tonation, and who adjusted his style to get the sound and effects he could hear in his head. Lawrence Brown was another trombone player with a tone all his own. Trummy Young used to play a beautiful horn, but after he went with Louis he went back and developed that rough way of playing. He got very disgusted and he used to tell me: "I've just lost all conception of my horn. If only I could get to some towns where I could go and jam someplace. I'm so sick of playing the same things over and over." It was the same with Tyree Glenn, who used to get over his horn beautifully with a good tone, but he got into a rut and tried to be a comedian. He still had the tone, that pretty little tone, but he didn't get over the horn as well as he did before.

Wardell Gray was with me about two years and he was a fine musician. Nobody ever ran over him and he made a lot of tenor players look up. He was just like Pres (Lester Young) in the way he always wanted to be playing his horn. He was a quiet person, as I remember him, and he didn't run around much. He used to read real serious books. In fact, he always seemed to be reading. He had some funny eating habits. He always carried a bottle of tabasco sauce with him, and he'd strip all the fat off bacon and put so much pepper on fried eggs you couldn't see them.

Billy Douglas was a wonderful trumpet player with a great future, but I think the whiskey got him. Sometimes he reminded me of Joe Smith, because he had that kind of soul and tone in his playing. Willie Cook was another fine trumpet in the band for several years, and at that time I think he was trying to play like Billy. He wrote some nice arrangements before I broke up the band in 1947, and he went on from there to Duke Ellington, who thought a lot of him.* Earlier I had guys like Freddy Webster and Benny Harris, who were on a modern kick, and also Shorts McConnell, who played the sensational trumpet solo on *Stormy Monday Blues*.

I first met Cliff Smalls in the South. Because he played piano as well as trombone, he was leery of talking to me, but I could see where he would be very valuable to me. When I was at the piano, he could be playing trombone, but when I was directing the shows with my big band, he would be at the piano. And he could *really* play the piano, because that was his first instrument. At rehearsal one day he showed me how he played some of Count Basie's numbers, and one we all liked was *Basie Boogie*. When we were playing the Apollo Theatre soon after he joined me, Basie's band was coming in the following week, and I had Cliff playing *Basie Boogie* all the week before. Basie caught me outside the theatre and you should have heard the language used! "What do you mean having that guy up there?" he wanted to know. "I just can't see anybody doing that! What am I going to play when I get there?" Of course, Basie and I were close friends, and it's something we talk and laugh about now. When I found out that Cliff could also arrange as well as play two instruments, I knew I'd made a good move.

That reminds me of another bandleader, Claude Hopkins. We used to sit in the barbershop and threaten one another, and pretend to be enemies. The barber would get in the act and pretend to be trying to pacify us. Claude would wear his deadpan expression and all the people there would think we were really quarreling, but we've always been the best of friends.

I was lucky with drummers in the band. Art Tatum used to call Wallace Bishop "Mr. Sandman," because of the way he played on our record of *Japanese Sandman*. After Wallace, I had Oliver Coleman, who had been in Ray Nance's little group, and then Alvin Burroughs. We called Alvin "Mouse," and he had played with Alphonso Trent and Walter Page out west before coming to Chicago.† You can hear what he did for the band on the Victor records we made in 1939 and 1940. When he left, I had Rudy Traylor for about a year, and then Shadow Wilson, who was another marvelous drummer. Chick Booth had not had much experience in big bands when he joined us, but if you can find the records we made in 1946, you'll hear how *he* kicked the band along.

I haven't said much about the band's singers after Billy Franklin was injured and left, but I always had a special interest in them. My auntie was the one who originally explained singing to me. She told me about vibrato and likened it to rippling waters. She said the higher you went, the more you were singing from your head. That's why so many vocalists used to hold their heads back and look at the ceiling. Louis Armstrong did that when he went to make a high note on the trumpet. He'd look up in the air. She also told me how a singer had to have control of his stomach. Most singers in the classical field have heavy, hard stomachs. It's not fat, but muscle from singing from there. Lois Deppe had it from singing deep, and so has Billy Eckstine now. He always had a nice upper register, but I showed him how to use his stomach for low notes and take advantage of the lower register. I learned a lot from Lois Deppe's teacher, because I had to be there to learn the scales he showed him, and I played those scales every day for his exercises in the upper and lower registers.

Among the singers I especially liked was Nat Cole—just as natural and smooth as could be. Frances Langford had a very smooth and lovely voice. She used to sing *I'm in the Mood for Love*. If you *saw* her singing, it made it even better, because she showed no effort at all. I just loved the way she sang. Lucille

---

* For more details of Cook's career and experiences with Hines, see *The World of Duke Ellington*.

† See Appendix, 1.

Hegamin, the blues singer, had that type of voice. It was very smooth and I always liked that kind of vibrato. Some people sound like a record running down if they have to hold the end of a note.

When we were in Detroit playing the Eastwood Gardens, all the youngsters were talking about a singer. "You want to hear *this* boy sing," they kept saying. So finally I did. I had him come up and sing *Stardust*, and he really sounded good to me. He was a handsome little boy with a very high voice, and I thought he'd make a great matinee idol. His name was Herb Jeffries, and he stayed with me quite some time before he went with Duke Ellington.

Then, later, I found Arthur Lee Simpkins in Augusta, Georgia. He was working in a bank at the time and he had a tremendous voice. Ida James, whom I mentioned before, won an amateur contest in Philadelphia, and that was where I found her.

Billy Eckstine was singing at the Club De Lisa in Chicago when I got him to join the band. He was a very handsome boy—still is—and he turned out to be one of my closest friends. If I may use the term, he was one of the first "balladeers." We had a lot of trouble getting him recorded. RCA said, "We want jazz. We don't want anybody singing ballads." The a. and r. man on the first 1940 session insisted that we have no singing, but while he was out to lunch we had Billy sing a couple of songs. The engineer was very nice about it and recorded them. We'd been playing the numbers on one-nighters, so we didn't need any music. After the session was over, the engineer asked the a. and r. man to listen.

"What do you think of that?" he said, after he'd played a side.

"It's good."

"What do you think of the voice?"

"It's a good voice. Who is he?"

"That's Earl's vocalist."

That a. and r. man raised Cain:

"I told you I didn't want any singing on the records!"

Then I talked to him and persuaded him to try one of the sides, to see what happened.

And that was the debut of Billy Eckstine on records, and when the public had the opportunity to hear him they felt just the way we did. Of course, he's much more of a pro now—a real master. Almost the reverse of this story happened at the end of 1940 when they wanted Billy to sing a blues, like he sometimes did on the road. *Jelly, Jelly* turned out to be one of our biggest hits.

When I was in New York, somebody told me about Madeline Green, a singer who had some kind of falling out with Benny Goodman. She was a very nice-looking girl, and she and Billy together made a great pair. We backed them up with the Three Varieties; and that reminds me that we had a trio earlier called the Palmer Brothers, who sang on our record of *Rhythm Lullaby*. They were three brothers, and the one who had the most life and spirit was crippled and had to use a cane. We used them at the Grand Terrace and took them on the road. Rather than have them walking on and off the stage, they sat right with the band with a microphone in front of them, so all they had to do was stand up, sing, and sit back down. That was in 1935 and they did a very good job for me, but it was expensive carrying them around and they ended up with Cab Calloway, who called them the Cab Drivers!

I put quite a few acts together while I was at the Grand Terrace. One was called Patterson and Jackson, two big heavy fellows. Both of them sang and were comedians. One wasn't doing so good in Detroit, and the other wasn't doing so good in Chicago, but by putting them together they turned out to have a terrific act. We put them on at the Grand Terrace and took them to the Apollo Theatre, where they were held over for another week after getting a standing ovation at every show.

I also put Son and Sonny together. Sonny was Ida James's brother, and when I took her as vocalist I took Sonny and his mother on the bus, too. When we got to Chicago, I put him with a boy who was working in a trio but didn't really have a name. They had two different styles of dancing, and they lasted quite some time as Son and Sonny. We carried them with us for quite a while, too.

Earl Hines, 1940.

I've told about how I met Sarah Vaughan elsewhere (see *Road Stories*). She was a big asset to the band. At first, she was so nonchalant. She didn't give a damn about *nothing* except Charlie Parker's music, and she loved that! I remember one night we had played a date in Chicago and she and I were out on the sidewalk trying to get a cab. It was late, and it was freezing cold. We stood there shivering. Very few cabs were around, and some passed and wouldn't stop.

"Get me a rock, Earl," Sarah said.

"What for?"

"I'm going to throw it through one of these plate-glass windows."

"Yeah?"

"Yeah! That'll bring the police. They'll take us to the station and we'll be able to get warm."

She meant it, too, but luckily a cab came by just about that time.

Another incident I always associate with her was when we played a concert at a college. The students had covered the orchestra pit with crepe paper and streamers. When I called her out to sing, I was standing at the microphone and I turned around to conduct the band in the introduction as she came out. I stepped back a little too far and fell through all the paper into the pit, carrying the mike with me. I just missed the organ and ended up among the music racks. It seemed as though I was going down for half an hour, but when I landed, there was Sarah, looking down with her poker face, and several of the guys clustered around her. Nobody said anything, so there was only one thing for me to do, and that was to get out of there and do the best I could without showing any pain, even though I was suffering for quite a while afterwards.

Of course, Sarah was wonderful in the band. All the gifts she showed then have carried her to where she is today, and, like Duke Ellington used to say, she is really "beyond category." When she left, there was no one around to take her place, but I was luckier with boy singers.

I think when I began to realize that big bands were not drawing as they did and were getting

Madeline Green.

out of reach economically was in Tulsa. When we went south with the band there would sometimes be eight or nine thousand people at a dance, and even as high as twelve thousand in Kansas City. In Tulsa they had big, new jukeboxes that played a hundred records, and there wasn't one big band on them. Before that we often had four or five sides on the jukeboxes. Here there was nothing but what they then called rhythm and blues, and this was what was going to turn into rock 'n' roll. We were playing an élite dance in an exclusive part of town. When we got there—and I had Billy Eckstine and Madeline Green with me—there were about five hundred people. After we got back to our hotel, we found there was a dance in a garage next door, and a drummer had a five-piece rock-'n'-roll group in there. He had a girl who played piano and sang. There must have been three thousand people outside as well as all those inside. You had to push your way to get in, and the weather was so hot it was just stifling inside, and then you couldn't move. That changed my mind about several things, and I said, "I'm through with the South with big bands." When I got back to Chicago, I decided to disband. I started to play as a single and do a little bit of everything. I made a record session with Sidney Bechet and Rex Stewart for RCA. Bechet was evil that day, but when we got to the studio he kept saying, "I'm going to do Hines's tune." I didn't know which one he meant, but he took out his clarinet and began to play *Blues in Thirds* with just Baby Dodds on drums and me. People all think of him as playing soprano sax, but he was also one of the best clarinetists around.

That session was in September 1940. The following month I got a wire from Benny Goodman asking me to join his band. My first impulse was to say I was ready, because I was a low, sick cat then with little work in sight and a lot of legal problems. I knew it would be admitting defeat, but people who believed in me, like Dave Dexter of *Down Beat* and Harry Lim, advised me against it. Those who thought I should join Goodman had some sort of axe to grind. Cootie Williams joined him a couple of months later, and a year or so after

that they tried to get Johnny Hodges to leave Duke and go with Raymond Scott.

This was when I came out of the Grand Terrace, after I'd taken Ed Fox to the union. The board of directors agreed that his contract with me was not valid. I was going to try to open a club and get Billy Eckstine to be like a floor manager, but Billy said, "No, let's have a band." He and Budd Johnson put their heads together and took my music. Budd said, "I'll let you hear the band. If you like it, how about taking a *new* band out?" After he'd rehearsed it for two weeks, it sounded *so* good! I was fortunate in getting a contract from a fellow out in California who said, "I can send you five thousand dollars in advance." That's all I needed. Right off the reel, I bought uniforms, and we started making new arrangements, and we went back out. There were many personnel changes in this band, of course, but it was probably the best and most successful I ever had.

Around this time I remember driving into Chicago with Billy Eckstine and Budd Johnson in the front, Dizzy Gillespie and two others in the back. I was speeding and was caught by the police.

"Play sick and groan," I said to Billy, "and we'll say we're hurrying to get you to the hospital."

"What we'll do," the policeman said, "is take you down to the station."

"What're you going to do?" Dizzy asked them. "Arrest me because I'm with this man?"

"Are you sick, too?" one of the policemen wanted to know.

"I am *now*!" Dizzy said, deadpan.

When I finally left the Grand Terrace, I wanted Billy Eckstine and me to do an act together, but styles were beginning to change. Dizzy, Charlie Parker and all of them were forming a little organization of their own. In fact, all of the "modern" musicians were getting together then, and even the vocalists were trying to sing in a way that related to what the musicians were doing. Billy was growing, had made a wonderful reputation, and thought it would be better to go out on his own. Later on, he decided to form a band. I think he was talked into it. Of course, a lot of

the members in my band wanted to go with
him, because he was much younger and
they'd been running around together. Billy
liked be-bop, but he wasn't that type of vocalist, and eventually he gave up the band because it was too much of a strain.

I was fortunate enough to find a young fellow by the name of Johnny Hartman, who was
a very good singer. We went into the Howard
Theatre, where Billy was working as a single
by this time. They had thought it a good idea
to bring us back together on the same bill.
When Billy heard Johnny he came to me and
said, "I don't know why you put this competition on me!"

"Well, Billy," I answered, "I've got to have
a vocalist of some kind."

After Billy had left me, in September 1943,
I decided what I needed was a complete
change of format, so I put together a string
section of girls. I had violins, a viola, a cello
and a harp, as well as girls playing guitar and
bass fiddle. Sarah Vaughan was my vocalist,
and we did a very good job, but transportation
was a big problem, especially through the
South. There were twenty-four people at one
time, and it was impossible to travel by train.
We couldn't get a bus big enough to take all of
us, because the harp, the bass, the drums and
all the baggage and clothing took up so much
room. If they took out some seats to make
space for the baggage, there were not enough
seats for everybody to ride comfortably. I was
trying to do something like Fred Waring did,
only with girls, and I hoped to find somebody
interested in that kind of organization, but the
time wasn't right for it and I had to let it go.

The outstanding player among those girls
was Angel Creasy, a violinist. We featured her
quite a bit. The harpist was very good. So was
the cellist, who married the band manager.
We also featured four of the girls singing as a
group we called the Bluebonnets.

By the time we got back to Chicago, bookings were getting spasmodic, and it was then I
was approached by one of the owners of the
Pershing Hotel out on 63rd Street and Cottage Grove.

"We have a club downstairs," he said, "and

Earl Hines and his orchestra, 1943. Left to right: (rear) Shorts McConnell, Benny Harris, Paul Cohen, Idrees Sulieman, Murray Dinofer, Lucille Dixon, Roxanna Lucas; Harold Clark, Wardell Gray, Thomas Crump, Johnny Williams, Scoops Carry, reeds; (front) Cliff Smalls, unknown, Gus Chappell, Benny Green, trombones; Lavilla Tullis, harp; Arlene Illidge, Angel Creasy, Helen Way, Lolita Valdez, strings; (foreground) the Bluebonnets: Ellen Solomon, Jean Parks, Anita San, Mary Beasley; and Earl Hines.

I think if we open it up and put your band in there, you could make it your home like the Grand Terrace."

It sounded like a good idea to me, so we went in there. Of course, I had already let the girls go. I had so much trouble with them. Some wanted long sleeves and some wanted short sleeves. They were not satisfied with their hotel reservations; and what with one thing and another it just got to be too much. So I went into the El Grotto with my regular band, but I told them I wanted a string section for special concert presentations. I brought strings out of the Chicago local, and business began to look good. In fact, we were

certs featuring the music of *Show Boat*, the works of Fats Waller, W. C. Handy, Duke Ellington, Cole Porter, Jerome Kern, and so on. Buggs Roberts could really write for strings, and I'm sure if his arrangements were heard now they'd be considered advanced and far ahead of their time. I had found two singers, nice-looking people, Dolores Parker and Essex Scott. My road manager decided we had to give Scott a name people could remember, so he became Lord Essex! I kept the band and the singers there until I ran into the red.

The club had about seven different entrances and exits, and we tried to close some

The Bluebonnets and Sarah Vaughan (right), 1943. Far right: Gus Chappell, Paul Cohen, Benny Green.

quite a sensation, and they finally sold me the club. Joe Louis had a club around the corner a few blocks away called the Rhumboogie.

Now I didn't actually have anyone to run the club, and I was trying to run the band and watch over the show. We put on special con-

of them, but the police department and the fire department said they had to stay open. We couldn't have people on all the doors, and the manager I finally got was girl-struck. Every time I'd look up, he was sitting around with some girls instead of watching business.

At one time we had a boy on the door who was responsible for charging a dollar admission to those who wanted to sit at the bar, and for collecting the cover charge from those who sat at the tables. One night we were trying to find change for fifty dollars, but nobody had it except the guy who collected tickets for the bar, and everybody wondered how in the world he got fifty dollars. People like him hated to see us go, for everybody made money there but me. Some nights, when the place was packed and jammed, we were supposed to have $2000 from the covers of $2.50 per person, but we never came up over $1000. "Where is it?" I used to ask. And "Where is

months until we went out on a tour to Canada and the Coast. It was on the way back from that that I had the accident in Texas that nearly cost me my eyesight.

Between April and August 1947, I lost $30,000 at the El Grotto. I thought I knew how to run a club! While I was doing that, Joe Louis lost $35,000 at the Rhumboogie!

My interest in boxing and boxers began in my father's little athletic club. I met Jack Johnson through my relatives when he was living on Fifth Avenue in Pittsburgh, but I was real young and couldn't have cared less. I remember my auntie saying, "This is the champion of the world," and I remember

it?" was all they would say in reply. Nobody could tell me.

The first time we were in the El Grotto we played to capacity business for nine weeks. Then I had Sonny Thompson bring a big band in. The next time, we were there eight

seeing him in his great big open touring car with that French beret that he wore all the time on his head. In later years, when Joe Louis was living in Chicago, he and I became very close friends. When I was in New York, I'd go out to his great, big camp at Pompton

Lakes, and we'd sit up on the fence and talk. Joe didn't have much education, but he was a very smart man in conversing with people of all professions. He'd talk to people connected with the judicial or the medical profession. Or, rather, he'd start them off and let them talk, and he'd remember all they said. So far as show business was concerned, he used to use me to find out where everybody was, who was established and who had a chance to make it. We'd sit on the fence till he was ready to go down for training, and I'd go down with him and use the medicine ball and all the things he had for training. It was great for me, and put me on a new trend, and I've been keeping it up, keeping in shape ever since.

I didn't get a chance to see Sugar Ray Robinson's fights, because I always seemed to be on the road, but he would come in the club wherever we were and want to sing a song. Ralph Cooper was recording people in 1953, and Sugar Ray and I made a record together. After that I did engagements with him—two weeks in Providence and two weeks in Boston. My group would go on first, and I'd act as m.c. and introduce Sugar Ray. He had a fellow who taught him to dance, and they'd close the show. He was supposed to come out with us on the Pabst Blue Ribbon Show one time. Something happened and he didn't, but he and I remained very good friends.

Above: Earl Hines and Muhammed Ali in Las Vegas, 1975.

Opposite: Earl Hines and his orchestra, 1946. Left to right: (rear) Gene Thomas (bass), Chick Booth, Cliff Smalls, Benny Green, Walter "Woogie" Harris, Gordon Alston, Palmer "Fats" Davis, Vernon Smith, Willie Cook, Arthur Walker; (front) Kermit Scott, Lloyd Smith, Scoops Carry, Buddy Hills, Wardell Gray, reeds; Bill Thompson, vibes; Earl Hines, conducting.

Right: Club proprietors Joe Louis and Earl Hines at the El Grotto, 1947.

Goodbye, Grand Terrace!

A LONG WAY
FROM THE LEADER HOUSE

While I was thinking what to do about the El Grotto, Joe Glaser came to Chicago. He'd written me before, but I hadn't paid any attention. This time, he came out by himself and we sat up in my office and talked.

"I'm getting an all-star band together, all bandleaders who have had bands and given them up—to play with Louis Armstrong. It's a good way to bring you together," he said, "and we might come up with something. You never know."

We made arrangements and I closed the club. The funny part was that the best I got out of that whole deal at the El Grotto was the whiskey. I had it up in my hotel room—every kind of drink anybody could think of. We didn't have any food, but we had enough whiskey for months!

I joined Louis in New York, worked with him four weeks at the Roxy Theatre, and then we went to Europe to play the Nice Festival in February 1948, where I met Hugues Panassié for the first time. When we got back, Joe Glaser asked me to stay on, and that was how I came to spend three years with that group. Everybody in the organization was wonderful when it started.

Big Sid Catlett, on drums, I knew from before when he worked with me in my club, and also when he was with Smack (Fletcher Henderson) at the Grand Terrace. Big Sid was a big man, knew his size, and was always afraid he might hurt someone, so he tried to keep control of himself. The only time he would rear up was when he thought someone was trying to take advantage of him or some of his friends. We were very close. He was a good drummer, a very good drummer, and he *never* lost tempo. Big as he was, and big as his hands were, he was the lightest person I ever heard on drums. If you wanted him to get loud, he could get as loud as any drummer there ever was, but he could also stay so soft you could hardly hear him at a distance. His rhythm was so dynamic. I shall never forget it. All the harm he did was to himself, never to anyone else. Trying to be nice to people who took advantage of him, and a few other worries he had, were the cause, I think, of his drinking as much as he did.

Jack Teagarden . . . you can't say too much about him. All he wanted to do was play his horn, and he never harmed anybody, but he wasn't a fellow who liked sports. He asked me any number of times about baseball. "Show me," he'd say. "Everybody raises so much Cain about baseball!" One day, when we were at the Oriental Theatre, he had a little locomotive steam engine, and he had it going downstairs in his dressing room. I was carrying a portable television around at the time, and we were all looking at the World Series, but his engine cluttered up the picture, so everybody was hollering, "Cut that thing off!" He was just disinterested and didn't know what it was all about when it came to baseball. He liked fooling with engines, especially anything pertaining to steam. His only habit was drinking, and he used to break little tablets of some kind into Coca-Cola and get real high off that. But he was a fanatic when it came to Bourbon whiskey! When we were in Italy making a picture for Josephine Baker and other stars, we went into town during a break. Jack asked Pugh the valet to get a fifth of whiskey, and Pugh found the only bottle in the store. The man got it down from a top shelf all covered with dust. Jack was so happy to get a bottle of American whiskey. He gave it to the valet to bring back, and as he got out of the car Pugh dropped it, right at the studio. Jack had nine conniptions! He just flipped and bawled the guy out. Apart from that time, I would say he was always just as nice as you'd want to find anyone.

I had known Barney Bigard before when he was with Duke Ellington. I hadn't worked with him much, but I'd been around socially with him. We sort of hit it off pretty well. He would complain a lot, but he didn't like going to the boss and telling *him*—he'd just tell us, all of us, about the things he didn't like. Other than that, Barney was a very nice fellow and a fine clarinet player.

Arvell Shaw, the bass player, was a youngster then and he felt a little out of place with us. I took up with him as much as I could, to help him in the way of living among traveling musicians. He wasn't married at the time and we did our best to keep him straight. He was just a happy-go-lucky fellow, and he didn't realize till later that he played as much bass as he did.

And Velma Middleton, the vocalist, was a happy-go-lucky girl who worshipped Louis. She was just another boy so far as we were concerned, and she fitted right in with the band, so everybody was happy.

As for Louis himself, he was a guy who always said he didn't want any responsibility at all. He wanted the agency to take care of his everyday life, and handle the band. He didn't want anything to do so far as the musicians were concerned, no hiring or firing. So they took all that away from Louis and just let him play his horn. When we were traveling in Europe, I was a little upset that he had so little time for us. I naturally remembered the years when we used to run around and hang out together. But later I found out that it wasn't *his* fault. He was a giant of jazz, a great personality, and he set a wonderful example and did wonderful things in Europe.

Cozy Cole joined the band when Big Sid died. So full of personality, and a good salesman, he was an excellent replacement. He and I soon began to run around and spend a lot of time together. We would rehearse with Arvell Shaw to get the rhythm together, and we ended up with a very good rhythm section that made us stand out. Cozy used to stutter a bit sometimes when he was disturbed about something, because he was thinking quicker than he could speak.

They had another bass player after Arvell. He wasn't much of a sociable type and he fell off the roof when a hotel we were in in Canada caught fire. Everybody was out on the street except me. Then Louis saw me coming. "He's all right!" he said. "I see his cigar!" They had my picture in the paper next day, coming out the hotel with my straw hat on and a cigar in my mouth. I was in shorts, with no socks on, and just sandals on my feet.

Another experience with that group happened early in the morning when we were traveling in the bus. We hit some sort of garbage truck, and all this filthy stuff went all over the windows and the bus. I didn't know what it was. I thought maybe we were dead, sure 'nough. We all had to go in the hospital, and everybody was examined, but nobody was hurt. It was a bad kind of excitement at that particular time of night.

We had a bus trip down to New Orleans in 1949 when Louis was King of the Zulus at the Mardi Gras. That was the first time I ever saw anybody made up like Louis was. He and Velma went on one of the trucks and it broke down downtown. When we left next morning, we found we were riding in a baseball bus. Louis had just been talking to the mayor of the city, and he didn't know exactly what was going on, but Hugues and Madeleine Panassié, who were with us, were very perturbed that someone as highly regarded as Louis was in Europe—and in the U.S.—should be riding in that kind of transportation. Of course, you must realize it was done by Frenchy the road manager, who looked at it, I guess, as just a way of saving quite a bit of money, although we were the ones who had to sacrifice.

When I left Louis in 1951, I quit in Richmond, Virginia, and I think he probably never really understood why I left. Of course, there were people around him I didn't like, who were always making sneaky kind of trouble. One of the guys who used to hang around went to Doc Pugh, Louis's valet, and told him that I'd said, "I don't want to play with these has-beens!" It was a lie, because I didn't think any of us were has-beens, but Louis was angry and didn't speak to me a whole month while we were at the Blue Note in Chicago. I found out what the trouble was, and when we got to Bop City in New York, here comes this same monkey again! I grabbed him and made him come with me to Louis's dressing room, and we had it out right then and there.

"Oh, that's all right, man," Louis said, grinning. "Forget about it."

"No, it isn't all right," I said, and I was still hot. "You didn't speak to me for a month!"

But that had nothing to do with my leaving.

It was because I didn't think the new contract they offered me was like it should have been. I didn't think I was greater than Louis, and I didn't think I had as much experience as he had, so far as going around the world was concerned, but I thought what I had contributed to the music business entitled me to more consideration than they offered. I had had a contract with seventy-five percent publicity and a good salary, but now they wanted to list me merely as a sideman. I thought they should have kept me with seventy-five percent publicity, but they were not going to, so that was my reason for leaving.

I had pretty tough dealing after that, maybe because Joe Glaser thought I shouldn't have left. They gave me a rough way to go. It never was pinpointed. I never knew why it was so hard to get engagements, even with other booking agencies. It was hard to break into some of the élite clubs, places where the agencies had, you might say, franchises on the clubs. Yes, it was pretty rough for me for a while.

I had decided to form a small group of my own, and I ran across a fellow in Los Angeles

Louis Armstrong, Jack Teagarden, Earl Hines.

who helped me get it together in 1952. I had Jonah Jones on trumpet, Benny Green on trombone, Aaron Sachs on clarinet and tenor, Tommy Potter on bass and Ocie Johnson on drums. Etta Jones and Aaron's wife, Helen Merrill, were the vocalists. It was a great band and each of those guys was wonderful. The only trouble I had was with Jonah. As the trumpet player, he was the guy responsible for carrying the melody, and I had to be on him constantly so that the other horns would know what we were doing.

"You must realize," I'd say, "that they have to know exactly what we're playing, and you're the trumpet and you have to carry the melody."

Of course, it was hard for Jonah to do. He just couldn't see that. He wanted to pick up his horn and start off blowing just the way he felt like blowing. After he got his own band, he always thanked me for making him realize that. I even made him stand out and sing, and he didn't want to do that either, but I kind of took all the scare off him. But he was a fine fellow to get along with—a lovely disposition—and very smart so far as musicianship was concerned.

Benny Green was so far advanced on his horn, and he used to go out constantly and jam with all kinds of guys until he got a good conception of how to play his trombone with ease and relaxation. No matter how hard we worked, he always had his horn with him and

was ready to play by day or night. He was always trying to find something different. He dressed very nicely and I thought a lot of him, but I was sorry when he got mixed up with the wrong crowd.

I used to see quite a bit of Ocie Johnson around Chicago, but nobody did anything for him, and I wanted to make sure he got credit for some of his ideas as an arranger. He had a nice little voice and he was a *good* drummer. (Before Ocie, I remember, I had Art Blakey on drums for a while—another good, strong drummer.) Ocie had his own ideas and he was very easy to get along with.

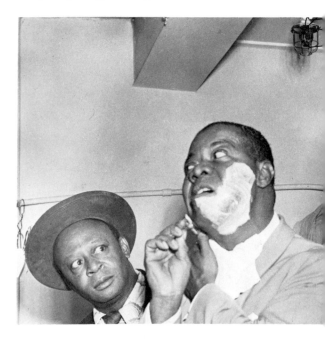

Helen Merrill had a small, soft voice, and didn't really know what her potential was, but I kind of coaxed her a little bit, and put her onstage with us to help both her and Aaron Sachs, her husband. It worked out well, too, although I had Etta Jones singing. They made an interesting contrast. Etta had a fine style, somewhere between Ella Fitzgerald's and Dinah Washington's. It was too bad she changed it, because I felt she had a great future. Rock 'n' roll came in, and when she changed I think she became confused for a time.

Anyway, that was a wonderful group, but it was too expensive, even at that time when if you paid a man $250 a week you were paying him a whole lot. After we left the Oasis in Hollywood, transportation began to eat up too much of the money, and I had to go for myself for a while. I tried again the following year with a septet that included Dicky Wells, Gene Redd, Jerome Richardson and Leroy Harris. It was another good and versatile group, but I faced the same problems with engagements and money, and I had to break that up, too. Musicians don't always understand what the leader has to pay out in commissions, transportation, taxes and other charges.

I was working at the Moulin Rouge in Las Vegas with a quartet when Joe Glaser said Doc Dougherty, the proprietor of the Hangover in San Francisco, had a proposition. I'd played there before for a short time with my group, but now he said:

"I'm having an all-star group as a house band, and I'd like you to take charge. I understand you've had bands before."

I agreed to his terms, but I didn't really know what I was getting into, because this was to be my first experience of Dixieland. What we played with Louis wasn't Dixieland.

We were supposed to open on a Friday night, and there was to be a rehearsal at noon.

Opposite, top: Louis Armstrong and Sidney Catlett.

Left: Louis Armstrong and Earl Hines with comedian Mantan Moreland.

Below: On tour. Left to right: Arvell Shaw, Earl Hines, Velma Middleton, Sidney Catlett.

Earl Hines, Kid Ory and Louis Armstrong.

When I got there, I saw all these elderly guys sitting around, and I said to the owner, "Doc, when're you going to have the rehearsal? Where are the musicians?"

"They're all here," he said.

"My goodness, what is this?" I thought as I looked at them.

But we all got up on the stand and, of course, I wasn't accustomed to the two-beat rhythm they wanted there, and I was out of line. Those guys realized it, too.

"All I want you to do is sit up there and chord," Doc said, "and play what you and they know."

The only three Dixieland numbers I really knew were *When the Saints Go Marching In*, *Tin Roof Blues* and *Panama*. When people told me, "Well, you're not a Dixieland pianist," I'd remind them there was no such thing as a Dixieland pianist. Dixieland bands were on the street. When they moved them inside, and got a piano player, all he did was chord, and most of the guys they got were blues piano players.

Nevertheless, every night seemed to be Saturday night at the Hangover. I went in for eight weeks, and then they asked me to stay three more months. At the end of that, Doc asked me to stay six months. When I agreed, he said, "Why don't you move out here?" So in 1956 I moved my family to San Francisco. I bought a home in Oakland a little later. I had married Janie Moses in 1947, and since we had two young daughters it was good for me to be home when they were growing up. I had a weekly radio show over KCBS, and after all those years on the road life at home seemed very comfortable.

I stayed in the Hangover five years, and I'm telling you that that was a long time! In the fourth year, we started doing gigs around the country. We didn't get too far with that, because we had nobody to represent us, but I was enjoying the music more. It hadn't taken me long to discover that those guys had a toe-tapping rhythm going. I changed the drummer and got Earl Watkins. I taught Pops Foster some new ideas in playing bass behind me, and got him away from the slap-bass. Be-

Tommy Potter at left; Art Blakey in foreground with Jonah Jones behind him; Earl Hines and Benny Green standing either side of unknown friend, 1952.

Earl Hines, Benny Green, Tommy Potter, Jonah Jones, Ocie Johnson, Aaron Sachs, 1953.

sides Darnell Howard on clarinet and Jimmy
Archey on trombone, we had a whole lot of
different trumpet players at different times,
like Henry Goodwin, Marty Marsala, Jackie
Coons, Ken Whitson, and one of my old
friends from Chicago, a beautiful musician,
Muggsy Spanier. And I ended up with Eddie
Smith, who had a really wonderful tone on
trumpet.

I would take time out from the Hangover
for special engagements, and in September
1956 I toured England as joint leader with
Jack Teagarden of a group that included Max
Kaminsky, Peanuts Hucko, Jack Lesberg and
Cozy Cole. We were a big success and later
that year I was voted top pianist in the Critics'
Poll of *Melody Maker*, the British music paper
that used to be rather like *Down Beat*. Such
polls may not mean too much, yet it gives you
a warm feeling to know you're appreciated.
The opposite of that had previously happened
to me in the U.S. I was asked what it would
be worth to me for my band to place first in
one of the best-known American jazz polls. I
guess I didn't pick my words carefully enough
when I refused to consider anything of that
kind, because for years after that my band was
not so much as listed in that magazine's polls,
not even when I had one of the hottest bands
in the country. And that is a matter of record!

Another engagement between months in
the Hangover was at the Embers in New York
towards the end of 1959. I had Calvin Newborn (Phineas Newborn's brother) on guitar,
Carl Pruitt on bass and Bill English on drums.
We were well received and a lot of piano
players came by. One night I particularly remember, Teddy Wilson, Eddie Heywood and
Erroll Garner were there, and we had a great
time reminiscing.

The following year I was at the Café Continental in Chicago with the same guys as at the
Hangover. We were twice held over, and altogether were there about three months.
When we got back to the Hangover, Doc
wanted a different deal. After all he'd made off
the band, he now wanted to pay the boys
scale. He was getting ready to retire, too, and
I told him the least he could do was to keep

them in there a year at the old rate. He wouldn't agree to that, so we ended up in another place called the Black Sheep, and we were there a year or so until bad management caused us to leave. After that I thought the best thing to do was to disband, because the musicians were getting pretty high salaries, and that kind of money just wasn't out there then.

I went on working as a single, running around here and there with a little trio until in 1963 I got involved with a partner in a club we called Earl Fatha Hines's Music Crossroads. It was in Jack London Square, Oakland, and it was an interracial thing, a mixed affair. My wife acted as hostess, and I had Japanese, Chinese, Jewish, Irish and Negro people working there. We got along like one happy family. We changed the concept of the night-club as a hangout and advertised it as "a place to bring your children." The police depart-ment and the people in Oakland were proud of the kind of club we had—except the busi-ness people in that area. When they began to realize I was a Negro owner, the squeeze was put on, and my attorneys thought it best for me to ease out while I could. I did just that.

Opposite: Club Hangover, San Francisco.

Below: Three from Chicago: Joe Sullivan, Earl Hines and Muggsy Spanier.

Someone had been telling the co-owner he could get him some go-go girls, and three weeks after I quit the place was raided.

We had an entertaining group in there with a very good little Japanese vocalist, and in 1964 I took it out on tour to the Sutherland in Chicago and Birdland in New York. But be-fore that something happened that changed the whole course of my career.

The Music Crossroads business dis-heartened me. I had made up my mind to get out of music and to open a store with my wife. Then I got a call from Stanley Dance in New York. I had met him in Europe and we had kept in touch by mail. He wanted me to come and play three solo concerts at the Little Theatre. Dan Morgenstern, the critic, and a friend of his named Dave Himmelstein, had got the use of the theatre for a series of Friday and Saturday jazz concerts. They opened with Coleman Hawkins and Stanley had suggested me to them for the following week. I was re-ally doubtful about going such a long way for such a short engagement. The money they had available was limited, and I had never played a solo concert before, but Stanley argued with me until I agreed to make it.

I had only a little time to rehearse with Ahmed Abdul-Malik on bass and Oliver Jack-son on drums. "I don't have anything written with me," I told them, "so all I can tell you is to follow me!" We just rehearsed *Tea for Two*, a *Fats Waller Medley* and *St. Louis Blues*. When I opened, I said to myself, "This is something new, and I've just got to get a cer-tain amount of energy and confidence together." But I was scared to death, although I'd had all that nightclub experience in the past forty years! One other thing I did. I asked for Budd Johnson on tenor saxophone. I'd always had confidence in him and thought he should have been recognized more than he was. So I set up the program for him to come in on the tail end of the concert, and that proved very fruitful and successful. But when I first went out and sat down at the piano, I don't know where the words came from.

"Ladies and gentlemen," I said, "I know you're looking for a concert, but just imagine you're in your living room, and you have a piano, and I'm there to play a few numbers for you."

That took all the strain off—people straining after what I'm going to do—and it sort of lifted me, too. I could hear a sigh of relief when they realized I had had stage experience, and that helped me an awful lot.

The first tune I thought of was *Memories of You*, which was written by Eubie Blake, the old, close friend who was the cause of my leaving Pittsburgh. I put everything I could into it, and the people applauded so much at the end of it that I couldn't think for a moment what to do next. I guess I was still scared, but I gathered confidence as I went along, and we just broke up the place both nights. All the critics were very kind, and the one I am especially grateful to is Whitney Balliett of *The New Yorker*.

He wrote about the concert, and then when I came back to New York later in the year to play at Birdland with my group he spent a lot of time with me. Stanley Dance had got me some record dates, and Charlie Carpenter had arranged for me to appear on a television show. Whitney came to the recording session at RCA, and a little later a long piece by him appeared in *The New Yorker*. It really opened doors for me, and from then on I had a new spirit, a new life.

I realized when I got out on the stage, and it was all me, the picture was changed, and there were things I wanted to do that I couldn't do. So when I went home, I really studied. I went into "my bag," as they say. The big band days had made me lazy, no doubt about it. Sometimes, all I'd do was make the introduction and then get off the stand! But I enjoy playing piano, and I got a kick out of the new role I found myself in.

Then Hugues Panassié asked me to tour France in 1965. He had always thought a lot of me, and he and his friends did everything in the world they possibly could to make the trip pleasant for me. Most of the concerts I played alone, but at some I was joined by my old friend and drummer from the Grand Terrace days, Wallace Bishop. Hugues made sure I

At the Hangover. Left to right: Darnell Howard, Pops Foster, Muggsy Spanier, Earl Watkins, Jimmy Archey, Earl Hines.

Earl Hines with basketball stars, 1954.

got the best publicity, and the whole tour was a big success and a wonderful experience for me. I stayed with him and his Madeleine at their house a couple of times. He was a guy who really knew wine, and it was a pleasure to see how much he enjoyed his favorite kinds— and food. He had 25,000 records in his house, and he seemed to know every note on those he liked. When he found how much I admired Joe Smith, he brought out records by Joe I'd never heard, and we spent hours listening to them. We had some little arguments about musicians whose playing he didn't like, but he helped me a lot by explaining what he thought I was doing right and what I was doing wrong on the records I'd made.

From France, I went to England and worked with Alex Welsh's band. They were such wonderful boys in that group. They were happy to do anything I wanted to do, and I was glad to see the friends I'd made there before like Sinclair Traill and Max Jones. When I got back to the U.S., I played a concert at the Pittsburgh Jazz Festival with Duke Ellington, The Lion, Mary Lou Williams,

Billy Taylor and other pianists. Duke and I even played a duet together! That same year I was elected to *Down Beat*'s Hall of Fame in its annual International Critics' Poll.

In 1966, I went back to Europe for another tour of piano recitals, and this time I took my wife and two daughters with me. I worked in a club in Rome for three weeks, and Mussolini's son Romano, who is also a jazz pianist, came in there almost every night. They gave me a tour all over the city and we saw all the sights, the cathedrals, the catacombs, the Colosseum and the Forum. The mother of the man who owned the club was a countess, and she was from England. She had met the Pope on several occasions, and in the meantime I had met a monsignor. So she arranged a little luncheon for the monsignor, my family and me, and I explained that it was my ambition to meet the Pope and shake his hand. When I had been in Rome before with Louis Armstrong, the whole band had been supposed to meet him, but the agent fixed it so that just Louis and Lucille went, not the rest of us. That was a big disappointment. Now at first the monsignor told us

Above: In Rome, 1966. Romano Mussolini at right.

Opposite: Leaving for Europe, 1966: Tosca, Earl, Janie and Janear Hines.

Below: "Fatha" Hines meets Pope Paul in Rome. His daughters, Janear and Tosca, are on the right with the monsignor.

how the Pope came out in the square on Sunday morning, and how we could get close enough to see him, but four or five days later he came back and said, "You have an audience with the Pope."

Now I became terribly nervous, more nervous than I had ever been before. I could hardly stand up. I couldn't imagine what I was going to do, and my wife felt the same way. We found out what we were supposed to wear—the children white dresses and white head scarves, my wife and I dark clothes, and my wife a dark head scarf. The monsignor took us to St. Peter's, the largest cathedral I ever saw in my life. So many stone steps, so many statues in side altars! An arm of some of those statues was as large as my whole body! And up on the ceilings, as far as you could see were paintings, the most beautiful by Michelangelo. I couldn't imagine how they were done.

The Pope was very kind and gentle with us, but I never felt so exhausted, so drained emotionally as I did when the audience was over.

Another experience in Italy that amazed us was when we went to Pompeii. There were one-way streets, phosphorous stones that lit up at night, hot water running through pipes, dogs turned to stone, loaded dice, people still sitting at a table where they died, and paintings that had been there since before Christ with ingredients in the paint that got brighter the more often they were rubbed.

Venice and the water taxis surprised us, too. My older daughter, Janear, was studying French then, and she helped out with the language when we got to Paris. My wife found it very expensive there when she decided to buy clothes for the children. And she had problems translating the money, even in England, unless Janear was with her.

When we got back from Europe, the first thing Stanley Dance told me was that I was going to Russia for the U.S. State Department in July on a six-week tour. He had been looking after my affairs while I was away, and I found they wanted me to take six musicians—black and white—and a girl singer. The group we eventually put together consisted of Budd Johnson on tenor, Bobby Donovan on alto,

Money Johnson on trumpet, Mike Zwerin on trombone, Bill Pemberton on bass, Oliver Jackson on drums, and Clea Bradford as vocalist. The official record on that tour was that we played 11 cities and gave 35 concerts to a total of 92,040 people. In a way we were too successful, because the Russians canceled our appearances in Moscow and Leningrad and sent us down south to the Black Sea. Nevertheless, it was one of the great experiences of my life, and somehow a lot of youngsters from those two cities managed to get down there to hear us. The authorities just didn't want their heads turned too much!

On arrival we had been met by a tour director, a big Russian, and a woman interpreter who was six months pregnant—nobody smiling. There was not much sympathy for women over there, and they seemed to do all the labor work as well as sweeping the streets. We used to complain about buses with no shock absorbers, but that interpreter rode 'em, holding onto the rail all the time.

We weren't impressed by the food in Moscow, where the boys managed to play in some jam sessions the very first night, but in Georgia it was more like Creole cooking in New Orleans, and very good. But it was awfully hot down there, and there was no air conditioning in our hotel. We found that a lot of the people didn't like the Russians at all, although they were careful how they talked because they were afraid it would get back.

We used to create quite a bit of excitement when we went shopping. Sometimes about a hundred people would follow us down to the store and watch us purchase whatever it was we wanted. Then they would follow us back to the hotel. When I was coming down the stairs to eat one time, a fellow was going up. He turned around, followed me into the dining room, sat right across from me, watched me eat my whole meal, and never said a word. When I got up, he got up and left!

The Russians treated us as well as we were treated in Europe, once they decided we were there for purely musical reasons, not political. At first, one of their officials wanted to give me information on how to run the band, but when he found I knew what I was doing he turned me loose and saw to it we had everything we wanted. He would even sub for me, go to the theatre when we hit town and see that the lighting, amplifiers and piano were right. In some towns we'd go to two or three places to find a very good piano, and when he asked for it they *had* to give it up! Our food was always the best available. If for some reason we didn't like it, all we had to do was tell him. He'd snap his fingers and everybody would jump to attention. I liked the ice cream in one place and asked if I could have another dish. He saw to it immediately, and from then on I had two dishes of ice cream wherever I ate.

We all had big rooms, but they liked to put me in an extra big one, because they thought that as leader I ought to be off by myself. They couldn't understand it that I was running around with the boys and that we were all together. Sometimes they'd come by and find us quietly playing pinochle. We'd have a drink or two and they'd join us. Then after what they'd been told about how Negroes were treated in the U.S., they could not understand it when they looked up at the bandstand and saw the two white boys bowing to me. Of course, it was just our way of acknowledging the master of ceremonies.

Before we got through, our tour director and the interpreter became very friendly. They used to laugh at everything we laughed at, whether they understood what we were laughing at or not. The interpreter liked to put electric bulbs in the boys' pockets, push up against them, and laugh when they exploded with a loud noise! Both of them came to the airport to see us off, and we all gave them presents.

Rehearsal for Russia, 1966. Left to right: Money Johnson, Mike Zwerin, Earl Hines, Bobby Donovan, Budd Johnson, Oliver Jackson, Bill Pemberton.

Earl Hines in bowling league competition.

I would have liked to continue working with
a group of that size, but back in the U.S. business in clubs made a quartet more practical,
and I had a very good one with Budd Johnson,
Bill Pemberton and Oliver Jackson.* In November I got a chance to put a big band
together once more when we played at the
Riverboat in New York with Ella Fitzgerald.
We had a lot of fun, and I had musicians in it
like Emmett Berry, Dud Bascomb, Jimmy
Cleveland and Eddie Barefield, besides Budd
Johnson. We went back the following year
with most of the same guys, plus Snooky
Young and Vic Dickenson, and I really got a
yen to have a big band again, but I knew it
was too difficult as an economic proposition.
The kind of musicians I liked either didn't
want to go out on the road or wanted too
much money.

From then on I nearly always worked with a
quartet, although I got another septet
together to tour Europe for Jean-Marie
Monestier of Bordeaux in 1968. (I just added
Bobby Donovan, Booty Wood and Money
Johnson to the quartet.) When Budd Johnson
left me in 1969, I got Haywood Henry, who
used to be with Erskine Hawkins, and he
plays all the reed instruments very well.
Bobby Mitchell, a trumpet player, took his
place in 1972, and Rudy Rutherford replaced
Bobby in 1974. Rudy is a first-class clarinetist,
and he is very versatile. He plays all the saxes
as well as flute.

For some engagements we needed a girl
singer, and I was lucky enough to meet Marva
Josie in 1968. She came to audition when we
were going into the Village Vanguard in New
York, and she had invested a lot of money in
special arrangements. She was quite surprised
when I said all I wanted to know was what
song she wanted to sing and in what key! She
is attractive, and I was impressed by her range
and style right away. In fact, I think she is one
of the most original talents I've discovered in
decades of show business. There are few
singers so versatile, and she can do anything
with her voice. Apart from occasional tours

* See Appendix, 5.

Marva Josie.

that I've made without the group, she has been with me ever since, and she's a very real asset wherever we work.

She had the right kind of musical background. Her father was a professional saxophone player and her mother the lead singer in a church choir. But in high school Marva was considered a bit of a weirdo because she preferred opera and the classics.

There was a whole lot of hard work behind the success she is today. She was born in Pittsburgh and first of all studied piano with a Miss Martin in Clarington. Then she studied privately with Marie Carter Hayes and Ralph Lewando in Pittsburgh, where she won a Gould-Lewando scholarship to Chatham College Opera Workshop. She also studied dramatic art with Olga Wolf and took languages at the University of Pittsburgh. She concentrated on Italian because she had opera in mind. After appearing in local musical productions, she made her professional debut in *Porgy and Bess* at City Center in New York, and then sang and danced in several off-Broadway choruses. She recorded for Polydor and United Artists, and has her own LP (*This Is Marva Josie*, TLP-4) on Thimble.

The year 1968 was also when I toured Japan for the first time. That was right after I played opposite Oscar Peterson at the Village Gate in New York. The following year he and I took our groups on a joint tour of South America. We left the day after I had played at Duke Ellington's seventieth birthday party in the White House. What a night that was! I shall never forget it.* But when I got back from South America, a terrific surprise awaited me.

Scott Newhall was managing editor of the San Francisco *Chronicle* and a very unusual person. He and his wonderful wife, Ruth, have been so generous to me and my family that I can never say too much about them. He has always got a helping hand out to someone trying to make his way in this unsettled world. Among his favorite piano players were Fats

Waller and Art Tatum, and he didn't like it at all when a great artist like Tatum passed away with very little recognition or financial support. Since I was the last of that group, he took it on himself to say, "This will never happen to Earl Hines!" And he went completely out of his way to make sure it didn't.

He and his capable secretary, Dolly Reed, organized a celebration at the Sheraton Palace Hotel in San Francisco, where he presented me with a terrific Steinway grand. When he unveiled it at the beginning of the evening, I could hardly believe my eyes. It is a magnificent instrument that was specially made in 1904 for Mr. Sherman of the original music firm of Sherman and Clay. As the plaque Scott put on it says, there is not another one of its kind. It's beautiful to look at and it has a beautiful soundboard. You have to hear its kind of aged-in sound to appreciate it, and I know that it is one of the greatest instruments I've ever played on. Even after I had had it home in my living room, I would come down in the morning and look at it and not believe it. I played it, of course, at the Sheraton Palace after Scott unveiled it. Mayor Alioto and Herb Caen, one of the Bay Area's leading critics, were both there, and they stayed the entire evening.

I just wish there were more Scott Newhalls to help those of us in the music profession. When he finally bought the home he had always wanted as a child, he had the family and me to stay several days. His friendship and help have meant so much to me.

Another real friend, whom I've already mentioned, is Stanley Dance. As I said, he was the cause of my not getting out of the music business at a time when I was threatening to hang up the gloves. It just didn't look

---

* For a description of this party, and Earl Hines's contribution to it, see *The World of Duke Ellington*.

Opposite, top: Earl Hines plays the Steinway grand presented to him by Scott Newhall at the Sheraton Palace Hotel in San Francisco.

Opposite, bottom: Earl Hines plays Scott Newhall's gift for the first time, 1969. The donor is fourth from left in foreground.

then as though there was any future for my kind of piano playing. I've never been what is commonly termed an Uncle Tom. I figured that if I had something to offer, I wanted it to be real, and I wanted to be accepted like other artists. Paul Whiteman loved my piano playing, and he would have liked me to join him, but he always had to qualify his admiration by saying, "If you were only white!" That stayed with me so long, and I didn't really understand what he was talking about until many years later. Then Stanley Dance sat down with me, and it was like a reprieve. He talked about different musicians and about my piano style, and how people really appreciated it. By this time he had been living in the U.S. several years, and what he also *knew* was how people still felt about me in Europe, where the public is very loyal. When I started to go there nearly every year, I soon found out how right he was. And I mustn't forget to mention his wife who, as Helen Oakley, used to come to the Grand Terrace when she was writing for *Down Beat*. She would criticize me for not featuring myself enough on the piano, and when she came in Trummy Young used to look at me and grin, as much as to say, "What will I do wrong tonight?" She knew so much about music and musicians, and was already one of the best critics around, so when she and Stanley married after World War II, that became some combination! Their friendship and support has been a comfort to me, and Stanley always gives up his time to take care of things when I'm away. He has acted as my representative on many occasions, but we never have had any kind of contract. He regards records as very important to an artist, and it is mainly due to his efforts that I have been able to make so many since 1964.

With his help and guidance, too, the last twelve years have been very active, and the group has worked steadily, so that sometimes the guys have come and asked me to take time off for a vacation. The world certainly became more aware of me, and for seven years I was voted top pianist in *Down Beat*'s International Critics' Poll.

Thanks to another good friend, Wilma Dobie,

I was made honorary president of the Overseas Press Club Jazz Club, and I have played for them several times, at one concert with Eubie Blake and Billy Taylor. On my seventieth birthday, the club put on a party for me at the Biltmore Hotel in New York, and so many old friends and musicians were there that I felt very moved. As soon as I came in the door, Clark Terry began playing *Happy Birthday* on his flugelhorn, and after that I guess a dozen different pianists played for me, beginning with Fats Waller's son, Maurice.

In 1971, I toured Italy, giving piano recitals and playing at the San Remo Festival. I went back in 1973 for festivals in Pescara, Verona and Spezia. The Italians really dig my style and I'm only sorry I can't speak their language better. I took the group to Japan and Australia in 1972, and back to Japan in 1974. But although it was a very busy time for us, 1974 was a *sad* year. Duke Ellington died and I played at his funeral service in the enormous Cathedral of St. John the Divine in New York. I really couldn't take it, and I had to go outside as soon as I had finished. I don't know who was the more upset, Count Basie, Stanley Dance, who delivered the eulogy, or me. I kept thinking of all the times we had been together, and how Duke would always have me up to play in the band if I went by when he was at the Rainbow Grill in New York. The last time, I had played *Things Ain't What They Used to Be*, and he liked it and hollered, "Give everybody in the house a drink!" I tried to put into words how I felt about that great man for *Stereo Review*:

Duke Ellington was the all-round greatest. As a bandleader, he had a stage presence that was just outstanding, and he always commanded the audience's respect. He was one of the greatest composers I know. His compositions pertained to everyday life, and he could translate into song whatever he saw. He had

Opposite: Earl Hines and Duke Ellington.

no equal as an arranger, and he had a vision of his own, which he pursued and proved without regard to all the other styles that came in and went out. A lot of people didn't realize how much piano he could play, but he was original and didn't copy anybody. Highly intelligent, he could talk with anyone—kings, queens, presidents, all kinds of artists—on their terms. There will never be another like him.

I think what made him so different as a pianist was that he was not just a stylist and an arranger, but a composer, too. I wish he had made more solo records, but I never forget how he could stimulate that band of his. Sometimes you might hear them playing at a dance before he arrived. Then he would come out and sit down at the piano, and the difference was like night and day. He had a lot of rhythmic drive.

We did two European tours that year and played the Nice and Montreux festivals. In August I went on a tour of South America with Teddy Wilson, Marian McPartland and Ellis Larkins. That was a unique experience. The contrasts in styles made the concerts very successful, and the impresario, Alejandro Szterenfeld, saw to it that we always had a good piano to play. I also appreciated the opportunity in Buenos Aires to see my good friend Eddie Fiore again. I met him when I went the first time with Oscar Peterson. He's very knowledgeable about jazz. In fact, I think he knows more about it than anybody else down there.

The big event for me in 1975 was a cruise on the *S.S. Rotterdam* to Nassau and Bermuda. I'd never been on a trip on a ship like that before, and I enjoyed it very much. It was what they called a jazz cruise. Besides my group, they had Dave Brubeck's, Mercer Ellington's, Dizzy Gillespie's, Carmen McRae's,

This page, top: Earl Hines and Oscar Peterson in Buenos Aires, 1969.

Opposite, top: On board the *S.S. Rotterdam*, 1975. Earl Hines and Dave Brubeck.

Right: Earl Hines, Harley White, Rudy Rutherford, Eddie Graham, on the *S.S. Rotterdam*, 1975.

Wild Bill Davis's, and the World's Greatest Jazz Band aboard, so it was just like a week-long party. I wish you could get the kind of service they had on that ship in hotels!

At the end of the year we went on another European tour with my old buddy, Benny Carter. This was organized by George Wein, who had previously been responsible for my appearing several times in his Newport festivals and at Nice. He's a pianist, too, so I always feel a bond between us. I guess he'd be playing more often if he didn't have so much business to attend to. That's a case of putting business before pleasure, which you have to do in life.

Right now, our schedule for 1976 * looks much the same as the last few years, except that one of the great events of my life took place on 17 May when I was invited to play at the White House after the state dinner for President d'Estaing of France. Marva Josie was to sing with me, and we were both invited to the dinner as well. I felt it was a great honor to sit at the same table as Mrs. Ford and the President of France. Next to me was Clint Eastwood, and I was surprised that he knew quite a bit about my career. After dinner, President Ford introduced me in the East Room, and I sat down at the same eagle-legged piano I played at Duke Ellington's birthday party. I began with *Rosetta* and *You Can Depend on Me*, and then went into *Boogie Woogie on St. Louis Blues*. After a couple of choruses of *Comme Ci, Comme Ça*, I segued into Charles Trenet's *I Wish You Love* and Marva Josie began to sing from the back of the room, using a cordless mike. It caused a sensation. Everyone, including Henry Kissinger, was turning around to find out where the voice was coming from. We'd developed this technique in clubs and always found it very effective. Budd Johnson did it with me originally, playing *It's Magic* on soprano saxophone out back somewhere and then coming down through the audience and onto the stand. Mr. Ford signaled to me for an encore, so we sang *Yellow Days* as a duet. This is a

great favorite with my brother-in-law, Arthur Fletcher, and his wife Bernice, who were both in the audience, Arthur being Deputy Assistant to the President for Urban Affairs. We got a lot of applause for that, and I was very pleased when the President held up his thumb for a second encore. Marva sang *Summertime*, really pulling out all the stops, and I interpolated *St. James Infirmary*, which a lot of people seemed to get a kick out of. We had a tremendous response from the audience, and both of the presidents and their wives said warm and complimentary things to us afterwards. Members of the White House staff told us there hadn't been so much enthusiasm after an entertainment for a long time, so we both felt awfully happy about the whole thing, and I knew it was a very big honor to play for the presidents of *two* countries.

Besides Marva and Rudy Rutherford, the group I've worked with since 1974 includes Harley White and Eddie Graham, both of them extremely cooperative musicians. Harley is a well-schooled bass player who constantly studies and advances. Eddie is a very gifted drummer who can put on an act that is a whole show in itself, and does. The great thing about this group is that all five of us are comfortable with one another. There's no temperament, no selfishness, no conflict of personalities, and I can't tell you what this means after all the years I've put up with that sort of thing. Everybody knows what he has to do and does it for the good of the group. We always have about six entirely different sets worked out and ready, so in any one night you never hear anything twice. Of course, I don't think a night goes by without a request for *Boogie Woogie on St. Louis Blues* or *Rosetta*, and I guess I'll have to play them until the end of my days, but we keep adding new

Opposite: At the White House, 1976, with Presidents Ford and d'Estaing and Madame d'Estaing.

---

* See Chronology.

things to the book that often surprise other musicians.*

It was a long way from the Leader House to the White House, but as I look back on my career I give credit to the friends who helped me, but most of all to my father, who set me on the right path. He told me that you can't carry on through life expecting something for nothing. You have to work for the good things, and when you get them the real enjoyment is in knowing you didn't work in vain. My father didn't like halfway measures at all, or people like quack doctors and shyster lawyers. "If you'll notice," he said, "they never get any further than that, and they usually end up behind the eight-ball."

Following his advice, I tried to go step by step in my piano playing. I learned to play it to begin with, studied it, and improved as I went along. With other musicians, I was never one for challenging, but I would ask them, "How do you do this?" or "How do you do that?" You can even learn a lot of things from people who can't read a note. When we were making a film in Hollywood with Louis Armstrong in 1951 called *The Strip*, the star of the picture, Mickey Rooney, loved to play piano, although he couldn't read, and there was a passage he used to make that was unbelievable. I never did figure out how he did it.

My father didn't believe in easy money and he was always reminding me that "all that glitters is not gold." He used to say that life was like the stage. The curtain goes up and there are all kinds of colors to catch your eye. Although costume jewelry and stage clothing are exciting to look at, you wouldn't wear them on the street if you were sensible. "It's the plain suit that stays right and lasts the longest," he would say. "A blue suit is a standard suit for a man, no matter what he does. He comes home, washes his face, takes a shower, puts on a white shirt and a blue suit, and he's a dressed man." Of course, there's a difference between everyday life and stage life. When George Raft was at the Grand Terrace, he told me not to buy expensive suits. "You're always

having them cleaned and pressed for stage appearances, anyway," he said, "so it's better to buy cheap suits and have more of them."

Although my father married again after my mother died, I was always his pet. He brought me something home in his lunch basket every day, but he would chastise me sure enough if I did something wrong. He really had very little to do with my half brother Boots and my half sister Nancy. They both played piano, and Nancy became a teacher and used my old books. It seemed as though the family became divided over the children, although I didn't realize it at the time. My father would come home, eat his dinner, say very little, and then maybe go out and take care of the garden. He always tried to get out of the house, and he'd go to a little club downtown where they played cards, and not come home till 11 or 12 P.M. when he thought everyone would be in bed. He'd get up in the morning, go to work, and we wouldn't see him all day.

When he died in 1956, I felt it very much. I flew home to Pittsburgh for his funeral.

(1973–76)

Earl Hines and his father, 1935.

TEATRO MASSIMO BELLINI
CATANIA

Sabato 23 novembre 1974 - ore 21

EARL HINES

Teatro esaurito in abbonamento

CONCERT

BENEFIT

MEMORIAL FUND

FOR ERECTION OF A NEW CHURCH

—— BY ——

LOIS B. DEPPE, Baritone

EARL HINES, PIANIST

AT EBENEZER BAPTIST CHURCH

Sunday Afternoon, March 23rd, 1924

3 P. M. Sharp

SILVER OFFERING

Programme

1.
{ (a) DOES'T THOU REMEMBER............................Gu..
{ (b) MEPHISTO SERENADE................................Gu..
Both Numbers from Opera Faust
Mr. Deppe

2
SILVER THREADS AMONG THE GOLD.......................Cornet S..
Leon Straughters

3
PAPER ON MODERNISM.....................................
Mr. Harry Jackson

4
YOUR EYES...Schnei..
HER EYES TWIN POOL....................................Burle..
{ O LORD, LET ME WEEP
{ LA CHIA CHIO PANGO..................................Han..
{ Sung in, "Italian"
Mr. Deppe

5
SAXAPHONE SOLO.....
Mr. Vance Dixon

6
PIANO SOLO...
Mrs. James Butler

Intermission

Remarks by Rev. Austin, Pastor of Ebenezer Baptist Church

7
ADAMASTOR, KING OF THE OCEAN...........................Meyerbe..
From Opera - La Africiana
DANNY DEEVER..Damros..
Irish Military Song
Mr. Deppe

8
REMARKS..
Mr. John Clark

9
SOMETIMES I FEEL LIKE A MOTHERLESS CHILD.............Burlei..
GO DOWN MOSES...Burleig..
LIL GAL..R. Johns..
Mr. Deppe

LOIS DEPPE

SINGER AND BANDLEADER

"I was born in Horse Cave, Kentucky, on 12 April 1897. My people moved out of there and came up into Indiana when I was about eighteen months old. Then they went to Springfield, Ohio, when I was six.

"My voice began to attract attention in Sunday school. One of the teachers, Mrs. Jackson, used to put on spring and fall festivals for the neighborhood kids, and she starred me, and I began to sing around town. I lived near a white boy with only one leg. He lost the other in an accident. We kids used to hop on the switch engines, and he fell off. His name was Albert Cain, and he had a phenomenal voice. We used to have singing contests in the backyard. Word of this got uptown, and they had us sing in the dining room of the Arcade Hotel. Then they had me sing out at the white country club. I'd sing pop songs of the day like *I Love You Truly*. I remember when they had a contest here in Chicago. You sent up the name of a song, and if they'd never heard of it, they sent you a special kind of card. They'd never heard of one I was singing, dressed up as an Indian, when I was nine years old:

> "*Big Chief Battle Axe,*
> *Love you true,*
> *All day long I gaze at you* . . .

"My mother and father separated and for stepfather I got a molder at Wickham's Piano Plate. He made piano plates, and I worked three weeks with him, but it was too hard for me. I had begun to take a real interest in singing, and I wanted to go to Cleveland to study with Bernard Landino, an Italian. I read all the musical magazines, and when I was sixteen I heard of Madame C. J. Walker. I had begun to get the urge to leave home, because I knew there was no outlet in a small town like Springfield. So I wrote to Madame Walker, and she asked if I would be interested in coming to Indianapolis and singing on a program she was giving in honor of Paul Laurence Dunbar, the great black poet. I went, and she took a liking to me. Then she asked if I would like to come to New York, and when she came to Springfield on one of her lecture tours she told my mother I would live with her family. So I went to New York, and she even got me a couple of lessons with Caruso's coach, Buzzi Pecci. That's when I first met Henry Creamer and Turner Layton. I was thrown in the company of people like Harry T. Burleigh, J. Rosamond Johnson and Melville Charlton, the great black pipe organist. Joe Jordan would come to the house, too. They were the associates of the wealthiest black woman in the world.

"Then Madame Walker told her daughter Lelia she was going to send me to Europe and spend a whole lot of money on my musical education. We were living in Lelia's house, which her mother had given her, on 136th and Lenox Avenue. They quarreled, and Madame Walker went off to Tuskegee until her home in Irvington was finished, leaving me behind.

Then the unpleasantries began, the things that would make me uncomfortable. So Rosamond Johnson asked why I didn't leave, and said they'd all help me. We went down to Wanamaker's store, where they had a big choir that used to sing from the balconies. I was introduced to the choir director and sang with the choir. They gave me a job running an elevator.

"I was nineteen when Henry Creamer and Turner Layton asked if I'd like to sing in a nightclub. After doing that, I wrote Mr. Lewis, the black impresario in Pittsburgh, who used to bring in black concert stars like Marian Anderson and Clarence Cameron White, the black violinist. This was before the jazz era, and people were still thinking more in terms of European concert artists. After doing a concert in Watts Street High School auditorium, they engaged me to sing at the Pitt Theatre with a big white chorus. They had a fifty-piece orchestra, and they were doing a southern story to tie up with the picture, and they wanted me to sing *Swanee River*. They liked me, and when the picture changed they showed *The Barrier*, a Rex Beach story. So they cast me as an Indian, and I sang *From the Land of the Sky Blue Water* and *Land of the North, I Hear You Calling Me*. Then one day the manager, Mr. Katz, called me to the office.

" 'I've got to let you go,' he said.

" 'What did I do?' I asked.

" 'You're just doing too good.'

" 'Well, what happened?'

" 'We've got this big chorus, and they've all said, "We're not going to work with that nigger no longer. He's doing all the solos." Now I can't lose my chorus just on account of you.'

"Next I sang with Ollie Reed in the ballroom of the Duquesne Gardens. He passed me as a Hawaiian in a white shirt, white flannel trousers and a lei around my neck. And Danny Norrell had a brass band downstairs in the ice-skating palace, and I would sing with him through a great, big megaphone. They'd put me 'way up in the rafters, and I'd turn the megaphone down and sing to the people from there.

"When my number came up, I was drafted, and I was in the Army from September 1918 to April 1919, but before that I'd heard a couple of kids playing at a rent party. They were in bloomer pants, like they wore in those days. A little boy named Harry Williams was beating on the drums, and the other was a tall, lanky kid from Duquesne named Earl Hines. (Those two, with Emmett Jordan on violin, were known as Earl Hines's Melody Lads.) It was the first time I heard Earl, and I still remember being amazed and saying, 'Listen to that kid play piano!'

"After the Army, the husband of Madame Anita Patti Brown engaged me to go to South America and through the West Indies on a concert tour with her, but when I got back there was practically nothing doing in Pittsburgh, so I went to work as a porter for a newspaper, the Pittsburgh *Press*. I'd rather work than beg, although my mother thought singing was silly and wanted me home. In all my career, she only heard me once!

"Then I started waiting tables in Collins Inn, doing what I'd seen the other waiters do, pouring out shots in the glass, hustling drinks. People kept asking me to sing, till one night I got tired of it and went out on the floor and sang *The World Is Waiting for the Sunrise*, singing around from table to table. I came back with my hands full of dollars, and I decided right there I was through waiting tables. I had been studying downtown with McClure Miller, who taught concert artists, but now it was nightclubs for me!

"In 1921 I went to the Sunset in Chicago, where the band was led by Dave Peyton. They paid me thirty-five dollars a week, but I'd been making almost as much in tips in Collins Inn as a waiter, so I returned to Pittsburgh and asked Collins for my job back. It was a big club, and black-and-tan shows were a novelty then, just as they were in Harlem, and white people went where the good black talent was. Besides Bob Cole and myself, there were five girls—seven entertainers taking their turns doing the tables.

" 'How much do you want?' Collins asked me.

" 'Eighteen dollars a week.'

" 'I wouldn't give it to you, Deppe, because you'd soon be making so much money here you'd be going into business with me.'

" 'Well, I'm not going to sing no more for nothing!'

"So I went up the street to Bowles and Clark who had the Leader House. They realized I was a drawing card, and all they had in there was a boy named Johnny Watters out of Toledo, Ohio, just playing piano.

" 'I can't work with him,' I said. 'I tried to, but he only plays in two keys. They're both sharps, and he can't transpose.'

" 'Do you know of anyone else you can get?' they asked.

" 'There's a kid named Earl Hines in Duquesne who plays the thunder out of a piano, but I don't know whether he can work here or not.'

"I was going to Miss Phillips, his aunt, to find out where he lived in Duquesne, and I was on my way up Center Avenue when here comes Earl walking down the street.

" 'I'm looking for you,' I said.

" 'Well, I'm in town now, staying with my aunt and going to Schenley High School.'

" 'You think your father would let you work in a nightclub?'

"We got hold of his father by telephone. By now I'd got quite a reputation in Pittsburgh, and he consented when I promised to look after Earl, who was only seventeen. I roomed at 1521 Wylie Avenue, and I got Earl a room right next to mine. The clubowners asked me how much he wanted, and I told them to give me twelve dollars and the boy fifteen. As I've told Earl time and time again, I needed him but he didn't need me. He had too much talent and someone had to bring it out. If it hadn't been me, it would have been someone else. Maybe I was just using psychology, to let him know he was making more than me, but soon everyone began talking about this kid with the new type of piano playing. I got stories about him and his picture in the papers, and before long he was the most popular young pianist in Pittsburgh. At that time a lot of pianists were just playing this chop style,

and boogie woogie, and ragtime. Earl had a *swinging* piano style, a terrific treble hand besides a great bass hand, which he has improved on down through the years.

"There was a little fellow we called Todelo, not quite a dwarf or a hunchback, but hardly over four foot tall. He played boogie-woogie-style piano, and Earl liked to hear him do that. Then there was another piano player named Dry Bread. I never knew his other name. This Johnny Watters I mentioned, who could only play in two keys, played ragtime piano, and Earl would stand around and dig him. But I think his biggest inspiration, and one of the most popular pianists in Pittsburgh in the early '20s, was Jim Thelman.* He had a terrific left hand and Earl had this great right hand. Earl used to stand behind him and watch him, and he copied his left hand. I can remember they got to the stage where they played so much alike that Thelman would sometimes say, 'Come on, man, take this off me! I'm tired.' And Earl would slip on the seat at the piano and take over without a break, and you'd think it was the same guy playing. Thelman drank a lot of whiskey and died at an early age. Night life, I guess, was just too much for him.

"There were times when Earl was inclined to loaf. In other words, just chords, you know. Not being a pianist, I didn't realize that a man got tired just swing-swing-swinging away all the time at the piano. But that's what the people were getting a kick from, his swinging syncopation. Sometimes I'd say, 'If you don't swing the piano, I'm going to push you off the stool and embarrass you for a never-mind!' And then he'd tear out. I think he appreciates that today, because that way of playing is what drew attention to him.

"By this time they'd changed the name of Collins Inn just down the street to the Paramount Inn. We'd have our windows all open, and I'd be sure I got near the window, so they could hear me sing a block and a half away. Then one day Earl asked, 'Do you think you could use my little drummer?' They said they

---

* Mr. Deppe insists that this is the right spelling.

couldn't afford to pay for a drummer, but we had a little kitty box and we split up our tips, and we got that little boy playing the drums with us.

"We were getting two meals a day at the Leader House, and where Earl and I lived the rooms were only four bucks a week. You could get a bowl of soup for a nickel. So we were eating good, and I was just carried away with this boy playing the piano, I'd never heard anyone of his calibre, doing what he was doing. He could play and read anything. One time he played the prelude from *Pagliacci* for me, and *The King of the Ocean* from Meyerbeer's opera *L'Africaine*.

"Previous to this, I used to go up the river and sing with a boy named Arthur Rideout, who gave me ten dollars a night. I bought a banjo so he could sell me as a musician. I'd hit a couple of notes and then get up and sing. I also bought a sax as a gimmick. Earl used to die laughing at me trying to play that C-melody horn.

"In 1921, Earl and I created a little excitement as a duo at Loew's Vaudeville Theatre. We were going over like a house on fire there. Earl had only one little blue suit at that time, and he used to press it every day with an old hot flatiron. Now you can always tell when he's going to play, because he'll set that right foot out and scoot back. He was very exuberant about making his first stage appearances, but at one show, when he set his foot out and rared back in his chair, the house began to laugh. I was standing beside the piano, wondering what in the world they were laughing at. When I turned round I saw his pants had split at the knee halfway down to the ankle. It was wintertime, and all his long underwear was showing!

"He and I were the first colored guys on radio in Pittsburgh, over KDKA at the big Westinghouse plant out at Turtle Creek. The broadcast caused a lot of excitement, especially in the colored neighborhood, because this was 1921. A lot of people had crystal sets, and there was a radio buff on Wylie Avenue who had loudspeakers sticking out his window. The street was all blocked with people,

and we were just mobbed when we came back. The numbers we did were *Isabel* and *For the Last Time Call Me Sweetheart*.

"Around this time a young boy named Vance Dixon came to town, a whale of a saxophone player. He wanted to get in with the young kids, and this gave me an idea. I'd sung in a big white roadhouse in Aspinwall called the Willows with Ollie Reed, so I went to see Mr. Saunders there and told him I'd got a band. When he heard Earl, Harry Williams on drums, Emmett Jordan on fiddle and Vance Dixon on sax, he said, 'All right, you boys sound good. How much do you want?' From then on we began to build.

"I think I got the idea for a band as far back as 1915 when I went to a vaudeville house in Pittsburgh where they had a white baritone singer. The curtain went up, and there he was standing in front of a fine big band of his own. Anyway, a few days after I got my band together, I ran into Roland Hayes, the great colored tenor, in a railway station early one morning. I was coming in from a concert.

" 'How're you doing, Deppe?' he asked.

" 'I've got a band now, a dance band.'

" 'Oh, you give up concerts?'

" 'Well, you know how it is . . .'

" 'Don't ever try to duplicate another man's success, Deppe. Figure out your own field and you're liable to be just as successful.'

" 'Well, I'm even singing in nightclubs.'

" 'You like to sing. Sing any place people want to hear you sing. Sometimes I wish I could do all kinds of singing like you're doing, and cover the whole field.'

"Most of the bands then were five or six pieces, and the dance promoters were packing five or six hundred people in a dancehall at a dollar a head. They were getting bands for thirty-five dollars—five dollars each and double for the leader. I decided to have a *big* band, nine men and myself.

" 'Deppe, who's going to pay you sixty-five dollars,' they asked, 'when we can get all we need for thirty-five?'

"So I went and rented dancehalls myself, and got placards and put 'em up around town. We had a Chinese Festival one time, and the placards had regular printing on top and what I thought looked like Chinese characters below. Another time we had an Orange Festival, with a whole lot of oranges and bananas.

" 'Don't ever give anything like that again in my dancehall,' the owner said. 'There was juice all over the place!'

"I'd go out of town to Homestead, Pennsylvania, and to Youngstown, Ohio, and rent dancehalls. I caught one of the big dance promoters asleep and got one of the biggest dancehalls in Pittsburgh, Labor Temple, for Easter Monday. I had my placards out for an Easter Monday Dance, and that's one day everybody wants to come out. I caught him another time and got Christmas Eve. Earl was getting popular as a son-of-a-gun, and people would all crowd around to hear this boy play piano.

"There was a fellow called Dan Cane who had a big Pierce-Arrow, and he hauled my band out of Pittsburgh. He was having a ball, because he got to travel, and we didn't have to pay him in front as we would have if we'd gone by train. We'd pay him *after* we played the dance. Eventually, Earl got his father to buy a big old twin twelve-cylinder Packard, and I got a big old Abbott-Detroit.

"After we stopped playing nightclubs, Earl and I were partners in the band, and we made Vance Dixon the director. I remember one night we played a date in Brownsville, sixty miles away, and we were back waiting for Earl and his part of the band at our headquarters, the Leader House. About 9 o'clock in the morning, his car came leaping and bumping up in front of the place. The tubes had blown and they'd stuffed rags and newspapers in the casings and tied the tires on!

"I think it was in 1923 I took Earl to New York to be heard, because to me he was already revolutionizing the style of piano playing. He was so different from all the rest of them. The only other guy at that time that I would say was great was Luckey Roberts. We went to his house, and we also met Fletcher Henderson, who was playing piano in Sam Wooding's band then. We had hoped to make a deal or at least be heard by the Black Swan

people, but our money was rather limited and after a few days in New York we could not stand the gaff much longer, so we returned home.

"The Starr Piano Company had a store in Pittsburgh where they sold pianos and Gennett records. The band had already gained quite a bit of popularity in the city, and the store manager contacted his people in Richmond and suggested they hear this band of mine and give us a chance to record. So on one of our western dance tours, we went to the Starr Piano factory. They heard the band and decided right there to record it.

"Now this was towards the end of Earl with the band. He met a girl named Baby, an entertainer, and when he was under the influence he married her. Baby Hines persuaded him to leave and go for himself, which was only logical. He organized a seven-piece band, but he was just a boy and the competition was too tough for him. He went in a place called Marian's Grape Arbor, but he didn't last in there too long. There were already five or six established bands around like French Hawkins's, Bob Dews's, the Broadway Syncopators (with Jim Thelman playing piano) and my band. The Broadway Syncopators and mine were the ones that made the scene the most. I asked Earl once why he didn't go home.

" 'Lois,' he said, 'I was really up against it after my band broke up. I was hungry, and when they wanted me to go to Chicago, I was ready to go any place. But when I got off out at Englewood Station with Vernie Robinson, the violinist, I said, "If this is Chicago, I'm going back home!" ' "

"Englewood was a suburb station, and he'd expected something like the big Union Station in Pittsburgh.

"After Earl left me, I made a trip out to Cincinnati, where Edgar Hayes was playing in the park, and hired him. He proved very hard to handle. He was temperamental and girl-weak. For a time, things went well. We played Derby Day in the Jockey Club at Churchill Downs, Louisville. Then I broke ice at Cedar Point, Sandusky, Ohio, where we were the first colored band ever to play. After that I went to the Ritz in Cleveland—a big white dining room where they danced—with a signed contract for over $1300 a week, and this was 1924. I was paying Edgar Hayes $125 a week, cutting out for myself about $165, and paying off $50 a week to my transportation man, because I owed him $1000.

"They had an all-white floorshow at the Ritz, and the owner told me all he wanted was for me to walk out in the middle of the floor and sing in front of my band. This started dissension among the boys. They thought they were doing all the work, because they were playing for dancing, and the band began to go to pieces. When the man gave a dinner for us at Thanksgiving, he asked what the matter was.

" 'I'll tell you what's the matter,' the banjo player said. 'There's too many men here begrudge Deppe his organization, and the fact that the marquee says *Lois B. Deppe and His Plantation Orchestra.*'

"I overheard one of their meetings, discovered what was happening, and made up my mind to leave. A lot of the instruments belonged to me, and I just took 'em to the pawnshop and sold 'em. 'I made this band with your help,' I told the musicians, 'but I'll be singing when you guys are forgotten!'

"A job had already been offered me in Columbus, Ohio, singing in the Empress Theatre with a pipe organ, so I went there and began to work. This was the end of me as a bandleader, although the guys found out where I was and Edgar Hayes came and said, 'Come on back. We were wrong. We'll do right.' The owner of the Ritz had given them two weeks' notice when my name came off the marquee.

"After I broke up the band, I tried to trace Earl and found he was in Winnipeg with Carroll Dickerson's band.

" 'Carroll owes me two hundred dollars, Lois,' Earl said, 'and if I can get the money I'll come back.'

"The next time I was in contact with him, he was in Long Beach, California, and he still hadn't got the money. I began to conclude that he didn't want to come back. He knew there had been contention in the band and that Vance Dixon had joined Sammy Stewart.

But Earl always condemned me, said I should have held on and got another pianist. Well, I had had enough of that trouble. One time I asked him how come he never offered *me* a job, and he said he always figured he could never offer the money he thought I was worth. Even when he was going over big at the Grand Terrace, he wasn't getting very much.

"When he first got to Chicago, Dave Peyton was regarded as an outstanding pianist, but the two who made Earl hustle were Teddy Weatherford and Jerome Carrington. They gave him some competition in the early days, but although I only heard Teddy Weatherford once, I knew he couldn't teach Earl anything. My wife is a pianist and she was playing at the Delphi Theatre then.

" 'Teddy Weatherford was good, and he had a beat, but there was really no comparison,' Mrs. Deppe* said. 'He played a different type of piano.'

"I stayed in Columbus from 1925 to 1927, when I went to Chicago to work at the Regal. Fletcher Henderson had me sing with his band at the Congress Hotel in Chicago. We were the first colored band ever to play there. Then he had me come to New York with him for a couple of weeks at the Roseland Ballroom. We did some gigs on the way, one in Harrisburg, I think. I wasn't a part of the band, but he paid me a hundred dollars a week just to sit up there and sing. Then I went into the Roxy Theatre for two weeks with the Hall Johnson Choir. While I was doing that, I auditioned for Flo Ziegfeld and Will Vodery—for *Show Boat*. 'Oh, you've got the voice all right,' they told me, 'but you're mulatto, not negroid enough.' They wanted Paul Robeson, but he had already signed a contract for twelve weeks in London, so they got Jules Bledsoe, a whale of a baritone and a fine pianist. Nevertheless, I did that part in *Show Boat* at the Municipal Opera, an open-air theatre in St. Louis, for J. J. Shubert in 1930, and again for Schwabb and Mandell in 1934, singing *Ol' Man River* both times.

---

* The former Marguerite Rosson, she was a graduate of Chicago Musical College and later concentrated on teaching.

"My theatrical career really began with a telegram from Lew Leslie. Don Heywood had told him in New York to get me for *Blackbirds*. I just packed up my things and went into rehearsals. We opened in 1927 at Elton's Theatre on 42nd Street. Songs in the show were *Diga Diga Doo*, *I Must Have That Man*, and the one I sang with Ada Ward as a duet, *I Can't Give You Anything But Love*. We'd walk out, take each other's hands, and I'd start singing—verse and chorus. Then she sang a chorus, and when she turned her back I put my arms around her waist, and we strolled back and forth across the stage, singing. That was all. No setting. Others in the cast were Adelaide Hall, Bojangles Robinson, Tim Moore (the comedian who played Kingfish in the Amos 'n' Andy movies), Mantan Moreland, Johnny Hudgins, Bessie Dudley, Lew McAllister, Snakehips Tucker, the Barrett Brothers and old man Rector.

"About the time the show was going to Europe, my first wife was about to have a baby. I had my passport and everything, but then my mother got frantic: 'Oh, suppose we get sick, and all that water between us . . . How're you going to get home?' I reminded her she hadn't carried on like that when I went to South America with Madame Patti Brown! My people had bought a farm and moved to the country, so I had to go and stay there till the baby came.

"I had been in the number one *Blackbirds* company, the Broadway company, but they had another company out on the road, so they took a boy from Baltimore who had been singing *I Can't Give You Anything But Love* on the road. Before *Blackbirds* closed, Fletcher Henderson had told me about a show called *Great Day*, and now he got me to sing for this man Vincent Youmans. I sang *Hallelujah* and *I'm Coming, Virginia* for him, and he asked how much I'd want. But he had a contract with Gilbert Holland, who I understood was getting two hundred a week. Youmans told Fletcher he'd give me sixty a week just to hang around the theatre a couple of weeks.

"The show opened in Philadelphia at the Garrett Theatre on a Monday, and the newspapers merely said that Gilbert Holland sang *Without a Song*. On Tuesday, the stage manager said Mr. Youmans wanted me to sing the next night. I stood in the wings and learned the lines—not many, just enough to cue me into the song—and they agreed to let me ad-lib 'em. *Great Day* closed the first act. In the second, when I came out to do *Without a Song*, I took nine curtain calls. The house was storming.

" 'Well, I'm thirty-two years old,' I said. 'Maybe I've finally arrived.' And I remembered how I used to go out to the barn when I was a kid and sing to the horses. My mother would ask what I was doing, and I'd say, 'Momma, I'm going to be a big singer one of these days!'

"I went downstairs to the men's smoker, and I heard Youmans on the telephone to his father: 'I took that fellow I was telling you about, and he tore my show upside down! I'm signing him to a five-year contract, and I'm going to make him the greatest colored baritone there is.'

"The colored kids in the show had been carrying me around on their shoulders. 'You go upstairs now, Deppe, to your own dressing room,' they said.

" 'No,' I said, 'I'm going to stay down here in the basement with you.'

" 'You're a star now,' they insisted, 'and we're proud of you.'

"So I went upstairs. And Harold Arlen came to my dressing room. He was singing in the choir. See, they had mixed singers, white and colored. Harold was crazy about the blues, and that's the reason he turned out to be a whale of a torch writer. He would always be hanging around Fletcher's band, or sitting on the stage at the piano, singing the blues or making up something. The story of *Great Day* was about a girl who fell in love with a cab driver in New Orleans. Fletcher and the band played in a cabaret scene where there was a lot of activity, and when they came off the stage they augmented the pit orchestra.

"After this opening, Youmans had me sign a run-of-play contract. We did two weeks at the Globe Theatre in Atlantic City, one at Asbury Park, and one at Long Branch, all in New Jersey. Then we shut down for the summer and I went home. We reopened for the fall theatrical season in Boston and played three weeks at the Colonial Theatre.

"Youmans was counting on *Great Day* having a long run on Broadway, but *Show Boat* beat us there. Both were stories of the South, and both featured a Negro baritone. We had a great musical score, but a bad story. McGuire, who was Ziegfeld's show doctor, came up from New York while we were in Boston. He straightened our show out and went back, but Youmans couldn't leave it alone. He kept fooling with the show till he messed it up again. He thought he could do what he did with *No, No, Nanette* in Chicago, where he kept doctoring and fixing it. When he took that to New York it became a big hit. So he thought he could both write and direct.

"They took Fletcher out of the show completely. That whole cabaret scene went. We opened at the Cosmopolitan Theatre on Broadway at 59th in New York the 17th of October 1929, and the show folded after six weeks. Youmans had signed me to a five-year contract. Although he lost over $350,000, three big song hits came out of that show—*More Than You Know*, which Marion Harris sang, and *Great Day* and *Without a Song*, which I sang.

"I went to work at Connie's Inn in Harlem. They had two shows a year there, and for each six months they'd get themselves a new band. While I was around they had Louis Armstrong, Fletcher Henderson, Russell Wooding, Luis Russell, Don Redman and Fats Waller. Fats wrote the music for a whole show, great songs like *Ain't Misbehavin'* and *Black and Blue*. Another I remember him writing at that time was *Stealin' Apples*. I recorded with Don Redman in 1931, and I was the first to sing *Trees* over the air—with Don's band.

"While I was in Connie's, I ran into Duke Ellington. We went to a place on 132nd Street—I think it was Mexico's Chili Parlor—and we sat there all morning till we both went to sleep. He was trying to talk me into leaving Connie's and going into the Cotton Club, but I told him I was satisfied where I was.

"Now the gangsters got to feuding. George Immerman, who owned Connie's Inn, had used his brother's name, Connie, for the place, and Connie got fooling with the gangsters. I know one night a fellow came in there to collect some money, and the next day it was in the papers that he had been found dead in the Harlem River. Then there was shooting around the front of the club, and a lady got hit at 132nd and Seventh Avenue, and she died.

The *Great Day* company, 1929. Harold Arlen is eleventh from the left in back row. On his left is Charlie Davis who staged the dances. Lois Deppe is immediately in front of him. In front of the last two ladies at right end of back row is Will Marion Cook with his arm around Avis

So people were scared of going there and the Immermans opened the Plantation on Lenox, somewhere between 125th and 130th. It had a glass floor with lights under it, and was quite a place, but it didn't last long because the Cotton Club gang came in and chopped it up with axes. So I went back to my ace in the hole in Columbus, where the man who owned the theatre told me I could return any time I wanted.

"I went to Chicago around this time, 1931, in *Hello, Paris*, a big white show out of New York with Chic Sales and W. C. Fields. They had a song in it called *Deep Paradise* that they thought would be another *Ol' Man River*, and I was singing the heck out of that song. Ashton Stevens said in his review that so far as he was concerned the show was over when I got through singing it, and they might as well ring down the curtain. Anyway, I was staying with Earl Hines at his place on the corner of 45th and Vincennes. We were having breakfast one morning when he happened to look out the window.

" 'Somebody ain't paid his dues on his car,' he said, laughing. 'Heh, heh, heh! They're towing it away.'

"He looked again and stopped laughing. It was his own Buick!"

"It was around 1937 that I really hit the night-club circuit," Lois Deppe resumed. "I went to Buffalo and sang at Ann Montgomery's Moonglow. After that I built up a circuit that consisted of the Three Sixes and the Plantation in Detroit; the Blue Grass at Cedar Gardens in Cleveland; the Cotton Club in Cincinnati; the Flame in Milwaukee; the Club Harlem in Atlantic City; the Harlem Casino in Pittsburgh; Rockhead's in Montreal. I always used to do sixteen weeks in Montreal, and there's a funny story about how I got to go there.

"I was singing at the Harlem Casino in Pittsburgh, and doing a characterization on *Water Boy* with a sledgehammer and a ball-and-chain on my leg. Gus Greenlee and Oscar Price owned the club. Greenlee and all of us were hustling then. We had old pieces of cabs running up and down Wylie Avenue. Homewood was where the big steel mills were, and after one or two in the morning the night life was running wild. People would get cabs and go out there and gamble, and visit the night-clubs 'way up till noon, till they wore themselves out. Now Oscar Price, for some reason, didn't like me, and one night he said, 'I've got a singer's going to run Deppe out of here!' It was a boy named Billy Reed, a fine singer, but

Andrews, who reputedly sang with Cab Calloway's band at one time. The famous comedy team of Running Wild, Miller and Lyle, are sitting in the second row from the front, in the middle of the picture, with singer Cora Green on their right.

he lasted just one week and went to Rock-head's Paradise in Montreal. A little later, I was in Buffalo at the Moonglow, and a boy named Lonzo Hunt went to the telephone and called Rockhead. 'I want you to hear this guy singing, long distance,' he said. Rockhead made me an offer and sent me a ticket. My visa was good for sixteen weeks and I stayed sixteen weeks. Rockhead had me back every winter for five years!

"Oscar Peterson was playing across from the Canadian Pacific Railway Station in Montreal, and he'd come to Rockhead's after he closed, and jam with the boys. I'd sing a couple of songs, cutting up, clowning. We'd talk, and when I'd ask him why he didn't go to the States, he'd say, 'I'm doing all right here. I'm with my wife and family, and I'm making two hundred dollars a week.' I think Count Basie talked to him, too, because when I went back one time he'd gone to New York to visit his sister, and somebody had persuaded him to stay.

"In 1944, I went to Chicago and met Marguerite, who is now my wife. She was looking *so* sad, because she had just buried her father. I invited her to meet my mother, and I think I was impressed by the fact that she was quite reserved, because I'd been around so many flamboyant women. As time went on, I began to talk about getting married again. I had been divorced, but she'd say she didn't want a husband who was always travel-ing and never home. We wrote letters, and fi-nally we were married on 29 May 1950. That summer a telegram came from Montreal for twelve weeks at Rockhead's, my sixth season. I went up there, but I got to thinking: 'I'm not going to lose *this* wife from being away from home all the time.' So after eight weeks I went home and just went to work—as a jani-tor. I never was too proud to work. I went to Oliver's Tavern in Lima twice, and once to the Club Flame in Milwaukee, and that wound it up. Now I just sing occasionally in churches.

"Well, now, I've been listening to Earl

Hines play the piano for over fifty years. I'll be seventy-five in April of 1972. I remember coming up to Chicago in the '20s when Earl was playing piano for Carroll Dickerson at the Sunset. People used to stop dancing and crowd around just to hear him play. As a con-cert singer, I'd had some very competent piano accompanists, and I found when I met Earl that he could read music very fluently. He played all the operatic arias, art songs and popular songs of the day that I sang. I pre-dicted that he'd be a world-renowned pianist and one of the most imitated in his field. I've heard pianists like Art Tatum and Oscar Peter-son, and lots of others who imitated his right hand, but in my opinion there isn't *any* pianist in his field who can do on the keyboard what he does with his hands. When he was here at the London House, for his last show he played with just bass and drums for forty minutes, and I heard him do things I'd never heard him do before. I asked him afterwards why he kept trying to make singers famous, and told him that what people were coming to hear was Earl 'Fatha' Hines, the world's greatest pian-ist.

"I like Earl like he was my son, and when Willie Randall had a birthday party for him, and all Earl's old musicians came to it, I walked out and sang a couple of songs with him. He started playing *The Siren Song*, and after that we did *For the Last Time Call Me Sweetheart*. Then I sat down and cried like a baby, thinking about the boy I met fifty-three years before, and how he was still playing that piano. Because Earl hasn't thrown his talent away! And when someone asked how a man of seventy-five could keep his voice, like I have, Earl turned to me and said:

"'Don't worry! It's something they can't take away from you. They can't borrow it, they can't buy it, and you can't loan it to 'em. It's yours!'"

(1969)

Lois Deppe died 26 July 1976.

Above: Earl Hines and Lois Deppe, 1951. *Below:* Lois Deppe singing *For the Last Time Call Me Sweetheart* with Earl Hines at Willie Randall's birthday party, 1971.

CHARLIE CARPENTER

LYRICIST AND MANAGER

"I was born and raised in Chicago. When I went to Hyde Park High School, there were about forty black kids there, the children of doctors, dentists and lawyers, people like that. My father was an ordinary guy, but I was a slicker. I had gotten tight with Alderman Jackson of the Third Ward at a time when they were trying to run all the black kids into Wendell Phillips at 39th and Calumet, in the heart of the black neighborhood. That's where Nat Cole went, and where George Kirby, whom I manage now, went. They didn't want me at Hyde Park High, but Alderman Jackson gave me a letter with his heading on it, and they had to take me. I was the only poor black kid there, and the other blacks didn't associate with me, although a few of the white kids did. I made the freshman football team and got my letter. Then the black kids wanted to talk to me and I didn't want to talk to them.

"When I was about twelve years old, I had met a little, fat, chubby kid named Louis Dunlap, who wanted to be a songwriter. He played ukulele very well and piano with two fingers. I had written a poem overnight and I got a gold star for it. After he read it, he started talking to me about Irving Berlin and people like that, and how I should come and try to write songs with him. I told him he was out of his mind, because I was an athlete. I loved athletics and played them all. But finally he got me to come by his house one Sunday, and his mother had homemade ice cream. I *loved* ice cream, too, and after I'd eaten some

of hers, he never could get rid of me again, and I started to write songs.

"Although she never knew I was alive, I was in love with a girl in high school when I was about sixteen. Then one day I saw an engagement ring on her finger and I asked her what was happening.

" 'Oh, nothing,' she said.

" 'But you're engaged . . .'

" 'No, my mother gave me that ring.'

" 'You're quitting school?' I asked.

" 'Yes, I'm going to dance with a group called the Regalettes at the Regal Theatre.'

"The Regal was just opening in Chicago, and when this girl walked out of school, it just tore me up. I'm a Leo and maybe that's why things hit me so hard inside, even if I don't show it. We didn't know about psychiatrists in those days, but I was flunking grades and my father was taking me to doctors to find out what was wrong. However, Louis Dunlap knew what the trouble was, because I confided in him. Now for over a year, whenever he and a friend of ours called Tip saw me, they'd start humming a tune of his. He could never understand why I'd write words for every other song he came up with, but not for this one. Maybe it's like grandmother says and everything happens for the best! After this girl had walked out of school, I was sitting in history class one day in a kind of trance, and the words for his song just flowed, one after another: *Though you say we're through, I'll always love you, you know you can depend on*

"Two little songwriters here, little Louis Dunlap and Charles Carpenter . . ." (Carpenter at right).

me . . . I walked in that night and gave Lap this lyric complete, and he almost had a fit. 'This is *it*, this is *it*!' he kept saying.

"I guess I was coming out of it then, because after blowing it and flunking all my subjects, I became a star in my junior year, and in my senior year I was All-City and All-State in Chicago at this school.

"Now since 1925 Louis Armstrong had been like a brother to me. He bought me my first Boy Scout suit. My folks used to take me with them on Saturday night to the old Vendome Theatre. My stepmother was crazy about the blues, and that's how I came to hear singers like Ma Rainey and Bessie Smith as a kid. Of course, I really wanted to go to the movies to see William S. Hart in action, and it was because I made a big fuss one night that I missed seeing Bert Williams, to my everlasting regret. But it was at the Vendome I first saw this cornet player stand up and sing. A girl came out on the little stage behind Erskine Tate's band and began to sing a chorus of *Big Butter and Egg Man*. She was Mae Alix and she looked like white. Then this fat guy with the cornet jumped up and said, 'Hey, mama, mama, I'm yo' big butter and egg man from 'way down in the South.' Later, I learned this was Louis Armstrong.

"He met Lil Hardin, who was a very big woman in Chicago, a graduate of the Chicago College of Music. She hadn't married him then, but she took him to a place called Dreamland on 36th and State, and she put his name above hers: *Louis Armstrong Featured with Lil Hardin's Band*. From there he went to the Sunset, where Earl Hines was playing piano in Carroll Dickerson's band.

"The reason I know all this is that I was born right down the street at 33rd and Calumet, and the Sunset was at 35th. A couple of guys named Ed Fox and Joe Glaser ran the Sunset. Now we kids used to go in through the back, and I still remember how we giggled when we saw the trumpet players using plungers to wa-wa with. In those days toilets were forever stopping up, and plungers were used to make the stuff go down.

" 'Oh, how can those guys use those filthy things?' we said.

"Then Joe Glaser would come in.

" 'All right, let's go!' he'd shout. 'Out, all you kids! Get outta here!'

"We'd run out, put our heads back in the door, and give him a razzberry. But Joe and I remained friends right up until the time of his death. One night, many years later at Basin Street East, he was with Joe Higgins and a few others.

" 'How long have I been knowing you?' he asked me. 'Since you were fifteen?'

" 'No, Joe, you've known me since I was twelve.'

"He turned to the people with him and said, 'Maybe you don't know it, but this man here is the most honorable, ethical man in the whole bleep business!' That made me feel very good.

"But going back to Louis Armstrong in Chicago, he'd often seen me standing around outside the Metropolitan Theatre when he was playing there. One night he walked up to me.

" 'Why do I always see you out here?' he asked. 'Don't you ever go in?'

" 'I'd like to,' I said, laughing, 'but I don't have the dime.'

(A dime was what it cost kids in those days.)

" 'Come in with me,' Louis said. He was always spontaneous and such a good-natured man. I went in with him to the dressing room, and he asked me if I was hungry.

" 'Well,' I said, 'I can't eat and go to the show at the same time, but I'll be hungry when I come out.'

" 'Tell you what,' he said, 'I'll wait for you. You just open the door and holler "Louis!" and I'll come on up and we'll go eat.'

"I did that, and he took me to a Chinese place. Up until that time the only Chinese food I had ever heard of was chop suey, so when we sat down and he asked what I wanted, I said, 'Chop suey.'

" 'Oh, you don't want chop suey,' he said. 'Get something good like shrimp egg fooyung.'

" 'Shrimp egg fooyung? What's that?'

" 'Waiter,' he said, 'bring us two orders of shrimp egg fooyung.'

"It was so good, and I still love it. You know how people like to go in a Chinese restaurant and dip in everybody's plate? To this day, I declare myself in front. 'If anybody thinks they may want some egg fooyung,' I say, 'then get two orders, because nobody gets any of mine!'

"My friendship with Louis started that night. All of us kids knew where he lived, at 441 East 44th Street.

" 'Why don't you come by the house when you aren't doing anything?' he told me a couple of times.

" 'Where do you live?'

" 'You know where I live!'

" 'I just asked you to see,' I said. 'Sure, we all know where you live.'

"He was a real nice guy, and he used to take me around just like you'd take your brother around.

"I think I first saw Earl Hines about 1926, out in the street with golf knickers on, shining his green Buick. At that time he lived between 44th Place and 45th Street on Vincennes, on the west side of the street. Then they built a new two-storey apartment across the street, and next to the apartment, starting at 44th Place, was a vacant lot big enough for a baseball field. The catcher had to stand under what turned out to be Earl's window. So his mother-in-law, Kathryn Perry's mother, would come out.

" 'Get out of here!' she'd say to us. 'Get away from here! Earl Hines is asleep. You're right under his window, making all that noise, and he has to sleep.'

" 'Well, why don't he sleep at night like everybody else?' we'd ask her. You know how cruel kids are.

" 'Because he works at night.'

" 'Why don't he get a job and work in the daytime?'

"Later on, she practically adopted me, and I always called her Mom or Ma, but we knew Earl would be in there fuming, and because of this none of us kids liked Earl Hines.

"After the Sunset, Louis, Earl and Zutty Singleton had made a pact not to work unless all three were hired. Next thing you know, Louis and Zutty had gone to work at the Savoy

Ballroom, where they didn't need a pianist. Soon after that, Earl caught the two of 'em together on the street.

" 'What you doing to me?' he asked. 'Here I'm mighty near starving to death!'

" 'It's rough out here,' Pops (Armstrong) said, 'and I gotta make them payments on the house. I had to get me a gig, so I went to work at the Savoy. And when he needed a drummer, Carroll Dickerson took Zutty, too. We tried to talk you in, but we stuck with you a pretty good while there, didn't we?'

"Earl had to admit they tried, and he was already well known in Chicago. Before this they'd had real cutting contests where, just to needle them, they used to get him and the other great pianist, Teddy Weatherford, playing against each other. They were both great in their era, but Teddy went off to China, and Earl took the piano out of the *bumptiddy-bumptiddy-bump* style, the way they had been playing it before him. Earl made the piano a solo instrument in jazz bands.

"After Louis and Zutty went to the Savoy, Earl went to the Apex Club with Jimmie Noone, and that's where he really became famous. People were amazed by his ability to know and accompany a singer. All piano players in those days had to play the intermission when the band was off and the singers went around the floor picking up tips. When the band came back, the piano player got a

Buck and Bubbles.

break, and they had to play without him. Earl had had experience with Lois Deppe, and he had innate ability as an accompanist. While working at the Sunset he had to accompany three or four different girl singers who were working in the show. They'd get about ten minutes each to sing during intermission, making the rounds of the floor to get their tips, which they'd split with the pianist.

"It was at the Savoy Ballroom that Louis was introduced to pot. There was no air conditioning in those days, and it was summertime and very hot inside the Savoy. So everybody was standing outside in the back, and I was right there, because I was always with Louis.

" 'I got a new cigarette, man,' a white arranger said to him. 'It makes you feel so good.'

" 'Yeah?' Louis said. 'Incidentally, where you been?'

" 'Well, I've been sick. I had the pneumonia.'

" 'You been sick,' Louis said, 'and you smoke this cigarette, huh?'

" 'Yeah, but I think it helped make me well.'

"So this guy lit it up, took a drag or two, and passed it around, and nobody would take it.

" 'Let me try it,' Louis finally said.

"So he tried it. It was pure marijuana, direct from Mexico, and it had an attractive odor, a little like the smell of those cigarettes people with asthma smoke. Later on, Mezz Mezzrow became Louis's supplier, and for five dollars you got a Prince Albert tobacco tin full of it. Buck of Buck and Bubbles used to go to Louis's house all the time then, but not Bubbles. They were typical of what you hear about stage teams. The minute they walked off the stage, one went one way and the other went another. They had different sets of friends, too, and Buck was Louis's friend. I met him at Louis's home in 1928, a year I'll never forget.

"Now Louis was getting a hundred dollars a week at the Savoy with Carroll Dickerson, but though he and Zutty were in the band they weren't drawing flies. Clarence Black had the other band there, but he had nobody that I remember ever became famous. All of a sudden, the Regal Theatre opened next door, and business dropped off pretty bad. Louis was getting bids from New York, but he didn't like New York. He'd been there before with Fletcher Henderson. 'This ain't for me,' he said, and split, and came on back to Chicago. The Regal and all that section there was owned by a wonderful old man named Englestein, and he offered Louis twenty-five dollars more a week to stay, so he was making more than anyone in the band, including the leader. But meanwhile Connie's Inn in New York kept after him, and eventually he went to play in the *Hot Chocolates Revue* there. The music for that show was written by Fats Waller and Andy Razaf. Earl Hines introduced me to Fats Waller when Fats was playing organ at the Metropolitan Theatre. We were coming up the alley from the Regal Theatre, where Earl's band was playing, and by this time I no longer disliked Earl for sleeping in the daytime! I told Fats what I was trying to do, and he was very nice to me and gave me some tips. Andy Razaf helped me, too, a few years later at the Grand Terrace.

"When Louis came back from New York with *Connie's Hot Chocolates*, he bought a Model A yellow two-door with a rumble seat. This was the time when he had a manager named Johnny Collins. One night Louis took me to the Grand Terrace, although I was not really old enough to go in there. That was the night I met Bing Crosby, who was singing with the Rhythm Boys for Paul Whiteman. They got through at 2 o'clock downtown, but the Grand Terrace stayed open till 4:30 to accommodate people like that. Years later I saw Bing on the Jackie Gleason show.

" 'I haven't seen you since 1928, Bing,' I said, 'and in 1928 I was pretty young, but I still remember you were tore up!'

"He looked at me and cracked up. 'I was what?' he asked.

" 'You were tore *up!*'

" 'I probably was, because in those days I was really putting it away.'

"Anyway, Louis and I would be driving

around in his little car, and he'd tell me to light up one of Mezzrow's cigarettes for him.

" 'Okay,' I'd say, but all I did was light it.

" 'Puff it,' he'd say, 'puff it! You want to write those songs.'

"He finally caught on to the fact that I was wasting it, because I never smoked till I was twenty-one, and I knew nothing about inhaling.

"I wasn't dependent on Louis, because I had a father who worked, a home, food and everything. But my father was never able to give me the kind of pocket money Louis just threw at me. He even paid for my graduation pictures from high school. I took him out to Hyde Park High once, and by that time we used to tell people we were cousins to stop them from heckling him. He came out to our dance with his horn, and in those days he played ten choruses on *Tiger Rag* at a very fast tempo. Louis looked at the drummer in the band and knew this kid was not going to be able to play even three choruses at that tempo.

" 'I play *Tiger Rag* 'way up here,' he said, clapping his hands for the tempo. 'Do you think you can keep up with me for ten choruses?'

" 'Yeah, yeah,' the drummer said.

" 'Well, if you can't, you don't have to play it that fast. We'll slow it down.'

"They might as well have slowed it down at the beginning, because by the sixth chorus the kid had already brought it 'way down. But Louis, with his kindness and understanding, dropped right down with him, and when he got through playing he gave the kid a hand and said, 'Wasn't that kid great?'

"After bringing Louis out there, I was really a big man in high school, because he was the only black male, outside of the singer George Dewey Washington, who had worked the Oriental Theatre downtown. One night, soon after that, he was playing some swanky cellar place, and he asked me if I wanted the car.

" 'Can you drive?'

" 'Yeah,' I said, although I had never driven in my life, but had just sat there watching him drive.

"Louis got out and said, 'Take the car, and when you're ready to go home, you go home with it. I'll come by in a taxi and pick it up after I've seen my little chick.'

"I drove off, and I've been driving ever since. You had to shift gears in those days, but in 1929 there weren't too many cars around even downtown, so I got away with it.

"He used to give me twenty dollars and the car to go down to the University of Illinois with Louis Dunlap and Tip, because my high school football season ended three or four games before the Big Ten ended. There were some black chicks down there we knew who had gone on from Chicago, and we liked to be around them although they were a little older than us. So he used to give us the car, and we'd drive down . . . about 175 miles, I guess.

"In 1930 Louis went to California to play with Les Hite's band, where he discovered Lionel Hampton playing drums. Hamp used to beat the big bass drum in the band that was sponsored by the Chicago *Defender*, a weekly black newspaper. It was very big in its time. Mr. Abbott, the editor-publisher, was a millionaire and had a home on 47th and South Park as soon as blacks could live there. Hamp had moved to California and Louis had him play vibraphone on a record. He also discovered Lawrence Brown, the trombone player, and had him on a record. When Lap, Tip and I heard these records, we said, 'Man, who is *that*?' as first Hamp and then Lawrence came up.

"Louis used to write me at least once a week, and as soon as he got back he called me and said, 'Come on over. I've got some records I want you to hear.' So Lap and I went over, and he was just ecstatic about *Song of the Islands*.

" 'What's the matter?' I said. 'I know it's pretty . . .'

" 'You don't hear nothing on there?'

" 'Yeah, I hear some people humming.'

" 'Those cats are *real* Hawaiians,' he said. 'I had real Hawaiians and violins on that record!'

"Man, he carried on! And around that time he asked me to go out on the road with him, but I explained that I couldn't until I finished school. He went out this time with his own band, with Zilmer Randolph on trumpet and Mike McKendrick on guitar. When he got back to Chicago, I was waiting for him to record *You Can Depend on Me*, which Zilmer had arranged for him. I cut school two days, the wrong days.

"While they'd been out, they'd been to New Orleans, where a cigar had been made called the Louis Armstrong Special. When he recorded *Lonesome Road*, he started ad-libbing, as he nearly always did when he made records. He never really went by what you put in front of him. Something else would hit his mind.

" 'Take that away,' he'd say. 'Let's try so-and-so. What was that I did the other night? How did I get into it?'

"The a. and r. man there, at Columbia Recording Studios on Canal Street, came out first and asked how he was going to do *Lonesome Road*.

" 'I'm going to do a little talking . . . I'll take the trumpet . . . maybe sing a chorus . . .'

"When he started making this record, he saw Louis Dunlap and me standing in the back smoking cigars, so he said, 'Two little songwriters here, little Louis Dunlap and Charles Carpenter . . . What do you think about that? They're smoking Louis Armstrong Special cigars!'

"Another day when I was there, he decided he was going to do *When the Saints Go Marching In*. Now this was 1931, and he started out singing the words. Then he sat down on a table, his legs swinging, and played ten of the most inventive choruses I ever heard in my life.

" 'How was that?' he asked the a. and r. man when he got through.

" 'Louis, I hate to say this, but I think you're a little ahead of your time with that song.'

" 'What do you mean? The Holy Rollers and everybody else do it in that tempo.'

" 'Yeah, Louis, but the masses are not too much aware of the Holy Rollers. I think they'd take my head off in New York if I sent this in.'

"So then Louis started doing *Chinatown*, and he did it the same way, sitting on the table, swinging his legs.

"When I went by Dunlap's house a couple of nights later, Lap opened the door for me. He was jumping up and down, waving a piece of paper. 'A telegram,' he said. 'Read it, read it!' I never will forget it. It was addressed to Mr. Louis Dunlap, 545 East 44th Place, Chicago, Illinois, and the message read: 'Recorded your little tune today. Hope you like it. Signed, Louis Armstrong.' He didn't know Dunlap very well, and we never were able to figure out how he knew where he lived, unless Zilmer Randolph knew and told him.

"I was kind of embarrassed, because I'd shown disappointment at the session, but I waited a couple of days and then went around to Louis's house, and sure enough he was still in town. He gave me another of the several lectures he gave me along the way, about being so quick to jump to conclusions, and how I should be more patient, because I had a long way to go, being just a little youngster not out of my teens. This was typical of Louis, and I learned an awful lot from him and that good old mother wit he had.

"He went away again, and the record came out and was a hit among black people. But before he left he had said, 'Okay, I'm ready to take you with me. You got no excuse now. What good you going to do in school anyway?' You see, he had come up in New Orleans as a waif, and he'd met all these people with degrees who were porters or amounted to nothing, although they had degrees. He figured I'd fare better with him, and he'd be able to pay me more.

" 'No, Louis,' I said, 'I gotta finish high school.'

" 'Well, when do you finish?'

" 'Next June.'

" 'Okay, you go ahead and finish.'

"In the meantime he told Earl Hines about me and asked him to look out for me.

" 'Let him run a few errands for you, like taking your suit to the tailor,' he said. 'Give him a dollar tip. He's a good kid, although I know I've spoiled him, throwing him ten and twenty dollars.'

"So I looked at Earl and Earl looked at me, and I'm saying to myself, 'I don't dislike him anymore, but have I got to be this close?' Anyway, I started going by his house, and Kathryn Perry's momma used to bake cakes. I'm telling you, I can taste 'em now! I would have loved Earl then because of the way his mother-in-law cooked cake!

" 'Well, son,' he said to me one day, 'I just found out I'm going on NBC in the fall of the year. They're going to be coming out here with all these songs, and you know I don't want to be bothered with it. Now you know a lot about this sort of thing, and you like to do it, so I want you to take care of all these publishers.'

"That's always been the thing about Earl. He would give you a chance, no matter who you were, give you your best shot at what you thought you could do. I felt I owed him something, and that's why I tried so hard to help him then and in later years. He would always delegate authority like that. The same applied to anybody who played or sang in the band. He'd always give you that big send-off and say, 'This is the shot you want—you've got it!'

"Although he and Kathryn went as Mr. and Mrs. Hines, he was chasing those chicks then! He was a chick-chaser all right, but he sat around and talked with me for quite a while.

" 'Son,' he said, 'you know everything in the book, and you love anything to do with songs, so why don't you make up the radio programs?'

" 'All right,' I said, and we started to heat up the airways in 1931. I'm picking songs, and Earl picked him a vocalist named Herb Jeffries who was lazier than Earl. One night I had to stand beside him and whisper the words in his ear, because he'd just walked in and couldn't find the words to a song that was already programmed. The radio show had started, so it was too late to change anything. I used to learn all the popular songs that I picked for Herb to sing. And I can brag, because I bet you I picked every hit song there was in those days. I even picked *Begin the Beguine* in 1935, I think it was, but I could not make Earl play it.

" 'Son, it's too long,' he said.

" 'It's going to be a hit, Earl.'

" 'Son, this goes on for ever,' he said, because nobody'd ever seen a double-chorus song then.

" 'It's made to order for Walter Fuller,' I said. 'He should sing it.'

"He was very stubborn, and I failed that time, although I think I was the only one ever able to make Earl do things he was determined not to. He did some very unwise things, too. Earl will tell it like it is sometimes when he ought to duck.

"Of course, he was as close to a genius as anybody in the profession would be. Consequently, he never had to practice. I have never seen Earl sit down, take a piece of music and practice on it with nobody around. Never, in all the years I've known him and been close to him! All he had to do was hear the music one time and he'd got it. They used to write those big, grandiose arrangements for the shows at the Grand Terrace, and in the beginning they didn't think Earl could read. One day they put the music up and asked, 'Are you going to get the piano player who used to play the show?'

" 'We don't need him,' Earl said. 'I'll play it now.'

" 'Yeah, Earl, but . . .'

" 'I'll play it,' he repeated, and he went right down it the first time. He can read as good as anybody, but he's lazy. Lester Young, whom I also managed later on, was like him. Lester had that ear and that genius. He heard it once and he had it. He could read a fly speck, but he didn't see the point of reading if he could hear it.

"When I was making those radio programs, I always said, 'Earl, you've got to have a solo in everything that's done, even if it's only a four-bar modulation. You've got to be heard, because *you* are what they're listening for.' He'd always get behind and start pushing somebody else. He's lazy, and he's awfully lucky.

"When Earl went to New York in the winter of 1932, they left me at the Grand Terrace because I had been making up those radio programs and selecting the songs. Clarence Moore's band was more or less in my charge, and Teddy Wilson was his piano player. He played so much like Earl, we used to give him a piano solo on almost every song. Now my knowledge and experience of music wasn't the greatest then, but I knew something was wrong from the frowns on the guys' faces. Teddy would go in at one tempo and come out flying. Everything would be picked up, and the drummer would be slamming on the drums trying to hold it. I asked Moore what was wrong after a couple of nights, and he said, 'He has trouble with tempo.' Later on, when Earl was living at 45th and South Park, he moved Teddy and his wife, Irene, into his house. I was Earl's valet then, and I saw this with my own eyes. Earl would have Teddy at the piano, teaching him how to keep time with his left hand, so that the tempo wouldn't pick up or decrease. For some reason, Teddy has never given Earl much credit. I don't know why. Nat Cole was different. I don't care where he was, if Earl Hines's name came up, Nat would say, 'Everything I am I owe to that man, because I copied him. Of course, through the years I've gotten away from him, but I'll never forget him, because he was my idol. He was always kind to me, and never too busy to say hello or to show me something.'

"It's hard to remember exactly, chronologically, but I think Reginald Foresythe came into the picture around 1932. He was accompanying a singer in the clubhouse at the Yankee Stadium, and after they broke up Earl was talking to him at the Grand Terrace. Earl always knew talent, and that's when he took him.

"There's a funny story before that, when they were working at the College Inn downtown. Reggie's father was English and his mother was West Indian, but he had grown up English. He *was* English. He even used to tuck his handkerchief up in his sleeve. Anyway, he sat down in the dining room at the College Inn to eat, and the headwaiter came over.

" 'I'm sorry, we can't serve you, Reggie,' he said. 'Negroes aren't allowed to eat in here.'

" 'How dare you!' Reggie said. 'How dare you have the audacity to call me a Negro! Must I show you my passport? I am an Englishman, and I will go straightway to the embassy and cause this place more trouble than you can stand!'

"So here was the star he'd traveled around the world with as an accompanist, eating in the kitchen, while they're serving Reggie in the dining room!

"He used to carry a cane, and I'd make fun of him and drive him nuts. But he had been brilliantly educated, and he sounded like he'd been to Eton or one of those schools. He used all those four-dollar words, and he was just so important and everything.

" 'Look at you American Negroes,' he'd say. 'You're my color, but you don't compare with me. You can't go here, you can't go there. I go anywhere I damn well please!'

"Everything was very English in the way he spoke and acted, and a lot of times I've thought of him and known he was right. He had the guts and the courage, some of which I think I assimilated, because I used to go places with Wallace Bishop, the drummer, where it was a borderline thing in a white restaurant. Sometimes, when we had sat down, we'd see Earl looking through the window, and then he'd come in with his big cigar.

" 'Hello, son! Mind if I join you?' he'd ask. 'What're you having, huh?'

"He explained how he felt about that kind of situation one time, and I give him credit:

" 'You went to Hyde Park High School, son. You went with all those white kids. Louis Fox, Ed Fox's son, went to the same school, a year behind you. You were the star of the football team, and for two or three years there wasn't another Negro on it. You just got used to white people, 'cause you were always around 'em.'

"Earl and I became very close through the years. He continued to give me more authority and let me do things. He didn't record *You Can Depend on Me* till 1940, I guess because he felt the opportunity had passed by, but in 1933 we had another song. They had brought in Valaida Snow, one of the most versatile women I've ever seen in my life. She played

Ed Fox.

an instrument in the band, she sang and she danced. The only thing she didn't do was impressions, but she did everything else. She found out Dunlap and I were writing songs, and she said she wanted us to write her show. She and Earl were going together, and she said, 'I'll make him help you.' And she did. We went to work to write her show, and the night it opened in 1933 was the night beer came in. I wrote a song called *Bubbling Over with Beer*. The verse was very good, and I never thought I'd forget it, but all I can remember now is a line about "I was waiting to drink with you." Jimmy Mundy wrote the arrangement and Valaida came out with the chorus girls, all with beer glasses. She sang and danced about five choruses at an awful fast tempo, and they wouldn't let her off. She came back, did the whole dance part again, went upstairs, and passed out. She was absolutely exhausted and we thought we were going to have to send her to the hospital. Val had to be in her middle thirties then, and that tempo was awfully, awfully fast.

"We also wrote a ballad called *Everything Depends on You*, which was quite appropriate to her, and she would come out and sing it. Another song was *I Want a Lot of Love*, and we must have had a couple of others. It was the best show they ever had. Dunlap and I, with Earl's help, wrote the whole thing, so guess what Mr. Fox, who ran the place, did then? He sent to New York for Paul Denniker and Andy Razaf to write the next show! I wasn't a kid, but I wasn't an old man, and that was heartbreaking to me. You say Ed Fox seems to be the villain in every interview you've done. Well, he *was*. He had a twenty-year contract on Earl. That was peonage, and Earl knew it, and he was trying to break out.

"Now we go out, and in 1934 or 1935 we played Loew's State in New York. I traveled as band boy. I was band boy, secretary, a little bit of everything. My grandmother had told me years before, 'Baby son, when you're on a job, learn everything you can about it, because you never know what you'll need to know.' So I was the leg man. I led the show.

"When we had played the Oriental Theatre

the first time in 1931, I think it was right after Duke Ellington. The husband of Ginny the vocalist came to me in the back and said, 'Mr. Fox said you should work the lights.' I didn't know what a stagelight was, but I went to the first guy I saw backstage and said, 'See all those lights up there? Who's in charge? Who runs them?' He called a guy whose name was Roy.

" 'What's your trouble?' he said. 'What can I do for you?'

" 'I'm supposed to work the lights for Earl Hines's show, and I don't know one of those lights from another.'

" 'Well, do you know the songs?' he asked. 'Do you know what's fast, what's slow, what it's about?'

" 'I know all of that,' I said.

" 'Okay,' he said, 'you just stand right here beside me and don't worry about a thing. We'll get him started. Then while he's working you explain what he's going to do next, and I'll figure out something fast to light it.'

"That was my beginning with lights, and it reminded me of when I got to New York and we were playing Loew's State. Sidney Pierpoint, the buyer, had to be in Baltimore opening day, but he came back the next day, Saturday. He watched the show before coming backstage, and then he wanted to know who lit Earl Hines's show.

" 'You know who lit your show, Mr. Pierpoint,' I said. 'There he is—your head electrician. I think he did a magnificent job. All we did was tell him what we were playing, and he lit it.'

"That guy's jaw dropped open. He could have fallen over. Mr. Pierpoint slapped him on the back and said, 'I knew I had the greatest crew in the world!'

"These were things I always used to do. Earl knew that I knew, just as George Kirby does now, but I didn't need any credit. Of course, that electrician was something. He said, 'Anytime you want to come into Loew's State, or bring somebody with you, come backstage and ask for me. You don't ever have to pay so long as I'm electrician here.' But I

didn't do it for that. It's like another of my grandmother's sayings: You throw the crumbs on the water, and sometimes a loaf of bread comes back.

"Eventually, Earl decided he was not going any further. He would go back home, break up the band, and not work until they re-negotiated that contract. He was getting $210 a week in the theatres then, but only $100 a week in the Grand Terrace, where scale was $45. Scale was even less in the Cotton Club then. Even for a black local, it was a problem. Chick Webb was walking along with Trummy Young and me one night, and he was trying to get Trummy to go with him.

" 'Man, my scale is thirty dollars,' he said, 'but I'll give you thirty-five.'

" 'Chick, I make forty-five in Chicago,' Trummy said quietly.

" 'What's an extra ten dollars, man? In New York, with records and this and that, you'll make so much over that you could forget about it!'

"Trummy wouldn't leave then, but when he did he went with Jimmie Lunceford, not with Chick.

"Fox came into New York while we were there, because he'd been hearing rumors. He didn't like the way Earl was talking. Fox sat down, and Earl was telling him how he wanted me as his right-hand man, how he didn't want Fox to have all the money—he was getting $3000 for the band—but just the commission he was entitled to. Fox didn't say anything and he went back to Chicago. When we got there, I found I was fired, and so was Dunlap, who had been acting as Earl's valet.

"Now Earl is standing on the corner in Chicago, looking as poor as Nat Cole used to look sometimes. But although Nat didn't have any money, Nadine would wash and starch his shirts, press his clothes and everything, and then he would come out sharp as a tack.

"Finally we hear Earl has been back in the Grand Terrace over a week, because most of the band hadn't backed him up. He hadn't said anything to Lap or me, so we went down to the club. Fox wanted to throw us out, but

Mrs. Fox, bless her heart, was very nice and talked to Dunlap and me, told us we should never have listened to Earl, and had a lot more to say.

" 'Well, maybe it isn't quite like that,' we said when we left. 'After all, he's got to eat, too.'

"Fox had Fletcher Henderson's band in the club after Earl, and when he decided to send Fletcher out on the road, he called me and wanted me to go out as road manager. Now in those days there had never been a black road manager of a major attraction like Fletcher. I was the first to do that. We went out on tour and came back. Subconsciously, I was getting ready to go to New York. I knew Fox was not going to let me work with Earl anymore, because we were a dangerous combination.

" 'Well, what happens now, Pop?' I asked him. Earl and everybody used to call Ed Fox 'Pop' at that time—Pop the Great White Father.

" 'You know business has been kind of heavy, and Dave is getting a little old,' he said. 'How would you like to be a headwaiter and work by the day?'

" 'I'd like it fine. What's the pay?'

" 'Thirty-five a week.'

" 'Yeah. I think I'd like that.'

"I wanted to scream, because that was an awful lot of money then. I knew I was going to get tips, and for almost a year I made a hundred dollars a week and saved up my money.

"Jimmy Mundy came to town in 1938 on a visit. He'd left us and gone with Benny Goodman in 1935. He used to do crazy things, and he had a yen to see a chick called Kelsey, so he got in his car and drove all the way to Chicago.

" 'When are you coming to New York?' he asked me. 'You know you'll starve to death in Chicago. You'll never write any songs here.'

" 'You know, you could be right.'

"It was August, so I got hold of Dunlap.

" 'Lap, let's go to New York,' I said.

" 'No, man, we can't go yet.'

" 'I've been asking and asking you to go to New York, and you've been putting me off. The Grand Terrace is closed for the summer. It's supposed to open up in September, but it can open up without me. I've got a couple of friends, Deke Watson and Orville Jones. They're tap-dancing now, but they want to sing. They worked the Grand Terrace and they told me they were going to New York to get 'em a quartet. They're going to call themselves the Ink Spots. Maybe I can get them to sing a song of ours. Let's take advantage of that!'

"But Lap wouldn't go, and he didn't think I was going. When Mundy pulled up at the house, I'd got my raggedy little bag, my one suit, an extra pair of pants, and a few shirts. So off we went to New York! I didn't have the money I should have had, because my father had married a young chick, and I had been taking care of my brother. The fifty or sixty dollars I had soon ran out. After I moved from Mundy's house, where I lived at first, I used to be so hungry! I got a little help from Jimmy, because he was arranging for Gene Krupa, whom I knew from Chicago. Gene had a song called *Bolero at the Savoy*, and he asked me to see if I could write words to it. We got a fifty-dollar advance, and that helped me pay the rent. I had moved in with Mundy's brother-in-law, and he paid the first week's rent, which was $4.50, and I paid it the next week and every week for the year he lived with me. But I got lucky. I got to copying for Elton Hill, who used to arrange for Krupa, too. He had so much he couldn't handle it all. I got six dollars an arrangement, and I used to copy four a week, so suddenly I was getting rich!

"Then Tommy Dorsey heard I was in New York and sent for me.

" 'That was a good song you wrote for Louis,' he said. 'You got any more of 'em?'

" 'Yes, I think I got one.'

" 'Did you write it all yourself? Where's your partner?'

" 'I'll bring him with me.'

"Henri Woode, the guy that wrote *Rosetta* with Earl, had a tune called *You Taught Me to*

Love Again. Shirley Ross, the movie actress, was on Tommy's show the day we demonstrated it, and she flipped. She used to come to the Grand Terrace whenever she was in Chicago.

" 'Do it again,' she said, 'do it again!'

" 'Just a minute,' Tommy said, 'let me ask him a couple of things. Have you got an arrangement on it?'

" 'No, but Henri can arrange.'

" 'Well, get me an arrangement and we'll do it.'

"He introduced it Christmas night, and the day after Christmas every publisher in New York was trying to get it. Tommy called and asked if we wanted to handle it ourselves, or whether we wanted him to.

" 'You handle it,' I said. He got us a $750 advance, and I never looked back!

"Then Earl Hines came into the picture again, and I became his personal manager. I picked all the songs and everything. The first time he came to the Apollo in 1938 after I'd moved to New York, he told me, 'Son, one of these days I'm going to get that contract with Fox busted, and then I want you to be my manager.' When he came back in 1939, he said, 'I think this year is going to be it.'

"Sure enough, Petrillo abrogated the contract, and I became the manager. I kept Earl out of Chicago a year till I had everything set like I wanted it, because I knew Fox was going to take us to court. When he did, I'd got Halpern, the lawyer of the William Morris agency. Fox was shaking like he had palsy. I even felt sorry for him when the judge said, 'Plaintiff, state your case.' It must have been cut and dried, because the judge jumped down his throat with four-dollar words. What he said, in effect, was, 'If you ever come back in my court again, I'll put you away for six months for contempt. Lincoln freed the slaves in 1863.' And Fox never bothered us again. We went back into the new Grand Terrace, booked by William Morris, and played it for a month. Fox had been the front man for Al Capone at the old Grand Terrace, but for some reason they threw him out after they moved to the new place, which was a little after I left in 1938.

"When I took over in 1939, Earl had booked himself from California to New York, and he'd only been sued twice. He lost a couple of contracts and missed two dates. I had met a lawyer named Chauncey Olman, and I paid him twenty dollars a month as a retainer. It was Chauncey, talking to Earl and me, who said, 'Having a manager like Charlie has never been done before, so we're going to write it into the contract with William Morris.' Usually you sign the artist and the manager's name isn't mentioned, and certainly not as having authority to do the negotiating. 'I better do this,' he said, 'because they might try to ignore Charlie.'

"We had a meeting at the William Morris office and they said they had never had a black personal manager. Now this was not a *road* manager but a *personal* manager. The gist of what they were telling us was, 'It's just never been done, and *we* are not going to do it!' Just about then, Earl turned to me and said, 'Son, let's go!'

"I think it was William Morris, Jr., who spoke up then. 'We are a booking agency,' he said, 'and if Earl wants him to be his personal manager, that's up to him. We don't pick personal managers.'

"So everybody got quiet. Harry Squires was sucking on his false teeth, and smiling that little smile of his. He'd been with us since 1931, I think. He was there when I first went out with Earl in the summer of '32. He went along with us and did the booking by telephone. Harry 'Telephone' Squires we named him. He was very fond of us, and he taught me so much. By this time I really knew the business. I took Earl from $250 to a guarantee of $650 a night. When we didn't go over $1000 I used to call Willie Randall, the road manager, and say, 'Man, you ain't going south with the money, are you?'

"George Dixon was the strawboss and Willie was the road manager. We called Willie 'Little Figures,' because he had studied accounting. I had taught Red the valet how to work the door, and he could do it as well as anybody living. Willie would go to the door, check up, and collect the money.

"Earl would never start out playing with the

band, and after intermission he might not be back for a set or a couple of numbers, but the minute it was time to hit, George Dixon hit. It was the same at the Grand Terrace. Earl would go back to the kitchen sometimes and fall right to sleep at a table. He wouldn't go to bed. Bed was like a jinx to him. I don't know why, unless he thought he was going to miss something! Now when I was in my early twenties I used to stay up like all day today, all night tonight, all day the next day, and all the next night, but Earl would outstay me. Of course, I never did drink. The Gold Coast crowd was what we poor South Side people looked up to. They'd come in the Grand Terrace so grand you couldn't touch them with a ten-foot pole. Two hours later they were calling each other every name under the sun, and pulling up their dresses—terrible! That turned me off drink. Then I used to watch Earl gambling with the waiters upstairs, and they used to steal his money, because he used to be nodding. I had sense enough not to say anything at the time. I didn't want somebody to stick a knife in me when I wasn't looking!

" 'Earl,' I'd say when we were alone, 'you keep nodding, and they're reaching over taking your money.'

" 'Oh, no, son. They wouldn't do that.'

" 'Don't tell me! I'm looking at 'em!'

"What broke up our playhouse was the Army. I managed Earl until 21 April 1942. I flew down to say goodbye in Shreveport, Louisiana, on the 20th. I was the first black to fly in and out of Shreveport, where Earl was working. I wanted George Dixon to meet me, and he and Omer Simeon were waiting down at the corner of the building.

" 'Come on up here, Dick,' I called.

" 'No way.'

"So I went down and met them.

" 'Look, you and I have got to go get my bags.'

" 'Well, we'll be here when you've got 'em.'

"So I went and got them and came on out. I've thought about that many times, even talked to George about it and the mentality of the whites in those days. They thought I was getting Mr. Charley's bags, a white man's bags, and never dreamed I was getting my own. When I went back to get on the plane, and George and Simmie were with me, they figured I'm walking along to Mr. Charley, and that I'm going to get to the foot of the steps and stop. When I got to the platform at the top of the steps, I turned around and waved to George and Simmie. Those white people were the funniest I ever saw in my life. Nobody had ever done this in Shreveport, Louisiana, and they were absolutely stunned.

"The Army just wrecked the whole thing. Willie Randall went next and then George Dixon, but Billy Eckstine and Louis Dunlap didn't have to go. We had Charlie Parker in the band, and I took Dizzy Gillespie after he had a little skirmish with Cab Calloway.

"It's a funny thing about Charlie Parker. In 1954, I had a show out and was company manager. It was booked out of New York as the Stan Kenton Jazz Show or something like that, and Cress Courtney said to me one day:

" 'I wanted to bet you on a fight, and I would have lost. Now I want to bet you something and I won't lose. I'll bet you Charlie Parker misses the show on you.'

" 'Cress,' I said, 'I don't want to take your money.'

"There were four or five shows Charlie could have missed and Cress wouldn't have known the difference, but he didn't miss one. He played every show, and they still don't believe it. This was not much more than a year before he died. He blamed my going in the Army for some of his troubles.

" 'When you used to go off to the Savoy, and they told me you were Earl Hines's manager, I'd never seen anything like that in my life,' he told me one time. 'I introduced myself and you talked to me. Then when Jay McShann was going back to Kansas City, you got together with Earl and he hired me. You were my crutch. Suddenly, I looked around, and you were in the Army. Now you know how sensitive I am. There were a couple of cats in the band using that stuff, and trying to get others to use. The next thing you know, I got in the dumps here and the dumps there, and I tried a little bit of this and a little bit of that. It just went from bad to worse, and then I was gone.'

"After I'd been in the Army a while, we sailed from Boston—in *The Explorer*, I never forget—to Greenock, Scotland. From there we went to Somerset in a real slow train on real hard seats. I think it took a day and a half! One day I went in a bar all by myself to get a soda—a 'mineral water,' I mean—and over the 'wireless' I heard that Fats Waller had died in Kansas City. It was as though something had pulled me in that bar at that time, and I was just stunned. I remember the last time I saw him alive, in a Pittsburgh hotel.

" 'You want some ribs?' he asked me.

" 'No, I'm not really hungry. I'll just eat some of yours.'

" 'Oh, no, you better get some of your own.'

" 'What are you going to get?'

" 'Five orders of ribs, two quarts of milk and a sweet potato pie. You sure you don't want anything?'

"He sent a guy out for them, and he ate all the ribs, all the pie, and drank all the milk. He wasn't lying. He wouldn't give me an eensty-weensty bit of any of those ribs.

"From England we went to France. I was a supply sergeant in a company hauling gasoline. We went into Belgium, back into France to Alsace-Lorraine, and then into Germany. When I got back from Europe, I went to Chicago to see my father and my folks. It was November 1945, and Earl was playing in the El Grotto, downstairs in the old Pershing Hotel. I went back for my job, and when he saw me walk in I could see he could have gone through the floor. In the meantime he had got Eric Illedge as manager and had married Janie, or was going to marry her. I talked to Illedge, Benny Green and Earl, and Earl knew the law, that he should take me back, but things were going down and he had got himself into a lot of hassles.

" 'Look, Earl, forget about it,' I said. 'I wish you all the best.'

"Pretty soon he wound up with Louis Armstrong. He had been carrying around all those fiddles and everything, which I wouldn't have let him do. I think I was the only one could control him. Before I went in the Army,

when we were at the Apollo, I told him, 'Whatever you do, *don't* do anything Ralph Cooper wants you to do!' When I was home on leave, I found out he'd gone out with Ralph doing the Pabst Blue Ribbon Show, playing camps for free and Pabst paying the tab. Ralph told Earl he was playing for scale like him, a hundred and some dollars a week, but I was told he was getting four hundred, and he left Earl stranded in Texas. Ralph had been an m.c. and he'd been in those black, quickie movies. At one time he'd been fairly big as half of Rector and Cooper. They were dancers, but they got into trouble when Eddie Rector brought a blonde into Chicago. This was in the '20s, and they got the thumbs-down routine from booking agents all over America after that, so Ralph had to go pretty much for himself then.

"Then again in 1952 I told Earl to get him a three-piece combo, or four pieces at the most. 'You'll get just as much,' I said, 'as you're going to get with eight pieces!'

"No, I can't play the piano anymore.'

" 'You're talking to me, Earl, to Charlie. You *know* I know. You can't play the piano? The style is yours, and that's what they want to hear.'

"Now the other night, at his seventieth birthday celebration in the Biltmore Hotel, he was really playing.

" 'Earl, you told me you couldn't play the piano in 1952,' I said. 'This is 1976. What was that you were just playing?'

" 'That was me, son!'

" 'Well, that's the same thing. In '52 you went out for $2500 and gave it all to the musicians. You could have got that for three people, because all they wanted to hear was you, anyhow.'

"Economics had hit Louis Armstrong in the '40s. That was why he went out with six pieces. He'd much rather have had a big band, but big bands were *passé*—they were gone.

"Well, I didn't work the whole of 1946. I had the 52-20 Club back of me. If you'd been a soldier, you got twenty dollars for fifty-two weeks in New York State. And my first check from *Frenesi*, which I wrote under the name of Ray Charles with Bob Russell, was for $3000. I was feuding with ASCAP and Johnny Mercer, a dear friend of mine, was trying to straighten it out. The name came from the fact that Martha Raye and I had been very close since 1934, when she used to come to the Grand Terrace after working at the Morrison downtown. She'd do her show with us, which consisted of *I'm in the Mood for Love* and *I Got Rhythm*. When Ralph Peer told me I had to have a *nom de plume*, I took her second name first, without the 'e,' and put my first name second. The white Ray Charles, who has the singers, was a friend of mine. He went to Hyde Park School, too, and he kids me all the time about taking the bows while I'm collecting the money. I don't think that's his real name either, because I believe he's Jewish and in school he was using his own name. The black Ray Charles I've never met, but I think that is his real name.

"I was feuding with ASCAP because I had been an 'associate' member since 1934. They wouldn't make me a full member because I was black, although I'd had a hit song and several others along the way like *You Taught Me to Love Again*.

"After *Frenesi*, a guy named Gilmore had come to me with a song by Bennie Moten with a tuba lead. He played me the original record and it was called *South*. Now this was in 1940, and you've got to imagine how I felt when Gilmore said, 'You write the words to this song, and you don't have to split the money. It's going to make as much as *Frenesi*, and it'll probably be around just as long.' I thought he was kidding, and I was about to crack up, but I went home that night and wrote the lyric to it, tongue in cheek. The next day Gilmore put the record on and began singing it in his monotone while tapping his feet.

" 'Yeah, this is it,' he said, while I was looking at him like he was going crazy. 'Draw up the contract,' he called to his secretary. Red Foley made a record of it, and it was a giant. Les Paul's wife recorded it. So did Count Basie. The last line shows you what imagina-tion songwriters have: *Don't you know you're next to Heaven down south?* Imagine me writing a line like that in 1940!

"After the war I became Lester Young's manager. When Cecil Irwin was killed in the 1935 bus accident, we played Minneapolis without a tenor and went on to the Main Street Theatre in Kansas City, where we were playing with the *four* Mills Brothers. John Mills was still alive then. Earl was having auditions when somebody told him about this tenor player with Basie, who was working in a basement place. Earl sent George Dixon to ask him to come to a rehearsal at the theatre. So Lester Young came backstage, and at that time he didn't drink anything but milk, and didn't even smoke cigarettes.

" 'What do you want to play?' Earl asked after they'd talked a bit.

" 'How about a little *Tiger Rag?*'

" 'What tempo?'

"Earl put it where he wanted it, and they lit out. Lester was holding his tenor out sideways, and it sounded like a soprano saxophone to me. I was from the Coleman Hawkins era, and I still remember him when he played at the Congress Hotel in Chicago with Fletcher Henderson in 1927, the first colored band to play downtown. I didn't really know what he was going when I heard him on the radio then, because I was singing songs like *My Blue Heaven*, and for me you had to have a melody. Jimmie Noone used to play that kind of saxophone now and then, and there was a guy in Sammy Stewart's band who played soprano. So that was the sound Pres seemed to have to me, but I knew he must have been doing something, because, man, all the cats were listening to him. They'd fall out and then come back with a riff. Pres played a whole lot of choruses, and he was fine. He and Earl went off and sat down and talked for fifteen or twenty minutes. When rehearsal was over, I went to Earl.

" 'Why doesn't he play soprano?' I asked. 'What he's doing is the funniest thing I ever saw. Why does he hold it out there like that?'

" 'Son, that's a peculiarity of his,' Earl said, 'and he does it to be different, I guess. What he's doing is 'way ahead of our time. The average musician playing tenor doesn't conceive of doing what he's doing, because they're all on the Coleman Hawkins thing, but one day . . .'

"Earl was always smart about things that had to do with music.

"After Basie came to New York in 1937, I'd see Pres off and on. We'd go around to the White Rose, and I asked him when he started drinking. 'Lady Day,' he said. 'I call Billie Holiday "Lady Day." I just started. I take a drink now and then.'

"When I came out of the Army, I heard about Lester Young working with five pieces and all the records he made. He was getting a thousand dollars a night, which was unheard of and ridiculous to me. The Gale agency was booking him, and the day after Christmas Frank Sands called me. He had been secretary for Harry Squires at William Morris when I managed Earl.

" 'I've got a job for you New Year's Eve,' he said.

" 'Man, I don't want to work.'

" 'You can't live off that 52-20 Club and what you saved for ever.'

" 'You could be right. What is it you got in mind?'

" 'It's just for one night,' he said, and he started laughing. 'I want you to go to Newark and manage Lester Young for one night.'

" 'Oh, no. Somebody else, not me.'

" 'Look,' Frank said, 'he's got a friend of yours in the band—Shorts McConnell.'

"The next day I went downtown and Frank Sands sold me a bill of goods. I thought about how nice Lester was, and Frank told me how everybody had been stealing from him.

"So I found myself riding the train into Newark with five of the funniest looking cats I ever saw in my life. Shorts was the one who played the trumpet solo on Earl's *Stormy Monday Blues*, and wanted to do it again, but I wouldn't let him. We're sitting on the train looking at each other, and I'm cracking up and they're cracking up. We went over to play this one-night dance and I figured there might be nobody there, but there were four thousand

people and we went into percentage. When Pres came out, I'd got everything figured out and gave him the money. He sat down in a corner and started counting. He made up six balls of bills, went to each musician and gave him a ball. He gave me one, and when I unwrapped it it was for twenty-five dollars! On the way way back on the train he sat down beside me.

" 'You know, I like the way you do things,' he said. 'I remember Earl Hines 'way back in Kansas City. He made a lot of sense in those days. You want to keep managing me?'

" 'I don't know,' I said, 'but we don't work without a contract.'

" 'I'm not going for that signing,' he said, 'but I just thought you might like to work with me after I go to Chicago.'

" 'You going to Chicago?' Right away I saw a free trip to see my folks.

" 'We play a couple of places on the way,' he said.

"I went with him, and when we came back to New York he sat beside me again.

" 'You know,' he said, 'I've been watching you and everything, and I've been thinking. You get your contract and I'll sign it.'

"So he signed it, and we were together ten years. I also picked up George Kirby along the way. Pres used to go out with *Jazz at the Philharmonic*, and that would take two or three months. And in the '50s I used to be out managing with big shows. I got Pres up to $1250 a week as a solo artist in the Birdland Show.

"I always knew I was in for trouble when I went in the back door at Birdland, and he'd be sitting right on the edge of his chair, rubbing his hands.

" 'Lady Carpenter,' he'd say, 'how are your feelings?'

" 'I'm fine, Lester.'

" 'I want you to know I'm not high tonight!'

"He was so high he was blind. He hadn't worked yet, hadn't perspired, hadn't started to show it. He had built up an immunity, but the heat would get to him. Contrary to what anybody thought, Lester was not a drug addict. He had musicians that used heroin and cocaine. The minute they drew that stuff out,

Pres would say, 'Out! When you get past a stick or a glass, you have passed Pres.' He never did anything but smoke pot or drink. Never. When he said, 'Out!' he meant for them to go to their room, because he didn't want them around him. A lot of people also used to think he was queer, but he was not. He was effeminate and his father didn't like him. He was never quite able to explain it, but he told the story about the time when his father had the carnival band, and got him up on the stand to play, and he couldn't read. His father talked awful bad to him in front of everybody, and told him to get off the stand. He went to his mother and never forgave his father.

"We had put him in the hospital, and his wife had care of him for six months, but he was too far gone. When he sat us down and talked to us, the doctor called it within two weeks. He said he'd live two years at most. It was hardening of the liver, cirrhosis."

(1976)

Banquet at the Theresa Hotel in Harlem for the band and friends from the show at the Apollo Theatre. Standing at left: Mr. and Mrs. Bob Crowder, fourth and fifth from left; Mr. and Mrs. Leroy Harris on their left next to Pee Wee Jackson and Wallace Bishop. Rudy Traylor is in front of the fire extinguisher. Seated at table on left, left to right, are: Scoops Carry, Mr. and Mrs. Budd Johnson, George Dixon, Louis Dunlap, Truck Parham, Willie Randall, Madeline Green, Charlie Carpenter. To right of table, Billy Eckstine is in the foreground and Joe McLewis is behind him. Earl Hines is at the head of the table.

GEORGE DIXON

TRUMPET AND SAXOPHONES

"My friend, George Dixon."

That is how Earl Hines always speaks of the man who, for many years, was the backbone of his band, as indispensable to him as Harry Carney was, in a different way, to Duke Ellington. Dependable and greatly talented as a player, he was also dependable as the leader's trusted confidant and strawboss of the band. The measure of his character lies in the fact that none of those who worked with him ever voice criticism of any kind. They all refer to him with respect, as a just and honorable man, and as a first-class musician.

Dixon was born in New Orleans in 1909. His father, the Rev. M. R. Dixon, was a Methodist minister. In due course, when the family moved to Natchez, George was taught violin by Sister Gerald, a Catholic sister to whom he gives much credit for his musical foundation. His father thought that he would play in church, but George already visualized making his living in music. The next of the minister's periodic five-year moves was to Pine Bluff, Arkansas. His son went to Arkansas State College in 1925 and began doubling on alto saxophone the following year, when he became leader of the college dance band. Having also learned to play trumpet, he decided to quit after one year at Arkansas State. He wanted to earn money to put himself through medical school, and he began "gigging around" Gary, Indiana, before moving into Chicago.

"I started entering amateur contests there," he recalled. "They used to have them in a lot of theatres, and they'd give cash prizes, like ten dollars for first place and five for second. So I'd play violin in one contest, saxophone in another, and trumpet in a third. Sometimes I'd go back and play all three instruments."

He auditioned for Sammy Stewart's band in 1928 and got the job on the strength of what was considered his unique skill in doubling on trumpet and alto saxophone. He had acquired enough experience by now to take his place beside musicians who were to make great names in jazz. The band included Bill Stewart and Kenneth Anderson, alto saxophones; Walter Fuller, trumpet; Kenneth Stewart, trombone; Alex Hill, piano; Ikey Robinson, banjo; Maurice Warley, bass; and Sidney Catlett, drums. Most of the arrangements were by Hill, who was occasionally replaced at the piano by the leader for a specialty.

"In those days, bands used to appear on-stage at all the big movie theatres," Dixon said. "The Oriental, the Marlboro, the Tivoli, the Chicago, and the Vendome at 31st and State, all put on a live show with a band. After working in Chicago we got an invitation to open a new theatre in Sammy's hometown, Columbus, Ohio, and we were there a year before going to the Savoy Ballroom in New York."

Chu Berry, the tenor saxophonist, was in the band when it left for New York, where Horace Henderson took Alex Hill's place at the piano. Dixon and Fuller were not at all enchanted by New York, and after another engagement, at the Arcadia Ballroom on Broadway, they were happy to return to Chicago and join Earl Hines at the Grand Terrace in 1929.

Apart from the brief period when Hines disbanded and Walter Fuller took a group into the Grand Terrace, Dixon was with Hines until 1942. Of the previous associates who had gone with Fuller, Dixon was the first to return—in St. Louis—to Hines, who was very glad to have him back.

The importance of radio on band fortunes made a big impression on Dixon at this time when so many direct broadcasts emanated from Chicago venues like the Aragon, the Trianon, the Sherman Hotel's Panther Room, the Black Hawk, the Edgewater Beach and, not least, the Grand Terrace. These broadcasts inevitably led to a demand for personal appearances in the U.S. and Canada.

"We covered all forty-eight states," Dixon remembered, "and I think we must have played every city in the country that had a theatre or ballroom big enough for a band like ours. We played at a presidential inauguration, at the Mardi Gras in New Orleans, and at the Kentucky Derby." Looking back on those days, when the band had to travel long distances by bus, Dixon had no complaints. "'I was young and couldn't have cared less about losing sleep," he said. "I had a ball. It was a wonderful way to see the country, too. One time, I remember, we played a date in Des Moines on a Saturday night and got to Detroit in time for another booking on Sunday evening."

He was in both the bus accidents that left such sad memories in the band. In the first, he believes Cecil Irwin was killed without ever knowing what hit him, because he was asleep with his head against the bus window. Dixon promptly commandeered a car, rushed the injured Trummy Young to hospital, and got to Iowa Falls a few minutes before Earl Hines and Kathryn Perry arrived there by train on their way to Minneapolis. When the battered band opened at the Orpheum that night, Kathryn Perry sang *I Never Had a Chance*, and moved the house to tears.

In the second accident, Dixon was thrown against the seat in front, but played his usual role in the evening show unaware his jaw was broken.

His memories of the Grand Terrace are many and various. The motto there, he said, was always, "Find out what they like and how they like it, and let them have it!" Among the intermission pianists he remembers were Frank Smith, Teddy Wilson, Leroy Gentry, Gene Rodgers and Jane Prater. He speaks of his own playing with reluctance, but is not displeased if his *baritone* saxophone work on *The Father Jumps* is mentioned. He wrote *Julia* for Billy Eckstine in the '30s, and he always played the sombre theme of *Deep Forest* on trumpet with distinction. His best-known alto solo is in the superb performance of *Number 19*, which Budd Johnson arranged. Familiarity with his alto and trumpet solos almost invariably suggests the name of his idol—Benny Carter. But what Dixon is perhaps most famous for—such is justice—are the shouts on the hit record of *Boogie Woogie on St. Louis Blues* as made in 1940. "Put out all the lights and call the law right now," he hollers, and then, a little later, "Play it till 1951!" As the performance draws to a close, he adds a final exhortation: "Don't quit now, Jack! Don't quit now!" The atmosphere and feeling of authenticity created by these shouts had much to do with the record's success. In fact, when an alternative take without Dixon's shouts was issued by RCA years later, there were many bitter complaints. He was also responsible for the equally authentic vocal directive to the guitar player on *Tantalizing a Cuban*—"Beat it out, Lemon!" He followed it with a comic but admiring commentary: "Yeah, now, Fatha!" as Hines began his solo; "Put me in the groove, Budd, and don't holler if I move!" before Budd Johnson's entry; and "Cool as a fool in a pool!" as the rhythm section took over to exit. Although less successful commercially, this loose, swinging record is an unpretentious gem.

Dixon's scrapbook offers convincing proof that the Hines band was one of the hottest in the country in the early '40s. Press clippings, taken at random, are full of statements like the following:

New York, 6 Feb., 1941. Earl (Father) Hines, whose great new band set an attendance record in its first appearance at the Fiesta Danceteria on Broadway last week, is the current rage among swing music fans and critics. A crowd of 1300 was on hand Saturday night to greet the famous Windy City piano star when he appeared on Broadway for the first time under the William Morris banner.

Baltimore, Md., 13 Feb., 1941. Earl "Daddy" Hines and his orchestra have broken all records at the Royal Theatre and are the talk of Baltimore. The first three days of this week the orchestra played to over 13,000 patrons.

Washington, D.C., 1 Mar., 1941. Earl "Fatha" Hines brought his famous Grand Terrace band here Saturday for an opening that outdistanced anything that has appeared in a Washington theatre in months. The orchestra came here from Baltimore where it triumphed at the Royal Theatre. In the latter house a new attendance record for the season was established.

St. Louis, 17 July, 1941. All kinds of records were shattered here on Friday night when Earl "Fatha" Hines, aided by Madeline Green, a favorite with local fans who recalled her work here while appearing with Jeter-Pillars orchestra at the ofay Club Plantation, showed up at Castle Ballroom at a dance sponsored by the Barcelonnas Social Club, one of the city's "live-wire" organizations.

Traffic was jammed and halted and more than that on busy Olive Street at Ewing as hundreds of dance addicts tried and tried in vain to gain admission to the hall. Officers had a real job on hand. Then the trouble started, but the crowd was good-natured and orderly. Some refunds had to be made. But it was all taken in good part.

Detroit, 24 July, 1941. Earl Hines and his orchestra broke the all-time record Monday, July 21, at the Graystone Ballroom in Detroit,

when they played to a jammed house of 6,593. The Sunday night before the Hines aggregation played for a record crowd at Cincinnati's Graystone. The crowd was so great (and so many other things) that the Mayor says he won't let Negroes dance there again.

Oakland, Calif., 11 Sept., 1941. Earl "Fatha" Hines broke the year's record for attendance at Sweet's Ballroom here during his Labor Day engagement.

Chicago, 11 April, 1942. Earl "Fatha" Hines brought his band to the Savoy Ballroom here in Chicago Sunday for an Easter dance and set a new attendance mark for the spot. On table tops, in red plush chairs and in the window sills, they danced and cheered for "Fatha." 'Twas homecoming for the largest crowd and merriest party Chicago had witnessed in months.

New York, 23 Jan., 1943. Earl Father Hines, his band and his show opened here on Friday to the most enthusiastic and largest crowd ever to greet an attraction at the Apollo. When the show opened Friday morning the house was packed and jammed and the lines outside extended to Seventh Avenue. And the same was true throughout the first three days of the run with Sunday presenting a situation that an extra performance failed to relieve.

Jacksonville, Fla., 4 Dec., 1943. Approximately 30,000 "Fatha" Hines dance lovers paid to hear their favorite leader during the week of November 21, it was announced this week. Starting with the official Victor Record ball at Camden, N.J., which attracted 10,000, the "Fatha" played to 6,000 the following night at the Golden Gate in New York City. Greenville, S.C., drew 3,000, the City Auditorium at Birmingham, Ala., had 3,700, the City Auditorium at Chattanooga, Tenn., had 2,900 on Thanksgiving Eve, and the City Auditorium in Atlanta, Ga., drew 4,400.

Under the headline HINES HITS BROADWAY AND TEARS IT APART!, Dave Dexter reviewed the band in *Down Beat* of 15 February 1941 and noted that "John Hammond, Mildred Bailey, Helen Oakley, Leonard Feather and all the others who were at the Fiesta opening seemed to agree" with Hines that the band was the greatest he ever had.

World War II played havoc with the band, as with so many others, and George Dixon went into the Navy for three and a half years in 1942. He was first at Great Lakes Naval Training Base, and then at the Naval Reserve Aviation Base in Memphis, where he directed a twenty-three-piece band. It was so well liked that he took it around the country to entertain at other bases. Back in Chicago once more, he decided to form his own quartet with Alvin "Mouse" Burroughs on drums. He had originally met this fine musician from Mobile in Kansas City, and had later learned to

appreciate him during 1938–40, when he was such a vital part of one of Earl Hines's best rhythm sections. (During his service years, Dixon caught the Hines band at the Paradise Theatre in Detroit, when Shadow Wilson had taken the place of Burroughs's able successor, Rudy Traylor. He was mightily impressed and found *that* rhythm section "almost perfection." Unfortunately, it was never recorded.)

Burroughs remained with Dixon's quartet until he died of a heart attack in 1950. They had played at the Circle Inn at 63rd and Cottage for four years before taking a job at the Club Silhouette on Howard Street for ten weeks. Then they worked at the Blue Heaven around the corner from the Circle Inn. After Burroughs's death, Dixon's doctor told him to

Left to right: Billy Eckstine, Franz Jackson, Earl Hines, George Dixon, Truck Parham. Seated saxophonists are Leroy Harris, Willie Randall and Scoops Carry.

quit working regularly at night, so he took a
civil service examination, passed, and became
an elevator operator at City Hall. From there
he went to the elevators at Police Headquarters, where he became chief elevator starter
after five years. He did not give up music,
however, but continued to play dates around
Chicago, leading groups of a size appropriate
to the occasion. Besides weddings, dances and
fashion shows, he played Summer Community
Concerts, which were presented free by the
Chicago Park District with Local 10.208's cooperation and a grant from the Music Performance Trust Funds. His reputation ensured
that he could get the best available musicians
in Chicago, and the personnel of his orchestra
for a typical concert at Harlan Park in 1973
was:

George Dixon, leader, trumpet and alto
saxophone;
Henderson Smith, Calvin Ladner, Fip
Ricard, trumpets;
Harlan Floyd, Joe McLewis, Kenneth
Stewart, trombones;
Nat Jones, Gordon Jones, Eddie John-
son, McKinley Easton, Moses Gant,
reeds;
Frank Smith, piano; Adam Lambert, gui-

tar; Lotus Perkins, bass; Eugene Miller,
drums;
Rudy Robinson, vocalist.

The program consisted of a judicious mixture
of jazz standards and contemporary songs:

Cavernism
Alfie
Cha Cha Cha
San Francisco
In a Mellotone
Lil' Darlin'
Just Cruisin' (vocal George Dixon)
Cleo (featuring Adam Lambert)
For Once in My Life
Millie
Things Ain't What They Used to Be
Fly Me to the Moon
Night Train
Tea for Two Cha Cha (featuring Nat
Jones)
That'll Just About Knock Me Out (featur-
ing George Dixon)
Shiny Stockings
Jeep's Blues (featuring Eddie Johnson)
Last Night

(1973)

Above: In front, left to right: Lois Deppe, Earl Hines, George Dixon. At back: Woogie Harris, Carl Pruitt, Vernon Smith. Lady unknown.

Opposite: Left to right: Roy Eldridge, Alvin Burroughs, Lotus Perkins, Rozelle Claxton, George Dixon.

WALTER FULLER

TRUMPET

Of all the many trumpet players who worked for him, Walter Fuller is the most closely identified with Earl Hines, perhaps because he was prominently featured as a soloist throughout most of the vital '30s, or perhaps because he stayed longer than most. He was audibly a disciple of Louis Armstrong as both trumpet player and singer, his virile drive and musicianship making him a very valuable asset to Hines.

He was born in Dyersburg, Tennessee, 15 February 1910. His father played mellophone, and his older brother, Wilbur, a professional musician, played trumpet. Walter also began on mellophone, but later switched to trumpet.

"Every year after school," he recalled, "I would travel with Dr. Stoll's Medicine Show through the states up as far as the coal region in Pennsylvania. I was twelve when that started, and a fellow from my hometown, a tuba player named Benny Stratton, was like my guardian and tutor. They had a very, very fine band, and they would carry me out to what they called the 'woodshed' and teach me, and make me study an hour each day. That went on all through the summer for three years.

"The last year, the owner of the show told Benny they would have to get rid of me. A girl in the show had gone to him and said some false things about me. I was very young, but I wrote my parents about it. Benny wanted to send me home, but I told him I was going on in to Chicago to my kinfolk. Some of my mother's people lived there, and I stayed with them for a while until I got together with a good friend from my hometown, and we found us a little apartment.

"This would be about 1925, and I began to play little gigs on the streets in Chicago. There'd be four or five of us kids, and we used to go around and play on different corners. Louis Armstrong was the talk of Chicago then, and years later I was so thrilled when they had me go down and play at the Royal Garden, the same place where he had played!

"Then I got a job in a five-piece band led by Emma Smith, a very fine pianist. She was the wife of the president of the union. Now I was still quite young and I had never heard about a musicians' union. When it got back to her husband—I never shall forget this—he came down and said:

" 'Young man, you be at the local when it opens up in the morning. You put up your money and get in!'

" 'Okay,' I said, and when the local opened up, I was there.

"I guess I was with Mrs. Smith about a year, and then Sammy Stewart was organizing a big band to take to the Savoy Ballroom in New York. He sent fellows down to ask if I would like to join. Sammy played piano, but he mostly conducted, and he eventually got Alex Hill as pianist and arranger. He also got Big Sid Catlett on drums, George Dixon on trumpet and, from out around Cincinnati, Chu Berry on tenor. It was a very good band in 1929 when we went to the Savoy and played opposite Chick Webb. We stayed there quite a while, until Sammy was planning on going downtown to the Roseland Ballroom, but I wanted to go back to Chicago, because I was a little bit in love. George Dixon left, too, and we went back in 1930, but Sid Catlett and Chu Berry stayed in New York, battled it out, and made good right there.

"When I got back to Chicago, I joined Irene Eadey at the Vogue. I think we were five pieces—piano, trumpet, guitar, bass and drums. Irene played good in those days. She had those little fingers going, and she would sit up there and play with a lot of drive. It was Prohibition time and the place was owned by gangsters. They were crazy about her. I remember it used to be so hot on the little bandstand that we'd always have a pitcher of beer up there. We'd drink it and just go back and get it filled up. That's what started me to getting fat—drinking beer.

"In 1931 I was approached by Earl Hines to join his big band at the Grand Terrace. I gave my notice in to Irene, and one night one of the gangster owners of the Vogue called me over to their table.

" 'Walter,' one of them said, 'we understand you want to leave the Vogue.'

" 'Yes, that's right, I'd like to go with Earl Hines at the Grand Terrace.'

" 'We have an interest in that, too, you know. You can't leave one of our places and go to another.'

" 'Oh, I didn't know that. I guess the best thing I can do is forget about it then.'

" 'Yeah.'

"About a couple of weeks later, Joe Fusco, one of the main bosses came in, and he called me over.

" 'I understand the boys told you you couldn't go with Earl Hines,' he said, laughing.

" 'Yep, that's the way it was.'

" 'Everything is straightened out. After you finish this week here, you can go ahead.'

"So that was how I came to join Earl. But I must say those people were very good to me. We used to make tips galore at the Vogue,

Walter Fuller.

and when my father passed away in Tennessee, Joe Fusco called me.

" 'Walter,' he said, 'I hear your father died. Is there anything you need?'

"I thought that was very nice, and I never forgot it.

"Earl gave me *Rosetta* to sing, and that piece just caught fire. In fact, I named my daughter Rosetta. She has three girls of her own now, and lives in Los Angeles. My wife and I just celebrated our fortieth anniversary. She was a dancer, one of the main dancers in the Regalettes at the Regal Theatre in Chicago. They traveled with Duke Ellington in a show for a while.

"I was with Earl's band when we had the accident out in Iowa. A big corn truck sideswiped the bus after we'd played a theatre date. Poor Cecil Irwin was killed, and Billy Franklin, our vocalist, had all the ligaments torn out of his arm. I had two sprained ankles, and Trummy Young had about the same thing. Our ankles were swollen up as big as watermelons.

"There was never any real dissension in Earl's band—a wonderful bunch of guys. Everybody got along just like brothers . . . George Dixon, Omer Simeon, Wallace Bishop, Jimmy Mundy . . . When a bunch of us went with Horace Henderson in 1937, it was because of Ed Fox, the manager at the Grand Terrace. He wasn't paying right. Different little things like that. We were with Horace about a year, mostly at Swingland in Chicago, and then we went back to Earl. He had a great band at that time, and in 1939 I recorded another vocal number that was quite a hit. It was *After All I've Been to You*. The following year, of course, he made his famous *Boogie Woogie on St. Louis Blues*, I sang on another big one, *You Can Depend on Me*, and Billy Eckstine recorded his first vocal with the band."

When the Grand Terrace reopened in September 1940, Fuller was the leader of a new big band. Many of his old associates were in the personnel, which was as follows: Fuller, trumpet and vocal; George Dixon, trumpet and saxophones; Milton Fletcher, Ed Simms,

trumpets; John Ewing, Ed Burke, George Hunter, trombones; Omer Simeon, alto saxophone and clarinet; Bob Crowder, Moses Grant, tenor saxophones; Rozelle Claxton, piano and arranger; Claude Roberts, guitar; Quinn Wilson, bass; Kansas Fields, drums. Plans for regular broadcasts from the club fell through, and Lionel Hampton's aspiring young band was brought in as a replacement for Fuller's by manager Joe Peterson, who was faced with the problem of gaining a reputation for the club comparable to that acquired at the old location.

"They had pulled me out from Earl's band and organized a big band for me to front," Fuller explained. "It was a fine band, and Duke Ellington and Billy Strayhorn had written a theme for me, but I never did get to use it, because at that time ASCAP and BMI had started their big feud. Jimmy Mundy had made a lot of arrangements for me, too, but I couldn't play them on the air for the same reason. So that ripped me right off. But I didn't really want a big band then. It was too much of a headache. Most of the guys went back with Earl. One person I should mention, who was in the show with us there, was Dinah Washington.

"Next I got a little group together and we went into the Capitol Lounge next to the Capitol Theatre. After we left there, we were booked into the Happy Hour at 16th and Nicollet in Minneapolis by Frederick Brothers, the agents. This was early in 1942, when I had Omer Simeon, Quinn Wilson, Buddy Smith on drums, Elmer Ewing on guitar, and Nelda Dupree as vocalist. Rozelle Claxton, who had been with Ernie Fields and Harlan Leonard, was on piano. We were the first black band to go there, and we stayed quite a while.

"We went back to Chicago, got a long engagement in Tony's Subway in Peoria, and then went out to Los Angeles and played both the Last Word and the Radio Room. It seems to me that we went back to Chicago, and then out to Peoria again, before we went to Kelly's Stables on 52nd Street for two or three months. Because they had more than one act in those clubs on the Street, we used to have

Left to right: Billy Franklin, Omer Simeon, Charlie Allen, Lawrence Dixon, Wallace Bishop, Earl Hines, Walter Fuller, Louis Taylor, Quinn Wilson, Darnell Howard, Cecil Irwin.

long intermissions, so all us musicians used to meet at a bar on the corner, where they had free eats, eggs, cheese and stuff, and you could get a shot for twenty-five cents. Billie Holiday was working right up the street from us, and the last time I saw her she was in that bar with her two big boxers. She used to call me 'Rosetta.' I used to go in where she was singing, and you didn't move when she was

on. You just stood right there, waiters and everybody, until she finished. I'm telling you, she used to gas me! She was wonderful people.

"I went back to Chicago around 1946, after we'd been in Kelly's Stables a second time, and this fellow from Frederick Brothers asked me if I'd like to go to San Diego in California. I told him some of my men had stayed in New

York and that I'd have to pick up a couple. I was able to get Preston Coleman, a wonderful bass player, and Buddy Smith, the drummer who had been in Minneapolis with me. I got a fellow out of Gary, Indiana, by the name of Montan Phillips on piano, and a girl singer who didn't last a week out there. There was a train strike on, and it seems as though it took us a couple of weeks, because they kept stopping, changing crews, and stopping again. Finally, we made it to Los Angeles and caught that little milk train out to San Diego. It was raining when we got there, and I think that was what discouraged Buddy Smith, because he sent his parents a telegram and told them to wire him that someone was sick, so he could get back home. After he'd gone, I got Charlie Blackwell out of Los Angeles on drums, and a tenor player named Eugene Porter, who had played with some big bands in the East like Don Redman's. Then someone told me about a girl called Marie Louise, who had won a talent contest on Al Jarvis's show. I brought her down to San Diego and trained her. She was a very beautiful girl and she made out real well. Later, when she went to Capitol and made all those records, they changed her name to Georgia Carr.

"I always did get my kicks from Louis Armstrong, and during the twelve years I was at the Club Royal in San Diego he would always come by if he had time. I remember when he came in with Velma Middleton and Barrett Deems. They stayed till 2 o'clock, and Pops got on the stand and sang, and Velma sang, and Barrett played the drums. The people just flipped and even now some of them will say, 'I was in the club, Walter, the night Louis Armstrong came to see you.' Louis was such a beautiful man. He never changed. One night, he was playing in a club here, and it was my night off, so my wife and I went out to see him. He happened to see us in the audience, and he put us in his song, right over the mike, singing about Ol' Walter Fuller and his Ida Mae, like in the Regal Theatre . . . Well, I never heard him when he sounded bad in *nothing*! Not Pops! It was a double tragedy for me the day he was buried, because my vocalist, Marie Louise—Georgia Carr—was buried that day, too. She was only about forty, but she had very high blood pressure.

"After the Club Royal, I was eight years at the Moonglow. Today it's the Walter Fuller Trio. I have Eugene Watson on piano and Hollis Hassell on drums. Hollis sings and we do vocals together. We've got so much material, offer lots of entertainment, and that's why we can stay on the job so long. Of course, you've got to carry yourself in a way that you're respected by your own musicians and your fellow men. I've never had a bad thing to say about *any* musician. Rather than say anything bad, I'll say nothing at all. It's a matter of liking people in general, too. I've been out to San Diego State College three times to give lectures to the kids. I don't need any notes. I tell them about the '20s and the '30s, and they always want to know about the things that happened in the gangster days. When they want to know about the chances of making a living in music today, I have to be very truthful with them. I think every kid should have music, because it's good for the soul, but I tell them not to be too impressed by the kids who strike it lucky. 'Get your music,' I say, 'but get your education first.' "

(1973)

QUINN WILSON

BASS AND ARRANGER

"Some relatives on my mother's side down in Jackson, Mississippi, were musically inclined, so I understand, but my mother moved to Chicago and married my daddy. I was born in Chicago on 26 December 1908 and began taking violin lessons when I was ten years old. I got on well, playing concertos and everything, but there were so many violinists in Chicago at that time that I figured I wouldn't be able to make any money in the concert field. I had a brother, a lot older than I was, who used to go over to Dreamland where Charlie Cooke was playing, and he was always telling me what a good violin player Darnell Howard was. So I tried to copy off Darnell, but I couldn't play jazz like he could. It was when I was returning from a music lesson, with my violin under my arm, that I saw Earl Hines for the first time. He was playing at the Sunset Café with Louis Armstrong, and I chinned up to look through the window and see them.

"When I went to high school, I wanted to get in the band and take some other kind of instrument. Charlie Allen, the trumpet player who died recently, was in the school ROTC band. He was a friend of mine and he handed me a tuba.

" 'What did you give me that for?' I asked. 'What am I going to do with three valves when I'm used to strings?'

" 'That's all right,' he said. 'I'll teach you.'

"So he taught me the fingering, and I took to tuba and went to town with it. The first professional band I played in was Art Sims's Wisconsin Roof Orchestra in Milwaukee. Jimmy McHenry, the drummer in it, was a friend of mine, and he asked if I wanted to go to Milwaukee with 'em. I was still in high school, but they'd pick me up Friday afternoon and we'd play Friday, Saturday and Sunday nights. Then they'd bring me back to school Monday morning. It got a little rough, but I left high school in the third year because we got another job in Milwaukee, six nights a week. The money went to my head! Sixty-five dollars was good money back in 1926.

"Then I had a chance to go into the Vendome Theatre where Erskine Tate's orchestra was playing for silent films, so I had to go back to my old band instructor at high school, and he taught me bass violin. I had to learn it in two weeks, because you got only two weeks' notice in those days. By the time I went in the theatre, I was playing string bass! It was easy really. The violin helped. My influences then were Wellman Braud—Duke Ellington's man—and Pops Foster. See, when they came up from New Orleans, that's when jazz bands started changing from tuba to string bass.

"After a time, I left Erskine Tate's band and went across the street to the Regal Theatre and Dave Peyton's orchestra. It was about twelve pieces, with violins, and we'd play in the pit for the silent news, and then we'd go onstage. Besides the Regal and the Tivoli, there were two or three other theatres in Chicago that had stage presentations. I stayed with Dave till I went to the Grand Terrace with Earl Hines in March 1931. Five of us left the Regal band to join him. The others were Darnell Howard, Omer Simeon, Louis Taylor and Wallace Bishop. I took the place of Hayes Alvis.

"I had started a little arranging while I was with Erskine Tate, and I did a lot more while I was with Earl. At that time, before television, those song publishers used to come by with brand new tunes. They'd get together with the arrangers, hand us the sheet music, and we'd arrange it for the band. Sometimes I'd have five or six arrangements to get out in a week. Cecil Irwin was there originally, and after he died Budd Johnson came in, but Jimmy Mundy was already there, and he did a lot of the arranging, too. Among the early ones I wrote and arranged were *Harlem Lament* and *Blue*. I did the arrangement on *That's a-Plenty*, and *Dominick Swing* was another I wrote. There was a ginmill in New York called Dominick's where musicians and theatrical people hung out. We had to get a swing tune together for a record session, and I just thought something up in my head and named it after Dominick.

"It was a good band Earl had at the Grand Terrace, and everybody got along beautifully. In fact, that was the first band I was in where everybody got along fine, and before we disbanded we had sixteen men. What I remember most are the big shows we had to play. When I started, Percy Venable was the production man and Lucky Millinder was his sidekick. After that, Valaida Snow brought in a big show. I mean it was a big production like you see on television, just like Hollywood, or like the Cotton Club—sixteen chorus girls, eight show girls, besides the acts. The audience was mixed, black and tan, no problem.

"As I remember, at the Grand Terrace we'd come in about 10:30, play a dance set for a half-hour, and then take a fifteen-minute intermission. After another short dance set, we'd play the first part of the show, which was in three sections. When that was over, we'd play another dance set and have another intermission. It would go like that all night, and after we'd played the third section and an-

other dance set, it was time to quit. Each section of the show would run about an hour and the shows were changed every five weeks. That meant a lot of rehearsing. In later years they used to have two different sections, and they'd repeat the first instead of having a different third section. That was all before the five-nights-a-week law. Guys now think working six nights is rough, but in those days I figured I was a musician and that I was *supposed* to work seven nights a week!

"I used to write arrangements for the shows and get twenty dollars for them. That was big money in the '30s, and I raised four daughters in the Depression. They all married and I wound up with thirteen grandchildren and sixteen great-grandchildren. On top of that, I've got a little boy eight years old!

"The gangsters were one reason why the job at the Grand Terrace was fun. They always liked to play, and those guys were funny. Earl went to sleep one night while he was eating at the dining table in the kitchen. His cigar was on the ashtray and it had gone out, so one of them put tabasco sauce on the end. When Earl put it in his mouth and lit it again, he got the taste of tabasco! Boy, you talk about guys being playful! They liked to give you a hotfoot, stick a match in the sole of your shoe, light it with another match and let it burn down to the end.

"We used to have big battles with Chick Webb at the Savoy in Harlem. How did we do? Not so good. Very few bands did good against Chick. He had powerful arrangements and a swinging little band. We had a swinging band, too, and special arrangements, but I don't know what happened at the Savoy. Duke used to say the same thing. Of course, Chick had the crowd back of him.

"I'll never forget the time Earl and Claude Hopkins had a Battle of the Pianos at the Roseland Ballroom in New York. They had baby grands back to back. Earl can play, I'm telling you, but if you want to hear him *really* play, just put him in competition. Like when we were at the Grand Terrace: there was an after-hours spot where we used to hang out after we got through, and he and the blind piano player, Art Tatum, used to hook up in the mornings. Earl was crazy about Tatum. I know there was a lot of Earl in Tatum's playing, but a lot of piano players took from Tatum, Teddy Wilson for one. There was a time, too, when Teddy Wilson sounded just like Earl. Another piano player I remember was Teddy Weatherford. I worked in the Green Room with him for a year, and I think he was closer to Earl than to Fats Waller, especially in the way he worked the left hand. But Earl could outplay him, and eventually Teddy left and went to China. Earl was crazy about Fats Waller, too, and in his young days Earl used to sit in at jam sessions around town.

"I knew Cecil Irwin well. He was wonderful, quiet, very talented and well schooled. He made several arrangements for the band in the Chicago Theatre, strings and all. I'm not sure where he got his musical education, but I believe it was in Chicago Musical College. I was in the accident when he was killed as well as in another terrible one in the Cumberland Mountains in Maryland, where Bish (Wallace Bishop) got his ankle sprained. Earl was there, too, because he rode the bus all the time with us. Nobody got killed in that one, but the bus went over a fifteen-foot embankment. There was an empty Coke bottle rolling loose in the aisle of the bus, and the driver turned and asked somebody to pick it up. The road turned, too, just about there, but he didn't turn the wheel. He just kept straight on, and we wound up at the foot of this embankment where there was a little creek and running water. The dust from the bus crashing down, the reflection of the red lights of the bus in the water, and the noise of the running water sounded like crackling fire, so somebody hollered, 'Fire!' Everybody rushed for the front, and Bish and I ended up in the door of the bus. They just trampled on Bish getting out, and I was upside down, on my head! At that, I was lucky. We didn't have anything but two-lane highways then, and the buses had governors so that sixty was about as fast as they could go.

"In later years, the jumps started getting

Quinn Wilson.

longer, as the bookings were further apart. We used to go out from the Grand Terrace about twice a year, usually leaving after New Year's for four or five months on the road. We'd come back, stay during the summer, go out again in the fall, and then come back for the holidays. It was all one-nighters and theatres—the Apollo in New York, the Royal in Baltimore, the Pearl in Philly (later, they moved the shows from the Pearl to the Lincoln), the Stanley in Pittsburgh . . . Most big cities had a theatre.

"I was crazy about that life. I *loved* it! I liked the traveling. I couldn't do it now, but when you're in your twenties it's all right. The first time we went out it was only for three or four weeks, and theatres, with maybe a couple of one-nighters. The *next* time, we had three or four months of one-nighters, and that's when we started going down south. The first part of the trip would be out east—Pennsylvania and New York—and then we headed southwest to Oklahoma and Louisiana. It was not until the last couple of years that we got to Georgia, Florida and Mississippi. It was all right. We stayed in colored hotels when we could find one. If we couldn't, we stayed with private families. Earl is right when he says we were the first Freedom Riders, but they seemed to treat us different from the home-town people. They figured because we were musicians we were educated. It was a hard life, but you got used to it, and you got to know people in different towns, and they'd look for you.

"Omer Simeon worked with me in Erskine Tate's band at the Vendome, and I've wonderful memories of him. He was a nice, quiet fellow, a very good musician, but he didn't get the recognition as an alto player he should have had. He was a fine first man in the section. He and I were on a record date with Jelly Roll Morton in 1927. They say now that Jelly Roll Morton was a 'character,' but he wasn't so far as I knew him. Maybe he changed in later years, but when I was making records with him he was very good, and I never had any trouble with him. I've heard people talk of his loud mouth, too, but I don't remember him that way. He was a talented man.

"I knew Milt Hinton, too, in Chicago, but I don't see much of him anymore since he's in New York. I'm the cause of his being in music. Milt, Lionel Hampton, Charlie Allen and Raymond Walters . . . oh, four or five of 'em lived on the same block! When I started taking violin lessons, the other kids wanted violin lessons, and Milt started taking violin from the same teacher. I knew Ray Nance, too, before he joined Earl. He and Oliver Coleman had a great little band at one time.

"I was with Earl till '39, when he disbanded, and Omer Simeon and I went with Walter Fuller and a small band for about a couple of years. Then I was at the Rhumboogie with Marl Young. Captain Walter Dyett was the leader there after Marl left. We had five brass, four saxes and four rhythm. Around 1946 I was with Little Sax Crowder's

combo. He had played tenor and arranged for Earl at the Grand Terrace. He retired from music, got in some other kind of business and went to Peoria, where he died. By that time I was playing at Jazz Limited, and I stayed there twelve years until it folded.

"I started jobbing around, but I took sick and had to go into the hospital for eight days. I had high blood pressure for one thing, and the ticker was getting kind of slow. The doctor took me off the tuba, which I'd been playing again, and told me to take it easy for a little while. So I figured I'd retire and go on Social Security.

"Meanwhile, Barrett Deems was in the Gaslight Club and he kept after 'em about getting a bass in there, and finally Joe Kelly, the leader, decided to try the bass out. So that's when I came out of retirement! It's five days a week at the Gaslight, six hours a night, seven on Saturday, and Sunday afternoons we play at Alfie's. Kelly plays trumpet; Bill Usselton, who used to be with Les Brown, is on tenor; Michael Ford is on piano, Barrett Deems on drums, and I'm on bass—five pieces. What we play is mostly jazz, and at the Gaslight we back the girls, who all sing.

"I stuck with upright bass a long time. Finally, I was working with a band in a club on the South Side where they had loud amplified guitar, loud tenors, and loud drums, so then I had to switch to Fender bass. I held out as long as I could! When I play it, I pick it almost like I would the upright bass, only I use one finger lightly, and that makes it sound more like an upright. Some of 'em use picks, and that gives it that guitar sound, and some of 'em get a long, dragging sound that's really ugly. I don't know whether it's what they want, or whether they hold a finger on the fingerboard too long. But I'm using the upright bass amplified now, and the Fender is sitting in the closet at home.

"I really feel a whole lot better since I'm back working. You've got to be active. I don't like that sitting in a rocking chair watching television re-runs."

(1974)

WALLACE BISHOP

DRUMS

"I was born in Chicago on 17 February 1906. I studied drums with Jimmy Bertrand, and he was my first private teacher. My mother took me by the Royal Gardens once to see Baby Dodds, who was playing with Joe Oliver at the time. When my mother asked him to give me some lessons, he said, 'I'm sorry, Mrs. Bishop, but I have too many girls to take care of!' I was about seventeen when I started work in a place called Funky London at 35th and State. The proprietress was named Mamie Ponce, and we had a trio—piano, clarinet and drums. The clarinet player was a fellow called Dodo, a very good clarinetist. I worked with Jelly Roll Morton in 1924 or 1925. We did a little tour of Indiana, Michigan and Ohio. He was working for MCA at the time, and I must say that he was a very good leader. Most people give him a bad reputation and say he bragged a lot. He bragged some . . . No, he didn't brag, because what he said was true. He was a very nice fellow. He paid you on time, and all you had to do was do his work, and that was all there was to it. I made records with him, too, with George Mitchell and Omer Simeon.

"In 1926, I went to Art Sims's big band in Milwaukee, and was with him about a year. After I got back to Chicago, I wanted to take a vacation. My mother asked me where I wanted to go, New York or New Orleans, and I chose New Orleans. At that time, I met Fate Marable, a pianist on the riverboats, and he offered me a job, but I couldn't take it because

I had promised Hughie Swift I would come and work for him back in Chicago after my vacation. I often regretted that, too, for I think it would have been a great experience for me.

"I worked with Hughie Swift at the Jeffrey Tavern in 1927, and then I gigged around until I got a job with Omer Simeon's brother, Al Simeon, a violin player, who worked at a place called the Farm, a roadhouse outside Chicago. From there I went with Erskine Tate from 1928 to 1931, when I joined Earl Hines. I had taken a fellow by the name of Ralph Cooper to New York to get a comedian called Billy Mitchell and some chorus girls. Then we drove back to the Grand Terrace. When we got there, the band was rehearsing. Earl had made some changes in the band and was auditioning other musicians. When I walked in, I saw George Dixon, Billy Franklin, Walter Fuller and, of course, Earl himself. So I got the job, because they were all my friends.

"I was with Earl until 1937, and it was a good job. The band was nice and the guys in it were friendly, and we all got along fine. I remember Jimmy Mundy bringing an arrangement to the band, and in those days the drummer kept straight rhythm, and didn't make any figures or anything. Mundy had the brass playing staccato, very fast, and George Dixon was sitting right next to me. So I kept my eye on George's music and played rim-shots with the brass. Mundy looked at me and said, 'What's going on up there?' I think I was the first one to start playing figures with the brass, because that was in '32, or no later than '33.

"The band was great, but we used to do six months of one-nighters every year, from east to west, north to south, all over the United States, traveling two or three hundred miles a day by bus. We'd get to the place just in time to eat something, change clothes, jump on the bandstand and play. Then we'd eat again, get in the bus, and travel the rest of the night and all day to the next job. Sometimes we'd have a day off, and then we could rest. It was tough, but we were young, and when you were about twenty-five years old you could do it.

"The Grand Terrace was also a hard job, and we had some real bad, tough shows to play. We'd go from 10:30 at night to 4:30 in the morning, seven nights a week, no night off. We had three shows to play, an hour to an hour and a half long each night, with chorus girls, dancers, singers and comedians. They were hard shows, but we had the best show band in Chicago, and we could take care of everything.

"When we had a new show the next night, we'd start rehearsing about 5 o'clock in the morning and wouldn't finish till about midday. We'd rehearse, and then maybe sit around and wait because the music wasn't ready. One time, I remember, it was snowing so hard you couldn't see across the street. When the show went on the next night, we'd have all the new arrangements, but sometimes we'd take one out of the book that the chorus girls knew, a nice swinging thing, for their speciality. We'd substitute it for the original, and when those girls heard it, how they would dance! They'd get encores for it. That was a *bad* band! I know any bands that came in there after we went out had a hard time, because those shows were so tough to play.

"I think Earl should have a big band again, because he really knows how to direct a band and get things out of men. He's a good leader. He was head of the band, but he never said, 'I'm the boss!' He'd tell you what you had to do, and he'd be polite about it, and everybody would cooperate. He's the greatest as a leader and a pianist. I can't compare him with Duke Ellington, because he doesn't write, compose and arrange like Duke, but he can play more piano than Duke. You can't compare him with Art Tatum either, because Art played a different style, but for swing . . . well, Earl's the swingingest cat I know. Fats Waller's was a different style, too—more bass, more stride. Of course, Earl can stride, too, when he wants to.

"I stayed around Chicago and worked with Jimmie Noone at the Yes Yes Club in 1941.

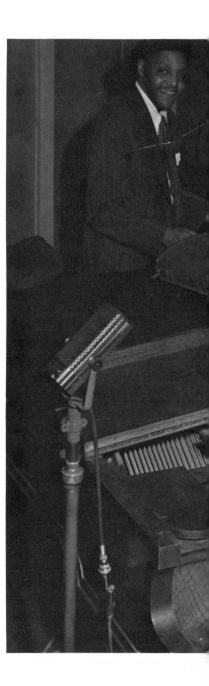

Later that year, I went to New York, the day of Pearl Harbor. I stayed there till 1949 and worked with Coleman Hawkins, Sy Oliver and John Kirby. In 1949 I met Buck Clayton one day on Seventh Avenue and 125th Street, and he asked if I wanted to go to Europe and play concerts for Hugues Panassié. I said yes and we left on 24th September and arrived in Paris on the 30th. I stayed in Paris about a year, but before that we made a concert tour in France and Switzerland. My last date was a big gala in Lausanne. There were three bands and one of the leaders asked if I wanted to work with him. He'd heard we were going back to New York the following week. I asked where we'd be working and he told me Switzerland. We went back to Paris and a few weeks later I returned to Switzerland and my new bandleader, Buddy Busen. We played in Basel and our last concert was in Zurich.

In Paris, 1949. Wallace Bishop, Buck Clayton, Barney Bigard, Earl Hines, Arvell Shaw.

While we were playing there, one of the men in the band, George Johnson, the alto saxophone player, asked me if I'd like to work with him in Holland, in The Hague. 'No,' I said, 'I'm going to New York.'

" 'Look,' he said, 'you can take the train from The Hague to Rotterdam, and it will only take a half-hour. You can get a boat from there to New York.'

" 'Fine!' I said.

"But after that job was over, he asked me to go to Amsterdam with him. I went there and played a few weeks until the band broke up. I took it over and got some work through our agent. We went to Switzerland, to Denmark, to Germany, and then back to Amsterdam for about six months until that band broke up, too. Before we went to Switzerland, I made some records in Paris with Willie 'The Lion' Smith for Hugues Panassié. I also recorded with Earl Hines, Buck Clayton and Barney Bigard there in 1949, and I got together with Earl again for a tour in 1967. I settled down in Holland, and I've been there ever since—for twenty-four years. It's my country, although I'm not working too much now.

"I think the musician of today is more sophisticated and has a better education than musicians of my time. They play and read well, and have been to universities like Berkeley and Juilliard. A trumpet player now will be able to arrange and play piano as well as his horn. They're good ensemble men, but they can't play jazz, real jazz . . . They're very good, but they don't have that feeling *together* like we used to have. When you joined a band in my day, you stayed there, because if it was a good band you were like a big family. Nowadays, musicians join bands, stay for two or three months, maybe a year, and then leave. I guess they have to do that, and there have to be changes. There are so *many* musicians. They're coming out of the universities like flies."

(1975)

Earl Hines and Wallace Bishop, Antwerp, 1965.

IRENE KITCHINGS

PIANO AND SONGWRITER

Irene Kitchings was born Irene Armstrong in Marietta, Ohio. While she was still an infant her mother moved to Muncie, Indiana, and Irene remembers attending kindergarten there.

"But I think I was playing piano even before that," she said. "My mother played, too, but my sister was not musical. There were only the three of us, so there was plenty of time for my mother to teach me the notes. Before long I was helping out at Sunday school.

"I went to live with an aunt in Detroit when I was about thirteen, and was still wearing woollen knee socks when I worked my first job. Aunt Dorothy had a detective take me to work and meet me when I got off in the morning. That was downtown at a place called the Metropole. Later I worked at the Royal Gardens, where the leader played violin, but I don't recall his name. I must have been about eighteen when I moved to Chicago. One of the first jobs they gave me was at the Book Store, where Sid Catlett was my drummer and Lester Boone played alto. The syndicate had everything sewn up at that time, and if Capone's fellows liked you, you could pretty well keep working. Everything was jumping right then. Louis Armstrong was in town. Earl Hines was at the Grand Terrace. Jimmie Noone was at the Nest and Johnny and Baby Dodds played somewhere on the South Side. Whole lots of people to hear!"

A short time later Irene Armstrong was asked to take a band into the Vogue. "I could add musicians," she recalled, "and I got Walter Fuller on trumpet, Johnny Grey on drums, and a boy we called Count on guitar. We had three horns as well. Afterwards, Fuller got a call from Earl Hines. He was excited, and I dug it, because Earl had a big name. But Walter nearly didn't get to go. He didn't understand that the people in charge at the Vogue were at the Grand Terrace, too. Right away they asked me real nice, 'You want your trumpet player to stay?' I had to smile and nod before he got his green light. It was kind of strange, but you were *family* if they liked you."

Although the personnel changed from time to time, she always fronted a band built around good musicians. Walter Fuller and Budd Johnson retain vivid memories of those times. "Renee was a star attraction. Not much bigger than a minute, but those fingers would fly over the keyboard," Fuller declared. "She was lively, and looked good, too."

The band retained its following and the bosses were pleased. For a nominal rent they offered Irene an eight-room house with garages attached. "Go out and furnish it, however you like," they told her, and Irene arranged for her sister to move in with her. Her mother was then living in Chicago, and she helped with the decorating and drapes. "I remember Duke's band was in town," Irene said, smiling. "Hearing I was housekeeping, Sonny Greer and Freddy Jenkins showed up one morning after the job to help me pick furniture. We even got a piano. Everything was just great, and it was some months before we found that the garages were stocked with sugar. They needed it to make the beer!

"When Fuller left, I hired Dolly Hutchinson on trumpet. Her mother, Pearl, played piano for Ethel Waters, and Dolly was really fine. She hadn't had much formal training, just what her mother taught her, but like Lady Day she had a natural ear. We had to keep a raccoon coat wrapped around her, because she felt the cold. Then when she'd screw down in her chair, she would be *gone*! She didn't play high, but had imagination and a great sound and beat. Kathryn Perry was with me, too. You couldn't imagine anyone so skinny and birdlike as she was then, but she could sing, loud and strong—an emotional singer. She played violin, too, just enough. But the Vogue got closed eventually, when the place was raided. There was a whiskey stash in the back. Then the syndicate figured they'd ready a new place, a lot fancier, and I decided while waiting that I might as well do something different.

"An older woman called Eloise Bennett asked Kathryn and me to work some gigs with her. She could dance, and sing a little, too. I played piano, Kathryn violin, and we'd finish up all three singing, and working dance routines as well. Our act was called The Three Classy Misses! We were booked into the Sunset, where Joe Glaser ran things and Cab Calloway was a single. It was quite a spot, and across the street was the Plantation featuring Josephine Baker. After a while, the Café de Paris opened. It was a beautiful place on 31st Street, and Percy Venable produced the show. Ethel Waters was the headliner, and we were the next featured act. I remember Zutty Singleton was drumming in the band there."

At the time she met Teddy Wilson, Irene Armstrong had formed yet another band. "We were working a small place on Cottage called the Cottage Café, and people who remember it kid me to this day, because I was advertised on the air as *Dark Irene*! They evidently thought that sounded fancy, and we were going over fine."

Certainly, the attraction must have been satisfactory, because later, when Irene and Teddy Wilson were married, their wedding present from the club was the piano she had used with a replica of the Cottage mounted over the keyboard. It was 1931 and Teddy Wilson was playing in a trio that came to Chicago from Toledo, with Melvin Banks on bass and Freddy Bryant on drums. They were working the Gold Coast, where Erskine Tate had the band.

"Getting off work early one morning," Irene remembered, "I stopped by this drugstore where lots of musicians and chorus girls congregated, and someone introduced Ted to me. 'You're strange here,' I told him, seeing that was how he felt. I invited him by my place any time he needed a piano to practice. Things happened fast after that. It was a month or two later that my cousin Callye accompanied Ted and me to City Hall. I think *she* had to get the ring. We hadn't got anything fixed up. A whirlwind affair."

After they were married, the new Vogue opened and Irene brought in an enlarged band, with Budd Johnson on tenor, and later his brother Keg on trombone. They were an

Irene Wilson.

instant success, and Irene remembered this as one of the best groups she ever led. "Ted had joined the union by then," she said, "and was working at a black-and-tan club called Dave's Place on 55th and Garfield. There were two unions at that time, and there was feuding. Later, Ted was with Eddie Mallory in a band that was contracted to perform regularly at a private club out of town, one the white union claimed as theirs. It got so bad that the boss ended up providing an escort to bring Eddie and the rest to and from work."

Irene remembered hearing a lot about Art Tatum from her husband, and going with him to meet Tatum when the latter was accompanying Adelaide Hall at the State Theatre. A short time before, the two men had played programs on two pianos which had been aired over WSPD. Her husband had loved Tatum so much that he would drive around Cleveland with him everywhere, going wherever he was to play. Tatum didn't let his bad eyesight bother him, and drove his car anyway.

Suddenly grave, Irene said she never imagined at that time that her world, like Tatum's, would darken. She was afflicted by Eale's disease, and her eyesight later failed.

Kathryn Perry and Irene Wilson, 1936.

"Art maintained his spirits though," she said, "and one of the things I'm proud to remember is that he recorded my *Some Other Spring* on one of his last albums. That was the first song I wrote after Ted and I broke up."

Benny Carter had heard Teddy Wilson in Chicago and brought him to New York in 1933 to play in the band he was taking into a Harlem club. At first, the Wilsons stayed with the Carters. "From that time on," Irene said, "I gave up performing. My mother-in-law disliked my working in public places alone, and Ted's career was more of a concern to me than my own." Then John Hammond succeeded in getting the American Record Company to record Wilson with Billie Holiday as vocalist. The sessions were under Wilson's name and they resulted in memorable music.

"At once, Lady and I were very close," Irene said warmly, "and we stayed that way till the day she passed. We met at the Hot Shot Club on Seventh Avenue. Benny Carter had said on the phone, 'There's a chick there I want you to hear.' It wasn't much of a spot, and I remember Billie wearing a lavender skirt and pink shirt, and looking like an overgrown child. She started coming up to the house after that to rehearse for the records. She often stayed with me, especially later when the break with Ted was not far off."

About this time the first Victor session featuring Benny Goodman, Gene Krupa and Teddy Wilson was released and occasioned much talk among musicians. From Chicago, this writer * sent Wilson the fare to appear with Goodman at a Rhythm Club concert in the Congress Hotel. "This was the trio's first public appearance," Irene said. "Right there Ted integrated Benny's band. In those days that was something!

"And some time after that," she went on, "I wrote *Some Other Spring*, my first number. *Ghost of Yesterdays, This Is the Moment, Pullin' Through* and the others all came out of that period after Ted and I split up. Even though I had quit playing, I had feelings, and they had to be expressed."

---

* Helen Oakley Dance.

Benny Carter was the first to recognize Irene Wilson's gift for songwriting. He listened one evening in her apartment as the changes evolved in the song she was working on. "Let's hear that again," he said. "And once more."

"Those changes are a little different," Irene explained, "and he made me play them one more time. Then he sat down, and it was all there. I was so moved. Next thing I knew, Lady Day had told Arthur Herzog about my number."

God Bless the Child was one of the songs Herzog and Billie Holiday had collaborated on successfully. With his lyrics for *Some Other Spring*, he demonstrated the same kind of affinity for Irene's music. "He's done all but one of my songs," she commented, "and I've never had to ask him to change a word. He and Lady were tight. The way she felt about race was never nasty, you know. If you were all right, that was it, and never mind color."

Billie Holiday was the first to record Irene's song. *Some Other Spring* has become a classic. Besides Benny Carter and Art Tatum, George Shearing made a striking version, and through the years instrumentalists like guitarist Charlie Byrd have demonstrated their appreciation of it. As a vehicle for singers, it has also enjoyed surprising popularity among such unrelated artists as Anthony Newley, Marianne Faithfull, Dakota Staton, Austin Powell of the Cats and the Fiddle, and Carmen McRae.

"Carmen had just graduated from high school when someone brought her to me," Irene remarked. "She could sing, and so I took her down for Lady to hear. For a long while, wherever we went, Carmen came along. She ended up recording most of my numbers, too."

At the time Irene started songwriting, living had become a problem. Without her husband, it was difficult to manage, and because he was striving to form and launch a band, money was scarce. "Aunt Dorothy was in Cleveland then, and when she heard I'd been ill, wanted me to join her for a while," Irene said. "But there were bills to pay, and the electricity in my apartment was off. Over the phone, John Hammond asked me, 'What are you doing, sitting up there in the dark?' He paid the bill, and that gave me a start. Then I threw a big party. I bought a hundred pounds of chitlins, and spaghetti and chicken as well. Duke's band was in town, and it looked like all of them came. Basie's musicians, and Count himself, were all there. They balled all night, and I cleared enough to break up my place."

The move was intended to be temporary, until Irene's health and spirits returned. But in Cleveland she met the man who represented the future. An Ohio State Youth Commissioner, Elden Kitchings was good for her state of mind, and they were married on 17 June 1946. "I never guessed that *Some Other Spring* might have been written for me," Irene said. "Elden lets nothing throw him. He keeps me smiling even now my sight is gone."

A new Hammond organ, a recent gift from her husband, has meant a lot to her. "I can play more on that thing than I ever could on piano," she said, laughing. "Once I sit at the keyboard, the blues can't catch me."

(1973)

Irene Wilson's orchestra at the Vogue with Stumpy Whitlock, trumpet, and Budd Johnson, reeds.

TEDDY WILSON

PIANO, ARRANGER AND BANDLEADER

"When I first heard *West End Blues* by Louis Armstrong and the Hot Five," Teddy Wilson said, "I was just amazed. I knew I had never heard that style of piano before—the melodic improvisation, the off-beat bass, the eccentric rhythm, and the ideas in the right hand like a trumpet would play.

"Even before I went to Chicago in 1931 and met him, I knew Earl Hines's work very well from recordings. But every night when I wasn't working, I would be down at the Grand Terrace listening to him. He was friendly with me, and he would let me sit in with the band while he was walking around the tables socializing with the guests. At jam sessions, after hours, I would always be looking over his shoulder. He appreciated that I was such a fan of his and was modeling my style after his. Then I wrote seven or eight arrangements for him. One of them was on *Chinatown*, and I took several choruses that Louis Armstrong had played on his record of it and orchestrated them for Earl's three trumpets. I think I did *Melancholy Baby* for him, too.

"I'd started arranging when I was in high school. I took a music major in theory while I was in college, and I did an awful lot of arranging when I was with the Speed Webb band. My brother Gus, who was fourteen months older, was doing a lot for Webb, too, and so was Vic Dickenson. We used to have Louis Armstrong and Bix Beiderbecke solos orchestrated for five brass in that band. Bix's ideas were wonderful for five-way harmony.

We also did some of Johnny Hodges's solos for the sax section. It was pretty exciting stuff for that day.

"When I came to New York, Benny Carter's was the first band I worked with, and Benny impressed me very much. You can hear that in the sax chorus on the arrangement of *Liza* I did for Willie Bryant. I did quite a bit of writing again when I had my own big band in 1939, and also when I had the small group at Café Society during World War II with Bill Coleman, Benny Morton, and Jimmy Hamilton. Later on, I had Emmett Berry and then Joe Thomas on trumpet.

"I never found arranging tedious. As a matter of fact, when I had my own big band, I'd get so wrapped up in it I'd write an arrangement and forget to put a piano solo in it. I'd write now if I had a group with horns. After the Café Society engagement, I rejoined Benny Goodman, and then I went into studio work and teaching at Juilliard, so there really wasn't much time for writing.

"Around 1957, Duke Ellington wrote *Tune Poem* for me. I don't think he ever did anything like that for anyone outside his own band before. The personnel of my group was Buck Clayton (trumpet), Sonny Pruitt (trombone—he also played good piano and tenor sax), Sam Most (clarinet, doubling on flute), Arvell Shaw (bass), Red Donovan (drums), and Joya Sherrill, who sang. We went out on a tour for Columbia Artists Management in a subscription series they called Community

Concerts. I think it was Peter Dean's idea to have a contrast after intermission with the group playing written music. Columbia paid Duke, of course, but I never knew what happened to the music after the tour."

Teddy Wilson was born in Austin, Texas, in 1912, and was six when his family moved to Tuskegee, Alabama. His father was head of the English Department and his mother chief librarian at Tuskegee Institute. He studied piano without much enthusiasm while in grade school, and then switched to violin, which he continued to play through high school, where he also took up clarinet and oboe. A young neighbor used to play popular songs on piano with "a smooth, melodic right, and full bass," and this interested Wilson enough for him to return to his original instrument when the school band required a pianist. Around this time, he began to listen to jazz carefully.

His father liked vocal music, and there were records about the house by Caruso and John McCormack as well as by blues singers like Bessie Smith and Trixie Smith. Wilson heard them, but his chief interest was already in instrumental music.

"The first records of importance to me were *Singin' the Blues* by Beiderbecke and Trumbauer, and King Oliver's *Snag It* featuring the famous Oliver break," he told Tom Scanlan in a *Down Beat* interview. "Later, with Tuskegee students, I heard *West End Blues* by the Armstrong Hot Five, with Earl Hines on piano, and Fats Waller's *Handful of Keys*. Now swing is not an objective word, but my conditioning of the swing feeling was the way Armstrong and Hines played on the Hot Five records—not the others, just Armstrong and Hines."

During his summer vacation in 1928, he went to Chicago and heard professional jazz live for the first time, as played by McKinney's Cotton Pickers and the bands of the Henderson Brothers, Fletcher and Horace. Coleman Hawkins, Buster Bailey, Jimmy Harrison and Joe Smith were with Fletcher, Benny Carter and Rex Stewart with Horace.

The Chicago experience was such that Wilson returned home determined to become a jazz musician, but his mother persuaded him to try college. He dutifully went to Talledega in Alabama for a year, and then left to begin his career as a professional player in Detroit.

He joined Speed Webb's band in 1929, at a time when it included his brother, Gus, on trombone, Roy Eldridge and Vic Dickenson. After gaining valuable experience in their company, he left in 1931 to take a job offered him by Milt Senior in a quartet in Toledo.

"Toledo was Art Tatum's hometown and he had been playing in that quartet before me," Wilson recalled, "but he got a radio show, a half-hour five days a week on WSPD, and it was a much better showcase for him than playing in a quartet with bass and guitar. He had a great gift for harmonic improvisation, and he would re-harmonize chorus after chorus on songs like *Body and Soul*, so the effect of bass and guitar was only to limit him. Neither he nor I had been to New York at this time, but we would go out together every night and make the rounds of after-hours places, playing on upright pianos until late morning and sometimes early afternoon.

"For command of the keyboard," and Wilson ran his hands left and right along an imaginary one, "I don't think Art Tatum has ever been equalled in jazz. He was a phenomenon. But strictly in terms of the jazz idiom, Earl Hines has it—the most powerful rhythmic drive, more so, I'd say, than Art or even Fats.

"Earl had this original concept of playing the piano rather like a horn, with an eccentric bass against it implying the rhythm, not playing on the beat like the stride pianists did—one, two, three, four, one, two, three, four . . . Earl would be playing between the beats with his left hand, which pianists are doing today.

"Originally, I'd been influenced by Fats Waller, and he sounded great playing by himself. But in a big band, with a rhythm section, Earl and his octave technique sounded wonderful. You could write backgrounds behind him just as you would for a trumpet or tenor sax. At that time, bands were playing in big dancehalls or clubs, not concert halls, and there was no microphone to amplify the piano, but with the octave technique he developed, Earl really stood out.

"He was a star on radio in those days, too, although he did not have such a big New York audience because of the time difference. When he was broadcasting from the Grand Terrace at midnight, it was already 1 o'clock in New York, and stations might be closing down there. But in the West and Canada he was tremendous.

"I heard him on television recently, and he was explaining how his style was influenced by piano and trumpet players in Pittsburgh before he got to Chicago. He and Louis Armstrong became friends, and I'm sure Earl influenced Louis just as Louis influenced him. They were thinking along the same lines.

Look how Billy Kyle and I stumbled on the same, identical format of playing piano, yet I grew up in Alabama and Billy grew up in Philadelphia. We never knew each other till we were both professionals.

"My style, you might say, evolved from three piano players: first, Fats and Earl on recordings, and then Tatum *live*, because Art hadn't begun to record when I came along."

After working in Chicago with Erskine Tate and François's Louisianians, Teddy Wilson went on tour in 1933 as pianist in a mediocre band led by Louis Armstrong. (A quarter of a century later, he told Tom Scanlan how beautifully Armstrong had played "with such a bad band behind him." Then he added, "I think Louis is the greatest musician that's ever been.") Returning to Chicago, he gained more

Left to right: Teddy Wilson, Eddie Heywood, Erroll Garner and
Earl Hines at the Embers, New York, 1959.

experience with Jimmie Noone, and Eddie Mallory, before playing once more at the Grand Terrace in Clarence Moore's group, which was substituting for Earl Hines who had gone out on tour with his band.

Hearing some brilliant piano in the course of a broadcast from the Grand Terrace, John Hammond called the station and found it was played by Wilson. He voiced his enthusiasm to Benny Carter, who had already heard the pianist in the Middle West. At his instigation, Carter went to Chicago and persuaded Wilson to come to New York, where Hammond immediately recorded him in both a small group and a big band under Carter's leadership. Following an engagement at the Empire Ballroom, the Carter band broke up and Wilson joined Willie Bryant's. He soon won a big reputation in New York.

The year 1935 was a vital one in his career, for after he had jammed with Benny Goodman and Gene Krupa at Mildred Bailey's house, the famous Goodman series of small-group recordings was initiated, beginning with this same trio on Victor. Thanks to John Hammond's help, Wilson also began to make an exciting series of records under his own name and as accompanist-leader for Billie Holiday. Jukeboxes were growing popular and prevalent, and Hammond was quick to realize their potential as a means to popularizing economically made jazz records. Those under Wilson's name, using six or seven musicians as a rule, featured most of the best soloists of the era, such as Roy Eldridge, Johnny Hodges, Benny Goodman, Ben Webster, Chu Berry, Frank Newton, Benny Morton, Buster Bailey, Jonah Jones, Buck Clayton, Lester Young, Henry Allen, Cootie Williams, Harry James, Lips Page, Benny Carter and Bobby Hackett, not to mention excellent musicians in the rhythm section like Cozy Cole, Sidney Catlett, Gene Krupa, Israel Crosby, John Kirby, Walter Page, Freddie Green, Milt Hinton and Jo Jones. The records were singularly consistent in their integrity and rhythmic lift, both of which obviously stemmed from Wilson himself.

On Easter Sunday, 1936, Goodman, Wilson and Krupa performed together publicly at a concert organized by Helen Oakley and sponsored by the Chicago Rhythm Club. Its success was such that Goodman decided to invite Wilson to join him on a permanent basis, with mutually beneficial results. Beyond its musical importance, the decision was of immense racial significance, and it led to much more integration in jazz. Wilson frequently rejoined Goodman in later years for jazz festivals and television appearances, and he has remained a respected and popular figure at home and abroad ever since. Unmarred by gimmicks of any kind, his neat, crisp and lucid playing has a timelessness uncommon in jazz.

In 1974, he toured Latin America with three other pianists—Marian McPartland, Ellis Larkins and Earl Hines.

"I guess I was with Earl more then than any time since I was in Chicago," he said happily. "It was a big success, and very enjoyable. They had good pianos down there, and after the concerts there were no drums or other equipment to pack and keep us hanging around. We'd each play a half-hour. Marian McPartland would open, and I'd follow. After a fifteen-minute intermission, Ellis played, and then Earl would finish it up. He'd bring all three of us out to take a bow. He's still my Number One Jazz Pianist!"

(1975)

MILT HINTON

BASS

Milt Hinton was born in Vicksburg, Mississippi, on 23 June 1910. He was an only child, a precious only child, since on his mother's side of the family there were thirteen brothers and sisters, only five of whom lived to adulthood, and none of them had children. His mother was sixteen when he was born, and his parents separated when he was three months old.

"All the efforts of our entire family were concentrated on *me*," he recalled. "My mother lived with her parents, and her brothers and sisters all contributed to my education. It was a musical family, and my mother was organist in the Ebenezer Baptist Church. There were choir rehearsals at home, and always singing. The black ministers were always telling the older people in the churches to try to get the children north to give them a better chance. As the ways of the South go, the people usually followed a river. We were on the Mississippi, so the first stop was usually Tennessee, and then into southern Illinois, and finally into Chicago.

"We migrated like this: In the year I was born, one of my mother's older brothers went to Chicago and got a job as a bellhop in a hotel. Chicago was a pretty raucous town in those days, and an efficient young man, a fellow with a fast eye, could be a bellhop and pick up quite a bit of change. My uncle got a *good* job and after a time he sent for his other brother. The two of them worked together, saved their money, and then sent for my mother and my aunt, leaving me with my grandmother and their youngest sister. This was after World War I, when the older brother had served in the Army and the younger one had been around the world in the Navy. The war had opened up employment opportunities, and when they had furnished an apartment, and got everything set up, they sent for the three of us, the last of the family.

"I have some memories of Mississippi, but not many good ones. It's surprising what stays in the mind of a child of seven or eight. When we'd get together for a family gathering, I'd sort of astound my mother. I could remember some of the streets, the first school I went to, the candy store I used to take my pennies to, and the old lady who ran it. But my schooling was more in Chicago.

"My mother bought my first violin on 18 July 1923. I was thirteen, and right across the street lived Quinn Wilson, who was about two years older, and who was to become a great bass player with the Earl Hines orchestra. He was doing very well on violin, and my mother heard him playing, so she asked him over to tune mine, gave him a quarter or something, and sent me to my first teacher. My mother had tried to teach me piano, but there always seemed to be a hassle somewhere along the line, and we would get a mother-and-son attitude going. But she was determined that I should play, which was why she bought the violin.

"Quinn and I went to the same school, and

he was a few grades ahead of me, so I set my sights on him. He was advanced enough to make the violin sound good when he came over to our place, and that made me want to strive to play better. By the time I got to the fifth or sixth grade, Quinn was graduating from eighth grade in grammar school, and for graduation exercises—I shall never forget—he played Schubert's *Serenade*. 'Gee, I must do this,' I said to myself.

"When I got to high school, Quinn was a lieutenant in the ROTC and was playing bass horn in the band. My sights were still set on him, so now I wanted to play bass horn. Major N. Clark Smith, a very fine gentleman, was musical director at Wendell Phillips High School, and quite a few famous personalities benefited from his tuition—Hayes Alvis, Lionel Hampton, and Nat Cole's brother, Eddie, who was also playing bass horn then. I wanted to get with fellows like that, so while playing violin in the school orchestra, I applied for the band and was given a tuba.

"Ed Burke, who later made his name as a trombone player, lived next door to me, and we went to the same violin teacher. The strings seemed to suit me more, but because Burke didn't make it so well with them, he switched to trombone in the school band. He stayed with that, and when Walter Barnes got the job at Al Capone's Cotton Club, he went in there with Barnes. I was still delivering 241 newspapers every morning for nine dollars a week, and Burke was making seventy a week, which is equivalent to four hundred now. In those days, people worked at the stockyards all week, eight hours a day, for twenty dollars a week, and took care of whole families with that.

"The Barnes band was the band to be in then. It wasn't special, but it was Al Capone's pet (he knew Barnes from somewhere), and the guys were making better money than Earl Hines's at the Grand Terrace, much better. Capone had opened up this tremendous club as a hangout for his boys, the whole syndicate. It was Prohibition time. They controlled all the liquor in Chicago, and they had nothing but money.

"I felt so terribly bad, up every morning at 4 o'clock with my newspapers. I thought myself as proficient as any guy in that Barnes band. I could read music, but I was still playing violin then, and violins were dead. Nobody was using them. So here would come Ed Burke, right down South Parkway, right down my route, driving his new car, just as I'm starting out with the newspapers. He'd wave at me, and stop the car to chat.

" 'Hello, Sporty,' he'd say, and that was what he always called me. 'Look, you got to get off that fiddle and get going, you know. Why don't you try trombone, Sporty?'

"He even bought a trombone and gave it to me. He didn't just lend it. Burke has always been like my own brother. He's been beautiful to me all my life. He tried to encourage me to get on something else, but I just couldn't comprehend the trombone. Finally, I got the bass violin, and then came the Eddie South period.

"In a way, it may have been unfortunate Burke got in the Barnes band. He played the trombone well when he was young, but he didn't go much farther. He didn't study music like I went on to do. He was making fabulous money, and he got married right away. But with me and some of the other boys, we began to go for the harmony and the theory. We wanted to define chords, and we wanted to write. Scoops Carry, and a bunch of guys like that, would get together. Someone would write an arrangement, and you'd be given a part, and you'd have to hum it. If you didn't read it right, you would be corrected. Then you might say, 'Okay, now you're so smart. Here's one for *you!*' And that way we all learned.

"It happened with quite a few bands that when they began to make a lot of money, especially when the guys were young, that they seemed to forget about the playing and become more concerned with the financial end of it. That is why I think we should subsidize young musicians some sort of way, so there won't be money problems, so they can dedicate themselves to the theory and techniques of the particular field they are in. I know that when I got through with my lessons at school, and some guys were out playing basketball, I'd be in the assembly hall with a little band, and we'd be trying to work out something. When I went to a dance, I didn't take a girl, because I didn't want to embarrass her. I would be standing right up front. How could I dance when Fletcher Henderson and his great musicians were playing? I can't dance to this day for that same reason. The minute I get on the floor, I'm listening to the band, and I forget what I'm doing, get out of step, and probably step on the girl's feet. When you start with this particular love for the music, it goes right through life with you.

"I studied violin for thirteen years and became pretty proficient, and I still have a great love for it. I got to play things like Mendelssohn's *Concerto in E Minor*, and I was concertmaster of the school orchestra. When I graduated, Ray Nance followed me as concertmaster. I was ahead of him just like Quinn Wilson had been ahead of me. It's a good thing when kids have someone a little older to follow and admire.

"Hayes Alvis was with Earl Hines before Quinn, and he mostly played bass horn. Earl was at the Grand Terrace at the time of the Lindbergh kidnapping, and I think that was the first time any orchestra was on nationwide network radio *all night*. They began to hook in networks to broadcast the news, and the only orchestra they had on was Earl's at the Grand Terrace. The news, of course, was of great concern to all Americans—this hero having such a terrible thing happen to his family. Yet sad as it was, the occasion was a tremendous break for Earl.

"When Quinn took Hayes Alvis's place, he doubled on bass violin and bass horn. There had already been a trend towards string bass in the '20s. Then, when Duke Ellington came through Chicago, Wellman Braud had shown his great dexterity on *Ring Dem Bells*. That tremendous two-beat he had just floored everybody, and we were all strictly sold. The horn had value before amplification, but after hearing Duke's band—which we always went back to—the rhythm section seemed to have more flow to it, even with the two-beat. Bass horn and banjo together were a little rigid and stiff. When Freddy Guy played guitar and Braud the string bass, Duke's rhythm section sounded so wonderful and fluid.

"With a good bass violin, the further you got away from it the better it was to hear it, even at the back of the hall. The first thing you heard when you hit the dancehall was the boom of the bass violin and the boom of the bass drum. I believe the bass sound carried

At Duke Ellington's seventieth birthday party in the White House: Earl Hines, Milt Hinton, Louis Bellson.

more then that it does now, for the simple
reason that we played two beats (to the bar),
which gave the strings more time to vibrate,
and you could hear the two different pitches.
Boom, boom, boom . . . the sound still rings
in my ears, this wonderful sound in the Savoy
Ballroom in Chicago, where I'd go to hear the
Ellington and Henderson bands.

"Fletcher kept John Kirby playing tuba for
quite a long time. He moved faster and got a
lighter sound on it, but even when he
switched to bass violin he kept a sort of influence from the tuba. He stayed with the two
beats a great deal, and he also stayed with the
one note, which is a very particular thing. If a
man plays one note, an F, and he plays four
beats of F, then you really hear this thing—
boom, boom, boom, boom. Whereas what we
do today—we walk. The bass being a low instrument, when you walk and play tone after
tone, they have a tendency to run into each
other. Unless you're close, or there's a mike,
you can't hear the separation of the notes.

"The way John Kirby stayed with the one
note gave you the definite identification of this
one note for the entire measure. It's just one
of the good things I remember about him, and
Charlie Shavers still likes that sort of playing
behind him. Being a bass player, I study each
musician I'm going to be associated with for
the night. You'd be surprised to see the happi-
ness, to see how a player's face lights up,
when you give him what he likes without his
having to ask for it. I can see Charlie Shavers
just *take off* when I give him that John Kirby
kind of thing, because he was associated with
it when he was happiest playing. Well, sure,
it's like your wife, who knows what type of
food you like. When she wants to please you,
she'll have it for dinner, and you'll be very
content. That's how it was with bands. We
were sort of married to each other in the organization, and during a period of search, trial
and error, playing and blowing together every
night, you struck up on a kind of happy me-
dium. There are great professionals today who
can do very well, but if they had a chance to
play together and really get to know each
other, it would sound *so* much better.

"It happens sometimes in the recording
business now. The producer may say, 'Gee,
these guys play well together!' And it's because we work together often, the same
rhythm section, the same drummer, the same
pianist, the same bass player, maybe two or
three dates a day. We fit each other and we
can do a little more this way, but we may not
know the particular styles and tastes of the
horns, and we're searching and groping, and
by the time we really find out, the session is
over!"

"I took up the bass violin in high school, and I
also played in the band Major Smith had
organized for the newspaper, the Chicago *Defender*. We used to play at festivals, picnics
and things like that for the newspaper. But I
was sort of handicapped in Chicago, because
there was really only one big band there, and
that was Earl Hines's, and his bass player was
Quinn Wilson. In my estimation, he played
much better. He was further advanced, a tremendous musician, a great writer, a good
arranger, and a pretty good pianist. There was
nothing much for me to do except little jobs in
out-of-the-way spots, and weekend and club
dates.

"Every summer, Earl Hines would break
up his band and the Grand Terrace would
close. There were clubs and roadhouses on
the outskirts of the city, and Darnell Howard,
the clarinet player, would take a segment of
the band and play at one of them, while
Walter Fuller might take another segment and
play in another. Then they would need two
bass players, so come the summer I had a job!
I think the first one I worked with was Darnell
Howard.

"Then Eddie South came back from
Europe, and at first he was going to organize a
big band. While I was still going to high
school, I used to deliver newspapers to his
mother, and when I went to collect for them
I'd see his pictures in her apartment. She told
me her son was a great violinist. By the time
he got back, I was known around Chicago as a
pretty decent young bass player, coming
along, and when Eddie asked Bob Schoffner

(trumpet) and John Thomas (trombone) about a bass player, they recommended me. His mother was quite happy to see her old newspaper boy playing with her son!

"The band rehearsed—fifteen pieces—and it was very good, but it seemed as though the time wasn't right for a big band with a Negro violinist standing in front playing ballads and pretty music like *Dancing on the Ceiling*. He was going to have it very sweet, and we rehearsed for many weeks upstairs right next to the Regal Theatre, and the band came around in beautiful shape with a wonderful sound, but for some reason the agency couldn't or didn't get bookings for it. Instead, they decided to put him into a small club, the Club Rubaiyat, on the North Side. It was very exclusive and seated only about sixty-five people. He had the group he brought back from Europe with him: Anthony Spaulding on piano; a guitarist; and Clifford King, a very cultured clarinet player, who was known as 'Clarinet' King. They decided to add a bass, and since I had been at the rehearsals, I got the job.

"We were together a year or so, and it was a very good thing for me. They were first-class musicians and Eddie was tremendously helpful to me, and to my dying day I can never thank him enough. I absorbed all the bowing, and he used to take piano copies of things like *Rhapsody in Blue* and *American in Paris*, and we'd play them, just our five pieces. I had to search out my part and memorize it.

"When Franklin Delano Roosevelt was nominated for the presidency the first time in 1932, we were playing at the Congress Hotel in Chicago, and that was where the nomination and convention took place. As an act, and billed as *Eddie South, the Dark Angel of the Violin*, we played the Keith and RKO circuits. We made tours of small towns, like all through Ohio, playing a few days here, a few days there. We went as far as Los Angeles and played the Ballyhoo Club. But Eddie didn't seem to have a lot of luck. This country wasn't prepared to accept his kind of continental, salon music then, although I think his was the first small group to play these plush hotel rooms in cities like Chicago and New York.

John Kirby's group had class and precision and musicianship, but Eddie's was before his, and it was even more delicate. When he augmented, he augmented with two or three violins, and there were plenty of people then as now who didn't like loud music. He could play jazz, but his whole being was artistic, and he didn't play the strictly hard swing like Stuff Smith.

"After two or three years, vaudeville fell off and theatres began to fade out, and that was Eddie's last stand so far as regular work was concerned. I still think there should be a place for a tremendous musician like him. It was one of the great regrets of my life not to see him have his just deserts.*

"During one of the periods we were laying off, Louis Armstrong left Chicago on his first big tour. He had been working at a place called the Show Boat and, because they wanted to follow him with another great trumpet player, they brought in Jabbo Smith from Milwaukee, and asked him to get a band. I remember he had Floyd Campbell, Jerome Pasquall, Cassino Simpson and Ted Tinsley (guitar). Jabbo did a tremendous job, but he was a handsome boy, quite a guy with the girls, and you could never get him there on time. I knew where he lived, and it was my duty, as a young member of the band, to call him, and go by, and try to get him to work. We hit at 10 o'clock, but he'd come in about 12 every night. And this was for Sam Beer, who was a partner in this Show Boat, and also one of the last owners of the Three Deuces.

"The last time I saw Jabbo was around 1951, when I was with Cab Calloway and we were playing a theatre in Newark. He showed up backstage, looking wonderful, and said he was living there. I don't understand why people haven't made more records of him, because he's the most fantastic man I've known in all my life—but quite unreliable. I've known many trumpet players, but I don't know of one I enjoyed listening to like I did him at the Show Boat. He had a mute that looked exactly like a doorknob—no bigger than that—and

---

* Eddie South died in 1962.

you couldn't see it when he put in the trumpet. He could play so very soft, but he was also the first I heard to play fast, fluid trumpet, like the kind Roy Eldridge started even before Dizzy Gillespie. Jabbo didn't make a feature of high notes, but he played high, and he had full mastery of his horn from top to bottom.

"At one time he played like Louis (Armstrong), because that was the style *everybody* copied, but then he branched out. So far as being accepted and everything, I think he reached his peak in Milwaukee. It was his town, the girls would fight for him there, and he was very happy. Chicago was all Louis Armstrong, but Milwaukee couldn't afford Louis.

"Jabbo was quite an egotist. I remember several occasions when he came into the Savoy when Louis was there, and he's say something like, 'Let me play something with you. I'll blow you down!' Of course, that was a joke in Chicago. You couldn't blow Louis down. But Jabbo was capable, and he tried several times, and they were always memorable to have been around and heard. To such an extent that when Louis left, they got him the job. And he goofed it, blew it! The club-owners and the patrons liked the band, be-cause it was good, but he didn't show up. He knew he could always go back to Milwaukee, so he floated back there. I truthfully can't ever remember seeing him drunk, and I never heard anything about narcotics in connection with him, but I do remember the women. He used to be with all kinds of beautiful girls.

"The next season, the manager called the same band back, but they gave it to Cass Simpson, who was a fabulous pianist. There were two trumpets, and one was Tick Grey, who had been with Louis; Ed Burke played trombone; and Scoville Brown played sax-ophone. We finally made the Regal, which was like playing the Palace Theatre in New York.

"After this band broke up, and Eddie South's touring days came to an end, I went into the Three Deuces with Zutty Singleton on drums, Cozy Cole's brother on piano, and Everett Barksdale on guitar. We played the jazz scene, but Art Tatum was the thing, playing 'intermissions' all alone. We were there a whole season, maybe six months, and it was at the Deuces I got with Cab Calloway."

(1961)

Cassino Simpson's band, winter of 1931–32. Left to right: (back) Ted Tinsley, Tick Grey, Richard Barnett, Milt Hinton; (front) John Thomas, Ed Burke, Claude Alexander, Guy Kelly, Franz Jackson, Cassino Simpson, Fred Brown, Scoville Brown.

FREDDY AND IRVING GOODMAN

TRUMPETS

Freddy Goodman:

"After visiting with one of his friends, my father was walking one day down a street on the West Side of Chicago. As he passed a synagogue, he heard music being played, so he went in and enquired if some of his family could learn to play there. He was told he should bring his sons over and they could furnish some instruments. Depending on our size, they would see what instruments were available. Harry, Benny and I were about seven, eight and nine years old then. The synagogue was called the Kehelah Jacob, and there Benny was given a clarinet. I wonder what it would have been like if he had been given a trumpet or violin? Harry was given a trombone, and when I joined, several weeks afterwards, I was handed an alto horn. Later on, I got a trumpet.

"This is how it all started. We didn't receive any instruction. We just played as best we could. Eventually we discovered it was possible to be tutored privately, and Benny went to the house of the old gentleman who ran the band, and there he received lessons. It was good of my father. With my mother, there were thirteen of us in the family that he had to provide for, so there was need for every cent he could earn. But he had vision, and really he was the foundation of it all. I regret he never lived to know it.

"It was perhaps a year or two later that a friend of ours spoke to us about Hull House. It was several miles away from our home, in a deprived neighborhood, and it was kept going, I think, by some sort of foundation, to help keep kids off the street and give them some sort of recreation. Miss Jane Addams was the principal, and as a result of a gift that had been made to her, Hull House was able to sponsor a band, the grant covering the cost of some seventy or eighty instruments, and uniforms. It was great for us, and we started going there a lot. We would make it on the streetcar, and at times we even walked.

"We were that young that we didn't know any of the other Chicago musicians. We weren't even aware of the fellows at Austin High, or the others. Nothing really happened until Benny played his first job. The old gentleman at the synagogue, whose name was Boguslawski, had a son called Ziggy, who was director at one of the big outlying theatres. People were just beginning to suspect that jazz might catch the public's fancy, and it occurred to the Boguslawskis that it might be a great idea to bring Benny down to the theatre to play. Late one afternoon, I saw the old man coming down our street, searching all around.

" 'Where's Benny?' he asked when he saw me.

" 'Practicing,' I told him, 'but I can get him.'

" 'I want him to come and play at the theatre tonight,' he said, 'the Central Park Theatre.'

"Benny rushed and cleaned up, and started off for the gig, still in knee pants. He was twelve, I guess, but not nervous. Benny was never nervous, really. And right then he was very pleased to be called on. Because he was so young, they didn't put him up on the stage. He played from where the leader of the pit band stood, from a sort of podium. The hit tune of the day was *When My Baby Smiles at Me,* the Ted Lewis thing, and Benny played it up—and broke it up, needless to say. Of course, we sat on through the movie, waiting for the second show. Several times Benny fell asleep, and when I woke him he would say, 'How's the story going?'

"At Hull House we weren't playing jazz. Most of the music was marches, small overtures, primer-type things. We were really only studying then, and most of the time we'd be rehearsing on the back porch. The way we first heard jazz was when we'd be passing a ballroom, coming home from seeing a movie maybe. We'd hear music. It would be real exciting, and we'd sneak in. I'll never forget the thrill I got listening to a trumpet player who used a wah-wah mute. One time Benny just jumped up onstage, grabbed the guy's clarinet, and started to play. He was a natural, that's all. He could do whatever he pleased, whatever he felt like playing, even then. He would just get aroused within.

"It must have been then that Murph Podalsky heard him. Murph fronted a small band and got quite a lot of work in those days. Benny could be hired because different musicians had already told him he ought to join the union. It wasn't associated with the A.F. of M. then, and it was hardly a real union, but more like a club. Anyway, Murph had a job four nights a week at a dancehall in Waukegan, about thirty-five miles outside Chicago, and he told Benny he wanted him. So Benny started making those gigs while he was still attending school. He began contributing to the family then, and I guess he's been doing it ever since.

"When he realized how much upright bass was in demand, Harry switched over from tuba, and about the same time he joined the club, the 'union' Benny was in. Then he played along with Murph as well, whenever Jim Lannigan, a great bass player, wasn't on

the job. It was about that time, too, we began meeting the rest of the guys like Bud Freeman, Jimmy McPartland, Davey Tough, Frank Teschmaker, and the others. Gene Krupa and I played our first job together out in Homewood, Illinois, although Gene had come on the scene a bit later, from Chicago's South Side. Jess Stacy was later still. He came into town from Ohio with Joe Kayser's band. Musicians like Eddie Condon, George Wettling and Floyd O'Brien were a real little community, knowledgeable right from the start, and kind of tough.

"Benny started going to an old German teacher named Franz Schoepp, who had taught at the Chicago Musical College. He was strict and Benny always gave him a lot of credit. Another thing he liked was that he had no racial prejudice at all. In fact, both Buster Bailey and Jimmy Noone, two of the best black clarinet players, studied with him. At one time Buster and Benny went for their lessons the same day, and Schoepp used to have them play duets together.

"Next, as I remember, Benny worked for Jule Stein, who had a band called the Blue Jackets. This was the M.C.A. man, not the songwriter. By then, we were hearing a lot about Ben Pollack, who played great drums. He was one of the first real, fine leaders, guys who could get around on their instruments. He was doing well out on the Coast when Gil Rodin came to Chicago and invited Benny to join the band. They played at a location in Venice, about a half-hour's ride out of Los Angeles, and the band included Fud Livingston and Glenn Miller. Benny was sixteen. They did so well that when they came back to Chicago in 1926 they expected another good reception, but somehow they couldn't do a darn thing. They couldn't even get a job!

"This was about the time when Louis Armstrong and Earl Hines had joined up and were playing together at the Sunset Café. Ben Pollack's band talked themselves into a stay at the Southmoor Hotel, and this is when all the musicians I've been talking of would make it down to the South Side several nights a week just to hear Louis and Earl. It was a ritual that every Friday night after work we'd all pile into the Sunset.

"Jimmy Noone was playing nearby, too, at a place called the Nest. And Johnny Dodds was another clarinet player Benny really appreciated. Baby Dodds, Johnny's brother, played fine drums, and he was George Wettling's inspiration. Davey Tough was crazy about him, too. Another place we'd go was Friars' Inn, where a great New Orleans trumpet player named Paul Mares had the band. He had Leon Roppolo on clarinet, and he was a guy you never wanted to forget. He set a pattern for everybody, and later on Fazola got that same sound. George Brunis was the trombone player, and this was the first white band to hit Chicago that I can recollect that came up with the New Orleans feel. Of course, in those days, the jazz groups didn't make a big hit. It was more a matter of musicians getting around to hear each other.

"The Eddie Condon record dates that came a bit later proved a big excitement around Chicago. I remember titles like *I Found a New Baby* and *There'll Be Some Changes Made*, which were among the first. Jimmy McPartland was on some of those sides, but another trumpet player who was really terrific, and who I think would have been very well thought of even today, was Muggsy Spanier. He influenced a lot of players, and in turn got his influence from Joe Oliver and Louis. He played with a kind of natural feeling, and he had a beautiful tone. I don't believe there was any other trumpet player to use a growl mute like he did. Bunny Berigan was the only other white guy with that kind of feeling.

"After they made their records, Condon and those guys were able to make it to the East, where they began to pick up occasional gigs. Joe Sullivan eventually got a job playing piano as a single at the Onyx Club on 52nd Street, and a lot of musicians used to congregate there for something to eat and drink, and maybe to sit in.

"When Ben Pollack took a vacation, and Harry and Benny came home for a visit, I was still gigging around town, but I'd begun to

have trouble with my lip. Since I was laying off, I went with them when they returned to New York. Our talk began to centre around Benny organizing a band for himself. He began to think seriously about it and, leaving Pollack, he started in doing radio work and building up his contacts. Things finally happened with Billy Rose opened up his supper club in 1934. Having dinner and seeing a show, all for $2.50, was a novel idea in those days. Benny decided to get a band together and audition for Rose. He was hired, and the job lasted several months. It helped get him started, and it gave him inspiration to hang on until he got that break with the National Biscuit Company's radio program.

"Outside of Harry on bass, and later my brother Irving on trumpet, the only Chicago musicians that Benny used in the band were Gene Krupa on drums and Jess Stacy on piano. But Benny's roots were in Chicago, and that was the musical background out of which he developed his style, and over the years he has never departed very far from that idiom. He may have embellished it, but so far as jazz was concerned, his language was the kind defined by Louis Armstrong, Earl Hines and Jimmy Noone."

Irving Goodman:

"In 1931, my brother Benny moved the family to New York. If my father had not died, I suppose we would have stayed in Chicago. Now we lived in Manhattan for a short period, and then we moved to Jackson Heights on Long Island. Benny automatically became head of the family when it came to making decisions, and he needed us near at hand, my mother and my younger brothers, Eugene and Jeremy. Besides Harry and Freddy, I was the only other one to take up music, and once we came east I started studying trumpet. Some fine musicians lived near us, and they were an inspiration. Bunny Berigan was not far away, and Glenn Miller lived right up the street. We used to see Adrian Rollini, too. He had a nephew who played drums and lived nearby, and Adrian would sometimes come out and play locally with him. He ran a small place of his own in New York which he called Adrian's Tap Room, and I got my first break when he hired me to come in and play occasionally.

"My whole life was the horn, and I used to practice every minute. After a while I was playing enough so that I could join Charlie Barnet's band, where I stayed about a year and a half. But the highlight for me of those days was the time I spent in Bunny Berigan's band (1935–38). Like everyone else, I was crazy about Bunny. He was with Benny only a short period, but whenever he was present it was another story. There haven't been that many guys could electrify Benny, but Bunny was certainly one of them. As a leader, he was great to work for. The whole band would do anything he wanted. It was like a real, happy family. His attitude was so great, too. Like when we played the boondocks, when it didn't really count, Bunny never let up. He always gave it everything he'd got. Another thing, he never acted like he was anything special. Maybe he didn't think he was. Music occupied his mind a lot, and he seemed to be able to inspire everybody to play a bit better than they ordinarily could. The way he beat off a tempo, and the sound he produced, got under our skins. It was so much fun, some of us were pretty near willing to work for nothing. And sometimes it nearly came to that! Bunny was never the businessman you needed to be then to head a band. But for a while we worked at the Pennsylvania Hotel in New York. I think Benny had put in a good word for us. We did a lot of guest appearances on the RCA show, too, but we had our share of lay-offs as well.

"Before he had the big band, Bunny had fronted a small group at the Famous Door on 52nd Street. Joey Bushkin was playing piano, and there was a tenor player named Forrest Crawford. They sounded great and the place was crowded every night with musicians who had come just to hear Bunny. Before that, he'd worked on staff at CBS, and every week he'd been featured on the Saturday Night Swing Show. Sometimes, of course, he was high, and what he would play was incredible. He made *I Can't Get Started* his theme, and that number could never belong to anyone else ever again.

"Later, I played with Benny's band, and with a lot of other bands, in the East and on the Coast, but those years with Berigan were the most enjoyable of my life. Besides being a nice person, sweet and lovable, Bunny was a musical giant."

(1973)

Irving Goodman.

JIMMY MUNDY

ARRANGER AND TENOR SAXOPHONE

"My father was a very fine baritone singer, and he used to play mandolin and bass violin in a trio. I *know* that's where I got my talent from. I was born in Cincinnati, and I studied violin for fifteen years, so you might say I was quite a well-schooled musician. I was in with the classics very seriously, and I gave several concerts, but how I got my real start was a funny thing. I used to play violin with a radical evangelist named Gene Wilson Becton. He was the first of his kind, I think, to carry an orchestra around, and we jazzed up the hymns. That was the attraction, and it brought out the young people to the churches. Eventually he fired me because he caught me making love to some broad, and I guess he thought that clashed with the religious activity. I could have apologized and gone back, but they say love makes the world go round, and I think I'd had it anyhow, so I didn't bother. Furthermore, I'd become rather attached to a young lady in Washington, so I stayed there. Becton later became a little too powerful, something like an early Martin Luther King, and eventually the gangsters did him in.

"Before he fired me, I had taken up the tenor saxophone. It was tenor with me right from the beginning. I never did play alto, although clarinet and soprano were my doubles. I dropped violin altogether, and I had a $1500 Boulanger, which was a very fine instrument. It wound up in the hock shop, and I never did retrieve it.

"I joined the White Brothers band in Washington, playing saxophone. Eddie White was on piano, Harry 'Father' White on trombone, and 'Sparks' White played alto, tenor and baritone saxes. That was a gifted family. Gene Price was on trumpet. There was a lot of talent in Washington. I remember another trumpet player we called 'Georgetown,' because he lived in Georgetown. His real name was Dan Brazier, or something like that. When Roy Eldridge came to Washington the first time, he was already a very exciting trumpet player, but Georgetown went home, got his trumpet, and ran Roy right out of the Crystal Caverns. I don't know what happened to him later, but I don't think he ever left Washington.

"When I joined the White Brothers, they were just amazed and appalled that I could go through their book the first night and read everything they had there. It was no big deal for me, because I was used to it, but at that time there were a lot of musicians who were as blind as bats, couldn't see, couldn't read. Later on, Tommy Myles, the drummer, took over the band, and it was while I was with him at the Crystal Caverns in Washington that Earl Hines came through. Earl heard a thing called *Cavernism* that I had written, and he flipped over it. He asked me to join his outfit, which I was very happy to do. That was my ticket to Chicago at the beginning of 1933.

"Contrary to some reports, the only band I worked with in Chicago was Earl's. Apart from the White Brothers' band and Tommy

Myles's, I also worked briefly with Duke Eglin in Washington. Trummy Young was in the Myles band, and I kept telling Earl about him till Trummy joined us later in 1933. I know Earl and Trummy often laugh and talk about how Helen Oakley used to pan the band a year or so later, but let's face it, the band was pretty bad for a time, and we *were* often out of tune.

"I didn't replace anyone in Earl's band. I was an addition, a fourth sax. The section was Omer Simeon, Darnell Howard, Cecil Irwin and myself. If I say it myself, I was a good, damn tenor player. I'll tell you what: anything I do, I do good. Well, if I can't do it good, I let it alone! I didn't play violin in the band because Darnell was already there, and he was a very, *very* good violin player. His musicianship was excellent and he was innovative at all times. The only thing was, he would sometimes get a little flat, and we used to give him hell about that. On sax, he wasn't on a par with Omer Simeon, who played lead alto. Omer was so wonderful. I used to compare him with Willie Smith of Lunceford's band. They had a lot in common, in their delivery and attack. It was beautiful how they played, and I idolized both of them. Omer never got the credit he deserved, and that goes to show you can't believe everything you read.

"We were always four saxophones while I was there. Later, when they hired a regular baritone player, every band had to have five. It was the same when they moved up to three trombones from two, and *everybody* had to have three. That was when I wrote *Fat Babes* to show off our three trombones, and when we went to record it it took almost the whole session to get it down.

"I don't think I did the arrangement on *Maple Leaf Rag*. I think Quinn Wilson— 'Kewpie Doll' as we used to call him—wrote that. He was the bass player and the first guy I ever met who had perfect and absolute pitch. You knock on the wall and he'd tell you what note it was. You ask him what voice you were speaking in, and he'd tell you. You go hit the piano to check it, and he was right. He never missed. He was unbelievable.

"It was while Reggie Foresythe was working with Earl that they got the Bechstein at the Grand Terrace. Reggie ordered it, and at that time I think it cost around $3500. Ed Fox went right up the wall! He called Reggie and everybody rotten so-and-sos—not a four-letter word, longer than that! Reggie had been there and gone before I arrived, but I heard about him and his very British style. That *Deep Forest* he wrote was a great theme song. He was quite an advanced musician, and he also did sophisticated numbers like *Serenade to a Wealthy Widow* and *Dodging a Divorcée*.

"The extraordinary thing about that Bechstein was how Earl would break strings in it. He had so much power in his left hand, and I'm sure he still has it. He could just flip with that left hand and a string would go. But sometimes, after work, Trummy and I would hammer it with our fists—wham!—trying to break a string, and we couldn't!

"How did I get into arranging? I started writing in Cincinnati and continued with Eddie White and Tommy Myles. I just picked it up, but I picked up fast. *Cavernism* was my first successful composition. Earl was really reluctant to let me go in 1936, and he pouted a little bit. Ed Fox called me a rotten so-and-so. Oh, yes, he was always the villain of the piece! He even used to call his wife and his sons rotten so-and-sos, too. That became a running gag around the Grand Terrace. Fox managed the club, but I think there was a close tie with gangsters. Whenever Capone or any of the boys came by, they got anything they wanted, and they took charge. Fox would be yassuhing and tomming all over the place. Some nights they closed up the club and nobody would come in but the Capone party. The whole show would go on just to entertain them. Ralph Capone did whatever had to be done, and Fusco was another of the lieutenants who belonged to the Family. Pretty Boy Floyd and John Dillinger used to frequent the Grand Terrace, too.

"When we were playing one night, Dillinger was dancing with some girl he had, and he accidentally stepped on another guy's foot. The guy got mad and wanted to fight him,

Earl Hines and his orchestra, 1935. Left to right: Louis Taylor, Lawrence Dixon, Walter Fuller, Warren Jefferson, Earl Hines, Trummy Young, Kenneth Stewart, Wallace Bishop, Jimmy Mundy, Budd Johnson, George Dixon, Quinn Wilson, Darnell Howard, Omer Simeon.

until somebody said to him, 'Man, don't you know that's John Dillinger?' You know, the guy fainted, right there on the floor!

"Cecil Irwin and I used to orchestrate the whole show for the band. Cecil was a great talent, a great writer. They'd call in Andy Razaf and Paul Denniker to do the composing and lyrics, and Leonard Harper was the choreographer. It was good experience, because we'd have to catch dance steps in the chorus routines, first this step, then that step. We had tip-top shows at the Grand Terrace at 39th and South Parkway. No money was spared on material and performances there. It was a beautiful place, lavishly furnished. The bandstand was quite elaborate, and the room was tiered, because I think it had been an old theatre.

"A lot of funny things happened on the road when I was with Earl, but he was not so flamboyant as Lucky Millinder, whom I was with later. Everything was more cut and dried with Earl, and I don't remember we ever ran out of

money. But I do remember when we were run out of Fort Lauderdale, Florida. The man didn't want to pay us, and he didn't. He told us to get the hell out of town, and we got the hell out of town! That was 'way back, when I first joined Earl, and lots of strange things happened when we went down south.

"Around '50 or '51, I was doing some writing for Lucky Millinder, and we were traveling. Lucky wasn't doing too well then. We had got to Cincinnati and were supposed to play Covington that night. We got to the bridge, and between nineteen guys we couldn't scrape up a dollar to get us and the bus across the Ohio into Kentucky. Lucky conned the toll collector into letting us over, and told him to come to the dance, enjoy himself, do whatever he wanted, and collect the dollar there. The guy finally relented, and he came to the dance, too. Knowing Lucky, I'd say he gave him five dollars, not just one.

"There was never a dull moment with Lucky. He was a great showman, but he couldn't read music, not one note. Yet you couldn't fool him—not about anything. He was a smart man and he had a terrific memory. If he heard anything one time, he'd got it and gone.

"When I left Earl to go with Benny Goodman in 1936, it was on an exclusive basis. Benny and I didn't get along too well, so I was always quitting, but then he would sweeten the pot. This went on quite a while, until 1939, when I had my own band for a time. I can't begin to remember who I arranged for in those days. You name 'em, I've done it. Besides Earl and Benny, there were Basie, Harry James, Gene Krupa, Tommy Dorsey, and even Vaughan Monroe, not to mention a whole lot of acts. I guess the biggest number, at least in terms of royalties, was *Swingtime in the Rockies*. I still get royalties from that, as well as from numbers I can't even remember. When I look at a list of those I did for Benny, I can't even remember some of the titles, but they keep on re-issuing records of them somewhere in the world.*

"I went out to California in 1941 and worked for Paul Whiteman till '43. He was doing the Gracie Allen show and other radio work, so I wrote for those shows as well as for the dance band he had then. It was playing at an old hotel in downtown San Francisco. I forget the name of the joint. I re-did part of *Rhapsody in Blue* for him—you know, modernized it—and Ferdie Grofé thanked me. In the interim, I had been going from one studio to another, and I think my movie work started off with Columbia and Rita Hayworth.

"When I got out there in California and they yelled for me to start doing some pictures, I didn't feel I was quite up to it. I did 'em anyhow, but I began studying with Dr. Ernst Toch at the University of Southern California. I lacked confidence in my own ability, and I wanted to improve my knowledge. I

needed to, and I've profited by the studying I did. I stayed out there till '48, when the musicals tailed off, and then I returned to New York and free-lanced. In fact, I've free-lanced most of my life. Morris Soloff wanted me to sign up with Columbia, but at the time I was making so much bread. Afterwards, I regretted not taking up his offer. It's the one regret of my life. The work was creative and innovative, and I'd be writing for anywhere from seven to forty pieces, according to the mood required by the film. The money was beautiful, too.

"Yes, I jumped past '43–45. I try to forget those years. I was in the Army.

"The last picture I did was in Europe with Charles Laughton, Franchot Tone and Burgess Meredith, and it received an Academy award.† I had one show on Broadway, where I did the compositions and orchestrations. That was *The Vamp*, with Carol Channing, in 1955. We got about fifty performances, and then it closed. The book was weak, but I got some good write-ups. Everybody's writing bold and brassy now, and that's what I was doing back in 1955. It was the same when Duke Ellington wrote the music for *Anatomy of a Murder*. That was criticized. He didn't disguise what it was by one iota, but they don't really like you to write jazz out there in Hollywood. I understand that when Quincy Jones went out there, they told him, 'We don't want any Basie stuff.' And he told them, 'Man, I gotta level with you; you won't get any Basie stuff!' Consequently, they didn't. They didn't know Quincy's ability, rated it cheap, but they found out fast.

"Anytime you're making arrangements for Basie, he'll say, 'Write me some blues.' So you just keep writing the blues over and over, the same twelve-bar phrase, as differently as you can. Jazz is based on blues, and the blues never left. They may have subsided, but they were always there. Anytime they seem dormant, they're just waiting to come back into their own.

"I don't use a piano when I write. It's not

---

* According to that definitive work, *B.G. on the Record* by D. Russell Connor and Warren W. Hicks (Arlington House), Goodman *recorded* over forty of Mundy's arrangements, among them *Madhouse*, *House Hop*, *Swingtime in the Rockies*, *Sing, Sing, Sing*, *Jam Session*, *Solo Flight* and *Fiesta in Blue*.

---

† *The Man on the Eiffel Tower.*

necessary. It would tie me down, because I'd start fooling around, playing something, and forget about writing. My wife used to think I was out of my mind the way I'd wake up whistling in the middle of the night, and then start writing. As you probably know, musicians are among the biggest thieves in the world. That includes arrangers. Anything I heard and liked, I'd use . . . a solo, an ensemble riff, or anything . . . I still do."

(1975)

Jimmy Mundy in 1958 with Jimmy Rushing (seated), and Nat
Pierce and Coleman Hawkins in background.

BUDD JOHNSON

SAXOPHONES, CLARINET AND ARRANGER

"My father played organ and trumpet, and conducted the choir at the New Hope Baptist Church in Dallas. He aspired to be a great musician, and he was really good. He could triple tongue with the trumpet, double tongue, and everything. Back when he was a boy, the Al G. Fields Circus offered him a job at twelve dollars a week, and that was a lot of money then. But his mother said, 'Oh, no! You're going to stay here and help me with the work, so I'll know where you are. You can help me pay these bills, too!'

"She was a very religious woman, so with his talents he naturally wound up in the church. He was great there, and he would preach sometimes. He also had a good job with the Studebaker firm in Dallas, Texas. He was self-educated—he didn't get any higher than the fifth grade—yet he was the first mechanic at the plant. When we went to automobile shows at state fairs, he would be in charge for Studebaker. He had worked for them before automobiles, when they were making wagons, the best wagons and buggies in the country. When he took a vacation, he'd get horses and one of the prettiest wagons, and we'd drive to the country to hunt and fish. I can remember him driving an electric car, too. He was so valuable to them that they didn't fire him during the Depression, when a lot of blacks lost their jobs. In fact, I can remember when he himself hired and fired. The automobiles used to come in by freight car, and he'd hire my brother and me, and other

people, and we'd go in there with hammer and chisel, and lay down on our bellies, and knock the supports away, and angle the autos out of the box cars, and take them to the plant, where he'd see they were ready. Sometimes, when there'd be an order for three or four cars to go to a little town, he'd get me to drive one. I was very young, but there was no law against it, and I made $1.25 an hour. He worked for them so long that, when they merged with Packard, they gave him a gold medal, like a badge, that entitled him to a job with Studebaker anywhere in the world, wherever they had a plant, and wherever he wanted to go.

"My father's name was Albert, and his father was named Albert, and I'm actually the third. My son is the fourth. My brother Keg and I used to joke about it. He'd say, 'Well, I'm the oldest son. Why aren't I Albert, Jr.?' But my father named him Frederick after a good friend of his, a German. I never knew too much about the family on my father's side, but I know his mother came from the West Indies, and he had two half brothers, and a half sister. I saw her only once, when my father passed away. He was about sixty-five, just eligible for Social Security, I remember.

"My mother's mother was stone African. She came from one of the plantations, and had seventeen children by the plantation owner's son, who was white. So I've got all shades of color! My mother was born in Tyler, Texas, and she had some first cousins—well, they were white really. She was always their favorite, and they loved her, and we used to go visit them. They had ranches of one thousand, two thousand, and five thousand acres, all around a little oil town. When I went down to my father's funeral, they had the body at our house, like a wake, and I went to my mother and said, 'Hey, Mother, what are all these white people doing here?' She told me they were my cousins. Some were blond, with blue eyes and everything. They're pretty well off, and most of them live in Los Angeles now.

"Yeah, that's something! And I don't remember having any trouble when I was a kid coming up in the South. My mother used to work for millionaire people, judges, and so on, and I used to go out there. You might say I was raised with the son and the daughter. I ate and played with them up to a certain age, and they never made me feel anything. If we did something wrong, their father would spank *all* of us. He was president of a bank in Dallas.

"I used to see my father's horn lying around the house, and I would pick it up and fool around with it. He paid for me to have piano lessons when I was eight years old, but I had found my own way of picking out songs on the trumpet. I would find the notes and write down the numbers of the valves, and whether they were open or I should push them down. One note might be the second and third valves, the next the first and second, or open. I couldn't read music, but I had an ear, and if I knew how the tune went, all I had to do was follow my code, and I could sort of play it.

"My brother Keg studied trombone at the time I was getting piano lessons, and my father taught him all about the embouchure and everything. To my memory, there were only about three teachers in town capable of really teaching music. I went to a man called Mr. Walton. There was also a Madame Pratt who taught piano. Her husband, Professor Pratt, was a teacher in the public school system. Their son played bass, but he went off to Omaha, Nebraska. Then there was an old New Orleans guy, a friend of my father's, Vernie Johnson, who played trombone. My father

sent my brother to him, down to Deep Elm, or Deep Ellum, as we called it. It was really Elm Street, but when it got close to the ghetto, they called it Deep Elm. That was where I first met Buster Smith, at Son Lewis's place.

"There were always a lot of us kids too young to go to dances when bands came to town, but they played matinées sometimes, and we'd slip around and stand outside and listen. We'd listen to records, too. Before we got instruments, I used to beat the devil out of my mother's washtubs and dishpans. We were like a glorified Tramp Band, but finally my mother got me a set of drums. I used to play for the kids to march in and out at recess in elementary school.

"I had put down the piano, because everybody told me, 'Man, you keep on playing that piano, you're gonna be a sissy!' It seemed all the piano players were gay, and I didn't want to be that, you know. But that was one of the saddest things in the world that ever happened to me, because I could have had a beautiful knowledge of piano. I was playing sheet music, and I knew the keyboard, but I cannot execute today. I can go to the piano and hit any chord you want me to hit, but I can't *play*.

"After Mother got me the drums, another boy got a banjo. My brother had an old trombone, and we had little pieces of old instruments for another friend. We started to practice and eventually we became the school band. There was no music director there at that time, but we began to get popular and play parties. We weren't getting any money, but we just loved what we were doing. Then there was a woman named Tillie Puckett, and she was slick. She had a little house and acted like a booking agent. She got our parents' consent, and after school was out she'd take us—the Moonlight Melody Six!—playing dances all around. She'd never pay us till we got back home, and then she'd say we'd have to go to the house and settle up. She'd have girls sitting around, and wine and homebrew that she made. She'd sell the wine to us, and try to sic the girls on us. By the time we got through, and she'd told us about transportation and paying for the car, we'd never have more than about forty cents each—after being out for three or four days! But it was great experience, and we were all thrilled. It didn't cost us anything to live, because we were all eating and sleeping at home.

"As we grew up, we stuck together, and we got better and better, until a drummer named Ernest Williams came along. He used to play with the Southern Serenaders, a band out of Tulsa, Oklahoma, that had a guy called Willie Lewis on piano and Big Chief Moore on trombone. There was another Willie Lewis from Fort Worth, who played saxophones and went to Europe. This one was also an arranger, and he ended up with Walter Page's Blue Devils. Well, Ernest Williams said he had a job for us on the outskirts of Tulsa. I was about thirteen or fourteen, and it was summertime, otherwise our parents wouldn't have dared let us go. We got a car and went off to this place. It was 'way on out of town, and there was a great big padlock on the door. So there we were— no money, no job—and I had just bought a saxophone and made room for a drummer in our band! I'd never played it, a Buescher tenor saxophone, and it was still in the box, but I was determined to play it. I always had a talent for instruments, and fooled with all of them. This boy we had on drums, John R. Davis, was considered about the second or third best drummer around then. In fact, he was sensational. He could flip the sticks and do everything. We had a good band and all kinds of novelties.

"We went into Tulsa, and although we hadn't any money, the man let us check into a room at a hotel. We were at least a dozen pieces, and this must have been about 1925. The Gonzel White Show was on tour with Pigmeat Markham, and we went down to beg for a job. 'Tell you what you can do,' they said, 'you can ballyhoo out in front of the theatre.'

"That's what we did, out on the street, just before the show went on, to attract the crowds. After the show was over, while they changed the house before the show went on again, we'd strike up and play our things.

They'd maybe pay like five dollars for the whole band for the whole day, and we were just getting enough to eat on. Finally, we got our parents to agree to pay somebody with a big car to take us all back to Dallas, and we went back to school.

"We stuck together and we went around, the Blue Moon Chasers, a bunch of kids. We copied everything off the record. We loved Red Nichols and His Five Pennies, and Fletcher Henderson's *Fidgety Feet*, and the Louis Armstrong Okehs when they began to come out. Later, I bought a bass saxophone, and I used to play everything Adrian Rollini played. Sammy Price, the piano player, wanted to play with our band, so he had his mother cut up a lot of food, make lemonade and everything. Then he invited us to his house so he could rehearse with us. We ate up Sammy's food, but he only rehearsed the one time as I remember, because he was a little too slow for us then.

"It was while I was with the Blue Moon Chasers that I first ran into the Blue Devils. A Mr. Brown, a sort of impresario, showed up with a big old Cadillac touring car, and he told our families he could take us out. We played to a lot of packed houses, and I remember one time when we played a dance in Guthrie. 'I don't know how in the hell all those people got in,' he told us afterwards, 'because I had police all around the joint, but they got in somehow. I managed to save us just fifty cents apiece.'

"We were lucky we got that job, because we were already sort of stranded. On the way down, we had seen big cabbage patches off to the side of the road—*huge* heads of cabbage— and we just admired the vegetation, but on the way back, with fifty cents apiece, we were thinking to ourselves, 'Now, wait a minute! How can we last? Man, we'd better stop on the way and pick up some of those heads of cabbage.' All we had to do was to get over the barbed-wire fence and get a few, which is what we did. The lady where we were staying understood our situation and felt sorry for us.

Opposite: Budd Johnson.

She put all the cabbage in a washtub, added some fatback, and did it up for us. We ate cabbage for about three days, until finally we had to get out of there, because we couldn't pay the woman any rent.

"My mother had relatives in Oklahoma, but I'd never called on any of them, because I didn't want them to know I was in bad shape and send me home. But when we got into Oklahoma City, I went to a dear friend of the family's who had the Hall Hotel on 2nd Street. 'Oh, my poor boy!' she said. She put me in a room and proceeded to get in touch with my mother, although I begged her not to. In the meantime, Jimmy Rushing's people had a restaurant right across the street, and he was seeing to it that all of us ate. His people were pretty well off, and they always had something going. We'd go over there every morning and eat waffles, pancakes, bacon and stuff for ten cents. Finally, the Blue Devils said, 'Okay, you little guys. It's almost time for you to be getting back to school. We're going to play a dance up to Slaughter's Hall, and we're going to give you the money and send you home.'

"So they played a benefit battle of music, between the Blue Devils and the Blue Moon Chasers. The hall was packed and they gave us all the money. They got a guy named Mr. Lemon, and paid him seventy dollars to drive us back to Dallas. When we got there, our parents gave him money to go on back. So that was quite an experience!

"William Holloway came through Dallas with his band, the Music Makers. He was a great saxophone player, strictly a tone man, and he taught me very much. He had played alto with Alphonso Trent, and then gone out on his own just as T. Holder did. He also had Ben Smith on alto, and Ben was another great musician. They had a guy named 'Fog' on tenor, and he could play, and read. (They called him that because he was so black.) They'd heard me, and they wanted me, because I could really take off by this time, but I couldn't read. I knew all the notes on the horn and I could see, but I couldn't put the time together fast enough to keep up. It was what

we called a big band then—three saxes, three brass, four rhythm. Now I'm sitting between Holloway and Ben Smith. Ben had been to Tuskegee and studied under Captain Dry. He played oboe as well as sax. He was also an architect and he designed the first boys' dormitory in Tuskegee. He used to take me every day, and everything was music. He and Holloway kept me right between them and worked on me, and I learned to read by a sort of picture system. I'd look at a whole line or a whole bar and memorize it, so that when I saw it again I could play it. One day they put out some new music, and it scared me to death, but all of a sudden I was reading!

"Ben Smith took the band over in 1927 and we went to a place called the Ypsilanti Club on the outskirts of El Paso, where we played for room and board and tips—no salary. We just played and rehearsed every day until my brother and I had an offer to join Eugene Coy and His Happy Black Aces in 1928. We joined him at a little town in Oklahoma where the Blackfoot Indians live. When we got there, Alan Durham, Eddie Durham's brother, and another brother who played bass were in the band, but the job only lasted two days. So now we set out in an old touring car for Amarillo, Texas, where Coy's people lived. It was about two hundred miles and there were ten of us with suitcases and instruments. Guys were riding on the fenders and everywhere. We had a dozen or more blowouts, and we had to pool all our change to buy second-hand tires. When we got to Amarillo, it was fifteen below zero. Coy took us to a place where there was a hotel with a restaurant and theatre downstairs. He got us two or three rooms and said this was his hometown and his family would stand for it. He went home, and his wife, Marge, who played piano, and his mother started putting on the pots for us.

"The next day, I went down to the theatre, and there was a guy sitting there playing piano for the silent movies. This was still 1928, and it was Ben Webster who was playing. We soon became friends, and we used to hang out with him every day. If we had a nickel apiece, we'd give it to Ben and let him go to the pool hall so he could win enough money for us to eat on. He was a pool hustler and very good with a cue.

"I remember Frankie Trumbauer was very popular then, playing that tune, *Singin' the Blues*, and Ben said to me, 'Man, I like the saxophone. Can you show me how to play it?' I told him I'd try, and I started, putting his fingers on the horn. I got him to play the low C, and showed him how to get the scale.

"Then they were opening up what I remember as the first nightclub in Dallas. T. Holder owned a lot of real estate, and he had this North Dallas club, the Thomason Hall, a dancehall, and he wanted the Johnson boys to be in the band there. They had sent to Chicago and got a show, and they had Jesse Stone to write the music and act as musical director. Jesse had spoken to a friend of ours, Arthur Alexander, who played saxophone and clarinet. He knew we were pretty proficient and all read music, but he had us come in a room one at a time for an aptitude test. He would put the music up on the piano, tell you to play it, and count. We all passed, so then he pulled out his music and we rehearsed for the show. T. Holder was the bandleader, and the band was known as T. Holder's Twelve Clouds of Joy.

"Holder had been in Tulsa with the original Twelve Clouds of Joy, and one night he ran off with the payroll and left them there. If those guys had found him, they would have killed him, but they made Andy Kirk the new head of the band because he had had a college education. Meanwhile, we became the Twelve Clouds of Joy *in Dallas*! We got Eddie Durham, who played guitar and doubled on trombone, and Eddie Tompkins, who later played trumpet with Jimmie Lunceford. My brother was on trombone, and Arthur Alexander and Booker Pittman played altos. Jesse Stone was on piano, Tresevant Sims played tuba, and John R. Davis was on drums. Holder stood out front and was the extra trumpet.

"The club didn't last too long and the band went out on tour. When Holder started stealing the money, we fired him and turned the band over to Jesse, who named it the Blue Serenaders. He was from Atchinson, Kansas, and he remembered some rich cats out of St. Joseph, Missouri, who used to book him, so we went there—about 340 miles from Oklahoma City. I must say it was a great band for its time, and the guys really played. Jesse was a writer *then*, and we had music on paper as well as heads. We had little Ocie Smith out of Oklahoma, a violin player like Stuff Smith. He had a horn on his violin back then, and he really wailed on it.

"Jesse used to be quite a ladies' man, and he knew this woman who had the Charleston Hotel. She let us have two rooms—seven of us to a room. The first three or four would get in the bed and sleep, and the rest of us would sleep on the floor or in chairs. But there was no work until I started to get a little gig here and there, working from 7 at night till 7 in the morning for $1.50. I had to bring every penny of it back, and Jesse would take it to buy crackers, cheese and baloney. Then we got a job broadcasting on the first radio station in St. Joseph, and we made a little money, enough to buy a car. We toured all through Iowa—Clarinda, Red Oak, Shenandoah—and on the way there was a horrible rain and floods. All the bridges were washed out in Shenandoah, and I was the guy driving the car. I broke the trailer that carried the instruments and suitcases. So we were stranded again! We stayed at a lady's house till we had spent all our money, and finally we got back to St. Joseph, flat broke. That was Coleman Hawkins's hometown and all his family were there. Jesse Stone's band was the first he ever played in, and Jesse had a cousin called Elmer Birch who used to watch Hawk all the time. Elmer played a whole lot of tenor and had a big sound, too.

"We finally got a job at a beautiful club about thirty-five miles outside Kansas City. Our old car was messed up by now, so Jesse borrowed another and took us over there two or three at a time. Once again we were playing for room, board and tips, but we did all right. The guy who owned the place had an old car he let us use to go into Kansas City and get our haircuts. We'd get around and meet the guys, and they started hearing about us, because by this time we had a great band. This was when I first met Count Basie. He said, 'I'm coming out there and jam with you guys.' We were playing all kinds of music, hard music, and when Basie and the cats came out and sat in, Jesse called the numbers. They couldn't get out of the first bar! I think we were the first black band that brought music on paper into Kansas City. The Alphonso Trent band had music, but they didn't live there. They loved us so much in Kansas City that later on we became like residents.

"One night, we got to gambling with the boss. Jesse took our tips and started shooting the dice. He broke the guy. It wasn't a whole lot of money, maybe three or four hundred dollars. Then he wanted to put up his car with the keys, but Jesse said, 'No, I don't want to do that . . . you've got to have your car.'

" 'Okay,' the boss said, 'then you're through!'

"So now we had to get out of there, and we went to a place on 13th and Lydia in Kansas City, which is why I wrote a tune called *13th and Lydia* when Booker Pittman recorded for Columbia many years later. So now we're all in this little apartment with nothing else in it, no linen on the beds or anything. We took whatever money was left to buy a whole lot of ham, cheese, baloney, crackers and stuff. After the first month, when the money ran out, we started sleeping in the park and using Street's Pool Hall for an address. I'd leave my horn there, too.

"Benny Moten and George E. Lee had the top bands in Kansas City then, and by this time we had met Lee and his cats. They had automobiles, and they were sharp, man! And they were working! So I took my horn, went to a rehearsal, and sat in George E. Lee's chair. He played tenor, too, and he liked what I did, and I got the job. So now I was making seven dollars a night, in 1928. I had to go out of town with them once for three days, and when I came back Jesse Stone, my roommate, was almost starved. I took him to a Chinese restaurant, and while we were waiting for our order, the only thing he could see was an

apple pie. 'Give me the pie,' he said, and he was so hungry he ate the whole pie before our food arrived.

"Finally, I got Jesse in the band. 'George,' I said, 'you need this cat. He's got all this music . . .' Jesse was teaching me to write and everything when George took him, too. Our old band just split up. Eddie Durham went with Bennie Moten, who had taken over Walter Page's Blue Devils, and Eddie started writing for Moten. My brother went to Minneapolis and a band led by Eli Rice, who also had Eddie Tompkins and Paul Webster. What a brass section that was! Buster Smith was with the Blue Devils, and besides alto sax he could play piano and write. The Charlie Parker style really came from him. Buster played with that lope as far back as I can remember, before Charlie was born. He used to play alto and clarinet—*yoo-ga, voo-ga*—'way back then. Of course, Frankie Trumbauer inspired a lot of cats, because he was the baddest cat back in those days, and everybody was trying to play his stuff. He was the boss of the alto like Hawk (Coleman Hawkins) was the boss of the tenor. So Pres (Lester Young) got a little held up with that Trumbauer style, because he used to play alto, and this style captured everybody. But Pres played two different styles at that time. He'd get up and play pretty on alto, and then he would really blow on the tenor, and this would break up the house. He was offered a job with McKinney's Cotton Pickers, but they wanted him to play alto, and he wanted Prince Robinson's chair. Prince was runner-up to Hawk at that time and everybody was asking, 'Who's the best? This guy or Hawk?' Well, Lester couldn't get Prince's job, but he was really an alto player. And don't forget how nicely he played clarinet—a very melodious clarinet.

"Battles of music were getting to be the thing, and we'd be throwing all this music at Bennie Moten. Eddie Durham hadn't been there long enough to put it on paper for them, and nearly everything they did was a head. I must say this though: they were RCA Victor's number one recording jazz band, and they sold more than anybody else for Victor at that time. But they were not really good till Bennie got the Blue Devils. They were really something. They had it all together. If you jumped on them, they'd blow you clear out of the ceiling. They had a guy called Billy Horn on alto, and another on tenor they called 'Chin.' They called him that because he had a long chin, but I never knew his other name. Then they sent for 'Hot Lips' Page, a young boy then. You could take Louis Armstrong, and put Page in there, and you couldn't tell them apart. He learned to play everything Louis ever played on a record, note for note, and with the same feeling. They say true individuality can never be captured, but it was *so* close. Then they had a guy called Simpson who used to take all the caps off his trumpet and just play on the stems. He was a good musician and he finally became a saxophone player, and a teacher.

"I traveled all over with George E. Lee. We'd go to Tulsa and play around there. Then we'd go down in Texas, all the way around, and then all the way up to North and South Dakota. We covered everywhere in that Midwest area. And I was making money! I was sharp, had eight or nine suits. One night, when we were working in Tulsa, Fletcher Henderson came to town. 'Man,' I said, 'I got to hear Coleman Hawkins!' George E. Lee, being such a great guy, said, 'We're going to cut our dance off an hour ahead of time, so we can get in and hear the last hour of Fletcher Henderson.'

"He was at a place called Dreamland Hall, and I worked my way through right up to the bandstand, till I was standing in front of Hawk. You know, young as I was, he gave me some attention when I let him know who I was. That is one of the reasons why I always respected this guy. I stood there and listened, and he really played. Rex Stewart had just joined the band then, and Fletcher didn't even have all the parts written for him. He was like the fourth trumpet. Once in a while he'd have specialties, and he'd get up and play, but most of the time he'd just sit there with his horn, because the parts hadn't been written for him.

"Hawk talked to me, and from that day on we were friends. He remembered me, and later, when he came to Chicago with Fletcher, we would hang out and drink whiskey. And he would always buy me a drink, too! When I eventually got to New York, I had an after-hours joint on 118th Street and Seventh Avenue. Minton's was in the middle of the block, and I was on the corner, on the fifth floor. I'd go down to Minton's and try to pull everybody from there to come on up to my place and drink some whiskey after Minton's closed. Hawk, Basie and Don Byas, all of 'em, used to hang out at my joint. There was nothing up there but drinking whiskey and listening to records. I had one bedroom, a little hall with a telephone, a kitchen and a living room. If you said, 'I've got a party and want a place for the night,' I'd say, 'Okay, there's some food, bacon and eggs and what not, so you can get your breakfast. Just be sure the door's closed and locked when you leave.' But this was 'way late, after I was married, about 1944.

"Going back to Hawk . . . nobody influenced me before him. It was definitely Hawk. I used to be able to play clarinet pretty well, and for clarinet I thought of Bechet and Buster Bailey. I loved Jimmy Harrison on trombone, and I could get some feeling from him. And, of course, I loved Louis (Armstrong). We all tried to play some of Louis's soul. I can hum some of his solos right now, note for note. Do you remember *Big Butter and Egg Man*? It was Louis and Hawk together with me.

"When Hawk left Fletcher Henderson, my brother was with the band, and they came to Chicago. Pres (Lester Young) had just joined, and everybody was saying, 'How the devil is he going to fit in that band?' Because he didn't have the vigor, the fire, or the power. He didn't fit there. And Pres dug it, I guess, before anybody else did, and he split. But that isn't taking anything away from his genius. Like I wouldn't wear a $150 straw hat out in a blizzard. I'd be out of line. However, it's a funny thing, because before ever we heard one another we played similar styles. Pres used to come and get me, wake me out of a deep sleep, pour whiskey down my throat, and say, 'Get up! So-and-so just came into town, and he's over there blowing. Let's go get him!' One guy in particular I remember—Georgie Auld. Pres said, 'Let's put him in the middle. You get on one side, and I'm going to be on the other, and we're going to blow him out of the joint!' That was Kansas City for you.

"Pres and I used to go to each other's rooms and say, 'Dig this. Here's what I learned today.' We'd show each other. When he hit a town where I was, he might come around and say, 'Look, I found out how to do all this in one breath.' We were eager then to show each other what we learned. There was no gap between musicians. I really never tried to copy Pres, until maybe later, when I may have thought I wanted to do something like he was doing.

"Ben Webster was still like a beginner in those days, because it hadn't been long since I showed him how to play the horn. He came to town in Jap Allen's band. Booker Pittman was in it, and they had Clyde Hart as arranger. Clyde used to take off McKinney's Cotton Pickers' stuff, and write the solos out note for note, and Ben would be playing Prince Robinson's solos as Clyde wrote them. But when Herschel Evans came through, he had made it, and he was blowing, *really* blowing. He was from Texas and he came out of a band from San Antonio that had a boy who played the sweetest alto you could ever want to hear. We called him Black Siki, and later on he played with Troy Floyd. I'm going back to the '20s now. Herschel went out to the West Coast, and even now, when I go out there, I seem to see all my classmates that are still living. The West Coast is just full of Texans!

"Herschel was definitely inspired by Hawk. He inspired all of us, really. I hadn't even heard of Lester Young when I first heard Hawk. A bit later, after Bechet and Buster Bailey, there was Benny Carter, and we never thought there could be anybody play more alto than Benny. Later still, Billy Eckstine used to say, 'Yeah, there is, a little cat named Charlie Parker.' 'Impossible,' I'd say, 'he can't possibly play as much horn as Benny Carter.'

"After I left George E. Lee and Kansas City, I went straight to Chicago, on 9 January 1932. My brother said, 'Come on up to Chicago, man. There's plenty of work here.' He was working at the Regal Theatre and doubling in a nightclub. I had no job, but I started looking around, taking my horn and jamming. The first band I remember playing in in Chicago was Ed Carry's. He was Scoops Carry's brother, an arranger and everything, but he got so he couldn't stand the music business and became a politician. We had a helluva band, the best guys around Chicago. Then I worked some with Cass Simpson, who played like Earl Hines. It must have been before that that I worked with Irene Eadey at the Vogue. I started going down to the Grand Terrace, taking my horn. While the band was taking intermission, Earl would stay up there on piano, and I would get up and play with him. 'This little cat can blow,' he said.

"He had Cecil Irwin, a great arranger, on tenor. When Cecil had to take off to do some writing, he'd get me to sit in his place, and he would pay me. I'd sight-read the book, because by this time I was quite a musician. 'Don't never come to Chicago if you can't read,' they used to say, and scare us to death in Kansas City. But I was prepared, and I had made up my mind I was going to join Earl's band when I used to hear it over the radio in K.C.

"By the time I got to Chicago, I had done some arranging and could write. But it was in Chicago that I took an orchestration and copied it all backwards. I thought I was being smart and that it would be *my* arrangement. It was as though instead of writing a sentence like, 'Born in Dallas, Texas, 14 December, 1910,' I had written, '0191, December 41, Texas, Dallas, in born.' I just took this stock arrangement, wrote everything backwards, and called it *Buckets*. Because it worked the other way, and the notes were right, and the harmony was good, I figured it had to be something very good and strange, but it didn't make any kind of sense, and I don't know why to this day. Since I've been dealing with twelve-tone compositions here of late, I know that that was what they reminded me of.

"Earl went out on the road in 1932, and I went with Clarence Moore when he took a band into the Grand Terrace. He was a very good violinist, wanted to be like Eddie South, and was almost as good. Teddy Wilson was in the band, and we used to broadcast. One night, a telegram came saying, 'Gee, Earl, you sounded beautiful tonight.' And it was Teddy all the time! Of course, Teddy idolized Earl, and I think he lived at Earl's house one time and studied with him. He idolized Art Tatum, too, and between the two there lies Teddy. At times now, when Earl sits down at the piano by himself, not trying to prove anything to anybody, just taking it easy and playing beautifully, you can hear where Teddy Wilson came from.

"I think it was in 1932, too, that I was in Eddie Mallory's band. We played at a place run by a big, tall, white-haired old Frenchman named Albert Burchet. It was really for millionaires, and it was on a plot of thirty-five acres. He had gondolas on the water, and little cabins where they could take the chicks. He put on exotic shows. He had Sally Rand, the fan dancer, and all kinds of acts from foreign countries. The music they threw up at us was like an education. They didn't have parts like we would write them in this country, and it meant a lot of transposing. Teddy Wilson, my brother and I hung out together all the time, and we could play this show music. White bands could play a good show, too, but they didn't have the jazz that we did when the dancing started. Sometime after we opened there, Burchet got a telephone message and called us up to the office.

" 'I'm going to lay my cards on the table,' he said. 'Here are contracts for all the bands that worked for me in the past five years, and I don't owe anybody a dime. Petrillo says if you're not off the job in thirty minutes, he's going to send gunmen out here to run you off. Now, I want to know how you feel about that.'

"We were in what was called forbidden territory for black musicians. Petrillo was president of Local Number 10, the white union, and he was really with the mob. Now this was 1932, and I was making sixty dollars a week with free meals as well.

" 'Man, we want to work,' we all said.

" 'Well, I'll tell you what I'll do. If you want to stay here, I'll send you home every night with some guys with guns, as far as your line.'

"That's what we did. We rode with these guys through Petrillo's territory on the North Side until we could get to the elevated and take the train home to the South Side. When we finally got a car, we had to lock all the doors and roll up the windows, because if they saw anybody black coming through the North Side, they tried to beat the hell out of them.

"We stayed on that job six months and never had any trouble, because Burchet had told Petrillo he'd meet force with force. That's usually the way, isn't it, if you speak up and perk up?

"Then one day, Teddy Wilson, my brother and I were lying around when we got a call from Mike McKendrick, a banjo player who was strawboss for Louis Armstrong.

" 'You cats like to play with Armstrong?' he asked.

" 'Of course . . .'

" 'Okay, we're going to have a rehearsal,' and he told us the time and the place.

"Zilmer T. Randolph was musical director and arranger for the band, and he used to write some hard music. It was a strange sort of band at that time, if I must say so myself. Z.T. played trumpet along with Elmer Whitlock, and Louis played solo and whatever else you wanted him to do. My brother was on trombone, a fellow named Little Al and George Oldham on altos, and myself on tenor. Teddy Wilson was on piano, and they sent for a New Yorker named Yank Porter, who had played shows like *Blackbirds* and was a pretty good drummer. Anyway, we got this thing together and went out on the road at forty dollars a week, which wasn't bad then. You could still get a room for fifty or seventy-five cents a night, and a meal for seventy-five cents. And of course, Louis kept us high!

"When we got to St. Louis to play a battle of music with the St. Louis Crackerjacks, they played first. When we got up on the stand, here come some little cats with this big stick they had rolled up in the shape of a baseball bat, small at the bottom and then growing out. On it they'd written in ink: *To the King of the Vipers, Louis Armstrong, from the Vipers Club of St. Louis.*

" 'Yeah, baby,' Louis said, 'look what we got! We'll smoke this. We'll have some mezz for dessert. You know, toppin' it off now!'

"We sat up there and smoked, and the cops kept the people away from us. When we got off for intermission, the Crackerjacks began with *Shine*, a number where Louis used to hit all those high C's, ending up on high F. But what Shorty Baker was doing with the Crackerjacks wasn't so strenuous. Instead of C's and then the F, he was hitting a G and ending on C, like a fourth or fifth away. Louis would have nothing to do with *that*, you know!

"As soon as we got back on the stand again, he said, '*Shine*.' And that night—I never heard it before and won't ever hear it again—Louis hit about 250 high C's, just *tch, tch, tch*, which will tear a man's chops to pieces. Man! Then he hit that high F, and held it, and made the walls tremble! The people just looked up at the roof. He wasn't going to take Shorty doing his number and getting a big hand for it!

"We went on touring, but then it got so we'd play one night and lay off two, and at the end of the week they'd pay off pro rata—forty dollars only if you worked *all* the week. Finally, when we were supposed to play Castle Farms in Cincinnati, we struck. They were changing buses there, and the old bus driver was going back to Chicago and was willing to take us, so we wouldn't have to pay any fare. 'Much as we like Louis,' we said, 'sorry, sorry.'

"It was the only way we could get at 'em, by refusing to play. Louis never would have anything to do with the band. He always had somebody else handling it, and would never come to our defense. We wouldn't budge out of the hotel. We had made up our minds, and when we said, 'No pay, no play,' they came through. But when we got back to Chicago, the band broke up and Louis went to Europe.

"That was certainly one of Louis's worst bands—a terrible band. When I was talking at a jazz club in Switzerland and told them how bad-sounding I thought it was, they didn't like me for it. But you couldn't get the right people to go out with him then, because everybody was trying to run the game. A lawyer named Collins had like power of attorney, and when Louis came back from Europe they split, but Collins took the car and everything Louis had. Of course, Louis was no businessman, but that's when he signed up with Joe Glaser. He trusted Joe implicitly. I heard that when Glaser died he left him a millionaire. He should have done, because I was told they had insurance on each other's lives.

" 'What you gonna do, Pops?' we'd ask him around this time, and he'd say, 'Well, there's a lot of cats want me to sign up with them.' Rockwell O'Keefe wanted to give him $5000 to sign with them. He'd been with them when he got into marijuana trouble in California, and they'd sent this Collins out to get him out of jail, but somehow Collins and his wife snatched Louis away from them. But now Louis began saying, 'I think I'm going to get with old Joe Glaser, because he ain't got nothin' and I can tell him what I want.' Joe had been a hustler, a slickster, around Chicago, and he had just come out of prison. His family always had that place called the Sunset Café, and there was income for him from that. So he got hold of Louis, this jewel, and they started to make it big, and Joe became a multi-millionaire.

"I think it was after I left Louis that I worked for Jimmie Noone, playing tenor and doing some writing for him. Then one night I got a call asking if I could join Earl Hines right away at the Orpheum Theatre in Minneapolis. They'd had a bus accident and Cecil Irwin had been killed instantly, and all the cats were messed up. Kenneth Stewart, the trombone player, and I went right out and joined the band at the theatre. That was 10 May 1935. I'll never forget the date. The cats were sitting up there on the stage, all bandaged up and everything. Omer Simeon had dots all over his face where the glass had been picked out, and

Trummy Young's leg was really messed up. But the show must go on, and that was my opening night with Earl Hines!

"I knew the whole book, because I had played it all before when I took Cecil's place. I had been supposed to join before that, but while they were on tour they got Jimmy Mundy on tenor. Earl had heard his arrangement of *Cavernism*, and he really dug it. We had no regular baritone player at that time—just four saxes—although George Dixon used to double on baritone. I would always alternate between tenor and alto with Earl. If he needed a first alto, I would switch over. We had a lot of doubles, and I used to fool around with all the instruments. I also started to arrange right away. Earl asked me to do *Deep Forest* over. Others I did over were *Blue Because of You*, *Rosetta* and *You Can Depend on Me*. I also wrote a lot of arrangements on pop songs, because all the soul brothers used to come in with their songs, to get them on the air, and they'd pay me and Mundy, and give us presents. We used to go down to the Grand Terrace and broadcast during the day as well as at night, so it seemed as though we were on the air all the time. When Mundy left in 1936 to go with Benny Goodman, I really started to take over, and I did all the show music.

"One night, when we were playing at the Grand Terrace, a waiter brought me a note from some people at a table who wanted me to have a drink with them. It was Gus Arnheim and his wife.

"'We just left Dallas and we were talking with your mother,' he said. (My mother was then in charge of all the maid service at the place where they stayed.) 'She told me she had two boys who played music, and that one of them was in Chicago with Earl Hines. Do you write, too?'

"When I told him I did, he asked me to play some of my things when I went back up. So I asked Earl to play a couple of my arrangements.

"'That's fine,' Arnheim said afterwards. 'We're opening at the Congress Hotel and we have a rehearsal at 11 tomorrow morning. Do

you think you could have an arrangement ready by that time?'

"I sat up all night and wrote that arrangement. I don't remember whether it was an original or not, but I should, because it was a turning point. Arnheim liked it and asked if I would join him and write for his band. I told him I already had a job, but he offered $150 a week, where I was only making $50. He asked me to talk to Earl about it.

"'Look, man,' I said to Earl, 'I've got a chance to make this money with this cat. What do you think?' Now here's why I always have liked Earl. He just said, 'Okay, if you want to go with him, go ahead!'

"So I joined Gus Arnheim's band, and guess who the piano player in it was—Stan Kenton! That's when we got tight. I remember buying a car in Minneapolis, and from there we drove to New York and opened at the Hotel New Yorker. Mickey Alpert heard the music and said he wanted me to do twenty arrangements for him. So I was really in the writing business. I was turning it out like crazy. This was in 1937. Finally, Arnheim decided he'd had it in the band business, and he went out to Hollywood and became president or vice-president of some bank there. I think he and his wife were millionaires—very wealthy people, anyway.

"I went back to Chicago and was with Horace Henderson for a while, just jobbing around. One night I got a call from his brother, Fletcher.

"'Cab Calloway just took Jeff (Hilton Jefferson) with him, and I need an alto player,' he said. 'We're going on the air in ten minutes. Get your alto and come on down to the Grand Terrace.'

"I got down there and grabbed the music to look it over. Wow! All those Benny Carter arrangements, sax solos, and everything. 'What am I into now?' I asked myself, looking at the different keys. I stayed with Fletcher in the Grand Terrace for a while, and then I went back to Earl.

"Ed Fox, who ran the Grand Terrace, wasn't paying Earl any money at that time, and Fox had a contract where his wife took

over if he died; if she died, the older son took over; and when he died, the next son. Earl got lawyers to break the contract, and when the judge saw it, he said, 'If you *ever* come in here with a contract like this—anybody—I'll put you all in jail!' The contract was so one-sided. Earl could never get any insurance, and he was just not a businessman. He was really burned up then, and he was worried. He did a lot of heavy drinking, and he was having problems with his common-law wife, Kathryn.

"After the split with Fox, part of the band went with Walter Fuller into the Grand Terrace. I had talked Billy Eckstine into coming with the band before this, and we stuck with Earl. 'You and Billy get the band together,' Earl said. This is when I organized the band, and we really set it up. We used to walk to rehearsals, and we'd fix red beans and rice to eat. We got Scoops Carry on alto, Truck Parham on bass, and Shorts McConnell on trumpet. We made Willie Randall the manager, because he was a beautiful businessman, and Leroy Harris was the treasurer. We put Charlie Carpenter up in the William Morris office to see they didn't book us on such long jumps that the bus company ate up all the money, and Charlie stayed in direct contact with the people there. We went out on tour and those were big years for the band and Earl. We had a great band, record hits, and Billy and Madeline Green as singers. Earl had more cash money than ever before in his life, but he soon blew it afterwards trying to run a night-

club in the Pershing Hotel. They stole him blind.

"I left Earl in 1942 when he wouldn't give me a raise. I knew what he was making, because I looked at the books every night. So I split and went to New York, where my wife was living and where my son was born in September. It was then that Billy Eckstine told Earl to send for Charlie Parker. We had tried to persuade him to come in the band on alto before that. When he got there, he didn't even have a tenor.

"I jobbed around until I ran into Al Sears. I knew him from when he used to come to Chicago with different groups. He had a band working uptown at the Renaissance Ballroom three nights a week. This went on till he had the opportunity to put a U.S.O. show together. We were honored to have the great Rubinstein on the bill with us—and Lester Young. Yes, Pres was in the band, so we had three tenors. Edgar Sampson, Marlowe Morris and a boy named Fats Green were in it, too. We went all over with this show, down south and everyplace, through Texas and Arkansas.

"Pres used to start all the crap games. He loved to shoot dice. As soon as he got up, he'd start a game. He'd stay with it, too, but he was always the first one broke. The first thing he did when he woke up in the morning was to take a drink. He'd drink all day long, and last thing at night he'd have that bottle up to his mouth. And when he went into a liquor

Opposite: Left to right: Leroy Harris, Willie
Randall, Budd Johnson, Madeline Green.

Above: Left to right: Thomas Crump, Budd
Johnson, Scoops Carry, Buddy Hills, Ernie
Wilkins. Woogie Harris is visible behind.

Right: Budd Johnson and Earl Hines in
South America, 1969.

store, he didn't just buy one bottle. He'd buy five or six.

" 'How can you drink so much like that, man?' I asked him once.

" 'Well, I never want to lose this feeling,' he said. 'This is the feeling I had when I made it with the horn, all the records with Basie and everything.'

"That was his philosophy, but, oh, the whiskey he used to drink! We had a lot of fun on the road until I got into a little demonstration down there. We happened to pull up in Little Rock, Arkansas, and my buddy, Howard Callender, got off the bus. He was a trumpet player, a Panamanian, and he used to be Lil Green's guy. He'd never been south before, and he made a mistake. He didn't read the signs, and instead of walking through where it said 'For Colored,' he walked through where it said 'For White.'

"We sat waiting in the bus a long time, and then all of a sudden here comes Howard, crying. He'd run into a bunch of cats who were fixing to bust his head.

" 'Wait a minute, man,' I said, 'I've lived in the South and that hasn't happened to me.'

" 'All you cats are scared down here,' he said. 'That's the reason things like this happen.'

" 'Well, I'm going to prove to you that I'm not afraid.'

"I had a .38 automatic on my hip, so I took it out and walked up to the white bus driver. 'All right,' I said. 'Let's get the hell out of here on this goddam bus. Drive it now!' You could hear a pin fall. Some of 'em up front were shaking, because we were in Arkansas, but Pres, who always sat in the extreme back seat, he didn't care. He hollered: 'Shoot your pistol, Buddy Boy! Shoot your pistol!'

"Al Sears fired me right there and put me off the bus. I had to wire my wife and have her send me fare to get home, but I had had to prove to Howard that all of us in the South were not afraid of white people, that they didn't kick us *all* around.

"I worked on 52nd Street with Dizzy Gillespie, Max Roach and Oscar Pettiford. Don Byas had been working with them and he thought he was going with Duke Ellington, so he gave me the job, but it was Al Sears who wound up with Duke instead. I was also with John Kirby's band about three months in 1945. What happened was that Buster Bailey and Kirby got into an argument when they were working in Baltimore, and Buster said he was going to quit. Charlie Shavers said they'd heard me play on Earl's *Jelly, Jelly,* and everybody thought I was a clarinet player. So they sent for me in New York, but I took my tenor as well as my clarinet. When I got there, they had made up and Buster wasn't going to leave. After I thought about it, I was glad, because I don't think I could have followed Buster. Kirby was a nice guy and he told me to stay and become the seventh man. I didn't have any music, but I took some home, and between Charlie and me we wrote fourth parts. After Baltimore, we went to Toronto, and then back to New York, where we made a record date and did numbers like *K. .C. Caboose.* I was in the band when Clyde Hart and Russell Procope were in it (Billy Kyle had gone in the Army), but by this time Emmett Berry had taken Charlie's place and Ram Ramirez was on piano. Anybody who could sit in that band and play that music had to be one hell of a musician, because they had some pretty hard music and you really had to play.

"When Billy Eckstine started off with his band, I was supposed to have been part of it. It was Billy's and my idea. Billy knew all the arrangements I had written for Earl, and I was going to write for him and be the band's musical director. For that, I was going to get twenty percent for my contribution. Billy Shaw was working for William Morris at this time, and they had signed Billy up and weren't going to have Budd Johnson get twenty percent. So they cut me out, and Dizzy (Gillespie) wound up being musical director, but the band got to be too undisciplined. They weren't making time, they weren't rehearsing, and the whole reed section were junkies. Billy Shaw was trying to get Billy Eckstine to take a screen test, because the Morris office people had their mind on movies. Shaw told me he wanted me to take over the band and go out on the road. I don't know whether B. wanted me to go or not, but I went out on the instructions of the New York office. I had to see they rehearsed, got out of hotels, and caught trains. This was 1945, and I got three hundred dollars a week whether I worked or not. We played a few places in California. At the Plantation Club, Sarah Vaughan was in the band and Billie Holiday was in the show. That was when we made the V-Disc for the Army. I stayed with that band till we got back east, and then I split. I'd had to take Dexter Gordon's place often, because he was messed up at that time. I rejoined later when they played the Golden Gate Ballroom, because Dex had got messed up again. All this time I was making arrangements for B. like *I'm in the Mood for Love*, which Bobby Tucker later blew up for strings, and he was recording for National. Gerry Valentine was writing stuff, too, like *Prisoner of Love*. B. really had a pretty good band at that time. He always loved be-bop, even if it didn't go with ballads. Yet he did more to save the blues. *Jelly, Jelly* was one of his biggest numbers. It was like Joe Williams, who always wanted to be a ballad singer, but his biggest thing was blues.

"When I first met B., he used to do m.c. work, a little tap dancing, and turning flips and things. He wasn't a musician. Earl and I practically taught him how to play trumpet and to read music. I remember Billy was working in Detroit when we pulled in there. He was staying at the Lovett Hotel and working downstairs in a place I think they called the Cotton Club. Everybody got a room but me, and Billy told me I could share his. He also told me he was trying to learn a little trumpet, and I started to show him something about it right then and there. We started talking and were good friends from then on. The next time I saw him, we were in Pittsburgh, and he came by the theatre to say hello. Then I saw him in Washington, D.C., where his sister taught school. In fact, he went to school there himself. He hung around with me then, and I went out to hear him sing for the first time.

" 'Man,' I said, 'why don't you come to Chicago? Nobody in Chicago can sing like you.'

" 'I hear they've got some great singers there. What would I do in Chicago?'

" 'You could get a job,' I said.

"He came to Chicago on the strength of my word, and started working for Mike De Lisa, while I worked to get him into Earl's band. The only way I got him in was by threatening to quit. Ed Fox didn't want him because Leroy Harris was singing in the band. Why did we need an extra singer? Anyway, that's how he got into Earl's band, as Billy will tell you. It's hard sometimes for people to remember things right.

"Like I heard Sarah Vaughan on television recently, and she was trying to remember how she was discovered by the Earl Hines band, and she didn't really tell it right. Billy Eckstine heard her on the amateur show at the Apollo Theatre, and broke his neck getting us to hear her. She got a week's work at the Apollo as a prize, and I went with Billy to hear her. Afterwards, we went straight to Earl. He dug it, too, and hired her right there.

"When she left Earl eventually, I was already in New York. I got her a job on 52nd Street, and then I had her with me in the Village at Café Society, working with J. C. Heard. That was where I introduced her to George Treadwell, and after that she didn't look back. He brought her up from seventy-five to five or six thousand a week. Although he had a tight contract, they eventually found a way to make him turn her loose for a little piece of money.

"Sarah has a lot of ability as a musician. She can sit down at the piano or organ, read the music, and play it. You can't beat natural talent. When you've got it, you've got it, and nobody can take that away from you. She can go up and down, but the more experience she has, the better she's going to sound. It takes experience to give you feeling to express. Nowadays, it seems as though there's always somebody to tell you what to do, how to do it, how to get to the public . . . They can do this because they control the media, but it used not to be like that. Nobody used to tell us what and how to play. You might sound bad sometimes, but that was all right, because you knew you were going to get 'em with the next tune. They would be waiting for you to create. Now you've either got to bop or be out in space. Those are almost the only kind of records you can buy today. And out of sight, out of mind. They can't find the kind of stuff we've recorded.

"Of course, I don't think stardom is everything. I've seen what happened to those who had their little burst of fame, the hardships that were created for their families. Stardom for a day . . . when you fall, it's such a hard fall. I never felt the way Don Byas did. He knew he could play better than most people, that he could go get his horn, find you, and blow you off the bandstand. I think you've got to have some of that ego to make you want to climb the stairs to stardom. There was a big change when the agencies went to work to cut out all the co-operative business in bands. They wanted to deal with just one man. In the old days, when we had those co-operative

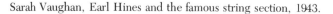

Sarah Vaughan, Earl Hines and the famous string section, 1943.

bands, we would change the leader every year, and the leader didn't get any more money, because after the transportation was paid for, the money was split equally between everybody.

"Maybe I've been a little lazy, but I used to beat the sidewalks and wear holes in my shoes running into those offices. I knew all the agents and everybody, and I used to hustle for record dates. 'I know you're a good musician,' they'd tell me, 'but the public don't know you.' Well, of course, these are new times, but at one time the public didn't know any-body. They had to make somebody. They had to give somebody a chance to do something!

"I always wanted to be known, but I don't know whether I ever felt I wanted to be a star. I can't tell you about that, but I know we used to do a lot of drinking, having a good time, and playing around, and we made a fair living. I've been lucky, and you've got to be a certain kind of person to make it the other way."

(1974)

The Little Theatre concert, 1964.
Left to right: Ahmed Abdul-Malik, Earl Hines, Oliver Jackson, Budd Johnson.

TRUMMY YOUNG

TROMBONE

"Trummy" Young was born in Savannah, Georgia, in 1912, and was christened James Osborne. His father, a railroad worker, was severely injured when a boiler exploded. The company for which he worked never paid any compensation to the family, and after suffering for nearly two years he died when his son was six. His wife, who had been a schoolteacher, sought to support herself, her son and two daughters, by sewing. A kind Jewish woman, for whom she sometimes worked, offered to take and raise her boy and one of the sisters. This benefactress had two children of her own of about the same age, and she later adopted another boy in similar circumstances. Racial prejudice at that time was such that her broadmindedness and charity did not escape criticism from neighbors. Undeterred, she tutored her charges at night when they began to work, so that they should not suffer from lack of schooling. To help the household expenses, Young got a job delivering groceries at an early age.

Savannah was a port, and "a good town" as he remembered it. Many musicians who were not born there, nevertheless made it their home. In the countryside around were numerous turpentine camps, and these attracted blues singers, who entertained the workers in the juke joints. On Saturday nights, all these people came into town, and Young soon became familiar with the basic blues. In fact, while still quite small, he used to lead one of the singers around. His name was Blind Wil-

lie, and after taking him to wherever he was to perform, the boy would find somewhere to rest until he was told, "It's time to take Willie home!"

There was only one musician in the youngster's family, an uncle who played trombone in Jim Europe's band, but music was in his blood, and by the time the following reminiscences were recorded in 1961, he was one of Louis Armstrong's famous "All Stars":

"I first started on trumpet in a school band in Richmond, Virginia. As a kid, I saw only street and parade bands. I thought trombones were more flashy, and I liked the sound of them. Trumpet was a little rough on me then, which it is for anyone starting, so I was glad to make a change. I had quite a few teachers in the beginning, but one fellow in particular came to our school from the Jenkins Orphanage Band. He played trumpet, baritone horn and trombone. His name was John Nick, and he's in Richmond now. I thought he was a wonderful musician. I've heard a lot of guys since, but he did some things I've never heard anybody else do. He was the first guy I heard who did lip trills, and he taught me how to do them. We also had a teacher at our school who came up on weekends. His name was John Scott, and he taught a little of everything on all the instruments. Naturally, he didn't have a great knowledge of them *all*, but he was very good on clarinet, his main instrument. He knew enough about the others to help us get started properly.

"I began to play professionally when I left school and went to Washington. I didn't know anyone there, and the first job I had was running an elevator. At first, I played with Frank Betters, a drummer who was also an undertaker. Sometimes there'd be just the two of us, drums and trombone; sometimes there'd be a tenor, and sometimes we'd have piano, too. We'd play little house parties and get maybe fifty cents apiece, drinks and something to eat. We just liked to play. This guy, the undertaker, and I didn't belong to any union then. We'd even go out on the beach and play for people. That was how I met Paul Jones, the tenor with Booker Coleman and His Hot Chocolates. He liked to go out with us, just to play his horn.

"I met Jimmy Mundy through him, although Jimmy was with another band then, Tommy Myles's, which I joined after I had been with Booker Coleman for a while. Booker had about twelve pieces, but Tommy's was the better band. Jimmy Mundy and Elton Hill were both writing arrangements for it. Garnet Clark was on piano, and just a kid. He never drank anything then, and he was a wonderful pianist with a nice little style. He could play, and he loved to play. You go by his house, and he would be playing all day. I never heard anything of his after he left the States, and I'd like to hear those records he made in Paris. Everything went wrong with him before he left. He just ran wild, but he could swing, and he could execute.

"Earl Hines met the whole Tommy Myles band when he was playing the Howard Theatre in Washington. They had a benefit there one night, and about six bands played. Earl was much impressed by Tommy's band, and to tell you truthfully, I thought Tommy had the better band. Earl had the name by then, but we had better arrangements by Jimmy and Elton. And Tommy could play some drums! It was too bad he was killed. Some jealous woman killed him, stabbed him to death. He gave me my nickname, a kind of abbreviation of trombone!

"Earl took Jimmy Mundy first, to play tenor and arrange. Jimmy was instrumental in getting me in the band in 1933. Later on, of course, Earl got Billy Eckstine, who had been singing with us while he was still in high school. It was a big kick for me to be with Earl. He was no businessman, but he gave you freedom to play, and he didn't bother you. If you were late, he just went on playing piano. I liked his playing. He swings, man, and he still can play! He was inspiring to work with, and I have to give him credit, because he helped me a lot. People used to say I was crazy, and ask what I was trying to do. One guy understood, and that was Earl, just as he did when Charlie Parker came along later. I had my first real chance to study when I was with him, because before that I hadn't had enough money. And Billy Franklin, the band's first trombone, also helped me very much.

"Jimmy Harrison was my first main influence, and I think he influenced quite a few other musicians. He was a tall, good-looking guy, and he worked hard on his horn. So far as I was concerned, he was *it*! I don't think anybody else could play as much as he did then. I heard Miff Mole, too. He was executing, but he has never actually been a jazz trombone. He has been a wonderful trombone player all through the years; he knew the instrument, he had a beautiful intonation, he could play sweet and he could play fast, but he never did too much of that *real* jazz.

"Then Louis Armstrong influenced me an awful lot, directly, not only through Jimmy Harrison. At different times I worked with several other trombone players and picked up a lot of little things from them. There was Briscoe with the Jenkins Orphanage Band, a left-handed player, originally from Kentucky. I thought he was wonderful. He could play any style. He could play jazz, he could growl, he could play sweet, and he could execute.

"I didn't have a chance to do much recording during the four years I was with Earl, but I was trying very hard, trying more or less for the trumpet style. I didn't worry too much about playing the instrument in the accepted trombone fashion, because I knew it had much greater possibilities than the way it was when I started. Jimmy Harrison had already shown me that, and I guessed there were things he hadn't thought of. Just like today, the kids will take it somewhere else, and ten years from now it will go another place. I think it should be like that. It's healthy. But a style is a style. It's not something you can get in a music store.

"I worked very hard on sound, as I do today, because sound is very important. The sound I went for was not as broad as was common at that time. Most of the big, broad sounds tend to be a little on the flat side. They're not brilliant. I always tried for a sharper, brilliant sound, but it meant work. Sound is something that's real buggy! In order to get a decent sound—and this I've been taught by those I studied with, and by any good musician I've talked with—a lot of long-tone study is involved, which is very monotonous, and it's hard to get a musician to sit down and do it unless he's dedicated, because he'd rather be moving. I deliberately cultivated that brilliant sound because it tied in with my conception. It's almost the opposite of Tyree Glenn's, which is big and soft, but note how wonderful he sounds on some of his recent records. They were commercial, and they were humorous. Tyree took my place in Tommy Myles's band, by the way.

"Talking of being humorous, I think the guy who has all the humor is Vic Dickenson. He is the most humorous trombone man I ever heard in my life. Dicky Wells has his own story, too. What I like about those two is that I *know* them in their playing. They're stylists. You can identify them, and there are not too many guys around that you can positively identify.

"Tricky? I thought Tricky Sam Nanton was the greatest thing that ever walked. That was my boy! When it came to swinging, I thought he could outswing anybody. I knew I never could play like him, and I never would try. I do a little light growl, but I don't work the plunger. I've never heard anyone approach him, and I've heard a lot of guys try it. Well, he *talked* like that! There was something in his throat that made it sound like a triad when he talked—he had three tones going. And he

played like that. It was an individual thing. He was the greatest ever lived on that stuff. No one else will ever play like that. There may be some great plunger man come along, but Tricky's chapter is finished.

"I really can't make comparisons with others who followed him, because so far as that plunger thing is concerned there was only the one guy, that's all. Al Grey's got his thing going, and he's wonderful. It's different, and I like the way he punches. I think I influenced him originally. I influenced Matthew Gee and Kai Winding. Just like when J. J. Johnson came along. I enjoy his work. What he does is very clean. From a technical standpoint, it's precise, exact, and he has very good command. By the same token, you might take a guy who didn't have such good command of the instrument, but he'd have a lot of soul. Soul is something else you don't buy in a music store. It's not for sale out there. It's there when you first get the instrument, and it's a matter of your learning enough to express some of that soul that's within you. Some guys learn the instrument well enough to do it, and others don't.

"There's no doubt in my mind that a lot of the younger musicians today are better than the older men. I am not speaking of *all* the old ones. I'm speaking in general. Everyone knows we had some wonderful older musicians, but never enough of them. The young ones have had more schooling—and they also had some trailblazers out ahead! The older guys had to create for themselves all the time by trial and error. You don't see kids today with busted up lips and things like that. The guys who did that know better now, and how to help them. The teachers have learned from the guys who ruined their lips to find out things.

"By 1937, I had had offers from several leaders, but I didn't want to leave Earl's band, because it was swinging and I had a lot of friends in it. I could have gone with Cab Calloway for more money, but I didn't think I could stand his hollering. When I got an offer from Jimmie Lunceford, his band was beginning to be a big success. Ray Nance advised me to leave Earl, and made sure I went by personally putting me on the train.

"Lunceford's band was quite different from Earl's. Punctuality and discipline were what I now had to adjust to, but it was a good move, because the Lunceford period really established me. Before that, no one knew about

jazz before Billy Eckstine came in. I always wanted to play with Chick, because he swung so much. I really went with Earl because Jimmy Mundy was already there and I figured I'd know somebody. I knew some of the guys with Chick, but not as well. Maybe I wouldn't have stayed with Chick too long, but I'd have

Earl Hines's musicians, 1937. Left to right: Leon Washington, Wallace Bishop, Trummy Young, Walter Fuller, Louis Taylor, Quinn Wilson, Darnell Howard, George Dixon, Lawrence Dixon, Kenneth Stewart, Omer Simeon, Willie Randall, Ray Nance.

me except a few musicians. I think Jimmie's arrangers must have dug my work at that time, because they certainly built some fine things around me. I imagine Jimmie told them what to do, too, because before that they never gave many solos to trombone. Do you remember *Think of Me Little Daddy*? I liked that one. The words were good. I think Ed Inge wrote the arrangement. It was always a ball recording with that band. We didn't make much money, but the guys enjoyed working together, and we rehearsed.

"It's a funny thing about that Lunceford period, because before I left Washington I was dickering with Chick Webb, and that was before I went with Earl. I often wonder what would have happened if I had gone to New York instead of Chicago. Chick had a good band then, before Ella Fitzgerald came in. In the same way, Earl's band used to play more

been around New York. It shows you the different roads you can take in life. But I wasn't unlucky with drummers. When Wallace Bishop broke his leg in the bus accident, Earl got Alvin Burroughs, who was living in Kansas City, or somewhere around there. He was one of the great drummers. He swung all the time. Then I had Crawford back of me when I was with Lunceford, and that was a pleasure, too. It's hard to find good drummers today, those who really back you up and are tasty with it. There aren't any Big Sid Catletts or Chick Webbs around.

"When I eventually left Lunceford, I went with Charlie Barnet, mainly for money. I didn't make too much with Lunceford, and the boys in his band were in pretty bad shape financially. Lunceford was not stupid by any means. He was a very intelligent man. You couldn't blame his manager, Harold Oxley, entirely. Jimmie must have condoned what went on, and you couldn't blame one and leave the other out. One day, we had a meeting on 135th Street at the YMCA to ask for more money. We put Willie Smith up as spokesman, and he told Lunceford. When Jimmie wanted to jump on him, we all said, 'No, no.' He called it mutiny and everything else, and he got angry in the process. 'You see my name up in front of this band,' he told us, 'not that of any of you guys.' He said he couldn't do any better, and that was that. The trouble started there and the guys began leaving one by one.

"Besides the money, Charlie Barnet was around New York most of the time, and I had an apartment there, which made it good. I stayed with him about a year, most of 1943. Then I was with Boyd Raeburn for about eight months. All the time I was recording with people like Don Byas, Dizzy Gillespie, Charlie Parker and Oscar Pettiford. We did a lot of records, even recording behind blues singers like Rubberlegs Williams. I made a session with Tony Scott and Sarah Vaughan. I did some with Georgie Auld; in fact, Erroll Garner was on the same date with Al Killian and Shadow Wilson. Then I worked with Tiny Grimes, John Hardee and Marlowe Morris. We were accompanying Billie Holiday on 52nd Street, and we played a few numbers on our own, but not many, because Art Tatum was also appearing at that club. Hell, they didn't need anyone else to play! He was doing all the playing that could be done, you know that.

"We rehearsed with Lady Day about three days before she opened. I think we had about thirty numbers, her tunes, with little intros and endings. Of course, you couldn't play loud, and I used the mute all the time. John Hardee was a wonderful tenor man. He's teaching chemistry in high school in Dallas, Texas, now. I saw him not long ago. He told me he got fed up with the music business, that it was a rat race. But John could play, and he could swing. I used to tell him on the bandstand, 'Man, you bring back memories of Chu!' And do you know what he'd say? 'That's good enough for me!'

"After that, as I remember, I was with Benny Goodman about eight months. We won't talk about that, but I never had any trouble with him. In fact, he dug my work. We had a photograph taken together one day, and he autographed it, 'To one of my favorite jazzmen.' That knocked me out. The only time he got real peeved was when we were at the 400 Club. I was behind with my alimony and they took me off the stand down to the alimony court. I paid it off and came back next night. Red Norvo, Slam Stewart and Teddy Wilson were in the band at that time.

"Next, I got a little band of my own. I picked them up in Washington and took them off to Chicago—John Malachi on piano, Tommy Potter on bass, Eddie Byrd on drums, and Leo Parker and Harry Curtis on saxes. They'd never been out of Washington before, and we worked for about four months. Ray Nance used to come by every night when he was in Chicago with Duke. He dug the little band. We played real soft to fit the club—tenor, alto, trombone and three rhythm.

"I went with Norman Granz and his *Jazz at the Philharmonic* until the latter part of 1946, and then spent a few weeks in Los Angeles. A group was getting ready to go to Hawaii—Gerald Wilson, Dexter Gordon, Red Callender and drummer C. P. Johnson—and I decided to join them. The gig didn't pay off properly, but I liked the place and stayed there. So did Red, for about a year. I got married there, and found I could get work and live fairly comfortably. I formed a six-piece band. Once I had a trumpet, but I changed back to alto sax. I found the combination of alto and tenor saxes, with trombone, is better for me. It shows off my horn and gives me a chance to do more. You can't just jam with a combo like that, or it would sound terrible, but it's good if you get some nice things worked out. I don't mean you have to have a lot of arrangements. You can still be loose. I love tenor and trombone unison. You remember it on the session with Hawk, Earl Hines and Joe Thomas? Don Byas and I did the same thing behind Dizzy on numbers like *I Can't Get Started*. I like that sound, and it's not hard to do. You can put it behind anything.

"Louis Armstrong heard me in Honolulu, and asked me to join him, which I eventually did in 1952. In the meantime, I had got Danny Barcelona out of high school to play drums in my group. He could play nothing but marches then, but I'd been having so much trouble with the previous drummer. He was from San Francisco, and talented, but he stayed drunk all the time.

"With Louis, I play what I'd call semi-tailgate. I don't go all the way. I try to fill in the spots, to complement what he's doing. Here I don't play a lead style. I've got to follow and support. I try to keep my tone brilliant. It helps fill out the little group, and it isn't necessarily a broader sound. If it's cutting through, that's the main thing. I may cut down on my sound, and most of the time I'm playing lower behind Louis. It just wouldn't work if I played high the way I used to. Then, too, I think my tone has improved some, because I've been working on it. Every day I do a little work on it, and I have better control of it now. I had a little tooth trouble, and in the process I had to change mouthpieces. I found I had to put a lot more work on this mouthpiece to get the brilliance I had on the other one. The mouthpiece I had on the album of Handy songs was not the same one I had on the Fats Waller album, and the work I had done on my teeth made a slight change in embouchure. Right now, I wouldn't care to record, because I'm in the process of bringing this mouthpiece round. The money doesn't mean anything. I never did make records for the sake of money, and I hope I never have to. You can't just think about money. You've got to try to make a good record. I'm going to wait and just keep working, because I've got the mouthpiece back I used on the Handy album.

"As a matter of fact, I gave Butter (Quentin Jackson) a mouthpiece like that for a Christmas present twenty-five years ago, a sterling silver mouthpiece. 'Man, you can't get that mouthpiece back,' he says. Al Mott—he's dead now—he made it. Lot of times the public doesn't know what a musician is going through. You can't go around explaining these things to 'em. You just go on and try to play.

You know what you can do, and what you aren't doing. Nobody else can tell you, because you're the first to know! I'm going to be real sharp when I make some more records. Say in a year from now.

"I don't consider myself a Dixieland player. Now, Ory's a great Dixieland player. A lot of guys playing Dixieland could learn a lot from him, because he has the timing for it and he knows those tunes. A lot of them have never been written down. We made an album with Louis a little while ago, for Audio Fidelity. A lot of the numbers, old King Oliver numbers, Billy Kyle and I didn't know. We had never heard them before, so Pops had to play them over for us a couple of times, and show us where the breaks were. He taught me some of the phrases on one of those tunes, and made it a lot easier for me.

"I did my best. I knew guys had done it, and any style is a challenge to me. There aren't many trombone players who make it right. Nobody plays Dixieland right like Ory. Vic Dickenson does a good job on it, but his is a more delicate, subtle style. Dixieland style is punch. It's got to come on out. It's got to build. Vic isn't by any means a strong trombone player. Now Dicky Wells, he's strong. But I don't think anyone really knows it outside of Ory. You just have to go in there according to how your feeling for it is. Some guys have a feeling for it, and some haven't. I never heard much Dixieland around my home. Most of the bands were jazz bands.

"I enjoy Louis and I try to keep him happy. He has got a lot of soul, more soul than anybody I ever met in my life. A lot of feeling. Naturally, you get tired of the same repertoire. Anyone would. But it's amazing to me the beauty he can put into those numbers night after night, always keeping that same beautiful feeling. You strive to go right along with that, and in the end I think it will help your playing. Pops is so dedicated. He picks up his horn every day, even if he does go over the same things. He doesn't care about being a guy you can put in a book. He just likes to play what he likes to play. What I don't understand is that he records so many different tunes, but when he goes out he just plays the

Trummy Young and Kid Ory in Hawaii, 1971.

same numbers. His explanation is, 'Well, as long as you're playing it well . . .' Which makes sense when you're playing for different people each night.

"Barney Bigard sounds a whole lot better than when he was with the band before. He'll surprise you. He's really playing. He's not drinking. It's hard to play decently when you're not sober. Even when you're always playing the same numbers, you've still got to be thinking, because it's very easy to forget what tune you're playing! You have a tendency to get too lax. I try to tighten up a few little things I do in the background behind

Louis. I make a little switch here and a little switch there. You have to figure out something that will fit and not get in his way. You can't be observed too much when you're doing that ensemble stuff. You have to help the rhythm along, and then you hold a note once in a while. Or that's the way I see it. That's one of the jobs with that tailgate style—helping the rhythm, helping to push it along. Every once in a while you come in on a harmony part and fill in the harmony, to fill up the open spots. While Louis is holding a note, you don't try to execute all over him. Barney doesn't play with me. He's got his own part going and that makes it better, more loose. If the clarinet plays along with me, that isn't how it's supposed to be in Dixieland. When Louis is doing a vocal, we may lay a little riff back of him once in a while, and that's all right. In Dixieland, if you can keep out of each other's way and have your own little thing going, it sounds much nicer.

"As for this business of re-making old numbers, I don't think there's ever anything like the original. Billy May asked me about those Lunceford re-makes, and he was a little peeved when I said, 'No.' Even Sy (Oliver) can't do it, and he made lots of the original arrangements. First thing, how can you recapture spirit? When you copy, there may be spirit, but it's a different spirit, and usually the copy is too precise. Even the tempos aren't the same. When people work together for a long time, they feel each other. Like Duke: how in the world would you ever record something like Duke's old band with Cootie (Williams), Tricky Sam, Barney and Sonny (Greer)? You might get technically better men, but how in the world could you get that sound on the old stuff Duke did? Man, the band will never see the day that could do it. It might play the notes, but Duke had a band of *individuals*. That's like the difference between Basie's old band and his new band. For precision and everything, Basie has a wonderful band today, but it isn't like that other band. Nobody can tell me it swings like the old one. It may have been a little sloppy, but that was partly what made the looseness. Today, it's *Ting!*, right together, but it doesn't have the thing Basie's band used to have. Where's he going to find another Herschel (Evans), people like that? Even Jack Washington—he wasn't a great musician, but he fitted that band. Of course, the present band has enthusiasm and is wonderful in its way. Basie has trained them like that. He knows what he's doing. He's no kid. He's been through it. What he had before in Buck Clayton, Harry Edison, Dicky Wells, Herschel, Lester, Walter Page and Jo Jones—that only happens once in a lifetime. Basie's original band wasn't over-arranged. More than half his book was

heads. It's a funny thing, but there's no arrangement going to sound like a head.

"You take *Swingtime in the Rockies*, which Jimmy Mundy did for Benny Goodman. It was just a head we used to do with Booker Coleman in Washington when Jimmy was still with Tommy Myles. We used to bust down the house with that. Just a head—*Hot Chocolate Stomp*, we called it. Jimmy wrote it down, and later on he went out on his own. Tommy Myles had a book full of arrangements, but we mostly had heads. We could out-swing them, though they were maybe cleaner than us.

"I've been very fortunate in my career. I've worked with some guys who played great jazz, like Louis and Earl. Although I intend to have a little group of my own again some day, I think I'm doing the next best thing to that now by working with Louis. As a brass man, I can still learn a lot from him. Nobody, but nobody, sounds like Louis. I always felt like that about him. His sound is so big and clear. Studying him, I've learned something about sound. He's certainly got the biggest sound I've heard, no two ways about that. After he was sick . . . say since January, he's been popping those high ones, and he hasn't been missing them, and he's had no lip trouble. What did happen might happen to anyone. Here's a man, sixty years old, hitting those high ones every night, all night, on all the tunes, even when another guy is maybe taking a solo. He's bound to get in trouble sooner or later, but he hasn't been in trouble for a long while now. When he's right, you can forget about him playing the same program, because he's making it and it's a wonderful thing. I hope I can just live to be sixty, let alone play as strong as he does, every night, and no guesswork. He loves to play. It's hard to get him off the bandstand."

(1961)

Parts of this interview originally appeared in *Metronome* and are reprinted by special permission of the publisher, Robert Asen.

WILLIE RANDALL

SAXOPHONES AND ARRANGER

"I was born in Chicago on 1 September 1911. My father had played violin and he always kept music in the home. We had the old-time Victrola and good, legitimate music, so I was well acquainted with the classical repertoire and symphonies. I guess it was because I had heard my parents talking about music from an early age that I decided I wanted to play violin when I was six or seven years old. My mother got me a three-quarter size, and I would practice with all the great symphonies and violinists—on the Victrola. When I was eight, my mother took me to study with W. L. Jackson, who had a music studio in the 35th block on State Street. Bobby Wall and Stanley Wilson were my chief instructors. I had a private lesson during the week, and on Saturday there was a class lesson when all the strings practiced together. I was there two years until I broke a student's bow and Jackson slapped my face. My mother went up and bawled them out, and that was the end of that!

"Then I started with Howard Offert, who was teaching string music in the University of Music at 37th and Michigan. I studied with him till I was twelve or thirteen, by which time I was in an intermediate group and had given a minor recital. He had had me seriously studying bowing techniques, exercises and double steps, and he told me I should go to a more advanced teacher. I was a teen-ager in high school, playing in the symphony orchestra there, and I felt I wanted to do more in music than the violin allowed, be-cause it wasn't recognized in the school dance orchestra. I got involved with saxophone after graduating from Wendell Phillips Junior High School in the ninth grade, where I had been associated with other violin students like Ray Nance, Edward Burke and Milt Hinton. We'd all been in the same classical orchestra, but Milt began playing tuba, Ray the trumpet and Ed the trombone. I know Ray and Ed were soon playing in the Major N. Clark Smith marching band. I believe Milt did, too, and what he was playing was not really a tuba but an E-flat helicon. He and a girl named Nell Matilda Ritchie were our best violinists, although Ray Nance was fine, too. Nell Matilda studied more extensively and went on to the American Conservatory. She is now supervisor of music on the Chicago Board of Education.

"After Wendell Phillips, I went to Crane High School, an all-boys school, where we had a little booster orchestra and where I really started playing saxophone. My father had bought me a Wurlitzer. I liked violin, but the only outlets for me were in straight music, and young people were going for fellows who played trumpet, saxophone and drums.

"I studied with George Pfeiffer at Wurlitzer. I already had a good musical background and all he really did was show me the fingering of the saxophone, and about breathing, and how to develop my embouchure. I took a lesson a week for six months. Finally, he told me, 'Well, Willie, there's no use you coming back, because the way you play now there's not much I can show you, and you've got your own motivation and peer group.'

"There have been improvements in saxophones since the early '30s—improvements in the mechanism that provide the musician with more flexibility, but it was still a matter of learning to produce the sound you wanted, just as Coleman Hawkins did, rather than of the nature of the instrument itself. If I'm truthful about the alto player that first impressed me, I have to say Wayne King. He had a very popular orchestra at that time, and that was all you could hear on the radio. But we had records at home, and I was also impressed by Frankie Trumbauer's playing on *Singin' the Blues*. That type of improvisation and solo playing really attracted my attention, and I well remember playing his solo along with the record. Of course, in later years my favorite alto players were Benny Carter and Willie Smith.

"I continued to study music through high school, playing saxophone with the booster band and violin with the symphony orchestra. When I went to Crane Junior College, I started serious study in theory and harmony. Later on, Captain Walter Dyett advised me to go to Vandercook on Washington Street. It's now a part of the Illinois Institute of Technology. He said the teachers there were recognized as the best, and he himself coached many famous musicians like Nat Cole, Ray Nance, Gene Ammons, Benny Green and Dorothy Donegan. I think he took Major Smith's place at Wendell Phillips before going to Du Sable High School, where he taught for more than thirty-five years. We all looked up to him and accepted his advice. So I added music at Vandercook to my academic studies at Crane Junior College.

"Around 1932, I joined the musicians' union on a dispensation of $12.75. We'd been playing house parties, but not as professionals. Ray Nance, Jesse Simpkins, myself and a dozen other musicians all joined at this special dispensation, and we were then eligible to work professionally. When I was called to some rehearsals with professional bands, I began to find out my shortcomings and to realize I wasn't quite ready. There's more to music than good academic training.

"About eight or ten of us left Chicago as part of a band with Haver's Minstrel Show. We did a weekend engagement in Milwaukee, and then found ourselves stranded! I didn't want to come home, and so I stayed in Milwaukee and met some very good musicians like Jabbo Smith and Stump Whitlock. Leonard Gay had a terrific band then, and there were so many good-sounding bands in the vicinity of Milwaukee and Madison. I was about twenty, and I'd left school, and that brought on a little conflict with my father and mother, because neither of them had wanted me to quit school. But I stayed around Madison about a year and went in to Chicago to see them every two months.

"Then I joined a band from Louisiana called the Louisianians. Their headquarters were in Eau Claire and I traveled all through Wisconsin with them. Prentiss McCarey from Chicago was on piano and Harry Cornell was playing bass. I think their drummer's name was Trotter. Anyway, we were eight pieces and we did dance dates and quite a few one-nighters through Iowa and in the Dakotas. We also did a few locations, including one at the French Casino in Madison. I really served my apprenticeship with them for about two years, and when I got back to Chicago I felt eligible to play with any of the local bands. I worked with Charles Elgar before joining Eddie South in the old Chez Paree. He had Lucius Wilson, Gordon Jones and myself playing saxophones, doubling on clarinet and flute. I played violin, too, and so did Milt Hinton, who was on bass, and we had Everett Barksdale on guitar—no brass. They had all foreign shows there. Leon Belasco, I think, had the house band, and we played the relief or interim part of the show. Eddie South was just terrific at this time, and my career as an arranger really began then. I wrote for his group, and I did most of his original compositions, like *Black Gypsy*. When he closed at the Chez Paree, I joined Dave Peyton at the Regal Theatre, playing saxophone and clarinet. I guess I was the youngest fellow in the pit there. Then a fellow named Mc-Swain came in from Minnesota, and he had a good twelve-piece band that didn't get much recognition, but I remember we were broadcasting over WKYW from, I think, the old Sunset Café.

"After that, I began writing a book for a group of a dozen musicians who practiced together once a week. It was a co-operative, sharing band. We had a nice repertoire of about twenty-five arrangements that I wrote. Franz Jackson and Dave Young were in that band, and when I left them to join Earl Hines I left the management and the whole book with Dave.

"Fletcher Henderson had come to Chicago and he needed some musicians. Buster Bailey was sick, and another man in the reed section was absent. So Scoops Carry and I were sent over as replacements until they arrived. Scoops and I had known each other since childhood, but it was Budd Johnson who was instrumental in getting me in Earl's band afterwards, because he knew of my ability to write. We had had another terrific band around Chicago from Kansas City. It was led by Jesse Stone, and he had twelve pieces and a wonderful book. They were all good musicians, but there was no work and they had a hard struggle. It was when he was with them that I first met Budd.

"Earl wanted arrangers because Jimmy Mundy had left to go with Benny Goodman, so I became an integral part of his band in 1936. We were doing these half-hour NBC broadcasts every night, and Ed Fox, the manager at the Grand Terrace, would tell me how many tunes he wanted us to play. He was getting his little taste! And the publishers were working with me. 'Will you see my tune is scheduled for Tuesday night?' is the kind of thing they'd keep asking. I was always under pressure, because I had to write four or five arrangements a week. It was sort of depressing in a way, because you seemed to be always backlogged. The arrangements had to be commercial enough to keep the publisher satisfied, and they had to be comparable to what Earl wanted. You couldn't go overboard in either direction; you had to keep everybody

happy. It was perpetual action, because I had to write for the shows, too. And when there were recording sessions coming up, there'd be new material to get ready for them. A lot of times, I didn't go home. I'd stay at the Grand Terrace and sleep there. Quinn Wilson, Budd Johnson and I did all the writing, but Quinn didn't get involved with the shows much. It was good experience for me, and the training I had had proved very beneficial then.

"Some of the material was original, depending on whether the producer was putting on original things, but most of the shows were built off currently popular music. Valaida Snow put on some of the finest shows the Grand Terrace ever had. She not only produced them, she starred in them. She had so much talent. She sang, danced, and played violin as well as trumpet.

"Omer Simeon was playing lead in the reed section when I joined it, and after he left we got Scoops Carry. When Leroy Harris came in to sing, he played alto, so in 1940 he and Scoops were playing altos and I was mostly playing tenor.

"I had left Earl with Pee Wee Jackson and Ray Nance in 1939 and joined Horace Henderson. Earl lost six or seven men about that time after a trip to the West Coast. I think they were really tired of traveling, and most of our one-nighters were in the South. Horace had a good reputation as an orchestra leader, and he played consistently throughout the Chicago area—not one-nighters but strictly week-stand engagements. When I joined him, we played the 5100 Club over on North Broadway, and the concession was given Benny Skoler for us to leave that club and open up the Rhumboogie for two weeks, and then go back to the 5100. We called Skoler the Little King because he had done so much for musicians and entertainers, and was very close to them. He'd had any number of clubs in Chicago, and kept so many musicians and show people working that he always had maximum support. It was an interesting experience working with Horace, but when Earl reorganized in 1940, I went back with him.

"I had a nominal amount of solo work, especially on one-nighters, but it was usually on

Reunion of the Hines alumni at Willie Randall's Chicago home in 1971. Left to right: (front) Franz Jackson, Leon Washington, Earl Hines, George Dixon, Willie Randall, Dave Young; (back) Leon Scott, Charlie Allen, Lois Deppe, Rostelle Reese, Rozelle Claxton, Joe McLewis, Kenneth Stewart, Walter "Woogie" Harris.

the sweet side, because Budd was taking all the stuff with any fire. Later on, besides arranging, I got involved in managing the band. Earl had a disagreement with one of his road managers while we were traveling, and I had to take over, so I was really doing a double job. When we got to New York, the William Morris agency asked me to stay in. Towards the end, it got a little hard, and I quit playing to some degree to manage and take care of some of the business. I had to arrange all particulars of transportation. Sometimes I had to leave the band and go on ahead, and make ar-

rangements for its arrival, and be ready to meet the bus when it got in. For a while we had Charlie Carpenter as liaison manager in New York, but I was with the band on the road, working directly with the William Morris agency. What I learned about the business and administrative side of music helped me with my own operation later.

"I stayed with Earl till 1942, when I went into defense work at the Sun Shipyard in Chester, Pennsylvania. By that time George Dixon was in the Navy, Leroy Harris had gone into service, and there were so many new members coming in that Earl practically had a new band. Transportation had become a problem for him. The armed forces had priority, and because he had to move the band by train it curtailed the number of one-nighters he could do.

"I remained in defense work two years, but I was able to keep contact with musicians because I worked the third shift, from midnight till 8 in the morning, for a long time. So I could go to New York for the weekend and come back Monday morning. Finally, I got on the day shift and became the first black supervisor at Sun Ship. They needed someone to work in shipfitting and berthing, so I took the examination. I had a knowledge of blueprints and was eventually moved to the production-and-control office.

"I went into the Air Force in February 1944, and I was at Warner Roberts Field near Macon, Georgia. When they knew I was a musician, I soon found myself back in music again. I was in Flying Varieties, the Army Air Force Music Show, and music soon became a full-time thing, because I was teaching music and co-ordinating music activities and entertainment for the officers' club as well as for the enlisted men, all of which involved my having an orchestra. I brought Jimmie Lunceford's band there to play for the enlisted men, as well as Earl's and Duke Ellington's. I wanted to get out from the service and I asked leaders like them to write my commanding officer and request my discharge. That was a mistake, because letters from such reputable musicians made them think I really was somebody, so they kept me there for morale work to the bitter end!

"I came out in '46 and found a new thing had happened in Chicago musicwise—be-bop. I went around all the joints and listened and found a whole new breed of musicians had come up through the war period. The big bands had been done away with, and where we had had half a dozen big clubs with bands of from ten to fifteen pieces, we now had numerous clubs with groups of four or five pieces. To me, what had happened was a lot of junk. A guy who couldn't do anything at all could go and play and say, 'This is be-bop!'

"I took my time evaluating the scene, and then got back to playing with those bands that had something to offer here. I wrote for Charlie Morrison at the Rhumboogie, where Ziggy Johnson was producing, for the band in the De Lisa, and for Larry Steele in the Bijou. I also became musical director for Floyd Campbell when he was in the Rhumboogie. My peer group of musicians came out of service and went right back together again, playing what we liked, what we thought was good music. The clubs survived and the be-bop bands and joints thinned out.

"One development after the war was the social club dance. Each club might put on two or three affairs a year, and in this way playing miscellaneous dance engagements became a thriving business for those who had what we called gig bands. When I put out a brochure in the '60s, I referred to somewhere between fifty and a hundred clubs that I had provided entertainment for. The kind of ballroom engagements we played when we went out on the road with Earl, doing one-nighters, had certainly diminished. Except for the big names, bands were looking for location work and staying in their own localities. The wages and expense of moving a big band made it difficult, and those bands still on the road at this time began to cut down in size. It was a matter of economics. If you stayed home and worked three nights a week, you were as well off as if you were on the road earning more, but with double the expense. Since we soon didn't have as many clubs where musicians could work full time, it meant that many of the fellows had to supplement their income with a day job and concentrate on night engagements over the weekend.

"There was a man named Herman Roberts who was in the taxicab business and wanted to own a nightclub. He knew of me as a musician, and he once gave a public dance in his garage at 66th and what is now King Drive, although at that time, around 1951, it was still South Parkway. One of the things I got into when I came out of the service was a co-operative group of veterans running cabs on South

Willie Randall and his orchestra. Left to right: (back) Frank Hooks, Harlan Floyd, Joe Mc-
Lewis, Eugene Bon Bon Miller, Rudy Martin, Earl Turner, Burgess Gardner, Calvin Ladner;
(front) Billy Atkins, Ronald Wilson, Clifford Clark, Willie Randall, Sylvester Hickman (bass),
Eddie Johnson, Everett Sands.

Parkway. I was accountant for the group, and that was how Roberts knew me, and knew he could use my talents. When he decided to build his Show Lounge, he told me, 'I'm going to rely on you to run it, to be my manager, my right-hand man.' The building went up, and after we expanded and put the hydraulic stage in, it got to be really big business. I knew all the booking agents in New York, and I took him there and we'd buy up our shows for three to six months in advance, using attractions like Louis Jordan and Arthur Prysock. Herman was successful with his nightclub and went into the motel business, and he retained my services as comptroller.

"I left him in '59, although I went back on a commission basis at different times to put in some new systems. During the '50s I had still kept playing with a small gig band, but the clients could see that George Dixon, Henderson Smith and Willie Randall were working together and taking turns as leader. So I took a period out and wrote about a dozen arrangements for a big band. I picked some fifteen to twenty musicians, told them what I was going to do, and went into rehearsing two or three times a week. They liked the music and the idea of a big band. I never fired anybody, but it was a matter of a guy moving himself out when he felt he didn't have what we needed. I got out a brochure saying I'd brought together a group of Chicago's top musicians, and sent it to two or three hundred people. Once the social clubs heard the band, they started saying, 'Well, Willie's got something new . . .'

"I made an investment of nearly $3000. It wasn't a big deal, but it was a lot for me then. I got all my music stands, cases and equipment, and fortunately I offset my investment within six months. I'd send out a mailing before Christmas, one around April, and another in August, because you have to hit people for the fall after the vacation period. I'd also send thank-you notes, reminders of past engagements, inquiries about future ones, and a calendar around the first of the year. These little tricks kept the big band moving, and I often played for big conventions during what would have been the slow period. Besides the big band, I'd provide little bands for some of the subsidiary rooms. We played mostly in Chicago, sometimes in Indiana, seldom any further away than Milwaukee or Aurora.

"I gained the respect of my men, because I paid them off before ever they blew a note. They knew they would pick up the check as soon as they came in and signed the payroll. They owned their uniforms, and we had four changes. Eddie Johnson was one of the guys

who picked them out. When it was time for us to have a new jacket, I usually got him and Rudy Martin to shop for us, because they both have good taste in clothes.

"Of course, this big band activity fell off when rock became the rage. Economics entered into it again, because with all their amplification rock groups needed only five or six pieces. Soon I had to cut down to six or eight, and I had to concentrate on writing arrangements that made eight men sound comparable to fifteen! There are certain ballrooms where it's mandatory to have a minimum number of twelve or fifteen men, and there are others where they like a full, big band although the minimum may be only eight.

"I've given concerts since 1963. They have always been Music Performers' Trust Fund Concerts, and I had the idea that they could be done in a jazz vein. I'd do numbers like *Sabre Dance* and *Moonlight Sonata* that way. We had a merger of the two unions that was ratified in '67, and from then on the number of my concerts definitely decreased. In our magazine, *Intermezzo*, you might see a musician's name listed as giving four concerts in a month with anywhere from twenty to thirty pieces, and the explanation always was that they were 'co-sponsored concerts.' It was never satisfactorily explained when musicians inquired. They knew the same amount of money was coming out of the Trust Fund. I'd gladly do some 'co-sponsored' concerts,' so that I'd have more work for my musicians.

"But I really have no gripes. I've got a substantial daytime job where I don't punch a clock. I'm in social work with the Department of Corrections, and I work with kids up to seventeen years old. I've got one of the finest drum and bugle corps in the city. It's all a matter of discipline and building character. There are fine young musicians coming up and I'm exposed to a lot of them. 'Willie, when do you have a rehearsal?' they worry me, asking. 'I just want to come by and sit and listen to your band!' "

(1971)

JOHN "STREAMLINE" EWING

TROMBONE

John Ewing was born in Topeka, Kansas, 17 January 1917. He was seventeen when he made his professional debut in a local band led by Richard Harrison. Four years later, he was in Chicago, in Horace Henderson's band, which included a number of musicians who had previously worked with Earl Hines.

"Walter Fuller, a good friend of mine, was with Horace then," he said. "So were Budd Johnson, Omer Simeon and 'Mouse' Burroughs. They had left Earl when he had some trouble with Ed Fox at the Grand Terrace, but they went back to him. I must have stayed with Horace about a couple of months longer, because I went to Detroit with him. When we get back to Chicago, he didn't have any work, and Walter Fuller and Milton Fletcher asked me if I wasn't ready to come on down with them at the Grand Terrace. So away I went and joined Earl Hines in November 1938. I wasn't too experienced then. In fact, I was really scared. Earl had a bigger name and more weight than Horace, and I was nervous. I could read, but I had more fear than anything else. The guys were beautiful to me. I couldn't have made it without people like Budd Johnson and Walter Fuller. They wouldn't let you quit. They knew I was scared and they just kept me going. 'Come on,' they'd say. 'You got it!'

"Trummy Young had been gone about a year when I joined, and the other two trombones were Ed Burke and Ed Fant. We had so much of a show to play that the lead was kind of split up between us, but I guess I had what was really the first book.

"Budd Johnson was the music director then. He was respected, and he was quite a guy. He rehearsed the band, and at that time we had to do a lot of rehearsing, because we were on the air twice a night, seven nights a week, and there were always new songs and new arrangements. That's how they plugged songs in those days, but I know the broadcasts also helped make me extremely nervous at first! I couldn't stand to look at a mike! We'd be on the air at 10:30 or 11, after the first show, and then again around 1 A.M.

"The first time I quit the band was really because I had gotten married and wanted to stay out of the Army. People told me 'If you get a defense job, you can stay out of it.' So we moved to Los Angeles in 1940, but the defense job didn't last long. I couldn't stand it, and I decided I'd rather take the Army. Meantime, I went back to Earl, and nothing ever happened, because I was classified 4-F. They thought there was a spot on my lung and that I had tuberculosis. That worried me, but it turned out that I didn't really have it. My prayers were answered.

"When I finally left Earl in 1942, I'd gotten tired of the road and all the traveling. Guys were getting drafted, coming and going so fast, and it was hard to keep a band together then. Anyway, I went to Chicago and stayed there a while.

"I think Earl Hines is one of the finest

235

Trummy Young, Earl Hines and Streamline Ewing at Disneyland, 1971.

leaders that have ever been. He's a dynamic man. He always encouraged you and always wanted you to feel a part *of* the band, not just someone who happened to be there. If there was something you could do, he gave you a chance to do it. 'Come on out front and blow,' he'd say.* But he led the way himself, because he certainly would put on a great solo. He didn't let anyone else bother him or get in the way of what he was going to do. You could do all you wanted to do, take as much time as you needed, and he'd still do what he was

going to do. He was easy to work for, and I never knew him to fire anybody while I was there. If he did, I didn't know about it. I've known guys to quit, and if he let somebody go, it was their fault. He was really about the best to work for that I've known. A lot of others were not so pleasant. And whatever he said he was going to pay you, he paid you. He doesn't owe me a dime! Only one time we had some trouble, and then it wasn't Earl's fault. Nobody in the band blamed him. He did his best, and we knew where the problem was. We were at the Grand Terrace and he just wasn't getting the money. He had a lot of problems with the people there. They were rough.

"Something else I remember about that

---

* Solos by Ewing with Earl Hines may be heard on the records of *Grand Terrace Shuffle, XYZ, Yellow Fire* and *Windy City Jive*. That on *Jeep Rhythm* by Jimmie Lunceford shows the influence of his predecessor, Trummy Young.

band was that it was a homey band. There were no cliques. There was no bunch of guys against another bunch over there. So it was enjoyable, and I don't know of anyone who worked with Earl who ever said anything disagreeable about him.

"He can certainly spot talent, especially in singers. I was in the band when Billy Eckstine joined, and I was there when B. made his first record. He had never heard his voice on a playback, and he came to me and asked what I thought of it. I told him I thought it sounded great, which it did.

"Some funny things used to happen when we were on the road. I remember when we were on tour in Montana. Every time we'd get some place where there was a stable, I'd get me a horse to ride. I got up early one morning in Helena, and Earl and some of the boys were already down in the hotel lobby.

" 'Where're you going?' they wanted to know.

" 'Horseback riding.'

" 'Well, we'll go, too!'

"There were Earl, Leroy Harris, Red the valet, and I'm not sure now who else. We went out to the stable and rented horses. The ride took us to the top of Mount Helena. Now, you know, if you'd never been on a horse before, or if you'd been off a horse for years, that had to be a tough ride! It took an hour or two to get to the top of the mountain, and coming down you had to kind of circle around. I do remember that Earl was *very* uncomfortable, and I doubt if he ever rode a horse again. He takes good care of himself, and keeps fit, but riding a horse is something else when you're not used to it. I've lived in Altadena for seven years, and it's zoned for horses, so now I have my own horse right there at home, and I still ride.

"After I had left Earl, I worked with Louis Armstrong a week in Chicago and a week in South Bend, Indiana. Luis Russell was his piano player then. After that, I remember being in a show with Lionel Hampton and Billie Holiday at the Regal Theatre in Chicago. Lionel had a wonderful band then, with people like Milt Buckner, Joe Newman, Joe Wilder, George Jenkins and Irving Ashby in it. I particularly recall Joe Wilder playing a beautiful solo behind Billie on one of her songs. Not long afterwards, I went with Jimmie Lunceford for about two years. Trummy Young had left him then, and I seemed to be following in his footsteps again. Later, I was with Cab Calloway for some time.

"I saw Earl again when he came out here (Los Angeles) around 1952 with a great little group. He had Jonah Jones, Benny Green, Aaron Sachs on clarinet, Tommy Potter on bass and Ocie Johnson on drums. They were at the Oasis. They played some Dixieland, which was kind of popular then, but they played other things, too, and Earl himself was as good as ever. He's always played good, and I've heard him on several television shows recently where he sounded wonderful. Last year, he had a small group at Disneyland with Trummy Young and Marshall Royal, and they were terrific. I was working out there, too, with Teddy Buckner.

"Streamline? When I was a teen-ager, I was real thin and skinny, and a drummer I was with gave me that nickname. It's stuck with me ever since."

(1972)

BILLY ECKSTINE

SINGER AND TRUMPET

This conversation took place on 28 November 1975, at the Plaza Hotel in New York. Billy Eckstine was appearing in the Persian Room, where he had invited Earl Hines and the author to dinner. To the audience's gratification, he persuaded his one-time leader to join him on piano for a lively performance of Jelly, Jelly. *Afterwards, in his suite, the two of them recalled the following incidents from their joint past. They reveal, I believe, why Billy Eckstine has always been so greatly liked and respected by jazz musicians of all persuasions.*

Eckstine: Do you remember the time, Gate, when we were in Americus, Georgia, and they turned off all the lights and threw firecrackers up on the bandstand? We were playing this white dance, and when the lights came on again there was *nobody* on that bandstand. They were great, big firecrackers, cherry bombs, and in those days you didn't know what the hell to expect!

Hines: The way they went off in that hall—boom, boom!—they might have been real bombs. And there was only one way in there, up those steps, remember?

B.E.: One way in, one way out! Oh, Lord, let me get out of here, I was saying to myself. Another time when we were down there, a bottle hit Leroy Harris right in the head. The funny thing about that was that Leroy was such a quiet little gentleman. He never had anything to say to anybody, and all of a sudden—bam!—a bottle hits *him* in the head. He just about passed out.

E.H.: How about the time, B., when we were on that train that had a jim-crow car? When we arrived in Washington, D.C., and I was getting off, I said, "Who's this cat under the car?" I saw B. and Scoops Carry standing there, but I didn't know what had happened.

B.E.: In those days they had segregated trains, and the black car was always right behind the coal car, so that all the dirt and dust would fly in on us. There was an old, rotten cracker in the coach behind us, and he did a lot of eating. When he got through with something, he'd open the door and throw his garbage into our section.

"Wait till we get to Washington," I told the guys, because when you got to Washington you'd left the South and were all right. When we got there, I jumped off the train and waited for this cracker. I was looking the other way as he got off, but I turned and said, "Man, what were you throwing all that stuff in on us for?" Then I hit him, and he slid backwards. I grabbed him and hit him again, and he started crawling under the train. "Please let me get up," he said.

"If you can stand up under there, you're gonna be a bitch," I said, "because I'm gonna whip your ass across the tracks and back under again!" Scoops Carry was waiting the other side, talking about, "Let me get at him, B., let me get at him!" He had bags under both arms and I remember asking, "What are you going to hit him with?"

Stanley Dance: I've heard stories about you mistreating pianos, too.

B.E.: Yes, another thing that used to make me mad was pianos. Here we come to some dance with Earl, the number one piano player in the country, and half the keys on the goddam piano won't work. So when we're getting ready to leave, I'd get some of the guys to stand around the piano as though we were talking, and I'd reach in and pull all the strings and all the mallets out. "The next time we come here," I'd say, "I'll bet that son-of-a-bitch will have a piano for him to play on."

E.H.: He used to have me so nervous! I never liked to say anything, because I was always thinking that I'd come back to one of these joints and they'd think I'd done it. But those guys of mine . . . they didn't care. And at that time we had an arsenal in the band. You had to have *something* then.

B.E.: Everybody had guns. We used to be riding down the highway, and we'd shoot

Billy Eckstine (at mike) with the Earl Hines orchestra, 1940. Left to right: (back) Ed Fant, "Rabbit," Joe McLewis, Alvin Burroughs, Hurley Ramey, Truck Parham; (front) Rostelle Reese, Russell Gillum, Pee Wee Jackson, George Dixon (doubling on baritone saxophone), Earl Hines, Franz Jackson, Scoops Carry, Willie Randall, Leroy Harris, Budd Johnson.

cows. We had nothing else to do on those long trips, and the guys would say, "Hey, B., wake up! There's some cows." So I'd roll down the window, and—bam!—a cow would fall over.

Joe McLewis and I set up a kind of mock fight at one time. It started as a gag, and we made it up over a bullshit argument. Earl was in on it.

"I don't give a goddam about him, and I'll do so-and-so and so-and-so," Mac would start off.

"Then I'll blow your damn head off," I'd say. "You can argue all you want, but I'm tired of hearing that kind of bullshit."

All this was in front of Shorts McConnell, who was a most complaisant little guy. "Come on, man," he'd say, "don't you guys talk like that." But we were building the argument up, and doing it on the bandstand, too, and Earl would be saying, "You all cut that out, you hear? You're working for me, and I don't want to hear any more about it."

Now we used to line up and get paid, and one day George Dixon was sitting at a desk paying off. Mac and I put Shorts in between us, and Mac was taller than I am. I pushed Mac from behind, and began:

"And another thing . . ."

"What're you talking about now?" Mac said, turning around and pulling out his knife.

Shorts was still right between us when I pulled out my pistol. He nearly died of fright, but he took off and ran through a cornfield.

E.H.: We were playing some outdoor event, and I had to send and find him in that cornfield.

B.E.: You remember when Shorts had that girl friend, Lorraine, and got married? Budd Johnson and I were talking to him.

"Man, you know what you ought to do?" I said. "You ought to go around and punch her right in the mouth. How are you going to let that woman run over you like that?"

Then we'd give Shorts another drink and Budd would say, "Sure, Shorts, I wouldn't take that if I were you."

We steamed him up so much, he went off and beat this girl. She came around, crying.

"Shorty has lost his mind," she said. And she left him.

"Man, Lorraine quit me," Shorts said when he saw us.

"You silly little so-and-so," we said.

E.H.: B., you may have forgotten the time we played the Paradise Theatre in Detroit. It was winter and cold as hell. The manager came to me and asked for us to do a little benefit for a Catholic place next door. He said all the bands that played the theatre did it, but it was segregated worse than Georgia, and you refused.

B.E.: Yes, I do remember. The son-of-a-bitch in there wouldn't even serve the guys coffee, cold as it was. I went in and asked for coffee.

"You want it to go?" he asked.

"No, I want to drink it now."

"You can't drink it here."

"Okay, give it to me anyway."

So he gave me this hot coffee in a container. When I started to take the top off, he said, "I told you you couldn't drink it in here."

"I ain't gonna drink it in here," I said, and threw it all over him.

E.H.: When that manager heard about it, he came to me and said we would never play the Paradise again, but after *Jelly, Jelly* came out, we were the first band to go in there!

That was like when we were in Cleveland and Dizzy (Gillespie) and some of them went in a restaurant that refused to serve them.

"We want some of those Equal Rights steaks," they said.

B.E.: "I don't know who'll serve you," the manager said.

"I used to be a waiter," I said. "I'll serve them." And I went behind the counter.

E.H.: Those guys! They were something! And they could all take care of themselves.

B.E.: I remember when we went someplace down south—maybe it was at the time I had my own band—and an old woman in a restaurant asked us:

"What do you motherfuckers want?"

"Hey, baby, don't you call me no motherfucker," Scotty said, looking her straight in the face.

"Let me tell you something," she said.

"You're a motherfucker till you die, and then you're a dead motherfucker!"

E.H.: That was something like the story you told me, Stanley, about you and Johnny Hodges.

S.D.: Oh, the time when Duke was playing a sacred concert at a church in the Bronx. Coffee and sandwiches had been provided downstairs for the band between rehearsal and the performance. Some of the parishioners were serving the refreshments. When Johnny and I went up a second time with our cups, a very old lady looked at us and said, "You motherfuckers want some more coffee, I suppose?" That put Johnny in a good humor for a week.

You've always given Earl a lot of credit, Billy. What was the most important thing you got from him?

B.E.: The main thing Earl taught me was showcraft. How to handle myself on stage.

E.H.: He used to bow like this. (*Demonstrates, bowing stiffly from the waist with fists clenched.*) "Who you gonna fight?" I'd ask him.

B.E.: Yes, I was so used to fighting then that I kept my fists balled up. And I'd run off the stage and run right back on. "Stay off, stay off a bit," Earl would say. "Make them want you." Shit, I was afraid they wouldn't be applauding when I got back!

E.H.: One time, when we went to record, and we had all those beautiful arrangements on ballads for B. to sing, the a. and r. man said, "Don't you have any blues?"

B.E.: On the road, especially in the South, we used to fill out the program with a lot of those Joe Turner blues, like *Cherry Red*; and things like *My Big Brass Bed*. In those days, too, the union allowed you to record more than four tunes if you hadn't used up the three hours. So Earl had me go out in the anteroom and write down the lyrics while he and Budd worked out a head arrangement with the band. That was *Jelly, Jelly*.

E.H.: By the time we got back to New York and the Apollo Theatre, the record was out, and when B. stepped out onstage and began to sing, "Hello, baby . . . ," the house just went wild. Chicks were yelling and hollering, "Yeah, yeah, yeah!"

B.E.: You remember that song, *Take Me, I'm Yours*? Don Redman wrote the arrangement. The band would play the introduction, and Earl would say, "And now Billy Eckstine . . . ," and I'd walk out to the mike. When we did it at the Apollo, there was some broad sitting near the front who shouted out, "I'll take you, you sweet motherfucker!"

E.H.: The whole house cracked up!

B.E.: I was singing *Sophisticated Lady* at Carnegie Hall last year in a concert with Count Basie, and some bitch 'way up in the gallery hollered, "Billy, you're making me come!"

"Maybe the lady isn't so sophisticated," I said.

S.D.: How did you and Earl first get together?

B.E.: Earl first heard me at the Club De Lisa in Chicago. That was a very late spot, and when the Grand Terrace closed they'd come up there. You see, I'd known Budd Johnson before in Pittsburgh, where I was born. He always tried to get me to come to Chicago. I left Pittsburgh in 1936, went to Buffalo for most of 1937, spent about three weeks in Detroit, and came on into Chicago in 1938. I was in the De Lisa about a year and a half before I went with Earl. Of course, I had been to school in Washington before that, and Jimmy Mundy and I had been in Tommy Myles's good little band there. Trummy Young and Tyree Glenn were in it, too, and Elton Hill, the trumpet player, who wrote all those things for Gene Krupa like *Let Me Off Uptown*. Many of the numbers that Mundy did for Earl and Benny Goodman were written for us when we were at the Crystal Caverns, like *Cavernism* and *Madhouse*. *Swingtime in the Rockies* was one we just called *C Sharp*. I wonder what Mundy is doing? I haven't seen him in fifteen years.

S.D.: It always seems strange to me, Earl, that Billy is by temperament just the opposite of what you expect a ballad singer to be. The fact that he was attracted to bop . . .

B.E. (*Laughs*): That's just the way things were. I was a singer, but I always thought of myself more as a musician, I like music period. And I've always appreciated the musical side more than just the showmanship. Willie Randall and Budd Johnson—Budd especially—taught me music, the scales, and how to read parts. Then, when I was with Earl, I sat up and played the fourth trumpet parts. All of that enhances what you can do as a singer. I never had vocal lessons, but I had lessons on trumpet from Maurice Grupp, the great breath-control teacher, which taught me how to breath as a singer.

E.H.: And when you play an instrument, it teaches you chord structure.

B.E.: You know what you can do. Like a cat

blessed with more of a voice, he would have been a great singer.

B.E.: Sure, and that's why I always felt very fortunate in being with him. Up to that time, Stanley, in the black bands, the singers were just there to bring up the instrumentals— unless it was a chick with a big ass or something. But with Earl, I had *carte blanche*. If I heard a song I liked, I didn't even have to go to him. I'd just go to Budd and have him write it up for me. That's the way Gate was. Earl believed in the *presentation* of an orchestra.

E.H.: When I went to the De Lisa, it was to get a dancer. Then Billy came out. "Who's this good-looking boy?" I asked. And then

Billy Eckstine with the Earl Hines orchestra in Oklahoma City, 1942.
Hines is between Madeline Green and Eckstine.

once told me you learn music not to know what to do, but what you can't do.

S.D.: Well, I was impressed with that solo you blew on *I'm Confessin'* tonight.

E.H.: To take the horn in the middle of your act like that, with no opportunity to warm it up, is *hard*.

B.E.: I stick the mouthpiece in my mouth before I begin, as you saw, but the metal is still cold.

S.D.: I always feel that if Earl had been

when he began to sing with that robust, baritone voice, I said, "Goddam, I'm going to try my best to get *him*! He'll kill everybody."

B.E.: It wasn't hard either, because I was making twenty-five dollars a week then!

E.H.: No, but I had trouble with the gangsters. They didn't want you to leave.

B.E.: They owned that De Lisa club.

E.H.: I had to speak to Ralph Capone about it, but when we went out on the road, it happened just like I knew it was going to happen.

All those chicks swarming around. I never saw anything like it in my life. There were so many goddam women, it made me feel young again! I had his left-overs. Tell you one thing, after B., all the bands tried to get good-looking boy singers.

B.E.: For a while, after Earl and I were together, every black band had a son-of-a-bitch singing like me. Buddy Johnson must have had five in a row, including Arthur Prysock.

S.D.: Before that, most black bands had male singers with high voices like Lunceford's Dan Grissom. What was the origin of that?

B.E.: I think Orlando Robeson started it. He

sang things like *Trees* with Claude Hopkins, and he would go higher than a dentist's drill. That used to bug the hell out of me, because I could never do it. My voice was too heavy, but I'd have had a fight every week if I'd begun to sound like a faggot.

E.H.: When Herb Jeffries was first with my band, he used to sing high—woo-woo—and we told him, "You got to come down from there, because we don't know what the hell you are!"

B.E.: Billy Strayhorn was the one that got him down when he did the arrangement of *Flamingo* for Duke, got him down into a range. Before that he mostly used to sing falsetto.

E.H.: Then he started to copy you. When I had B. and Madeline Green, I really had a couple of the best-looking matinée idols.

B.E.: What a beautiful girl she was! I remember telling her that we ought to put our money together and save it. But we had a regular casino at the back of the bus. The guys put flashlights on coathangers so we could gamble all night long as we went down the highway. Madeline would give me her money to "save," and I'd go right back and blow it. When Earl and I broke up, she came to me and said, "Where's my money?" She went to Earl about it, but he said he couldn't get in the middle, couldn't do anything about it.

E.H.: But B. was luck*eeey*! He used to break the band all the time. He even broke that guy from Texas.

B.E.: Don Robey, when he was traveling with us. He was supposed to be a slick gambler, but he didn't give me credit for knowing what I was doing. I broke him on the bus, and he told Earl, "Don't you bring that son-of-a-bitch down here no more!"

E.H.: Billy had taken so much money off him that they had to start gambling again on the platform at a railroad station. When he got some of his money back, he took the next train and got the hell out! I remember when they broke Scoops Carry, too. Scoops was going to send some money home to his Jo-Jo, but they took it before the dance, and he was the saddest-sounding saxophone player that night I ever did hear. After the dance, he won most of it back, but they kept on till he lost it again.

S.D.: What games did you play?

B.E.: Blackjack, craps, poker, everything.

E.H.: He was just lucky, and he loved to gamble.

B.E.: I gambled *all* the time. They got me once though, at the State Theatre in Hartford, Connecticut. We were gambling, gambling, gambling all day long there, until I was broke, and I hadn't even got a room yet.

"Man, give me some money so I can get a room?" I asked McLewis.

"Broke son-of-a-bitch ain't supposed to have no room," he said. "Get out of here, man! Stop hangin' around the table. Your breath smells!"

So finally I slept in the theatre in a big trunk they used as a bass case. Rats and everything were running around there, so I got up and got a big stick they used for pushing windows up and down, and I lay there in the case with this stick to beat the rats off when they tried to come over the side.

E.H.: That was the damnedest band I ever had!

S.D.: Right then, it must have been about the hottest band in the country.

B.E.: Yes, we had the best musical band. We come into a theatre, we had a show aside from the swinging. We were a Chicago band, a Midwestern band, and when we came into New York they used to lay for us. But we'd shake them off like they were nothing, whoever they put on us. We had so much entertainment. I remember when we went into the Savoy opposite Erskine Hawkins. They were saying that Earl depended on Billy, but after they got through with *After Hours*, Earl would come back with *Boogie Woogie on St. Louis Blues*, and tear it *up*.

E.H. And after Jimmy Mitchell finished with *Cherry*, here'd come Billy with *Jelly, Jelly.* *Tuxedo Junction* was their big hit then, and each time they played it we'd follow with something different, like *Grand Terrace Stomp*. Erskine tried to get the crowd back with *Tuxedo Junction*, but they played it so many times that one little cat, who'd been standing between the stands and listening all night, finally asked them, "Don't you know anything but *Tuxedo Junction*?"

B.E.: That was some kind of band we had then, and we were all like brothers. Hey, I've got to get dressed for the next show!

(1975)

Above: Dizzy Gillespie (left), Earl "Fatha" Hines and Billy Eckstine at Wolf Trap.

Opposite: Earl Hines, Billy Eckstine, Dizzy Gillespie and Bobby Tucker at Wolf Trap, 1976.

FRANZ JACKSON

TENOR SAXOPHONE, CLARINET AND ARRANGER

"My mother played a little bit by ear. I wouldn't exactly say she was a musician, but she loved to listen and was very sensitive to music. What started me off was just hearing a fellow play saxophone. I went to one teacher, Jerome Pasquall, who used to be with Fletcher Henderson. At that time he had just gotten out of Boston Conservatory, and he was real fresh. When he came to Chicago, I think he worked with Charlie Cooke at the White City. My mother met him somewhere and told him about me, and he agreed to teach me.

" 'You take the sax,' he said, 'and I can teach you faster, and it's a more popular instrument. Then you can pick up on the clarinet. It's just a matter of getting the technique.' That's what I did. I really went into the book with clarinet after I had learned to read and to know what I was doing with chords. He used to play the piano, and then I'd get off, and he'd say I was playing such-and-such a chord. I had a pretty good ear and could follow things, because when I first got the horn I couldn't afford to pay for it and lessons, too. So I had started working on it and playing by ear.

"My father had died when I was quite young, and my mother had three children. She had to struggle you know. Fortunately, she had a profession, an unusual skill. She was a dressmaker and she passed for white. That was the only way she could make a living, for at that time a colored woman could only do kitchen work and jobs like that.

"The first group I played with, and got a little money from, was on a boat that ran from Jackson Park to the Pier, here in Chicago. They used to pass the hat around. It was no great thing, and I wouldn't call that a professional start. When I really got hired was with Al Wynn, Punch Miller and Albert Ammons. We used to get on a truck and go around advertising those excursions that went to New Orleans and Memphis. That was really my first job, and playing saxophone. Clarinet was such a hard instrument, and saxophone kept on growing in popularity. Unless you could really blow clarinet, the guys wouldn't tolerate you, and I couldn't play it that well then.

"My main influences were Coleman Hawkins, of course, and Johnny Hodges and Benny Carter. I also used to try to get that solo Frankie Trumbauer played on *Singin' the Blues*. I was impressed by it, and I used to listen to his records, and I tried to work with that song. On clarinet, I liked Barney Bigard very much.

"The first big band I was with was Shuffle Abernathy's out of Milwaukee. I went up there with Scoville Brown. He was playing tenor and I was playing alto then. Eddie Tompkins, the trumpet player later with Jimmie Lunceford, was the best-known musician to come out of that band. They were reading music, and this was the first band that ever played my arrangements.

"The reason I got into writing was because I had been working with François Moseley, and his band didn't read any music. Punch Miller,

Fat Howard and Silas White were in it, and we learned everything by ear. When a guy left, our little head arrangements were all messed up. I made up my mind if ever I had a band that wasn't going to happen to me. So I started studying arranging. You know, youth . . . you like to know everything you can about what interests you. I went to the library and read one book after another. Then, when I went to the Chicago Musical College for a year and a half, it extended what I knew, and I learned how to write without a piano, solfeggio, and all that. I took harmony and counterpoint, and it was money well spent. Pleasurable, too. When I get into something, man, I really chew it! Of course, I was working around during that time.

"Back in '26 and '27, there were big bands like Charlie Cooke's, and the musicians in them were very sharp. They'd come out of

François Moseley's band, 1927. Left to right: Gideon Honore (piano), Franz Jackson, Leon Washington, François Moseley, Sylvester Birch (banjo), Silas White, trumpet players unknown.

little theatres at times, but jazz musicians were found just here and there. You had to contend with the fact that most of these guys couldn't read parts, and that put them in the category of working in those roadhouses and joints they had around Chicago. I played in them a long time before I started reading a score. When I did start, it sort of fell into place. The job with Abernathy was a chance for me to read.

"In 1931, I think it was, I joined Cass Simpson's band. He'd spent a lot of time with Bernie Young's band in Milwaukee, and I think he studied a lot there. He was pretty exotic. I mean in the way he would innovate with that band. When we started, we had some funny little arrangements, and we rehearsed. We were at Sam Beard's Showboat on State Street, and we were on the air almost every night. Cass had about twelve pieces and he'd just pass the parts of a stock out and say, 'Come on, we're going to play this! And he'd pass out choruses on anything. I particularly remember that happening with *Sweet and Lovely*. I thought it was the darnedest tune, because it had a lot of changes in it that were unusual. It wasn't like passing out choruses on *I Got Rhythm*. And he'd get at that piano and play—mostly kind of like Fats Waller then, you know—and it didn't make any difference what *you* or the band were playing. He was playing so much back there! He was like Art Tatum. He used to say, 'Now I'm going to play like so-and-so.' He could sound like Earl Hines or anybody. Finally he blew it! It was paresis. When he made an album in the asylum, he was just a shell of what he really was, and people weren't interested.

"The next job I remember was with Carroll Dickerson. He was an old bandleader who had the band at the Savoy Ballroom in Chicago, and he'd gone to New York and come back. Bob Shoffner and Kenneth Anderson were rehearsing a band. They had arrangements, and it was a good tight band, but they couldn't get any work, so Carroll took the whole group over. Kenneth Anderson quit and I took his place. I was doing well then, working those small joints, not working with any bands. As I said, musicians were either one way or the other at that time. Either they could read music, or they had to have it explained. Gangsters were running everything. You didn't make a big salary, but you got your money every night, because the next night the joint's liable to be burned up, or gone, or closed, or padlocked across. You got three or four dollars a night with a meal, and the tips you made. You could pick up anything in tips in the Prohibition period, because you never knew who'd come in. There might be four or five parties during the night, and you could make seventeen or eighteen dollars a night, which was good then, a week's salary for some people. You might be paying two dollars a week for a room, and you could get a meal for thirty-five cents. So I was doing well, helping my mother out, going to school, and going to work in these clubs Fridays and Saturdays. The competition in those days came from those mechanical machines that had the drums and violin in them. They were in the joints to be played when there were no musicians. Of course, when the talking pictures came out, the musicians got thrown out of the theatres, but until then they had been working in clubs after the theatres closed. Working in ballrooms was second-class for pay as compared with theatres, although top musicians played in ballrooms, too. Theatres were rated top because you did an afternoon show, maybe two shows in the evening, and that was all your work.

"The job with Carroll Dickerson didn't last long. I played a while with Frankie Jaxon, and then there was another group headed by Eddie King, a piano player. Bob Shoffner was on trumpet, James Thomas on banjo, Kenneth Stewart on trombone, Fred Avendorph on drums, Fred Brown on alto and clarinet, and I played tenor. Things were really rolling that time, and we were getting theatre dates. Eddie King, Fred Brown and I were with Reuben Reeves in 1933. Reuben was a trumpet player who had been with Cab Calloway, but he left him, came back to Chicago and formed his own band. We went around, tried to scuffle, but never got anywhere. There was just nothing around to be had, although we did that record date for Vocalion. They were all my arrangements—*Zuddan, Mazie, Yellow Fire* and *Screws, Nuts and Bolts*—and I was still under the Barney Bigard and Johnny Hodges influence. The band had ability, but you've got to have some connections, and that's still true today. Even then, a big band was no small amount of money, but nothing like the money it takes today. You could go out on the road and make it on ten dollars a night. Some of us were working in little nightclubs and rehearsing with Reuben Reeves in the daytime. But he just didn't get the breaks, and there weren't the jobs during the Depression.

"I think it was in 1934 that I was at Swingland on Fifth Street. The place had a lot of different names, but that was what it was called then. Bill Lyle played bass and violin, Sidney Catlett was on drums, and Prentiss McCarey on piano. (Prentiss works quite a bit with me now.) Next I remember being with Jimmie Noone at the same time Fletcher Henderson

was at the Grand Terrace. We used to broadcast, and then they used to broadcast. Benny Goodman would come in whenever he was in town, because he liked Jimmie's playing. Jimmie told me how, when he was going to a teacher, Benny would come in and the teacher would have them play duets. Jimmie would play clarinet with the saxes in this band, which had Eddie Pollock on alto, myself on tenor, Leon Scott on trumpet, William Anderson on bass, and Bill Winston, a very good drummer. Chu Berry came down there, seeking me out, and we had a jam session right on the air. 'Oh, what the hell!' Jimmie said, and didn't try to stop us.

"He was a typical New Orleans guy. They've all got their little ways. It's not only that the musicians are suspicious, but they're very flaky in their temperaments. I don't know why they're so sensitive. It's just their way, I guess, but I could name Blanche Thomas, Preston Jackson, who works with me now, François Moseley, Guy Kelly and Charlie Du Gaston. One thing I recall as outstand-

Earl Hines and his orchestra, 1941. Left to right: (front) Earl Hines, Franz Jackson, Scoops Carry, Willie Randall, Leroy Harris, Jimmy Mundy; (middle) Ed Fant, George Hunt, Joe McLewis; (back) George Dixon, Tommy Nixon, Benny Harris.

ing about Jimmie was that he had to have a
lead going all the time when he took his solos.
That is *true* New Orleans style. It's an ensemble style. The man taking a kind of solo is
doing it while the others are also playing. Chicago style began with Louis Armstrong and
the Hot Five, with those soloists picking
spots, and ensembles in between.

"Now in 1937 I was with Roy Eldridge at
the Three Deuces. Chu Berry had left
Fletcher Henderson to go with Cab Calloway
and Ben Webster had taken his place. Ben
had debts or some trouble, and he left the
band, just cold—bam! I had always wanted to
play the Henderson book, and I just went on in
there and sat down and started to play. I
wasn't asked: I just took the job! And I got as
much as I could out of it, about fifteen
months. I learned all the arrangements, and
found out I really knew 'em one night in Bun-
kersville, West Virginia. I never will forget
the place! I got tired and had slept all night on
the bus. There was nothing to do in the morning, and I fooled around. It slipped up on me,
and I got drunk. They set the book up for me
that night, because I couldn't manage it myself, and I found I knew all the arrangements
subconsciously.

"Fletcher wasn't too much of a leader, but
he was a man you respected for his arranging
ability. I got tired of the band and the traveling, because I was recently married, so I quit
in Kansas City. Then I went back to Roy Eldridge at the Arcadia Ballroom in New York in
1939, still playing tenor, because he had
Prince Robinson, and Prince had a very good
style on clarinet. I liked to hear him better
than I liked to hear myself. I liked that jumping style he played, the way he kicked it. I
worked with Roy off and on, and I made New
York my base till 1950, but I joined Earl
Hines in 1940.

"It was a hot band. The guys were all sharp,
all young fellows. Not that being young makes
you sharp, but they all wanted to do something, and they played that way. It was a wild
band doing wild things, but it was sharp musically, and there was no sloppiness so far as the
playing was concerned. It was very pleasurable. If you wrote an idea for them, they'd

Franz Jackson, 1966.

rehearse it, and, man, that's all there was to it! There wasn't a whole lot of teasing. A guy might say, 'Come around to my room, and I'll give you some lessons.' At that stage in the business, for fellows in their twenties, that was very good. There was nobody telling them they were no good, or that they were not playing their horn well.

"This was the time when Earl had Billy Eckstine and Madeline Green, and the band was real hot. We were traveling on the strength of *Boogie Woogie on St. Louis Blues* and Billy's singing. The union had broken the contract Ed Fox had that made Earl like a slave to him and his heirs, and now Earl was out on his own. He didn't have a whole lot of money, because he'd never been able to accumulate anything. It was like Basie and Louis at different times: they were slaves to a booking agent or a manager.

"It was one of the best bands Earl had, but I'd heard them 'way back in the Grand Terrace and at the Regal Theatre, and they were kicking then. I don't know about the records, but I heard them in person, and his bands were good. The only reservation I had was that I thought the reed section could be a little brighter. Not that they didn't have good men in it, like Omer Simeon, but I just had a different idea of how reeds should sound. Alvin Burroughs was on drums when I was there, and he was just perfect for that band.

"Earl asked me to go back after I left in 1941, and I went and played one night, but I just couldn't take it. They had a lot of arrangements that I still wrote for them, but my mental attitude was wrong. It was during the war, and I just didn't want to be in a big band and running to catch trains. It was different when you walked from your hotel room to the bus with your bag. You had to travel by train now, you had to travel light, and you had to get cabs everywhere. Getting around was hard, and it got on my nerves. Also, there was the draft, and it got to be almost like you were a criminal. You were moving so fast that the only people who knew where you were were those you wrote to, like your mother or your wife.

"After Earl, I worked with Fats Waller in a little pick-up band around New York. I was in about the last big band he went out on the road with. I don't remember how I happened to get into that. Probably hanging around on the street, or something like that. I enjoyed playing with him and I enjoyed listening to him. I've always liked piano, from working with Earl and also with James P. Johnson while I was around New York. I played with James P. in Carnegie Hall once. I got where I *loved* that stride style, and almost tried to play it myself. It knocked me out. Fats and James P. were *it* when it came to stride, no doubt about that.

"I was working with Red Allen and J. C. Higginbotham in some New York club when Cootie Williams began to form his big band. I probably would have stayed where I was, but I wasn't very satisfied with Red and he wouldn't let me play any saxophone either. I found myself with Cootie and didn't quite know how I got there. They wanted me to work and write for the band. 'I don't want to go through all these changes again,' I said to myself. 'Writing—I did that years ago! And I've been on the road with Fletcher and Earl.' By this time I was pretty seasoned. I'd play around New York, catch bands as they came in, and write arrangements for them. I was interested in promoting my own self, and not anybody's band. So when I found what they wanted me for with Cootie, I just didn't want to be bothered. But Pearl Bailey was working for him then, and I did write some arrangements for her vocals.

"After that, Pete Brown had some jobs and wanted me to write for the band, but I could never get anything out of him and we never did get together much. Then I was in Boston with Frankie Newton, Vic Dickenson and Arthur Herbert. Arthur played drums in Coleman Hawkins's big band for a while, and he had a shuffle along with his beat that I liked. And Vic . . . he had a beautiful style on trombone.

"Then in 1944 Roy Eldridge got together a big band and tried to make it, but we never quite hit it off. We played the Apollo and had some success with the record of *Fish Market*. Another one we made never came out. It was

Frank Newton's band in Boston. Franz Jackson (standing, left), Frank Newton and Vic Dickenson (seated, right).

my arrangement of *St. Louis Blues*, played at a very fast tempo.

"I was at Ryan's with Wilbur De Paris for a long time, still playing saxophone. Everybody was enthralled by tenor at that time, and I really didn't play clarinet much till I got my own band. Even when I was with Jimmie Noone I didn't play it, because that man played such pretty clarinet I just wanted to listen. And Wilbur wasn't playing Dixieland then. That came later, after Omer Simeon had taken my place.

"Then I got with Jesse Stone for a U.S.O. tour of the Pacific. He played piano and he was a jazz musician, but he wasn't a soloist. He wrote jazz arrangements and he would adjust himself to anything that was necessary to be done, just as I did. One tour led to another, and work is work. My wife was the singer with the group when we went to Europe, and we stayed in Sweden a year. Because Europe didn't hold great things for me—I liked Japan more—I had to do something. So I bought a bassoon, but I got the wrong type, the French system. There's nothing wrong with it, but it's like the Albert system, and over here everybody plays the German system. I never felt any ideas on it. I think there are possibilities, but not in the

type of music we're playing now, which is loud and funky. I've played first bassoon with the De Paul University Community Symphony for fourteen years. It's a sombre instrument. I wrote a little something for it with a string background when I was working around here with a Mr. Elder, whose classical group played in schools three or four times a month. It gave me a place to express myself.

"After I had returned to Chicago, things began slowing down. I had a seven-piece band, and there weren't many places that would carry that size band. I started cutting down and doing shows with different size groups. Then I realized a certain type of thing was needed, and nobody was doing it. The way it really happened with me was that George Lewis came to play in a club with a band out of New Orleans. When George got sick, they asked me to take his place. I'd gone through that kind of music in my younger days, so there was nothing unusual in it for me. After they went back home, the club-owner wanted me to get some young musicians and train 'em to be like George Lewis's. There are people who think the sun rises and sets in that category of music. It didn't mean anything to me, although I found I enjoyed it. People think you're restricted, but there's a

Franz Jackson and the Original Jass All-Stars. Left to right: Joe Johnson (piano), John Thomas, Bob Schoffner, Richard Curry, Bill Oldham, Lawrence Dixon, Franz Jackson.

lot of freedom in it. Anyway, I told the man I didn't want to start with young musicians, because I didn't want to go through that. 'It's hard to teach somebody to have the feeling,' I said, 'or what's supposed to be done. I'll take some old heads, bald heads, guys that were *there*, and all they'll have to do is recollect.' That was the beginning of the Original Jass All-Stars in 1957. I had Bob Shoffner on trumpet, Al Wynn on trombone, Joe Johnson on piano, Lawrence Dixon on banjo, Richard Curry on drums, and Bill Oldham on tuba. The music was so natural to them, it seemed they couldn't play anything but two-beat. We were a success at once. We played for years at the Red Arrow, Jazz Limited and the Old Town Gate, and we made six or seven albums. In 1967 we did a three-month U.S.O. tour of the Far East; in 1968 we went to Alaska and the Aleutians for seven weeks; and we also did a four-week tour of the Bahamas.

"I will not let people put me in a New Orleans basket on clarinet. I pick up the tenor and play it. To hell with it not being typical of New Orleans. You get a lot of that shit, you know. But I don't give a damn, and I'm not going to put the tenor away anymore. I put it away for years until I started to use it again on the U.S.O. shows. I needed a heavy horn, and the clarinet is a lacy thing. You need to have someone else playing to be effective on it, and a lot of times I couldn't get people to play like I wanted. So I had to get my tenor, something I could really bark with!

"Right now, I'm studying classical guitar for my kicks. You know what made me do that? There was an altogether different viewpoint in the contemporary music the guys were putting down. We were looking at things harmonically, and with these guys everything seemed to be horizontal. That didn't make so much difference, because in harmony you learn those kinds of progressions. But theirs was out harmony, not like what we'd been doing at all. Before the war, music had reached a peak, and all the bands were playing good music, with good voicing and good taste. Then, bam, the war came! The bands broke up and they started pushing those little singing groups, because there was no dancing and they had filled the places up with chairs. That was the way rock rolled in. And because there was no dancing, and they didn't want any entertainment, the jazz guys started playing *everything* as innovative as possible."

(1974)

DIZZY GILLESPIE

TRUMPET AND BANDLEADER

"My father was a brickmason. He had the first bass violin I ever saw. I was only ten when he died, but they tell me he used to play a whole lot of instruments, like the clarinet, the mandolin, and the piano as well. He used to play for dances, but he couldn't support his big family of nine as a musician down there in Cheraw, South Carolina.

"There was a lady next door who had been a schoolteacher, and through her I knew how to read, how to write, and how to count before I went to school. They found I was too advanced for the primer and moved me into First Grade. Next thing, I was moved into Second Grade and had caught up with my older brother. I know that was *embarrassing!* I was the youngest in the family and I used to get him into trouble all the time. I used to fight anybody, big, small, white or colored. I was just a devil, a strong devil. I could whip all the guys my brother's size, but I could never whip him. I guess he knew my secrets. Guys his size and a little bigger would cross the street when they saw me coming. One day I followed him and he told me, 'Go on back!' I sneaked up on him again and we started fighting. He hit me in the stomach, and that *hurt,* so I picked up a stick and threw it at him. He put up his hand and I saw blood coming, and I thought I had put his eye out. So I ran home, and my mother beat me and beat me, and after that we didn't have many fights. When you're hot-tempered, you're liable to pick up anything, and down there there was always an axe lying around for chopping wood.

"When they first made up the band in my junior high school, I was too small to get a horn. I had to wait until all the big guys got theirs, and then all there was left was a trombone. My arms were so short then I couldn't get down to the last position, but I wanted to be in the band anyway, so I messed with the horn.

"There was a boy next door—James Harrington—whose father bought him one of those long trumpets. I asked him if I could practice on it. 'Yes, sure,' he said, 'we can practice together.' So I was going between his house and mine like a tennis ball. Eventually, when I could play pretty well, they decided to let me have a trumpet at the school.

"After I'd been playing for a time—and we only played in B flat then—I began to get pretty popular. Every year in school, we'd have a little minstrel show, with a small orchestra and little girls dancing. There was a girl called Ruth Jones who had short hair and reminded me of Nina Mae McKinney. She was one of the stars and she had personality. Miss Alice Wilson, our teacher, would have my cousin and two others sing. She had taught them harmony. I used to play with just piano and drums, and one way and another I thought I had quite a lot of experience.

"Then one day Sonny Matthews called. He was a marvelous pianist who got away up north. I ran into him later in my career, but I

254

think he's dead now. He was up near Albany for some years. He could play! He had been telling them about this little 'G'lipsy' boy who played trumpet, and I went down to his mother's place with the school horn. (I never had one of my own until I went north. We were so poor. My father had saved money, but when the Depression came a guy in the bank made off with everybody's money.)

" 'What do you want to play?' Sonny asked me.

" 'You name it,' I said.

" 'You know *Nagasaki*?'

" 'Yeah.'

" 'Okay, let's play.'

"So he started playing in C and I couldn't find the first note.

" 'Wait a minute! What're you doing?'

"I figured he was wrong. I could play only in B flat, but from that time on I said, 'Boy, I'm going to learn how to play in those other keys.'

"So I taught my piano player how to comp. The bass player had only one string, so I made a mark on the fret where B flat was, where F was, and E flat, and then turned the thing until it got to B flat. It's like the guitar players down south do. They put a fret in to change keys, and then just go on playing the same thing.

"There were some good musicians in Cheraw then. I remember a trombone player named Bill McNeil. He was in his twenties and he reminded me of J. C. Higginbotham. If he had lived, and had come up here, I think he would have been great. He was playing rough gutbucket in those days, didn't know one note from nothing, but he had the feeling. The white people said he was a Peeping Tom, killed him, and put him on the railroad track.

"Wes Buchanan, the bandleader, was a little short guy and a very good dancer. His instrument was the bass drum! There were several reasons why he was the leader. His mother had a little money, because some of her sons had been killed in World War I, and she had a pension from the government. They always had enough to eat—that's what having 'a little money' meant then. Also, he had one

of those blue suits which cost $22.50 and which everyone who was working wanted to have. I never have heard anyone since play the bass drum in a jazz orchestra like this guy. He'd sit and play it with one knee up against the head. Whenever he wanted to get a different sound, he'd move his knee forward or back, just like some guys do today with their elbow. That was in 1930. I told Art Blakey I'd like to have him come on a record date just to play bass drum, with another drummer. The younger guys don't know anything about playing bass drum. If anybody in the world did, it was Chick Webb! You can do a whole lot with your hand, and I could show Art Blakey or Max Roach how to do it. I'm not sure now whether Wes used his other hand for cymbals, but probably he did when he was marching. There are things you can do with your hand you can't do with your foot. When it gets too fast with your foot, it gets to be nerves, dynamic tension, but with your hand you can keep rhythm and make accents anywhere you want. It's more sensitive, and you can get more variation of sound.

"Later, I got a scholarship to Laurinburg Institute, a boarding school in North Carolina. The son of the president had been a trombone player, and the dean's son a trumpet player. When they left, a girl from my hometown, who was in the nursing school there, recommended me and a boy named Norman Pope to take their places. Besides the music, I was on the football team. The reason I went after football was to get on the training table. I was always hungry, and when they told me the guys with the piled-up plates were being trained as athletes, I said, 'That's for me!' I stayed there in the summer, too, and worked on the farm and plowed. I didn't like that too much, but it was part of the deal. It meant that I didn't cost my mother anything, and sometimes I could send her money home.

"I remember one day I was sleeping on top of one of the Ford trucks when they thought I was plowing. There was a waterfall nearby, and the hotter the weather the colder the water was. The football coach was in charge of the students that stayed in the summer, and

somebody told him where I was. He got a
bucket of this ice-cold water—and *sloosh*! I
came to swimming!

"I didn't get through the last year. I was so
busy with music and football that I hadn't time
to study, and I blew physics. It meant I had to
stay another whole year to get my diploma.
Cheraw was only twenty-eight miles away, so
one day I set out for home, walking and hoping to get a ride on a truck. The country there
was horrible, horrible. I stopped at one of
those country stores because I was hungry. I'd
been walking two or three hours, and I asked
for some cheese and a loaf of bread. A loaf was
only a nickel then, and I remember how we
used to buy one, split it all down the side, and
spread a nickel can of baked beans all the
length of it—a baked bean sandwich! Anyway,
there were all these white guys sitting around
the stove, spitting tobacco on the floor, and
they looked around and saw me.

" 'Hey, I'm talkin' to you, nigger!'

" 'Yessir.'

" 'You know how to dance?'

" 'Nossir.'

" 'No? C'mon, you know all niggers know
how to dance. Don't you know how to dance?'

" 'Nossir.'

"One of the guys reached in his pocket,
grabbed his pistol, and shot down by my feet.
I danced. They made me dance. Talk about
buck dance! I buck-danced in and out of
there. They were having fun, but they would
kill you, too.

"My mother had moved to Philadelphia that
winter while I was in school, but she had
wanted me to stay down there and finish. The
school didn't know where I was, but when I
eventually got to my aunt's place I found a boy
who was driving north, and he said I could go
with him. When I walked in on my mother,
she was surprised.

" 'This is the end of *that* for me, too,' I said.

"That was 1935 and I was so glad to be up
there. I hadn't a horn until my brother-in-law
bought me one. He bought it in a pawnshop
and it didn't have a case, so I had to carry it
around in a paper bag. That's when guys
started calling me 'Dizzy.' First, I was the

Dizzy Gillespie.

dizzy trumpet player with the paper bag, and
then it was shortened and shortened to Trumpet Dizzy, Trumpet Diz, and Diz. Before that
I had been John Birch, although my name was
John Birks. I think that was because there was
a sanctified preacher called Elder Birch in
Cheraw, about a half-block from my house,
and every Sunday night the white people
would be out in their cars listening to them
shouting in there. Johnny Birch played the
bass drum, Willie Birch the snare drums, and
they had tambourines . . .

"A long time later, the mayor and all of
them gave me a day in Cheraw. We had a
parade—and what was unheard of—I played
an unsegregated concert in the Armory. I'm
sure I was the first Negro to play in the Armory, segregated or unsegregated.

"When I went back again, it was a big deal.
They had some buildings called Gillespie
Court, and a street—a crooked street—called
Dizzy Gillespie Drive. We went around all
the old places, and I went over to see Miss
Alice Wilson, who had been my teacher. We
invited her to the Newport Jazz Festival when
I did a concert for George Wein. George flew
her and a companion up, lodged them at the
Americana, and that was really very nice. A

lot of people do nice things, but news of bad things travels a thousand times faster than news of good things. And nobody's interested when you say something nice about someone.

"When I first went to New York in 1937, I was a pretty good dancer. I believe I was the only musician in the 400 Club. They used to have those exhibitions Tuesday nights, and that's where they took Whitey's Lindy Hoppers from. The girls there used to like to dance with me, because I could throw 'em up and everything like the Lindy Hoppers did. A lot of musicians can't dance, can't even keep time. When our new music came out in the '40s, some people said to me:

" 'We can't dance to it.'

" 'What! What do you think I'm doing out front there?'

"Billy Shaw, the agent, came and told me about other people saying the same thing.

" 'You come to the theatre, daddy, and you'll see,' I said, because I was dancing all over the stage. Of course, we did play a lot of fast tempos, but I always created dances to the music. Just like the people who say they're dancing the bossa nova now. When I dance that, it's the samba—although not *really* the samba.

"When they had white dances in my home-town up over the drugstore, I was often the only colored guy there. There would be bands like Neely Plumb and His Georgia Tech Ramblers. They had arrangements before I ever saw arrangements. I wouldn't play, but they'd call me out, and I'd dance, and they'd give me money. I always danced. I was an entertainer. I didn't just start doing it when I came up north.

"And I always had a feeling for Latin-American music. When I joined Teddy Hill's band at the Savoy in 1937, Mario Bauza was playing first trumpet with Chick Webb, and Mario liked me and helped me. In fact, Chick Webb liked me, too. He used to let me sit in Taft Jordan's place and take solos, and I think I was the only one he used to let sit in like that. Of course, I could read very well by that time. A couple of years later, Mario was with Cab Calloway and knew he wanted a solo

trumpet. So one night he sent me down to the Cotton Club in his place. He told me to let Lammar (Wright) take all the first parts and then, when it came time for a solo, to blow. Cab didn't know me, and I didn't even report—just put on the uniform and sat down! I could play fly then from being in Teddy Hill's band, so when I took my solos Bill Robinson and the chorus girls were looking back at me—'Who's that?' In those days, the solo trumpet would accompany soft-shoe routines and so on, and I *stood up* when it was my turn!

"Rudolph, Cab's valet, was a good friend of my wife's, and she was working hard then and was tired, so she told Rudolph:

" 'Rudolph, you've *got* to give him a job!'

"So a couple of weeks later, when I was in the Apollo with Teddy Hill, I got a call from Rudolph at the Cotton Club.

" 'Come down!'

" 'Yeah, what do you want?'

" 'Come on down here, fool!'

" 'Bring my horn?'

" 'Yeah, bring it.'

" 'Okay.'

"So I went down there and started that night, although I still hadn't met Cab or asked what the salary was. Cab had several numbers like *Cuban Nightmare* in the book. I went for them right away and got to take solos on them. After I left Cab and went to form my own band, I told Mario, 'I want one of those tom-tom beaters.' That's what I called the conga drummers then.

" 'I've got just the guy for you,' Mario said.

"He had—Chano Pozo, the best.

"When I went to Kenya, years later, the musicians there were playing something so similar to the calypso.

" 'Hey, you-all been listening to the West Indians?' I asked.

" 'Look, we were here first,' they said. 'When calypso came into being, we were already over here doing it!'

"Now I've lived through maybe three generations of our music and changes in its style. It was funny for me to hear some of the things Bud Powell played when he was in my band.

Before that, I'd played with Earl Hines, and I'd hear Bud play things that Earl had already played. Billy Kyle was Bud Powell's main source of inspiration until Charlie Parker came along, and Billy Kyle was directly influenced by Earl Hines. I'm sure Bud appreciated the contribution of Earl Hines, but it takes time for a musician to become adult enough to look back and see how these things developed. In

were several stops on the way before I joined Earl Hines in 1943. I went to Levaggi's in Boston with Ella Fitzgerald right after Chick Webb died. Teddy McRae was in charge of the band then. I went with Claude Hopkins for a while, and then with Les Hite. I made that record of *Jersey Bounce* with Hite, and it has a very definitive solo in my style of that time. But Hite had a drummer called Oscar

Earl Hines and his orchestra, 1943. Left to right: (back) unknown, Gus Chappell, Benny Green, Shadow Wilson, Jesse Simpkins, Connie Wainwright, Julie Gardner; (front) Dizzy Gillespie, Benny Harris, Gail Brockman, Shorts McConnell, Earl Hines, Sarah Vaughan, Thomas Crump, Goon Gardner, Scoops Carry, John Williams, Charlie Parker.

Bud's case, you might say Billy Kyle was musically like his father, Earl Hines like his grandfather. In the same way, there's a definite connection between Louis Armstrong and me, but in between there's Roy Eldridge. It's hard to explain how styles evolve. You start out playing, trying to play exactly like somebody else. Then you come to a point where you're digging into somebody's complex style, and you yourself advance, and you become aware, and move into an evolutionary period when you play less and less like the other guy. You build on top of what you have learned from him.

"After I left Cab Calloway in 1941, there

Bradley, who was like a studio drummer. He used to do ratamacues and paradiddles, and rip on my solo. I told him what he could do with his drums and where he could put 'em! So we were playing the Apollo, and when I got up and played, this nigger went into his rappata. I sat right down. Les Hite looked at me, and I guess it seemed screwy to him, but after leaving Cab Calloway, and nicking Cab in the ass, I had a reputation then, a reputation that took me out of the draft! Other bandleaders didn't mention my name. 'Dizzy, that's Dizzy,' was all they would say.

"By 1942, I was in Lucky Millinder's band. Lucky would fire anybody in the world. He fired himself one time. 'Yeah,' he said, 'you're fired, Lucky!' He would fire you to assert his authority, and then give you more money before the two weeks' notice was up. We were at the Savoy, and I was having lip trouble.

"Randy Brooks told me about a Dr. Irving Goldman, who had cut his lip across, taken out a cyst, and sewed his lip back up. Some months later, Randy came back, blowing

stronger than he had been before. Now at that time the East Side was prejudiced against blacks, and I didn't even know where East 73rd Street was. But I found it, and Dr. Goldman put me in a little room as soon as I came in. I thought I was a V.I.P. or something. I was dumb, yes, until I saw in the paper where an Indian diplomat was traveling down south in Texas, and they put him behind a curtain. When the diplomat found out they thought he was a nigger, he hit the ceiling! Diplomatic wires burned from Nairobi to Afghanistan to China . . .

"Well, Dr. Goldman starts looking at my lip and says, 'Uh-huh.' Then he grabbed it and

took a tiny little file—like you file your nails with, but very tiny—and went deep down in my lip. Raw! You don't know what raw is! Then he put some white stuff around it, and I went right back to work and played on it. (I once had galloping pneumonia, and later pleurisy, and still played, didn't even miss a matinée all week.) Eventually, the hole started healing outwardly, but for a while it would crack.

"That was like the time when Butter (Jackson) and Keg (Johnson) were in Cab's band. They bought these sterling silver mouthpieces and cruised me into buying one for thirty-five dollars. After paying that money, I made up my mind I was going to play that mouthpiece if it killed me, which it nearly did. I was in misery with it all the time. Mouthpieces are strange. You don't go around trying to find the right mouthpiece for yourself, but you may just happen on one, put it to your lip, make an attack on it—and you can tell immediately that that's your mouth. Sometimes you get one that has what the last one had, and more. That's beautiful, because you find you can do what you weren't able to do with your embouchure before. Of course, I play from somewhere up in my right nostril. People walk up to me and say, 'Ah, you have half a moustache!'

" 'If you will observe closely,' I reply, 'you will see that it is a mark from the trumpet embouchure.' And their eyebrows go up.

"A guy named Al Cass in a little town in Massachusetts makes my mouthpieces now. He has also perfected the best oil for the trumpet. It's clean. You can put it in your mouth and it doesn't taste like oil. The only trouble is, I've now got so much of it. My wife, Lorraine, says, 'You must be an Arab, all that oil hanging around here. Call him up and tell him not to send anymore. You're got enough to last the next ten years.'

"But going back to Lucky Millinder and my lip trouble . . . Lucky went around telling everybody I'd lost my chops, and I was on my last week's notice when he came to me and asked if I would stay, and how much I would want.

" 'No, Lucky,' I said. 'I've got a job. I'm playing at the Down Beat in Philly.'

"It was Nat Stevens's place, a little club on 11th Street, and nice. Red Rodney was a kid then, and he couldn't get in, but sometimes he'd sneak up the stairs, and I'd see him looking—until they put his ass out of there. Stan Levey and Buddy De Franco used to come by, until one night in 1943 when Earl Hines came through town. Billy Eckstine and Shadow Wilson were with him, and they cruised me.

" 'Man, you come over here to Earl Hines,' they said.

" 'Oh, I'm having a good time here.'

"Well, they put it on me, and I went out to hear Earl, and that's when I joined his band. By then, he wasn't playing the Grand Terrace, but he was traveling all over the country. Next, they got Charlie Parker, but they didn't need an alto player, because they already had Scoops Carry, who played alto and clarinet, and Goon Gardner, who played alto. Thomas Crump played tenor, like Lester Young, and Johnny Williams was on baritone. So Earl got Charlie a tenor to play.

"As you say, people talk about the Hines band being 'the incubator of bop,' and the leading exponents of that music ended up in it. But people also have the erroneous impression that the music was new. It was not. The music evolved from what went before. It was the same basic music. The difference was in how you got from here to here to here . . . Naturally, each age has got its own shit.

"Art Blakey claims I wrote *Night in Tunisia* on a garbage pail in Houston, Texas, but that's a lie, because I was . . . well, sitting down at the time. I think I started it when I was with Benny Carter, making some of those little kinescopes. Like Carmen McRae, I never could pass a piano. If there's a piano between her and where she's going, she's *got* to touch it. She's a lover! Or that's what I call a lover. When you like somebody, when you're in love, and you pass by 'em, you've just got to . . . And that's all that's needed sometimes, when things are really things of the heart. My wife is a good example of doing things strictly from the heart, right *out* of the heart. No frills, no nothing. That's the way she does things. She won't attempt anything she can't finish. That was one of the main lessons I learned from her. If you're going to help somebody, help them all the way—no strings attached.

"Anyway, I was sitting at the piano and after hitting this chord, a D minor, I said to myself, 'Boy, that's a nice change.' And the melodic line of *Night in Tunisia* was in that chord. Sometimes you hit the E flat with it, sometimes the A—E flat and A, like a flatted fifth. I had to write a bridge for it, of course, and I didn't have a name for it till Earl Hines gave it that title. Tunisia was on everybody's mind at that stage of World War II.

"Earl Hines has got class. He is one of the classiest jazz musicians, like Duke Ellington and Coleman Hawkins. Younger musicians who are aware of the unfolding of our music, they look to these guys. Earl would stay apart, by himself, but, man, the biggest thrill among the guys in the band would be to get one of his chicks! Most bandleaders are targets for getting the needle, but especially Earl, because of his class. Actually, you see, the guys were *undermining* his class. But Earl Hines is a true bandleader. He doesn't let anything come between him and what he calls a certain level of perfection. Leaders like him are real classy *every* time you see them, ready to act, to perform, right then. I guess if you went into his bedroom, he'd jump up, the original Mr. Clean, and he'd never get messed up or nothing.

"Right, there's no recorded documentation of the period when I was with Earl, because of the union ban on recording then. I would suggest that a guy like John Collins or John Simmons could tell more about how the bop style evolved than I do. How did Charlie Parker and I affect one another? Look, it was a mutual non-aggression pact, a matter of mutual respect for one another, of respect for the other's creativity. We each inspired the other. It was like the flash or spark when two stars converge. I'd met him some time before 1943 in a hotel room in Kansas City with Buddy

Anderson, a very fine trumpet player who was with Jay McShann. Charlie Parker's playing took on a decided change after he met me, and my playing took on a decided change after I met him. That's the way it was. You can tell how I'd been playing from the records of *King Porter Stomp* and *Blue Rhythm Fantasy* that I made with Teddy Hill in 1937, and *Hot Mallets* with Lionel Hampton two years later.

"I'll never forget the record date Billy Eckstine had at National after he left Earl. He had me write one of the arrangements, for the *Good Jelly Blues—Jelly, Jelly*, you know. Talking about be-bop, we were *beeeee*-boppin' behind him! He'd got all those dudes together for the date—and didn't we have a bunch of them! I'd been used to writing all sixteenth notes, and they didn't know how to read it, no way! But when I brought my arrangement to the rehearsal, I brought my voice along with it, too.

"When Miles Davis first came around, he was enthralled with my conception of har-

mony and Freddie Webster's conception of sound. All three of us were really tight, but Miles was torn, absolutely torn.

" 'That note,' he'd say to me, 'where'd that note come from?'

" 'The piano,' I'd answer. 'You've got to learn to play the piano, or you don't know where the notes come from.'

"A musician is supposed to have many gears, and his gears are supposed to last his lifetime. When Charlie Parker and I met, it was like shifting to another gear. I respect Miles Davis's spunk in not playing anything he has played before, although I don't believe in disowning your grandfather or turning your back on what went before. Maybe I'm just unhip enough not to dig that, but I always try to distinguish between reality and fantasy. That's the biggest problem, because things can look awful real and yet be phoney."

(1963 and 1975)

CLIFF SMALLS

PIANO, TROMBONE AND ARRANGER

Cliff Smalls was born in Charleston, South Carolina, on 3 March 1918. His mother died when he was young, and he was brought up by his father and two stepmothers.

"My father played several instruments," he recalled, "and he taught quite a few guys around town—trombone, small fiddle, piano. He was like a jack of all trades. My brother played fiddle and my father started me off on trombone. I was a very skinny kid, and every time I got sick my mother would say, 'It's nothing but that horn, nothing but that

horn . . .' I learned how to play the B-flat scale from him, and that's about all, before he switched me over to piano.

"There was a band around town called the Royal Eight, and while I was in high school I used to play weekend jobs with them. That went on until the Carolina Cotton Pickers came through. They were a band that started out from the Jenkins Orphanage in Charleston, and I was still in my teens when they stole me out of school. They had a piano player named Slim (I never can remember his other name), and he could play, but he couldn't read at all. He was very good, and he played more or less in the Earl Hines style, because Earl was *it* then, around 1935.

"A trombone player in the band called Hawk told them about my reading. His real name was Julius Watson, but they called him that because he was so fast. (Later on, he played with the Sunset Royals, and he is in New York now, but he no longer plays.) The big thing with the bands in those days was the out chorus, where the brass made a figure and the reeds answered them. But before you started a solo, they'd always have you take a break to make your own entrance to it, and that was where Hawk was *fast*.

"Anyway, he had me go to this dance in the hall where they were playing, and they had a piano part written out on—I'll never forget the tune—*Did You Ever See a Dream Walking?* I sat down and played it, and from then on I started working with them around town till they were going away on a trip. They didn't tell me how long we were going to be away, and I just asked my father if I could go to Wilmington to play with the band.

" 'Yeah, that's all right,' he said.

"So we went off to play this dance, and then they started distributing us around to different houses. I didn't know why. I had thought we were going home afterwards, but that was where we were to stay before going on to other towns. I guess I was about seventeen then, but I was crying all night, because I knew my stepmother was going to kill me. When the band went on and on, the guys kept telling me:

" 'What you crying for? Everything's going to be all right.'

"Finally, we got back home, and I eased into the house. When they asked how the band was doing, I didn't lie. I told them everything.

" 'Well, he seems to be interested in music,' my stepmother said. 'He doesn't seem to be getting into any trouble either, and it beats staying around here.'

"So I kept going with that band.

"There was a gentleman by the name of Mr. Roseborough who had had charge of them at Jenkins's, as well as when they went out on their different tours, when they passed the hat around where they played. After they decided to stick together and make a regular orchestra of it, he made it a co-operative group. He got them a house where they could cook and sleep, and that was how they really got started.

"When I joined them, the trumpets were Ken Anderson, Joseph Williams and Thad Seabrook; the trombones were Julius Watson and Leroy Hardison, and when Mr. Roseborough died Hardison took over the managing. The alto saxes were Pepper Martin and Booker T. Starks; the tenor saxophone was Julian Bash, who also came from Charleston, like Julian Dash who was with Erskine Hawkins. Eugene Earl played tuba at that time, and Otis Walker was on drums. A guy named Wesley Jones used to sing many of Cab Calloway's things like *Minnie the Moocher*, and since he was up front he used to call himself the conductor, but there wasn't really anything to conduct.

"All our jobs were in the southern area at that time. Different bands operated in different areas. Around Pensacola, for instance, you'd find Harley Toots's band, or Smiling Billy Stewart's, or the Sunset Royals. There was another band led by Ray Shep, and out in Texas there were Don Albert's and Boots and His Buddies. That was where we ran across Eddie Heywood, who wrote a couple of arrangements for us, one of them on *Rosetta*.

"When we eventually went north, we got as far as the Howard Theatre in Washington, D.C. Willie Bryant fronted the band, and Pearl Bailey was in the show, but she wasn't the big star then she is now. From there we went to the Royal in Baltimore, and that was about as far north as we got. We didn't make it to the Apollo in New York, but we wound up in Kansas City at a nightclub called Scott's Theatre Restaurant. They'd have regular shows there, chorus girls, and all that. It was a pretty popular place at the time. Charlie Parker was around town then, and so was 'Little Dawg,' a trumpet player with Harlan

The Carolina Cotton Pickers. Left to right: Thad Seabrook, Joseph Williams, Leonard Graham, trumpets; Kate Woodard, drums; Lou Williams, Ernest Zeke Vann, John Vaughan, Harold Clark, reeds; Eugene Earl, Leroy Hardison, trombones; Laverne Barker, bass; Wesley Jones, vocalist; Jimmy Edwards, guitar; Cliff Smalls, piano. (Purvis Henson, tenor saxophone, was absent when this picture was taken.)

Leonard. They used to make all the jam sessions, and some of those sessions would begin Friday night and carry right through till Blue Monday. That was before Charlie was with Jay McShann or Earl Hines. Tommy Douglas, the alto player, also had a band. But we were just a bunch of kids trying to make it, and fortunately this guy kept us in his club for quite some time.

"Pha Terrell, the singer, was very big with Andy Kirk in those days, but every time Kirk went to California they seemed to have some kind of misunderstanding, and Pha didn't get to go. Then someone got the bright idea of putting Pha in front of the Carolina Cotton Pickers, and sending us out to the Coast so that he could clean up. That's how *we* got to California. We worked at the Lincoln Theatre first. Bardu Ali had the pit band and he got

into some kind of dispute with Pha. So when it was his turn to play, he would put on a young kid with a big, heavy, Paul Robeson-like sound, singing Pha's hits. It was Arthur Walker, who was later with Earl Hines. When it came our time, we were out on the stage. Wesley Jones was still 'conducting,' and Pha would be announced, come out and do his tunes, and from then on the girls had him. Pha was mad with us when we went back to Kansas City.

"He was a big, beautiful guy, happy-go-lucky, soft spoken, always complaining about his feet, an ex-boxer. I've seen people get him wrong because of that falsetto singing he did. They thought he was a fag. I never forget one morning in Georgia when we were eating breakfast. Some girls came in, and they were so excited to see him. 'Oh, oh, Pha Terrell!'

they were crying. Now, you know, there's always one cutie-pie in every town, and the one here was soon having some nasty things to say.

" 'Well, so long as he don't bother me—fine,' Pha said. 'But if he comes over here and starts something, that's it!'

"Finally, this guy wound up over where we were, still opening his mouth. One punch from Pha and they had to take him outside.

"By the time we went to California, the band was very good, and I had learned to write. Earlier, when we were in Florida, we had an alto player named Charlie Jacobs. He had been to Jenkins's, too, but after he got out he went to school and started arranging. Then we got him in the band, and we had some pretty good arrangements by him. He left later and went back to Mobile, which I think was his wife's home. (I saw him again there years afterwards when I was with Earl Hines.) After he'd gone, I wanted to write so bad, and I used to sit up at the piano at night and try to figure out the notes and the syncopations, and everything like that. But I didn't know anything about the transposition of the instruments. The first thing I tried was *Marie*, and I never forget when I passed the parts out.

" 'What is *this*?' the guys said. They made me feel so bad. They just picked up the music and threw it over their shoulders or down on the floor.

" 'Wait a minute!' Hawk the trombone player said. 'Don't you-all do that. We've got to help him. Maybe he's the guy that's going to save us one of these days. Let him see what you do.'

"So Pepper Martin came over to the piano and said, 'My instrument is alto, and your A is my F sharp. I'm a step and a half below you, you know. And the tenor is a step above you. Your A's a trumpet's B. And the trombone's just like the piano; the note's the same, only you write them in bass clef.'

"I went home that night, took all the parts, did exactly what he told me, and brought them back the next day. Although we were laying off at the time and only rehearsing, the guys frowned—'What, *again*!' We passed the

parts out, and it wasn't a top-notch arrangement, but everybody could play it. From then on I couldn't keep a pencil out of my hand. We recorded a dozen or so sides in 1937, but so many of the things we played then were heads. When new musicians kept coming in the band who didn't know the arrangements, they started asking me to write them out, so that they wouldn't be stumbling around too long.

"When we were in Dallas one time, the first trombone bought a brand new horn, case and everything from a junkie for twenty dollars. He gave his old horn to the second trombone, who didn't want to carry two horns, so he asked me, the piano player, to carry one of them for him. I went down to a music store one morning and bought one of the books by Otto Langley my father used to teach me from. Back in the hotel, I put it on the bed and had the horn playing the B-flat scale. After a time there was a knock on the door, and the whole band was out there. 'Man,' they said, 'this guy must be some kind of genius. Just got the horn two or three days ago and he's playing it already!' They didn't know about the tuition I'd had, and I never told them. I didn't really know that much about the horn, but I was trying, and I was coming along fine, playing goose eggs (whole notes).

"Now after we left California, we went back to Scott's in Kansas City, because that was like a regular job for us. We could go out on a trip and come back to it. I started going to a music school there. In the band, I used to pick up the trombone, play the channel or something with the other guys, put the horn down, and go back over to the piano. Earl Hines's manager and some of his guys saw me doing this when they were in town, and one night Earl himself came in.

" 'Gate, here's that kid I was telling you about,' the manager said.

" 'Yeah,' Earl said. 'Well, tell him to come up to the room tomorrow and let's talk!'

"They had the same idea: 'Man, if we get this guy, we can have him playing the piano when Earl's not there.' But when the manager spoke to me about it, I thought he was crazy.

" 'Are you kidding?' was all I said.

Earl Hines and Count Basie.

"Next morning, I was going to school at the conservatory in Kansas City, Kansas, and I was catching the bus at Versailles Street and Royal. I had forgotten all about going to see Earl at the hotel when Eric Illedge, the manager, came by in a cab. He was big and strong, a pretty rugged guy who had managed a basketball team before.

" 'When you come back from the school,' he said, 'be sure to stop by the hotel.'

"They explained they were opening at the Apollo in New York in two weeks on a Friday, and that they wanted me there on the Thursday for a rehearsal, but I still paid Ellidge no mind.

"That particular Friday, when I came back from school, Leroy Hardison, the manager of the Carolina Cotton Pickers, was in the hotel lobby with the president of the colored union in Kansas City, and they were arguing like dogs. They'd got the manager of the club, which also owned the hotel where we were staying, and the two of them were giving Hardison hell. Eric had called the union president and told him to put me on the next plane out. In the end, Hardison said, 'To heck with it!' He took me back to my room and told me to start packing. So I started throwing things in my bag, and we didn't have too many to travel with at that time, anyway! He took me out to the airport and put me on the plane. When I got to the Apollo next morning, I found that Tom Whaley, who later was Duke Ellington's copyist, had been up all night writing a full trombone book.

"So there I was, in the summer of 1942, sitting up on the Apollo stage in Earl Hines's band with a first trombone book in front of me that I could do nothing with—nothing at all! But what Earl really wanted me for was to play *Basie Boogie*. That was Basie's big hit at the time, and I could break it up playing that. Basie came backstage and called Earl all kinds of names. 'Man, that's my biggest hit, and you've got this so-and-so playing it,' he said. 'Are you crazy?' But I imagine he was mostly kidding, because he and Earl were good friends.

"Earl used to introduce me as his protégé. 'I've got a surprise for you,' he'd say, 'my protégé, Cliff Smalls, and he's going to play a tune for you, one I'm sure you've heard before.' The band would go into the introduction, and then they'd turn me loose. He featured me on piano on other tunes as well. It was a great band, and I stayed with it till it broke up. I never played much solo trombone in it. I was playing parts in the section, and every now and then I'd have eight bars. Earl wanted someone to be playing the piano until the people came in, and then he would come out. I wrote arrangements for him, too. *Blue Skies* was one, and a lot of people used to comment on another I did on *Wagon Wheels*.

"When I joined him, he had Gail Brockman playing first, Jesse Miller, Shorts McConnell, and Dizzy Gillespie for the trumpet section. The trombones were Benny Green, Gus Chappell, a guy by the name of Scotty, and me. The saxes were Scoops Carry, Goon Gardner, altos; Thomas Crump, Charlie Parker, tenors; and John Williams, Mary Lou's ex-husband, on baritone. Connie Wainwright, a little short fellow, was the guitar player. Paul Simpkins was the bass, and Shadow Wilson was on drums.

"Dizzy and Charlie used to have these cute little unison things they would play behind Sarah Vaughan when she was singing, but the guys used to fan 'em off then because they were so different. They were playing *Night in Tunisia* before I joined. Dizzy can write. He's terrific with a pencil, and he did several things for Sarah like *East of the Sun*. I could recognize his things in the book from the penmanship. Earl had some popping bands and this was one of them, but somehow he never had enough credit for them. Of course, Billy Eckstine was the other singer, and I can remember several times when we were on the air, so maybe some of those broadcasts will still show up on records. Everybody had solos in that band, and Dizzy and Charlie got theirs, but they were not big stars then, although they were playing the way that made them famous. In some of the towns we played, musicians would be standing at the side of the stand, looking at each other like it was crazy. Which it was—then.

"Although Charlie played tenor all the time he was with the band, it sounded like he was still playing alto, because he'd always have an alto style. His sound wasn't like Lester Young's. I wouldn't say he had a fuller sound, either. It's hard to explain exactly, but it was his *own*. What was amazing about him was that all he would have on the bandstand, besides his horn, would usually be a pipe, a cigarette lighter, a pack of chewing gum, or something like that. Now Earl had two tremendous books—a society book, and a book for regular gigs, one-nighters. Charlie used to sit on his book, with all those reed choruses and everything in, all the time. Everybody else got their music out, but he was *sitting* on his! He'd remember it all. When we got a new tune, he might look at it a couple of nights, but after that it wouldn't come out of his case any more.

"We had played a string of theatres and were about to go south, playing one-nighters, when Billy Eckstine left. He was very big then, and I guess he figured he should have his own thing. Dizzy and Charlie Parker went with him, but Sarah Vaughan stayed. To offset Billy's going, Earl hired an all-girl string section, a girl harpist, a girl guitarist, Lucille Dixon on bass, and four more girls who sang and were called the Bluebonnets. I got two guys in the band from the Carolina Cotton Pickers, a trumpet player called Ed Reese, whose real name was Leonard Graham, and a tenor player from Texas, Harold Clark. (Crump went out to California, and the last time I saw him he was in San Francisco. He was a good tenor player, played the book, the changes and everything right *all* the time.) Wardell Gray came in on alto at first. Scoops Carry, the strawboss, didn't like Wardell or Harold. I think he wanted to bring in some of his own buddies, and I'll never forget a rehearsal at the old Nola Studio. Scoops took the numbers at tempos almost twice as fast as we usually played, and Wardell and Harold just *ran* through them, right straight through them.

" 'See what you got?' John Williams cried. 'I've been here all the time, and they're playing them better than I am!'

In Cleveland, 1944. Cliff Smalls at the piano with Chick Booth, drums; Woogie Harris, trombone; Billy Douglas, trumpet; and Kermit Scott, Lloyd Smith, Scoops Carry, John Williams and Wardell Gray, reeds.

Earl Hines and his orchestra, 1943. Left to right: (front) Dizzy Gillespie, Jesse Miller, Gail Brockman, Shorts McConnell, trumpets; Earl Hines; Charlie Parker, Goon Gardner, Scoops Carry, John Williams, Thomas Crump, reeds; (rear) Cliff Smalls, Scotty, Gus Chappell, Benny Green, trombones; Shadow Wilson, drums; Connie Wainwright, guitar; P. O. Simpson, bass.

Earl Hines's brass, 1945. Left to right: (rear) Willie Cook, Marion Hazel, Fip Ricard, Palmer "Fats" Davis; (front) Gordon Alston, Woogie Harris, Benny Green, Cliff Smalls.

Ira Pettiford addresses his trumpet. Gus Chappell, Rudy (?), Sparrow (?), Cliff Smalls, trombones; Palmer "Fats" Davis, Arthur Walker, Willie Cook, trumpets; Lucille Dixon, bass; Earl Hines; Harold Clark, tenor saxophone.

"But from then on, there were a lot of changes, a lot of different guys, because World War II was on. We had good trumpet players like Willie Cook and Fats Palmer. Ira Pettiford, Oscar's brother, was in the band for a time. I remember he was with us when we played the Plantation in St. Louis. He was a very learned guy, but he used to drink his ass off. He'd break it up when he came out to play his solo. He'd spit at his trumpet, blow some, stop, spit at his horn, and then play again. Arthur Walker, the singer, came in from California, and he was strong on trumpet, had good chops, and could play very high. Then there was Billy Douglas, a trumpet player who was *really* something else. He had his own style and was just phenomenal. John Thompson, a very good saxophone player, was in the band when we started going back to Chicago. After Shadow Wilson, we had an ofay who didn't make it too long, but then we got Chick Booth, and he was a very good big-band drummer. There were a flock of good guys around then.

"We had a lot of trouble with pianos when we were on the road doing one-nighters, and piano players used to leave a little sign on them to tip you off. There was a girl called Jackie, who played with the Sweethearts of Rhythm, and a couple of other friends of mine, whose sign I'd always recognize. I'd walk up to the bandstand, see the sign, and tell the man:

" 'The piano's no good.'

" 'How do you know? You haven't even touched it.'

"Then I would play a little, and maybe he could hear how bad it was himself. Sometimes we'd really wreck a piano after a dance, so they'd get another before the next group came in. The owners would think the place was being vandalized by somebody from outside. They hire somebody like Earl, and a band like his, and pay out the money, but why would they think we were going to sound good with a really bad piano?

"When we were playing the El Grotto in Chicago, Buggs Roberts did most of the arrangements for the concert-type things Earl was presenting in the club. Buggs was tremendous. His voicing was terrific and he made the band sound so full. He was from St. Louis originally, and he had been writing for George Hudson's band, which upset New York when it went there. His whole sax section was playing Coleman Hawkins's *Body and Soul*, and I think Buggs wrote that for George. Ernie Wilkins, who was also with the same band and from St. Louis, wrote the arrangements for Earl's Fats Waller concert, if I remember right.

"When Earl had his Gershwin concert, everybody came by to hear him do *Rhapsody in Blue*. Art Tatum, Nat Cole, Sonny Thompson and, I think, Stan Kenton, were in the place that night, but they were disappointed when they found Earl *conducted* on *Rhapsody in Blue* and didn't play piano. They had figured he was going to do it *up*! But they all went on upstairs and started jamming. Sonny Thompson is a terrific piano player, and he and Tatum lost everybody, until Nat Cole decided he wasn't going to play any more piano. I went home, got some sleep, and found they were still at it when I came back next morning about 12 o'clock!

"In these concerts at the El Grotto, Earl always featured a little group that consisted of Bill Thompson on vibes, Rene Hall on guitar, Gene Thompson on bass, Chick Booth on drums, and myself on piano. We'd pick the tempo up fast, pass the solos out, and it was quite a unique thing—a pity it could not last.

"I remember very well a night when the band played a prom at Michigan State. There was a huge pit in front of the stage, big enough to take about a hundred pieces. They had flowers everywhere for this affair, and they had covered the pit entirely with decorative paper, all twined together and tacked to the stage, with roses and flowers pinned on it. Earl was wearing a white tuxedo, with blue bow tie, blue cummerbund and blue shoes. He was clean! His band was sharp, too, and he had his girls and all with us. Sarah Vaughan was going to sing *You Go to My Head*, and he made one of his enormous introductions. The Four Bluebonnets sang their little interlude, and then when Sarah began . . . 'You go to my head' . . . Earl was supposed to bring the band in. So he jumped up . . . and disappeared! He went through the paper! It was all dusty down there, but those big football players jumped in, picked him up, and put him back on the stage in nothing flat. He had dust all over his white tux, and when he gave us the down beat everybody was so busy laughing that not a note came out. Not one note! That was hilarious, but he was lucky he didn't break his neck. I think there was an organ down there, and that broke his fall.

"Another incident I remember happened after Earl had that bad automobile accident in Texas and nearly lost an eye. We were wondering how we were going to play the date. The people kept looking for him, and the manager and Scoops Carry would say, 'Oh, he'll be here, he'll be here . . .' But to me they were saying, 'Cliff, you'll have to play the piano! When it came time to hit, time for the dancing, we arranged that all the guys were on the stand talking to one another. 'Okay, this is it,' Scoops said, and I went over to the piano and played the little thing Earl used to call the attention of the guys. They all came over to the piano and tuned up individually. I had my back to the people, but they could see my fingers flying, and they were calling, 'Hey, Earl!' or 'Hi, Fatha!' You know, we made it through that whole dance, and never said anything about Earl not being there. After the first set, I went across the stand like I was giving somebody hell for doing something wrong, and all the guys stood around me. Then I went back and played another set. We got out of there without any trouble.

"When Earl had to break up the band, we were in Chicago and Johnny Harman was the vocalist. Johnny had me get the rhythm section together to back him on a radio show every Saturday that was run by a popular disc jockey named Benson. About this time, Billy Eckstine was looking for a piano player, and a friend of mine in Kansas City had heard me on the radio.

" 'Why don't you get my buddy?' he asked Billy.

"So Billy called me in Chicago, asked what I

was doing, and arranged for me to meet him at the Paradise Theatre in Detroit. I stayed with him a long time, until we got to Bop City at 49th and Broadway in New York. Another friend of mine overheard a conversation there among the people who were running affairs at the club. Billy was crazy about me, and he wasn't there, but they were talking about the curiosity value of the name Eckstine to bring

in a lot of white customers. They were fixing to hire Hugo Winterhalter then to make B. really big and push him to the top. What they said about me was, 'Look, there's no doubt what *he* is when he walks out. It'll never work with him.' What they meant was that I was too dark.

"Soon after that I went with Earl Bostic, who was hot then. We had an accident in 1951, and I broke a leg and put my right hip out of place. He had fallen asleep, and we hit an oil truck. I was in bed a year and three months. They put both legs in a cast and left the bones to knit back as well as they could. After two months in the hospital, my wife took me home and looked after me. After nine and a half months, they took the right leg out of the cast, and soon they were able to push me up on crutches, with the cast still from my armpit all the way down my left leg. The first time I got out of bed, they asked where I wanted to go, and I said to the piano. But I had no strength at all in my fingers and I couldn't play, and the tears just started coming out of my eyes. The doctor came by and gave everybody hell, said they'd probably injured me for life. Even now, if I make a mistake, which I don't very often, I tend to think back to that accident, and for a long time I'd find myself hating Earl Bostic. Of course, he

to come and tote me out to the car and slide me into the back seat. It was fun just to get out of the house after being in bed all that time. They'd get me into the place and up onto the piano stool in the club in New Jersey where we worked two or three months.

"Al Sears was another who did me a great favor after the accident. He flew me to Toronto, and they drove up and met me at the

Left to right: Cliff Smalls, unknown newspaperman, Art Tatum, Sonny Thompson, Earl Hines.

didn't do it intentionally, but he never came to see me, not one time. His wife came, and brought my horn back to me, but she wasn't in the house a half-hour.

"There were certain musicians they wouldn't let come to see me. In fact, only seven came. Arnett Cobb was one, and he had been badly injured himself. He used to hobble in. 'Hold your head up,' he'd say. 'Hold it up if you're going to talk to me!' And Eddie 'Cleanhead' Vinson, who lived just around the corner, he came. 'He's gonna play with me,' he'd say. They were trying to build my confidence. The guys I had played golf with were usually the ones who made me laugh. They'd tell me about this one doing that, and how that one cheated, and I used to like the gaiety of it.

"After the right leg had been taken out of the cast, a bass player named Gene Groves, and Dickey Thompson, the guitar player, used

airport with the station wagon. I still had all that harness on, and he used to dress and undress me, because I couldn't do it myself. All the guys in that band were good to me. They'd come to my room at night, call me, or check to see if I wanted to go to the bathroom. 'Look, man, don't worry about it,' they said. 'We'll take care of you.' They were like father and mother to me, and they never complained. I'll never forget them: little, short Rudy Powell, the alto player; Jumpin' George the drummer; Buddy Smith the singer; Eli Robinson the trombone player; Shad Collins on trumpet; Bennie Moten on bass; and Al on tenor.

"When they took me out of the cast altogether, they put a brace on the left leg, which I could unlock at the knee so that I could sit down at the piano. I was moving around pretty good with a cane when I met Benny Green at a party for Billy Eckstine and

Charlie Parker—the last time I saw Charlie alive. We were talking about old times with Earl, and Benny asked if I could play piano. 'Yes,' I said, 'and my horn, too.' I had asked my doctor if I could do some dates with Benny, and while I was out with him the doctor died. I never did bother another doctor about that leg, because they had been talking about operating on it. It won't bend all the way, but nobody would know that now if I didn't tell about it.

"Next, I went out on the road with Paul Williams. He had four saxes and five brass, and we were playing rhythm and blues. Clyde McPhatter was in that show, and he was hot as a firecracker then. He hired me and I stayed with him quite some time, until Brook Benton took me away when Clyde wasn't working much. I stayed with Brook longer than anybody, about seven and a half years. We'd just come back from overseas when George Rhodes, who played piano for Sammy Davis, cut a tendon in his hand changing a tire. Reuben Phillips had him call me. I was all ticketed to go with Sammy, but my oldest son talked me out of it, and out of staying with Brook Benton, because Smokey Robinson and The Miracles were looking for a conductor and arranger.

" 'You know who Smokey Robinson is?' my son asked me.

" 'No.'

" 'Well, he's got more money than those other guys put together.'

"I didn't know that he and Barry Gordy had started Motown in a garage. I was thinking, too, that when George Rhodes's hand got better they wouldn't want me, but Sammy really wanted him to conduct and to have someone else play piano. Anyway, Smokey and The Miracles made me an offer I couldn't refuse, one where they were talking to me on a yearly basis, about what I would be making when we were working and how much it would be when we were off. I'd never had a job like that before. They were a group of singers, a beautiful bunch of guys, and I enjoyed working with them. They carried a drummer, a guitar, bass and conga, but I didn't play piano very often. I was with that group three and a half years.

"Somewhere in between these different jobs, I was with Ella Fitzgerald for three or four months, with Herb Ellis on guitar and Gus Johnson on drums. I also often worked with Reuben Phillips at the Apollo Theatre. We were good friends and played golf together. Whenever I came off the road, he would try to get me to stay with his band, so we could play golf! 'Cliff Smalls is back in town,' guys in the band used to say. 'Look out, piano players!'

"After I left Smokey Robinson and came back from Detroit, Candy Ross called and told me Sy Oliver was fixing to organize another band. I wanted to stay in New York to be with my kids. Now you might say that I had been away from the piano for seventeen or eighteen years. Playing for singers, all you do is make an introduction and accompany them. You don't really get to play as a soloist. Sy had already tried three or four other piano players, and he called me because they didn't make it. When I sat down at the piano, I played an introduction to *My Blue Heaven* that Ed Wilcox had taught me years before when I was with the Carolina Cotton Pickers. Sy asked me to do it again, and then I played a couple of other things, and that's how our association began in 1970. On and off, I've been working with him ever since. I've written one or two things for his group, and when he looked at what I'd done on *On Green Dolphin Street* recently, he laughed and said, 'You're like all piano players. You put too much in!' "

(1974)

(Cliff Smalls can be heard to advantage on several Master Jazz records, notably on his own *Swing and Things*, 8131, and on Buddy Tate's *The Texas Twister*, 8128.)

DICKY WELLS

TROMBONE AND ARRANGER

"After being with the Savoy bands, I went with Earl Hines in 1954—my last regular group. For versatility, that was about the best small band I ever worked with. I replaced Benny Green, one of the greats, who had been in Earl's last big band. Jonah Jones had been playing trumpet, and it was a musician's band, but before I joined there had been a certain amount of confusion because of the progressive element, who didn't want to play Dixieland. We played a bit of everything, including Dixieland, which Earl taught us. We didn't play much of the music we recorded on that Nocturne album, because when it got down to music most of the houses we played didn't want it. All through Canada, Earl broke records which are still standing. He's such a tremendous showman. There'd always be a pile of requests on the piano. He'd go into a Dixieland house and say:

" 'Bear with us, friends, but we've got a request for so-and-so.'

"It would be some progressive-type number, and he'd bring the house down, although no one there had really wanted it. In a progressive room, he'd do the same thing, play *Muskrat Ramble*, and maybe say, 'I don't like it any more than you do.' The people would accept it, and that was his way of keeping the band flexible.

"We had Morris Lane on tenor then. He had a big, fat sound. We were going out to the Hangover in San Francisco, a Dixieland house, and Earl told Morris to be sure to get a clarinet.

" 'Yeah, Gates, I'll get it,' Morris said. 'Don't worry about nothin', Gates.'

"Opening night, he didn't have it.

" 'Get the clarinet next week, Morris,' Earl said.

" 'Yeah, okay, Gates. A little short, you know, but everything will be all right.'

"The boss there liked Morris and Morris was playing a couple of beautiful tenor solos. The place had been a Dixieland joint for years, with a clarinet every day of the week, but the boss said:

" 'That boy plays so fine, Earl. Don't bother him.'

"So he never did get the clarinet.

"Earl liked everybody to stay neat and sharp, and he had two or three uniforms for us. He gave me the keys and told me to see they took the uniforms off before they left. I had to hang on Gene Redd to see he took his off. Then I would lock them all up. Redd had been with Bostic before. He was a fine trumpet player, but he was sold on vibes.

"That was the way to keep Earl happy—to stay neat. I haven't heard him say anything to anyone yet about playing his instrument. That was *your* job, and he expected you to take care of it, but for Heaven's sake stay neat! He'd tell you it didn't cost anything to shine your shoes.

"Of course, he was forever trying things. I remember he came through here with girl violinists and everything one time, and when he had big bands, new things were always being tried out. In this little band—and I remember

273

Shadow Wilson, God bless him, was with us for a time—there was so much variety that you never got bored. Jerome Richardson would sing a couple of songs, and so would Earl.

"Earl would dedicate a number to the memory of Fats Waller every night. He won't let him die. He'd play *Honeysuckle Rose* and tell how Fats wrote his songs, on a tablecloth in London, and so on. They used to be regarded as rivals, but Earl was crazy about Fats, idolized him. He'd be talking and playing, and the crowd loved his spiel, and he'd do it to give us a rest. He'd tell us to go out for a half-hour or more, and carry on working himself. Sometimes, when he knew the house, he'd look at his watch and say, 'Make it an hour.' We'd go out on the street, come back, and they wouldn't want him to stop. He was a hell of a showman. You listen a while and he could sell you Brooklyn Bridge. He'd tell us to sit down, and he'd be telling people about James P. Johnson, and he'd have his left hand going, and after a time he'd bring us in on a number. The time went quickly that way. It was a kick working for Gate, and he always paid us as much as he could.

"Then we went out with the Harlem Globetrotters for several months. It wasn't actually the basketball players. They always had several acts to entertain in the intervals—jugglers, acrobats, trick cyclists, a singing ex-basketball star, and what not—and we accompanied these acts, and played several numbers on our own. We went all through the West, played at the halls where they had basketball. It was a show—no basketball at all. Abe Saperstein had got together about thirty people who had entertained with the Trotters that way, and it was his way of giving them some income in the off-season. Sometimes we might play to an almost empty house, but he didn't seem to care.

" 'It serves a purpose,' he'd say.

"We were supposed to go for six weeks, but we stayed three months, and on the whole did good business.

"Earl has a way of playing that makes *you* feel like playing, but we had to prod him into

doing all those numbers he was famous for. When we got on to *Piano Man*, he'd remind us how it became *Drummer Man* later, with the same melody. He didn't get any royalties or even, he'd say, a 'thank you.' He's inspiring to work with and I think he's at his best in a small band. A big band restricts him, although I must say he led some of the finest big bands through the '30s and '40s.

"One night at The Hangover, some cat kept calling out for *Royal Garden Blues* and Earl didn't hear him, but Carl Pruitt, the bass player, did, and Carl answered him:

Left to right: Earl Hines, Carl Pruitt, Shadow Wilson, Leroy Harris,
Jerome Richardson, Dicky Wells, Gene Redd, 1954.

" 'Man, you come on up here and play it if you want it. Damn it, we're going to play what we want!'

"So Earl says, 'What's that noise going on over there?'

" 'This man keeps yelling what he wants us to play,' Carl says.

" 'Man, we've got to play what the people want,' Earl says.

"We found out later Carl was arguing with a man from one of the big newspapers in 'Frisco. Afterwards, the guy met Carl, liked him, and told him:

" 'You don't tell me. We're supposed to tell you what we want. We pay you.'

" 'I guess you're right,' Carl admitted.

"Pruitt is a good musician, very concerned about his sound, and he had had a tremendous variety of experience with trios, small groups, big bands, and even the symphony. He has worked with Earl Hines several times and I think there's a good understanding between them.

"We had a lot of fun with that band. It was swinging group, especially when Shadow Wilson was in it. I found that Earl had quite a name in Canada. Maybe they hadn't forgotten all those broadcasts he used to do from the Grand Terrace. We played Montreal, Quebec, Toronto, London and Vancouver. The people up there have different taste in music. They want more melodies and they make more requests. That can be inspiring, too, because it means you play a lot of different numbers besides the regular program.

"Earl doesn't like to argue. He gets upset if anyone argues about money. He may have troubles, but he doesn't let you know it. Earl told one of his guys once, 'You may have holes in your shoes, but don't let the people out front know it. Shine the tops!' But I guess he got tired of the road and the hassles like anyone else, and that's why he enjoyed spending more time in his own home, and with his family, in San Francisco. I am glad he has been recording more, because he can *really* play that piano."

"While we'd be sitting around in the dressing room between sets, we'd sometimes get into some big arguments and discussions. One I remember while I was with Earl Hines went something like this:

" 'Hello, square!'

" 'Say, dude, what's your definition of a square?'

" 'One who falls for that I-can-do-more-for-you-than-your-wife-can jive.'

" 'Or one who goofs off his pay by the way of Sportsville—chicks, gambling, et cetera.'

" 'Yeah, and how about the cat who's over the hill and still thinks he's young, and keeps chasing teen-agers till he's damn near hung?'

" 'Then there's the educated square who's too smart for his own damned good.'

" 'How about the one who thinks he's the slickest in the land, until he winds up handcuffed to the po-lice man?'

" 'I'll tell you two of the squarest. There's the one who believes everything she tells him. Watch those club meetings! There's more than one kind of club. Dig Webster. The other one follows her to dig her happenin's. This cat's an FBI square, and he's passed the point of no return.'

" 'Well, there's also the unconscious square. I asked a dear friend of mine why he split from his old lady. He said that all the time he had been registering Mr. and Mrs., he should have been registering Mr. and Mr. You know, when Shorty George is in the act, it's hard to determine who the square is until Shorty is caught.'

" 'Don't forget the one who says, "Man, I know my girl is different. She doesn't fool around." '

" 'What about the one who thinks *you* are a square, and comes back for another handout, thinking you've forgotten the others which he never paid back?'

" 'Or the one who digs only himself?'

" 'Or the one that never goes to church and tries to heckle you because you do?'

" 'There's always the barfly square who thinks he has it made with a babe after tightening her wig. He's about to say, "Let's split!" when she's saved by the bell. "Oh, here come some of my girl friends," she says. "Excuse me a minute." She makes it over to the other side of the bar. Then, with one of her friends, she heads for the conference room or city outhouse, and from there he gets word she has been taken ill and they will have to take her home. "But she said she will see you next Saturday," her friend says. "Okay," the square answers, "I'll be here." '

" 'So let's just say a square is one who's so square he can't roll.'

" 'To be a square and not know it is one thing, but to be a square and know it is something *else!*'

" 'I must have been a square gangs of times and didn't know it.'

" 'Junior, I suppose at times we all have been.'

" 'Right.' "

(1971)

The first section of the above appeared in *The Night People* and is reprinted by permission Crescendo Publishing Co., Boston (© 1971 by Stanley F. Dance).

ROAD STORIES

During 1969 Earl Hines was playing a three-week engagement at the London House in Chicago, and old friends frequently came to see him in his suite at the nearby Executive House. George Dixon and Leon Washington were there one afternoon, and the latter had brought two bottles of a strange Greek beverage that was singularly effective in loosening tongues and provoking outrageous reminiscences. Eventually there was so much boisterous laughter that long sections of the "conversation" I was trying to tape were rendered indecipherable. Moreover, some of the stories were too scandalous or damaging to print, but what remains has considerable humor and illustrative value.

Although Leon Washington was with Earl Hines less than two years, a lasting bond was forged. Indeed, he seemed to me to be a typical, Chicago-reared Hines associate— bold, confident, efficient, good-humored, outspoken, friendly, yet strongly individual. Not all of Hines's men were like this, of course. Nevertheless, there was a type peculiar to his band, as though the musicians were touched by something while they were in it. It may not emerge in the stories printed here, but in person Leon Washington, Trummy Young, Charlie Carpenter, Billy Eckstine, Jimmy Mundy, George Dixon and Quinn Wilson, for example, have something in common beyond music. Perhaps it is a matter of generation rather than experience, but the men of the

Lunceford band of the '30s similarly seemed to have acquired a distinguishable manner and attitude towards life. That was true, too, of the Erskine Hawkins band, whose musicians had something like a family relationship. The musicians in Count Basie's bands of the '30s and '50s also had distinct, recognizable characteristics, a way of being rather like that of their counterparts with Earl Hines. The exception that could prove the rule was Duke Ellington's band, where a man might recognizably be of it, but could not really be typed, because Ellington always *wanted* only one of a kind.

I had intended to interview Leon Washington at the first opportunity, but he died, alas, before I could return to Chicago. He was an excellent musician with a style on tenor saxophone that at times brought the great Chu Berry's to mind. Details of his career given in John Chilton's invaluable *Who's Who of Swing* show that he was born in Jackson, Mississippi, in 1909. Three years later his parents moved to Chicago where he was taught first clarinet and then tenor saxophone. His first known professional work was with pianist Zinky Cohn in 1926. After gigging in Chicago, he joined Bernie Young in 1931. Engagements followed with Carroll Dickerson, Louis Armstrong, Fats Waller and Jimmy Cobb before he joined Hines in 1937. From 1938 onwards, he was in the Red Saunders band which worked at the Club De Lisa for eighteen years. He continued to free-lance around Chicago, playing and writing arrangements, even after he took a job as business agent for Local 10.208.

George Dixon: We had a whole lot of nicknames in the band. Willie Randall was called "Little Hog." And Leon Washington here, he was "Tow Head." That was the name they put on his music.

Leon Washington: A girl in Florida gave me that name when we were playing a dance. "I want that tow-headed so-and-so," she hollered. "He's my man, he's my man!" The whole band heard it and that name stuck with me from then on—Tow Head.

G.D.: And Louis Taylor, one of the trombone players, we called "Zilch." I don't know why.

L.W.: Another trombone player, Kenny Stewart, we called "Rev.," because he looked like a preacher. But he was just the opposite.

G.D.: He studied theology, too.

L.W.: That's right. He studied theology, but every town we went he'd find out if there was a bookie. He'd look him up, because he had to put his bet in before he'd go to bed.

G.D.: John Ewing was just "Streamline" because he was thin and skinny. Darnell Howard was "Bonzo." And Omer Simeon was "Graf," short for Graf Zeppelin. He had those wide shoulders, and the Graf Zeppelin was making news at that time.

L.W.: The name we gave Ray Nance was "Little Dipper," because he was short and small. That was the name we used to write on his music . . .

G.D.: How's he doing, do you know? He has an uncle on the police department that asks me all the time if I hear anything about Ray.

Stanley Dance: He has a regular job at the Gaslight Club in New York, and he's made some records recently.

G.D.: That's good. You know, his mother knew about his habit 'way back when we were in California in 1937. She used to send him literature about dope. We were staying at that hotel on Central, the Dunbar, and he'd throw it out on an adjacent roof. I remember one time I made him climb back out on the roof and get it.

"Man," I said, "at least read the mail from your mother!"

"Aw, she's a square," he'd say.

L.W.: I didn't know Ray was that heavy on the stuff. I really didn't.

G.D.: Remember when we left San Antone going to the Coast? Ray had bought thirty dollars' worth of it then.

L.W.: I remember this guy coming up to me in Lexington, Kentucky, and making me a ridiculous offer. "You're full of jive," I told him, but he came back with a great, big sack of pot, and I put it in the back of the bus. Every day I'd take it out and look at it, and separate it, treating it right there in the bus as we were going up and down the highway. That shows how far we'd got, because we could all have been put in jail. The cats were smoking up all that stuff, but George and them didn't want to say anything.

Earl Hines: You know what they did to me one day? I used to sit at the right side in front, and after the bus left I'd take my pipe out and smoke. Sometimes I was the last one awake, sitting there smoking and thinking, because everybody would start dropping off asleep after about fifty miles. Well, this time I put my pipe on the window and went to sleep myself. While I'm asleep, some of these cats emptied out the tobacco and put pot in instead. When I woke up, I took my pipe again and lit it. It tasted funny, but I thought it was my mouth or something I ate, and I kept on smoking and smoking. It's got to be my mouth, I thought. Then we pulled into a gas station and I said, "I'm going to get something to eat now." Everybody got out, and someone yelled, "C'mon, Fatha!" I let out the funniest, giggling laugh. I was laughing like hell, and I almost fell off the bus because I couldn't find the steps.

L.W.: Yeah, there we were layin' out on the sidewalk . . .

E.H.: And I'm laughing at *them*! I didn't know what was wrong, but I felt *gooood*, just sitting there floating! It wasn't till about a year afterwards that Scoops Carry told me what happened. "You lousy dogs!" I said. But they lay on the sidewalk till they cracked up. They had to go behind the joint, they were laughing so much!

G.D.: When I was in the Navy, the head of our special services came in and said, "Dixon, we got a lot of money, and if we don't use it we'll have to send it back into the Navy Department. So we ought to have a big dance. I want you to see if you can get 'Fatha' Hines, because he came here and played for us free. It doesn't matter what the charge is, we'll pay it." I called the office and they told me, "No, Earl's not available, but we can get you Del Courtney or Billy Eckstine." So I told them we'd take Billy Eckstine, and we booked the date. When Billy came in, they gave me two buses to go to the hotel and pick the band up. On the way out I said, "Billy, when we get there tell Mr. Baird you want me to go out with you for about a week, because one of your men has had to go back to New York. That'll get me some time off." Billy said, "Okay," and he grabbed this lieutenant at the base. "Sure," the lieutenant said, "I'll make out the pass. How long you want to be gone?" So I got out and made a date with them, but it's a wonder that bus didn't go straight up in the air, they were so high in there!

E.H.: We heard about it . . . everybody . . . all over the country.

G.D.: Well, I left them and went back to the base, and it wasn't a week later I read that the bus driver went off and left 'em in Kansas City. He said he couldn't take it any longer.

E.H.: Our driver called me one time. "What's the matter?" I asked.

"I can't go no further, Earl. I'm sick as a dog. I can't see. I don't know what it is they got."

So I went back and said, "Well, if you've got to smoke it, sit at the back and open the window!" But it was kind of cold, and they had all the windows closed. The smoke was going up front, and it was night, and those brakes were screeching! Eventually, I had to more or less fumigate the bus before the driver would go back in there.

G.D.: Those bus drivers had to put up with a lot. You remember the time when we'd been rolling all night and we got to a little town

called Crossbill, Tennessee? Joe was driving the bus—Joe with the Newark Bus Company—and he pulled up to a restaurant. The guys started waking up, and then it was, "Bring me a coffee!" Or, "Bring me a ham-and-egg sandwich and a coffee!" Or, "Bring me two hamburgers and a coffee!" So Joe went in to get all these things, and he came out with one tray full and went back in and got another. Just then the sheriff walked up in his overalls and stopped in front of the bus.

"I'll give you niggers just fifteen minutes," he said.

"Well," Joe said, "we just trying to get something to eat."

"Fifteen minutes, and then get out of town!"

E.H. (Laughing): I don't even remember that one.

G.D.: Another night we were playing a colored dance in Tuscaloosa, Alabama, and a lot of white students who knew the band from Chicago came down. Jerry Jerome, the saxophone player, he was a student down there. They came up to the stand, speaking to you, Earl, and they brought up some of the girls and introduced them. Then this one-eyed sheriff walked in, and I remember he was in overalls, too.

"Is this thing on?" he asked.

"Earl, he wants the mike," I said, and you turned it on and gave it to him.

"The dance is over," he said. Then he turned to us and said, "You niggers, don't even stop to eat! Get out of town right now!"

E.H.: You never knew what you'd run into down there.

G.D.: That's the point I'm coming to, because from there we went to Montgomery, Alabama, to play a country club. We got there early and parked. Just before the dance, we were back there changing clothes, and two fellows came in. One had a basket and he said, "Which one's Earl Hines?" We pointed to him, and this fellow said, "I'm the Mayor of Montgomery and this is Police Chief So-and-So. We want you-all to have a drink. We know the stories that get out about bands coming down here, and we want you to know you're welcome. And if *any*body bothers you in *any* way, just contact one of us. We'll be right here to-night." So we got the glasses out and we all had a drink.

E.H.: A basket of whiskey!

L.W.: Well, you meet some nice and some that ain't. You never knew what would happen. You remember that dance in Texarkana, Arkansas, when the stand was shakin' and rockin', and we were scared to death it was going to collapse with the weight of all of us up there. The place was packed, but there was no money in the box. All the people had to do was pull a board off somewhere and walk into the dance. Five thousand people, and a hundred dollars at the most in the box!

G.D.: That's like when we were playing a lit-tle coal-mining town in Cumberland, Ken-tucky, 'way back. We got in there and were standing around waiting. Earl told me to see the promoter and collect the money. I went to him and he said, "Well, I don't have it all." I told him I had to collect the balance on the contract, and he said, "You'll have to wait until the people come." When I told Earl this, he said, "No, no, if we can't get the money, the orders are not to play." So we started packing up, and then a policeman in a khaki uniform came up.

"Where y'all goin'?"

"We're going," Earl said, "because we can't get our money."

"Oh, no! These people made all the prepa-rations for this dance tonight, and you're going to play!"

"But they don't have the money," Earl re-peated.

"I don't care if they don't," the cop said. "You ain't going to take that bus out of here. Get this stuff unpacked and get back on the stand. This is a white folks' dance and they've been preparing for it for a whole three months, so you're gonna play!"

We played—and we got the money.

E.H.: You remember the way Billy Eckstine and Joe McLewis used to scare Shorts Mc-Connell?

G.D.: That time in Topeka, Kansas, when we were sitting in the back of the dancehall. I had the payroll and was getting ready to pay off when Joe and Billy started arguing.

"I'll cut your fucking throat," Mac says, pulling his knife.

"Just keep on pulling that knife," Billy says, pulling out his .45. "Come on!"

There I was with all this money, and Shorts didn't see Mac laughing as I did, and he was gone—gone down the highway! He was new in the band and they worked this gag up on the bandstand, too.

"I'm a friend of his and a friend of yours," Shorts would say to Mac, all sincere, "and I don't want any part of this quarrel."

But Billy would go up to him then and say, "What the fuck you talking to that cat for?"

"Look, Billy," Shorts would say, "I'm new and I want to make good in the band, but I'm nervous all the time."

E.H.: I was sitting on the sidelines and I could hardly keep a straight face. He'd come to me and say:

"Mr. Hines, I think you better . . . there's going to be a fight."

"What kind of fight?"

"Those two fellas . . . I don't know . . ."

"Well, you go on back to the bandstand and don't worry about it."

G.D.: We were in Georgia someplace on the Fourth of July. They turned the lights out and threw one of those firecrackers among us.

E.H.: They threw one of those bombs right in front of the stand and ran the ticket-taker away from the hall. The guys were mad for a whole week.

E.H.: I'm not a cross person. My disposition stays the same. The only thing I ask of a man is to be on time and to be able to do his work.

L.W.: That goes a long way back. Be on time and be able to play. Get as drunk as you want when you leave off work.

E.H.: That's right. I used to get drunk with everybody else. I don't give a damn how drunk you get, but when you come back the next night be able to play the music. And that's all I ask for now.

G.D.: I spent thirteen years with him and if anybody knows him I know him. No greater guy to work with . . .

L.W.: The guys used to say, "Earl, I ain't

never seen no bandleader just stay around with the cats all the time. You supposed to be up . . ."

E.H.: Shit! I'm going to stay with my guys. I'm going to hang out with them, you know. That's what they couldn't understand when I took the band to Russia. "Why's he sitting with them?" they asked. They gave me a great big old room and I said, "Ain't you got another room close to the boys?"

G.D.: Stanley, he was always riding the bus with us.

L.W.: You know when Freddy Webster was supposed to join Count Basie? When Count asked what his price was he said, "After you've paid the rest of those motherfuckers, you and I split fifty-fifty!" He was serious. He wasn't kidding. He was going down then though, and he died shortly after that. It was during the war. He got a beautiful tone, and there was such a shortage of good musicians then.

Did you hear about his buddy, Pee Wee Jackson, who also played trumpet? It was in all the papers. He stole a milk truck in Cleveland at 5 o'clock in the morning and drove it around the streets in a respectable neighborhood, blowing taps and bugles, waking people up. There were big headlines: GABRIEL BLOWS HIS HORN! The police got him. He got sick after that and finally died. He was drinking two fifths of wine a day.

G.D.: When we used to go down south, he wouldn't touch a thing. Then he'd come back to New York and have his big celebration. He'd get some Duff Gordon sherry and just have a little sip, and laugh at us drinking.

E.H.: He wouldn't touch a drop.

L.W.: Then he really turned.

E.H.: I never knew that.

L.W.: Oh, he was a basket case . . . every day!

E.H.: When I first went to Europe, Hugues Panassié told me a story about Sandy Williams, the trombone player who used to be with Chick Webb. He was over there with Rex Stewart, and there was a festival in some little French town. Sandy was wandering around with his horn, drinking and having a

ball. He got on a train with some other musicians, and nobody knew where Sandy was. They made an announcement over the loudspeaker that they were going to cut off some cars, and one part of the train was going to one place, the other part somewhere else. So this monkey was sitting up there and he didn't pay no 'tention to what the people said. When he got ready to go back and see the guys in his band, he found they were not there, not on his train at all. Sandy got off at the first stop. All he had was his horn; his bags were on the other part of the train. He couldn't talk French and the people couldn't talk English. He didn't know what to do. The only thing he thought of was to go out in the middle of the street and blow his horn. He kept blowing it till the police came up. One of them spoke a little English.

"Where did you come from?" he asked.

"I don't know."

"Where are you going?"

"I don't know."

"How did you get here?"

"On the damn train!"

"Well, what ticket do you have?"

"I didn't buy a ticket."

"How did you get on the train?"

"I was already on the train," Sandy said, and now he was getting mad. "I'm already on the train and the next thing I know I don't know where my people went."

"What people?"

"I'm with a band."

"Well, where's the band?"

"I don't know."

"*What do you know*? I'm trying to help you. You're with a band, but you don't know where you came from, you don't know where you're going, and you have no ticket. Who shall we talk to?"

"I don't know."

They sat around with him for a while until Sandy said, "You know Hugues Panassié? There were some people there who had friends connected with Panassié's Hot Club, and they said, "We'll find some musicians who might know this fellow." So soon one of Panassié's guys showed up.

"Oh, you're Sandy Williams," he said.

"Yeah," Sandy said. "Who the hell are you, man?"

"Where are you going?"

"Don't *you* start that! I'm in a group, and next thing I know I'm up here, and I don't know where I'm going."

So this guy phoned Panassié, and they put Sandy on the line, and Panassié told him, "Stay right there! Don't move!" And they came and got him.

L.W. (*Laughing*): That's funny, man! Don't know where he came from and don't know where he's going . . .

G.D.: You know what Billy Eckstine is playing now? He told me that it was when he was home sick he saw his son playing guitar. He picked it up one day and started working on it. He got to play very well, all the keys and everything.

E.H.: That's wonderful. I'd like to hear him.

L.W.: He plays *Love for Sale*, plays beautiful changes with it.

E.H.: Maybe he should have played that in the first place. You see, Leon, when he joined the band I put him in the musicians' union, because whenever I got a singer—and every time I turned around—there'd be a damn agent from AGVA trying to make him join and sign a contract. So I had Billy play trumpet. George and all of them would stand up there and hit B flat, *da-dah*! And Billy would be standing right there with them. We get to New York and here comes this agent saying, "Look, you got this singer . . ."

"Now, wait a minute," I said, "the man's a musician."

"What're you talking about?"

"Well, just stay here," I said, and he saw Billy standing with the trumpet players making one note, *da-dah*. "Now what're you going to do about it?" I asked him.

Same way with Sarah Vaughan. I had her playing on a second piano. "She's a musician," I said, "and the union supersedes. You have to keep out of it."

You know how I first heard her? June Clark and I were drinking all day, and Ella Fitzgerald was singing with some kind of quar-

tet behind her—four boys—and I said, "June, let's go see Ella. I've got to go before I go to bed, because I'll never be able to get up tomorrow and go!" So before Ella came on, they brought out this girl who had got a week's engagement at the Apollo Theatre for winning the amateur contest the past Wednesday. Sarah was standing there, flat-footed, no personality at all. And I was so high, I said to June, "Is that girl singing, or am I drunk or what?"

"No, that kid is singing, boy!"

So we went backstage, and she was sitting on a Coca-Cola box. June walked up to her.

"I want you to meet Earl Hines," he said.

"Who, me?" she said.

"Would you be interested in going with a big band?" I asked.

"*Eee-yuh*," she said, not believing me.

When I brought her down to the Nola Studio, the guys looked at her, and after Madeline Green being with us, they all thought the same thing:

"Goddam, Gate must have lost his mind!"

She looked like home-made sin, you know, but I told 'em how she could sing, and after they heard her they all put their arms around her.

S.D.: Did her personality change?

E.H.: See, Sarah's spasmodic. Well, she's gone through so damn much. Now she's got control of her voice. She can sing her country ass off, and she does lovely little things. I heard her when she was at the Fairmont in San Francisco. We were sitting at a front table, my wife, myself and our two kids, and I felt kinda bad, because she hadn't known we were coming. She said she was nervous because her former boss was out there. But, oh, I was so proud of her! She's got a helluva range now, can hit that top and come back down. She's got phrasing, she embellishes, and, ooh, man, this girl is terrific!

G.D.: You remember that time when we were down in Washington and Lionel Hampton's guys were sitting in their bus? They'd just heard Ol' Hamp had got a new singer. They thought a great, big, beautiful girl was going to walk out, and when they saw Dinah Wash-

Left: Sarah Vaughan, 1943.

Below: Sarah Vaughan and Earl Hines, 1973.

ington everybody covered their head up. Except Slappy White. He talked to her, and was nice to her, and it paid off for him.

E.H.: Those cats covered their heads, but they didn't know how Dinah could sing. "Aw, hell," they said, "he's got another dud." They bitched, covered their faces, and went back to sleep, but when her first engagement came around the same cats said, "The bitch can wail, can't she?" That was how they talked, but Slappy was the only one that had been nice to her.

G.D.: What was this Billy Eckstine was telling me about Monterey? He said he got out on the stage and sang a number you had forgotten about.

E.H.: Yeah, *When I Dream of You*. And that monkey never did record it, although he sings the hell out of it! It's a very simple thing, but it takes somebody with a voice to sing it, because of the range. I wrote the first lyrics, and then I had Charlie Carpenter write another set. But Billy and all of them liked the lyrics I wrote better.

S.D.: Who sang it when you recorded it?

E.H.: Johnny Hartman.

S.D.: You don't seem to believe in playing your own numbers.

E.H.: Yeah, I do, but at a place like the London House you have a problem. The waiters told me that when Oscar Peterson, George Shearing and Ahmad Jamal were in there, they were constantly cussing the people out. They used to stop playing altogether when the talking got too bad. The people will not keep quiet when you start to play piano. You sit up there trying to play something, and there's a party right under you going yah-yah-yah, talking business. I don't say anything anymore. The only time I made a remark is when the girl comes out to sing. I hear that Mr. Kelly's is different.

L.W.: For one thing, there are no obstructions. You can see from anywhere, because the stage is in the centre, and the house is known to be quiet.

E.H.: Now there's where I could play any number of tunes! When the people are listen-

ing, you can concentrate better, and get some feeling into the music. When I'm trying to beautify a tune with different chords, it's very distracting to have someone right next to you saying, "Well, I told her yah-yah-yah . . ." In the last show, early in the morning, when there are fewer people, you get more consideration and you can concentrate.

L.W.: Like Wednesday night, when I was there.

E.H.: Yeah. Some of the different houses I've played in, like the Embers in Indianapolis—why, it's beautiful! And in Louisville, they have signs flashing each side of the stand that say, "Quiet Please."

L.W.: Well, they demand quiet up at Mr. Kelly's.

E.H.: But Chicago is really a city of transients and conventions. People come in that have never been in a nightclub. "Let's go in there and eat," they say. I've seen them go through a whole business transaction without ever looking up to see who's playing. It's a doggone shame. They don't know what's going on.

G.D.: It's not only hard on performers; it's hard on those who come to hear you.

E.H.: That's what I always tell 'em. It almost develops into an argument. I ask those who are not interested to have some consideration for the others who want to listen.

G.D.: There's another problem with kids. All they know is the garbage disc jockeys pump to them over the radio.

L.W.: I never thought I'd live to see the American public accept the kind of music they do today.

G.D.: I took my band over to Waller High School. They had two rock bands, and they wanted each of them to play a half-hour, and then for us to play an hour before intermission. They tuned all the guitars up and turned up the amps as loud as they could. It was real crazy, and the kids were just screaming. They ran us out of the hall. We couldn't stand it. A few kids asked when we were going to start. They said, "We're so sick of this noise!"

E.H.: They said that to you?

G.D.: Yeah, some of 'em, and when we were playing one of those dreamy things we could see we were getting to them, but then others would start shouting: "Hey, come on! When y'all going to rock?"

Another time we were over at Ridge Park for a teen-age thing, and there was a group called Four Days and a Night, four white fellows and a colored fellow. They had a big Chinese gong, and everybody had a mike. After they had turned up the volume, one of them was standing there with a baseball bat, and this guy would turn around and hit the gong anywhere, at random, no meter, anytime, and laugh along with all the kids. Another guy had crash cymbals and was beating them all off the beat. Now if that bat had had felt on it it would have been bad enough, but it was just a bare baseball bat. I waved to this guy and said, "When you get through, come out. I'll be outside!"

(1969)

THE 1946 BAND: CAPSULE BIOGRAPHIES

Extracted from the publicity manual, these provide further facts about the band's members during the confused period following World War II.

TRUMPETS:

Vernon Smith, a former Clark College collegian, played with various combinations in Atlanta to get tuition money. Smith is married to Dolores Parker, the band's female vocalist, and is father of a three-year-old girl. He joined the band to lead the trumpets in June 1946 after his discharge from the armed forces. Smith, the band's amateur photographer, has worked for Tiny Bradshaw and Fletcher Henderson.

Arthur Walker of Los Angeles, California, is the band's featured baritone singer and trumpeter. He was discovered by the "Fatha" back in 1944 in a small nightclub in Los Angeles singing and playing in his unusual style. Walker has also played with the Roy Milton and Bardu Ali bands on the Coast.

Palmer "Fats" Davis joined Earl in 1943 after making the rounds with Benny Carter, Teddy Hill, Edgar Hayes and Joe Bostic. "Fats" is from Philly, Pa.

Willie Cook of East Chicago, Indiana, joined Earl in 1943 after working with King Perry, Claude Trenier, the 'Bama State Collegians and Jay McShann's band.

TROMBONES:

Clifton Smalls, leader of the band's rhythm quartet during the *Ol' Man River* number of Earl's *Show Boat* concert, came to him after fledging in the Carolina Cotton Pickers orchestra in 1943. Smalls, who arranges and relieves Earl at the piano, was taught music by his father. A native of Charleston, S.C., where he led his high school band, he has further studied music at Kansas City Conservatory and the Chicago Conservatory.

Walter Harris, from Pittsburgh, Pa., besides adding a tower of strength to the band's terrific trombone section, is also noted for his other sidelines. Three of them are cooking, printing and tailoring. Harris joined Hines in 1944 after having worked with Fletcher Henderson, Terry Stelle and numerous combinations in the Pittsburgh area.

Joe McLewis of Chicago, debuting again with Earl after two and a half years in the Army, has worked in the band at various intervals since 1937. He believes the present Hines aggregation is the best he has worked with.

Benny Green of Chicago, also a recent Army returnee, came to Hines in 1942 from Horace Henderson and other local band spots.

SAXOPHONES:

George "Scoops" Carry, featured alto sax and clarinetist, is also the band's rehearsal leader and leader when the "Fatha" steps off the stand. "Scoops," a former University of Iowa collegian and member of Kappa Alpha Psi Fraternity, is a native of Chicago. He was leading his own group when discovered by the "Fatha" in 1940. He formerly worked with Roy Eldridge and Fletcher and Horace Henderson's bands.

Lloyd Smith of St. Louis, Missouri, is also featured along with Carry in the band's saxophone section. Smith plays alto sax, clarinet and flute. He came to Hines in 1944 after having worked with nearly every bandleader in St. Louis.

Braxton Patterson of Buffalo, N.Y., joined the band in San Francisco in June 1946 on discharge from the Navy. He formerly worked for Noble Sissle, Ralph Williams, and the McRae Brothers.

Scoops Carry.

Arthur Walker.

Lord Essex.

Dolores Parker.

John Thompson, a Chicago lad, was playing with Tiny Bradshaw when his draft board called him. Recently discharged after two and a half years service, he joined Hines on the Coast a few months ago.

John Williams, baritone and alto sax, joined Earl in 1942. He says his fame lies in the fact that he was married to Mary Lou Williams, noted pianist, for fifteen years. A former bandleader in Memphis before breaking up his group to work eleven years with Andy Kirk, Williams joined Cootie Williams, and then came to the "Fatha's" fold.

RHYTHM:

Wild Bill Thompson, featured vibes and tympany soloist, joined the band in June 1945. Thompson, Smalls, Booth and Thomas comprise the personnel of the band's zany swing quartet. A former drum-beating bandleader, Bill was discovered by Earl while working with his own small combo in Miami, Fla.

Eugene Thomas, featured bassist in the *Show Boat* concert, joined the band in 1944 after two years with Noble Sissle.

Chick Booth of Erie, Pa., who joined Earl in 1943, is a drummer graduate from the small combo school of fame. His terrific drive and kick set the pace for the beat of the new Earl "Fatha" Hines band.

VOCALISTS:

Dolores Parker of Chicago, Ill., retired from the music world three years ago when her husband, Vernon Smith, was called into the service, and her youngster, Sharon, began to call for all her attention. Dolores's start in show business began with her winning an amateur contest in 1939 at the Regal Theatre in Chicago. After a spot on a radio program was offered, she began seriously to consider singing as an avocation. In 1942 she was a member

of the Rhythm Debs, Fletcher Henderson's girl singing group. She joined Earl "Fatha" Hines in 1945.

Lord Essex, considered the owner of one of the more pleasing voices in show business today, was discovered by Hines in Oakland, Calif., while working at the El Capp Club as a

member of the duo of Hunter and Scott. Born in Texas, but reared on the Coast, Scott (as he was then known) attended school and studied music out there. While working with Hunter, their repertoire consisted of over 2000 numbers, Scott's job calling for him to sing all the romantic ballads, current popular, and some semi-classics, when the customers demanded.

Left: At the Regal Theatre, Chicago, week of 17 August 1945.

Below: An El Grotto concert.

Opposite, bottom: Ford, Harris and Jones, Three Maniacs of Rhythm, with Earl Hines orchestra.

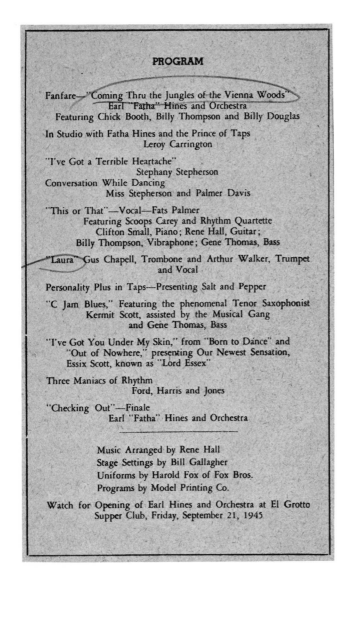

PROGRAM

Fanfare—"Coming Thru the Jungles of the Vienna Woods"
Earl "Fatha" Hines and Orchestra
Featuring Chick Booth, Billy Thompson and Billy Douglas

In Studio with Fatha Hines and the Prince of Taps
Leroy Carrington

"I've Got a Terrible Heartache"
Stephany Stephenson
Conversation While Dancing
Miss Stephenson and Palmer Davis

"This or That"—Vocal—Fats Palmer
Featuring Scoops Carey and Rhythm Quartette
Clifton Small, Piano; Rene Hall, Guitar;
Billy Thompson, Vibraphone; Gene Thomas, Bass

"Laura" Gus Chapell, Trombone and Arthur Walker, Trumpet
and Vocal

Personality Plus in Taps—Presenting Salt and Pepper

"C Jam Blues," Featuring the phenomenal Tenor Saxophonist
Kermit Scott, assisted by the Musical Gang
and Gene Thomas, Bass

"I've Got You Under My Skin," from "Born to Dance" and
"Out of Nowhere," presenting Our Newest Sensation,
Essix Scott, known as "Lord Essex"

Three Maniacs of Rhythm
Ford, Harris and Jones

"Checking Out"—Finale
Earl "Fatha" Hines and Orchestra

_____

Music Arranged by Rene Hall
Stage Settings by Bill Gallagher
Uniforms by Harold Fox of Fox Bros.
Programs by Model Printing Co.

Watch for Opening of Earl Hines and Orchestra at El Grotto
Supper Club, Friday, September 21, 1945

Earl "Fatha" Hines
Presents His Piano, Orchestra and Strings
in
Concert on Cole Porter's Compositions

SECTION I

1. **BEGIN' THE BEGUINE**
   Featuring Lord Essex, supported by Clifton Small, Piano; Lloyd Smith, Oboe; Willie Cook, French Horn
2. **I GET A KICK OUT OF YOU**
   Featuring Arthur Walker, Vocal
3. **I'VE GOT YOU UNDER MY SKIN**
   Featuring Janet Sayre from Boston Conservatory of Dancing
4. **MY HEART BELONGS TO DADDY**
   Featuring Delores Parker, Vocal
5. **JUST ONE OF THOSE THINGS**
   Featuring Ford and Harris in their nonsense
6. **WHAT IS THIS THING CALLED LOVE**
   Featuring Melrose Colbert, Vocal, supported by Ephraim Garcia Cello; Lloyd Smith, Oboe and Scoops Carey, Alto Sax
7. **NIGHT AND DAY**
   Featuring Lord Essex, supported by Delores Parker and Melrose Colbert and the Strings

SECTION II

1. **MEDLEY—FASCINATIN' RHYTHM, LADY BE GOOD, LIZA**
   Featuring Thomas Crump, Tenor; John Jackson, Tenor; Fatha Hines and the Trombone Section
2. **GOODY**
   Featuring Melrose Colbert
3. **EMBRACEABLE YOU**
   Featuring Benny Green, Trombone; Thomas Crump, Sax and the Trumpet Section
4. **SPEAKEASY**
   Featuring Janet Sayre, sensational Terpsichorean
5. **LOVE WALKED IN**
   Featuring Fatha Hines, Vernon Smith; Fats Palmer, Willie Cook, Lord Essex, Lloyd Smith, Scoops Carey
6. **SOONER OR LATER**
   Featuring Delores Parker and Thomas Crump
7. **FORD AND HARRIS**
   Fastest Act in Show Business
8. **SONATA—GIRL I MARRY**
   Featuring Lord Essex
9. **RHAPSODY**
   Featuring Clifton Small and Entire Band

CLUB EL GROTTO

PRESENTS

STAR TIME

MR. HINES	It's Show-Time
Introduced by Melotones	
Keep Jumping	Scoops Carey, Chick Booth and Grottoettes
In Studio	Mr. Hines and Lord Essex
Guitar Lament	Rene Hall
Indian Number	Martina D'Arcy and Grottoettes
Quartette	Melotones
Maniacs of Rythm	Ford-Harris-Jones

FINALE (1st Section)

SECOND SECTION

Ensemble Number	Grottoettes
"Exclusively For You"	MR. HINES, Janie Moses, Fats Palmer, Lord Essex, Martina D'Arcy
C Jam Blues	Kermit Scott, Tenor Eugene Thomas, Bass
Quartette	Melotones
MR. HINES' Compositions	Arthur Walker
"In Your Heart"	"Furlough Blues"
Maniacs of Rythm	Ford-Harris-Jones
FINALE	Honky Tonk Train
Featuring Clifton Small	

APPENDIX

1. "Alvin Burroughs was playing with Alphonso Trent around 1930, a young boy. He had good hands and an unorthodox style, and he had a snare drum that maybe needed a new head, but he got a beautiful sound. Who cares *how* you make a sound and effects as long as you get 'em? He did. The last time I saw Alvin, he was at the Grand Terrace with Earl Hines, and he was a great asset to Fatha. That was a wonderful rhythm section, and Earl Hines is still one of the bosses today. He plays piano as though he owns it, and when you hear men like Teddy Wilson and Oscar Peterson, they all have a touch of the old Fatha there, somewhere. He's always been a nice guy, and a lot of fellows took advantage of him. I remember when he was broadcasting from Chicago, if you turned a notch on your radio you'd hear Claude Hopkins from New York. That's what we used to do all night when we had a chance."

Drummer Jimmy Crawford to the author, 1961.

2. "In 1943 I heard the great Earl Hines band which had Bird in it and all those other great musicians. They were playing all the flatted fifth chords and all the modern harmonies and substitutions and Dizzy Gillespie runs in the trumpet section work. Two years later I read that that was bop and the beginning of modern jazz. For me it hadn't had a name. The band never made recordings.

"By that time I was already into (for that time) very modern music—Schönberg, Berg, Stravinsky—and what was so exciting about the Hines band was that they were playing harmonies and complex rhythms and textures that I already knew from classical music. Although what was new in jazz was forty years old in classical music, they discovered it on their own route. Imagine how bored I was with Dixieland music, which was all one-four-five, and if you got a seventh chord you were in heaven already! *These* guys were coming out with bitonal chords (though Ellington had been doing it ten years before that); this was a whole new age of discovery in jazz. There were great bands—Boyd Raeburn, Gerald Wilson, Herman, Kenton."

Gunther Schuller, composer, conductor and author, interviewed by Richard Buell, Boston *Phoenix*, 14 November 1972.

3. Typical programs by the Hines band in 1943, as detailed by George Hoefer in *Down Beat* (25 April 1963), included:

Good Enough to Keep (arr. by Budd Johnson)
Easter Parade (vocal by Howard Scott)
Intermezzo (violin solo by Angel Creasy)
I've Heard That Song Before (arr. by Dick Vance)
As Time Goes By (arr. by Dick Vance)
Taking a Chance on Love (arr. by Don Redman)
It Started All Over Again (arr. by Don Redman)
Stormy Monday Blues (arr. by Bob Crowder)
Down by the Old Mill Stream (unison band vocal, solos by Gail Brockman and Benny Green)
This Is My First Love (arr. by Dizzy Gillespie, vocal by Sarah Vaughan)
Down Under (arr. by Dizzy Gillespie)
Night in Tunisia (arr. by Dizzy Gillespie)
Second Balcony Jump (arr. by Gerry Valentine)

Hoefer quoted tenor saxophonist Charlie Rouse as saying: "When bop first started to happen in my life, it was all coming from the Earl Hines band." Arranger Neal Hefti added, "I thought it was the greatest thing I'd ever heard, and if the band had been able to record, maybe I'd still think so."

4. "My lip went bad after a year in the Hines band. They swung so hard and played so much.

"The Hines band had no cliques in it. Everyone hung out together. It was a real close-knit organization. There was never any animosity. We used to get to Bird when it looked like Earl was going to fire him for goofing; fourteen ganged up on him in one room."

> Trumpet player Benny Harris in *Bird* by Robert George Reisner (Citadel Press, New York, 1962).

5. "Earl is a very difficult person to play with. His sense of timing is uncanny; he's got practically perfect time on that piano, and that means that *you've* got to do everything perfectly. What he plays with his right hand is altogether different than what he's playing with his left. You can take your pick—you can go with the left hand or go with the right. I generally go with the right, because that left hand goes all over!

"Hines has counter-motion going, and all kind of counter-rhythms, so whatever you do has got to be right in there, because if you ever get *off*, it's going to be so noticeable, and it's going to be a great struggle to get back where it is. Your timing has got to be good, and you've got to have a melodic ear."

> Drummer Oliver Jackson interviewed by Valerie Wilmer, *Down Beat*, 14 December 1967.

6. "At the start of my playing, I was a big Earl Hines fan. I still *am*, in fact. I heard him play a few months ago, and he scared me. I was astounded that this man, at his age, is still a strong, powerful player—and doesn't sound dated. Like, he was doing up-to-date tunes; he did a thing on *Scarborough Fair* that just laid me out—the arrangement as well as what he played. He just keeps on going. When you see people like him, it makes you feel like: 'Wow, I got a lot of time to go.'"

> Pianist Junior Mance interviewed by Les Tomkins, *Crescendo*, October 1974.

Alvin Burroughs.

CHRONOLOGY

Much of the following was compiled from contemporary newspapers, magazines and trade sources by the late Walter C. Allen and given to the author for the purpose of assisting the preparation of this book. It was typical of Allen's constant generosity and unselfish research. His original object was to establish the Hines band's itineraries during the '30s and '40s, but in doing this he came up with a great deal of additional and useful data, which I have supplemented with information already in my possession, some of it derived from Earl Hines's memorabilia. Dates of engagements from 1965 to 1975, for example, were mostly drawn from programs or the relevant union contracts.

The chronology does not pretend to be complete, but to provide a guide to sources, to the activities of Hines and his different groups over a period of fifty years and to serve a purpose in relating many incidents in the preceding stories to time and place. Among the odd facts to emerge is that the significance of the phase when Dizzy Gillespie and Charlie Parker were in Hines's band was not publicly recognized until *after* they had left. There is virtually no mention of it in the contemporary sources examined.

ABBREVIATIONS:
For Sources:

AA	Baltimore *Afro-American*
AGE	New York *Age*
AN	New York *Amsterdam News*
BBD	*Billboard*
CA	*California Eagle* (Los Angeles)
CD	Chicago *Defender*
CG	Cleveland *Gazette*
CT	Chicago *Tribune*
DB	*Down Beat*
IM	*International Musician*
JI	*Jazz Information*
MB	*Memorabilia* (Earl Hines and Stanley Dance)

MET	*Metronome*
NJG	Norfolk (Va.) *Journal-Guide*
NYT	*New York Times*
OW	*Orchestra World*
PC	Pittsburgh *Courier*
PT	Philadelphia *Tribune*
ST	Savannah *Tribune*
VAR	*Variety*

For Places:

APO	Apollo Theatre, New York
AUD	Auditorium
BR	Ballroom
GT	Grand Terrace, Chicago
TH	Theatre

1905
Born in Duquesne, a suburb of Pittsburgh, Pa., 28 Dec.; his father a trumpet player, his stepmother an organist.
1914
Begins to study piano, first with Emma D. Young of McKeesport, and then with a German teacher named Von Holz, his intention being to become a concert pianist.
1921
Encounters jazz at a Pittsburgh club while still in high school; forms a trio with a violinist and a drummer and is hired by singer Lois Deppe to accompany him at the Leader House; influenced by three local pianists—Toodle-oo (Toad-lo or Toadlow), Johnny Watters and Jim Fellman—and rhythmically by a banjoist named Burchett.
1922
Joins Lois Deppe's big band, with which he tours and records for Gennett.
1924
Forms first band, which includes Benny Carter and his cousin, Cuban Bennett; then goes to Chicago and works as a single entertainer in Elite No. 2 Club.
1926
Tours with Carroll Dickerson's band.

1927

With Louis Armstrong at the Sunset Café, Chicago. Later at Apex Club with Jimmie Noone.

1928

Records classic performances with Louis Armstrong and Jimmie Noone, and piano solos for QRS and Okeh labels.

Rehearsing orchestra to open new café in Chicago in a few weeks; called to New York two weeks ago to make records for QRS; is husband of popular entertainer and violinist, Kathryn Perry. **CD** *22 Dec.*

Opens GT last week, S. Parkway, Chicago (Ed Fox mentioned). **CD** *29 Dec.*

1929

At GT; ten pieces. **CD** *9 Mar.*

At GT. **CD** *27 Apr.*

At GT; William Mitchell, now first cornet, improves section; was formerly with Charlie Cook Orchestra at Café de Paris. **CD** *20 July*

At GT; personnel: Shirley Clay, George Mitchell, trumpets; William Franklin, trombone; Toby Turner, Cecil Irwin, Lester Boone, reeds; Earl Hines, piano; Claude Roberts, banjo; Hayes Alvis, tuba; Benny Washington, drums. **OW** *Sept.*

Cecil Irwin still with Earl Hines at GT. **CD** *19 Oct.*

1930

At GT; same personnel as in Sept. **OW** *Feb.*

Hines accompanies Ethel Waters on piano, Grand TH, Chicago. **CD** *26 Apr.*

In St. Louis last week with orchestra. **CD** *3 May*

GT closes for summer. **CD** *7 June*

To appear Duquesne Gardens, Pittsburgh, Monday, 23 June, with eleven-piece Victor recording orchestra; Lois Deppe, vocal. **PC** *14 June*

Personnel given as before, plus George Dixon (trumpet and violin); brief Hines biography. **PC** *21 June*

Wheeling, W.Va. **PC** *12 July*

Photo; returns to Pythian Temple, Pittsburgh, Monday. **PC** *19 July*

Hines fails to appear without guarantee. **PC** *26 July*

Back in Chicago from tour; same personnel as in June. **CD** *6 Sept.*

Cecil Irwin, tenor sax. **CD** *11 Oct.*

At GT. **CD** *15 Nov.*

1931

At GT; Hayes Alvis, bass. **CD** 10 Jan.

Review of broadcast from GT over WSBC. **VAR** *25 Feb.*

At GT. **CD** *11 Apr.*

Darnell Howard and Omer Simeon in band. **CD** *18 Apr.*

At GT; Omer Simeon, "red hot sax." **PC** *25 Apr.*

Savoy Ballroom, Chicago, 30 May. **CD** *30 May*

At GT; Ben Washington and Lawrence Dixon in band. **CD** *13 June*

At GT; Charley Allen ("Old Ironlips") replaces Shirley Clay. **CD** *20 June*

GT closes for summer. **CD** *4 July*

To play Savoy BR, Chicago, 9 Aug. **CD** *8 Aug.*

Cecil Irwin, sax. **CD** *15 Aug.*

To reopen GT 7 Sept.; rumored that Franklin, George Dixon and Simeon will join Don Redman. **CD** *22 Aug.*

Irving Mills takes over management of Hines band at GT; to reopen there 4 Sept. **VAR** *25 Aug.*

Returns to GT 3 Sept. with Franklin, Dixon and Simeon in band. **CD** *5 Sept.*

GT opens with Earl Hines. **BBD** *19 Sept.*

Cecil Irwin, arranger. **CD** *26 Sept.*

At GT; Wallace Bishop, drums. **CD** *17 Oct.*

Hines band succeeds Duke Ellington at GT; features "Jabbo" on cornet. (?) **PT** *22 Oct.*

Regal TH, Chicago, week of 21 Nov. **CD** *21 Nov.*

Cecil Irwin, arranger; Lawrence Dixon, banjo, guitar and cello. **CD** *28 Nov.*

At GT. **CD** *5 Dec.*

On radio WEAF, New York. **AN** *Dec.*

Fourth season at GT; Billy Franklin, baritone, featured. **OW** *Dec.*

1932

At GT with thirteen pieces. **CD** *2 Jan.*

To Pythian Temple, Pittsburgh, with eleven pieces, 18 Feb. **PC** *23 Jan.*

Out of GT, to tour ten weeks; Moten band into GT. **CD** *23 Jan.*

On eastern tour; to Pittsburgh 18 Feb. **CD** *30 Jan.*

Leaves GT; to Pittsburgh 16 Feb.; Charlie Allen, cornet. **CD** *6 Feb.*

Cornets: George Dixon, Walter Fuller, Charlie Allen. **CD** *13 Feb.*

Photo of band (no names); in Pittsburgh 2–4 Mar. **PC** *13 Feb.*

Pearl TH, Philadelphia. **PT** *18 Feb.*

A hit in Philadelphia. **CD** *27 Feb.*

Band with GT Revue to Howard TH, Washington, D.C., week of 27 Feb. **AA** *27 Feb.*

Howard TH, Washington, D.C.; next week Lafayette TH, New York. **AGE** *5 Mar.*

Lafayette TH, New York, week 5 Mar. (photo). **AN** *2 Mar.*

Savoy BR, New York, 10 Mar., sixth anniversary, opposite Chick Webb. **PC** *12 Mar.*

Personnel at Lafayette TH, New York: Charlie Allen, Walter Fuller, George Dixon, trumpets; William Franklin, Louis Taylor, trombones; Omer Simeon, Darnell Howard, Cecil Irwin, reeds; Hines, piano; Lawrence Dixon, banjo; Quinn Wilson, bass; Wallace Bishop, drums. Managers: Ed Fox, William Bryant, T. Lyons. Band members given party by Lafayette TH management. **CD** *19 Mar.*

Return to GT, replacing Clarence Moore band. **CD** *19 Mar.*

Return to Chicago and GT last Saturday. **CD** *26 Mar.*

To double Oriental TH, Chicago, one week. **CD** *16 Apr.*

Same personnel as last (Walter Barnes's column). **CD** *16 Apr.*

Savoy BR, Chicago. **PC** *28 May*

GT closes for summer; band to Detroit for a week. **CD** *28 May*

In Indianapolis; Billy Franklin, trombone and vocal. **CD** *4 June*

To play Stanley TH, Pittsburgh, this week. **PC** *11 June*

Pythian Temple, Pittsburgh, 12 June. **PC** *11 June*

Lafayette TH, New York, week of 18 June. **AGE** *18 June*

To play Rockland Palace, New York, opposite Noble Sissle, 2 July. **N.Y. Tattler** *23 June*

To play Trenton, N.J., Sunlight Elks, 27 June. **PT** *23 June*

In Hartford, Conn. **CD** *9 July*

In Atlantic City, N.J. **PC** *16 July*

Sunset Park, Williamsport, Pa., 19 July. **MB**

In St. Louis one week, then to Kansas City. **CD** *18 Aug.*

On tour, same personnel as last. **CD** *20 Aug.*

In Knoxville; then to New Orleans; return GT 1 Oct. **CD** *3 Sept.*

Was at Wisconsin TH, Milwaukee; met Don Albert in Texas. **CD** *10 Sept.*

One-nighter in Cincinnati. **CD** *17 Sept.*

In Houston and St. Louis. **PC** *24 Sept.*

Back in Chicago, at Savoy BR, 9 Oct. **CD** *1 Oct.*

Ad. for opening at GT, 3955 S. Parkway, Chicago. **CD** *8 Oct.*

Opens at GT 14 Oct. **CD & PC** *8 Oct.*

At Oriental TH, Chicago. **CD** *4 Nov.*

Photo of band. **PT** *17 Nov.*

At State-Lake TH, Chicago. **CD** *3 Dec.*

Broadcasts from GT. **AA** *17 Dec.*

To leave GT 3 Jan. to tour. **CD** *24 Dec.*

1933

Joins MCA. **PT** *12 Jan.*

Standard TH, Philadelphia, week of 21 Jan. **PT** *19 Jan.*

In Dayton and Columbus, Ohio. **PC** *21 Jan.*

Lafayette TH, New York, week of 11 Feb. **AGE & AN**

To play Chester, Pa., 22 Feb. **CD** *11 Feb.*

New Strand BR, Baltimore, 24 Feb. **AA** *25 Feb.*

In Providence, R.I. **CD** *4 Mar.*

In Roanoke, Va. **CD** *11 Mar.*

At Savoy BR, Chicago, 19 Mar. **CD** *18 Mar.*

Returns to GT 22 Mar.; photo of band with Omer Simeon, etc.; Valaida Snow featured. **CD** *25 Mar.*

To play in St. Louis. **CD** *20 May*

Hines suspended for playing non-union café in St. Louis. **CD** *17 June*

Suspended for year by union for playing non-union dance in Danville, Ill. Hines appeals. **AA** *24 June*

MCA drops Hines. **CD** *1 July*

Hines claims prejudice on part of St. Louis whites. Suspension lifted after two days. **AA** *1 July*

Back on radio from GT. **CD** *29 July*

Back on air; okay again with union. **AA** *5 Aug.*

At GT; Leonard Harper produces shows. **CD** *8 Aug.*

At GT. **CD** *25 Nov.*

On road about 1 Jan. **CD** *23 Dec.*

1934

Fifth year at GT. **MET** *Jan.*

To play Durham, N.C., 2 Feb. **PC** *20 Jan.*

Fisk University, Nashville; whites mock band at jim-crow dance. **PT** *1 Feb.*

To tour South; band at Paramount TH, Nashville, recently; Carroll Dickerson band into GT. **MET** *Feb.*

To play Savoy, Pittsburgh, 8 Feb. **PC** *3 Feb.*

In Montgomery, Ala.; "battle" with 'Bama State Collegians. **CD** *10 Feb.*

To Municipal AUD, Savannah, 5 Mar. **ST** *22 Feb.*

Malone's Alcazar, Albany, Ga., Tuesday. **CD** *17 Mar.*

Lafayette TH, New York, week of 17 Mar. **AGE & AN**

Still on tour. **MET** *Apr.*

Lincoln TH, Philadelphia; photo of band. **PT** *5 Apr.*, **CD** *14 Apr.*

Strand BR, Philadelphia, 23 Apr. **PT** *19 Apr.*

Regal TH, Chicago. **CD** *5 May*

Long article; biography to date. **AA** *12 May*

Personnel: Walter Fuller, vocal and trumpet; George Dixon, vocal, sax and trumpet; Louis Taylor, trombone; Billy Franklin, vocal and trombone; Omer Simeon, Cecil Irwin, saxes; Darnell Howard, sax, clarinet, violin and trumpet; Jimmy Mundy, sax, piano and violin; Earl Hines, piano; Lawrence Dixon, guitar and cello; Quinn Wilson, tuba, string bass, accordion, violin, piano; Wallace Bishop, drums, chimes, tymps, bells, vibes; Herbert Jeffries, vocal; Irwin, Mundy, Wilson, arrangers; Ed Fox, manager. **AA** *12 May*

Back at GT; signs Trummy Young, trombone, ex-Hardy Brothers Orchestra. **CD & AA** *19 May*

Plans to replace one man with New York musician thwarted by Local 208, which objects to "letting out" a local man. **CD** *26 May*

Darnell Howard, saxophonist and radio expert. **CD** *23 June*

Palace TH and GT, Chicago. **CD** *7 July*

At GT. **MET** *July & Sept.*

Still at GT. **CD** *27 Oct.*

Darnell Howard, saxophonist. **CD** *22 Dec.*

1935

To Savoy BR, Pittsburgh, 14 Jan. **PC** *12 Jan.*

Out of GT; replaced by Carroll Dickerson band. **AA** *19 Jan.*

To tour. **MET** *Jan.*

Band on tour; expects to be out of Chicago eight months. **DB** *Mar.*

Harlem Opera House, New York, week of 19 Jan. **AGE & AN**

Lincoln TH, Philadelphia, week of 25 Jan. **PT** *24 Jan.*

Palace TH, New York, this week. **AGE** *9 Feb.*

Jazzland Dance Hall, Pennsauken, N.J., 3 Mar. **PT** *21 Feb.*

Recently at Palace TH, New York; opens at Harlem Opera House week of 8 Mar. **PC** *23 Feb.*

Harlem Opera House, New York, week of 9 Mar. **AGE & AN**

Ten-day tour of New England. **DB** *Mar.*

On tour. **CD** *23 Mar.*

To Welch, W.Va., 3 Apr.; Charleston, W.Va., 4 Apr. **PC** *30 Mar.*

Back at GT. **AN** *4 & 11 Apr.*

Ed Fox to rotate Hines, Henderson, Ellington and Calloway bands at GT during summer rather than close. **CD** *4 Apr.*

At Savoy BR, Pittsburgh, 12 Apr. **PC** *6 Apr.*

In Kansas City. **PC** *4 May*

Jimmy Mundy leaves to join Benny Goodman as arranger; will make $150 a week; Willie Randall replaces him; Milton Fletcher replaces Warren Jefferson. **CD** 9 *May*

Cecil Irwin killed when bus collides with corn truck eight miles northwest of Nevada, Iowa. Franklin, Fuller, Young, Taylor, Simeon and Bobby Frazier injured. Band plays date in Minneapolis that night, 3 May. **PT** 9 *May*

Cecil Irwin killed in crash; Walter Fuller, Trummy Young, James ("Jug") and Louis Taylor play in bandages same night in Minneapolis. Bus had left Des Moines; accident occurred 2:00 A.M., 3 May. **DB** *June*

Hines escapes accident, having traveled by rail. Band had just completed four-day engagement at Orpheum TH, Des Moines, on 2 May and left there early Friday morning of 3 May. **AA & PC** 11 *May*

In Apollo TH, New York, week of 31 May. **AGE & AN**

George Dixon, trumpet. **AGE** 8 *June*

At Frolic TH, Birmingham, Ala. **CD** 6 *July*

To Savoy BR, Chicago, 4 July. **PC** 6 *July*

Savoy BR, Chicago, Sunday, 14 July. **CD** 13 *July*

To Regal TH, Chicago, week of 26 July. **CD** 20 *July*, **PC** 27 *July*

To open at GT, 10 Sept. **CD** 3 *Aug.*

Personnel: George Dixon, Walter Fuller, Warren Jefferson, trumpets; Louis Taylor, James Young, Ken Stewart, trombones; Omer Simeon, Darnell Howard, Jimmy Mundy, Budd Johnson, reeds; Earl Hines, piano; Lawrence Dixon, guitar; Wallace Bishop, drums; Arthur Lee Simpkins, Kathryn Perry, vocals; Mundy, Johnson, Hines, "hot" arrangers; Jefferson and Wilson, "sweet" arrangers. **DB** *Aug.*

To Savoy BR, Chicago, 7 Sept. **CD** 31 *Aug.*

Opens at GT last Thursday, 26 Sept.; Arthur Simpkins, vocal. **PC** 28 *Sept.*

Review of GT show; Earl Hines's fourteen-piece band, featuring Walter Fuller; Adelaide Hall; Pops and Louie; Alice Whitman; George McClennon, clarinet and comedy. **BBD** 28 *Sept.*

Budd Johnson replaces Cecil Irwin, killed in accident. **DB** *Aug.*

At GT; Arthur Simpkins, vocal. **CD** 26 *Oct.*

Back at GT, broadcasting over WMAQ. **DB** *Oct.*

Comparisons drawn between Hines and Tatum piano techniques. **DB** *Oct.*

Carroll Dickerson at GT. (Possibility of error here.) **BBD** 28 *Sept.*, 2 *Nov.*, 9 *Nov.*

Hines at GT according to BBD, same issues into 1936. **BBD** 2 *Nov., etc.*

Hines husband of Kathryn Perry. **AA** 9 *Nov.*

At GT a few weeks more. **CD** 28 *Dec.*

1936

Fletcher Henderson to open at GT 26 Jan.; Hines to tour. **CD** 11 *Jan.*

Hines entertains forty stage and society notables at De Lisa Winter Gardens in honor of Duke Ellington and Ivy Anderson; Hodges, Bigard, Brown, Carney, Greer, and Mr. and Mrs. Jack Hylton present. 23 Jan. **CD** 25 *Jan.*

Henderson and Hines bands both present at opening, 26 Jan. **CD** 25 *Jan.*

Hines band to leave Friday for Alvin TH, Pittsburgh; then Lincoln TH, Philadelphia, Loew's State and Apollo TH, New York. **CD** 1 *Feb.*

Opens tour in Pittsburgh. **AA** 8 *Feb.*

At Lincoln TH, Philadelphia, week of 7 Feb. Kathryn Perry featured. **CD** 15 *Feb.*

At Loew's State TH, New York, last week. **AN & BBD** 22 *Feb.*

At Apollo TH, New York, 21–28 Feb.; Franklin to rejoin 1 Mar. **CD** 22 *Feb.*

At Savoy BR, Chicago, 15 Mar.; returns to GT 22 Mar. for six weeks; Fletcher Henderson to return when Hines leaves. **CD** 14 *Mar.*

To return to GT 29 Mar.; Henderson popular there and held over; Hines and Ed Fox patch up differences. **CD** 21 *Mar.*

Will return to GT; Sammy Dyer, producer of floor show; Hines band at Savoy BR, Chicago, last Sunday. **AA** 21 *Mar.*

Hines subbed at GT last Monday, while Fletcher Henderson played at Graystone BR, Detroit. **CD** 28 *Mar.*

GT, Chicago. **BBD** 11, 18, 25 *Apr.*

Riverside TH, Milwaukee. **BBD** 23 *May*

Apollo TH, New York, week of 5 June. **AN** 6 *June*

Personnel: Walter Fuller, Milton Fletcher, George Dixon, trumpets; James Young, Ken Stewart, Louis Taylor, trombones; William Randall, Darnell Howard, Omer Simeon, Albert Johnson, saxes; Earl Hines, Lawrence Dixon, Quinn Wilson, Wallace Bishop, rhythm. **AA** 6 *June*

Mystic Knight Club, Youngstown, Ohio, prom, 19 June. **PC** 20 *June*

In Cleveland, en route to Detroit. **AA** 20 *June*

In Flint, Mich.; on road another two months, after which will replace Fletcher Henderson at GT. **CD** 11 *July*

In Norfolk, Va. **PC** 18 *July*

Band in car crash near Cumberland, Md.; Wallace Bishop, George Dixon, Darnell Howard slightly injured. **CD** 25 *July*

Bus collides with telephone pole in Cumberland, Md.; lands in small creek; Hines knocked unconscious; 2:00 A.M., 28 July. **DB** *Aug.*

In Jacksonville, Fla.; to replace Fletcher Henderson at GT 1 Sept. **CD** 25 *July*

Band in another bus accident; no injuries. **CD** 1 *Aug.*

In South Bend, Ind., 3 Aug. **PC** 1 *Aug.*

Played Sky Club, Toronto, in Aug. **MET** *Sept.*

Bus crash near Baltimore, 6 Aug.; no serious injuries. **PC** 8 *Aug.*

In Cincinnati 10 Sept. **CD** 5 *Sept.*

Tour to Texas. **PC** 5 *Sept.*

Dance at A & M College, Tallahassee, Fla., 3 Oct. **CD** 3 *Oct.*

Lincoln TH, Philadelphia. **PT** 15 *Oct.*

Howard TH, Washington, D.C. **AA** *31 Oct.*

Ida James, local girl singer, age seventeen, joins band. **PT** *5 Nov.*

Apollo TH, New York, week of 6 Nov. **AGE & AN**

Count Basie had replaced Fletcher Henderson at GT in Nov.; Hines to replace Basie 4 Dec. Alvin Burroughs, drums, replaces Wallace Bishop. **CD** *21 & 28 Nov.*, **PT** *3 Dec.*, **AN** *12 Dec.*

1937

Jimmy Mundy, ex-Hines band; staff arranger for Benny Goodman; wrote and arranged *Cavernism*. **PT** *14 Jan.*

At GT. **MET** *Jan.*

To close at GT 24 Jan.; to tour; Ida James, vocalist. **CD** *16 & 23 Jan.*

GT closes "forever" 24 Jan.; to be rebuilt as theatre; new location sought. **DB** *Feb.*

Leaves closed GT; at Decatur, Ill. **PC** *6 Feb.*

On tour in Ohio; Budd Johnson leaves to arrange for Gus Arnheim band. **CD** *6 Mar.*

Apollo TH, New York, week of 5 Mar. **MB**

Nixon Grand TH, Philadelphia, with Ida James. **PT** *11 Mar.*

Ray Nance and Leon Washington now in band, having replaced Milton Fletcher and Budd Johnson respectively. **CD** *27 Mar.*

In Durham, N.C.; itinerary for southern tour. **CD** *3 Apr.*

In Little Rock and Texas. **PC** *24 Apr.*

Opens Sebastian's Cotton Club, Culver City, Calif., 27 Apr. for four weeks. **CD** *17 Apr.*, **VAR** *5 May*, **BBD** *15 May*

Willie Randall arranges for Hines. **CD** *29 May*

Personnel at Sebastian's Cotton Club: Dixon, Fuller, Nance, trumpets; Young, Stewart, Taylor, trombones; Simeon, Randall, Howard, Washington, reeds; Hines, Dixon, Wilson, Bishop, rhythm; Ida James, vocal. **TEMPO** *May*, **MET** *June*

Leaves Sebastian's 21 June. **PC** *5 June*

Returns to Los Angeles. **PC** *3 July*

Tours Coast, returns to Chicago in Aug. **TEMPO** *Aug.*

Finishes in Seattle, 21 July; tour east to Chicago. **CD** *17 July*

Back in Chicago. **CD** *31 July*

Darnell Howard, Omer Simeon, Walter Fuller, Young, Bishop, and Lawrence Dixon leave Hines. New personnel: Leon Scott, George Dixon, Nance, trumpets; Taylor, Stewart, Ed Fant, trombones; Leon Washington, Pinky Williams, Randall, Leroy Harris, reeds; Hines, Hurley Ramey, Wilson, Oliver Coleman, rhythm. **CD** *7 Aug.*

To appear opposite Fletcher Henderson at Tomlinson Hall, Indianapolis, 27 Aug., and at Graystone BR, Detroit, 30 Aug.; photo with Henderson, signing contract. **CD** *21 Aug.*

Drew 4000 at St. Joseph, Mo., last week. **CD** *28 Aug.*

At Riverview Park, Des Moines. **BBD** *18 Sept.*

Tour in Iowa, S.C. and Minn.; recent "battle" with Fletcher Henderson at Graystone BR, Detroit; 4700 at-

tended. To Oriental TH, Chicago, week of 24 Sept. **PC** *11 Sept.*

Budd Johnson replaces Pinky Williams; Trummy Young now with Jimmie Lunceford; Ray Nance with Horace Henderson. **CD** *25 Sept.*

Report of "battle" at Indianapolis with Fletcher Henderson, 27 Aug. Personnel as CD 7 Aug., except Claude Adams on guitar, not Ramey. **DB** *Oct.*

Returns to GT 1 Oct. **CD** *25 Sept. & 2 Oct.*

Opened at GT last Friday night, 1 Oct.; Dorothy Derrick, Ada Brown, George Dewey Washington in show. **CD** *9 Oct.*

Into GT at new location for first time, following date at Oriental TH, Chicago. **AA** *9 Oct.*

At GT; new revue; Dorothy Derrick, vocal. **CD** *13 Nov.*

Louis Armstrong to open at GT 28 Jan., replacing Hines. **CD** *11 Dec.*

1938

Oliver Coleman, drums. **CD** *8 Jan.*

Opens at State-Lake TH, Chicago, 28 Jan. **CD** *15 Jan.*

Leaves GT 28 Jan.; Leroy Harris, Ida James, vocalists. **PC** *22 Jan.*

At Savoy BR, Chicago, 30 Jan. **CD** *29 Jan.*

At Apollo TH, New York, week of 18 Feb. **CD** *26 Feb.* *& AN*

At Mercantile Hall, Philadelphia, 4 Mar. **PT** *17 Feb.*

At Loew's State TH, New York. **CD** *12 Mar.*

Review of show at above. **VAR** *16 Mar.*

On Dixie tour, itinerary given. **CD** *2 Apr.*

Temple Roof, Baton Rouge, La., 18 Apr. **VAR** *16 Mar.*

Opens in Jacksonville, Fla., for ten days, 29 Mar. **PC** *19 Mar.*

In Greenville, Miss., 29 Apr. **CD** *14 May*

In St. Paul; to N.D., 21 May. **CD** *28 May*

Private party, Wisconsin Club, Milwaukee, 13 July. **VAR** *6 July*

Returns to Chicago; will replace Fletcher Henderson at GT later in month. **CD** *16 July*

Opens at GT, 29 July; Leroy Harris, vocalist. **CD** *30 July*, **AA** *6 Aug.*

Three themes used for radio programs: *The Father Steps In*, *Cavernism* and *Deep Forest*. Personnel: George Dixon, Pee Wee Jackson, Freddy Webster, Ray Nance, trumpets; Louis Taylor, Kenneth Stewart, Joe McLewis, trombones; Willie Randall, Leroy Harris, Budd Johnson, Leon Washington, reeds; Hines, piano; Claude Roberts, guitar; Quinn Wilson, bass; Oliver Coleman, drums; Ida James, vocal. **DB** *Aug.*

Nance, Leroy Harris, Oliver Coleman, in band. **CD** *20 Aug.*

Six men on notice from Hines: Johnny Hartfield, Gail Brockman, Ray Nance, trumpets; Oliver Coleman, drums; Scoops Carry, alto; and "Fleming." Following men to leave Horace Henderson, whose band is not working, to join Hines: Walter Fuller, Milton Fletcher, Omer Simeon, Budd Johnson, Alvin Burroughs, and one other. **PC** *8 Oct.*

Changes in personnel; gets six men from Horace Henderson. From 13 Oct.: Dixon, Fletcher, Fuller, trumpets; Burke, Taylor, McLewis, trombones; Simeon, Randall, Harris, Johnson, reeds; Hines, Roberts, Wilson, Burroughs, rhythm. (Ed Burke was sixth man from Henderson.) **CD** *8 Oct.*

At Savoy BR, Chicago, 20 Nov., opposite Tiny Parham. **CD** *19 Nov.*

1939

Broadcasts from GT over WENR and WMAQ almost daily, 1–11 Jan.; first broadcast by Henderson, 12 Jan. **CT**

Closed at GT Wednesday, 11 Jan. **CD** *14 Jan.*

Apollo TH, New York, week of 20 Jan. **APO notes**

At Howard TH, Washington, D.C. **AA** *4 Feb.*

In Greenville, Miss., 16 Feb. **CD** *4 Feb.*

At Savoy BR, Monroe, La., 17 Feb. **CD** *18 Feb.*

To Cain's BR, Tulsa, Okla., 6 Mar. **CD** *4 Mar.*

To Lincoln, Neb., 10 Mar. **IM** *Mar.*

To Frog Hop, St. Joseph, Mo., 11 Mar. **BBD** *4 Mar.*

To Skylon, Sioux City, Iowa, 12 Mar. **BBD** *4 Mar.*

At Orpheum TH, Memphis, this week. **CD** *1 Apr.*

East Market Gardens, Akron, 11 Apr. **PC** *18 Mar.*

Opened at GT and first broadcast on 20 Apr.; last Henderson broadcast from GT 18 Apr. **CT**

At GT to mid-June. Notes

Apollo TH, New York, week of 16 June. **APO notes**

In New York; to tour Me., Baltimore, Richmond, New Brunswick, N.J., etc. **CD** *15 July*

Tour of South; itinerary given. **CD** *22 July*

At Temple Roof Garden, Baton Rouge, 7 Aug. **BBD** *22 July*

Playing Texas and Miss., 8–11 Aug. **CD** *5 Aug.*

In Greenville, Miss., 16 Aug. **BBD** *5 Aug.*

At Mecca Club, Galveston, 17 Aug. **BBD** *5 Aug.*

Olmos Club, San Antonio, 18–19 Aug. **VAR** *16 Aug.*

At Cotton Club, Austin, 21 Aug. **BBD** *19 Aug.*

In Evansville, Ind., 28 Aug. **VAR** *16 Aug.*

At Riviera BR, Lake Geneva, Wis., 30 Aug. **BBD** *19 Aug.*

At AUD, Kansas City, 8 Sept. **BBD** *19 Aug.*

Oriental TH, Chicago, week of 30 Sept. **CD** *30 Sept.*

To Rhythm Club, Natchez; George Dixon's native city. **BBD** *7 Oct.*

At Lion's Club, Ann Arbor, 7 Oct. **SWING** *Oct.*

At Eagles' AUD, Buffalo, 11 Oct. **SWING** *Oct.*

Apollo TH, New York, week of 13 Oct. **APO notes**

Into GT, 29 Oct. **CD** *28 Oct.*

Personnel at GT: Fuller, Dixon, Fletcher, Ed Simms, trumpets; Ed Burke, John Ewing, Joe McLewis, trombones; Simeon, Harris, Johnson, Robert Crowder, reeds; Hines, Roberts, Wilson, Burroughs, rhythm. (Close at GT 23 Dec.) **DB** *1 Oct.*, **CD** *4 Nov.*

Savoy BR, Chicago, **CD** *2 Dec.*

1940

GT closes, Jan. **DB** *1 Feb.*

Savoy BR, New York, 11 Feb. **BBD** *27 Jan.*

Apollo TH, New York, week of 16 Feb. **APO notes**

Brooklyn Palace TH, New York, 24 Feb. **BBD** *27 Jan.*

Opens at Blatz Hotel, Milwaukee, for eleven days, 12 Mar. **JI** *29 Mar.*

Tune Town BR, St. Louis, 2–4–7 Apr. **VAR** *6 Mar.*

Pilgrim AUD, Houston, 1 May. **PC** *20 Apr.*

Rockland Palace, Miami, 12 May. **PC** *27 Apr.*

Opens Roseland BR, New York, for five weeks, 24 May. **PC** *18 May*, **IM** *June*

Apollo TH, New York, week of 21 June. **APO notes**

Kathryn Perry divorced; Hines to marry Ann Jones Reed, showgirl previously wife of producer Leonard Reed; band playing new Hines composition, *Ann.* **PC** *29 June*

Regal TH, Chicago, 19 July. **CD** *20 July*

Hines breaks with Ed Fox. **CD** *10 Aug.*

Walter Fuller, trumpet, opens at GT mid-Sept. with George Dixon, Milton Fletcher, Ed Simms, trumpets; John Ewing, George Hunt, Ed Burke, trombones; Omer Simeon, Bob Crowder, Moses Grant, reeds; Rozelle Claxton, piano and arranger; Claude Roberts, guitar; Quinn Wilson, bass; Kansas Fields, drums. **DB** *1 Oct.*

Hines plans his own café. **CD** *7 Sept.*

Hines plans Studio Club at 3522 Michigan, Chicago. **DB** *15 Sept.*

To Savoy BR, Chicago, 22 Sept. **CD** *21 Sept.*

Benny Goodman negotiating with Hines for him to join as pianist and Billy Eckstine to take over Hines's band, which has several forthcoming Chicago dates; Budd Johnson, Scoops Carry, Willie Randall, John Ewing mentioned as in band. **PC** *5 Oct.*

Hines tells of breaking contract with "cigar-puffing Ed Fox"; could do nothing without Fox's approval; Fox booked band and took much of profit from tours; union found contract unfair and broke it; Hines let most of old band go and found new men while waiting out closing out of old contract. Budd Johnson rewrote the book. Hines turned down offer from Benny Goodman last fall, although it was Goodman's offer that caused him to go to union and fight Fox. Now with William Morris office. No regrets. **MB** *June (1941)*

Hines plays in Harry Lim's jam sessions at Hotel Sherman, 6 & 13 Oct. **JI** *25 Oct.*

To Savoy BR, Chicago, 19 Oct. **CD** *12 Oct.*

Ed Fox sues Hines for breach of contract. **AA** *26 Oct.*

Leaves for West Coast tour 20 Oct.; Hot Springs first stop; opens at Paramount TH, Los Angeles, 14 Nov. for two weeks. Personnel: Harry "Pee Wee" Jackson, Rostelle Reese, Emmett Berry, trumpets; Joe McLewis, John Ewing, Ed Fant, trombones; Budd Johnson, Willie Randall, Leroy Harris, Scoops Carry, Franz Jackson, reeds; Hines, Hurley Ramey, Truck Parham, Alvin Burroughs, rhythm; Leroy Harris, Billy Eckstine, Madeline Green, vocalists. Hines's marriage and cocktail lounge "indefinitely postponed." **JI** *25 Oct.*

From Dallas to Shreveport, 28 Oct.; to tour Calif. **CD** *2 Nov.*

Rainbow BR, Denver, Wednesday 16 Nov., in from San Antonio; to Salt Lake City, 17 Nov. **BBD** *16 Nov.*

In Oakland, Calif.; personnel as in JI 25 Oct. except Russell Gillam, trumpet, replaces Berry, and no Franz Jackson listed. **PC** *23 Nov.*

In Hollywood recording. *2 Dec.*

Little work available on West Coast. **CD** *14 Dec.*

GT closes owing Walter Fuller's band $600; Ed Fox not to be found; to reopen under Ralph Buglio's management. **DB** *1 Jan.*

George Dixon returns to Hines in St. Louis, from Walter Fuller's band; Dixon played alto sax on *Number 19* and trumpet lead on *Blue Because of You*. **PC** *21 Dec.*

Duquesne Gardens, Pittsburgh, 31 Dec. **MB**

1941

Apollo TH, New York, week of 10 Jan. **APO notes**

Opens Fiesta Danceteria, New York, for four days, 30 Jan. Personnel as below except Ed Simms in place of Benny Harris. **PC** *8 Feb.*

Royal TH, Baltimore. Personnel: Pee Wee Jackson, Tom Enoch, Benny Harris, George Dixon, trumpets; Ed Fant, George Hunt, Joe McLewis, trombones; Scoops Carry, Leroy Harris, Budd Johnson, Franz Jackson, Willie Randall, reeds; Earl Hines, Hurley Ramey, Truck Parham, Alvin Burroughs, rhythm; Billy Eckstine, Madeline Green, vocals; week of 7 Feb. **AA** *15 Feb.*

Boston, 14 Feb. **MB**

Portland, Me., 15 Feb. **MB**

Savoy BR, New York, 16 Feb. **VAR** *12 Feb.*

Howard TH, Washington, D.C., week of 17 Feb. **MB**

Metropolitan TH, Morgantown, W.Va., 18 Feb. **VAR** *12 Feb.*

Basle TH, Washington, Pa., 19 Feb. **VAR** *12 Feb.*

Neal's Savoy BR, Knoxville, 4 Mar. **MB**

Liberty Club, Valdosta, Ga., 5 Mar. **VAR** *26 Feb.*

Sunset AUD, W. Palm Beach, 7 Mar. **VAR** *5 Feb.*

Two Spot Club, Jacksonville, 10 Mar. **VAR** *5 Feb.*

Apollo BR, Tampa, 12 Mar. **VAR** *5 Feb.*

Harlem Square Club, Miami, 16 Mar. (Same venue shown as 9 Mar. in VAR of 5 Mar.) **VAR** *5 Feb.*

Windsor Club, Ft. Lauderdale, 17 Mar. (Same venue shown as 16 Mar. in VAR of 5 Mar.) **VAR** *5 Feb.*

Pickwick Club, Birmingham, 20 Mar. (See next entry.) **VAR** *5 Feb.*

Orangeburg State College, Orangeburg, S.C., 20 Mar. **VAR** *26 Feb.*

AUD, Macon, Ga., 21 Mar. **VAR** *26 Feb.*

Tuskegee Institute, Ala., 22 Mar. **VAR** *26 Feb.*

Palmetto Park, Augusta, Ga., 24 Mar. **VAR** *12 Mar.*

Armory, Durham, N.C., 26 Mar. **VAR** *12 Mar.*

Armory, Charlotte, N.C., 27 Mar. **MB**

Community Center, Greenville, S.C., 28 Mar. **VAR** *26 Feb.*

Bayshore Pavilion, Buckroe Beach, Va., 31 Mar. **VAR** *28 Mar.*

Albert AUD, Baltimore, 1 Apr. **VAR** *26 Feb.*

Savoy BR, Pittsburgh, 2 Apr. **VAR** *26 Feb.*

Ambassador BR, Philadelphia, 3 Apr. **VAR** *19 Feb.*

Jefferson TH, Auburn, N.Y., 4–6 Apr. **VAR** *19 Feb.*

Trianon BR, Cleveland, 7 Apr. **VAR** *12 Feb.*

Moonlight Gardens, Canton, Ohio, 11 Apr. **BBD** *12 Apr.*

Waldemeer Park, Erie, Pa., 12 Apr. **VAR** *19 Feb.*

Rudy Traylor, drums, replaces Alvin Burroughs. John "Streamline" Ewing, trombone, replaces Ed Fant. **DB** *1 May*

Savoy BR, Pittsburgh, 14 Apr. **VAR** *26 Feb.*

At Stanley TH, Pittsburgh, last week. **VAR** *5 Mar.*

Nu-Elms BR, Youngstown, 16 Apr. **VAR** *5 Mar.*

Apollo TH, New York, week of 18 Apr. **VAR** *12 Feb.*

At Apollo TH; photo of band. **MET** *May*

On tour: New York to Canada to La. **PC** *31 May*

Palace TH, Brooklyn, 3 May. **VAR** *19 Mar.*

Warehouse, Petersburg, Va., 5 May. **VAR** *9 Apr.*

Armory, Richmond, Va., 6 May. **VAR** *9 Apr.*

Cotton Club, Dayton, Ohio, 10 May. **VAR** *7 May*

Hines drew 600 at Cotton Club, Dayton, 11 May. **VAR** *21 May*

Olympia Park, Pittsburgh, 12 May. **BBD** *12 Apr.*

Foot Guard Hall, Hartford, Conn., 16 May. **VAR** *19 Mar.*

Freddie Webster, trumpet, replaces Benny Harris. **DB** *15 June*

To Cleveland from Pittsburgh. **CD** *24 May*

Grand TH, Canton, Ohio, 20–21 May. **VAR** *23 Apr.*

Pine Bluff, Ariz., 27 May. **MB**

Manhattan Center, New York. **VAR** *7 May*

Mecca Temple, New York, 29 May. **VAR** *7 May*

Howard TH, Washington, D.C. **CD** *31 May*

Owenisia Country Club, Chicago, 21 June **BBD** *14 June*

Savoy BR, Chicago, 22 June. **BBD** *14 June*

Hines names Louis Armstrong, Duke Ellington, Coleman Hawkins, Benny Goodman and Tommy Dorsey five greatest musicians in jazz history. **DB** *15 July*

Mort Maser, arranger of *Everything Depends on You*, *Sally Won't You Come Back* and *It Had to Be You*. **DB** *15 July*

Spur Inn, Karnak, Ill., 24 June. **BBD** *14 June*

Legion Stadium, Pine Bluff, Ariz., 26 June. **BBD** *14 June*

Aristocrat Club, Little Rock, 27 June. **BBD** *14 June*

Automobile Bldg., Dallas, 29 June. **BBD** *14 June*

Palace Park, Shreveport, 30 June. **BBD** *14 June*

Tour: Tex., La., Miss., Mo., Ark. and Tenn. **PC** *5 July*

Murphy Skating Rink, Alexandria, La. **BBD** *14 June*

AUD, Galveston, 2 July. **BBD** *14 June*

AUD, Houston, 3 July. **BBD** *14 June*

Temple Roof Garden, Baton Rouge, 4 July. **BBD** *14 June*

Blue Moon, Bunkie, La., 5 July. **BBD** *14 June*

Rhythm Club, New Orleans, 6 July. **BBD** *14 June*

Castle BR, St. Louis, 11 July. **BBD** *14 June*

Paradise BR, Nashville, 13 July. **BBD** *14 June*

Tour: Ind., Ohio, Wis., Miss., Mo., Kan., Okla. and Tex., 17–31 July. **PC** *19 July*

Graystone BR, Detroit, 21 July. **BBD** *9 Aug.*

English Village, Tulsa, 26 July. **BBD** *5 July*

Palladium, Portland, Ore., 7 Aug. **IM** *August*

Paramount, Los Angeles, week of 21 Aug. **VAR** *1 Oct.*
Balboa Park, San Diego, 29 Aug. **DB** *1 Sept.*
Sweet's BR, Oakland, 31 Aug.–1 Sept. **DB** *1 Sept.*
Elk's Lodge, Los Angeles, 4 Sept. **BBD** *6 Sept.*
Civic AUD, San Jose, Calif., 6 Sept. **BBD** *6 Sept.*
Natatorium Park, Spokane, 20 Sept. **BBD** *4 Oct.*
Worland, Wy., 24 Sept.; 1085 attended. **VAR** *1 Oct.*
Opens at GT 3 Oct., with Madeline Green and Billy Eckstine. **CD** *27 Sept.*, **PC** *4 Oct.*
Personnel: Pee Wee Jackson, Jesse Miller, William Johnson, George Dixon, trumpets; Joseph McLewis, George Hunt, Nat Atkins, trombones; Scoops Carry, Leroy Harris, Willie Randall, Franz Jackson, Budd Johnson, reeds; Hines, Hurley Ramey, Truck Parham, Rudy Traylor, rhythm; Billy Eckstine, Madeline Green, vocals. **CD** *25 Oct.*
Above personnel, but Tommy Enoch, trumpet; no Miller or Johnson. **DB** *1 Nov.*
Six-piece reed section in back-cover photo. **DB** *1 Nov.*
Hines wins first round in court suit by Ed Fox for breach of contract. **CD** *25 Oct.*
Leaves GT 30 Oct.; starts tour at Gary, Ind.; to Pittsburgh 7 Nov. **CD** *25 Oct.*
Ivory BR, Uniontown, Pa., 5 Nov. **BBD** *18 Oct.*
Golden Gate BR, New York, 2 Oct. **AN** *15 Nov.*
Memorial AUD, Raleigh, N.C., 5 Dec. **MB**
Durham, N.C., 6 Dec. **MB**
Municipal AUD, Savannah, 8 Dec. **MB**
Brunswick, Ga., 9 Dec. **MB**
Cherokee Ranch, Augusta, Ga., 10 Dec. **MB**
City AUD, Albany, Ga., 11 Dec. **MB**
Delmar Casino, Augusta, Ga., 12 Dec. **VAR** *10 Dec.*
Nashville, 14 Dec. **MB**
AUD, Knoxville, 15 Dec. **VAR** *10 Dec.*
Ziegfeld Skating Rink, High Point, N.C., 16 Dec. **VAR** *10 Dec.*
Henderson, N.C., 17 Dec. **MB**
Community Center, Greensboro, N.C., 18 Dec. **VAR** *10 Dec.*
Township AUD, Columbia, S.C., 19 Dec. **VAR** *10 Dec.*
Madrid BR, Harrisburg, Pa., 25 Dec. **VAR** *10 Dec.*
Franz Jackson leaves. **MET** *Jan. 1942*
1942
Strand BR, Philadelphia, 8 Jan. **VAR** *31 Dec.*
Royal TH, Baltimore, week of 16 Jan. **VAR** *31 Dec.*
Apollo TH, New York, week of 23 Jan. **VAR** *31 Dec.*
Brookline Country Club, Philadelphia, 31 Jan. **BBD** *21 Feb.*
Roseland BR, Taunton, Mass., 2 Feb. **VAR** *31 Dec.*
Howard TH, Washington, D.C., week of 15 Feb. **CD** *28 Feb.*
Memorial Hall, Dayton, Ohio, 28 Feb. **CD** *28 Feb.*
Paradise TH, Detroit, week of 6 Mar. **BBD** *17 Jan.*
Review: Johnson, Eckstine, Green mentioned. **MET** *Mar.*
Lincoln BR, Columbus, Ohio, 13 Mar. **VAR** *4 Mar.*
Coliseum, Cleveland, 16 Mar. **VAR** *4 Mar.*
Strand BR, Philadelphia, 20 Mar. **VAR** *4 Mar.*

Royal Windsor BR, New York, 21 Mar. **Var** *4 Mar.* & **AN**
Turner's Arena, Washington, D.C., 22 Mar. **VAR** *4 Mar.*
Armory, Fairmont, W.Va., 23 Mar. **VAR** *4 Mar.*
Coliseum, Cleveland, 25 Mar.; drew 1500. **VAR** *1 Apr.*
Paris BR, Milwaukee, 28 Mar. **VAR** *25 Mar.*
Palais Royal, South Bend, Ind., 29 Mar. **VAR** *25 Mar.*
On tour for William Morris agency. **DB** *15 Mar., 1 & 15 May*
Eastwood Park BR, Detroit, 4 Apr. **MB**
Savoy BR, Chicago, 5 Apr. **VAR** *25 Mar.*
Armory, Louisville, 6 Apr. **VAR** *25 Mar.*
Castle BR, St. Louis, 8 Apr. **VAR** *25 Mar.*
Municipal AUD, Kansas City, 9 Apr. **VAR** *25 Mar.*
Casa Loma, Tulsa, 10 Apr. **MB**
Blossom Heath, Oklahoma City, 11 Apr. **VAR** *25 Mar.*
Armory, Junction City, Kans., 7–8 May. **BBD** *2 May*
Frog Hop BR, St. Louis, 9 May. **VAR** *6 May*
Skylon BR, Sioux City, Iowa, 10 May. **VAR** *6 May*
BR, Watertown, S.D., 11 May. **BBD** *2 May*
Arkota BR, Sioux Falls, S.D., 12 May. **BBD** *2 May*
Municipal AUD, Moberly, Mo., 15 May. **BBD** *2 May*
Chermot BR, Omaha, 16 May. **BBD** *2 May*
Tro-Mar BR, Des Moines, 17 May. **BBD** *2 May*
Earl Hines of Baltimore (presumably a different man) opens with band at Comedy Club, Baltimore, 5 June. **AA** *6 June*
Band's itinerary: Ohio, Va., D.C., Pa., N.Y., Mich., and Ontario. **PC** *13 June*
Tune Town BR, St. Louis, 2–8 June. **VAR** *6 May*
Skating Rink, Richmond, Va., 24 June. **BBD** *13 June*
Lincoln Colonnades, Washington, D.C., 25 June. **BBD** *13 June*
Olympia Park, Pittsburgh, 26 June. **BBD** *13 June*
Junction Park, New Brighton, Pa., 27 June. **BBD** *13 June*
AUD, Buffalo, 28 June. **BBD** *13 June*
Graystone BR, Detroit, 29 June; breaks record. **BBD** *13 June*
Palais Royal, Toronto, 30 June. **BBD** *13 June*
Cotton Club, Dayton, Ohio, 2 July. **BBD** *13 June*
Strand BR, Philadelphia, 4 July. **VAR** *1 July*
Carr's BR, Baltimore, 5 July. **VAR** *1 July*
Apollo TH, New York, 10–16 July. **VAR** *1 July*
Chestnut Street Hall, Harrisburg, Pa., 22 July. **VAR** *15 July*
Memorial Hall, Kansas City, 25 July; 2000 people. **MB**
Joe Louis visits from Ft. Riley during Kansas City one-nighter and says, "The Father sounds terrific." **DB** *15 Sept.*
Recreation Bldg., Ft. Worth, 27 July. **MB**
Earl Hines band to break up? **AA** *1 Aug.*
Sunset BR, Carrolltown, Pa., 1 Aug. **VAR** *29 July*
Rosedale Beach, Millsboro, Del., 3 Aug. **VAR** *29 July*
Convention Hall, Philadelphia, 27 Aug. **VAR** *29 July*
Savoy BR, New York, opposite Cootie Williams, 30 Aug.; attendance 4258. **VAR** *2 Sept.*
Jerry Blake, Gale Brockman, Ed Knox and Benny Green

respectively replace Randall, Dixon, Jackson and McLewis, who have been drafted. **DB** *1 Oct.*

Howard TH, Washington, D.C., week of 18 Sept. **VAR** *7 Oct.*

Hines in jam session organized by critics Feather and Goffin at New School, New York, with Bill Coleman, Bobby Hackett and Pete Brown. **DB** *15 Oct.*

Apollo TH, New York, week of 9 Oct. **VAR** *7 Oct.*

Golden Gate BR, New York, fall dance, 17 Oct. **AN** *10 Oct.*

Paradise TH, Detroit, week of 23 Oct. **VAR** *7 Oct.*

In Detroit (at Paradise) band included George Dixon, Shorty McConnell, Scoops Carry, Budd Johnson, Shadow Wilson. **PC** *21 Nov.*

Fays TH, Philadelphia, week of 12 Nov. **PT & AN** *28 Nov.*

Ritz BR, Bridgeport, Ct., 22 Nov.; 1212 attend. **VAR** *25 Nov.*

Golden Gate BR,, New York, 25 Dec. **AN** *19 Dec.*

1943

Apollo TH, New York, week of 15 Jan. **APO notes**

Royal TH, Baltimore, week of 22 Jan. **VAR** *23 Dec.*

Robbins TH, Warren, Ohio, 2 Feb. **VAR** *27 Jan.*

Paradise TH, Detroit, 5–11 Feb. **VAR** *27 Jan.*

AUD, Dayton, Ohio, 13 Feb. **VAR** *27 Jan.*

Savoy BR, Chicago, 14 Feb. **VAR** *27 Jan.*

Judy Gardner, accordion; Shorts McConnell, trumpet; Angie Gardner, alto sax; Jesse Simpkins, bass, in band at Savoy BR, Chicago, where three shootings occur in hour on Valentine's Day. **DB** *1 Mar.*

Tune Town BR, St. Louis, 23–29 Feb. **VAR** *27 Jan.*

Ashland Ave. AUD, Chicago, 27 Feb. **CD** *13 Feb.*

Adams TH, Newark, 4–10 Mar. **BBD** *30 Jan.*

"Sure, I taught Jess Stacy, Joe Sullivan, Whitey Berquist, and Teddy Wilson how to play when I was at the Sunset. We were just kids then," Hines is quoted as saying. Sarah Vaughan came to band right out of Apollo TH amateur contest "about three months ago." **DB** *15 Apr.*

Fays TH, Philadelphia, 12–18 Mar. **BBD** *30 Jan.*

Dance for Mass. State Guard, Boston, 20 Mar. **CD** *8 Mar.*

Howard TH, Washington, D.C., 2–8 Apr. **BBD** *30 Jan.*

Lincoln Colonnades, Washington, D.C., 11 Apr. **VAR** *31 Mar.*

Memorial AUD, Buffalo, 18 Apr. **VAR** *31 Mar.*

Apollo TH, New York, 23–29 Apr. **APO notes**

Golden Gate BR, New York, opposite Louis Jordan, 8 May. **AN** *1 May*

Municipal AUD, Kansas City, 19 and 21 June; drew 3500 each day. **VAR** *23 June*

Apollo TH, New York, 9–15 July; Sarah Vaughan, vocal. **APO notes**

Town Hall, Philadelphia, 16 July. **BBD** *10 July*

Manhattan Center, New York, 17 July. **BBD** *10 July*

Tic Toc Club, Boston, 18–24 July. **BBD** *10 July*

Palace TH, Brooklyn, 25 July. **BBD** *24 July*

Renaissance BR, New York, 25 July. **AN** *17 July*

Howard TH, Washington, 30 July–5 Aug. **IM** *Aug.*

Royal TH, Baltimore, 6–12 Aug. **IM** *Aug.*

Winston-Salem, N.C., 13 Aug. **BBD** *7 Aug.*

Logan, W.Va., 14 Aug. **BBD** *7 Aug.*

Johnson City, Tenn., 16 Aug. **BBD** *7 Aug.*

Goldsboro, N.C., 17 Aug. **BBD** *7 Aug.*

AUD, Charlotte, N.C., 19 Aug. **BBD** *7 Aug.*

Riverside Beach, Charleston, S.C., 20 Aug. **BBD** *7 Aug.*

Roosevelt Hotel, Jacksonville, Fla., 21 Aug. **BBD** *7 Aug.*

AUD, Macon, Ga., 23 Aug. **BBD** *7 Aug.*

McIntyre Gymnasium, Brunswick, Ga., 24 Aug. **BBD** *7 Aug.*

AUD, Albany, Ga., 25 Aug. **BBD** *7 Aug.*

Wrightsville Beach, Wilmington, N.C., 28 Aug. **BBD** *7 Aug.*

Some men into Army; forms mixed band. **AN** *11 Sept.*

Adds twelve girls to band. **PC** *11 Sept.*

Adds females; band now twenty-three pieces. **CD** *4 Sept.*

Apollo TH, New York, 17–23 Sept.; string section, total of twenty-three instrumentalists and five singers. Cancels southern tour to reorganize band after losing about six men to draft; Eckstine is 1-A. **VAR** *1 Sept.*

Adds four female violins, bass, guitar and harp. **IM** *Oct.*

Photo of band: four trumpets, four trombones, five reeds, piano, bass, guitar, drums, three violins, cello, harp. Paul Cohen, trumpet; Murray Dinofer, drums; Angel Creasy, Helen Way, Lolita Valdez, violins; Ardine Loving, cello; Lavilla Tullos, harp; Roxanna Lucas, guitar; Lucille Dixon, bass. **MET** *Oct.*

Manhattan Center, New York, 25 Sept. **BBD** *25 Sept.*

Fays TH, Philadelphia, 1–7 Oct.; new orchestra; seventeen men, eleven girls. **PT** *2 Oct.*

Turner's Arena, Washington, D.C., 10 Oct. **BBD** *25 Sept.*

Dropping three brass; now nineteen instrumentalists. **VAR** *6 Oct.*

Strand TH, Baltimore, 11 Oct. **BBD** *9 Oct.*

Paradise TH, Detroit, 29 Oct.–3 Nov. **BBD** *9 Oct.*

Book-Cadillac Hotel, Detroit, 12 Nov. **BBD** *23 Oct.*

Fays TH, Philadelphia, week of 14 Nov. **PT**

Club Madrid, Louisville, 22–28 Nov. **BBD** *30 Oct.*

Public Hall, Cleveland, 1 Dec. **BBD** *30 Oct.*

Howard TH, Washington, D.C., week of 3 Dec. **BBD** *30 Oct.*

Bayshore Pavilion, Hampton, Va., 10 Dec. **VAR** *1 Dec.*

City Armory, Durham, N.C., 11 Dec. **VAR** *1 Dec.*

Two-Spot Club, Jacksonville, Fla., 20–26 Dec. **VAR** *1 Dec.*

South St. Casino, Orlando, Fla., 27 Dec. **VAR** *22 Dec.*

Club Windsor, Ft. Lauderdale, 28 Dec. **VAR** *22 Dec.*

Harlem Square Club, Miami, 29 Dec. **VAR** *22 Dec.*

Elite TH, Winter Haven, Fla., 30 Dec. **VAR** *22 Dec.*

1944

City AUD, Macon, Ga., 3 Jan. **VAR** *22 Dec.*

AUD, Atlanta, Ga., 4 Jan. **VAR** *22 Dec.*

Municipal AUD, Birmingham, 5 Jan. **VAR** *22 Dec.*

Brookley Field, Mobile, Ala., 8–10 Jan. **VAR** *22 Dec.*

Regal TH, Chicago, week of 21 Jan. **CD** *22 Jan.*

Apollo TH, New York, week of 18 Feb. **APO notes**

Town Hall, Broad and Race Sts., Philadelphia, 10 Mar.; featuring Sarah Vaughan. **PT** *4 Mar.*

Loew's State TH, New York; twenty-two pieces, strings, harp, etc. **VAR** *5 Apr.*

Earle TH, Philadelphia; sixteen pieces; Betty Roche, Jesse Perry, vocals; review. **VAR** *12 July*

Apollo TH, New York, week of 14 July. **APO notes**

Review: Willie Cook and three other trumpets; three trombones; five reeds (including Scoops Carry, clarinet; Wardell Gray, tenor sax; Lloyd Smith, flute); Hines, piano; Cliff Smalls, trombone, doubling piano; Rene Hall, guitar; Lucille Dixon, bass; drums. **MET** *Aug.*

Savoy BR, Chicago, Sunday, 7 May. **CD** *6 May*

Plays "Star Spangled Banner" at Tic Toc Club, Boston, to avert racial clash. **AA** *12 Aug.*

Savoy BR, Chicago, Sunday, 10 Sept., opposite Eugene Wright band. **CD** *2 Sept.*

Orpheum TH, Los Angeles; sixteen pieces; Betty Roche and Jesse Perry vocalists; week of 29 Sept.; review. **VAR** *4 Oct.*

Booked into Club Plantation, Los Angeles, in Oct., after Count Basie. **BBD** *15 Oct.*

Down Town TH, Chicago, week of 1 Dec.; Butterbeans and Susie on bill. **CT** *1 Dec.*

Hines sued by American Guild of Variety Artists for firing seventeen-year-old singer, Jesse Perry. **VAR** *6 Dec.*

1945

Apollo TH, New York, week of 5 Jan. **APO notes**

Review of Apollo TH appearance: Wardell Gray, Kermit Scott, Fats Davies, Arthur Walker and vocalist Essex Scott featured. **MET** *Feb.*

Review of Apollo TH appearance. **DB** *1 Feb.*

Recorded series of solos to be transcribed and published in folio by Robbins, Feist & Miller **MET** *Jan.*

Hines names *Tantalizing a Cuban, Boy with Wistful Eyes, I Got It Bad* and *Boogie Woogie on St. Louis Blues* favorite own records. **MET** *Feb.*

Sharon Pease analyzes the Hines piano style and illustrates it with *My Monday Date.* **DB** *1 Feb.*

Schedules "Evolution of Jazz" concert at Carnegie Hall, New York, 6 Feb., for benefit of NAACP. **BBD** *3 Feb.*

University of Louisville School of Music; band plus lecture on music; 13 Feb. **VAR** *14 Feb.*

National TH, Louisville, week. **VAR** *14 Feb.*

Opens Opera House, Newark, 23 Feb. **IM** *Feb.*

Opens at El Grotto, Chicago, 2 Mar. **BBD** *3 Feb.*

At El Grotto. **DB** *15 Mar.*, **AA** *31 Mar.*

El Grotto, 6412 Cottage Grove, Chicago, till 4 Apr.; held over till new show opens 6 Apr. **CD** *24 Mar.*, **BBD** *17 Mar.*

El Grotto; seventeen pieces, featuring Scoops Carry, Kermit Scott, Eugene Thomas, Chick Booth. **CD** *10 Mar.*

After playing to capacity nine weeks at El Grotto, closed 2 May. Sonny Thompson with sixteen-piece band takes over. **DB** *1 May*

Club Plantation, St. Louis, 5–25 Apr. **BBD** *17 Mar.*

Hines cancels talk and concert at University of Louisville

since Negro students would not be admitted. **BBD** *28 Apr.*

Savoy BR, Chicago, 13 May. **CD** *5 May*

Scoops Carry, with Hines for eight years, now assistant leader and personnel manager. **PC** *12 May*

Apollo TH, New York, week of 22 June. **APO notes**

Returns to El Grotto, Chicago, 25 July. **CD** *26 May*

Café Society, Knoxville. **CD** *23 June*

Regal TH, Chicago, week of 17 Aug. **CD** *18 Aug.*

Pershing BR, Chicago, 14 Sept. **CD** *8 Sept.*

El Grotto, Chicago. **CD** *22 Sept.*, **CD** *6 Oct.*

1946

At El Grotto, Chicago, till Apr. **CD** *5 Jan.*, **CD** *26 Jan.*

At El Grotto (20 Feb.); review; eighteen pieces; Dolores Parker and Essex Scott, vocals. **VAR** *27 Feb.*

Pershing BR, Chicago; Urban League benefit; 15 Mar. **CD** *16 Feb.*

At El Grotto eight months; will tour. **CD** *23 Feb.*

Leaves for tour, Canada to Calif. **CD** *23 Mar.*

Opens Orpheum TH, Los Angeles, 23 Apr. **BBD** *23 Mar.*

Review show at Orpheum TH, week of 23 Apr.; features Hines, Clifford Smalls, pianos; Scoops Carry, alto sax; Chick Booth, drums; Lord Essex Scott, Dolores Parker, vocals. **BBD** *4 May*

Swing Club, Oakland, Calif., from Orpheum. **PC** *11 May*

Hines in car accident near Houston in July; serious head injuries necessitating eye operation. Ken Anderson wrote arrangements for band and the book, *Earl Hines Piano Styles.* **DB** *26 Aug.*

Apollo TH, New York, week of 30 Aug. **AN** *Aug.*

Howard TH, Washington, D.C., and Royal TH, Baltimore. **CD** *7 Sept.*

Regal TH, Chicago, week of 27 Sept. **CD** *28 Sept.*

Pershing BR, Chicago, 20 Oct. **CD** *19 Oct.*

Rio Casino, Boston. **PC** *16 Nov.*

Rehearses at Nola Studio in New York; almost completely recovered from accident; concert routines on *Show Boat, Porgy and Bess, Rhapsody in Blue,* plus Handy, Cole Porter and Waller medleys; arrangers Buggs Roberts, Shep Shepherd and Tadd Dameron. **DB** *2 Dec.*

Personnel includes: Lloyd Smith, alto, flute, oboe, clarinet; Willie Cook, trumpet and French horn; Braxton Patterson, tenor and trumpet; Clifton Smalls, trombone and piano; Bill Thompson, vibes; Chick Booth, drums; Essex Scott, Dolores Parker, vocals; Vernon Smith, trumpet; Wardell Gray, Joe McLewis, Kermit Scott and Druie Bess replaced respectively by John Thompson, Gordon Austen, Braxton Patterson and Benny Green. **CD** *7 Dec.*

Opposite, top: Kermit Scott, tenor saxophone, with the Earl Hines orchestra in Cleveland, 1944.

Opposite, bottom: Sonny Thompson welcomed to the El Grotto, 3 May 1945.

1947

Apollo TH, New York, week of 7 Mar. **APO notes**

Opens at El Grotto, Chicago, 31 Mar. or 1 Apr.; has six violins. **CD** *1 & 8 Mar.*

Hines buys El Grotto nightclub in Pershing Hotel. **DB** *9 Apr.*

To St. Louis for a week. **CD** *19 Apr.*

Still at El Grotto, Chicago. **CD** *21 June*

To join Louis Armstrong in California? **CD** *9 Aug.*

Buggs Roberts to Koch's Hospital, St. Louis, with chest condition. **DB** *10 Sept.*

Four quintet recordings for Vita "last month"; include *Mandy Make Up Your Mind* and *I'm a Little Blackbird.* **DB** *24 Sept.*

Apollo TH, New York, week of 5 Sept. **AN** *5 Sept.*

Regal TH, Chicago, week of 26 Sept. **DB** *24 Sept.*

Records twenty sides with organist Bob Wyatt for Sunset in Dec. **DB** *14 Jan.*

1948

At Riviera, St. Louis, with Essex Scott and Scoops Walker (sic). **CD** *3 Jan.*

Joins Louis Armstrong; to Nice Festival, 22–28 Feb. **MB**

Apollo TH, New York, week of 19 Nov. Fall theatre tour with thirteen pieces including Joe Garland (director) and Gus Johnson (drums). **AN** *Nov.*

1949

On tour with Louis Armstrong; intends forming twelve-piece band. **DB** *25 Mar.*

Still with Louis Armstrong. **DB** *26 Aug.*

Apollo TH, New York, week of 18 Nov. **APO notes**

European tour with Armstrong's All-Stars. **MB** *Nov.*

1950

Sharon A. Pease re-analyzes the Hines piano style and illustrates it with transcribed *Rosetta.* **DB** *3 Nov.*

1951

Armstrong angry when Hines quits him in fall. **DB** *22 Feb.*

1952

Opens at Blue Note, Chicago, in Feb. with Jonah Jones, trumpet; Benny Green, trombone; Sol Yaged, clarinet; Tommy Potter, bass; Art Blakey, drums; Etta Jones, vocalist. **DB** *22 Feb.*

The Oasis, Hollywood. **DB** *18 June*

Opens at The Capitol Lounge, Chicago, 14 Nov. **DB** *19 Nov.*

1953

Snookie's, New York, 23 Feb.–15 Mar. **DB** *11 Feb.*

Personnel at Snookie's as before, but Aaron Sachs and Ocie Johnson respectively replace Yaged and Blakey. **DB** *8 Apr.*

Hi-Hat, Boston, 8 Apr., with Vernon Smith, trumpet; Benny Green, trombone; Aaron Sachs, clarinet; Carl Pruitt, bass; Ocie Johnson, drums; Etta Jones, vocalist. **DB** *20 May*

Rendezvous, Philadelphia. **DB** *6 May*

Palm Gardens, Columbus, Ohio, 20–26 May. **DB** *20 May*

The Jazz Scene Today as viewed by Hines. **DB** *15 July*

Regroups, now has quartet. **DB** *12 Aug.*

Blindfold Test with Leonard Feather. **DB** *23 Sept.*

1954

The Hangover, San Francisco, 15–28 Feb. **DB** *27 Jan.*

Peps, Philadelphia, 16–20 Mar.. **DB** *24 Mar.*

Birdland, New York, 15–28 Apr. **DB** *7 Apr.*

Plans eleven-piece band with Penny Lynn, vocalist. **DB** *19 May*

Crescendo, Hollywood, with Gene Redd, trumpet and vibes; Dicky Wells, trombone; Jerome Richardson, tenor saxophone; Leroy Harris, baritone saxophone; Paul Binning, bass; Hank Milo, drums. **DB** *14 July*

Howard TH, Washington, 3–9 Sept. **DB** *8 Sept.*

Peps, Philadelphia, 18–23 Oct. **DB** *20 Oct.*

Saperstein's, Chicago. **DB** *29 Dec.*

1955

On tour, Kan., Mo. and Colo. **DB** *23 Mar.*

Crystal Lounge, Detroit, 22 May. **DB** *27 July*

Moulin Rouge, Las Vegas, to 17 July with Morris Lane, tenor saxophone; George Bledsoe, bass; Ed Bourne, drums. **DB** *10 Aug.*

The Hangover, San Francisco, 5 Sept.–30 Oct., with Darnell Howard, clarinet; Jimmy Archey, trombone; Ed Garland, bass; Joe Watkins, drums. **DB** *19 Oct.*

1956

At the Hangover, Izzy Rosenbaum, bass, replaces Garland. **DB** *8 Feb.*

Pops Foster, bass, replaces Rosenbaum; Henry Goodwin, trumpet, added. **DB** *25 July*

Hines returns to Pittsburgh for his father's funeral. **DB** *31 Oct.*

1957

Jackie Coons, trumpet, replaces Goodwin at the Hangover; band plays benefit for San Francisco Symphony. **DB** *21 Mar.*

Muggsy Spanier, trumpet, replaces Coons; Hines rehearsing big band. **DB** *18 Apr.*

Nat Cole pays written tribute to Hines. **DB** *2 May*

Ken Whitson, trumpet, replaces Spanier at the Hangover. **DB** *11 July*

Earl Hines and Jack Teagarden tour Britain with Max Kaminsky, trumpet; Peanuts Hucko, clarinet; Jack Lesberg, bass; Cozy Cole, drums. 28 Sept.–13 Oct. **MB**

Hines voted top pianist in *Melody Maker Critics' Poll.* **MB**

1958

Presents big band with Ernestine Anderson, vocalist, in San Francisco Civic AUD, 4 May; Hines signs for fourth year at the Hangover, where Muggsy Spanier returns to the band. **DB** *15 May*

1959

The Hangover reopens 16 Jan.; band with same personnel indefinitely. **DB** *19 Feb., 28 May & 9 July*

The Hangover to close 31 Oct. for two months while Hines tours. **DB** *3 Sept.*

Appears at Monterey Jazz Festival with Vernon Alley, bass; Mel Lewis, drums. **DB** *12 Nov.*

At the Embers, New York, until 3 Jan., with Calvin

Old friends: Earl Hines and Benny Carter.

Newborn, guitar; Carl Pruitt, bass; Bill English, drums. **DB** *24 Dec.*

1960

At the Town Tavern, Toronto, for two weeks. **DB** *18 Feb.*

Reopens at the Hangover with Eddie Smith, trumpet; Jimmy Archey, trombone; Darnell Howard, clarinet; Pops Foster, bass; Earl Watkins, drums. **DB** *17 Mar.*

Café Continental, Chicago, with above group until 6 Nov. **DB** *27 Oct.*

Held over at Café Continental until 3 Dec. **DB** *24 Nov.*

1961

Held over at Café Continental until 28 Jan. **DB** *5 Jan.*

Review of performance at above. **DB** *2 Feb.*

At Black Sheep, San Francisco. **DB** *25 May*

At Black Sheep, San Francisco. **DB** *17 Aug.*

At Basin Street, Chicago, to 3 Sept. **DB** *14 Sept.*

At Colonial Tavern, Toronto, with sextet. **DB** *9 Nov.*

Sextet back at Black Sheep, San Francisco, after three-month trip that included Chicago, Detroit, Joplin, Toronto and Phoenix. **DB** *23 Nov.*

1962

Hines takes over direction of Grover Mitchell's rehearsal band, adding some of his arrangements to the book; Arthur Walker, trumpet, involved; sextet still at Black Sheep. **DB** *15 Feb.*

Big band performs at Happy Valley Inn, Lafayette, Calif.; Hines and Pops Foster deliver lecture at Oakland Public Library. **DB** *1 Mar.*

Big Boy Goudie, clarinet, replaces Darnell Howard at Black Sheep. **DB** *12 Apr.*

Concert at AUD Santa Monica, Calif.; series of Sunday concerts at Lafayette initiated 1 April. **DB** *26 Apr.*

At Black Sheep, San Francisco. **DB** *13 Sept.*

Monterey Jazz Festival with Rex Stewart, Benny Carter, Ben Webster and Stuff Smith, 21 Sept. **DB** *8 Nov.*

Colonial Tavern, Toronto, 1–27 Oct. **DB** *11 Oct.*

1963

Claremont Hotel, Oakland, with sextet three months, Feb.–May. **DB** *28 Feb.–25 Apr.*

Music Crossroads, Jack London Square, Oakland, opened in September. Hines partner in enterprise; plays in trio; shows feature international talent. **DB** *2 Jan.*

1964

Concert at Little Theatre, New York, with Budd Johnson, tenor saxophone; Ahmed Abdul-Malik, bass; Oliver Jackson, drums, 7 Mar. **MB**

Sutherland Lounge, Chicago, with Ayaka Hosokawa, vocalist; Tommy Smith, organ; Vi Redd, alto saxophone; Ray Fisher, drums. **DB** *24 Sept.*

At Birdland, New York, with above group. **DB** *3 Dec.*

1965

Village Vanguard, New York, with Coleman Hawkins, tenor saxophone; George Tucker, bass; Oliver Jackson, drums; week of 7 Mar. **MB**

European tour, piano recitals, 16 Mar. to 15 May. **MB**

Appears at Pittsburgh Jazz Festival with Duke Ellington, The Lion, Billy Taylor, Mary Lou Williams and other pianists, 20 June. **MB**

Village Vanguard, New York, with Budd Johnson, saxophones; Gene Ramey, bass; Eddie Locke, drums; 29–30 June. **MB**

Concert at Museum of Modern Art, New York, 1 July. **DB** *26 Aug.*

Newport Jazz Festival appearance, 2 July. **DB** *12 Aug.*

Named to Hall of Fame in *Down Beat*'s International Critics' Poll. **DB** *9 Sept.*

Lennie's-on-the-Turnpike, West Peabody, Mass., with Tony Texiera, bass; Alan Dawson, drums; end of July. **DB** *9 Sept.*

Down Beat Jazz Festival, Chicago, 13–14 Aug. **DB** *26 Aug.*

Tours colleges in South in Ford Music Caravan; returns to Village Vanguard, 9 Nov. **DB** *4 Nov.*

1966

Village Gate, New York, ten days from 7 Jan. **MB**

European tour, piano recitals, from 21 Jan. to 28 Apr.; Hines and family received by Pope Paul VI. **MB**

Lennie's-on-the-Turnpike, West Peabody, Mass., two weeks from 6 June. **MB**

At Museum of Modern Art, New York, 1 July. **DB** *11 Aug.*

Opens six-week tour of Russia for U.S. State Department 8 July with Money Johnson, trumpet; Mike Zwerin, trombone; Bobby Donovan, alto saxophone; Budd Johnson, tenor saxophone; Bill Pemberton, bass; Oliver Jackson, drums; Clea Bradford, vocalist. **DB** *11 Aug.*

Played 35 concerts in 11 Soviet cities to a total of 92,040 people. **DB** *3 Nov.*

Colonial Tavern, Toronto, two weeks from 21 Aug. **MB**

Living Room, Cincinnati, week of 26 Sept. **DB** *3 Nov.*

London House, Chicago, with trio, three weeks from 4 Oct. **MB**

Leads big band at the Riverboat, New York, for two weeks from 7 Nov. and accompanies Ella Fitzgerald with it. **DB** *17 Nov.*

Personnel of band for above engagement: Emmett Berry, Dud Bascomb, Al Bryant, George Triffon, trumpets; Jimmy Cleveland, Elmer Crumbley, Mike Zwerin, Benny Powell, trombones; Bobby Donovan, Eddie Barefield, Dave Clark, Budd Johnson, Howard Johnson (baritone saxophone), reeds; Bill Pemberton, bass; Jackie Williams, drums. **MB**

Ad Lib, Milwaukee, week of 21 Nov. **MB**

Basin Street West, San Francisco, two weeks from 28 Nov. **MB**

1967

Olympic Hotel, Seattle, three week beginning 6 Feb. with Budd Johnson, Bill Pemberton, Oliver Jackson, and Lori Harper, vocalist. **MB**

Davey Jones's Locker, Minneapolis, week beginning 27 Feb. **MB**

European tour in *Jazz from a Swinging Era* package, four weeks from 9 Mar. **MB**

At Shepheard's, New York, 10 Apr., opening attended by Soviet delegates to U.N. and other diplomats. **DB** *18 May*

Signs "lifetime" contract to appear at The Factory, San

Francisco. (This subsequently proves valueless.) Heads big band at the Riverboat, New York, two weeks from 22 May. **DB** *29 June*

Personnel for above engagement: Emmett Berry, Snooky Young, Irving Stokes, Richard Williams, trumpets; Vic Dickenson, Henderson Chambers, Jimmy Cleveland, trombones; Rick Henderson, Bobby Donovan, Budd Johnson, Russ Andrews, Howard Johnson (baritone saxophone), reeds; Bill Pemberton, bass; Oliver Jackson, drums. **MB**

Colonial Tavern, Toronto, two weeks from 12 June. **MB**

Newport Jazz Festival, 30 June. **MB**

Al Hirt Club, New Orleans, two weeks from 3 July. **MB**

The Showboat, Washington, two weeks from 31 July. **MB**

Wins DB International Critics' Poll as pianist. **DB** *24 Aug.*

At Lennie's-on-the-Turnpike, West Peabody, Mass., two weeks from 28 Aug. with Budd Johnson, Bill Pemberton and Oliver Jackson. **DB** *16 Nov.*

Monterey Jazz Festival, 15–17 Sept. **DB** *16 Nov.*

London House, Chicago, three weeks from 26 Sept. **MB**

1968

Colonial Tavern, Toronto, three weeks from 15 Jan. **MB**

Olympic Hotel, Seattle, three weeks from 5 Feb. **MB**

Village Vanguard, New York, two weeks from 27 Feb. **MB**

Colonial Tavern, Toronto, two weeks from 1 Apr. **MB**

Marco Polo, Vancouver, two weeks from 22 Apr. **MB**

Jazz Workshop, Boston, week of 20 May **MB**

Byrd's Nest, Silver Spring, Md., two weeks from 27 May. **MB**

Theatrical Grill, Cleveland, two weeks from 10 June. **MB**

Village Gate, New York, with Oscar Peterson, week of 1 July. **MB**

Tour of Japan, from 1 Sept. **MB**

London House, Chicago, three weeks from 30 Sept. **MB**

European tour, five weeks from 24 Oct. with Money Johnson, trumpet; Booty Wood, trombone; Bobby Donovan, alto saxophone; Budd Johnson, tenor saxophone; Bill Pemberton, bass; Oliver Jackson, drums. **MB**

Departure for Europe of *Jazz from a Swinging Era* tour, March 1967. Left to right: Vic Dickenson, Roy Eldridge, Earle Warren, Oliver Jackson, Bill Pemberton, Budd Johnson, Earl Hines, Buck Clayton and Sir Charles Thompson.

The Lighthouse, Los Angeles, two weeks from 25 Nov. **MB**

Colonial Tavern, Toronto, two weeks from 9 Dec. **MB**

1969

Tropicana, Las Vegas, two weeks from 3 Jan. **MB**

Olympic Hotel, Seattle, three weeks from 3 Feb. **MB**

Colonial Tavern, Toronto, two weeks from 24 Feb. **MB**

Plaza Hotel, New York, two weeks from 25 Mar. **MB**

Performs at Duke Ellington's seventieth birthday party in the White House, Washington, 29 Apr. **MB**

South American tour with Budd Johnson, Bill Pemberton, Oliver Jackson, and the Oscar Peterson Trio, 1–17 May. **MB**

Presented with Steinway grand by Scott Newhall of San Francisco *Chronicle* at special celebration in San Francisco, 26 July. **MB**

Wins *Down Beat*'s International Critics' Poll as pianist. **DB** *21 Aug.*

Top of the Plaza, Rochester, two weeks from 22 Sept., with Haywood Henry, saxophones and clarinet; Larry Richardson, bass; Khalil Mhadi, drums; Marva Josie, vocalist. **MB**

Colonial Tavern, Toronto, two weeks from 6 Oct. **MB**

The Embers, Indianapolis, week of 20 Oct. **MB**

London House, Chicago, three weeks from 19 Nov. **MB**

Plaza Hotel, New York, two weeks from 9 Dec. **MB**

1970

Royal Sonesta Hotel, New Orleans, three weeks from 19 Jan. **MB**

Colonial Tavern, Toronto, two weeks from 2 Mar. **MB**

Olympic Hotel, Seattle, three weeks from 30 Mar. **MB**

Theatrical Grill, Cleveland, two weeks from 25 May. **MB**

Sheraton Motor Inn, Battle Creek, week of 8 June. **MB**

Regency Hyatt House, Atlanta, three weeks from 15 June. **MB**

Holiday Inn, St. Joseph, Mich., week of 6 July. **MB**

Emerson's, Washington, D.C., two weeks from 13 July. **MB**

Lambertville Music Circus, N.J., 26 July. **MB**

Encore Room, Pittsburgh, week from 27 July. **MB**

Wins *Down Beat*'s International Critics' Poll as pianist. **DB** *20 Aug.*

Concord Festival, Concord, Calif., 21 Aug. **MB**

Colonial Tavern, Toronto, two weeks from 21 Sept. **MB**

Midtown Plaza Hotel, Rochester, two weeks from 5 Oct. **MB**

Hines becomes honorary president Overseas Press Club Jazz Club, New York, and performs at first concert with Maxine Sullivan, 9 Oct. **MB**

European tour, 19 Oct.–28 Nov., with Haywood Henry, Larry Richardson, Khalil Mhadi and Marva Josie. **MB**

Ronnie Scott's Club, London, 30 Nov.–12 Dec. **MB**

1971

Colony Steak House, Phoenix, three weeks from 4 Jan. **MB**

Winnipeg Inn, Winnipeg, two weeks from 25 Jan. **MB**

Bayshore Inn, Vancouver, three weeks from 15 Feb. **MB**

Olympic Hotel, Seattle, three weeks from 29 Mar. **MB**

Colonial Tavern, Toronto, two weeks from 19 Apr. **MB**

Landmark, Kansas City, three weeks from 3 May. **MB**

Lennie's-on-the-Turnpike, West Peabody, Mass., week of 31 May. **MB**

Mr. Henry's, Washington, D.C., week of 15 June. **MB**

Continental Plaza, Chicago, four weeks from 21 June with Bob Mitchell, trumpet; Larry Richardson, bass; Tony Johnson, drums; Marva Josie, vocalist. **MB**

Frog and Nightgown, Raleigh, two weeks from 19 Aug. **MB**

Disneyland, Anaheim, Calif., two weeks from 6 Sept. **MB**

El Matador, San Francisco, two weeks from 23 Sept. **MB**

La Bastille, Houston, ten days from 8 Oct. **MB**

Harrah's, Tahoe, week of 28 Oct. **MB**

Landmark, Kansas City, two weeks from 8 Nov. **MB**

Delmonico's, New York, two weeks from 22 Nov. **MB**

Tour of Italy, including San Remo Festival, solo performances, 2–27 Dec. **MB**

1972

New Jersey colleges, week of 24 Jan. **MB**

At Kennedy Center, Washington, D.C., with Earle Warren, alto saxophone; Wilbur Little, bass; Rudy Collins, drums; Marva Josie, vocalist, 6 Feb. **MB**

Blues Alley, Washington, D.C., week of 7 Feb. **MB**

Records for MPS with Jaki Byard, 14 Feb. **MB**

Bayshore Inn, Vancouver, three weeks from 28 Feb., with Bob Mitchell, trumpet; Milan Rezabek, bass; Bill Moody, drums; Marva Josie, vocalist. **MB**

Sheraton Cadillac, Detroit, 6–8 Apr. **MB**

Univ. of Illinois, Champlain, 22 Apr. **MB**

Univ. of California, Berkeley, 23 Apr. **MB**

London House, Chicago, three weeks from 24 Apr. **MB**

Theatrical Grill, Cleveland, two weeks from 15 May. **MB**

Dinkler's Motor Inn, Syracuse, two weeks from 29 May. **MB**

Frog and Nightgown, Raleigh, week of 15 June. **MB**

Tour of Japan and Australasia, 5–31 July, with Mitchell, Rezabek, Moody and Marva Josie. **MB**

Wins *Down Beat*'s International Critics' Poll as pianist. **DB** *17 Aug.*

The Savarin, Toronto, two weeks from 11 Sept. **MB**

Maryland Inn, Annapolis, week of 25 Sept. **MB**

Esquire Show Bar, Montreal, week of 2 Oct. **MB**

Dinkler's Motor Inn, Syracuse, three weeks from 9 Oct. **MB**

Blues Alley, Washington, D.C., week of 30 Oct. **MB**

Half Note, New York, two weeks from 6 Nov. **MB**

Pzazz, Burlington, Iowa, two weeks from 4 Dec. **MB**

Manor, Vail, Colo., week of 27 Dec. **MB**

1973

Laval Univ., Quebec City, 25 Mar. **MB**

Solo concert at New School, New York, 27 Mar. **MB**

Dinkler's Motor Inn, Syracuse, three weeks from 2 Apr. **MB**

The Savarin, Toronto, two weeks from 24 Apr. **MB**

Frog and Nightgown, Raleigh, week of 15 May. **MB**

Olympic Hotel, Seattle, two weeks from 22 May. **MB**

Earl Hines and Truck Parham, 1971.

Redondo Beach, Calif., two weeks from 5 June. **MB**
Maryland Inn, Annapolis, two weeks from 19 June. **MB**
Newport Jazz Festival, New York, 4–7 July. **MB**
Festivals in Pescara, Verona, Spezia, Italy, 14–17 July.
MB
Ravinia Festival, Chicago, 2 Aug. **MB**
Wins *Down Beat*'s International Critics' Poll as pianist.
DB *16 Aug.*
Michael's Pub, New York, two weeks from 7 Aug. **MB**
Just Jazz, Philadelphia, week of 18 Sept. **MB**
Jazz Power, European tour, three weeks from 2 Oct. **MB**
Dinkler's Motor Inn, Syracuse, three weeks from 23 Oct.
MB
Royal Box, Americana Hotel, New York, three weeks
from 13 Nov. **MB**
Solo concert at the Smithsonian, Washington, D.C., 18
Nov. **MB**
Blues Alley, Washington, D.C., week of 11 Dec. **MB**
1974
Shelly Manne's, Los Angeles, two weeks from 15 Jan.
MB
Miyako Hotel, San Francisco, three weeks from 28 Jan.
MB
Olympic Hotel, Seattle, two weeks from 18 Feb. **MB**
Michael's Pub, New York, four weeks from 5 Mar. **MB**
Dinkler's Motor Inn, Syracuse, three weeks from 1 Apr.
MB
Blues Alley, Washington, D.C., two weeks from 22 Apr.
MB
Colonial Tavern, Toronto, week of 6 May. **MB**

Islander Lodge Motel, Stockton, Calif., week of 14 May.
MB
Harvey's, Lake Tahoe, two weeks from 21 May. **MB**
Plays at funeral service for Duke Ellington in Cathedral
Church of St. John the Divine, New York, 27 May. **MB**
Tropicana, Las Vegas, three weeks from 4 June. **MB**
Newport Jazz Festival, New York, 28–29 June. **MB**
European tour including Montreux and Nice festivals,
1–27 July. **MB**
Meadowbrook Music Festival, Rochester, 2 Aug. **MB**
Merriweather Post Pavilion, Columbia, Md., 4 Aug. **MB**
Latin-America tour; solo piano concerts with Teddy Wil-
son, Marian McPartland and Ellis Larkins; 8–27 Aug.
MB
Nugget, Reno, 3–17 Sept., with Rudy Rutherford, clari-
net; James Leary, bass; Bunky Wilson, drums; Marva
Josie, vocalist. **MB**
Miyako Hotel, San Francisco, four weeks from 18 Sept.
MB
Solo performance at Marin College, San Francisco, 13
Oct. **MB**
Playboy Club, Los Angeles, week of 14 Oct. **MB**
European tour, 26 Oct.–28 Nov. **MB**
Japanese tour, 2–16 Dec. **MB**
1975
Playboy Club, Phoenix, week of 17 Feb., with Rudy
Rutherford, clarinet; Harley White, bass; Eddie Gra-
ham, drums; Marva Josie, vocalist. **MB**
Margarita's, Santa Cruz, Calif., 28 Feb. **MB**
Great American Music Hall, San Francisco, 1 Mar. **MB**

Playboy Club, Atlanta, two weeks from 3 Mar. **MB**
Concert, Sarasota, Fla., 17 Mar. **MB**
Column's Restaurant, West Dennis, Mass., week of 24 Mar. **MB**
Blues Alley, Washington, D.C., two weeks from 31 Mar. **MB**
Dinkler's Motor Inn, Syracuse, two weeks from 14 Apr. **MB**
Tropicana, Las Vegas, four weeks from 2 May. **MB**
S.S. *Rotterdam* cruise to Nassau and Bermuda, week of 7 June. **MB**
Sandy's, Boston, week of 17 June. **MB**
Playboy Club, Montreal, 22 June. **MB**
Rainbow Grill, New York, three weeks from 23 June. **MB**
Newport Hall of Fame concert, Carnegie Hall, New York, 4 July. **MB**
Nice Festival, France, 15–28 July, with Harley White, Eddie Graham and Marva Josie. **MB**
Maryland Inn, Annapolis, two weeks from 5 Aug. **MB**
Playboy Club, Los Angeles, week of 18 Aug. **MB**
Harvey's, Lake Tahoe, two weeks from 26 Aug. **MB**
Eldorado, Reno, two weeks from 9 Sept. **MB**
The Lighthouse, San Diego, week of 22 Sept. **MB**
Earl Hines Day at Howard Univ., Washington, D.C., 1 Oct. **MB**
Overseas Press Club Jazz Club concert at Biltmore Hotel with Eubie Blake and Billy Taylor, 2 Oct. **MB**
College concerts, New Brunswick and Nova Scotia, 3–4 Oct. **MB**
Statler-Hilton, Buffalo, two weeks from 7 Oct. **MB**
Cuts four piano rolls for Q.R.S., 15 Oct. **MB**
European tour, 24 Oct.–22 Nov., with Benny Carter, alto saxophone; Harley White, bass; Eddie Graham, drums; Marva Josie, vocalist. **MB**
Columns Restaurant, West Dennis, Mass., week of 1 Dec. **MB**
Copley Plaza Hotel, Boston, two weeks from 8 Dec. **MB**
Addresses music students at Harvard Univ., 16 Dec. **MB**
Seventieth birthday party at Biltmore Hotel, New York, 29 Dec. **MB**
1976
Bicentennial Concert, Denver, 31 Jan. **MB**
Maryland Inn, Annapolis, four weeks from 3 Feb. **MB**
Ratso's, Chicago, week from 2 Mar. **MB**
Concert, Palace Theatre, Manchester, N.H., 12 Mar. **MB**
Dinkler's Motor Inn, Syracuse, three weeks from 15 Mar. **MB**
Blues Alley, Washington, D.C., two weeks from 5 Apr. **MB**
Statler-Hilton Hotel, Buffalo, three weeks from 20 Apr. **MB**
Broadmoor Hotel, Colorado Springs, three weeks from 10 May. **MB**

White House, Washington, D.C., following state dinner for President of France, 17 May. **MB**
The Longhorn, Minneapolis, week from 1 June. **MB**
Concert, Tower Park, Kansas City, 5 June. **MB**
Japanese Centre Theatre, Bimbo's, San Francisco, 9 & 10 June. **MB**
Concert, Omaha, Nebr., 12 June. **MB**
New Showboat, Silver Spring, Md., week from 15 June. **MB**
Madeline Green died in Cleveland, Ohio. **DB** 9 *Sept.*
Sandy's Revival, Beverly, Mass., week from 22 June. **MB**
Piano Recital, Newport Festival, Waterloo Village, Stanhope, N.J., 27 June. **MB**
Concert, Wolf Trap, Vienna, Va., with Billy Eckstine and Dizzy Gillespie, 27 June. **MB**
El Matador, San Francisco, week of 29 June. **MB**
Louis Armstrong Birthday Celebration, New Orleans, 4 July. **MB**
Cactus Pete's, Jackpot, Nevada, week from 5 July. **MB**
Harvey's, Lake Tahoe, two weeks from 12 July. **MB**
Lois Deppe died in Chicago, 26 July. **MB**
Concerts-by-the-Sea, Los Angeles, week from 27 July. **MB**
Playboy Club, Los Angeles, two weeks from 2 Aug. **MB**
Inverness Festival, Inverness, Calif., 15 Aug. **MB**
Ritz-Carlton Hotel, Chicago, five weeks from 30 Aug. **MB**
Michael's Pub, New York, three weeks from 5 Oct. **MB**
S.S. *Rotterdam* cruise to Nassau and Bermuda, week from 23 Oct. **MB**
Hyatt Regency Hotel, Phoenix, two weeks from 8 Nov. **MB**
Copley Plaza Hotel, Boston, two weeks from 22 Nov. **MB**

Errors are inevitable in such a compilation, but it is hoped that some at least can be rectified with the help of readers in future editions. Detailed discographies of Earl Hines's recordings in the standard works by Delaunay, Rust and Jepsen valuably complement this chronology. His many broadcasts and television appearances are almost a subject in themselves, but three television specials deserve particular mention: Ralph Gleason's *Jazz Casual* interview with the pianist in San Francisco; Charles Nairn's hour-long film of Hines alone at Blues Alley in Washington for British ITV in 1975; and another of equal length filmed later in that year showing the whole group in action at the Statler-Hilton Hotel in Buffalo.

Fatha and friends at the Rainbow Grill, 1975. Left to right: (back) Teddy Wilson, Earl Hines, Cleo Laine, Eubie Blake, Marva Josie, Horace Silver, Johnny Dankworth; (front) Mel Davis, Junior Mance, Roland Hanna, Eddie Heywood.

How the Grand Terrace and the Sunset Café looked in 1976! (Photographed by Lois Deppe.)

BIBLIOGRAPHY

Essays of a General Character on Earl Hines's Career and Music:

The Fatha! by Barry Ulanov, MET, Feb. 1945.

Bouquets for the Living by Ralph J. Gleason, DB, 8 Feb. 1952.

The Father! by Barry Ulanov, MET, Jan. 1945.

He Played Trumpet on the Piano by Stanley Dance, *Melody Maker*, 17 Dec. 1955.

Earl Hines by John S. Wilson in *The Jazz Makers* edited by Hentoff & Shapiro, 1957 (Rinehart).

Father Knows Best by Dick Hadlock, DB, 30 Oct. 1958.

Earl Hines on Bird by Dick Hadlock, *Jazz Review*, Nov. 1960.

Earl Hines in the 1940s by George Hoefer, DB, 25 April 1963.

Bringing Up "Fatha" by Russ Wilson, DB, 6 June 1963.

Earl Hines by Hugues Panassié, *Bulletin H.C.F.*, March 1965.

Le Spectacle Earl Hines by Madeleine Gautier, *Bulletin H.C.F.*, April 1965.

The Resurgence of Earl Hines by Dan Morgenstern, DB, 26 Aug. 1965.

Earl Hines by Richard Hadlock in *Jazz Masters of the '20s*, 1965 (Macmillan).

Earl "Father" Hines by Milton "Mezz" Mezzrow, *Bulletin H.C.F.*, April 1966.

Hines '66 by Jean Arnautou, *Bulletin H.C.F.*, May–June 1966.

Sunshine Always Opens Out by Whitney Balliett in *Such Sweet Thunder*, a reprint of the important *New Yorker* profile of 2 Jan. 1965, 1966 (Bobbs-Merrill).

The Grand Return of Earl Hines by Martin Williams, IM, March 1968.

Fatha Knows Best by Al Van Starrex, MR., July 1970.

A Monday Date by Siegfried Mohr, *Jazz Hot*, No. 263, 1970.

Earl Hines by George T. Simon in *The Big Bands*, 1971 (Macmillan).

Earl Hines by Félix Sportis, *Le Point du Jazz*, Sept. 1971.

Earl "Fatha" Hines by Stanley Dance, *Stereo Review*, Jan. 1974.

Alive and Very, Very Well by Grover Sales, *San Francisco*, April 1974.

Portrait d'un Piano Bien Tempéré by Daniel Nevers, *Jazz Hot*, No. 307, 1974.

Hines: Stretching Out a Little by Max Jones, *Melody Maker*, 7 Dec. 1974.

Earl "Fatha" Hines on the Road by Jeffrey Robinson, *TWA Ambassador*, March 1976.

Earl "Fatha" Hines by Leonard Feather in *The Pleasures of Jazz*, 1976 (Horizon).

Recording for M-G-M in 1960.

A REPRESENTATIVE LP DISCOGRAPHY

All the records listed are American except those where a single capital letter in parenthesis, immediately following the record label, indicates country of origin, thus: (A) Australia, (E) England, (F) France, (I) Italy, (J) Japan. Not all of the albums are currently in catalogue, but most can be obtained through specialist dealers.

Like other major jazz figures, Earl Hines has been the victim, in the U.S. and in Europe, of unscrupulous record bootleggers. Their products are not listed here. Quite apart from the moral issue, they are generally inferior in terms of both quality and performance.

A MONDAY DATE (1923–28) Milestone 2012

YOUNG LOUIS THE SIDEMAN (1927) (Hines on two tracks) Decca DL-9233

LOUIS ARMSTRONG & EARL HINES (1928) (2 discs) Smithsonian Collection R002

AT THE APEX CLUB (with Jimmie Noone) (1928) Decca DL-9235

YOUNG EARL HINES (1929) RCA (F) FPM1-7023

THE INDISPENSABLE EARL HINES, VOL. I (1929–39) RCA (F) 731.065

57 VARIETIES (1928 piano solos plus others from 1932 and 1950) CBS (F) 63364

EARL HINES & HIS ORCHESTRA (1932–37) Jazz Archives JA-2

SOUTH SIDE SWING (1934–35) Decca DL-9221

HINES RHYTHM (1933–38) Epic EE-22021

THE INDISPENSABLE EARL HINES, VOL. II (1939–40) RCA (F) 741.041

THE INDISPENSABLE EARL HINES, VOL. III (1940–42) RCA (F) FPMI-7000

THE FATHER JUMPS (1939–45) (2 discs) RCA Bluebird AXM2-5508

CLASSIC JAZZ PIANO (1939–41) (Hines on four tracks) RCA LPV-543

MASTER MUSICIAN (with Sidney Bechet) (1940) (2 discs) (Hines on five tracks) RCA Bluebird AXM2-5516

ALL STAR SESSION (with Cozy Cole and Coleman Hawkins) (1944) (Hines on four tracks) Trip 5538

HAWKINS & HINES (1944) (as above plus four tracks with Charlie Shavers) Mercury Int. (E) 5516.21034

PRE BOP (1944) (Hines on four tracks) Bob Thiele Music 0940

EARL HINES ET SON GRAND ORCHESTRE (1945–46) Vogue (F) CMD INT 9733

SWING INTO BOP (1945–46) (as above plus two tracks) Xanadu X-111

EARL HINES & HIS ORCHESTRA (1947) Bravo 134, Pickwick 127

EARL HINES IN PARIS (with Buck Clayton and Barney Bigard) (1949) GNP Crescendo 9010

NEW ORLEANS NIGHTS (with Louis Armstrong) (1950) Decca DL-8329

SATCHMO ON STAGE (with Louis Armstrong) (1950) Decca DL-8330

I LOVE JAZZ (with Louis Armstrong) (1950) (Hines on one track) Decca DL-74227

SATCHMO IN PASADENA (with Louis Armstrong) (1951) Decca DL-8041

EARL FATHA HINES & JONAH JONES (1952) (Hines on four tracks) Crown 5422

EARL FATHA HINES (septet) (1954) (duplications and further titles on Coronet CX2-250 and Tiara 7524) Everest FS-246

ANOTHER MONDAY DATE (1956) (2 discs) Prestige P-24043

PARIS ONE NIGHT STAND (1957) Philips (F) BBL-7222

EARL'S BACKROOM & COZY'S CARAVAN (1958) (Hines on three tracks) Felsted (E) FAJ-7002

SWINGIN' THE '20s (with Benny Carter) (1958) Contemporary S-7561

LIVIN' WITH THE BLUES (with Benny Carter and Barbara Dane) (1959) Dot 3177

EARL'S PEARLS (1960) M-G-M E-3832

A MONDAY DATE (1961) Riverside 398

EARL "FATHA" HINES (with Ralph Carmichael Orchestra) (1963) Capitol ST-1971

SHOWCASING EARL "FATHA" HINES (1964) Virgo 1003

THE REAL EARL HINES (1964) Focus 335

UP TO DATE WITH EARL HINES (1964) RCA LSP-3380

"FATHA" (1964) Columbia JCS-9120

THE MIGHTY FATHA (1964–66) (2 discs) Flying Dutchman FD-10147

GRAND REUNION, VOL. I (with Coleman Hawkins and Roy Eldridge) (1965) Limelight 86020

GRAND REUNION, VOL. II (with Coleman Hawkins & Roy Eldridge) (1965) Trip 5557

EARL HINES & ROY ELDRIDGE AT THE VILLAGE VANGUARD (1965) Xanadu 106

TEA FOR TWO (1965) Black Lion 112

HINES '65 (1965) Master Jazz 8109

JAZZ AT BLACK LION (1965) (Hines on one track) (2 discs) Black Lion (E) 2661-006

PARIS SESSION (1965) Ducretet Thompson (F) 300V.140

THE JAZZ PIANO (with Duke Ellington, Billy Taylor, etc.) (1965) RCA LSP-3499

ONCE UPON A TIME (with Johnny Hodges) (1966) Impulse A-9108

STRIDE RIGHT (with Johnny Hodges) (1966) Verve V6-8647

DINAH (1966) RCA (F) 431.023

JAZZ MEANZ HINES (1966) Fontana (E) STL-5378

AMERICANS IN EUROPE (1966) (Hines on two tracks) Fontana (E) STJL-916

BLUES AND THINGS (with Jimmy Rushing) Master Jazz 101

JAZZ FROM A SWINGING ERA (1967) (Hines on five tracks) (2 discs) Fontana (E) DTL-200

SWING'S OUR THING (with Johnny Hodges) (1967) Verve V6-8732

FATHA BLOWS BEST (with Buck Clayton) (1968) Decca DL-75048

AT HOME (1969) Delmark 212

MASTER JAZZ PIANO, VOL. I (1969) (Hines on two tracks) Master Jazz 8105

MASTER JAZZ PIANO, VOL. II (1969) (Hines on two tracks) Master Jazz 8108

QUINTESSENTIAL EARL HINES (1970) Chiaroscuro 101

EARL HINES IN PARIS (1970) Musicdisc America (F) 6107

FATHA & HIS FLOCK ON TOUR (1970) M.P.S. 749

IT DON'T MEAN A THING (with Paul Gonsalves) (1970) Black Lion (E) BLP-30153

LIVE AT THE OVERSEAS PRESS CLUB (with Maxine Sullivan) (1970) Chiaroscuro 107

MASTER JAZZ PIANO, VOL. III (1971) (Hines on two tracks) Master Jazz 8117

MASTER JAZZ PIANO, VOL. IV (1971) (Hines on two tracks) Master Jazz 8129

MASTER JAZZ PIANO, VOL. V (1971–72) (Hines on two tracks) Master Jazz 8135

MY TRIBUTE TO LOUIS (1971) Audiophile 111

HINES COMES IN HANDY (1971) Audiophile 112

HINES DOES HOAGY (1971) Audiophile 113

HINES PLAYS ELLINGTON, VOL. I (1971) Master Jazz 8114

NEW ORLEANS TO CHICAGO (1972) (one side by Hines, the other by Armand Hug) Swaggie (A) 1294

HINES PLAYS HINES (1972) Swaggie (A) 1320

SOLO WALK IN TOKYO (1972) Columbia (J) NCP-8502

TOUR DE FORCE (1972) Black Lion 30143

HINES PLAYS ELLINGTON, VOLS. II & III (1972) (2 discs) Master Jazz 28126

QUINTESSENTIAL CONTINUED (1973) Chiaroscuro 120

BACK ON THE STREET (with Jonah Jones) (1973) Chiaroscuro 118

WALTZING MATILDA (1973) Swaggie (A) 1338

EARL HINES PLAYS GEORGE GERSHWIN (1973) Swaggie (A) 1339

EARL HINES PLAYS GEORGE GERSHWIN (1973) (2 discs) (entirely different from Swaggie 1339) Carosello (I) 23017/18

AN EVENING WITH EARL HINES (1973) (2 discs) Chiaroscuro 116

QUINTESSENTIAL '74 (1974) Chiaroscuro 131

A BUCK CLAYTON JAM SESSION (1974) Chiaroscuro 132

EARL HINES PLAYS COLE PORTER (1974) Swaggie (A) 1345

WEST SIDE STORY (1974) Black Lion (E) 30170

HINES '74 (1974) Black & Blue (F) 33.073

DIRTY OLD MEN (with Budd Johnson) (1974) Black & Blue (F) 33.084

GIANTS IN NICE (with Barney Bigard) (1974) RCA (F) FXL1-7156

TRIBUTE TO LOUIS ARMSTRONG (with Davenport, Dickenson, Bigard) (1974) RCA (F) FXL1-7159

FIREWORKS (1974) RCA (F) FXL1-7160

PIANO PORTRAITS OF AUSTRALIA (1974) Swaggie (A) 1350

EARL HINES IN NEW ORLEANS (with Wallace Davenport) (1975) (2 discs) UP International (I) 5057/58

EARL HINES PLAYS DUKE ELLINGTON, VOL. IV (1975) Master Jazz 8132

HOT SONATAS (with Joe Venuti) (1975) Chiaroscuro 145

LIVE AT THE STATLER-HILTON, BUFFALO (1975) Improv 7114

EARL HINES AT SARALEE'S Fairmont 1011

THE SOUND OF CHICAGO, JAZZ ODYSSEY, VOL. II (1923–40) (3 discs) (Hines on five tracks) Columbia C3L-22 (Produced by Frank Driggs and annotated by John Steiner, this provides a good general picture of the Chicago scene. The accompanying booklet contains many rare and valuable photographs.)

Top, left: Recording for Contact in 1964, observed by Bob Thiele and Stanley Dance.

Top, right: Recording for Flying Dutchman with Johnny Hodges, 1970.

Bottom, left: Recording for Ducretet-Thompson in Paris the album that won the Arthur Honegger Award for Jazz in the French Grand Prix du Disque, 1965.

Bottom, right: Recording for Swaggie in Australia, 1972.

INDEX

Note: Page references to illustrations are in *italics*.

Abdul-Malik, Ahmed, 111, 219
Abernathy, Shuffle, 246, 248
Adams Theatre, 70
Addams, Jane, 193
Adrian's Tap Room, 196
After All I've Been to You (song), 168
After Hours (song), 244
Aiken, Gus, 22, 90
Aiken, Philip, 69
Ain't Misbehavin' (Waller), 138
Alexander, Arthur, 207
Alexander, Claude, *192*
Alfie's (nightclub), 174
Al G. Fields Circus, 202
Ali, Bardu, 263, 285
Ali, Muhammed, *101*
Alioto, Joseph L., 120
Alix, Mae, 49, 61, 143
Allen, Charles, *66*, 76, 77, *169*, 171, 174, *231*
Allen, Gracie, 200
Allen, Henry, 186
Allen, Jap, 210
Allen, Red, 251
Alpert, Mickey, 213
Alston, Gordon, *101, 268*
Alvis, Hayes, 57, *60*, 62, 172, 188, 189
American in Paris (Gershwin), 191
American Record Company, 181
Ammons, Albert, 246
Ammons, Gene, 229
Anatomy of a Murder (film), 200
Anderson, Buddy, 260–61
Anderson, Ivie, 88
Anderson, Kenneth, 160, 248, 262
Anderson, Marian, 132
Anderson, William, 249
Andrews, Avis, 138
Ann (song), 74
Apex Club, 46, 55–56, 145
Apollo Theatre, 65, 70–71, 93, 154, 162, 173, 217, 241, 251, 257, 258, 265
Arcadia Ballroom, 161, 250
Archey, Jimmy, 110, *113*
Arlen, Harold, 137, 138
Armstrong, Lil Hardin, 53, 143
Armstrong, Louis, 23, 35, 58, *90, 105–8*, 179
    "blue vein society" and, 68

Budd Johnson and, 204, 209, 211–12
Charlie Carpenter and, 80, 143–48, 156
at Connie's Inn, 138
first meeting of Hines and, 45
Gillespie influenced by, 258
Hines with band led by, 103–5, 114, 128
John Ewing and, 237
Leon Washington and, 277
playing style of, 90–92, 250
at Show Boat, 191
at Sunset Café, 47–54, 62, 63, 86, 171, 194–95
Teddy Wilson and, 183–85
Trummy Young and, 221, 225–27
Walter Fuller and, 166, 170
Arnheim, Gus, 77, 213
ASCAP, 157, 168
Asen, Robert, 227
Ashby, Irving, 237
Atkins, Billy, *233*
Audio Fidelity Record Company, 225
Auld, Georgie, 210, 224

Badge, Laura, *27*
Bailey, Buster, 184, 186, 194, 209, 210, 216, 230
Bailey, Mildred, *66*, 74, 162–63, 186
Bailey, Pearl, 251, 262
Baker, Josephine, 104, 180
Balaban Theatre, 67
Balliett, Whitney, 112
Ballyhoo Club, 191
Bamville (show), 30
Banks, Melvin, 180
Barcelona, Danny, 225
Barefield, Eddie, 119
Bargy, Roy, 66
Barker, Laverne, *263*
Barksdale, Everett, *192*, 229
Barnes, Walter, 70, 188
Barnet, Charlie, 196, 223, 224
Barnett, Richard, *192*
Barrett Brothers, 137
Barrier, The (film), 132
Bascomb, Dud, 119
Bash, Julian, 262
Basie, Count, 92, 182, 208, 227, 265, *265*, 277
    Budd Johnson and, 208, 209

Charlie Parker and, 89
at Duke Ellington's funeral, 122
Freddy Webster and, 281
Jimmy Mundy and, 200
Lester Young and, 157, 158
Oscar Peterson and, 140
Basie Boogie (Basie), 92, 265
Basin Street East (nightclub), 144
Bauza, Mario, 257
Beach, Rex, 132
Beard, Sam, 248
Beasley, Mary, 97
Bechet, Sidney, 95, 209, 210
Becton, Gene Wilson, 197
Beer, Sam, 191
Begin the Beguine (song), 149
Beiderbecke, Bix, 48–49, 183, 184
Belasco, Leon, 229
Bellson, Louis, *189*
Bennett, "Cuban" Theodore, 29–30
Bennett, Eloise, 180
Benson (disc jockey), 270
Benton, Brook, 272
Berigan, Bunny, 195, 196
Berlin, Irving, 142
Berquist, Whitey, 48
Berry, Chu, 160, 166, 167, 186, 249, 250, 277
Berry, Emmett, 119, 183, 216
Berry Brothers, 64
Bertrand, Jimmy, 175
Betters, Frank, 221
Bigard, Barney, 104, *177*, 178, 227, 246, 249
Big Butter and Egg Man (song), 49, 143, 209
Bijou (nightclub), 232
Birch, Elmer, 207
Birch, Sylvester, *247*
Birchett, Harold, *21*, 28–29
Birdland (nightclub), 111, 112, 158
Bishop, Wallace, 67, *68*, 71, 92, *159, 169*, 172, 175–78, *177, 178*, 199, *223*
    Charlie Carpenter and, 150
    on French tour, 112
    injured in bus accidents, 69, 76, 173, 223
    leaves band, 77
    Walter Fuller and, 168
Black, Clarence, 54, 146
Black and Blue (Waller), 138
Blackbirds (musical), 137, 211

Black Forest Overture, 46
Black Gypsy (song), 229
Black Sheep (nightclub), 111
Blackwell, Charlie, 170
Blake, Eubie, 15, 22, 30–31, *31*, 52, 64, 112, 122, *311*
Blakey, Art, 106, *109*, 255
Bledsoe, Jules, 136
Blind Willie (blues singer), 220
Blue (Q. Wilson), 172
Blue Because of You (song), 213
Bluebonnets, 96, 97, *98*, 266, 269
Blue Devils, 204, 206, 208, 209
Blue Grass (nightclub), 139
Blue Heaven (nightclub), 163
Blue Jackets, 194
Blue Moon Chasers, 204, 206
Blue Note (nightclub), 105
Blue Rhythm Band, 62
Blue Rhythm Fantasy (song), 261
Blue Serenaders, 207
Blues in Thirds (song), 56, 95
Blue Skies (song), 266
Blue Yodel No. 9 (song), 58
BMI, 168
Body and Soul (song), 184, 269
Boguslawski, Ziggy, 193
Bolero at the Savoy (song), 153
Boogie Woogie on St. Louis Blues (song), 56, 79–80, 126, 161, 168, 244, 251
Book Store (nightclub), 179
Boone, Lester, 57, *60*, 179
Booth, Chick, 92, *101*, 267, 269, 287
Boots and His Buddies, 262
Bop City (nightclub), 105, 270
Bostic, Earl, 270–71, 273
Bostic, Joe, 285
Bradford, Clea, 116
Bradley, Oscar, 258
Bradshaw, Tiny, 285, 287
Brassfield, Frank, *21*
Braud, Wellman, 171, 189
Brazier, Dan "Georgetown," 197
Broadway Syncopators, 22, 135
Brockman, Gail, 266, *267*
Brooks, Randy, 259
Brother, Can You Spare a Dime? (song), 64
Brown, Anita Patti, 132, 137
Brown, Dave, *41*, 42, 45
Brown, Fred, *192*, 248
Brown, Lawrence, 91, 147
Brown, Les, 174
Brown, Pete, 251
Brown, Scoville, 192, *192*, 246
Brown, Silas, *21*
Brown, Stanley, *41*
Brown, Thornton, *21*
Brown and McGraw, 48, 49
Brubeck, Dave, 91, 124, *124*
Brunis, George, 195
Bryant, Freddy, 180
Bryant, Willie, 66, 183, 186, 262
Bubbling Over (song), 65
Bubbling Over with Beer (Carpenter), 151
Buchanan, Wes, 255
Buck and Bubbles, 58, *145*, 146
Buckets (song), 79, 210
Buckner, Milt, 237
Buckner, Teddy, 237
Buell, Richard, 290
Burchet, Albert, 211

Burke, Edward, 77, *79*, 168, 188, 192, *192*, 228, 235
Burleigh, Harry T., 131
Burroughs, Alvin "Mouse," *79*, 92, 163, *165*, 223, 235, *239*, 251, 290, *291*
Burroughs, Shug, 35, 46–47
Busen, Buddy, 177
Bushkin, Joey, 196
Byas, Don, 209, 216, 218, 224
Byrd, Charlie, 182
Byrd, Eddie, 224

Cab Drivers, 93
Caen, Herb, 120
Café Continental, 110
Café de Paris, 180
Café Society, 183, 217
Cain, Albert, 131
Callender, Howard "Red," 216, 224
Call Me Happy (song), 89
Calloway, Blanche, 49–50
Calloway, Cab, 49–50, 73, 93, 139, 180, 248, 250, 262
   Dizzy Gillespie and, 155, 257–59
   Hilton Jefferson and, 213
   John Ewing and, 237
   Milt Hinton and, 191, *192*
Campbell, Floyd, 191, 232
Cane, Dan, 22, 23, 135
Capitol Lounge, 168
Capone, Al, 61–62, 154, 179, 188, 198
Capone, Ralph, 198, 242
Cara, Mancy, *40*
Carlisle, Una Mae, 73
Carmichael, Hoagy, 49
Carney, Harry, 160
Carolina Cotton Pickers, 261–66, 272, 285
Carpenter, Charlie, 80, 112, 142–59, *143*, *159*, 214, 231, 277, 284
Carr, Georgia, 170
Carrington, Jerome, 136
Carroll Dickerson's Charleston Revue (show), 40
Carry, Ed, 210
Carry, Scoops, 89, 97, *101*, *159*, 163, 210, 214, *215*, *239*, 249, 260, 266, *267*, 278, 286
   Billy Eckstine and, 238, 243
   capsule biography of, 286
   Cliff Smalls and, 270
   Milt Hinton and, 188
   Willie Randall and, 230
Carter, Benny, 161, 210, 213, 229, 246, 285, *305*
   Cliff Smalls and, 260
   on European tour, 126
   at Grape Arbor, 29–30
   Irene Wilson and, 181–82
   Teddy Wilson and, 183–84, 186
Carter, Jack, 63, 65
Caruso, Enrico, 131, 184
Cass, Al, 259
Castle Ballroom, 162
Catlett, Sidney, 103, 104, *107*, 160, 166–67, 179, 186, 223, 249
Cavernism (Mundy), 197, 198, 213, 241
Cedar Point, 135
Channing, Carol, 200
Chappell, Gus, 97, 98, 266, *267*, *268*
Charles, Ray, 157
Charlton, Melville, 131

Cherry (song), 244
Cherry Red (song), 241
Chez Paree, 229
Chicago Rhythm Club, 186
Chilton, John, 277
Chinatown (song), 148, 183
Christopher Columbus (song), 72
Circle Inn, 163
C Jam Blues (song), 70
Clark, Clifford, *233*
Clark, Garnet, 221
Clark, Harold, *97*, *263*, 266, *268*
Clark, June, 282
Claxton, Rozelle, *165*, 168, *231*
Clay, Shirley, 57, *60*
Clayton, Buck, 177, *177*, 178, 183, 186, 227, 307
Cleveland, Jimmy, 119
Club De Lisa, 93, 232, 241, 242, 277
Club Flame, 139, 140
Club Harlem, 139
Club Royal, 170
Club Rubaiyat, 191
Club Silhouette, 163
Cobb, Arnett, 271
Cobb, Jimmy, 277
Cohen, Paul, *97*, *98*
Cohn, Zinky, 277
Cole, Bob, 18, 132
Cole, Cozy, 104, 110, 186, 192
Cole, Eddie, 188
Cole, Nat, 92, 142, 150, 152, 229, 269
Coleman, Bill, 183
Coleman, Booker, 221, 227
Coleman, Oliver, 77, 92, 174
Coleman, Preston, 170
College Inn, 150
College Room, 72
Collins, Harry, 28, 31, 33, 36, 38, 39
Collins, John, 146, 260
Collins, Shad, 271
Collins (lawyer), 212
Collins Inn, 18, 28–30, 132, 133
Columbia Artists Management, 183
Comin' in Home (song), 89
Comme Ci, Comme Ça (song), 126
Community Concerts, 183–84
Compton, Glover, 34, 36
Condon, Eddie, 194, 195
Congaine (Hines), 26
Connie's Inn, 138, 146
Connor, D. Russell, 200*n*
Cook, Willie, 91–92, *101*, *215*, *268*, 269, 285
Cook, Will Marion, *138*
Cooke, Charlie, 171, 246
Coons, Jackie, 110
Cooper, Ralph, 70, 100, 156
Cornell, Harry, 229
Cosmopolitan Theatre, 138
Cottage Café, 180
Cotton Club (Cincinnati), 139
Cotton Club (New York), 48, 62, 138, 139, 152, 188, 257
Courtney, Cress, 155
Courtney, Del, 279
Coy, Eugene, 206
Coy, Marge, 206
Crawford, Forrest, 196
Crawford, Jimmy, 290
Creamer, Henry, 131, 132
Creasy, Angel, 96, 97

Crosby, Bing, 146
Crosby, Israel, 186
Crowder, Bob, 89
Crump, Thomas, 97, *215*, 260, 266, *267*
Crystal Caverns, 197, 241
Cuban Nightmare (song), 257
Curry, Richard, 253, *253*
Curtis, Harry, 224

Dance, Stanley, 111, 112, 116, 120, 122, 239, 241–44, *315*
Dancing on the Ceiling (song), 191
Dankworth, Johnny, *311*
Dash, Julian, 262
Dave's Place, 181
Davis, Charlie, 138
Davis, John R., 207
Davis, Mel, *311*
Davis, Miles, 261
Davis, Palmer "Fats," *101*, *268*, 269, 285
Davis, Sammy, 272
Davis, Wild Bill, 126
Davison, Wild Bill, 91
Dean, Peter, 184
De Franco, Buddy, 260
Deems, Barrett, 170, 174
Deep Forest (Hines and Foresythe), 74, 75, 161, 198, 213
Deep Paradise (song), 139
Denniker, Paul, 151, 199
De Paris, Wilbur, 252
Deppe, Lois, *20–21*, 30, 56, *130*, 131–40, *138*, *141*, *165*, 231, *311*
    "blue vein society" and, 13
    Hines as accompanist for, 15–17, 21–23, 25–28, 146
    singing style of, 92
Deppe, Marguerite Rosson, 136, 140
Desmond, Paul, 91
Dew, Bob, 135
Dexter, Dave, 95, 162
Dickenson, Vic, 119, 183, 184, 222, 225, 251, 252, *307*
Dickerson, Carroll, 34, 38–47, 54, 136, 140, 143, 145, 146, 248, 277
Did You Ever See a Dream Walking? (song), 262
Diga Diga Doo (song), 137
Dillinger, John, 198–99
Dinofer, Murray, 97
Disneyland, 237
Dixon, George, *60*, *66*, *68*, 70, *71*, 76–78, *79*, *159*, 160–64, *163*, *165*, 199, 213, *223*, 231, *239*, 240, *249*, 277–85
    in bus accident, 69
    Charlie Carpenter and, 154–55
    Lester Young and, 157
    in Navy, 231
    Wallace Bishop and, 175
    Walter Fuller and, 166–68
    Willie Randall and, 234
Dixon, Lawrence, 67, 68, *68*, *71*, 76–77, *169*, *199*, *223*, 253, *253*
Dixon, Lucille, 97, 266, *268*
Dixon, M. R., 160
Dixon, Vance, 18, *21*, 27, 134–36
Dobie, Wilma, 122
Dr. Stoll's Medicine Show, 166
Dodds, Baby, 95, 175, 179, 195
Dodds, Johnny, 179, 195
Dodging a Divorcée (Foresythe), 74, 198

Dominick Swing (Q. Wilson), 172
Dominique, Natty, 45, 50
Donegan, Dorothy, 229
Donovan, Bobby, 116, *117*, 119
Donovan, Red, 183
Dorsey, Jimmy, 48
Dorsey, Tommy, 48, 90, 153–54, 200
Dougherty, Doc, 107–8
Douglas, Billy, 91, *267*, 269
Douglas, Tommy, 263
Down Beat (nightclub), 260
Draper, Julian, 77
Dreamland (nightclub), 34, 171
Dreyfus, Sam, 45
Drummer Man (song), 274
Dudley, Bessie, 137
Du Gaston, Charlie, 249
Dunbar, Paul Laurence, 131
Dunlap, Louis, 69, 80, 142–43, *143*, 147, 148, 151, *159*
Dunn, Johnny, 50–51
Dupree, Nelda, 168
Duquesne Gardens, 132
Durham, Alan, 206
Durham, Eddie, 207, 208
Dutrey, Honoré, 42, 45, *51*, 54
Dyett, Walter, 174, 229

Eadey, Irene, 46, 74, 167, 210
Eadey, Joe, 46
Earl, Eugene, 262, *263*
Earl Fatha Hines's Music Crossroads, 111
East of the Sun (Gillespie), 266
Eastwood, Clint, 126
Eastwood Gardens (nightclub), 93
Eckstine, Billy, 82, 155, *159*, *163*, 223, 238–44, *239*, *242*, *245*, 251, 266, 277, 282, 284
    Budd Johnson and, 210, 214, 216–17
    Cliff Smalls and, 270, 271
    Dizzy Gillespie and, 260, 261
    George Dixon and, 279
    record debut of, 93, 168
    Shorts McConnell and, 280
    singing style of, 86, 92
    starts own band, 95–96
    Trummy Young and, 221
Edison, Harry, 227
Edwards, Jimmy, *263*
Eglin, Duke, 198
Eldridge, Roy, *165*, 184, 186, 192, 197, 250, 251, 258, 286, 307
Elgar, Charles, 229
El Grotto (nightclub), 73, 96–99, 101, 103, 156, 269
Elite No. 1 (nightclub), 47
Elite No. 2 (nightclub), 31, 33, 36–38, 45, 47
Ellington, Duke, 16n, 85, 98, *122*, 176, 227, 241, 243, 260, 277, 290
    Al Sears and, 216
    Barney Bigard and, 104
    in elevator accident, 70
    film score by, 200
    first meeting of Hines and, 26
    funeral of, 122
    Hayes Alvis and, 62
    Herb Jeffries and, 93
    Irene Wilson and, 179, 182
    Johnny Hodges and, 95
    on origins of bop, 90n
    at Pittsburgh Jazz Festival, 114

Ray Nance and, 88, 224
Regalettes and, 168
Sarah Vaughan and, 94
seventieth birthday party for, 120, 126, *189*
Teddy Wilson and, 183
Wellman Braud and, 171, 189
Willie Cook and, 92
Willie Randall and, 232
Ellington, Mercer, 124
Ellis, Herb, 272
Ellison, Kittens, 36–37
Elton's Theatre, 137
Embers (nightclub), 110
Empire Ballroom, 186
Empress Theatre, 136
Englestein (theatre owner), 146
English, Bill, 110
Entertainers Club, 34, 39, 48
Essex, Lord, 89, 98, *287*, 288
Europe, Jim, 220
Evans, Herschel, 210, 227
Evans, Stumpy, 45, 47, 51
Everything Depends on You (song), 79, 89, 151
Ewing, Elmer, 168
Ewing, John "Streamline," 77, *79*, 168, 235–37, *236*, 278

Faithfull, Marianne, 182
Famous Door (nightclub), 196
Fant, Ed, 235, *239*, 249
Farm roadhouse, 175
Fat Babes (Mundy), 198
Father Jumps, The (song), 161
Fats Waller Medley, 111
Fazola (clarinet player), 195
Feather, Leonard, 163
Fellman, Jim, 18, 19
Fidgety Feet (song), 204
Fields, Ernie, 168
Fields, Kansas, 168
Fields, W. C., 139
57 Varieties (song), 52
Fiore, Eddie, 124
Fish Market (song), 251
Fitzgerald, Ella, 106, 119, 223, 258, 272, 282
Flamingo (song), 243
Fletcher, Arthur, 126
Fletcher, Bernice, 126
Fletcher, Dusty, 70, 71, *71*
Fletcher, Milton, *71*, 77, *79*, 168, 235
Floyd, Harlan, *233*
Floyd, Pretty Boy, 198
Floyd, Troy, 210
Foley, Red, 157
For the Last Time Call Me Sweetheart (song), 134, 140, *141*
Ford, Betty, 126
Ford, Gerald, 126
Ford, Michael, 174
Foresythe, Reginald, 74, 150, 198
Foster, Pops, 109, *113*, 171
Four Step Brothers, 58
Fox, Ed, 61, 62, 80, 150–54, *151*, 168, 198, 230, 235
    contract with Hines invalidated, 95, 213–14, 251
    influence of waiters on, 65–66
    opens Grand Terrace, 57–58

Sunset Café run by, 45, 50, 143
    tours arranged by, 64, 67
Fox, Louis, 150
François's Louisianians, 185
Franklin, Billy, 57, 60, 66, 69, 76–77, 92,
    168, 169, 175, 221
Frazier, Bobbie, 69
Frederick Brothers agency, 168, 169
Freeman, Bud, 194
French Casino, 229
Frenesi (Carpenter and Russell), 157
Friars' Inn, 195
From the Land of the Sky Blue Water (song),
    132
Fuller, Walter, 66, 68, 71, 166–70, 167,
    169, 190, 199, 214, 223
    Charlie Carpenter and, 149
    George Dixon and, 160–61
    injured in bus accident, 69, 76
    Irene Wilson and, 179
    John Ewing and, 235
    Quinn Wilson and, 174
    Wallace Bishop and, 175
Funky London (nightclub), 175
Fusco, Joe, 167, 168, 198

Gale agency, 158
Gardner, Burgess, 233
Gardner, Goon, 260, 266, 267
Garner, Erroll, 1, 110, 185, 224
Gaslight Club, 174, 278
Gay, Leonard, 229
Gee, Matthew, 222
Gentry, Leroy, 161
Gerald, Sister, 160
Gershwin, George, 56
Ghost of Yesterdays (I. Wilson), 181
Gillespie, Dizzy, 89–91, 95, 192, 245,
    254–61, 256, 258, 266, 267, 290
    Budd Johnson and, 216
    with Hines's band, 89–90, 95, 155, 240,
        266
    on jazz cruise, 124
    Trummy Young and, 224
Gillespie, Lorraine, 259
Gillum, Russell, 239
Giscard d'Estaing, Valery, 126
Glaser, Joe, 45, 50, 103, 105, 107, 143–44,
    180, 212
Gleason, Jackie, 146
Glenn, Tyree, 91, 222, 241
God Bless the Child (Herzon and Holiday),
    182
Go, Go (show), 26
Golden Gate Ballroom, 217
Goldman, Irving, 259
Gonzel White Show, 204
Goodman, Benny, 48, 93, 193–96, 224, 249
    Cootie Williams and, 88, 95
    Jimmy Mundy and, 77–79, 153, 200, 213,
        227, 230, 241
    Teddy Wilson and, 181, 183, 186
Goodman, Eugene, 195
Goodman, Freddy, 193–95
Goodman, Harry, 193, 194
Goodman, Irving, 195–96, 196
Goodman, Jeremy, 195
Goodwin, Henry, 110
Gordon, Dexter, 217, 224
Gordy, Barry, 272
Graham, Eddie, 124, 126

Graham, Leonard, 263, 266
Grand Terrace, 57–58, 60–66, 72–76, 79,
    85–86, 88, 93, 95, 102–3, 112, 122,
    128, 136, 146, 149–50, 152–55, 157,
    161, 168, 171–72, 174, 176, 179, 183,
    185, 188–90, 198–99, 210–11, 213–14,
    230, 235–36, 241, 249, 251, 276, 290,.
    311
Grand Terrace Stomp (song), 244
Grand Theatre (Chicago), 35, 36
Grand Theatre (Philadelphia), 70
Grant, Moses, 168
Granz, Norman, 224
Gray, Wardell, 91, 97, 101, 266, 267
Graystone Ballroom, 162
Great Day (musical), 137–38
Green, Benny, 97, 98, 101, 106, 109, 229,
    237, 266, 267, 268, 271–73, 286
Green, Big, 45
Green, Cora, 139
Green, Fats, 214
Green, Freddie, 186
Green, Lil, 216
Green, Madeline, 82, 89, 93, 94, 95, 159,
    162, 214, 215, 243, 251, 282
Greenlee, Gus, 139
Green Room, 173
Greer, Sonny, 26, 179, 227
Grey, Al, 222
Grey, Johnny, 179
Grey, Tick, 192, 192
Grimes, Tiny, 224
Grissom, Dan, 243
Grofé, Ferdie, 200
Groves, Gene, 271
Grupp, Maurice, 242
G. T. Stomp (song), 80
Guy, Freddy, 189

Hackett, Bobby, 91, 186
Hall, Adelaide, 137, 181
Hall, Rene, 269
Hall, Tubby, 40, 41–42, 45, 51
Hallelujah (song), 137
Hall Johnson Choir, 136
Halpern (lawyer), 154
Hamby, Willie, 47, 49, 50, 51
Hamilton, Jimmy, 183
Hammond, John, 162, 181, 182, 186
Hampton, Lionel, 147, 168, 174, 188, 237,
    261, 282
Handful of Keys (song), 184
Handy, W. C., 98, 225
Hangover (nightclub), 107–11, 113, 273
Hanna, Roland, 311
Happy Hour (club), 168
Hardee, John, 224
Harding, Buster, 89
Hardison, Leroy, 262, 263, 265
Harlem Casino, 139
Harlem Globetrotters, 274
Harlem Lament (song), 172
Harlem Opera House, 70
Harman, Johnny, 270
Harper, Leonard, 199
Harrington, James, 254
Harris, Benny, 92, 97, 249, 290–91
Harris, Leroy, 77, 79, 107, 159, 163, 214,
    215, 230–31, 237–38, 239, 249
Harris, Marion, 138

Harris, Walter "Woogie," 101, 165, 215,
    231, 267, 268, 286
Harrison, Jimmy, 184, 209, 221
Harrison, Richard, 235
Hart, Clyde, 210, 216
Hartman, Johnny, 96, 284
Has Anyone Seen My Corinne? (Howard), 29
Hassell, Hollis, 170
Haver's Minstrel Show, 229
Hawkins, Coleman, 23, 158, 201, 207–10,
    224, 229, 246, 260, 269
    Arthur Herbert and, 251
    Fletcher Henderson and, 26, 157, 184
    Little Theatre concerts by, 111
    Wallace Bishop and, 177
Hawkins, Erskine, 78, 119, 244, 262, 277
Hawkins, French, 135
Hayes, Clifford, 58
Hayes, Edgar, 135, 136, 285
Hayes, Jimmy, 34, 36
Hayes, Marie Carter, 120
Hayes, Roland, 134
Hayworth, Rita, 200
Hazel, Marion, 268
Heard, J. C., 217
Hefti, Neal, 290
Hegamin, Lucille, 25, 92–93
Hello, Paris (show), 139
Henderson, Fletcher, 25, 65, 72, 189–90,
    204, 246, 249–50, 285–87
    Budd Johnson and, 213
    Charlie Carpenter and, 153
    Coleman Hawkins and, 26, 157, 184, 209
    Lois Deppe and, 135–38
    Louis Armstrong and, 146
    Sidney Catlett and, 103
    Willie Randall and, 230
Henderson, Horace, 77, 184, 213, 230, 235,
    286
Henry, Haywood, 119, 160, 168
Henson, Purvis, 263
Herbert, Arthur, 251
Herzog, Arthur, 182
Heywood, Don, 137
Heywood, Eddie, 110, 185, 262, 311
Hickman, Sylvester, 233
Hicks, Warren W., 200n
Higginbotham, J. C., 251, 253
Higgins, Joe, 144
Hightower, Willie, 41, 42, 45
Hill, Alex, 160, 166
Hill, Elton, 153, 221, 241
Hill, Teddy, 257, 261, 285
Hills, Buddy, 101, 215
Himmelstein, Dave, 111
Hines, Baby, 28, 135
Hines, Earl, 7–128, 17, 37, 40, 59, 87, 90,
    94, 114, 118, 121, 123–25, 169, 215,
    270–71, 274–75, 277–85, 311
    as accompanist, 54–55
    Alvin Burroughs and, 290
    at Apex Club, 55–56
    athletic prowess of, 12–14
    awards to, 120–22
    with band led by Armstrong, 103–5, 114,
        128
    Benny Carter and, 305
    Benny Goodman and, 194–95
    on big bands, 80–81
    Billy Eckstine and, 163, 238–44, 239,
        242–43

Hines, Earl (*continued*)
  birth of, 7
  "blue vein society" and, 68
  Budd Johnson and, 79–80, 210–17, *215*
  Carroll Dickerson and, 38–47, *41*
  Charlie Carpenter and, 80, 143–46,
    148–58
  Charlie Parker and, 89
  Chicago underworld and, 35–36, 46–47,
    58, 61–62
  childhood of, 7–12, *11*
  Cliff Smalls and, 262–70, *272*
  at Collins Inn, 28–30
  Count Basie and, *265*
  on death of Ellington, 122–24
  Dicky Wells and, 273–76
  Dizzy Gillespie and, 89–91, 95, 258, 260,
    290
  at El Grotto, 98–103
  at Elite No. 2, 31, 33, 36–38, 45, 47
  Eubie Blake and, 30–31, *31*
  first marriage of, 28
  first meeting of Armstrong and, 45
  first recordings by, 26
  first trip to New York of, 26
  Franz Jackson and, *163*, 250–51
  George Dixon and, 160–63, *163*
  at Grand Terrace, 57–66, 72–76, 95
  at Hangover, 107–11, *110–13*
  introduced to jazz, 15–16
  Irene Wilson and, 179–80, *181*
  Jimmy Mundy and, 197–200
  Joe Louis and, 98–100, *101*
  John Ewing and, 235–37, *236*
  at Leader House, 16–21, 30
  Lois Deppe and, 16–23, 25–28, 56,
    132–36, 139, 140, *141*, 165
  on marijuana users, 84–85
  meeting of Pope and, 114–16, *115*
  Milt Hinton and, 187–90, *189*
  Muhammed Ali and, *101*
  photographs of Armstrong and, *105–8*
  photographs of orchestra and, *66–68, 71,
    78–79, 96–97, 100, 199, 223, 249,
    258–59, 267*
  piano concerts by, 111–14, 122, *219*
  piano roll recordings of, 56
  Quinn Wilson and, 171–74, *173*
  recording of Armstrong and, 52–53
  at recording sessions, *311, 312, 315*
  on relations with band, 85–98
  on Russian tour, 116–17, *117*
  Sarah Vaughan and, *218, 283*
  small groups led by, 105–7, 119–20
  at Sunset Café, 45–48, 50–54
  Teddy Wilson and, 183–86, *185*
  on touring South, 81–84
  tours arranged by Ed Fox for, 66–72
  trained as barber, 13, 14
  travel accidents of, 69–70
  Truck Parham and, *309*
  Trummy Young and, 221–24, 227, *236*
  Wallace Bishop and, 175–76, 178, *176–78*
  Walter Fuller and, 167–68
  at White House, 126, *127*
  Willie Randall and, 230–32, *231*
  at Wolf Trap, *245*
Hines, Hilton, 27
Hines, Janear, *115*, 116
Hines, Janie Moses, 109, *115*, 156
Hines, Joseph "Boots," *32*, 128

Hines, Nancy, 27, *32*, 128
Hines, Tosca, *115*
Hinton, Milt, 174, 186–92, *189, 192*, 228,
  229
Hite, Les, 147, 258
Hodges, Johnny, 91, 95, 183, 186, 241, 246,
  249, *315*
Hoefer, George, 290
Holder, T., 207
Holiday, Billie, 158, 169, 181, 182, 217, 224,
  237
Holland, Gilbert, 137
Holloway, William, 206
Honeysuckle Rose (song), 82, 274
Honore, Gideon, *247*
Hooks, Frank, 233
Hopkins, Claude, 92, 172, 243, 258, 290
Horn, Billy, 209
Hot Chocolates Revue (show), 146
Hot Chocolate Stomp (song), 227
Hot Mallets (song), 261
Hot Shot Club, 181
House of Blue Lights (nightclub), 73
Howard, Bart, 29
Howard, Corinne, 29
Howard, Darnell, 22, 67, 68, 71, *71*, 76–78,
  77, 169, 171, 190, *223*, 278
  Carroll Dickerson and, 45
  at Hangover, 110
  Horace Henderson and, 77
  Jimmy Mundy and, 198
  Quinn Wilson and, 172
Howard, Fat, 247
Howard Theatre (Chicago), 96
Howard Theatre (Washington), 70, 262
Hucko, Peanuts, 110
Hudgins, Johnny, 137
Hudson, George, 269
Hughes, Isaiah, 12–13
Hull House, 193, 194
Hunt, George, *249*
Hunt, Lonzo, 140
Hunter, Alberta, 65
Hunter, George, 168
Hutchinson, Dolly, 180
Hutchinson, Pearl, 180
Hylton, Jack, 84

I Can't Get Started (song), 196, 224
I Can't Give You Anything But Love (song),
  137
I Found a New Baby (song), 195
I Got It Bad (song), 89
I Got Rhythm (song), 157, 248
Illedge, Eric, 156, 265
Illidge, Arlene, 97
I'll See You in C-U-B-A (song), 15
I Love You Truly (song), 131
I'm Coming, Virginia (song), 137
I'm Confessin' (song), 242
I'm in the Mood for Love (song), 92, 157, 217
Immerman, Connie, 138–39
Immerman, George, 138–39
I Must Have That Man (song), 137
In a Mist (Beiderbecke), 49
I Never Had a Chance (song), 161
Inge, Ed, 223
Ink Spots, 153
Irwin, Cecil, 57, *60*, 63, *67*, 76, 79, *169*, 172,
  198–99, 210
  death of, 69, 77, 157, 161, 168, 173, 212

Isabel (Roberts), 26, 134
It's Magic (song), 126
I Want a Lot of Love (Carpenter and
  Dunlap), 151
I Want Some Molasses (Roberts), 26
I Wish You Love (Trenet), 126

Jackson, Franz, 89, *163, 192*, 230, *231, 239,
  246–53, 247, 249, 250, 252, 253*
Jackson, Oliver, 111, 116, *117*, 119, *219*,
  291, *307*
Jackson, Pee Wee, 77, *159*, 230, *239*, 281
Jackson, Preston, 249
Jackson, Quentin "Butter," 225, 259
Jacobs, Charlie, 264
Jamal, Ahmad, 284
James, Harry, 186, 200
James, Ida, 88, 93
James, Sonny, 93
Japanese Sandman (song), 92
Jarvis, Al, 170
Jaxon, Frankie, 248
Jazz at the Philharmonic, 158, 224
Jazz Limited (nightclub), 174, 253
Jefferson, Hilton, 213
Jefferson, Warren, *68, 199*
Jeffrey Tavern, 175
Jeffries, Herb, 80, 93, 149, 243
Jelly, Jelly (song), 93, 216, 217, 238, 240,
  241, 244, 261
Jenkins, Freddy, 179
Jenkins, George, 237
Jennings, Mrs., 12
Jerome, Jerry, 279
Jersey Bounce (song), 258
Jockey Club, 135
Johnson, Albert, 202
Johnson, Budd, 68, *71*, 76, 77, 79, 95, 119,
  126, *159, 199*, 202–19, *205, 215, 239,
  307*
  Billy Eckstine and, 240–43
  George Dixon and, 161
  Gus Arnheim and, 77
  Irene Wilson and, 179, 180, *182*
  John Ewing and, 235
  in piano recitals, 111
  Quinn Wilson and, 172
  on Russian tour, 116
  Willie Randall and, 230, 231
Johnson, C. P., 224
Johnson, Eddie, *233*, 234
Johnson, Endicott, 82
Johnson, George, 178
Johnson, Gus, 272
Johnson, J. J., 222
Johnson, J. Rosamond, 131, 132
Johnson, Jack, 30, 99
Johnson, James P., 73, 251, 274
Johnson, Joe, 253, *253*
Johnson, Keg, 180, 202, 203, 259
Johnson, Money, 116, *117*, 119
Johnson, Ocie, 106, *109*, 237
Johnson, "Toodle-oo," 16*n*
Johnson, Vernie, 203
Johnson, Ziggy, 232
Jones, Ann, *74*
Jones, Broadway, 26
Jones, Etta, 106
Jones, Gordon, 229
Jones, Jo, 186, 227
Jones, Jonah, 91, 106, *109*, 186, 237, 273

Jones, Max, 114
Jones, Orville, 153
Jones, Paul, 221
Jones, Quincy, 200
Jones, Ruth, 254
Jones, Wesley, 262, 263, *263*
Jones Boys, 63–64
Jordan, Emmett, 15, 18, *21*, 30, 134
Jordan, Joe, 131
Jordan, Louis, 234
Jordan, Taft, 257
Josie, Marva, 119–20, *119*, 126, *311*
Julia (G. Dixon), 161
Jumpin' George (drummer), 271

Kaminsky, Max, 110
Katz (theatre manager), 132
Katz Theatre, 67
Kayser, Joe, 194
K. C. Caboose (song), 216
Keith theatre circuit, 39
Kelly, Guy, *192*, 249
Kelly, Joe, 174
Kelly's Stables, 168, 169
Kenton, Stan, 213, 269
Keppard, Freddy, 35
Kern, Jerome, 98
Killian, Al, 224
King, Clifford "Clarinet," 191
King, Eddie, 248
King, Wayne, 229
King Porter Stomp (song), 261
Kirby, George, 142, 152, 158
Kirby, John, 177, 186, 190, 191, 216
Kirk, Andy, 207, 263, 287
Kissinger, Henry, 126
Kitchings, Elden, 182
Kitchings, Irene, 179–82, *181*
Krupa, Gene, 153, 181, 186, 194, 195, 200, 241
Kyle, Billy, 185, 216, 225, 258

Ladner, Calvin, *233*
Lafayette Theatre, 67, 70
Laine, Cleo, *311*
Landino, Bernard, 131
Land of the North, I Hear You Calling Me (song), 132
Lane, Morris, 273
Langford, Frances, 92
Langley, Otto, 264
Lannigan, Jim, 194
Larkins, Ellis, 124, 186
Last Word (nightclub), 168
Laughton, Charles, 200
Layton, Turner, 131, 132
Leader House, 16–21, 23, 30, 128, 133, 135
Lee, George, E., 208–10
Leonard, Harlan, 168
Lesberg, Jack, 110
Leslie, Lew, 137
Let Me Off Uptown (Glenn), 241
Levey, Stan, 260
Lewando, Ralph, 120
Lewis (impresario), 132
Lewis, George, 252
Lewis, Son, 203
Lewis, Ted, 194
Lewis, Willie, 204
Liggins, Mrs., 36
Lim, Harry, 95

Lincoln Theatre, 70, 263
Little Al (saxophone player), 211
Little Dawg (trumpet player), 262
Little Theatre, 111–12
Livingston, Fud, 194
Liza (song), 183
Loew's State Theatre, 151, 152
Loew's Vaudeville Theatre, 134
Lombardo, Guy, 63, 66
London House, 140
Lonesome Road (song), 148
Louis, Joe, 98–100, *101*
Louisianians, 229
Love for Sale (Bechet), 282
Lucas, Roxanna, 97
Lunceford, Jimmie, 85, 91, 198, 243, 277
  Eddie Tompkins and, 207, 246
  John Ewing and, 237
  Trummy Young and, 77, 152, 222–24, 227, 236*n*, 237
  Willie Randall and, 232
Lyle, Bill, 249

McAllister, Lew, 137
McCarey, Prentiss, 229, 249
McConnell, Lorraine, 240
McConnell, Shorts, 92, *97*, 158, 214, 240, 266, *267*, 280
McHenry, Jimmy, 171
McKendrick, Mike, 148, 211
McKinney, Nina Mae, 254
McKinney's Cotton Pickers, 184, 208, 210
McLewis, Joe, 77, *79*, *159*, *231*, *233*, *239*, 240, 244, *249*, 280, 286
McNeil, Bill, 255
McPartland, Jimmy, 194, 195
McPartland, Marian, 124, 186
McPhatter, Clyde, 272
McRae, Carmen, 124, 182, 260
McRae, Teddy, 258
McShann, Jay, 155, 261, 263, 285
Madden, Owney, 62
Madhouse (song), 241
Make Believe (song), 89
Malachi, John, 224
Mallory, Eddie, 181, 186, 211
Mance, Junior, 291, *311*
Maple Leaf Rag (song), 198
Marable, Fate, 175
Mares, Paul, 195
Marian's Grape Arbor, 135
Marie (song), 264
Marie Louise, 170
Markham, Pigmeat, 204
Marsala, Marty, 110
Martin, Dr., 14
Martin, Pepper, 262, 264
Martin, Rudy, *233*, 234
Matthews, Sonny, 254
May, Billy, 227
Mazie (song), 249
Melancholy Baby (song), 183
Memories of You (Blake), 112
Mercer, Johnny, 157
Meredith, Burgess, 200
Merrill, Helen, 106
Metropole (nightclub), 179
Metropolitan Theatre, 144, 146
Mezzrow, Mezz, 146, 147
Middleton, Velma, 104, *107*, 170
Milenberg Joys (Morton), 34

Miley, Bubber, 26
Miller, Eugene "Bon Bon," *233*
Miller, Glenn, 194, 195
Miller, Jesse, 266, *267*
Miller, McClure, 132
Miller, Punch, 51–52, 246, 247
Millinder, Lucky, 57, 172, 258–60
Mills, John, 157
Mills Brothers, 63, 157
Milton, Roy, 285
Minnie the Moocher (song), 262
Minton's (nightclub), 89, 209
Miracles, The, 272
Mr. Kelly's, 284
Mitchell, Billy, 61
Mitchell, Bobby, 119
Mitchell, George, 57, *60*, 175
Mitchell, Jimmy, 244
Mole, Miff, 90, 221
Monestier, Jean-Marie, 119
Monroe, Vaughan, 200
Montgomery, Ann, 139
Moonglow (nightclub), 139, 140, 170
Moonlight Melody Six, 203
Moore, Big Chief, 204
Moore, Clarence, 149, 186, 211
Moore, Tim, 137
Moreland, Mantan, *107*, 137
More Than You Know (song), 138
Morgenstern, Dan, 111
Morris, Marlowe, 214, 224
Morris, William, Jr., 154
Morrison, Charlie, 232
Morton, Benny, 183, 186
Morton, Jelly Roll, 34, 36, 47, 55, 174, 175
Moseley, François, 246, *247*, 249
Most, Sam, 183
Moten, Bennie, 157, 208, 209, 271
Mott, Al, 225
Moulin Rouge, 107
Mundy, Jimmy, 68, 72, 86, 151, 197–201, *199*, *201*, 249, 277
  Benny Goodman and, 77–79, 153, 200, 213, 227, 230, 241
  Quinn Wilson and, 172
  Trummy Young and, 221, 223
  Wallace Bishop and, 175
  Walter Fuller and, 168
Music Makers, 206
Music Performers' Trust Fund Concerts, 234
Muskrat Ramble (song), 273
Mussolini, Romano, 114, *115*
My Big Brass Bed (song), 241
My Blue Heaven (song), 157, 272
Myles, Tommy, 197–98, 216, 221, 222, 227, 241
My Monday Date (song), 53, 56

Nagasaki (song), 255
Nance, Ray, 77, 83, 88, 92, 174, 189, 222–24, *223*, 228–30, 278
Nanton, Tricky Sam, 222
NBC (National Broadcasting Company), 63, 75
Nest (nightclub), 55, 179, 195
Newborn, Calvin, 110
Newhall, Ruth, 120
Newhall, Scott, 120, *121*
Newley, Anthony, 182
Newman, Joe, 237

Newport Jazz Festival, 256
Newton, Frank, 186, 251, *252*
Nicholas Brothers, *74*
Nichols, Red, 204
Nick, John, 220
Night in Tunisia (Gillespie), 90, 260, 266
Nixon, Tommy, 249
No, No, Nanette (musical), 138
Noone, Jimmie, 55–56, 145, 157, 176, 179, 186, 194–95, 212, 249, 252
Norrell, Danny, 132
Norvo, Red, 224
Number 19 (song), 161
Nuts and Bolts (song), 249

Oakley, Helen, 122, 163, 186, 198
Oasis (nightclub), 107, 237
O'Brien, Floyd, 194
Offert, Howard, 228
O'Keefe, Rockwell, 212
Oldham, Bill, 253, *253*
Oldham, George, 211
Old Town Gate (nightclub), 253
Oliver, Joe, 45, 175, 195
Oliver, King, 23, 34, 45, 48, 55, 184, 225
Oliver, Sy, 177, 227, 272
Oliver's Tavern, 140
Olman, Chauncey, 154
Ol' Man River (Kern), 136, 285
Olsen, George, 84
On Green Dolphin Street (song), 272
Onyx Club, 195
Oriental Theatre, 80, 103, 147, 151
Original Jass All-Stars, 253
Orpheum Theatre, 212
Ory, Kid, *108*, 225, *226*
Overseas Press Club Jazz Club, 122
Oxley, Harold, 223

Pabst Blue Ribbon Show, 156
Page, Billy, 30
Page, Lips, 186, 209
Page, Walter, 92, 186, 204, 208, 227
Palmer Brothers, 93
Panama (song), 15, 109
Panassié, Hugues, 103, 104, 112, 114, 177, 178, 281–82
Panassié, Madeleine, 104, 114
Pantages theatre circuit, 39–40, 42, *43*, *44*, 45, 48
Paradise Theatre, 240, 270
Paramount Inn, 133
Parham, Truck, *159*, *163*, 214, *239*, *309*
Parker, Charlie, 95, 208, 210, 214, 221, 258, 267, 272
    Charlie Carpenter and, 155
    Dizzy Gillespie and, 89–90, 260–61, 266
    Sarah Vaughan and, 94
    Trummy Young and, 224
Parker, Dolores, 98, 285, 287, *287*
Parker, Leo, 224
Parks, Jean, 97
Pasquall, Jerome, 191, 246
Patterson, Braxton, 286
Patterson, Pat, 10, 16
Patterson and Jackson, 93
Paul, Les, 157
Paul VI, Pope, 114–116, *115*
Pearls, The (Morton), 55
Pearl Theatre, 67, 70, 173
Pearson, Ted, 75

Pecci, Buzzi, 131
Peer, Ralph, 157
Pemberton, Bill, 116, *117*, 119, *307*
Perkins, Lotus, *165*
Perry, Kathryn, 63, 65, 69, 144, 149, 161, 180, *181*, 214
Perry, King, 285
Peterson, Joe, 168
Peterson, Oscar, 120, 124, *124*, 140, 284, 290
Petrillo, James Caesar, 154, 211
Pettiford, Ira, *268*, 269
Pettiford, Oscar, 224
Peyton, Dave, 34, 35, 54, 132, 136, 171, 229
Pfeiffer, George, 228
Phillips, Montan, 170
Phillips, Reuben, 272
Phillips, Sadie, 15, 27
Piano Man (song), 274
Pierce, Nat, *201*
Pierpoint, Sidney, 152
Pittman, Booker, 207, 208, 210
Pitt Theatre, 132
Plantation Club (Chicago), 34, 48, 50, 55, 180
Plantation Club (Detroit), 139
Plantation Club (New York), 139
Plantation Club (St. Louis), 89, 269
Plumb, Neely, 257
Podalsky, Murph, 194
Poet and Peasant Overture, 46
Pollack, Ben, 194, 195
Pollock, Eddie, 249
Ponce, Mamie, 34, 175
Poor Little Rich Girl (song), 50
Pope, Norman, 255
Porgy and Bess (Gershwin), 120
Porter, Cole, 98
Porter, Eugene, 170
Porter, Yank, 211
Potter, Tommy, 106, *109*, 224, 237
Powell, Austin, 182
Powell, Bud, 258
Powell, Rudy, 271
Pozo, Chano, 257
Prater, Jane, 161
Pratt, Madame, 203
Price, Oscar, 139
Price, Sammy, 204
Prisoner of Love (song), 217
Procope, Russell, 216
Pruitt, Carl, 110, *165*, 274–75
Pruitt, Sonny, 183
Prysock, Arthur, 234, 243
Puckett, Tillie, 203
Pugh, Doc, 104, 105
Pullin' Through (I. Wilson), 181

Radio Room, 168
Raeburn, Boyd, 224
Raft, George, 128
Rainbow Grill, 122, *311*
Rainey, Ma, 25, 143
Ramey, Hurley, 77, *239*
Ramirez, Ram, 216
Rand, Sally, 211
Randall, Willie, *71*, 77, 89, 140, *141*, *159*, *163*, *215*, 223, 228–34, *231*, *233*, *239*, 249, 278
    Billy Eckstine and, 242
    Budd Johnson and, 214

    Charlie Carpenter and, 154, 155
Randolph, Zilmer T., 148, 211
Raye, Martha, 157
Razaf, Andy, 146, 151, 199
Rector, Eddie, 156
Red Arrow (nightclub), 253
Redd, Gene, 107, 273
Redman, Don, 16*n*, 22, 26, 84, 138, 170, 241
Reed, Billy, 139
Reed, Dolly, 120
Reed, Ollie, 132, 134
Reese, Ed, 266
Reese, Rostelle, *231*, *239*
Reeves, Reuben, 248
Regalettes, 142, 168
Regal Theatre, 54, 65, 136, 142, 146, 168, 171, 192, 210, 229, 237, 287
Renaissance Ballroom, 214
Rhapsody in Black (show), 64
Rhapsody in Blue (Gershwin), 46, 56, 74, 191, 200, 269
Rhodes, George, 272
Rhumboogie (nightclub), 77, 98, 99, 174, 230, 232
Rhythm Club, 181
Rhythm Debs, 288
Rhythm Lullaby (song), 93
Ricard, Fip, 268
Rice, Eli, 208
Richardson, Jerome, 107, 274
Richardson, Walter, 63, 74
Rideout, Arthur, 13, 134
Ring Dem Bells (song), 189
Ristina, 70
Ritchie, Nell Matilda, 228
Riverboat (nightclub), 119
Roach, Max, 216, 255
Roane, Happy, 26
Roberts, Buggs, 89, 98, 269
Roberts, Claude, 57, *60*, 77, *79*, 168
Roberts, Herman, 232–34
Roberts, Luckey, 16, 25–26, 135
Robeson, Orlando, 243
Robeson, Paul, 136
Robey, Don, 243
Robinson, Bojangles, 19, 25, 30, 54–55, 58, 63, 137
Robinson, Eli, 271
Robinson, Ikey, 160
Robinson, Mary, 27
Robinson, Prince, 208, 210, 250
Robinson, Smokey, 272
Robinson, Sugar Ray, 100
Robinson, Vernie, 28, 29, 31, 34, 135
Rockhead's Paradise (nightclub), 139
Rodgers, Gene, 161
Rodin, Gil, 194
Rodney, Red, 260
Rogers, Jimmy, 58
Rollini, Adrian, 195–96, 204
Rooney, Mickey, 128
Roosevelt, Franklin Delano, 191
Roppolo, Leon, 195
Rose, Billy, 195
Roseborough (manager), 262
Roseland Ballroom, 136, 167, 172
Rosetta (Hines and Woode), 56, 76, 126, 153, 168, 213, 262
Ross, Candy, 272
Ross, Shirley, 154

Rouse, Charlie, 290
Roxy Theatre, 103, 136
Royal, Marshall, 237
Royal Creolians, 70
Royal Eight, 261
Royal Garden Blues (song), 274
Royal Gardens, 175, 179
Royal Theatre, 70, 90, 162, 173, 262
Rushing, Jimmy, *201*, 206
Russell, Bob, 157
Russell, Luis, 138, 237
Rutherford, Rudy, 119, *124*, 126

Sachs, Aaron, 106, *109*, 237
St. James Infirmary (song), 126
St. Louis Blues (song), 111, 252
St. Louis Crackerjacks, 211–12
Sales, Chic, 139
Salt Peanuts (song), 90
Sampson, Edgar, 214
San, Anita, 97
Sands, Everett, *233*
Sands, Frank, 158
Saperstein, Abe, 274
Saunders, Red, 277
Savoy Ballroom, 36, 54, 55, 144–46, 160,
    162, 166–67, 172, 190, 191, 244, 248,
    257, 258, 273
Scanlan, Tom, 184, 185
Schiffman, Frank, 71
Schoepp, Franz, 194
Schoffner, Bob, 190–91
Schuller, Gunther, 290
Schwartz, Dutch, 62
Scott, Essex. *See* Essex, Lord
Scott, John, 220
Scott, Kermit, *101*, *267*, *302*
Scott, Leon, 77, *231*, 249
Scott, Raymond, 95
Scott, Tony, 224
Scott's Theatre Restaurant, 262, 264
Seabrook, Thad, 262, *263*
Sears, Al, 214, 216, 271
Senior, Milt, 184
Serenade to a Wealthy Widow (Foresythe),
    74, 198
Shavers, Charlie, 190, 216
Shaw, Arvell, 104, *107*, *177*, 183
Shaw, Billy, 216, 257
Shearing, George, 182, 284
Shep, Ray, 262
Sherrill, Joya, 183
Shine (song), 212
Shoffner, Bob, 248, 253, *253*
Shorter Brothers, 21
Show Boat (musical), 89, 98, 136, 138, 285,
    287
Show Boat (nightclub), 191
Show Lounge, 233
Shubert, J. J., 136
Siki, Black, 210
Silver, Horace, *311*
Simeon, Al, 175
Simeon, Omer, *67*, 68, 69, *71*, 76, 77, *79*,
    169, 198, *199*, 212, 223, 230, 251, 278
    Charlie Carpenter and, 155
    Horace Henderson and, 77, 235
    Jelly Roll Morton and, 175
    Quinn Wilson and, 172, 174
    Walter Fuller and, 168
    Wilbur De Paris and, 252

Simmons, John, 260
Simmons, Red, 50
Simms, Ed, *79*, 168
Simpkins, Arthur Lee, 93
Simpkins, Jesse, 229
Simpkins, Paul, 266
Simpson, Cassino, 191, 192, *192*, 210, 248
Sims, Art, 171, 175
Sims, Tresevant, 207
Singin' the Blues (song), 184, 207, 229, 246
Singleton, Zutty, 45, 53–55, *53*, 58,
    144–46, 180, 192
Siren Song, The (song), 140
Sissle, Noble, 15, 22, 30–31, 64, 286, 287
Skoler, Benny, 230
Smalls, Cliff, 92, *97*, *101*, 261–72, *263*, *267*,
    268, 285–86
Smith, Ben, 206
Smith, Bessie, 143, 184
Smith, Buddy, 168, 170, 271
Smith, Buster, 203, 208
Smith, Eddie, 110
Smith, Emma, 166
Smith, Frank, 161
Smith, Henderson, 234
Smith, Jabbo, 191–92, 229
Smith, Joe, 20, 22, 23, 30, 52, 90, 91, 114,
    184
Smith, Lloyd, *101*, *267*, 286
Smith, N. Clark, 188, 190, 228
Smith, Ocie, 207
Smith, Stuff, 207
Smith, Trixie, 184
Smith, Vernon, *101*, *165*, 285, 287
Smith, Willie "The Lion," 34, 56, 178, 198,
    224, 229
Snag It (song), 184
Snow, Valaida, 63–65, 150–51, 172, 230
Soloff, Morris, 200
Solomon, Ellen, 97
Some Other Spring (I. Wilson), 181, 182
Son and Sonny, 93
Song of the Islands (song), 147
Sophisticated Lady (song), 241
South, Eddie, 78, 188, 190, 192, 211, 229
South (song), 157
Southern Serenaders, 204
Southland (nightclub), 34
Spanier, Muggsy, 48, 110, *111*, *113*, 195
Spaulding, Anthony, 191
Squeeze Me (song), 15, 16
Squires, Harry, 68–69, 154, 158
S. S. Rotterdam (ship), 124
Stacy, Jess, 48, 194, 195
Stanley Theatre, 173
Stardust (Carmichael), 49, 93
Starks, Booker T., 262
Starr Piano Company, 135
Star Theatre, 27
State Theatre, 243
Staton, Dakota, 182
Stealin' Apples (Waller), 138
Steele, Larry, 232
Stein, Jule, 194
Stelle, Terry, 286
Stevens, Ashton, 139
Stevens, Nat, 260
Stewart, Bill, 160
Stewart, Kenneth, *68*, *71*, 76, 77, 160, *199*,
    212, 223, *231*, 278
Stewart, Rex, 70, 95, 184, 209, 281

Stewart, Sammy, 34, 45, 68, 136, 137, 160,
    166
Stewart, Slam, 224
Stewart, Smiling Billy, 262
Stone, Jesse, 207–8, 230, 252
Stormy Monday Blues (song), 92, 158
Stratton, Benny, 166
Strayhorn, Billy, 168, 243
Strip, The (film), 128
Sulieman, Idrees, 97
Sullivan, Joe, 48, *111*, 195
Sullivan, Maxine, 30
Summertime (Gershwin), 126
Sunset Café, 34, 36, 45–48, 50–54, 56, 57,
    63–65, 77, 86, 132, 143, 144, 146, 171,
    180, 194, 212, 230, *311*
Sunset Royals, 262
Swanee River (song), 132
Sweet and Lovely (song), 248
Sweethearts of Rhythm, 269
Sweet's Ballroom, 162
Swift, Hughie, 175
Swingland (nightclub), 168, 249
Swingtime in the Rockies (song), 200, 227,
    241
Symphonian Serenaders, *20–21*

Tack, Annie, 35
Take Me, I'm Yours (song), 241
Tantalizing a Cuban (song), 161
Tate, Erskine, 34, 35, 47, 66, 72, 143,
    171–73, 175, 180, 185
Tatum, Art, 73, 92, 120, 140, 192, 224, 269,
    271
    Irene Wilson and, 181, 182
    Teddy Wilson and, 173, 181, 184, 211
Taylor, Billy, 114, 122
Taylor, Louis, *66*, 68, 69, *71*, 76–78, *169*,
    172, *199*, *223*, 278
Taylor, Lovey, 32, 34, 36, 37, 39
Tea for Two (song), 41, 111
Teagarden, Jack, 91, 103–4, *105*, 110
Templeton, Alec, 84
Tennessee Ten, 22
Terrell, Pha, 263–64
Terry, Clark, 70, 122
Teschmaker, Frank, 194
That's a-Plenty (song), 172
Thelman, Jim, 133, 135
There'll Be Some Changes Made (song), 195
Thiele, Bob, *315*
Things Ain't What They Used to Be (song),
    122
Think of Me Little Daddy (song), 223
13th and Lydia (B. Johnson), 208
This Is the Moment (I. Wilson), 181
Thomas, Blanche, 249
Thomas, Eugene, *101*, 287
Thomas, Joe, 183, 224
Thomas, John, 191, *192*, *253*
Thompson, Bill, *101*, 269, 287
Thompson, Charles, *307*
Thompson, Dickey, 271
Thompson, Gene, 269
Thompson, John, 269, 287
Thompson, Sonny, 99, 269, *271*, *302*
Three Classy Misses, 180
Three Deuces (nightclub), 191, 192, 250
Three Sixes (nightclub), 139
Three Varieties, 93
Tiger Rag (song), 52, 147, 157

Tin Roof Blues (song), 109
Tinsley, Ted, 191, *192*
Toadlow (pianist), 16
Toch, Ernst, 200
Tomkins, Les, 291
Tompkins, Eddie, 207, 208, 246
Tone, Franchot, 200
Tony's Subway, 168
Toots, Harley, 262
Tough, Davey, 194, 195
Traill, Sinclair, 114
Traylor, Rudy, 92, *159*, 163
Treadwell, George, 217
Trees (song), 138, 243
Trenet, Charles, 126
Trenier, Claude, 285
Trent, Alphonso, 92, 206, 208, 290
Trotter (drummer), 229
Trumbauer, Frankie, 49, 184, 207, 208, 229, 246
Tucker, Bobby, 217, *245*
Tucker, Snakehips, 137
Tullis, Lavilla, 97
Tune Poem (Ellington), 183
Turner, Earl, *233*
Turner, Joe, 241
Turner, Toby, 57, *60*
Tuxedo Junction (song), 244
Twelfth Street Rag (song), 56
Twelve Clouds of Joy, 207

Usselton, Bill, 174

Valdez, Lolita, 97
Valentine, Gerry, 217
Vamp, The (musical), 200
Vanderhurst, Sammy, 48
Vann, Ernest Zeke, *263*
Vaughan, John, *263*
Vaughan, Sarah, 86, 94, 96, *98*, 217, *218*, 224, 266, 269–70, 282, *283*
Venable, Lucius, 57
Venable, Percy, 45–47, 57, 58, 62, 172, 180
Vendome Theatre, 35–36, 49, 143, 171, 174
Very Thought of You, The (song), 64
Village Gate (nightclub), 120
Village Vanguard (nightclub), 119
Vinson, Eddie "Cleanhead," 271
Vodery, Will, 136
Vogue (nightclub), 167, 179, 180, 210
Von Holz (piano teacher), 10, 15

Wagon Wheels (song), 266
Wainwright, Connie, 266, *267*
Walker, Arthur, *101*, *263*, *268*, 285, *286*
Walker, Lelia, 131
Walker, Madame C. J., 131
Walker, Otis, 262
Wall, Bobby, 228
Waller, Fats, 49, 52, 72–73, 98, 120, 122, 173, 176, 277
 at Connie's Inn, 138, 146
 death of, 146, 274
 Franz Jackson and, 251
 Teddy Wilson and, 184, 185
 Trummy Young and, 225
Waller, Maurice, 122
Walters, Raymond, 174
Walton (piano teacher), Mr., 203
Ward, Ada, 137
Waring, Fred, 96

Warley, Maurice, 160
Warren, Earl, *307*
Washington, Buddy, 57, *60*
Washington, Dinah, 106, 168, 282, 284
Washington, Geneva, 63
Washington, George Dewey, 147
Washington, Jack, 227
Washington, Leon, 77, *223*, *231*, *247*, 277–85
Water Boy (song), 139
Waters, Ethel, 25, 54, 58, 73, 88, 180
Watkins, Earl, 109, *113*
Watson, Deke, 153
Watson, Eugene, 170
Watson, Julius "Hawk," 262, 264
Watters, Johnny, 18, 19, 133
Way, Helen, 97
Weather Bird Rag (song), 52
Weatherford, Teddy, 34, 35, 37, 45, 63, 136, 145, 173
Webb, Chick, 152, 167, 172, 223, 255, 257, 258, 281
Webb, Gus, 184
Webb, Speed, 183, 184
Webster, Ben, 186, 206–7, 210, 250
Webster, Freddy, 92, 261, 281
Webster, Paul, 208
Wein, George, 126, 256
Wells, Dicky, 91, 107, 222, 225, 227, 273–76, *275*
Wells, Johnny, 55
Welsh, Alex, 114
West End Blues (song), 183, 184
Wettling, George, 194, 195
Whaley, Tom, 52
When I Dream of You (Hines), 284
When My Baby Smiles at Me (song), 194
When the Saints Go Marching In (song), 109, 148
White, Clarence Cameron, 132
White, Eddie, 197, 198
White, Harley, *124*, 126
White, Harry "Father," 197
White, Silas, 247, *247*
White, Slappy, 284
White, "Sparks," 197
White Brothers band, 197
White City (nightclub), 246
Whiteman, Paul, 49, 66, 74, 122, 146, 200
Whitey's Lindy Hoppers, 257
Whitlock, Elmer, 211
Whitlock, Stumpy, *182*, 229
Whitson, Ken, 110
Wilcox, Ed, 272
Wilder, Joe, 237
Wilkins, Ernie, *215*, 269
William Morris agency, 68, 69, 154, 158, 214, 216, 231
Williams, Bert, 143
Williams, Carrie, *41*
Williams, Cootie, 88, 95, 186, 227, 251, 287
Williams, Ernest, 204
Williams, Harry, 16, *21*, 30, 132, 134
Williams, Joe, 217
Williams, Johnny, 97, 260, 266, *267*, 287
Williams, Joseph, 262, *263*
Williams, Lou, *263*
Williams, Mary Lou, 114, 266, 287
Williams, Paul, 272
Williams, Ralph, 286
Williams, Rubberlegs, 224

Williams, Sandy, 281
Willows roadhouse, 134
Wilson, Alice, 254, 256
Wilson, Gerald, 224
Wilson, Gus, 183, 184
Wilson, Irene, 179–82, *180–82*
Wilson, Lucius, 229
Wilson, Quinn, 67, *68*, *71*, 76–77, 79, 168, *169*, 171–74, *173*, *199*, 223, 277
 Jimmy Mundy and, 198
 Milt Hinton and, 187–90
 Willie Randall and, 230
Wilson, Ronald, *233*
Wilson, Shadow, 92, 163, 224, 260, *267*, 269, 274, *275*
Wilson, Stanley, 228
Wilson, Teddy, 46, 73–74, 110, 124, 150, 161, 180–81, 183–86, *185*, 290, *311*
 Art Tatum and, 173, 181, 184, 211
 Benny Goodman and, 224
Windear, Phil, 12, 16
Winding, Kai, 222
Windy City Jive (song), 89
Winston, Bill, 249
Winterhalter, Hugo, 270
Without a Song (song), 137, 138
Wolf, Olga, 120
Wood, Booty, 119
Woodard, Kate, *263*
Woode, Henri, 76, 153–54
Wooding, Russell, 138
Wooding, Sam, 135
Woods, Rev., 10
World Is Waiting for the Sunrise, The (song), 132
World's Greatest Jazz Band, 126
World War II, 65, 89, 90, 163
Wright, Lammar, 257
Wynn, Al, 246, 253

Yellow Days (song), 126
Yellow Fire (song), 89, 249
Yes Yes Club, 176
You Can Depend on Me (Carpenter and Dunlap), 80, 126, 148, 150, 168, 213
You Go to My Head (song), 269
Youmans, Vincent, 137, 138
Young, Bernie, 248, 277
Young, Dave, 230, *231*
Young, Elzy M., 18
Young, Emma D., 10
Young, James Osborne "Trummy," 66, 68, 69, *71*, 72, 76, 122, 161, 168, 212, 220–27, *223*, 226, 235, *236*, 277
 Jimmie Lunceford and, 77, 152, 222–24, 227, 236n, 237
 Tommy Myles and, 198, 241
Young, Lester "Pres," 91, 149, 157–58, 186, 208–10, 214, 216, 260
Young, Marl, 174
You're Lucky to Me (song), 73
You Taught Me to Love Again (Woode and Carpenter), 153–54, 157
Ypsilanti Club, 206

Zanzibar (nightclub), 84
Ziegfeld, Flo, 136
Zuddan (song), 249
Zwerin, Mike, 116, *117*